An Exposition of Galatians
A Reading from the New Perspective

Third Edition

Don Garlington

Wipf and Stock Publishers
Eugene, Oregon
2007

An Exposition of Galatians*: A Reading from the New Perspective*
Third Edition

By Garlington, Don

Copyright©2007 by Garlington, Don

ISBN: 1-59752-779-3

Printed by Wipf & Stock Publishers, 2007
199 West 8th Ave., Suite 3
Eugene, Oregon 97401

All rights reserved. No part of this publication may be reproduced, stored in a retrieval system, or transmitted in any form or by any means, electronic, mechanical, photocopying, recording, or otherwise, without the prior permission of the publisher and author. The only exception is brief quotations in printed reviews and articles. (First rights belong to the original publishers of the articles herein published.)

Library of Congress Cataloging-in-Publication Data

Garlington, Don, *An Exposition of Galatians: A Reading from the New Perspective,* Third Edition
p. cm.

To all those who have listened patient to my lectures on Galatians,
and especially to my esteemed teacher and friend,
James D. G. Dunn

TABLE OF CONTENTS

Preface to the Original Edition	vii
Preface to the Second Edition	ix
Preface to the Third Edition	xii
Introduction	1
Galatians Chapter One	41
Galatians Chapter Two	103
Galatians Chapter Three	177
Galatians Chapter Four	235
Galatians Chapter Five	291
Galatians Chapter Six	355
Bibliography	397

PREFACE TO THE ORIGINAL EDITION

The present commentary seeks to be a kind of "halfway house" between highly technical and popular treatments of Galatians. Its purpose is to make the exposition as "user friendly" as possible with only as many technicalities as necessary to accomplish that end. For this reason, grammatical and textual observations have been kept at a minimum and are mainly confined to the footnotes, and all Greek and Hebrew words have been transliterated. The emphasis of the work is decidedly theological, with attention focused on the salvation historical argument of Paul's letter.

Galatians has become even more controversial than ever these days with the advent of the "New Perspective" on Paul in his relation to contemporary Judaism. The present commentary assumes a modified form of this "New Perspective" as its framework of interpretation, and for this reason a premium has been placed on the letter's historical context as attested by the literature of Second Temple Judaism. It must be added, however, that far from being inimical to the foundational concerns of the Reformation, the reading of the Galatian letter proffered herein is fully supportive of the great mottoes of the Reformers themselves: *Sola Scriptura*, *Sola Fide*, *Sola Gratia* and especially *Solus Christus*, and all the more as the present work endeavors to honor an oft-neglected slogan of the Reformation—*Ad Fontes* ("to the sources"). Hence, the subtitle: *A New Perspective/Reformational Reading*. As providence would have it, this "New Perspective" commentary on Galatians was completed on Reformation Day!

In order to cut to the chase as regards the exposition of the text itself, and to facilitate easier reading, I have largely refrained from arguing with other points of view, and such argumentation is normally confined to the footnotes. Other matters germane to the text of Galatians have been placed in the section notes at the end of some units of exposition. References to secondary literature are hardly exhaustive, with the ever-growing body of work devoted to Paul in general and Galatians in particular. In a work of this sort, it was my judgment to cite only as many sources as necessary to document the various exegetical decisions and to provide the reader with other avenues of information.

As will be evident, I am particularly indebted to the commentaries of Dunn, Witherington and Martyn, as well to such excellent and insightful studies as those of Ciampa (*Scripture*), Cummins (*Paul*) and Hafemann ("Paul"). In places, I have quoted or referred to these and others at some length, in order to bring to the readers of this commentary the best of what I have learned from such scholars.

My sincerest gratitude, as ever, goes to my wife, Elizabeth, who graciously and carefully proofread the entire manuscript and uncovered numerous mistakes—confirming again what a bad typist I am! She, however, is not responsible what mistakes may remain. As always, my sons, Robert and Thomas, have been gracious and understanding in allowing me to be "cloistered" during the production of this book.

A special word of thanks goes to Mr. Jim Tedrick of Wipf & Stock for his patient guidance in turning the manuscript into a book.

Normally, biblical quotations are from NIV, with others as noted. All abbreviations conform to *The SBL Handbook of Style: For Ancient Near Eastern, Biblical, and Early Christian Studies* (eds. Patrick H. Alexander, et al. Peabody: Hendrickson, 1999). In the text of the commentary, all secondary literature is cited by abbreviated titles only, with full information provided by the bibliography.

59 Shoredale Drive
Toronto
Ontario
M1G 3T1
Canada

Reformation Day, 2002

PREFACE TO THE SECOND EDITION

The second edition of this commentary is issued with numerous corrections and clarifications, updating of secondary literature and further reflections on several passages, most notably Gal 3:20; 3:22-25 and 4:21-31. The introduction has been restructured and expanded, so as to include discussions of Anatolian folk belief and the role of Pauline rhetoric in Galatians. In one or two cases, lengthy footnotes have been rendered into section notes. In other cases, bibliographical references have been moved to footnotes, so as to keep the text of the commentary as uncluttered as possible.

I take the occasion to reiterate and emphasize three elements from the preface of the first edition. First, this exposition is intended as a kind of "half way house" between highly technical and popular treatments of Galatians. Its chief design is to fill a gap for pastors and students. For this reason, I have sought to distill the contributions of various scholars, which otherwise would be mostly inaccessible to the "rank and file" of New Testament students. In keeping with this goal, I have attempted to draw upon the most relevant of the secondary sources, without attempting to provide anything like an exhaustive accounting of literature. Among many treatments of Galatians, ready sources of bibliography are the commentaries of Betz, Dunn, Martyn and Witherington, as well as the bibliographies to R. B. Hays, *Faith* and Nanos (ed.), *Debate*.

Second, although I have assumed a modified form of the "New Perspective" as a framework of interpretation, it must be stressed that far from being inimical to the foundational concerns of the Reformation, the reading of Galatians herein submitted is fully supportive of the great mottoes of the Reformers themselves: *Sola Scriptura, Sola Fide, Sola Gratia* and especially *Solus Christus,* and all the more as the present work endeavors to honor an oft-neglected slogan of the *Reformation-Ad Fontes* ("to the sources"). Hence, the retained subtitle: *A New Perspective/Reformational Reading.* To some, this combination of terms may appear to be an oxymoron, if not a genuine paradox. How can the New Perspective and the Reformation coexist? But the wording is quite deliberate and expresses my conviction that the former poses no actual threat to the latter. Indeed, I am taking as my point of departure the famous *obiter dictum* of the Puritan pastor, John Robinson, that new light is always breaking forth from the Word of God. And whatever light springs from God's Word can never threaten the life, health and stability of the Church of Christ. If Paul's passion in the Galatian letter was to (re)preach *Christ only*, as opposed to the Messiah envisioned by Jewish tradition, then Christians of all stripes must recall that *ecclesia reformata ecclesia reformanda est*— "the Reformed church is always reforming itself."

Third, I have quoted or referred to various scholars at some length, in order to present to my readers the best of what I have learned from other sources. In so doing, I have attempted to make this commentary a study-tool, particularly for pastors and students.

Once again, I am much indebted to Mr. Jim Tedrick for his invaluable assistance in the production of this book.

59 Shoredale Drive
Toronto
Ontario
MIG 3Tl
Canada

July 30, 2004

PREFACE TO THE THIRD EDITION

The third and final edition of this commentary is issued with the inevitable corrections of typing errors, some rearrangement of paragraphs and other technical adjustments, but mainly with the benefit of having lectured through Galatians once more and the opportunity of perusing the most relevant of the recent literature devoted to this epistle. In the process of teaching one is always taught; and I have endeavored to bring to the readers of this exposition the fruit of classroom discussion, along with a good deal of renewed thinking on the epistle as a whole. This has resulted in some restructuring of the format of the commentary plus added references to primary and secondary literature. But as much as anything else, I have been forced to test certain assumptions in the light of the constant flow of scholarship dedicated to Paul's letter. Especially conspicuous in this regard is a rewriting of the comments on Gal 2:15-3:29, taking into account Paul's use of the "partisan *ek*" as it bears on the question of justification (a forthcoming article explores this in more depth). I must add that in the process of "iron sharpening iron," numerous insights and refinements can now be presented because of an intensive two day study of Galatians in the "upper room" of Bath Road Baptist Church, Kingston, Ontario, in April of 2006.

The subtitle of this "ultimate" version of the commentary has been changed to: *A Reading from the New Perspective*. The original subtitle, *A New Perspective/Reformational Reading*, was intended to make a point, namely, that the "New Perspective on Paul" has never been inimical to the foundational concerns of the Reformers. That point having been made, I prefer now to stress that this work has been informed and enriched by the insights into Second Temple Judaism stemming from E. P. Sanders, as taken up, modified and applied to the letters of Paul by such scholars as J. D. G. Dunn, N. T. Wright, Kent Yinger, Richard Hays and Nancy Calvert-Koyzis, to mention just a few.

In keeping with the original design of this work as a "halfway house" treatment of the text, I have engaged a selected portion of the most recent secondary literature, without at all endeavoring to be exhaustive. Likewise, the character of this book as a study-tool for pastors, missionaries and students has been retained, meaning that I have distilled, mainly in the section notes, the best of scholarship that has come to my attention on various points: exegetical, hermeneutical and theological. For this reason, I have not hesitated to quote at length from those who have gone before, particularly when source materials are not readily at hand for many readers.

I have opted to retain the method of documentation employed in the previous two editions. That is to say, most citations of secondary literature are inserted parenthetically into the main text, while others are placed in the footnotes. This way, neither text nor footnotes are overburdened with references. Once more, all abbreviations conform to *The SBL Handbook of Style: For Ancient Near Eastern, Biblical, and Early Christian Studies* (eds. Patrick H. Alexander, et al. Peabody: Hendrickson, 1999). In the text of the commentary, all secondary literature is cited by abbreviated titles only, with full information provided by the bibliography.

For a final time, my heartiest thanks go to Mr. Jim Tedrick and Mr. James Stock of Wipf & Stock Publishers for their kind consideration and their willingness to accommodate this expanding project.

Certainly not least, my deepest gratitude is due to my son, Robert, for his invaluable technical expertise in rendering the manuscript into a book.

It is hoped that these pages will continue to receive a welcome among those who love the Pauline gospel of freedom in Christ.

59 Shoredale Drive
Toronto
Ontario
M1G 3T1
Canada

Remembrance Day, 2006

INTRODUCTION

The purpose of this introduction is to focus attention on the historical/theological issues that formed the context of the Galatian letter and gave rise to its issuance on the part of Paul. Questions such as authorship, date, place of writing and destination are of interest in themselves. But apart from authorship, there continues to be uncertainty on all these points, and it is unlikely that any unanimity will ever be reached (cf. Betz, *Galatians*, 9-12).[1] Besides, the resolution of these issues is hardly indispensable to the interpretation of the epistle's biblical-theological content. Discussions can be found in the introductions to each of the commentaries cited throughout this work, to which I would add, among many others, R. E. Brown, *Introduction*, 467-82; Gorman, *Apostle*, 183-226; Hansen, *DPL*, 323-34; Carson/Moo, *Introduction*, 456-78; deSilva, *Introduction*, 493-526; Martin, *Foundations*, 2.145-58; Guthrie, *Introduction*, 450-71.[2] Overviews of the theology of the letter can be found in Dunn, *Theology of Galatians*; Thielman, *Theology*, 262-75; Marshall, *Theology*, 209-35; Johnson, *Writings*, 327-40.

---

[1] My inclination is to think that the letter was directed to the churches of South Galatia and dates from c. AD 48-49 (as per Martin, *Foundations*, 2.151-52).

[2] On Paul the letter writer, see Gorman, *Apostle*, 74-97 (with further literature); Doty, *Letters*, 21-47; Roetzel, *Paul*, 69-92; Cousar, *Letters*, 23-45; Aune, *Environment*, 158-82; Stirewalt, *Paul*; Richards, *Paul*; Witherington, *Paul Quest*, 99-115; cf. Stowers, *Letter Writing*. Methodological questions pertaining to the letter are addressed by Silva, *Explorations*, and Wright, "Exegesis and Theology." Galatians has been subjected to various structural studies, such as Boers, *Justification*. The broader missionary context of Galatians is set by Hultgren, *Gospel*; O'Brien, *Gospel*; Bolt/Thompson (eds.), *Gospel*; Köstenberger/O'Brien, *Salvation*, 161-201; Schnabel, *Mission*, vol. 2; id., "Israel;" Schnelle, *Paul*, 111-20; Hofius, "Paulus;" Scott, *"Imago Mundi;"* id., *Paul*. Paul's place within the social and religious setting of the Mediterranean world is explored, among many, by Sampley (ed.), *Paul*; Schnelle, *Paul*, 57-86, 138-45; Neyrey, *Paul* and Malina/Neyrey, *Portraits*. The last two are recommended with some qualification. See my "Review Article" of Neyrey's *Paul*, along with T. L. Carter's critique (*Paul*, 80-86). Numerous rhetorical and historical issues are addressed by Nanos (ed.), *Debate*. An oft-discussed matter is the relation of Galatians to Paul's trip to Jerusalem as related in Acts 11:27-30 and especially the "apostolic conference" of Acts 15. See the discussions of Witherington, *Grace*, 13-20, and Schnelle, *Paul*, 121-32. The section note to 2:1 likewise offers a reconstruction.

EXPOSITION OF GALATIANS

Occasion and Purpose of the Letter

The letter to the Galatians mirrors the first major crisis in the life of the infant church. The issue is simply stated: according to Acts 15:1, certain Jewish Christians were insisting that unless Gentile converts to Christianity are circumcised according to the custom of Moses, they cannot be saved. But this demand on the part of former Pharisees, now reckoned among the Christian community, was extended beyond circumcision to the observance of the whole law of Moses (Acts 15:5; cf. Gal 5:3). In short, according to the "circumcision party," anyone wishing to join the ranks of the people of God from the outside must conform to the normal procedure prescribed for proselytes—circumcision and commitment to Israel's Torah.[3]

Luke terms this company "believers," presumably because its adherents accepted Jesus as the Messiah and came to recognize that the age of the Spirit had arrived with him. Nevertheless, in focus and commitment, these people apparently brought their Pharisaic presuppositions over into their Christianity. According to that set of assumptions, Israel's law was eternal and unchangeable,[4] and the Messiah himself was conceived of as a servant of the Torah. His job was to preserve intact the values of God's covenant with Israel and to eliminate all opposition to the contrary (as classically affirmed by *Psalms of Solomon* 17-18).[5]

In the Acts narrative, the insistence on circumcision and the law represents the climax of a story, namely, the struggle for Gentile equality in the assemblies of Jesus the Christ. The issue is posed by Boice (*Galatians*, 409):

---

[3] See Schürer, *History*, 3.150-76; Donaldson, *Paul*, 54-65.

[4] For example, *Bar* 4:1; *2 Apoc. Bar.* 77:15; *1 Enoch* 99:2; *Wis* 18:4; *Jub.* 1:27; 3:31; 6:17; Josephus, *Ag. Ap.* 2.277; Philo, *Vit. Mos.* 2.3, 14. See further W. D. Davies, *Torah*; Banks, "Role;" Garland, "Defense," 178-79.

[5] Gorman would appear to attribute too much to the circumcisers in writing that they did not deny the importance of Christ's death for sins. As we shall see, they were, in point of fact, ashamed of the cross and would have considered it, in Bruce's words, a "blasphemous contradiction in terms" (*Galatians*, 166). See on 1:4. However, Gorman is certainly right that their christology was not centered on Christ's cross but on his role as a teacher of the law (*Apostle*, 189-90). Similarly, Hays thinks that the other missionaries did presumably speak of the cross. But again, it is difficult to conceive that they gloried in it as Paul did. Even so, Hays is accurate in writing that the opponents did not interpret the cross as the apostle did, as "the apocalyptic termination of the old world of religious symbolism and obligation" (*Galatians*, 343).

INTRODUCTION

> When the gospel was being preached primarily to Jews by Jews, the development of the church progressed smoothly. But as the ambassadors of Christ pushed out into largely Gentile communities and the gospel began to take root there, questions arose regarding a Christian's relationship to the law of Moses and to Judaism as a system. Was the church to open her doors wide to all comers, regardless of their relationship to the particularized traditions of Judaism? Were her boundaries to be as wide as the human race? Or was she to be only an extension of Judaism to the Gentiles?

By the time the "apostolic conference" of Acts 15 concludes, the apostles and other participants arrive at a consensus: Gentiles are not to be burdened unnecessarily by the Mosaic regulations; they need only abstain from immorality and idolatry (see Witherington, *Acts*, 460-67). Effectively, they said, being Christian does not hinge on first becoming Jewish. Paul's letter to the Galatians marks the early stages of the controversy. The party whose positions were finally rejected by the Jerusalem church was actively engaged in missionary activity for a number of years. Whatever name it might have borne, it is this same basic group that followed Paul around on his travels and attempted to counter his law-free gospel to the Gentiles with its "other gospel" of Christ plus "the works of the law." For Paul, such a "gospel" was unconscionable, simply because "a supplemented Christ is a supplanted Christ" (Hendriksen, *Galatians*, 112).

> For Paul, Christ is everything or nothing. Either God has inaugurated the new, eschatological age of the Spirit through Christ, or not. Either justification, or life in the Spirit, is received by faith, or not. Either cruciform faith expressing itself through cruciform love is the essence of covenantal existence, or not. Either this is all of grace, or not. *Whereas for the circumcisers Christ is necessary but not sufficient, for Paul Christ is either sufficient or else not necessary* (Gorman, *Apostle*, 216, italics his).

Much has been written on the identity of the opponents and their theology.[6] But after all is said and done, Paul's antagonists in

---

[6] For example, Martyn, *Galatians*, 117-26; Schütz, *Anatomy*; Howard, *Crisis*, 1-19; Dunn, *Theology of Galatians*, 8-12; Brinsmead, *Galatians*; Ellis, *Prophecy*,

Galatia conceived of themselves as Jewish Christian missionaries, whose goal was to bring the nations into captive obedience to Israel's king, in fulfillment of such OT passages as Ps 2:8 and Gen 49:10.[7] In their view, they were only attempting to promote the promise to Abraham of a multitude of descendants by bringing Gentiles under the dominion of the law, as supported *prima facie* by such prophetic texts as Isa 2:2-4; Mic 4:1-3; Zech 14:16-19.[8] Galatians, therefore, is Paul's response to the efforts of the other missionaries to bring Gentiles who have turned to Christ under the dominion of the law, in order to "complete" their conversion to the God of Israel. Referring to Gal 2:11-21, Garland puts it this way:

> The incident in Antioch bears witness to the fact that many Jewish Christians saw themselves as simply a renewal movement within Judaism and regarded newly converted Gentiles as proselytes who needed to be circumcised and to adhere to Jewish mores if they were to become fully certified as members of the covenant community ("Defense," 167).

As far as these preachers were concerned, faith in Jesus of Nazareth as Messiah is well and good—this much is fundamental

---

80-115, 116-28; Georgi, *Opponents*; Sumney, *Opponents*; Gunther, *Opponents*; Nanos, *Irony*, 110-92; Calvert-Koyzis, *Paul*, 86-93; Rapa, *Meaning*, 81-94. Nanos exposes some of the weaknesses of the traditional designations of the group in question. Nevertheless, terms such as "Judaizers," "circumcision party," "Jewish Christian missionaries, "other missionaries," "opponents," "rivals," "antagonists," "the men from James," and "Teachers" (Martyn) are retained and used interchangeably. Hays' objections to "Judaizers" have some basis (*Galatians*, 185). Yet even with his qualification of the participants in the Galatians controversy, Paul's opponents were endeavoring to compel Gentiles to "live as Jews," as Peter inadvertently was doing (2:14).

[7] De Boer ("Quotation," 383, n. 53) prefers to speak of this company as "Christian-Jewish" evangelists rather than "Jewish-Christian," because they took their theological point of departure from the Mosaic law rather than from Christ. Whatever we call them, De Boer is certainly correct in this regard.

[8] The commentary proceeds along the traditional line that Paul's antagonists were in fact "Jewish Christian missionaries," whose conception of the place of the law in the messianic age differed from that of Paul (on the designation "Jewish Christian," see Cummins, *Paul*, 94, n. 1). The thesis of Nanos (*Irony*) that the "influencers," as he calls them, were representatives of local synagogues attempting to win the Gentile Galatians to non-Christian Judaism is intriguing but hardly convincing. While respecting Nanos' position, Das rightly concludes that the "they group" in the letter is comprised of Jewish Christians in the Galatians' midst, not non-Christian Jews (*Paul and Jews*, 17-29). See the further critique of Carson/Moo, *Introduction*, 465, n. 25.

INTRODUCTION

to everything else, because every Jew of the Second Temple period knew that the religious life was first and foremost a matter of reliance on God. This axiom of faith in Judaism is amply confirmed by the literature of the predestruction period, which is replete with references to faith in Yahweh.[9] However, it is equally clear from these sources that faith always assumed a *nationalistic bias*. That is to say, belief in the God of Israel was always to be accompanied by a steadfast commitment to the Torah, which gave concrete expression to the will of the Lord of the covenant. In brief, the law was given to regulate the life of the believing community, and genuine faith was always sensitive to the "household rules" put in place to guide the faithful in their walk in the ways of the Lord.

Given such a set of assumptions, Paul's opponents in Galatia were more than glad to have "outsiders" join the ranks of God's people—but under the proper conditions. Those conditions are well illustrated by the book of Judith. According to Jdt 14:10, the Gentile Achior believed in the God of Israel, was circumcised, joined the house of Israel and remained steadfast all his days. For these "Judaizers," it was self-evident that God was ready and willing to receive believers in God's Messiah; but such faith could never remain alone—it had to be attended by "the works of the law" (see on 2:16) in order to be valid. But Paul disagreed, and disagreed vociferously. In light of what God has done in Christ in the fullness of the time (Gal 4:4), the law has served its purpose in salvation history, the dividing wall of hostility between Jew and Gentile has come down (Eph 2:14), and God has now received all who place their trust in Christ irrespective of ethnic distinctives and devotion to the law of Moses. In a nutshell, the only distinction that postdates the resurrection of Christ is faith versus unbelief.

By way of an important qualification, however, it should not be supposed that Paul was a Marcionite before Marcion, even though he has some very radical things indeed to say about the law in this letter. It is not that he conceives of Israel's Torah as an evil

---

[9] Garlington, *Obedience*. Similarly, Schnelle correctly maintains that there existed in ancient Judaism the fundamental conviction that God is merciful, good and loving to his creatures (*Paul*, 283). Commenting on the Qumran *Hymn Scroll*, Schnell writes that the confession of guilt points to dependence on God's righteousness and mercy, which he will reveal in the judgment. "God's righteousness leads to obedience to the law, but without thereby making it a matter of earning merit before God. Rather, God alone grants the devout assurance of salvation that comes from their belonging to the chosen people" (ibid., 459). Cf. my *Obedience*, 266-67.

of some sort. Rather, he seeks to address an attitude that would keep the law around after its goal has been realized—Christ (Gal 3:23-25; Rom 10:4).

> Paul's most basic problem with the Law is that it is obsolete and therefore following it is no longer appropriate. It is not the rule of the eschatological age and it is not to be imposed in the new creation which is already coming to be. If Christ came even to redeem Jews out from under the yoke of the Law, if the Law was a pedagogue meant to function only until Christ came, if the Law was "set aside" as 2 Cor. 3.11 says, then it is a mistake, indeed a serious mistake to go back to keeping it, or in the case of Gentiles to begin to submit to it in any form or fashion. The Law had an important function and role to play in the divine economy, but the rule of the Mosaic Law has had its day and ceased to be. But it is not just the anachronism that bothers Paul about insisting that Christians, whether Jews or Gentiles, must keep the Mosaic Law. What bothers him most is that keeping the Law implies in Paul's mind that Christ's death did not accomplish what in fact he believes it did accomplish. To submit to the Mosaic Law is to nullify the grace of God (Gal. 2.21) and to deny that justification or righteousness, whether initial or final, comes through the death of Christ.[10]

deSilva writes to similar effect:

> Paul's polemic against "works of the law" is not a polemic against "good works," as this is commonly but erroneously understood. Rather, Paul opposes the continued observance of a boundary-maintaining

---

[10] Witherington, *Grace*, 354. Witherington adds: "We may sum up by saying that for the Christian Paul, the Mosaic Law was a good thing, something that came from God, but that it was limited—limited in what it was intended to and could accomplish, limited in the time-span for which it was meant to be applicable, and limited in the group to which it was meant to be applied (namely Jews and converts or adherents to Judaism). It was but one form of the *stoichea* ["elements"], and it was something Christ's coming had rendered no longer in effect. The people of God were no longer to be under the Guardian now that the eschatological age had broken in and those in Christ could be new creatures and walk in the Spirit" (ibid., 355-56). Such a consideration should temper Schnelle's assessment that in Galatians the law has no revelatory function and is portrayed in an entirely negative light (*Paul*, 288-89). For its day, the law did indeed have revelatory value, but that day is past.

INTRODUCTION

> code, not only in the observance of the more obvious differentiators like circumcision, kosher laws and sabbath, but also as *an entire body of laws given to Israel as a mark of her distinctiveness and separation from the Gentiles....* It is not in maintaining the ethnic identity of Israel (through such "works of Torah") that we are conformed to God's character or brought in line with God's purpose, but only through faith in Jesus, which results in the life of the Spirit being born in us so that we are born to life before God. Paul certainly expects the Spirit to produce all manner of "good works" in the life of the disciple (Rom 2:6-11; 6:12-13, Gal 5:13-25, Eph 2:10) (*Introduction*, 505, n. 9, italics mine).

Carrying on from these observations, it follows that *the law cannot justify because it was never intended to justify.* In other words, the inability of the law to justify is rooted in eschatology. There is, one might say, a teleology of the law; that is, its sole reason for being was to point Israel and all humanity to Christ, in whom God had always purposed to vindicate his people.[11] In his study of the weakness of the law, Bayes takes issue with the traditional view that the law's inadequacy to justify resides in anthropological failure (the famous suppressed premise). He rightly maintains that this explanation of the law *in Galatians* misses the point.

> For Paul, the law can be described as weak in respect of justification simply because it was not given by God for the purpose of justification, but rather as an interim provision pointing forward to the Christ, in whom justification would become a reality. To seek justification by the law, therefore, as the Galatians were mistakenly trying to do, is to attempt to direct the law towards an end for which it is essentially unsuited by the purpose of God.... Moreover, the power which the law did possess according to Galatians is not its ability to convict of sin, but its epochal purpose as a pointer to Christ designed to keep God's people hoping for His coming.[12]

---

[11] Cf. Rappa, *Meaning*, 167. This is where the term coined by Peter Enns is so helpful. According to Enns, the whole of the OT is "Christotelic" (*Inspiration*, 154). As regards righteousness, and everything else, Christ is the goal (*telos*) of the law (Rom 10:4).

[12] Bayes, *Weakness*, 138. The entire discussion of pp. 125-74 is stimulating and useful.

The core issue of Galatians thus boils down to a simple but profound choice—*Christ or the Torah*.[13] From Romans 14, it is clear enough that Paul was willing to allow Jewish Christians (and others) to practice the law as a matter of personal lifestyle, if they chose. But he drew the line when Torah observance was made the indispensable condition for entering and remaining within the people of God. In short, he repudiated the law as the "Jewish gateway to salvation" (Räisänen, *Paul*, 177-201). At one time, the community of the saved was in fact constituted of circumcised and law-observant people. But with the coming of Jesus the Messiah, who himself began to relax the Mosaic strictures (e.g., Matt 8:3; Mark 7:18-19; Luke 7:14; 13:10-17; John 5:9b-18), the demand of the Jewish Christian missionaries for circumcision and law-obedience is not only obsolete, it actually impedes access to God and is tantamount, no less, to idolatry and apostasy (see on 3:10-13; 4:8-10). As Witherington again so aptly puts it:

> The Gospel of grace proclaims the acceptance and acceptability of both Gentiles and Jews on the basis of trust in the faithful work of Jesus Christ which justifies (or sets right) sinners, and not on the basis of works of the Mosaic Law. Therefore works of the Mosaic Law are not merely unnecessary or redundant. If they are pursued by those who are Christians as the proper manner of Christian living, as if Christians were obliged to obey the Mosaic covenant's requirements, they amount to a fall from grace, a devaluation of what Christ accomplished on the cross. The origin, character and content of the Gospel determines the origin, character and behavior of the people of God, who are Jew and Gentile united in Christ and his finished work on the cross (*Grace*, 90).

At this juncture, it is important to underscore that the bottom line issue in Galatians is *soteriology*. Sanders is doubtlessly correct to maintain that "Paul's argument is not in favor of faith per se, nor is it against works per se. It is much more particular: it is against requiring the Gentiles to keep the law of Moses in order to be 'sons of Abraham'" (*Paul, the Law*, 19). He adds further that "we have become so sensitive to the theological issue of grace and merit that we often lose sight of the actual subject of the dispute" (ibid.).

---

[13] Gordon, "Problem;" Hubbard, *Creation*, 199-200.

INTRODUCTION

Thus, the subject of Galatians is "the condition on which Gentiles enter the people of God" (ibid., 18). Nevertheless, much more is at stake than a sociology or group identity, one enclave distinguishing itself from another. If the topic under discussion is "how to enter the body of those who would be saved," then "the topic is, in effect, soteriology" (ibid., 45, 46). Cousar speaks to the same effect: "The issue under debate, raised by the agitators' demand for circumcision, was basically soteriological, how God saves people" (*Galatians*, 61).[14] See Acts 15:1.

This affirmation of soteriology as lying at the root of Galatians is a necessary corrective to N. T. Wright's otherwise excellent treatment of justification and righteousness language in the Paul. Wright maintains that justification and, consequently, the subject matter of Galatians, does not tell one how to be saved; it is, rather, a way of saying how one can tell that one belongs to the covenant community, or, in other words, How does one define the people of God?[15] To be sure, such issues are to be judged in light of the covenant context of "the righteousness of God" and similar ideas. On this, Wright is undoubtedly correct, and in this regard the ensuing exposition is much in his debt. Indeed, Galatians does address the question, "Who is a member of the people of God" (*Paul*, 121). Likewise, it is true that "justification, in Galatians, is the doctrine which insists that all who share faith in Christ belong at the same table, no matter what their racial differences, as together they wait for the final new creation" (ibid., 122).

This much said, it must be countered that Wright has constructed a seemingly false dichotomy between the identity of the people of God and salvation. It is closer to the mark to say that Galatians does have to do with entrance into the body of the saved, meaning that to belong to the new covenant *is* to belong to the community the of saved.[16] Therefore, justification does indeed tell us how to be saved, in that it depicts God's method of saving sin-

---

[14] All this is seconded by Hubbard (*Creation*, 200). However, Hubbard mistakenly relegates the unity of the people of God in Galatians to a topic of secondary status.

[15] Wright, *Paul*, 119, 120-22, 131; id., *Perspective*, 122.

[16] In this regard, Hafemann is correct in insisting that the context of Paul's usage of "works of the law" is the contrast between the two covenant eras within the history of redemption, not (merely, I would say) a material or socio-ethnic contrast. "Hence, to continue to maintain allegiance to the old covenant once the new has arrived not only denies the saving efficacy of Christ's work, but also leads at times to a false boasting and ethnically based 'legalism' [I prefer "nomism"] as a by-product" ("Spirit," 178, n. 24).

ners—*by faith* in Chris*t*, not *from* works of the law—and placing them in covenant standing with himself.[17] If justification is *by faith*, then in point of fact a method of salvation is prescribed: one enters into the realm of salvation *by faith*.[18]

It is just because the bedrock of Galatians is soteriology, and it is just because Paul sees defection from Christ to the law as taking place "so quickly" in the Galatian congregations that he writes with an intense awareness of the plight of his "children" in the gospel who are in danger of forsaking their Lord for what effectively is no better than their former bondage to pagan deities (4:8-10). In plain terms, the letter is written to avert the apostasy in Galatia. No wonder, Paul's passions are white hot in this letter.

Todd Wilson's study of the apostasy motif in Galatians is brilliant and significant in many regards. Wilson begins with the question of J. L. Martyn, What time is it (see below)? Instead of pursuing this issue as such, he poses a related question, Where are the Galatians? That is to say, what is their current position *vis-à-vis* the beginning and end of their pilgrimage of faith. His answer is that they are in the wilderness, somewhere between Egypt and the promised land. But the problem is that they, like the Israel of old, are in danger of forsaking the Lord and returning their old master. In particular, Wilson develops the apostasy/idolatry theme in relation to the issues of freedom and bondage. His conclusion is:

> After having been miraculously delivered from servitude through an Exodus-like experience in Christ (1.4; 3.13; 4.4-5; 5.1), the Galatians are now contemplating a return to Egyptian-like bondage. Paul is at pains, therefore, to exercise whatever moral leverage he can over the situation, thus colouring his rebukes and warnings with language that evokes the Israelites' own tragic wilderness defection and disinheritance.[19]

---

[17] I am setting aside the traditional rendering of "*by* works of the law" in favor of "*from* works of the law," for reasons to be clarified in the commentary on 2:16 and subsequent passages.

[18] A very telling consideration is that "righteousness" and "salvation" are placed in synonymous parallel in passages in the Prophets and the Psalms. See on 2:16.

[19] Wilson, "Apostasy," 570 (cf. Smiles, *Gospel*, passim). Keesmaat's monograph on the exodus traditions in Galatians proceeds along the same lines as Wilson. Note as well the exploration of the wilderness/apostasy motif in the Corinthian correspondence by Oropeza: *Paul* and "Apostasy." By means of rhetorical analysis, T. Martin contends that the apostasy would have been to paganism, not Judaism or a Judaistic form of Christianity ("Apostasy"). But while his conclusions

INTRODUCTION

The Message of the Opponents and Paul's Reply

Apart from what can be reconstructed respecting the presuppositions of the other teachers from historical sources, we are dependent on Paul himself for information about his opponents' positions. Although there are limitations to the method, any interpretation of Galatians inevitably resorts to a certain amount of "mirror reading" of the text.[20] That is to say, judging from what Paul actually writes about his antagonists, certain factors can be deduced, running the whole gamut from the certain to the incredible (Barclay, "Mirror Reading," 265-66). While commentators will continue to debate the precise demands made on the Galatians by the Jewish Christian missionaries, in the main these are not so difficult to discern. Nor is Paul's reply difficult to determine. As Gorman writes, Paul responds to the Galatian crisis by telling a series of stories—"Stories about himself, about Christ, about the Galatians and their experience of the Spirit, about God, about the Law, about biblical characters like Abraham and Hagar and Sarah, and about life together.... These stories all serve his main purpose of dissuading the Gentile Galatians from being circumcised."[21]

Before descending to particulars, it will be useful to have an overall appraisal of Paul's antagonists. Here Gorman is particularly helpful (*Apostle*, 190). He observes that because the circumcisers seem to have embraced a comprehensive vision greater than the mere desire for Gentile circumcision, the most apt moniker for them may be "covenantal nomists," individuals who believed that keeping the Law was the way to express and maintain their covenant status. More specifically, Gorman proposes that the circumcisers were "messianic covenantal nomists," since it is probable that they affirmed Jesus as Messiah. As messianic covenantal nomists, the circumcisers would have believed: (1) that through Messiah Jesus the God of Israel was graciously inviting Gentiles to the covenant; (2) that entrance into the covenant was gained by faith in the Messiah followed (for males) by circumcision; and (3) that

---

fail to carry conviction (see Martyn, *Galatians*, 21, n. 26), he is not wrong to draw a parallel between Paul and the prophets of Israel, who brought divine lawsuit against Israel for breach of the covenant. "Both the prophets and Paul exert pressure on the unfaithful partner to return to covenant faithfulness" ("Apostasy," 94).

[20] See Barclay, *Obeying*, 37-45; id., "Mirror Reading."

[21] Gorman, *Apostle*, 192; cf. Hays, *Galatians*, 189-90.

God expected his covenant people to live distinctive lives of holiness in which they observed the Law of God.

The main thrust of the circumcisers' message was a critique of Paul. According to Gorman:

> They seem to have found his apostleship dubious, his message deficient, and his ministry dangerous. They likely claimed that his message and ministry originated in himself and had the sanction of neither Jerusalem nor heaven. His truncated gospel offered the Gentiles the Jewish Messiah without bringing them into the realm of the covenant and Law that the Messiah embodied. His emphasis on the cross and Spirit without circumcision and the Law had generated unnecessary persecution from Jewish leaders and, through them, from pagan mobs and government officials (*Apostle*, 192).

In view of their self-perceived mission, Gorman wisely cautions that some benefit of the doubt ought to be granted to their motives.

> They were not antichrists opposing Jesus' messiahship. Nor were they legalists, teaching a doctrine of salvation by works, as many traditional interpretations have presented them. They were—like Paul—Jews who affirmed God's gracious election and covenant, Jesus as the Messiah, and the inclusion of the Gentiles in the covenant—only on terms that differed significantly from Paul's (ibid.).

The Demand for Circumcision

If anything is obvious from the letter itself, it is Paul's resistance of the "gospel of circumcision" as preached by the Judaizers (on the significance of circumcision, see on 2:3; 5:2-3, 6; 6:12-13, 15, with literature). At a pivotal point in the historical narrative of chaps. 1-2, his repudiation of circumcision for Gentiles is for the very purpose of preserving "the truth of the gospel" for the Galatians (2:5). The opponents, for their part, were simply following suit with the requirements of both the Abrahamic and Mosaic covenants.

Foundational to their thinking was God's own word of command to Abraham (Gen 17:9-14):

> And God said to Abraham, "As for you, you shall keep my covenant, you and your descendants after you

INTRODUCTION

> throughout their generations. This is my covenant, which you shall keep, between me and you and your descendants after you: Every male among you shall be circumcised. You shall be circumcised in the flesh of your foreskins, and *it shall be a sign of the covenant between me and you.* He that is eight days old among you shall be circumcised; every male throughout your generations, whether born in your house, or bought with your money from any foreigner who is not of your offspring, both he that is born in your house and he that is bought with your money, shall be circumcised. *So shall my covenant be in your flesh an everlasting covenant. Any uncircumcised male who is not circumcised in the flesh of his foreskin shall be cut off from his people; he has broken my covenant.*" (RSV)

That this "sign of circumcision" was not to be trifled with by later generations is underscored by that strange passage, Exod 4:24-26:

> At a lodging place on the way the LORD met him and sought to kill him. Then Zipporah took a flint and cut off her son's foreskin, and touched Moses' feet with it, and said, "Surely you are a bridegroom of blood to me!" So he let him alone. Then it was that she said, "You are a bridegroom of blood," because of the circumcision. (RSV)

deSilva calls to mind that the Word of God had further spoken of a time when the unclean and uncircumcised would no longer be permitted entrance into the assembly of Israel (*Introduction*, 502-3). According to Isa 52:1:

Awake, awake,
  put on your strength, O Zion!
Put on your beautiful garments,
  O Jerusalem, the holy city;
for the uncircumcised and the unclean
  shall enter you no more. (NRSV)

Likewise, Ezekiel (44:9), in prophesying of the heavenly temple, declares: "Thus says the Lord GOD: No foreigner, uncircumcised in heart and flesh, of all the foreigners who are among the people of Israel, shall enter my sanctuary." (NRSV)

With all these and a score of other biblical passages Paul's antagonists in Galatia were thoroughly familiar. From their standpoint, remarks Barclay, "The opponents could argue that the only way for the Galatians to secure their identity as members of God's people and recipients of his promises was by accepting circumcision: the present half-way status was valueless" (*Obeying*, 54-55). To this Ehrman adds:

> Paul's opponents may simply have argued that while the covenant was now open to all who believed in Christ, God had not rescinded the rules of the covenant itself: it was an "everlasting" covenant, that is, one that would not be changed. Those who wished to belong to it must be circumcised, as God had said from the very beginning (*New Testament*, 306).

Apart from the Scriptural arguments forwarded by the opponents, Barclay helps us to understand why Gentiles would ever be inclined to submit to circumcision, especially given the disdain in which the practice was held in the Greco-Roman world (as tantamount to castration). As Christians, the readers of the letter would have been in a precarious social position. They had abandoned the pagan temples and, as a consequence, would have experienced social dislocation. "To dissociate oneself from the worship of family and community deities would entail a serious disruption in one's relationships with family, friends, fellow club members, business associates and civic authorities" (*Obeying*, 58). By accepting circumcision, the Galatians would have a recognizable group with which to identify (Philo makes this very point in *Spec. Laws* 1.9.51-52).[22]

> Although Jews may not have been popular, at least the Jewish religion had a long-established pedigree; it was not a suspicious novelty like the Christian movement. By becoming proselytes the Galatians could hope to identify themselves with the local synagogues and thus hold at least a more understandable and recognizable place in society. The adjustments required for this move were minor compared to their Christian conver-

---

[22] Cf. Das, *Paul and Jews*, 167, and see further the discussion of Galatians and Anatolian folk belief below.

INTRODUCTION

sion: the resocialization was a relatively straightforward matter.[23]

Additionally, it might have been argued that the Jerusalem apostles were themselves all circumcised Jews, meaning that if the Galatians wanted to identify with them, the "pillars" of the church (2:9), they too would have to become circumcised. The agitators would have pressed the case that the Christian movement involved Jewish identity, and for Gentiles that necessitated circumcision.[24]

But notwithstanding the various arguments drawn from the Hebrew Scriptures and the example of the mother church in Jerusalem, for Paul the rules of the game had changed: circumcision now means nothing—all that counts now is the new creation and faith working through love (5:6; 6:15). The Mosaic covenant, with its entrance rite of circumcision, has passed off the scene and has given way to a new covenant. As for the covenant with Abraham, itself signed and sealed by circumcision (Rom 4:11), it has found its realization in Christ, the true seed. As the ensuing exposition will affirm, Paul places his premium not on the Sinai covenant but on the bond with Abraham that preceded Sinai by 430 years (3:17). That state of affairs commenced with Yahweh's promise: "I will bless those who bless you, and him who curses you I will curse; and by you all the families of the earth shall be blessed" (Gen 12:3). Later, in anticipating the return of Abraham's seed from exile, the same Yahweh declares (echoing Gen 12:3): "At that time I will be the God of all the families of Israel and they shall be my people" (Jer 31:1).

Given, then, the eschatological realization of these promises of a household of God, the children of Abraham are now to be defined by their connection with Christ, not the mark in the flesh called circumcision (see on 3:29). So adamant is Paul on this point that circumcision for him is an exit ritual out of Christ, not an en-

---

[23] Barclay, *Obeying*, 60. Adams seconds Barclay's proposal and adds that the Galatians may have viewed themselves as an inferior group that needed to be assimilated to a superior group (*Constructing*, 222-24).

[24] Barclay, *Obeying*, 59. Fredriksen has shown that some later rabbinic authors allow for the possibility of "righteous Gentiles," mainly those who had abandoned idolatry. She concludes that such people would be admitted into the eschatological kingdom as Gentiles, as those saved graciously, "Apart from the works of the law" ("Judaism," 236-47). Even so, her sources considerably post-date Galatians and form a "minority report" on the subject. Certainly, in Paul's lifetime circumcision was high on the agenda of the opponents and served as the *sine qua non* of admission into the kingdom.

trance rite into the community of God's people (see on 5:3). In view of all these factors, we are not necessarily surprised that in one place Paul goes so far as to suggest that since his rivals have such a keen interest in removing foreskins, they should go all the way and emasculate themselves (5:12)!

Observance of the Law

If circumcision was axiomatic for the other missionaries, then the Torah *in toto* certainly was. The importance of law observance for any Jew of Paul's day goes without saying.[25] The Judaizers would have been guided by the working principle of the Mosaic covenant as voiced by Lev 18:5: "So you shall keep My statutes and My judgments, by which a man may live if he does them; I am the Lord" (NASB). The same perspective is evident in the recurring refrain of Deuteronomy: "This do and live" (Deut 4:1, 10, 40; 5:29-33; 6:1-2, 18, 24; 7:12-13; cf. 29:9, 29; 30:2, 6, 8, 10, 11, 16, 20; 31:12-13; 33:46). Given that the context of doing the law is the covenant graciously established at the time of the Exodus, the point of Lev 18:5 is hardly that of Israel having to earn God's favor or obtain life by performance. Rather, the people would continue to live in the land and enjoy the abundant blessing of God if they remained within the parameters of the law and turned away from idolatry—this is to "do the law" (see on 3:12). Therefore, the fundamental premise of the Jewish Christian missionaries was that all who would seek to be vindicated as the faithful people of God in the final judgment must assume the yoke of the law and live as Torah observant Jews. But what we must understand is that for them this was not a burden or another form of bondage (in contrast to Paul). Rather, *the law is the good news, it is the gospel.*[26]

In socio-theological terms, the crux of the Galatian controversy can be posed as one of boundaries. To modify somewhat T. L. Carter's analysis, the issue at stake is what boundaries now demarcate the people of Christ. Paul's Jewish Christian opponents defined the boundaries essentially in terms of law observance. In Carter's words, "Those who adhered to the Jewish works of the law could be classified as righteous insiders, while those who did not, including Paul and his uncircumcised Gentile converts, belonged outside, in the class of sinners" (*Paul*, 85-86). Appropri-

---

[25] See, e.g., Barclay, *Obeying*, 60-72; Dunn, *Jesus, Paul*, 216-25; id., *Theology of Paul*, 354-59; id., "Issue," 298-305.

[26] See Martyn's important discussion, *Galatians*, 121-22, 134-35.

ately, then, it would be the "insiders," not the "outsiders," who would be vindicated as the Lord's own in the day of judgment.

It is over against such a conception of the law that Paul says several things in reply. (1) The final judgment has already taken place in Christ, one does not have to wait until the consummation of this age. (2) Torah observance has nothing to do with one's ultimate vindication: only faith in Christ counts (see on 2:16). For him, the law has fulfilled its function of pointing to Christ (3:23-25) and for that reason can never be the measure of one's fidelity to God. Paul would have given his hearty assent to one of the great mottoes of the Reformation—*sola fide*. (3) The long-expected new exodus has now occurred; the new Israel has returned from exile.[27] However, this is an exodus that has delivered the people of God from *the bondage of the Torah* (see on 1:4; 2:4-5; 3:23-25; 4:1-11; 5:1-12)! What a different conception of the law than that entertained by the Judaizers, and what a different reading of the story of Israel! For Paul, that story has reached its climax in Christ, but in such a way as to mark a startling discontinuity between the ancient people and the community of the new age.[28]

To be sure, Paul has his own "boundary markers." But for him they are *Christ, his cross and the Spirit*. As far as he is concerned, the "insiders" are those who "in Christ" share in the eschatological age of the Spirit, which is entered solely on the basis of faith in Christ. His Gentile converts are, however, under attack from infiltrators preaching a false gospel of circumcision (1:7; 4:17; 5:7; 6:12). "Paul responds by redrawing the boundaries to emphasise that those who are under the law are sinful outsiders, because they still belong to the present evil age and are under the power of sin" (Carter, *Paul*, 86. See the entire discussion of pp. 86-123.).

As Carter further explains, in the context in which Paul lived and worked, the main boundary markers that set observant Jews apart from Hellenistic culture were abstention from participation in other cults, separation at meals, male circumcision and sabbath observance (I might add purity laws) (ibid., 92). However, not all Jews rejected Hellenistic culture: some embraced it while remaining self-consciously Jewish, whereas others became assimilated to the point of losing their Jewish identity.[29] The boundaries separat-

---

[27] See Keesmaat, *Paul*; W. D. Davies, *Engagements*, 123-40.
[28] See throughout Wright, *New Testament*; id., *Jesus*; and Hays, *Faith*, xxxv-xxxviii. The place of Israel's story in Galatians (and Romans) is debated back and forth in B. W. Longenecker (ed.), *Dynamics*.
[29] See Barclay, *Jews*, 138-80, 336-68 and 104-12, 321-26 respectively.

ing the Jewish community from the Hellenistic world were thus constantly subject to erosion, and Paul's insistence that Gentile believers need not observe food laws, circumcision and sabbath would have led to his being perceived by his fellow Jews as someone who had abandoned his Jewish identity and assimilated to Hellenism. Those who opposed Paul thus perceived him as a traitor, which is why Paul suffered persecution for the cross of Christ (5:11). Those who opposed Paul in Jerusalem, Antioch and Galatia were, therefore, attempting to reinforce the boundaries between Judaism and Hellenism by insisting on circumcision, food laws and sabbath observance.

Apart from the law's twofold function as a wall of separation between God's people and the outside world and as guarantor of ultimate vindication, it was none other than the Torah that served to keep in check the impulses of the flesh. As noted above, the primary biblical injunction was that Israel was to walk in the law and enjoy life as a result (Lev 18:5, et al.). The nation was to be holy as God himself is holy (Lev 19:2; 20:26). deSilva points to certain post-biblical texts that preserve and promote this "prime directive" to Israel (*Introduction*, 503-4). Besides the *Letter of Aristeas* and the works of Philo, 4 Maccabees provides an instructive illustration. According to this specimen of Jewish literature, unchecked by the Torah, including the dietary regulations, "The passions of the flesh would clamor louder than the reasoning faculty, derailing a person's commitment to virtue and ability to walk in line with virtue" (ibid., 503).[30] He then comments that this is precisely the kind of argumentation that the rival teachers would have had ready at hand when they encountered the Galatian converts, "Still painfully at the mercy of their fleshly impulses and desires." This is why "the rival teachers presented the Torah as the best trainer in virtue, the way to perfection in terms of ethical progress, a proven discipline for mastering the 'passions of the flesh'." By way of counterbalance, then, Paul would have to demonstrate that the Galatians had already received everything necessary to rise above such passions and embody the virtues God sought for his people (ibid.,

---

[30] On this dimension of 4 Maccabees, see further deSilva, *Apocrypha*, 359-69. In later rabbinic theology, it was just the Torah that was given to counteract the "evil inclination" (*yetzer harah*) in human beings. On the "evil inclination," see W. D. Davies, *Paul*, 20-35; Moore, *Judaism*, 1.479-96; Schechter, *Aspects*, 242-92; Montefiore/Loewe, *Anthology*, §§757-811; Urbach, *Sages*, 471-83; Str-B, 4.1.466-83. For the tradition that the Torah was given to counteract the evil *yetzer*, see Montefiore/Loewe, *Anthology*, §§326-32. At more length, see my *Faith*, 129, n. 86.

504). In brief, what they needed, and had in fact received, was the Spirit.[31]

The Vision of the Messiah

As stated above, the core question of Galatians is the choice between Christ and the Torah. At the end of the day, the overarching issue is differing visions of the Messiah, that is, *christology* with its manifold implications. For Paul, the article of standing or falling of the church is Christ himself. This means that, both in Galatians and in Paul generally, even more basic than *sola fide* is *solus Christus*. Paul's method of argumentation in this letter, as in all the others, is historical. His is not a topical discussion of faith and works or of legalism versus grace. Rather, his point is that continued devotion to the Torah exalts the law above Christ and is tantamount to idolatry; it is like being in bondage all over again. Effectively, the message of Galatians is encapsulated by the central statement of Colossians: Christ must have the preeminence in all things (1:18). Gaventa says it so well:

> Although the issue that prompts Paul to write to Galatian Christians arises from a conflict regarding the law, in addressing that problem Paul takes the position that the gospel proclaims Jesus Christ crucified to be the inauguration of a new creation. *This new creation allows for no supplementation or augmentation by the law or any other power or loyalty.* What the Galatians seek in the law is a certainty that they have a firm place in the *ekklēsia* of God and that they know what God requires of them. It is precisely this certainty, and every other form of certainty, that Paul rejects with his claim about the exclusivity and singularity of Jesus Christ.[32]

That christology is at the heart of Paul's controversy with the circumcision party is underscored by the relation of the Messiah to the Torah in the theology of the rival evangelists. Martyn very

---

[31] deSilva is right in subtitling his chapter on Galatians: "Walking in Line with the Spirit."

[32] Gaventa, "Singularity," 159 (italics mine). Similarly, Hafemann concludes that the essential distinction between Paul and Qumran (and I would say Judaism more broadly considered) is not the law per se nor the nature of the eschatological community as such, but his understanding of the person and work of Christ and their impact on both the law and the nature of the people of God ("Spirit," 188-89).

helpfully distills the thinking of the opponents as regards the Christ of the law. The Teachers (Martyn's consistent designation for this group) viewed Jesus as the completion of the ministry of Moses:

> They view God's Christ in the light of God's law, rather than the law in the light of Christ. This means in their christology, Christ is secondary to the law.... For them the Messiah is the Messiah of the Law, deriving his identity from the fact that he confirms—and perhaps even normatively interprets—the Law. If Christ is explicitly involved in the Teachers' commission to preach to the Gentiles, that must be so because he has deepened their passion to take to the nations God's gift of gifts, the Spirit-dispensing Law that will guide them in their daily life.[33]

The issue of the Holy Spirit is addressed in the relevant portions of the commentary.[34] Suffice it to say here that the law teachers were insisting that the gift of the Spirit is insolubly linked to the Torah. And given the contexts in which the Spirit is promised to an Israel returned from exile (e.g., Isa 4:2-6; 11:1-2; 32:15; 42:1; 44:3; 61:1; cf. 63:11; Ezek 36:26-27; 37:14; 39:29; Joel 2:28-29), they were proceeding consistently with a face value reading of the Prophets. In a nutshell, for them Torah and Spirit are conjoined twins, and it was just the role of the Messiah to keep intact what God had united from of old. To be sure, Paul and his competitors both held to an apocalyptic world view in which the Spirit had been quenched until the time of the end; and both believed that the end had arrived with Jesus of Nazareth, who has inaugurated the age of the Spirit. But the radical difference between the two was the place of the law now that the Spirit has been outpoured. In this regard, Paul is 180 degrees away from the opponents. His conception of the relation of law and Spirit is based on his experience of the eschatological Spirit. As Fee explains, for Paul the line is not from the Old Testament to the New but from his experience of the Spirit as God's empowering presence back to the Old (*Presence*, 915).

It is precisely to this experience that Paul appeals in 3:2: "This is the only thing I want to find out from you: did you receive the Spirit by the works of the Law, or by hearing with faith" (NASB)?

---

[33] Martyn, *Galatians*, 124-25. Likewise, De Boer, "Quotation," 383, n. 53.

[34] Systematic treatments are provided by Fee, *Presence*, 367-471, 803-903; Lull, *Spirit*; Cosgrove, *Cross*; Williams, "Justification;" Schnelle, *Paul*, 284-86.

INTRODUCTION

Therefore, Who really possesses the Spirit? This is the crucial question and lies at the heart of Paul's dispute with the other missionaries. For the circumcisers, it is the law-people who have the Spirit, and only the Torah can guarantee the blessings of the Spirit (Cosgrove, *Cross*, 87-114). But, in such conspicuous contrast, for Paul the Spirit brings an end to Torah observance.[35] Perhaps the most trenchant commentary is provided by the apostle himself: "Now the Lord is the Spirit, and *where the Spirit of the Lord is, there is freedom*" (from the law) (2 Cor 3:17).

The New Perspective on Paul

All of the above data serve to reinforce the conviction that, in order to understand the conflict between Pauline and Judaistic Christianity, it is vital to have historically accurate views of the place and function of the law within the Judaism of the first Christian century. The traditional approach to the subject, in commentaries on Galatians from the Reformation onward, has been to read Paul's controversy with Judaism and the Judaizers in the light of Luther's struggle with medieval Catholicism. According to that interpretation, in Galatians Paul sharpens his sword against a system of works-righteousness legalism that sought insure standing before God on the basis of personal merit, a kind of "justification by decency."[36] However, since the appearance of E. P. Sanders' *Paul and Palestinian Judaism* in 1977, a "New Perspective" on Paul in relation to his contemporaries has emerged.[37] The phrase was

---

[35] Fee, *Paul*, 101-3. Gorman, then, is quite right to entitle his survey of Galatians: "The Sufficiency of the Cross and Spirit" (*Apostle*, 183-226). "Whereas the circumcisers may be called messianic covenantal nomists, Paul, we may say, is a *cruciform covenantal charismatic*. He is focused on the crucified Messiah whose death unleashes the age of the Spirit, by whom believers fulfill the covenant through cruciform faith and love—apart from circumcision and the Law" (ibid., 191, italics his).

[36] Bruce, *Flame*, 336, writing of the soteriology of Pelagius. Rapa's recent work defines "legalism" as "insistence on *Torah* observance as the means to become 'complete' Christians, or to 'gain favor' with God; i.e., the necessity to *do* something in order to become God's children" (*Meaning*, 168). It seems to me that the two italicized words, *Torah* and *do*, are the most telling. The Judaizers were not insisting that the Galatians do "something," but specifically that they engage in "Torah" observance. To be sure, Paul's opponents wanted these people to become "complete Christians," but that is not the same as "gaining favor." It is, rather, honoring the Torah as it constituted faithfulness to the God of Israel.

[37] The New Perspective and matters relating to it, such as Paul and the law, Paul's relation to his fellow Jews and justification/righteousness, have been surveyed

coined by James Dunn ("New Perspective," as reprinted in *Jesus, Paul*, 183-214).[38] For good reason, Moisés Silva calls the "New Perspective" the "Sanders/Dunn trajectory" ("Law," 341).

The now famous phrase employed by Sanders to bespeak his understanding of the Judaism of the Second Temple and rabbinic periods is "covenantal nomism."[39] According to Sanders:

> Covenantal nomism is the view that one's place in God's plan is established on the basis of the covenant and that the covenant requires as the proper response of man his obedience to its commandments, while providing means of atonement for transgression.... Obedience maintains one's position in the covenant, but it does not earn God's grace as such.... Righteousness in Judaism is a term which implies the maintenance of status among the group of the elect (*Paul*, 75, 420, 544).

In one place, he summarizes his position under the following points:

> (1) God has chosen Israel and (2) given the law. The law implies both (3) God's promise to maintain the election and (4) the requirement to obey. (5) God rewards obedience and punishes transgression. (6) The law provides for means of atonement, and atonement results in (7) maintenance or reestablishment of the covenantal relationship. (8) All those who are maintained in the covenant by obedience, atonement and God's mercy belong to the group which will be saved. An important interpretation of the first and last points is that election and ultimately salvation are considered to be by God's mercy rather than human achievement (ibid., 422).

---

many times. See, with responses pro and con, Thompson, *New Perspective*; Westerholm, *Perspectives*, 3-258; id., "New Perspective;" Carson/Moo, *Introduction*, 375-85, 470-72; deSilva, *Introduction*, 518-19; O'Brien, "Justification;" Kruse, *Paul*, 27-53; Koperski, *Paul*; Kuula, *Law*, 5-33; Das, *Paul and Jews*, 1-16.

[38] The many and various works of Dunn devoted to the New Perspective are documented in the bibliography. Note most recently the collection entitled, *The New Perspective on Paul: Collected Essays*.

[39] Strangely overlooked is Longenecker's *Paul*, which predates Sanders by thirteen years. Longenecker had already spoken of a "reacting nomism" that characterized the Judaism of Paul's day (ibid., 78).

INTRODUCTION

Dunn further clarifies Sanders' outlook:

> This covenant relationship was regulated by the law, not as a way of entering the covenant, or of gaining merit, but as the way of living *within* the covenant; and that included the provision of sacrifice and atonement for those who confessed their sins and thus repented.... This attitude Sanders characterized by the now well known phrase "covenantal nomism"—that is, "the maintenance of status" among the chosen people of God by observing the law given by God as part of that covenant relationship.[40]

To these explanations, I would add that "covenantal nomism" can be summarized under three basic propositions. (1) Israel became the people of God by his electing grace as manifested in the Exodus. (2) The covenant forms the context of law-keeping. In other words, Israel is bound to keep the law not in order to earn salvation, but in order to maintain her side of the covenant bond. Thus, the stress falls not on legalism but on fidelity to the covenant and preservation of the community. (3) Sanders, therefore, epitomizes his understanding of Jewish religion with the phrases "getting in" and "staying in." One "gets in" the covenant by being born into the Jewish community, which was formed in the first place by the electing grace of God. One "stays in" the covenant by keeping the law, not perfectly and certainly not for the purpose of establishing a claim on God, but out of a sincere intention to remain loyal to the God of grace. And if one sinned, God has provided the sacrifices to atone for sin and restore one to his standing within the community.

Dunn builds on Sanders' construction of predestruction Judaism, but levels the criticism that "Sanders' Paul hardly seems to be addressing Sanders' Judaism" ("New Perspective," 121). In other words, the Paul of Sanders takes his countrymen to task for precisely the same reason that Luther did! Dunn thus distances himself from Sanders' Paul by defining the apostle's phrase "the works of the law" not as a generalized principle of obedience for the purpose of earning salvation but as those works done in response to the covenant in order to maintain the bond between God

---

[40] Dunn, *Romans*, 1.lxv. See additionally his *Theology of Paul*, 335-40.

and Israel (the works of "staying in").[41] Dunn does maintain that "the works of the law" encompasses the whole Torah, but within the period of the Second Temple certain aspects of the law became especially prominent as the boundary and identity markers of the Jewish people: prominently circumcision, food laws, purity laws and sabbath.

Dunn has frequently been misrepresented on this point, as though he restricts "the works of the law" to the "boundary markers" without allowing that the whole Torah is in view when Paul employs the phrase.[42] But just the opposite is the case. He states, in point of fact, that circumcision and the other ordinances were *not* the only distinguishing traits of Jewish self-identity. However, they were the focal point of the Hellenistic attack on the Jews during the Maccabean period. As such, they became *the acid tests of one's loyalty to Judaism.* "In short...the particular regulations of circumcision and food laws [et al.] were important not in themselves, but because they *focused* Israel's distinctiveness and made visible Israel's claims to be a people set apart, were the clearest points which differentiated the Jews from the nations. The law was coterminous with Judaism" ("Works," 526).[43] That there is a darker side to Paul's deployment of "works of the law" is not to be doubted, especially as the phrase intersects with others such as "under sin," "under law" and the "curse of the law" (see the final section note to 2:16). Nevertheless, such works pertain to practices commanded *by the Torah*, not works in the abstract or works generalized beyond their specific function of *regulating the covenant with Israel*. Given that the law is a "package deal," "the works of the law," as much as anything, mark Jewish ethnic identity and

---

[41] This understanding of "works of the law" has recently been confirmed by Abegg's study of 4QMMT, in which the equivalent Hebrew phrase, *miqsat maasē ha-torah*—"some of the works of the law"—is found ("4QMMT") (see on 2:16).

[42] Dunn justifiably issues a note of protest in *Theology of Paul*, 358, n. 97. This frequent misrepresentation of Dunn has been perpetuated as recently as Das, *Paul*, 155-60 (seconding Fitzmyer, *Paul*, 23); Esler, *Galatians*, 183; Carson/Moo, *Introduction*, 466. This is why I have added italics to the quotation from David deSilva as quoted above (*Introduction*, 505, n. 9). See also on 2:16.

[43] This essay is likewise reprinted in *Jesus, Paul*, 215-41. See further Dunn's "Yet once more." Hafemann is right that "the works of the law" have reference to what the (whole) law itself commanded or enjoined rather than an isolated subset of the law, such as ethnic distinctives and ritual purity ("Spirit," 178, n. 24). That the law is coterminous with Judaism is actually affirmed by Das, who writes that the Mosaic law and the covenant were considered to be two sides of the same coin, e.g., Sir 39:8; *Pss. Sol.* 10:4; *Mek. Bahodesh* 6 (on Exod 20:6) (*Paul and Jews*, 43, n. 65, with other literature).

INTRODUCTION

symbolize comprehensive obedience to the obligations of the Sinai covenant (see on 2:16).

As expected, not everyone is happy with this reading of the Judaism of Paul's day and, consequently, with the more recent evaluation of the law in Paul, especially as it has a bearing on issues such as justification. Since 1977, tons of literature have rolled off the presses in response to various aspects of this "Sanders-Dunn trajectory."[44] Nevertheless, the ensuing commentary assumes a modified form of this "New Perspective" and seeks to expound Galatians within its framework.[45] No doubt, Paul would have been adamantly opposed to any scheme of self-salvation based on human performance (passages such as Rom 4:4-5; Eph 2:8-9; Titus 3:5 have direct applicability). Nevertheless, it is the underlying assumption of this work that historically he has in his sights the works of fidelity to the Mosaic covenant ("staying in") which would stand one in good stead on the day of judgment. In this regard, the Reformers were correct that if justification is not by Jewish tradition, then it is not by church tradition either. Salvation is not by "religion," however conceived. This is the hermeneutical "significance" or application of the historical issue at stake: only Christ can save, not religion or tradition. Christ must be, in the familiar phrase, a "personal savior." When Paul became a Christian, he left "religion" and came to Christ.

---

[44] Mention can be made of only a few recent volumes: Schreiner, *Law*; Stuhlmacher, *Revisiting*; Das, *Paul*; Kim, *Perspective*; Gathercole, *Boasting*; Westerholm, *Perspectives*; Carson/O'Brien/Seifrid (eds.), *Justification*, esp. vol. 2. I have responded in some detail to vol. 1 of these two books (*Defense*, 59-105). In particular, I have sought to demonstrate that Mark Seifrid's bifurcation of creation and covenant as pertains to righteousness ("righteousness Language") is illegitimate. Another category of literature is comprised of works that offer some criticisms of the New Perspective and yet agree in the main that Paul does not take issue with a merit-based system of soteriology (e.g., Kuula, *Law* [note pp. 65, 73]). In principle, this applies to Avemarie's much cited *Torah und Leben*. Avemarie postulates that in the rabbinic materials there is a tension between God's grace and the works required of Israel. But even so, Avemarie does endorse "covenantal nomism" as an appropriate description of Tannaitic Judaism (ibid., 584).

[45] The modifications are set out in my "New Perspective" (= *Defense*, 1-28). Frequently, Sanders and other have been criticized for not recognizing the variegated nature of Second Temple Judaism. Actually, this is not true, because no leading advocate of the New Perspective is unaware of the diversity factor in the sources. See, for example, Dunn, *Partings*, 18; Garlington, *Obedience*, 263-64. In any event, Wright is correct to insist that variety is no excuse for smuggling back in an anachronistic Pelagian, semi-Pelagian or medieval works-righteousness vision of Judaism (*Perspective*, 109).

What Time Is It?

Modern scholarship has increasingly come to recognize that in Paul generally and in Galatians in particular there is a decided apocalyptic element (the movement is chronicled by Matlock, *Unveiling*). As a simplified definition of Apocalyptic, we might call it the hope of a new heavens and a new earth: it is the new creation breaking into the old (as per Isa 65:17-25).[46] The latter Jewish apocalyptic movement took over this dimension of the prophetic message and exaggerated its essential elements in order to make a point, namely, that although this age and the age to come are hopelessly in conflict, God will eventually overwhelm the evil powers and usher in the age of bliss.[47]

> Apocalypticism sees world history in the grip of warring forces, God and Satan, the spirits of truth and error, light and darkness. The struggle of God with man, and of man with sin, evil, and death becomes objectified into a cosmic struggle. The world, captive to evil powers and principalities which have been given authority in the era of divine wrath, can be freed only by the divine might. But the day of God's salvation and judgment dawns. The old age has moved to its allotted end and the age of consummation is at hand, the age of the vindication of the elect and the redemption of the world.... In short, the apocalypticist lives in a world in which the sovereignty of God is the sole hope of salvation, and in the earnestness of his faith and the vividness of his hope he is certain that God is about to act. The faithful will be given the gift of salvation (Cross, *Library*, 69, n. 3).

Martyn in particular has explored the apocalyptic outlook of Galatians and has asked the appropriate question, What time is it?[48]

---

[46] It should be clarified that "apocalyptic" is to be taken as a theological concept rather than a designation of a literary genre (cf. Matlock, *Unveiling*, 311). Paul did not produce an "apocalypse," but his theology of the fulfillment of the prophetic Scriptures in Christ bear the character of an apocalyptic theology.

[47] Handy overviews of Apocalyptic may be found in Wright, *New Testament*, 280-338; Dunn, *Unity*, 310-16.

[48] Martyn, *Galatians*, 97-105; id., *Issues*, 111-123. See further Dunn, *Theology of Galatians*, 46-52; Beker, *Paul*, passim; Hall, "Arguing;" Das, *Paul and Jews*, 34-36; Gorman, *Apostle*, 21-23; Wright, *Perspective*, 50-58; Segal, *Paul*, 158-61; and

INTRODUCTION

As noted in the commentary, Galatians contains certain bracketing ideas that provide an interpretive key to its contents. One of these ideas is a powerful apocalyptic signal. According to 1:3, Jesus gave himself to rescue us from "the present evil age;" and a closing declaration is that what counts is the "new creation" (6:15). In between, Paul constructs a series of what Martyn calls "apocalyptic antinomies," or polar opposites, that is, forces or qualities characteristic of each age respectively. These have been set in motion by the sending of God's Son and the Spirit of his Son.[49]

On the one side are such entities as sin, death, the law and the flesh; on the other are Spirit, life, justification and freedom. Martyn points out that at several crucial points in the letter Paul uses the noun "revelation" (*apokalupsis*) and the verb "reveal" (*apokaluptō*) to describe the end-time reality inaugurated by Christ and the Spirit (e.g., 1:13, 16; 3:23; 6:14). Most striking of all is the sequence of antinomies developed in the story of Hagar and Sarah in 4:21-31 (see Martyn, *Issues*, 25). Thus, the whole of Galatians is set within the framework of a new era which has come to displace the old.[50] One day that displacement will be complete, but for the time-being the two are in conflict, as evident particularly from 5:17: "The desires of the flesh are against the Spirit, and the desires of the Spirit are against the flesh; for these are opposed to each other, to prevent you from doing what you would" (RSV).

In sum, Paul's response to his afflicted converts is predicated upon the fundamental conviction that

---

especially De Boer's important discussion, "Quotation," 373-75. De Boer notes that in apocalyptic there is a decided spatial element. This serves to illuminate Gal 4:26: the "above Jerusalem." For further literature, see ibid., 373, n. 10.

[49] The drawback to Martyn's apocalyptic hermeneutic is his claim that Paul's depiction of God's apocalyptic invasion of the cosmos in Christ "banishes any trace of pre-Christ linear salvation-history" ("Events"). Given the endeavors of the rival missionaries, Martyn reasons that Paul's insistence on the singularity of the gospel of necessity had to be anti-salvation history (ibid., 176). In so saying, Martyn seems to have disregarded the story of Israel that underlies so much of the Galatian letter, especially the exodus traditions.

[50] See Cummins, *Paul*, 106-9; B. W. Longenecker, *Triumph*, 35-67; Silva "Structures." Hubbard is right that the continuity between the apocalyptic and Pauline paradigms is evident in that both provide the answer to the human dilemma. The discontinuity between the two consists in the way that each respectively analyzes the causes of the dilemma. Whereas apocalyptic authors stress extrinsic factors (Satan and the Gentiles), Paul singles out intrinsic phenomena (sin and the flesh) (*Creation*, 238). His distinction is accepted with the qualification that in Galatians (and Romans) "flesh" is associated with the extrinsic factor of the law, which made so many provisions for that dimension of human nature.

through Christ and the Spirit they are participants in the now inaugurated reign of God, even if they must still do battle with the dying vestiges of the old age—a sphere which they have left behind and to which they must not return.[51]

The question, What time is it? is a two-edged sword in Paul's hands. On the one side, his answer, as Wright observes, is radically different from the Jewish answer. "As a Pharisee he would have answered: we are living in the last days before the great act of God within history to defeat the pagans and liberate Israel. As a Christian he answered: we are living in the first days after the great act of God within history to defeat sin and death and liberate the whole cosmos" (*Paul*, 141). Or, phrased somewhat differently, "*The one true God had done for Jesus of Nazareth, in the middle of time, what Saul had thought he was going to do for Israel at the end of time*" (ibid., 36, italics his; cf. Fitzmyer, *Pauline Theology*, 8-11). What time is it? then, marks the main difference between Judaism and Christianity.

On the other side, Paul, in Galatians, is not combating non-Christian Judaism but rather a group of individuals who confessed Jesus as the Christ and believed that the age of the Spirit had dawned with him. To this extent they were "Christians" (as indicated by Luke's ascription to them of the predicate "believers" in Acts 15:5). However, they were Christians of a different stripe than Paul. Their conviction was that the advent of the Messiah, the servant of the Torah, and his Spirit effected no change in the way God had always identified and received his people within the covenant relationship. They were still to be bounded by the law and find their self-definition by remaining within its parameters. That to Paul such was a wrongheaded conception goes without saying. In Thielman's estimation (*Theology*, 268):

---

[51] Cummins, *Paul*, 108. Cummins ably distills the entire Galatian crisis as seen from the vantage point of this apocalyptic setting: "Paul's reaction to the contentious Galatian scenario is governed by a Jewish apocalyptic conceptual schema—as typified by Daniel 7-12 and its response to the archetypal Maccabean crisis—but as now radically reworked through Christ and the Spirit; that is, those (afflicted) Galatians conformed to their eschatological redeemer, Messiah Jesus, and demarcated by the long-suffering Spirit comprise the people of God who even now participate in the inaugurated new creation. Conversely, those drawn to the Agitators and their coercive 'non-gospel' of circumcision and Torah-obedience are embracing a Jewish way of life no less bankrupt than their former Gentile idolatry, and so again become enslaved to the old sphere ('world', 'flesh', 'man')" (ibid., 114).

INTRODUCTION

> By turning back to the era of the Mosaic law, however, the Galatians and their teachers have started a futile attempt to swim against the current of salvation history. They have denied the obvious—that God's inclusion of Gentiles into 6 people by faith in Christ is the fulfillment of his promise to bless all the Gentiles through Abraham—and have instead claimed that Abraham's inheritance can only be realized through the law, and thus through Jews and Jewish proselytes (3:18). By reintroducing the law, they have regressed in time to the period of the law's curse and have decided to live under that curse rather than under God's eschatologically provided remedy for it (3:10-12). They have preferred life under a child-minder to adult life (3:24), life under trustees and guardians to life as the grown son who has come into his inheritance (4:1-7), and life in an enslaved, earthly Jerusalem to the eschatological life of the heavenly Jerusalem (4:25-26). For the Galatians, such a life is no better than their life under the idolatrous practices of their former pagan religions (4:8-10). To regress to the Mosaic law is, in short, to desert God (1:6) and to be cut off from Christ (5:4).

Hays, then, is quite right that "Galatians is not an anti-Jewish text. It is, rather, a manifesto against distortions of the gospel introduced by *Christian* preachers who *subordinate the law to Christ*" (*Galatians*, 195, first italics his, second mine). Therefore, to draw upon Witherington:

> Paul's letter to the Galatians is neither antinomian in character nor is it an attack on legalism. It is a salvation historical argument about *recognizing what time it is, and what covenant God's people are and are not now under*. The Law of Christ is not the Mosaic Law intensified or in a new guise. It is the new eschatological dictums appropriate for those living as new creatures albeit in an already and not yet situation (*Grace*, 345, italics mine).

From this vantage point, the specific answer to the question, What time is it? or, more pointedly, What is the character of this time? signals the distinction between Pauline Christianity and the religion of the law teachers. For the latter, Israel's election remains bound to the Torah; but for Paul election and eschatology have now been reconstructed around the Jesus the Messiah and the Spirit (Wright, *Perspective*, 135-50).

The question respecting the character of the time, in turn, has an obvious bearing on another question, What is Galatians "all about?" In brief, it is "about" Christ and the Spirit who displace the law, thus enabling Paul to redefine what descent from Abraham and sonship to God and mean in the eschatological "now." Or, as Garland writes so ably ("Defense," 180):

> As a result of Christ's work, things have changed. Paul uses intricate arguments to persuade the Galatians that they have made a serious error in submitting to the influence of the troublers who promote the status quo with their emphasis on works of law and ultimately nullify the grace of God. From a Jewish perspective, they are the radical arguments of an extremist who has lost his senses. Is it any wonder that the one who wrote these words had the synagogue's punishment of thirty-nine lashes inflicted on him at least five times (2 Cor. 11:24) and that he earned Jewish animosity almost everywhere he went? But his arguments stem from the revelation he received about Christ (1:12) whose death and resurrection have transformed this present evil age so that wholly new possibilities await those of faith. Why return to the old order and its regimen that leads only to curse and death? Freedom, justification, and life are promises now fulfilled in Christ which extend to all humankind.

Galatians and Anatolian Folk Belief

From the sociological point of view, it would be extremely helpful to pinpoint the geographical locale of the Galatian churches. But even with relative uncertainty, we may assume that the readers had come under the pervasive influence of the emperor cult and, in all probability, had experienced firsthand the worship of the Anatolian Mother Goddess. The first mentioned is discussed in the commentary (see on 1:22 and the first section note to 4:8-11); and here the latter will occupy our attention.[52]

In particular, we will follow (with some modification) Arnold's discussion of why the Galatians were "so quickly" abandon-

---

[52] See S. Elliott, *Cutting*, as summarized in her "Mother;" Arnold, "Folk Belief;" Thielman, "Folk Belief."

ing Christ for the Torah ("Folk Belief"). The commentary on 1:6 will suggest that that the adverb "quickly" has Israel connotations, in that Paul echoes Exod 32:8; Deut 9:16; Judg 2:17, all three referring to Israel's abandonment of Yahweh for idols. But apart from this salvation-historical impact of "quickly," there are decided sociological reasons why Paul's readers were prepared to surrender so readily to the Jewish Christian missionaries. In a nutshell, the Judaizing gospel offered in principle what these former pagans had given up in their worship of the Mountain Mother and other deities of the Anatolian region.

Arnold begins by summarizing S. Elliott's thesis respecting Gal 4:21-5:1 (see the introduction to 4:21-31). Paul developed the story of Hagar and Sarah because it would communicate so powerfully to his Anatolian readers. In short, just as Jews under the old covenant live in slavery to a mother (Hagar) corresponding to a mountain (Sinai), in a similar fashion, the Galatians also once lived in slavery to a mother (the Anatolian Mother Goddess) who corresponded to a mountain. The solution, then, is for the Galatians to reject both mountain mothers and live in the freedom that Christ provides.

But while the great Mountain Mother played a central role in the popular piety of Anatolia, she was not the only deity worshipped throughout the land. This is where a study of inscriptional evidence over the past century comes into play. To a considerable degree, these inscriptions have illuminated the popular religious beliefs of the people of this region. To cut to the chase, Arnold explains that these are commonly referred to as "confessional" inscriptions. In his view, however, a more accurate designation for this genre of inscriptions would be "propitiatory" or "appeasement" inscriptions. Each of them is essentially a monument (stele), erected to appease one or more of the local deities who have been offended and, as a consequence, have struck the worshipper with some kind of serious malady as a punishment. The only recourse for the afflicted person is to admit the error to the deity and pay to have a stele set up to praise and honor the power of said deity.

There is little doubt that the propitiatory steles engendered a climate of respect and fear of the gods. The very notion of erecting monuments—"religious billboards"—in public places to be read by all who passed by would certainly have added to this climate of fear. The power of these deities was displayed for all to see by proclaiming their power to punished people who did not give heed to their purity requirements, ritual observances, or who sinned in some other fashion. It could be that the spread of Christianity in the region had led to the erection of a greater number of these inscriptions, in order to solidify the rule of the territorial gods in a given area against the competing new religion. In any event, the practice of constructing propitiatory steles, along with the beliefs that they represented, was part of the traditional mentality and practice of the local peoples.[53]

All this paves the way for understanding why the Galatians were so susceptible to the message of Paul's opponents. As Arnold explains, the missionary opponents must have spoken persuasively and with some degree of (biblical) logic to support their case. But was there anything more than this that predisposed the Galatians to their message? No doubt, some of the Galatians were already proselytes and Jewish sympathizers prior to their conversion. This may very well have inclined them to accept the gospel of the opponents, who wanted to reclaim the Torah for these new Christian communities. But there may be something more than this. There were a few key features of their pre-conversion religious lives that may very well have attracted them to the form of the gospel preached by the rival missionaries who came to "correct" what Paul had proclaimed to them initially. These "extra-biblical" attractions (my phrase) may be reduced to the following.

(1) *The obligation to fulfill cultic requirements to maintain a favorable standing with the deity.* When the opponents came insisting on circumcision and other rites of Judaism as essential for these new believers to observe, their teaching would have resonated with the experience the Galatians had with the gods in their pre-Christian practice. Performing the proper rites, not neglecting religious obligations, keeping the appointed festival times, keeping one's vow, and maintaining ritual purity was vital to keep from experiencing the judgment of the gods. To disregard any of these obligations could lead to the anger of the god and divine punishment. The Galatians would have been particularly sensitive to the

---

[53] Arnold notes that these inscriptions are located in the approximate context of the Christian communities that Paul planted in central Anatolia, both chronologically and geographically. Although none of the inscriptions were discovered in the Galatian cities, there is reason to believe that the same kind of piety exhibited by the western Anatolian inscriptions would have characterized the worship of the Gentiles in central Anatolia. This is rendered more likely by the fact that the deities mentioned in the inscriptions were worshipped in both the northern and southern Galatian cities. Perhaps the most prominent deity of the propitiatory inscriptions, a lunar god, had a major cult center in Antioch of Pisidia. The relevance of these inscriptions for describing the folk piety of central Anatolia is further strengthened if it is correct to infer that this form of piety had its roots in indigenous Anatolian and Hittite beliefs and practices.

maintenance of ritual purity, so as to prevent the anger of the gods. Infractions of ritual purity often carried stiff penalties.

If the readers of Galatians entered the Christian community from a background of needing to maintain strict adherence to cultic requirements, the message of the Jewish Christian missionaries would have resonated well with them. Their deeply ingrained sensitivity to the importance of observing cultic requirements of the gods would have made the Galatians susceptible to the demands of the Judaizers. They had lived every single day of their lives fearing the consequences of sinning against the objects of their worship. Against this backdrop, Paul's gospel would have been unprecedented good news of extraordinary and even incredible freedom. And when the Jewish Christian missionaries came with their message about the cruciality of Torah observance to please God and obtain salvation, it would have been discouraging to the Galatians, but it would have made sense nonetheless. That is how they already assumed they would need to respond to a deity.

(2) *The obligation to perform good works to maintain a favorable standing with the deity.* A fairly stringent moral code characterized many of the religions of central Anatolia during the Roman period. Numerous monuments depict the Anatolian gods Hosios ("Holy") and Dikaios ("Just") carrying a set of scales and a measuring rod to weigh and measure the deeds of their worshippers. These deities, along with other local gods and goddesses, sought to compel the observance of a wide range of ethical behavior. They took grave offense at thievery, sexual improprieties, acts of hatred and bitterness, violence and witchcraft. When these deities became aware of the infractions against their moral law, they often exacted a harsh and immediate punishment against the violator.

The central Anatolian deities maintained a moral code that was not to be trifled with. Although there was no written law in cultic books for people to read and learn, the steles stood as firm reminders of the kinds of moral offenses that could result in stern punishment from the local gods. Undoubtedly, there was a sensitivity among Anatolian peoples not to overstep these moral boundaries for fear of offending these deities and bringing divine wrath upon themselves. Those from this area who became Christians upon hearing Paul's gospel would certainly have retained this sensitivity. Good behavior as a means of averting the awful punishing wrath of the deity may very well have been part of the religious belief-structure these new Christians would have brought with them into the church.

My only qualification is that Paul's "works of the flesh" (5:19-21) bear an uncommon resemblance to the prohibitions found in the Anatolian inscriptions and other Greco-Roman literature. Paul had his own set of ethical requirements, and they were not to be trifled with either. Nevertheless, the tone of the inscriptions and their detailed attention to moral infractions find a ready parallel in the law of Moses. Such an analogue would make all the more relevant Paul's identification of the Torah as "the elements of *the world*" or the old creation (4:3) and devotion to it as tantamount to the service of pagan deities (4:8-10).

(3) *The Pauline gospel, the gospel of the opponents and the temptation to defect.* "Sin" is one of the outstanding features of the inscriptions. In a very real sense, the wages of sin were death—not as the forfeiture of life in the hereafter but as severe physical punishment and even death. According to Arnold, for people converted from the central Anatolian cults, the Pauline gospel must have provided an exhilarating experience of freedom. Paul brought them the message of a loving and merciful God who has finally and forever forgiven their sins. Rather than pay for their sins in the present life, Paul shared with them the good news that a propitiatory act had already taken place. The Lord Jesus Christ "gave himself for our sins" (1:3-4). This simple but profound fact would have been revolutionary in the lives of the Galatians. No longer would they need to fear vengeful deities striking them down for any particular infraction and sin. They could live in the freedom of life in Christ (5:1).[54]

Although it is true that the God of Paul's proclamation exhibits an anger toward sin that leads to the death of the sinner, and that this anger needs to be turned away, propitiation had already taken place in the death of Jesus Christ on the cross nearly 20 years earlier in Judea. Paul's letter emphasizes the fact that he publicly portrayed the crucifixion of Jesus Christ to the Galatians when he first brought to them the gospel (3:1). It would have been startling news

---

[54] Thielman ("Folk Belief," 3) is quite right that the problem for first-century apostles and evangelists in pagan contexts lay not in convincing their audiences that they were sinful and that their sin made the gods angry. Human sin and the wrath of the deity was something they understood well. For Thielman, Arnold is precisely correct when he asserts that the gospel would have come to the Galatians as a great relief. Paul told them that they need not fear the gods, for there is one God, and in his love for his creatures he has provided the final atonement for offenses against himself. He has done this through the death of his own Son. He only asks his creatures to receive this free gift in faith and to devote themselves to his praise along with others who also believe.

to each of the Galatians to realize the truth about the Son of God "who loved me and gave himself for me" (2:20). Furthermore, Paul's gospel brought a sharp judgment on their former deities, upon whom they had lavished their devotion. They were "by nature" not gods at all; they were only weak and miserable "elements" (4:9).

The death of Jesus, then, provided them with an absolute freedom from the cultic requirements and moral code of the gods they once worshipped. This death also has significant implications for the Galatians' relationship to the Mosaic law, which the Jewish Christian missionaries were attempting to assert as essential for these new Christians. The death of Jesus not only brought redemption for Gentiles held in slavery by the gods of this world but as well redemption for Jews under the old covenant. The Galatian Gentiles could now experience freedom from the requirements of their former gods and their punishments, in addition to freedom from the requirements of the Jewish law as a means of initiation into and maintenance of the new covenant.

Given this remarkable good news that Paul shared with these central Anatolian Gentiles, who had formerly given their allegiance to a variety of vindictive gods and goddesses, How is it possible that they could so quickly turn away to a law observant form of the gospel? The answer, in brief, is that when the other missionaries came to the Galatian communities and asserted their objections to Paul's gospel, the nature of their objections would have resonated well with the Galatians, given the structure of their former belief-system. Their insistence that the Galatians be circumcised would have been a discouraging blow to them after the freedom of the Pauline gospel from such ritual obligations. Nevertheless, it would have made sense to them, based on the similarity of the Judaizers' demands to the structure of their former convictions, according to which the gods pressed particular cultic requirements for the forgiveness of sins.

The thought of freedom from cultic requirements, in Paul's preaching, was indeed radical, and was probably thought to be too good to be true. This, coupled with the Scriptural arguments advanced the opponents, were proving to be compelling to the Galatians. Hence, the opponents' emphasis on careful Torah observance would have struck a responsive chord with such people, who were accustomed to following specific cultic laws and the moral code of their gods. A nomistic orientation was part of their pre-Christian experience and stood behind their concept of sin, as illustrated by the propitiatory inscriptions. One wonders about the degree to which the Jewish Christian missionaries knew the pre-Christian backgrounds of the Galatians, as well as the extent to which they "contextualized" their own message in order to persuade them to observe the Torah. In any event, their method of dealing with sin was not dissimilar to that of the Anatolian deities as celebrated in the inscriptions.

(4) *The religiosity of the propitiatory inscriptions and contextualization in Galatians.* There are a few other features of Galatians that suggest that the kind of religiosity expressed in the propitiatory inscriptions is something Paul may have been aware of when he wrote this letter. Among these are witchcraft, castration, supernatural revelation and angelic mediation, all of which find points of contact in Galatians.

Arnold appropriately concludes there are three groups of people to be considered in interpreting Galatians in its socio-rhetorical context: Paul, the Jewish Christian missionaries and the Galatians themselves. Scholarship has extensively explored the first two sets of participants in the discussion, but has not adequately explored the third. The propitiatory inscriptions from Asia Minor, as well as a variety of other Anatolian inscriptions, provide us with an opportunity to explore aspects of the belief-structure of these central Anatolian peoples in more detail. The result is a better composite picture of the pre-Christian beliefs and practices of the readers that helps us understand how they could give credence to the Torah-oriented teaching of the other missionaries who followed Paul to Galatia.

My reaction to Arnold's thesis is that while it may require qualification in a couple of areas, he is right that the deep-seated concern of the Galatians to maintain favor with the gods through scrupulous observance of cultic requirements and the performance of good works would have inclined them to accept the message of Paul's opponents "so quickly."[55]

---

[55] Thielman ("Folk Belief") advances two qualifications in particular. One is that only two of the one hundred twenty-four inscriptions cited by Arnold come from the first century. However, Thielman agrees that Arnold has identified a "pattern of religion" that is common to so many inscriptions, over such a long period of time and through such a wide swath of Anatolia, that he is justified in using them to paint the background of Galatians. But mainly, Thielman proposes that the avoidance of persecution may have been the prime mover in the Galatians' acceptance of the Judaizing message. In brief, Paul's readers could have escaped the wrath of the Romans state by identifying themselves with a recognized religion, Judaism, that, like its pagan counterparts, offered sacrifice to the emperor.

Even so, concedes Thielman, this scenario certainly does not need to replace the background for which Arnold has argued so helpfully. It is important to keep

INTRODUCTION

Galatians and Pauline Rhetoric

An "ever burgeoning" field of research of late has been Paul's presumed dependence on the canons of Greco-Roman rhetoric, exemplified prominently by Quintilian. This rhetorical reading of Galatians has particularly influenced the commentaries of Betz and Witherington.[56] My own judgment is that while Paul likely had some acquaintance with rhetorical methods, the categories have been greatly overworked, and the results have proven to be largely artificial. Hays offers a balanced and common sense assessment: "Paul was not slavishly following a rhetorical handbook on how to write a deliberative speech, but was employing rhetorical strategies that were simply in the air in his culture. A knowledge of how such strategies worked may occasionally help us to see how the argument is put together."[57]

Martyn's analysis of the role of rhetoric is succinctly enlightening. While Galatians does, in fact, reflect some training in rhetoric on Paul's part, it is doubtful that he would have recognized as his own any of the modern structural analyses of his letter (*Galatians*, 20-21). If we assume, Martyn argues, that the letter must conform essentially to the recommendations of the ancient rhetoricians, we will put it into a straightjacket, concluding that it is fo-

---

in mind that the propitiatory monuments of ancient Anatolia are primarily the products of individual piety and only secondarily expressions of the accepted religion of the region. Those who erected them did so because the god, in his wrath, had struck them, their wives, their husbands or their children. This means that if we are going to use the monuments to understand the appeal of the Judaizers, and to help us explain why Paul equates the former idolatry of the Galatians with their new interest in the Mosaic law, then Arnold is probably right. Both the indigenous religion and the Judaizers may have insisted that individuals conform to the gods' revealed requirements or face the danger of their personal curse, whether in the near future or in the eschaton.

[56] See further Nanos (ed.), *Debate*, 3-196; Aune, *Dictionary*, 418-25; deSilva, *Introduction*, 508-10; Witherington, *Paul Quest*, 115-27; Forbes, "Paul;" Ramsaran, "Paul;" Gorman, *Apostle*, 83-85; Hester, "Structure;" Rapa, *Meaning*, 101-22; Wenham, *Story*, 18, n. 2.

[57] Hays, *Galatians*, 189. To the same effect is Martyn, *Galatians*, 20-27. In the same vein, Schnelle points to 2 Cor 11:6, Paul's admission that he was "untrained in speech," with the counsel that "Paul incorporated rhetoric as one element of his cultural environment, but it did not become the determining factor in his line of reasoning" (*Paul*, 273). The definitive challenge to scholarly opinion that Galatians is cast in the mold of the rhetorical handbooks is provided by Kern, *Rhetoric*.

rensic, deliberative or epideictic, whereas impressive arguments have been advanced to the contrary (ibid., 21).

Martyn conceives of Galatians as a "repreaching of the gospel." In the epistle, Paul is enabled to do on parchment what he could not do in person. Moreover:

> The oral communication for which the letter is a substitute would have been an argumentative sermon preached in the context of a service of worship—and thus in the acknowledged presence of God—not a speech made by a rhetorician in a courtroom. Specifically, Paul's sermon would certainly not have been a defensive speech delivered in a metaphorical court of law with the Galatians sitting as judges, considered by Paul competent to decide the case (ibid., 21).

Paul's "epistolary sermon," as I would call it, is a reproclamation of the gospel in the form of an evangelistic argument. As Martyn writes, rhetoric can serve the gospel, but the gospel itself is not fundamentally a matter of rhetorical persuasion, because the gospel has the effect of placing at issue the nature of argument itself. That is to say, since the gospel is God's own utterance, it is not and can never be subject to ratiocinative criteria that have been developed apart from it (ibid., 22). It follows, then, in the body of the letter, that Paul shows relatively little concern with observing rules set out in the standard teaching of rhetoric. Rather, Paul concentrates his attention on reproclaiming the gospel in light of the Teachers' message, taking into account the ways in which their attacks on him distort the gospel, and considering as well the ways in which their exegetical treatments of Abrahamic traditions are misleading the Galatians (ibid., 23).

At heart, what the Galatians need from Paul is not a "persuasive" and "hortatory" argument as to what they were to do to remedy their situation. They need to be taught by God, so that they see the cosmos that God is bringing into existence as his new creation. Their need of that vision is what determines the nature of Paul's rhetoric. Thus, because Paul's rhetoric presupposes God's action through Paul's words, this rhetoric proves to be more revelatory and performative than hortatory and persuasive. Paul is constructing an announcement designed to wake the Galatians up to the real cosmos, made what it is by the fact that faith has now arrived with the advent of Christ (ibid., 23).

INTRODUCTION

In short, Paul is concerned in letter form to repreach the gospel in place of its counterfeit. Rhetorically, the body of the letter is a sermon centered on factual and thus indicative answers to two questions, "What time is it?" and "In what cosmos do we actually live?"

The better part of wisdom lies, then, in the thesis that, although it contains passages that partially support both of the major rhetorical analyses...the body of the letter as a whole is a rhetorical genre without true analogy in the ancient rhetorical handbooks of Quintilian and others. *Fundamentally...it is a highly situational sermon* (ibid., 23, italics mine).

Outline of The Letter

Introduction (1:1-10)
   A. Greeting (1:1-5)
   B. The Curse of the New Covenant (1:6-10)

Paul's Autobiography as Paradigm (1:11-2:21)
   A. The Divine Origin of Paul's Gospel (1:11-12)
   B. Paul's Former Life in Judaism (1:13-14)
   C. Paul's Conversion/Calling and Its Immediate Results (1:15-17)
   D. Paul's First Visit to Jerusalem (1:18-20)
   E. The Aftermath of the Jerusalem Visit (1:21-24)
   F. Paul's Second Visit to Jerusalem (2:1-10)
   G. The Incident at Antioch (2:11-14)
   H. Summary and Transition (2:15-21)

The Argument from Scripture and Salvation History (3:1-4:31)
   A. The Spirit and the Gospel (3:1-5)
   B. Faithful Abraham (3:6-9)
   C. The Curse of the Law (3:10-14)
   D. The Law and the Promise (3:15-18)
   E. Why the Law? (3:19-22)
   F. The Sons of God and the Seed of Abraham (3:26-29)
   G. Heirs and Sons of God (4:1-7)
   H. Don't Become Slaves Again (4:8-11)
   I. A Personal Appeal (4:12-20)
   J. The Story of Hagar and Sarah (4:21-31)

Freedom in the Spirit (5:1-6:18)
   A. The Call to Freedom (5:1-6)

EXPOSITION OF GALATIANS

    B. Run the Race (5:7-12)
    C. The Responsibilities of Freedom in the Spirit (5:13-6:10)
       (1) Freedom Means Love (5:13-15)
       (2) Spirit Versus Flesh (5:16-26)
       (3) Freedom in Service to Others (6:1-10)
    D. The Last Word (6:11-18)

GALATIANS CHAPTER ONE

INTRODUCTION (1:1-10)

A. Greeting (1:1-5)

Paul's opening words to the Galatians are, at the same time, both typical and atypical of his letters. The paragraph is typical in that Paul identifies himself as an apostle of Christ, names the letter's recipients and confers upon them the apostolic benediction of grace and peace. Yet it is atypical because his customary thanksgiving is lacking altogether. He simply addresses "the churches of Galatia," without any complimentary qualifiers (in contrast to Rom 1:8-12; 1 Cor 1:4-5; Eph 1:1; Col 1:2). Even with all the theological complexity attached to "churches" (*ekklēsiai*), his salutation is still terse and should have alerted them to his dissatisfaction with them. This is why he turns immediately to the crisis that has caused him such alarm. It is, then, only for lack of a better term that the opening can be called a "greeting." In addition, this "greeting" is unusual because of the presence of its doxology. Four matters are of importance in Paul's opening.

(1) His assertion of the divine origin of his apostleship. The fact that he was commissioned directly by God the Father and the Lord Jesus Christ precludes any human intermediaries or authorities who might place an imprimatur upon his mission, most notably the original apostles and/or the church in Jerusalem. Paul's office is in no sense indirect, dependent or secondary.

(2) The death of Christ. Paul is concerned to stress the cross from the outset because of the way it must have been downplayed by the Judaizers. It had to be emphasized as a matter of great moment that Christ's death took place "according to the will of our God and Father," not as an afterthought on the part of God, an accident of history or even a tragic mistake on the part of Israel. By the time Paul ends this letter, he will declare the cross to be an object of boasting (6:14).[1] And here, at the outset, he does not hesitate to place the ignominious cross at the heart of what God had

---

[1] Note that these references to the cross bracket the letter and provide an important framework of interpretation. In a very real sense, Galatians is about the cross. In a similar manner, Paul's phrase "the obedience of faith" brackets the Roman letter (1:5; 16:26) and informs us that his most famous missionary epistle is about faith's obedience among the nations.

purposed in Christ for the "ends of the ages" (1 Cor 10:11). As Wright puts it eloquently:

> The cross became, for Paul, the fullest possible revelation of both the love and the justice of God, and then, in its outworking, the extraordinary saving power of God, defeating the powers that held people captive in pagan darkness and breaking the long entail of human sin. The crucifixion and death of Jesus...is not merely added on to Paul's Christology but the point where it is all going, or, from another viewpoint, the point where it all began.... The cross is the place where Paul sees God's justice fully displayed; his Christology, seen as the revision of Jewish-style monotheism, is the context within which we can best understand it (*Perspective*, 96)

The Judaizers, for their part, refused to endure persecution for the sake of the cross (6:12). But for Paul the cross is glorious (6:14) and, along with the resurrection, signals the turning point of salvation history, the portal from BC to AD (Cullmann, *Christ*). For Paul, no cross, no gospel.

(3) The threefold mention of God the Father. If we read this greeting in the light of the whole epistle, the repeated reference to the Father is intended to pave the way for one of its outstanding motifs, namely, the adoptive sonship of believers in Christ. Thus, our Father is none other than the Father of the Lord Jesus himself. It is the Father who has lavished grace upon us in his uniquely beloved Son (Eph 1:6).

(4) The apocalyptic outlook. Hansen ("Paradigm") has demonstrated that the whole opening is placed within an apocalyptic framework. That is to say, with the death and resurrection of Christ, the old world has passed away and now has been superseded by a new creation. Corresponding to the letter's subscription (6:11-18), the focus of the introduction is on Paul's end-of-the-world and new creation experience by his identification with the cross of Christ. Paul's example for the Galatian believers is a demonstration of the way to bring about the abolition of the old world order of divisions between "circumcision and uncircumcision" and the inauguration of the new creation of unity in Christ through their own personal appropriation of the cross of Christ.

> All of these elements of the rebuke-request structure of Galatians point in the same direction: they feature

GALATIANS CHAPTER ONE

> Paul's participation in the apocalypse of Jesus Christ which guarantees the inclusion of Gentile believers in the people of God. The emphasis on the apocalyptic event of the cross has a social purpose: to protect the freedom and unity of all believers in the new creation in Christ. Paul presents himself as a paradigm of the apocalypse (ibid., 154).

When examined in light of the whole letter, Paul's opening contains everything in a nutshell. In it, he telegraphs in advance the major themes with which he will deal throughout the letter. As such, it corresponds to the epistle's final paragraph (6:11-18), which in its own way also serves to distill the content of the whole.

1 Paul, as customary, states his name to the readers. But he is not merely Paul, he is Paul the apostle. The very term "apostle" places Paul within the company of the original disciples of Jesus. Paul thus identifies himself with the Twelve, who were "sent out" by Jesus to preach (Matt 10:2; Mark 3:14; 6:30; John 13:20; 20:21).[2] Without unduly pressing the etymology of *apostolos*, it is nonetheless true that the apostles were *sent* and commissioned by the risen Jesus, and to that end were endued with the Holy Spirit. Particularly telling is John 20:21-23. After bestowing "peace" on the disciples (the very "peace" Paul confers on the Galatians), Jesus fixes the role of the apostles as those, who, like himself, are sent: "As the Father has sent me, I am sending you" (John 20:21). Jesus is thus portrayed as the "apostle" of the Father (in fulfillment of Isa 61:1), and the Twelve in turn are his "apostles." It is not accidental that those thus sent receive the Holy Spirit (John 20:22) and are granted the authority to forgive and retain sins (John 20:23; cf. Matt 16:19).

As far as Galatians is concerned, the question, Who really possesses the Spirit? is crucial and lies at the heart of Paul's controversy with his opponents. By calling himself an "apostle," he implicitly claims the Spirit and denies the same claim to his antagonists who, no doubt, were insistent that the Spirit was procured precisely by Torah observance. Moreover, Paul is implying that he has actually been sent by Christ, whereas the Judaizers are like the false prophets of Jeremiah, who have run without being sent (Jer

---

[2] On Jesus and the Twelve, see McKnight, "Jesus." Ridderbos shows that the apostles were "taken into the redemptive counsel of God about the sending of His Son" (*History*, 13). This means that the sending of the Son is incomplete without the sending of the disciples.

14:14; 23:21; 27:15; cf. 2 Cor 10:13-18). A possible echo of Jeremiah here is strengthened by the certain allusion of Gal 1:15 to Jer 1:5, where Paul likens himself to the prophet (as well as to Isaiah [Isa 49:1]). Also, the "false brothers" of Gal 2:4 easily translates into the "lying prophets" of Jeremiah.

Paul immediately qualifies that as an apostle he was "sent not from men nor by man, but by Jesus Christ and God the Father." Dunn points out that the phrases hang together as a single concept, namely, "Apostle-not-of-men-nor-through-man-but-through-Jesus-Christ." He continues with the observation: "The fact that Paul puts the negative part of the definition first strongly suggests that he was rebutting and rebuking an alternative way of defining his apostolic status" (*Galatians*, 25). S. K. Williams discerningly observes that although Paul typically introduces himself as an apostle, nowhere else does he feel compelled to assert that he is *not* an apostle because of a human being. "That he does so here is this letter's initial clue to one of his principal concerns: what the ultimate source of his authority and his gospel *is* and what it is *not*" (*Galatians*, 34).

Apparently, some in Galatia were affirming what Paul here denies, namely, that his commissioning was from human beings ("men") or an individual human being ("man"), such as Peter, James or even Ananias (Acts 9:10-17). This is why Paul is compelled in 1:11 to assert in emphatic terms that his gospel is not to any degree human. It is possible that the reference is to Paul's sending by the church in Antioch (Acts 13:1-3); but it is more likely that the "men" in question are the Jerusalem apostles, especially as Paul, in the immediate context, seeks to distance himself from Jerusalem. Witherington objects to the familiar reading that these "men" are the Jerusalem apostles because, he says, the opponents certainly would *not* have objected to an apostleship derived from Jerusalem (*Grace*, 71).

Without, however, abandoning the traditional approach, Witherington's insight helps to sharpen the focus on the actual issue respecting Paul's apostleship. The Judaizers could very well have had Jerusalem in mind—and their precise complaint is that Paul has betrayed the mother church by removing Torah observance from his gospel. In their view, Paul is a renegade apostle who needs to be brought under the discipline of Jerusalem. Thus, it was not Paul's claim to apostleship as such that was under fire but rather that he had proven disloyal to the people who were the source of his commissioning. To a Gentile church that probably stood in awe of Jerusalem, this would have been a compelling argument. No wonder, then, Paul is quick off the mark in this letter to counter such a misrepresentation of the origin of his apostleship.

In staking his claim to a divine, not human, source of his apostleship, Paul uses two prepositions interchangeably: "from" (*apo*) and "through" (*dia*). Technically speaking, the first indicates source and the second instrumentality or agency. Thus, as to its origin and the medium of its bestowal, Paul's apostleship is "from above," not "from below." Since there could be no higher source or instrumentality of sending than God the Father and the risen Lord Jesus Christ, all human agents are rendered superfluous. As Paul continues to write, both prepositions are merged into one in the phrase "*through* Jesus Christ and God the Father." Likewise, in 1:3, "from" does service for both prepositions ("*from* God the Father and the Lord Jesus Christ").

Paul's choice of words would seem to suggest two things simultaneously. One is that in the first clause of 1:1 he distinguishes himself from the false apostles, who did not receive a commission from Christ, while in the second he ranks himself with the Twelve, who were in fact commissioned by the Lord himself. Second, Paul's assignment of these prepositions to God and Christ respectively signals a high christology on his part: Christ is equally the source and agent of his gospel *as the Father*; and it was this conjunction of God and Christ which summed up Paul's basic hope for his converts. Like the Jewish teachers, Paul believes that there is only one God; yet this one God has identified himself by his act in Jesus Christ, making that act the "primal mark of his identity" (Martyn, *Galatians*, 85). Moreover, in Paul's letters, this Jesus is accorded the status of God himself (Rom 9:5; Phil 2:6-11; Titus 2:13; cf. 2 Pet 1:1) (M. J. Harris, *Jesus*); and the confession of Jesus as Lord becomes the Christian equivalent of the *Shema* (1 Cor 8:5-6 = Deut 6:4) (Wright, *Climax*, 120-36).[3]

The person of Christ was a critical issue for Paul: "If Jesus Christ were not fully divine, he could never have redeemed us from the curse of the law or freed us from the power of sin by his

---

[3] Note how in Titus 2:13 and 2 Pet 1:1 the Godhood of Christ is supported by the famous Granville Sharp Rule: when two nouns (or participles) are connected with the preposition *kai* ("and") as proceeded by only one definite article, the two nouns are equivalent to each other (see Dana/Mantey, *Grammar*, 147; Porter, *Idioms*, 110-11), though the "Rule" applies only in the singular not the plural (Porter, *Idioms*, 111).

death on the cross" (George, *Galatians*, 81).[4] Although Paul does not actually say so, he may be hinting that his view of Christ is higher than that of his opponents. If they were at all typical of first-century Jews, a *divine* Messiah would not have been a necessity for them. Indeed, the very idea that a human being could be identified with God would have been a stumbling block. It was only required that the Anointed be able to "get the job done" by restoring the fortunes of Israel.[5]

Notable in 1:1 is Paul's mention of the resurrection.[6] At first glance, it might seem as though a reference to the resurrection is redundant, if not entirely out of place, in this greeting. Why should Paul call the Galatians' attention particularly to the resurrection at the outset of the epistle? A number of answers come to mind.

(1) Like the Jerusalem apostles, Paul himself has seen the resurrected Christ, albeit on the Damascus Road (*Gentile* territory) rather than in Jerusalem and its environs—and it is none other than the exalted Christ who has commissioned Paul directly and immediately to preach the gospel, as well as the other apostles. If witness to the resurrection was a condition of apostleship (Acts 1:22), then Paul *is* on a par with the original twelve disciples of Jesus. It is in just these terms that he puts the question to the Corinthians: "Am I not an apostle? Have I not seen Jesus our Lord" (1 Cor 9:1)? In Paul's particular case, his witness to the resurrection has resulted in a commission to be a light to the Gentiles (Dunn, *Jesus, Paul*, 89-107). He and Jerusalem may traverse different turf in their respective ministries, but Paul's testimony to Christ is equally valid to that of the Twelve and can be sustained independently of them. Perhaps implicit is Paul's dismissal of his opponents, who themselves would have readily acknowledged their linkage to Jerusalem and the derived character of their missionary outreach. After all, they were "the people *from James*" (Gal 2:12). On the other hand, the opponents would have criticized Paul at just this point, that he refused to admit to his own dependence on Jerusalem.

---

[4] Paul's christology in all its aspects continues to be explored. Accessible treatments can be found in Schnelle, *Paul*, 410-54; Hurtado, *Lord Jesus*, 79-153; Dunn, *Theology of Paul*, 182-293.

[5] This is not the place to pursue Paul's vision of Jesus as Messiah. The literature is voluminous, to be sure; but a useful starting point is Wright, *Perspective*, 42-50; 91-96; id., *Climax*, 18-136.

[6] On the resurrection in Galatians, see Bryant, *Christ*, 143-61; Wright, *Resurrection*, 219-25.

(2) Jesus' resurrection marks the turning of the ages by inaugurating the messianic era.[7] Williams notes that in the context of Jewish apocalyptic expectations Paul would have viewed the resurrection of the Crucified One not as an isolated event but as inaugurating the new age.[8] Such is the "good news" he preached (*Galatians*, 44). As the inauguration of this new age, his death and resurrection correspond to those oracles concerning the captivity and restoration of the tribes of Israel, the nation's own death and resurrection (e.g., Isa 26:19; Ezek 37:1-14; Hos 6:1-2).[9] As risen, Christ is the representative man who embodies Israel in himself and brings the covenant to its climax. His resurrection accomplishes the return from exile, when the definitive forgiveness of sins was to be conferred, evil was to be dealt with decisively and the people of God were to be reconstituted (notably Ezekiel 36-37). See the second section note to this verse. It is particularly the reconstitution and reconfiguration of Israel that features so prominently in Galatians. All this has been realized in principle because we have been raised with Christ and made to sit with him in the heavenly places (Eph 2:6).

(3) It is by means of the resurrection that Christ has rescued us from "the present evil age" (1:4) by defeating death itself. A fitting parallel is 1 Thess 1:10: like the Galatians, the Thessalonians "turned to God from idols to serve the living and true God" and were taught to await his Son from heaven, "Whom he raised from the dead—Jesus, who rescues us from the coming wrath." An important corollary to deliverance from this age is the *liberty* for which Christ died and rose again, a liberty inclusive of the newfound freedom to do the will of God (5:13-6:10). Such liberty is one of the most notable motifs of this letter (2:4-5; 3:23-29; 4:1-11, 21-31; 5:1-12, 13).[10]

(4) A dominant motif of the letter is "the gospel of the promise," a promise that God the Father fulfilled to Abraham in the person of Jesus by raising him from the dead (Acts 13:26-39). In the central portion of the letter (chaps. 3-4), Paul will develop the promise motif in terms of the gift of the Spirit who has now been

---

[7] On the centrality of the resurrection in Paul, see Gaffin, *Resurrection*; Wright, *Resurrection*, 209-398.

[8] The OT and Apocalyptic materials are canvassed by Wright, *Resurrection*, 85-206.

[9] See McKnight, "Jesus," 218-20; Gowan, *Theology*.

[10] On liberty in Paul, see Schnelle, *Paul*, 538-45; Chamblin, *DPL*, 313-16; Dunn, *Liberty*.

given to the church in Christ apart from the law. Paul thus breaks the mold of the Jewish expectation by insisting that the Torah has nothing to do with the fulfillment of God's promise to Abraham.

(5) Jesus is vindicated by the Father after death had done its worst. He was condemned by his own people as the reprobate of Deut 21:18-23 (Matt 11:19; Luke 7:34; cf. John 1:11); but the resurrection proved him to be innocent of their charges, indeed, to be entirely faithful to his covenant commitment as the Servant of Yahweh (in fulfillment of Isaiah 50). It is in this sense that he was vindicated (justified) by the Spirit (1 Tim 3:16; cf. Rom 1:4) when he was powerfully raised from the dead. The circumcision party would have agreed that Christ was vindicated by the resurrection, but would have disagreed that the cross was within the plan of God. At best, as far as they were concerned, the cross was a mistake on Israel's part, rectified when God raised his Son. That is why Gal 1:4 (3:13) is adamant that in his death Christ *gave himself* (voluntarily on the cross) for our sins. An appropriate cross-reference is Rom 3:25, according to which Christ was destined to be the propitiation for sin.

2 As Paul pens this letter, he is not alone: there are "all the brothers with me" (cf. Phil 4:22). Paul is not the only one who espouses the gospel to be championed within the pages of this epistle, nor is he the only one cognizant of the divine origin and independent status of his apostleship. He does not name these "brothers," but there are, nonetheless, quite a few ("all") who are prepared to back up his claims. "If the Teachers are telling the Galatians that he still stands virtually alone in his perception of the gospel, Paul will emphasize that, as he writes, the Pauline circle of preachers is a group of some size" (Martyn, *Galatians*, 85). His message, then, is far from an oddity or personal idiosyncrasy. His apostleship was from God and Christ, but he did not work in isolation from others. Betz notes that the emphatic "all" here is unique to Paul and indicates that he writes as the spokesman of a group which is solidly behind him (*Galatians*, 40). A recognition that Paul had a "support group" does not elevate these people to the status of a human sanction of his authority. (Noticeably absent, however, is any mention of Barnabas).

That Paul should call his supporters "brothers" reflects much more than an early Christian convention whereby believers identified and addressed one another as members of a "brotherhood."[11] Quite pointedly, "brothers" (*adelphoi*) evokes Jewish usage (e.g., Exod 2:11; Deut 3:18; Neh 5:1; Isa 66:20; Tob 1:3; 2 Macc 1:1; 1QS 6:10, 22; CD 6:20-7:2). As such, Paul uses the term to make a statement: the members of God's eschatological family—Gentiles as well as Jews—are the heirs of the fellowship of Israel and now assume the identity of the saints of old (Eph 2:11-22). A similar phenomenon appears in Rom 1:5-7, where Paul lifts from the OT various titles and predicates of Israel and applies them directly to *all* of the members of the Roman church (Garlington, *Obedience*, 238-42). The point would have been all the more telling for the Galatians if at least some of the "brothers" supportive of Paul were themselves Gentiles who refused to submit to the yoke of the Torah.

"To the churches of Galatia." The singular of the word translated "churches" (*ekklēsiai*) is common in the LXX for the "assembly" (*qahal*) of Israel, a solemn gathering of the nation before Yahweh (e.g., Deut 4:10; 18:16; 23:1-2; 31:30; Josh 9:2; Judg 20:2; 1 Chr 28:8; Mic 2:5; cf. Heb 12:23).[12] A closely related concept is that of the "holy convocation" (*mikra qōdesh*). This Hebrew phrase is rendered by the LXX as both *klētē hagia* (Exod 12:16; Lev 23:2, 3, 4, 8, 24, 27, 37; Num 28:25) and *epiklētos hagia* (Num 28:18, 26; 29:1, 7, 12). This is the assemblage of the "holy ones" or "saints."

By tapping into such a well-known term for the people of God, Paul suggests a number of things simultaneously. (1) A direct line can be drawn from Israel to the (mainly Gentile) Galatian "assemblies," thus underscoring the essential unity and *continuity* the people of God within the trajectory of salvation history.

(2) His "assemblies" are dominantly Gentile and, unlike the former Israel, no longer define holiness in terms of a Mosaic standard (e.g., Neh 13:1; Lam 1:10; 1QSa 2:3-4; CD 12:3-6). In keeping with Zech 14:20-21, the extension of the "assemblies" beyond ethnic Israel corresponds to the extension of holiness beyond the normal "holy places" of Israel. In this regard, there is a measure of *discontinuity* between old and new covenants.

(3) If the Galatians are the "assembly" (*qahal*) as they stand, then there is no need for them to become anything other than what

---

[11] The notion of brotherhood in non-Jewish/non-Christian circles was certainly extant in the world of Paul's day. See Harland, "Identity."

[12] See Burton, *Galatians*, 417-20; Schmidt, *TDNT*, 3.527-31; Müller, *TLOT*, 3.1118-26; Coenen, *NIDNTT*, 1.291-96; Schnelle, *Paul*, 560-62.

they were when Christ accepted them in the gospel. If only these believers would come to grips with their true identity, they would resist the pressure to become a gathering characterized by the "old things" which have now passed away in Christ (2 Cor 5:17).

(4) The "assembly" of Israel has become the "assembl*ies*" of Christ. The LXX characteristically uses the singular of the noun, but Paul—quite conspicuously against the backdrop of the Greek OT—uses the plural and celebrates this as a desirable state of affairs. Once the worshipping "assembly" expands beyond the borders of Palestine, the various "assemblies" become the individual manifestations of the new "assembly universal." Yet it is the very plurality of the local Christian gatherings that intensifies Paul's alarm as he dispatches this epistle, because more than one of his churches is in danger of capitulating to the Judaizing influence.

3 Although Paul has intimated in no uncertain terms that he is less than pleased with the situation in Galatia, he is, nevertheless, compelled to confer upon these congregations the apostolic benediction of "grace and peace" from God the Father and the Lord Jesus Christ. These words are not so much a wish as a pronouncement that the Galatians, for all their deficiencies, are blessed with God's grace and peace. For this reason, he can still address them as "brothers" in v. 11. It would appear that Paul's benediction corresponds to that which Moses was to convey to Aaron and his sons, namely, that the Lord would "be gracious" to Israel and give her "peace" (Num 6:24-26). "Grace" and "peace" here refer to God's covenant favor toward his people. Paul thus blesses the new Israel in the same manner as the priests blessed the old (cf. Rom 15:16, where Paul likens his ministry to priestly service). But there is one major difference: "Paul extends this covenant favor, once reserved exclusively for Israel, to his Gentile congregations" (Matera, *Galatians*, 38).

It is just this newly reconfigured people, the "Israel of God," who receive the corresponding benediction of "grace and mercy" at the end of the letter in 6:16. This datum raises the intriguing possibility that the whole of Galatians can be conceived of as a kind of *inclusio*; that is, the letter is bracketed by Paul's blessing of the latter-day Israel, who have become the recipients of covenantal grace and peace in the person of Christ (cf. John 1:17). Therefore, they must remain within God's favor as manifested *in Christ* in this era of "grace" (5:4; cf. 2 Cor 6:2) and not incur the "curse" (*anathema*) of the new covenant by departing to "another gospel" (1:7-9).

GALATIANS CHAPTER ONE

"Grace" (Greek *charis* = Hebrew *hesed* and *hēn*) is God's covenant love and fidelity for Israel,[13] now actualized in the gospel for a new Israel (6:16). Given this definition, "grace" is God's self-giving to Israel or his marriage-covenant with his people (Torrance, *Grace*, 15). If God gives himself to Israel in a marriage-like relationship, then he commits himself to the maintenance of his bond with her. The classic passage is Exod 33:19-34:9, especially in context, the worship of the golden calf, Exodus 32.[14] After Israel had so quickly forsaken Yahweh for an Egyptian idol (Exod 32:8; Deut 9:16), the Lord declares nonetheless: "I will have mercy on whom I will have mercy, and I will have compassion on whom I will have compassion" (Exod 33:19). Thereafter, he reveals his name to Moses: "The LORD, the LORD, the compassionate and gracious God, slow to anger, abounding in love and faithfulness" (Exod 34:6). Yahweh's name is the revelation of his character as the God who forgives sin and is gracious, "Maintaining love to thousands, and forgiving wickedness, rebellion and sin" (Exod 34:7). As Wright states so aptly:

> The word "grace" is a shorthand way of speaking of God himself, the God who loves totally and unconditionally, whose love overflows in self-giving in creation, in redemption, in rooting out evil and sin and death from his world, in bringing to life that which was dead. Paul's gospel reveals this God in all his grace, all his love (*Paul*, 61).

This reminder of grace is especially appropriate for these readers because they, like the exodus generation, were in danger of "so quickly" deserting *their* Lord, Jesus (1:6).

Accompanying "grace" is "peace." The Greek word rendered "peace" (*eirēnē*) is the equivalent of the Hebrew *shalōm*, a greeting exchanged by Jewish people from of old. *Shalōm* stands for well-being, wholeness and prosperity in every realm of life. Yet there is a more profound salvation-historical underpinning to the term, one especially appropriate for Paul's greetings to all his churches but to the Galatians in particular. Originally, "peace" was the blissful condition of the creation before sin. Later, the Prophets of Israel portray the coming age of salvation precisely in terms of "peace,"

---

[13] See Glueck, *Hesed*; Clark, *Hesed*; Snaith, *Ideas*, 94-130; Torrance, *Grace*, 10-20.

[14] See Piper, *Justification*, 78-89; Hafemann, *Paul*, 189-254.

a time when the lion and the lamb will dwell together and war will be no more (Isa 2:4; 11:6-9).[15] In short, "peace" is a return to the paradise of the Garden of Eden, as procured by the work of the Messiah (e.g., Isa 9:6-7; 32; 52:7; 57:19; Ezek 37:26; Hag 2:9; cf. Num 6:22-26). In this age to come, "peace" will once again characterize the earth, when Israel's exile is ended and the nation returns to the land (e.g., Isa 32:15-20 = Rom 5:1).[16]

In view of recent studies of Paul in relation to the Roman empire (see below on v. 22), it is altogether probable that Paul is issuing a challenge to the Roman claim to have procured worldwide peace by virtue of military might (the *Pax Romana*). The true peace-giver, for Paul, is not the emperor but the Lord Jesus Christ, whose kingship is "not of this world" (John 18:36) (see Wengst, *Pax Romana*).

By conferring this peace on the Galatians, Paul intimates that the "Prince of Peace" (Isa 9:6) as proclaimed in *his* gospel has in principle restored the creation (Rom 5:1; 1 Cor 2:9 = Isa 64:4; 65:17; Eph 2:17; Col 1:20; cf. Luke 2:14). His resurrection has already brought about the rebirth of the universe and has procured for his people an indescribable hope for the future attended by "joy unspeakable and full of glory" (1 Pet 1:8 [KJV]). If the Galatians have any appreciation of what Christ has done, they must not exclude themselves from this glorious future (cf. 2 Thess 1:9) by turning away to the alternative "gospel" of the Judaizers. They must see themselves for what they really are. Uncircumcised and non-kosher though they may be, *they* are the restored Israel of God.

Just as important, the prospect of peace is far from an abstract ideal projected into the distant ages. It is, rather, the hallmark of the church here and now (Eph 2:14-17; 4:1-7; Col 3:15), so much so that Paul could coin the phrase "the gospel of peace" (Eph 6:15). If we may read the beginning of Galatians in the light of its ending (chaps. 5-6), peace was precisely what was lacking in Galatia. Rather than the order and harmony of God's "very good" creation (Gen 1:31), chaos was beginning to dominate the Galatian scene. Instead of peace, there was "biting and devouring" (5:15), the "works of the flesh," especially hatred and its attendant attitudes (5:19-21), conceit, provocation, envy (5:26) and harsh treatment of offenders (6:1-5). In brief, "They [Paul's readers] have not

---

[15] On the complex of ideas associated with the age to come see, Gowan, *Eschatology*.

[16] See McKnight, *Vision*, 229-33; Beale, "Background," 37-38.

understood the implications of the Gospel of grace and instead of peace there is strife, and quarrels and divisions exist in these assemblies" (Witherington, *Grace*, 76). They were not allowing the "peace of God" to guard their hearts and minds in Christ Jesus (Phil 4:7). As a result, the "God of peace" (Phil 4:9) was not with them. As Witherington further observes, these divisive actions and beliefs are traceable to submission to circumcision and the Mosaic law on the part of certain Christians in the assemblies, thus separating them from the others (ibid.).

Such "grace" and "peace" are "from God our Father and the Lord Jesus Christ." By mentioning the Father first, Paul is not constructing a hierarchical order. Rather, the intention is to rank Jesus *along with* God. "Paul calls Jesus Christ by the title Lord in order to say that his cosmic rulership is on a par with that of God, although even as Lord he remains the Son of God the Father" (Martyn, *Galatians*, 88). Paul's very application of the title "Lord" (*kurios*) has tremendous christological implications. *Kurios* is the Greek word that, in the LXX, normally translates the divine name Yahweh.[17] Moreover, the lordship of Jesus, in the setting of the Roman empire, provided an all-powerful impetus to Paul's missionary message: *only Jesus is Lord—Caesar isn't!* See the third section note to this verse, the section note to 1:6 and the comments on 1:22.

The lordship of Christ is the corollary of his resurrection and exaltation. His vindication after suffering and death consisted in God's bestowal on him of the name that is above every other name (Phil 2:9-11 = Isa 45:23; cf. Heb 1:4, 13 = Ps 110:1). Paul thus views Jesus' lordship in terms of his dominance over the creation which God had intended for Adam.[18] Paul invokes the lordship of Christ, as noted above, because former pagans living in Greco-Roman society needed reminding that Christ, not Caesar, is Lord. Yet we should recall that Paul's earliest converts on non-Jewish soil were adherents to Diaspora synagogues, schooled in the traditions of Israel. Consequently, the lordship of Jesus has a special bearing on those who were being pressured, if not intimidated, into the common Jewish belief that the Messiah would be the servant of the law and would thus preserve intact the old theocratic societal values (Martyn, *Galatians*, 124-25). The fact that Christ is Lord means that he is free to change the very Torah itself and to accept

---

[17] See Dunn, *Galatians*, 32-34; Pietersma, "Kyrios."

[18] Dunn, *Galatians*, 33; id., *Christology*, 108-10.

without distinction all who come to God through him. Jesus, then, is to receive the preeminence, not the Torah (cf. Col 1:8).

4 If grace and peace emanate from the Lord Jesus Christ, it is on the basis of his finished work. This is why Paul marks him out as the one "who gave himself for our sins to rescue us from the present evil age, according to the will of our God and Father." As Hays strikingly puts it: "The gospel is about *Jesus Christ's gracious self-giving* for our sake, and that self-giving must be understood as an apocalyptic rescue mission" (*Galatians*, 202, italics his). For Christ to "give himself" (see also Rom 4:25; 5:8; 8:32; Gal 2:20; Eph 5:2, 25; 1 Thess 5:10; 1 Tim 2:6; Titus 2:14; Mark 10:45; cf. 2 Cor 5:21) means that the cross was a deliberate and pre-meditated action on his part, not a "Plan B" when "Plan A" failed, not an accident, and not a mistake that could only be rectified by resurrection. Rather, all this transpired "according to the will of our God and Father." Paul is entirely in line with Jesus himself, who declared that he had power to lay his life down and power to take it up again (John 10:15-18; 15:13). Paul, therefore, embraces the cross as his glory (6:14), unlike the rival teachers, who shun the cross, believing the idea of a crucified Messiah to be a "blasphemous contradiction in terms" (Bruce, *Galatians*, 166). In Luther's famous phrase, Paul's theology is truly a "theology of the cross" (*theologia crucis*).

Christ's self-sacrifice has a particular importance within the argument of Galatians (2:19-20; 3:23-36; 4:1-7, 8-9; 5:1; 6:14).[19] As in some of Paul's other letters (e.g., Rom 3:25; Eph 2:14-22), his pronouncements about the death of Jesus have to do with the removal of the barriers between Jew and Gentile. So, the gloves are off from the outset of the letter. Not only would the Judaizers have denied that the death of Jesus was necessary for redemption, they would have been scandalized by the proposition that his death has broken down "the dividing wall of hostility" (Eph 2:15) between Jews and Gentiles. Even more novel for them was the notion that the death of the Messiah should be a substitutionary sacrifice "for our sins."[20] This pronouncement that Christ died "for our sins" corresponds to Mark 10:45, which in turn echoes Isa 53:5, 12 (cf.

---

[19] On the background of sacrifice in Paul's letters and his development of a sacrificial theology, see Hengel, *Atonement*; Lyonnet/Sabourin, *Sin*; Finlan, *Background*.

[20] On Christ's substitutionary and atoning death, see Schnelle, *Paul*, 443-51; Cousar, *Theology*, and the section note to v. 5. Also relevant is McKnight, *Jesus*.

Rom 4:25), the self-sacrifice of the Servant of Yahweh on behalf of the transgressions of his people (Ciampa, *Scripture*, 51-59). Such a conception of the death of Christ is taken for granted by evangelical Christians. Nevertheless, the proposition that the Messiah would die as a sin-offering was apparently unknown to the Judaism of Paul's day. It would seem that the connection between the animal sacrifices of Israel and an atoning Messiah was not made.

As Hengel points out, the expression "die for," referring to the Messiah "dying for" sins (or sinners), is striking because it has no parallel in the OT or in the Semitic sphere (*Atonement*, 49). Furthermore, states Hengel, although there are analogies between Jewish and even Greco-Roman conceptions of atonement, the NT goes beyond contemporary parallels and represents the sacrifice of Christ as the eschatological act whereby the Son of God has reconciled apostate creatures with their Creator (ibid., 73-74).

The purpose of Christ's substitutionary death "for our sins" was "to rescue us from the present evil age" and thus usher us into the "age to come." The present age is evil because it is idolatrous, engulfed in the worship and service of the creature rather than the Creator. This era of world history is under the dominion of "the god of this world" (2 Cor 4:4) as headed by the first Adam (Rom 5:12-19). (Shockingly, Paul will later place the law within this "present evil age.") Left to itself, this age is hopeless and helpless. But God has not left the world to itself, because he purposed to redeem the creation in the fullness of the time (4:4).

In accordance with this purpose, the Prophets anticipate a new creation to take place when the people of God return from exile (e.g., Isa 2:2-4; 25:6-12; 26:19; 35; 60; 65:17-25; Ezekiel 36-37). This hope for the end-time was taken up and intensified by the Jewish apocalyptic movement (e.g., *Jubilees*; *Joseph and Aseneth*; 4 Ezra 7:50, 113; *2 Apoc. Bar.* 31:5; *1 Enoch* 91:15-17).[21] But the "clout" of Paul's statement is that the anticipated "age to come" has already arrived with the first advent of Christ (1 Cor 10:11). Believers, because they share the risen life of Christ and partake of his Spirit, have already entered the resurrection age (Rom 6:4-11; Eph 2:5-7; Col 3:1-3 = Isa 26:19; Ezek 37:1-14; Hos 6:1-2).

This is Paul's "inaugurated eschatology," which represents a radical breach with what he had believed as a Pharisee: *"The one true God had done for Jesus of Nazareth, in the middle of time, what Saul had thought he was going to do for Israel at the end of*

---

[21] See respectively Hubbard, *Creation*, 11-25, 26-76.

time" (Wright, *Paul*, 36, italics his). Wright adds: "The Present Age and the Age to Come overlapped, and he was caught in the middle, or rather, *liberated* in the middle, liberated to serve the same God in a new way, with a new knowledge to which he had before been blind." Thus, Paul was not just living in the last days: "He was living in the *first* days—of a whole new world order" (ibid., 37, 50, first italics mine, second his). Therefore, to say that we have been delivered from the present evil age means that the "not yet" has become for us the "already." Nevertheless, the "present evil age" is still with us, thus creating the period of overlapping ages in which we currently live.

Since we participate in this age and are affected by it, the sacrificial self-giving of Christ is the final answer to the problem of all our moral failure and guilt. And his epoch-making sacrifice is all-encompassing in its effects, including both objective and subjective elements. Objectively, we have been delivered from the old aeon and brought into a new historical era, a new order of existence. Subjectively, since we have experienced newness of life in this "new world order," we need no longer be dominated by the evil spiritual powers of this age.[22] Elsewhere, Paul can speak of the death (and resurrection) of Christ as delivering his people from the dominion of sin, death and condemnation (Rom 5:9-10; 6:1-11). After paying the sin-debt incurred by us because of our involvement in the idolatry of this age, he rises in newness of life and bestows his Spirit so that we may finally and fully be released from the grip of evil and rebellion against God when we assume the likeness of his resurrection body (Rom 6:5-6; 8:11; 1 Cor 15:42-50; Phil 3:20-21).

The verb "rescue" or "deliver" (*exaireō*) signifies a release from the power of someone or something (Acts 7:10, 34; 12:11; 23:27; 26:17). In this setting, it assumes a specific reference to Israel's deliverance from bondage in the exodus (cf. Acts 7:34).[23] Ironically, in Gal 4:5, the more or less synonymous verb "redeem" (*exagorazō*) has reference to Israel under the law (cf. Col 2:20). Without saying so directly, Paul is paving the way for the salvation-historical portion of the letter (chaps. 3-4), in which he will identify the law as a state of bondage and even equate it with idolatry. As Romans 6-8, Galatians places the law in the era of sin and death. The age of the Torah is no less than the "present evil age"

---

[22] On newness as an eschatological and ethical concept, see Hoch, *All Things New*.

[23] See Wilson, "Apostasy," 555.

(Dunn, *Theology of Paul*, 128-61). The Judaizers may have believed that the age to come had arrived in Jesus of Nazareth. But even so, they would have been convinced that the law pertains to the messianic age, not just to the pre-eschatological state of affairs. Paul is thus 180 degrees away from his opponents when it comes to the place of the law in the age to come.

Christ's work of redemption was accomplished "according to the will of our God and Father." It is no accident, remarks Dunn, that Paul rounds off his opening paragraph with his focus once again on God. "It is his way of underscoring his conviction to his Galatians readers that what was at stake in their dispute was nothing less than the will and purpose of God for his world, and that Paul's gospel looked to no other source and no other validation" (*Galatians*, 37). Moreover, against the backdrop of the OT and predestruction Judaism, an added reference to the Father would evoke his role as the redeemer and restorer of his people. Christ's finished work "according to the will of our God and Father" is nothing other than the redemption and restoration of a new covenant community from bondage and the re-creation of all things (the emphasis on God as the Father-Creator is found in Deut 32:6; Isa 43:6-7; 64:8; Jer 3:19; Mal 2:10; cf. Rom 11:36; 1 Cor 8:6).[24]

Wilson ("Apostasy," 554) provides confirmation by calling attention to the fact that in Paul's day the designation "Father" was neither commonplace nor without emotive power. Most pointedly, in the OT and Jewish tradition, "Father" was associated with the exodus: the Father was the Redeemer, as per Isa 63:15-16.[25]

Look down from heaven and see,
  from thy holy and glorious habitation.
Where are thy zeal and thy might?
  The yearning of thy heart and thy compassion
  are withheld from me.
For thou art our *Father*,
  though Abraham does not know us
  and Israel does not acknowledge us;
thou, O LORD, art our *Father*,
  our *Redeemer* from of old is thy name. (RSV)

---

[24] The figure of the potter and the clay is likewise an image for God as creator: Ps 2:9; Isa 29:16; 41:25; 45:9; Jer 18:1-11; Sir 33:13; *T. Naph.* 2:2, 4; 1QS 11:22; 1QH 1:21; 3:23-24; 4:29; 11:3; 12:26, 32; 18:12; cf. Wis 15:18.

[25] He cites Deut 32:5-20; Isa 1:2; 64:4-12; Jer 3:12-19; 31:9; Hos 11:1-2, 10-11; *Pss. Sol.* 17:27; *Jub.* 1:24-25; *T. Judah* 24:3; 3 Macc 6:3, 8; Tob 13:4; Sir 4:10; 23:1, 4; 1QH 9:33-6. See additionally Ciampa, *Scripture*, 40-2.

This identification of Father and Redeemer, however, did not originate with Isaiah, because already in Exod 4:22-23 we find: "And you shall say to Pharaoh, Thus says the LORD, Israel is my first-born son, and I say to you, Let my son go that he may serve me; if you refuse to let him go, behold, I will slay your first-born son." Accordingly, "Father" very naturally connects with the verb "deliver" (*exaireō*) (ibid., 555-56).

With this stress on the Father's role in redemption, Paul underscores again the self-giving of Christ is no accident. Very likely, he echoes Isa 53:10: "Yet it was the LORD's will to crush him and cause him to suffer, and though the LORD makes his life a guilt-offering, he will see his offspring and prolong his days, and the will of the LORD will prosper in his hand." The "will of our God and Father" thus entails a (pre)determined purpose to subject his Son to suffering and death as a sin-offering, but thereafter to exalt and vindicate him. The Galatians themselves are "his offspring" as his days have been prolonged by virtue of resurrection; and it is through Paul's gospel exclusively that the will of the Lord is prospering in his hand.

5 The revealed will of God can only lead the apostle to praise this God: "To whom be glory for ever and ever. Amen." This doxology, unique to Paul's opening epistolary paragraphs, is the natural complement to the will of God the Father. Williams explains: "The effect of ascribing eternal *glory* to the One whose *will* is being implemented by Jesus' efficacious death is to establish the firm *theological* parameters of everything that follows and, at the same time, subtly to reinforce the claim of verse 1 that the authority with which Paul writes derives ultimately from God" (*Galatians*, 35). Dunn concurs: "Since the normal epistolary introduction had been disrupted by lifting his readers' eyes from the immediacy of their own situation to the eternal purpose of God, no more fitting conclusion could be found" (*Galatians*, 37). Therefore, the "amen," by which Jews would commonly affirm the truth of an assertion, is much more than liturgical. It is the seal of Paul's heartfelt confirmation and commitment to this conviction.

"Glory" (Greek *doxa*) corresponds to the Hebrew *kabōd*, the "splendor" of God or the manifestation of his attributes, which results in the honor, reverence and submission due to him as the Majesty of the universe. Paul's verbless doxologies (in Greek) are more than a wish ("to whom *be* glory"); they are, rather, statements of fact ("to whom *is* glory"). God is glorious by definition.

Not only does glory belong to him, he is "the glory" (Rom 9:4; cf. John 1:14; Jas 2:1 [in Greek]), the *shekinah* of Israel, the nation's most treasured possession. Paul's precise point, then, is that the God who is the glory has now chosen to dwell in the midst of the nations; no longer is he confined to one people only (contrast Sir 24:5-8). In this regard, the doxology invites comparison with a famous passage in pre-Christian Jewish literature, Bar 4:2-4:

Do not give your glory to another,
  or your advantages to an alien
    people.
Happy are we, O Israel,
  for we know what is pleasing to
    God. (RSV)

Here, a Jewish author emphatically urges his coreligionists not to share their glory with foreigners. The "glory" was a preeminent and unmistakable token of the Israel's election: no other peoples have this. At one time, Paul would have agreed; but on the Damascus Road he came to realize that to confine "the glory" to Israel would be to nullify the purpose of God when he made a covenant with Abraham. Therefore, Paul has reshaped election around Christ and the Spirit, the "boundary markers," I would say, of the new covenant/new creation (Wright, *Perspective*, 108-29).

This residence of the glory in lands beyond Israel is in keeping with the expectation that there would be an end-time manifestation of the *doxa* to all nations (Luke 2:32). Moreover, in obvious contrast to Baruch, Isa 56:5-7 envisions the time when outsiders to Israel will actually become priestly servants of Yahweh:

I will give in my house and within my walls
  a monument and a name
    better than sons and daughters;
I will give them an everlasting name
  which shall not be cut off.
And the foreigners who join themselves to the LORD,
  to minister to him, to love the name of the LORD,
    and to be his servants,
every one who keeps the sabbath, and does not profane it,
  and holds fast my covenant—
these I will bring to my holy mountain,
  and make them joyful in my house of prayer;
their burnt offerings and their sacrifices
  will be accepted on my altar;
for my house shall be called a house of prayer

for all peoples. (RSV)[26]

Section Notes

1 It has been proposed that the office of apostle is modeled on the Jewish institution of the *shaliah*, which itself is related to the Hebrew verb *shalah*, "to send." In the rabbinic period, the *shaliah* was a legal representative of a person of substance, who was "sent" to act as the authoritative representative of that person (Rengstorf, *TDNT*, 1.414-20; Schmithals, *Office*, 98-110; Barrett, *Signs*, 12-14; id., "Shaliah;" Spicq, *TLNT*, 1.188-89; Lightfoot, *Galatians*, 93; Bruce, *Galatians*, 72; George, *Galatians*, 78-79; Mußner, *Galaterbrief*, 46-47; Schlier, *Galater*, 26-28; McKnight, *Galatians*, 48-49). However, there were notable differences between the Jewish concept of *shaliah* and the Christian idea of apostle (Longenecker, *Galatians*, 3; Witherington, *Grace*, 70-71). Therefore, while the identification of the two is tempting, it must remain an open question, particularly given that the rabbinic materials postdate the NT. As apostle, we refer to Paul as a "missionary." However, Barton is right that "missionary" is a word of ours but not native to Paul himself. Rather, Paul draws on metaphors such as planter, builder, father, mother, nurse and priest, each of which captures something of how he saw his work ("Paul").

1 The "climax of the covenant" or "return from exile" motif factors in the exposition of Galatians. Outstanding contributions to the theme have been made by Wright, *New Testament*; id., *Jesus*; id., *Climax*, 137-56; Scott, "Tradition;" id., "Works of the Law;" id. (ed.), *Exile*; Dempster, "Geography;" Evans, "Exile;" Knibb, "Intertestamental Period;" id., "Damascus Document;" Pate, *Communities*; id., *Reverse*. The degree to which Second Temple Jews were aware of a continuing exile is disputed, especially since the textual evidence is not uniform (e.g., Bar 4:36-37; 5:5-9 versus Jdt 4:1-5; 5:17-19; Josephus *Ant.* 4.8.46.344; 10.7.3.112-13; 11.1.1.1-4). For references pertaining to the debate, see Das *Paul*, 153-55; id., *Paul and Jews*, 38.

In any event, whether Paul's contemporaries were aware of a continuing exile or not, effectively the nation was still in bondage until the appearance of another Moses who would lead them on a new exodus of redemption. As far as Galatians is concerned, the exile has in fact been reversed with the liberation of the people of God from the bondage of the law (see on 3:22-25; 4:8-11). Das may be right that Paul's opponents considered the exile to be at an end because of Israel's devotion to the law

---

[26] Comments Oswalt: "God had not chosen Israel and given them all that he did in order to shut out the world, but to bring in the world. All of Israel's separation from the world was in order to keep Israel from being absorbed into the world and thus loosing the ability to call the world out of itself into the blessings of God. But should Israel ever come to believe that its separation was so that Israel could keep her God and his blessings to herself, then all was lost" (*Isaiah*, 2.460-61).

since the return from Babylon. But so ironically, the nation's rejection of Jesus the Messiah has brought about a *new exile* for the majority of the Jewish people (*Paul and Jews*, 38, n. 55; see also Seifrid, *Christ*, 168-69).

3 Yahweh's "peace," in the prophetic hope, stands for his eschatological deliverance of Israel from her enemies and his recreation of all things. From the NT's perspective generally, peace is the promised final "salvation" which has now transpired historically through Jesus Christ. See Mußner, *Galaterbrief*, 49-50; Ciampa, *Scripture*, 48-50; McKnight, *Vision*, 229-33; Von Rad/Foerster, *TDNT*, 2.405-6, 412-15; D. J. Harris, *Shalom!* A virtual synonym of "peace" is "rest" (Herbert, *Throne*, 159-63). In Gen 2:1-3, God's own rest provides the paradigm of Adam's rest to be enjoyed after the completion of his mandate to subdue the earth (Gen 1:28). With Adam's fall, however, "rest" undergoes a semantic shift and likewise becomes synonymous with the "salvation" (= new creation) procured by Christ (cf. the use of Ps 95:8-11 in Heb 3:7-4:13). See Lincoln, "Sabbath."

3 Addressing the issue of Jesus' lordship, Wright reconstructs the setting in which Paul predicates *kurios* of him. "It should...be apparent that the proper contexts for this term...are its Jewish roots on the one hand and its pagan challenge on the other. Taking them the other way around for the moment: the main challenge of the term, I suggest, was not to the world of private cults or mystery religions, where one might be initiated into membership of a group giving allegiance to some religion's 'Lord.' The main challenge was to the lordship of Caesar, which, though 'political' from our point of view as well as in the first century, was also profoundly 'religious.' Caesar demanded worship as well as 'secular' obedience: not just taxes, but sacrifices. He was well on his way to becoming the supreme divinity in the Greco-Roman world, maintaining his vast empire not simply by force—though there was of course plenty of that—but by the development of a flourishing religion that seemed to be trumping most others either by absorption or by greater attraction. Caesar, by being a servant of the state, had provided justice and peace to the whole world. He was therefore to be hailed as Lord and trusted as Savior. This is the world in which Paul announced that Jesus, the Jewish Messiah, was Savior and Lord" ("Paul's Gospel," 168). In this light, Phil 2:6-11 greatly gains in significance as Paul's manifesto that the one seated on the throne of imperial Rome is not *kurios* after all; it is Jesus, the one to whom every knee is to bow. So very interestingly, Wright notes that this "hymn" has exactly the same shape as some imperial acclamations naming Caesar as both the "servant" of the state and its "lord." Thus, "Jesus, not Caesar, has been a servant and is now to be hailed as *kyrios*" (ibid., 174).

4 Hengel shows that the death of the cross was so horrible that it was hardly mentioned in polite Roman society (*Crucifixion*, 22-38). On the cross, see further Green, *DJG*, 147-48; id., *DPL*, 197-99; O'Collins, *ABD*,

6.1207-10; Schnelle, *Paul*, 429-34; Cousar, *Theology*; Brown, *Death*, 2.900-1198. It is in this setting that the "foolishness" (1 Cor 1:18) of Paul's gospel stands out in stark relief: "The heart of the Christian message, which Paul describes as 'the word of the cross'...ran counter not only to Roman political thinking, but to the whole ethos of religion in ancient times and in particular to the ideas of God held by educated people" (ibid., 5. See further Hengel, *Atonement*, 65-75.). For this reason, Wright can add that "God has reversed the world's values. He has done the impossible. He has turned shame into glory and glory into shame. His is the folly that outsmarts the wise, the weakness that overpowers the strong" (*Paul*, 47). The scandal of the cross was no less pronounced for Judaism, evoking, as it did, Deut 21:23 and Yahweh's curse on the disobedient (see below on 1:8-9 and 3:10-13).

5 The expression "to give his life," in Mark 10:45, matches the same formula in later Jewish usage (*nathan naphshō*) which is predicated of Moses and David, who gave themselves sacrificially on behalf of the Torah (see Schlier, *Galater*, 32; Phillips "Paradigms"). The notion of substitutionary atonement is rooted in the sacrificial system of the Mosaic covenant. Sin is conceived of debt, which can only be paid by the substitution of one life for another. Because the life was in the blood of the sacrificial victim (Lev 17:11, 14), this life had to be extracted violently in order to compensate for the sin-debt of the worshipper. It is frequently claimed that since Paul uses the preposition *huper* (or possibly *peri*, depending on the manuscript reading followed [see Longenecker, *Galatians*, 8]), not *anti*, there is no clear idea here of a substitutionary atonement. However, this appeal is vacuous, because Christ could not have died "for" our sins in any meaningful sense unless he died "in the place of" the sinner. Both the debt and the guilt of sin require propitiatory sacrifice. This is especially evident in Gal 3:13: Christ became a curse "for (*huper*) us." Cf. 1 Cor 15:3. Longenecker is right that in the relevant Pauline texts the vicarious idea of "in the place of" is connoted by *huper* (*Galatians*, 8). The phrase "for our sins" is thus a compact way of saying that Christ died with a view to the forgiveness of our sins by offering himself as a substitute. Some commentators cite 1 Kgs 16:19 (LXX), according to which Zimri died "because of" (*huper*) his sins, not as an atonement for them. However, the context of this verse is decidedly different from Gal 1:4, and the usage is clearly exceptional, nor normative.

Some scholars maintain that the propitiatory death of Jesus in the NT originates in pre-Christian Jewish circles which produced such documents as 2 Macc 7:32, 37-38; 4 Macc 1:8, 10; 6:27-29; 9:6; 13:9; 16:25; 17:21-22; 18:3. It is true that in these passages Jewish martyrs gave their lives for the sake of their fellow Israelites. But the point is that the martyrs died in the hope that their deaths would be accepted so that the entire nation did not have to perish at the hand of its enemies. The deaths of the martyrs may have been expiatory in the sense that wrath was averted from Israel (4 Macc 17:22). Even so, the thought is not that of dying "for the sins" of others in the sense that forgiveness is conferred on the individual by means of their sacrifice. This is only to be expected given that the sacrificial system existed for this purpose. Therefore, Paul's declarations that Christ died "for our sins" represent a radical step beyond martyrdom as traditionally conceived (on which, see Pobee, *Persecution*, 13-46). For him, Jesus takes the place of the sacrificial cultus of Israel. See further Hultgren, *Gospel*, 60-69. Bailey has argued that *hilastērion*, in Rom 3:25, represents Jesus as the Mercy Seat ("Mercy Seat"). See Bailey's summary of his thesis in *TynBul* 51 (2000), 155-58.

Nevertheless, these observations on the atonement do not negate the insightful work of Cummins (*Paul*), to which reference is made at numerous places in this exposition. Cummins contends that the apocalyptic conceptual framework of Galatians sets the stage for Paul's inversion of the Maccabean crisis, whereby Christ is represented as Israel's (unexpected) eschatological redeemer, whose death effects a reversal of the cause for which the Maccabean martyrs gave themselves (see, ibid., e.g., 123). Both Paul and his mission were dramatically transformed when God revealed his son "in him" (Gal 1:15-16a). Explains Cummins: "This encounter may be seen as representing a radical reworking of the Jewish messianic expectations based on Daniel 7:13-14 with regard to a redeemer/ruler who would rescue and vindicate afflicted Israel, and inaugurate God's glorious rule. It was expected that Israel's vindication would include its now condemned enemies' astonished recognition that those whom they had formerly persecuted—not least as embodied in their righteous representative(s)—were in fact the now exalted saints/sons of God. However, in God's disclosure of Jesus 'in Paul' this 'great reversal' is itself reversed. Here and now (not at the future judgement) it is Paul, the exemplary zealous Jew, who realizes that the one whom he had been persecuting—by means of his pursuit of Jesus' followers—was in fact Israel's (and the nations') Messiah and Son of God. The rejected and martyred Jesus now occupied an exalted role within the divine economy, and those conformed to him (whether Jew or Gentile) constituted the 'Israel of God' rescued from the evil age/sphere, who even now had a share in the glorious reign of their representative redeemer" (ibid., 123).

The effect of Cummins' work is that a drastic role reversal is seen to be at work in Galatians. "Whereas the Jewish community [including, I would add, the Jewish Christian missionaries] could readily have invoked the Torah-obedient Maccabeans as their ideal...the Christians would have laid claim to the martyred and exalted Messiah as their exemplar" (ibid., 138). Because of Antiochus IV Epiphanes' archetypal assault upon the Jewish way of life some two hundred years before Paul, the most zealous members of the Jewish community would have been determined to uphold the Maccabean ideal of an undivided commitment to Torah/Israel/God, not least in the face of the competing claims of the rival Christian community. By contrast, according to Cummins, Paul conceived of himself as a martyr ready to suffer and die not for Judaism but for the martyred and now exalted Jesus, the one who has put an end to

Jewish separation and distinctiveness—a radical reconfiguration of martyrdom indeed. The whole martyr tradition, then, in Paul has been christologically redeployed and applied in the Galatian context.

This being so, it was inevitable that there would be Jewish Christian conflict over competing claims as to what it meant to be the faithful people of God, who ultimately would be vindicated by him. "The Jewish community was constituted according to God in Torah, and its exemplars would have numbered the Torah-obedient Maccabean martyrs. The Christian community was constituted according to God in Christ, and its leading figures comprised those faithful to him. Indeed, to compound the complexity and controversy, the Antiochene Christians would have claimed that it was precisely in and through his martyred and exalted servant Christ—and their conformity thereto—that God had now fulfilled Torah, manifested his covenant faithfulness to Israel (not least to her martyrs), and inaugurated the long-awaited resurrection life of the kingdom" (ibid., 160).

Not all of Cummins' parallels between the Galatian situation and the martyrs have been automatically endorsed, and indeed in some cases he appears to be stretching the point, but frequently I have passed them on for consideration. Certainly they are always stimulating and well worth weighing. The only major qualification, if it is that, of Cummins' work is that the death of Christ in Paul goes beyond martyrdom to embrace his identity and function as the substitutionary sin-bearer "for our sins" (1 Cor 15:3).

B. The Curse of the New Covenant (1:6-10)

If Paul's displeasure with the Galatians was more or less subliminal in the opening paragraph, here it becomes so obvious that no one could miss the point. His indignation, however, is far more than annoyance with a recalcitrant group of disciples. If Paul is blunt—even to the extreme—it is because the stakes are so very high. Nothing less than the curse of the new covenant and the loss of eternal life will result if these people fail to heed his warnings and obey the "other gospel" of his opponents. As the writer of Hebrews was later to say, "How shall we escape if we ignore such a great salvation" (Heb 2:3)? No wonder, Paul's customary thanksgiving is lacking in Galatians. Because the Galatians were in the process of departing from the gospel of Christ, there could be no thanksgiving. Instead, a curse—that of the new covenant—is pronounced upon anyone who brings another message.

6 Paul begins this section by expressing his amazement: "I am astonished…" (or "appalled"). Williams and others may be right that the readers would have recognized in the verb "astonished" (*thau-*

mazō) a formula typical of a particular kind of Hellenistic letter, according to which an author would indicate dismay at the behavior of the letter's recipients. "The tone of such letters," Williams remarks, "Was one of disappointment and reproach, but often a note of confidence was obvious in an appeal to correct the offending conduct." He further notes that if the bearer of this letter had not given the Galatians an indication of Paul's displeasure, then they could no longer be in doubt when they read: "I am astonished" (*Galatians*, 38)! In any event, the seriousness of the situation was such that to mince words would have been to imperil the souls of these people (3:1 is even stronger).

The occasion of his astonishment is the rapidity of the Galatians' movement away from the gospel of Christ: "You are *so quickly* deserting the one who called you...." He may mean "so quickly" after his original preaching to them or after the arrival of the opponents in Galatia. Either way, Paul likely echoes Exod 32:8 ("They have been *quick* to turn away from what I commanded them and have made themselves an idol cast in the shape of a calf") and Deut 9:16 ("When I looked, I saw that you had sinned against the LORD your God; you had made for yourselves an idol cast in the shape of a calf. You had turned aside *quickly* from the way that the LORD had commanded you"). After the exodus, Judg 2:17 brings the same indictment of the people when they were settled in the land: "Yet they would not listen to their judges but prostituted themselves to other gods and worshiped them. Unlike their fathers, they *quickly* turned from the way in which their fathers had walked, the way of obedience to the LORD's commands."

Paul thus depicts the Galatians in Israel-like terms. As the exodus generation (and that of the Judges) so suddenly deserted the Lord for idols, so also the Galatians, the latter-day "Israelites" (6:16), are in the process of repeating Israel's apostasy: they are "quickly" deserting the one who called them.[27] "They were making the very mistake of the first Israelites in abandoning the covenant almost before it had been ratified" (Dunn, *Galatians*, 40). In blunt terms, *the Torah is the Galatians' golden calf!* Here Paul anticipates 4:8-11, in which the stunning assertion is made that life under the Torah is no better than the bondage of pagan idolatry. This warning stands at the head of the letter because of the magnitude of the issues involved. George puts it vividly: "Galatians is a tornado warning!" Although none of God's true people will finally fall away, "There is no such thing as 'eternal security' for a local

---

[27] See further Ciampa, *Scripture*, 71-77; Wilson, "Apostasy," 557-59.

congregation that has lost its first love (Rev 2:1-7)" (*Galatians*, 84).

Paul views their in-progress defection as a "desertion" under fire, a changing sides, a serious defection from a cause. This departure is especially ironic given that the same verb "desert" (*metatithēmi*) was used centuries before to depict the apostasy of Jews from their covenant faith (2 Macc 4:46; 7:24; 11:24). "Ironically," comments Hays, "Paul sees the Galatians act of turning *toward* law observance as a similar act of defection" (*Galatians*, 204). The Galatians' potential apostasy is from "the one who called you in the grace of Christ." "Grace" is God's covenant love for Israel (see on v. 3). Such grace has now been localized and (re)focused in Christ (cf. John 1:16-17), who has formed a new covenant community. He has built *his church* (Matt 16:18). Accordingly, *his church* has been reconfigured after himself and no after longer Israel's Torah.

The Judaizers must have acknowledged the messiahship of Jesus, but for them the Torah was still the embodiment of God's covenant love. Jesus, for them, was a servant of the Torah, in keeping with the common messianic outlook of Second Temple Judaism. But for Paul grace now assumes the "shape" of Christ. It is to such a newly re-formed congregation (*ekklēsia* = *qahal*) that God has called the Galatians. As the Israelites of old had been called to enter and then maintain Yahweh's covenant, so now the church of Jesus Christ has been summoned to embrace the "obedience [perseverance] of faith," with himself as the Lord of the new covenant. If, then, the Galatians defect from Paul's gospel, they will desert *"the God who called them into existence as part of his new creation, the church"* (Martyn, *Galatians*, 117, italics his).

It is "in" such grace that they were called. The preposition "in" (*en*) denotes location. "God's grace is the space into which he has called the Galatians" (Martyn, *Galatians*, 109). Or, as Betz explains, "in" provides a "definition of the situation before God enjoyed by those who were called." Because they are called "in grace," Christians are "in peace," "in hope" and in the state of "holiness" (*Galatians*, 48).

In their disregard of the God who called them "in the grace of Christ," the readers are flirting with "another gospel." In its own way, "another (or "different") gospel" identifies the central issue of the letter. What is at stake in the Galatian churches is what earlier was at stake when Paul visited Jerusalem (2:1-10) and when Peter traveled to Antioch (2:11-14), namely, "the truth of the gospel" (2:5, 14).

Before attempting to understand what "another gospel" is, it is necessary to have biblical ideas of "gospel." To be sure, the "gospel" (*euangelion*) is the "good news" of salvation in Christ. Nevertheless, the OT background of the term is frequently overlooked. Five passages are crucial: Isa 40:9; 41:27; 52:7; 61:1-2; Joel 3:5 (LXX).[28] In all five, an announcement is made that Israel's captivity is at an end and that the people will embark on an exodus from Babylon, just as the wilderness generation had originally come out from Egypt, the "house of bondage." Wright points out that the Isaiah passages, in the broader context of Isaiah 40-66, speak to the issue of Yahweh's return to Zion and his enthronement there, when the nation itself would return from its captivity. Thus, the "good news" has specific reference to Israel in exile, when the Lord would bare his arm and deliver his people in a new exodus of deliverance. "The 'good news' or 'glad tidings' would be the message that the long-awaited release from captivity was at hand."[29]

Additionally, Dickson ("Gospel," 217-20) points to the Psalms as a significance source of "gospel." Ps 40:9-10; 68:11-12; 96:1-2 all proclaim the "good news" of the Lord's deliverance of his people. Psalm 96 in particular exhibits a strong dependency on Isa 40:10; 44:23; 49:13; 44:23; 52:7; 55:12; 59:19; 60:1; 62:11. Notably, the "new song" of Ps 96:11-12 corresponds to the "old song" of Exod 15:1-21: both are celebrations of Yahweh's salvation from the hands of Israel's oppressors; both are songs occasioned by an exodus experience.

By his use of "gospel," then, Paul is the latter-day herald announcing that the new Israel has been delivered, not from Egypt, Babylon or any other human power but Satan; and, as he will say so shockingly later, from the law! As such a herald, Paul follows in the footsteps of Jesus, who himself proclaimed that Isa 61:1-2 was fulfilled in his preaching of the kingdom of God (Matt 11:5; Luke 4:17-21; 7:22). That there should be a deliverance above and beyond the original Isaianic vision is confirmed by the fact that certain crucial features of the anticipated release had not as yet been

---

[28] The theme is picked up in Second Temple literature by *Psalms of Solomon* 11; 1QH 18:14-15; 11QMelch 15-25.

[29] Wright, *Paul*, 41; id., "Gospel." Wright defines Paul's gospel as "the announcement that the true god has acted in fulfilment of his promises, sending the Messiah to die and be raised, and so ushering in the new world order in which the false gods are confronted and confounded and their adherents summoned to a new and liberating allegiance…" ("Gospel," 239).

fulfilled (note how the post-exilic Prophets still anticipate a coming day of the Lord even after the restoration to the land).

If such is the biblical significance of "gospel," then "another gospel" must propound a message that represents a reversal of liberation and bondage. Paul apparently coined the phrase "another gospel" because the Jewish Christian missionaries probably used "gospel" for their own message, and just as probably claimed that their proclamation stemmed from Isa 40:9; 41:27; 52:7; 61:1-2; Joel 3:5 (see the first section note to this verse). But their "gospel" for Paul was anything but release from captivity; it was, in point of fact, a return to slavery. Their "different gospel" is the message that God's grace is restricted to the members of the chosen people who live within the parameters of the Torah, thus making Jewish identity paramount and indispensable. Paul is confident of this because, from the vantage point of fulfillment in Christ, he has experienced the "glad tidings" as deliverance from law (the year of Jubilee = Isa 61:1-2 = Lev 25:8-24). He must not allow the alternative message of the opponents to stand because Gentiles could not and would not be accepted as they are. They would have to become "honorary Jews" in order to enjoy the benefits of redemption.

7 Having stated that the Galatians were moving toward "another gospel," Paul hastens to qualify that there is not really "another gospel." In vv. 6b and 7a two forms of the Greek adjective "other" are placed in service. The former is *heteros* and the latter is *allos*. The classical distinction between the two is that *heteros* means "another of a different kind," while *allos* mean "another of the same kind." Such a distinction would be appropriate here: there is indeed a gospel of a "different kind," but there could never be a gospel "of the same kind." But before hastily concluding that such is the case, it is to be noted that in 2 Cor 11:4 (certainly parallel in thought to the present passage) *allos* and *heteros* are used interchangeably: "another (*allos*) Jesus," "another (*heteros*) spirit," "another (*heteros*) gospel" (cf. 1 Cor 12:9-10). This interchange of terms would tend to confirm the thesis that in the Greek of Paul's day the two were used synonymously (J. K. Elliott, "*Heteros*").

But whether or not Paul observes the niceties of classical Greek, what is clear is that he will not acknowledge any legitimate alternative to *his* gospel (cf. Rom 2:16)—which is the *only* "gospel of Christ" (the phrase is ambiguous: either the gospel with Christ as its sole object or with Christ as its originator, or, very likely, both). The "gospel" of his opponents is qualitatively distinct to his own, even though they may apply the same word to their teaching (probably evoking Isa 40:9; 41:27; 52:7; 61:1; Joel 3:5; and perhaps the LXX of Ps 67:12). According to Martyn, "He means they are turning it around 180 degrees, changing it into the not-gospel. Paul has no intention of seeking a compromise formulation which might lie somewhere between what he calls 'gospel' and that to which the Teachers give the same name" (*Galatians*, 112).

What there are, rather, are "some people [who] are throwing you into confusion and are trying to pervert the gospel of Christ." For Paul, this "other gospel" is a "perversion" of "the gospel *of Christ*." "Pervert" (*metastrephō*) is "a forceful word, denoting a radical change, as of water into blood, fresh water into salt, or feasting into mourning, or daylight into darkness" (Dunn, *Galatians*, 43, referring to the LXX of Ps 77:44; Joel 3:4; Amos 8:10; Sir 39:23; 1 Macc 9:41; Acts 2:20; see also Jas 4:9). "The idea is not merely a twisting of the gospel, but of giving it an emphasis which virtually transformed it into something else" (Guthrie, *Galatians*, 63). The real gospel was being transmuted into a proclamation that focused on the Torah, not on Christ and his cross.

Effectively, this "other gospel," instead of delivering people from bondage, has returned them to a different kind of bondage, slavery to the law. Such, according to Paul, was the precise intent of the rival missionaries: they were desirous of this very state of affairs (literally, they were "willing" [*thelontes*] to pervert Christ's gospel). "Their intent," comments Ridderbos, "Was to overturn the gospel that had Christ as its content and to live out an opposing principle. This happens when the cross of Christ is no longer recognized in its all-sufficiency.... Then the gospel is turned upside-down and robbed of its strength" (*Galatians*, 49).

Those who enunciate such a "gospel" are "troublers" (see further 5:10; 6:17). The verb "trouble" (*tarassō*), rendered "throwing you into confusion" by NIV, means a pronounced agitation, such as an upheaval of water (John 5:7). In the NT, it has reference mainly to mental/psychological disturbance, consisting in excitement, perplexity or fear (Matt 2:3; John 14:1; Acts 15:24). Acts 15:24 is especially relevant, because it makes precisely the same point as Paul: "Since we have heard that certain persons who have gone out from us, though with no instructions from us, have said things to *disturb* (*etaraxan*) you and have unsettled your minds" (NRSV). The Galatians thus found themselves in a state of chaos rather than the peace to which they had been called in Paul's gospel (see on v. 3).

Additionally, Paul may be alluding to Achar, the "troubler of Israel" (1 Chr 2:7).[30] If so, he is implying that the Judaizers are the disturbers of the new Israel and apostates on a par with Achar. The irony would be even more intense if "troublers" is an oblique reference to the Gentile rulers and Jewish apostates who were "troubling" Israel's faithful during the Maccabean crisis.[31] Paul's designation of the Teachers as "troublers" has implications for his relations with Jerusalem. As Bligh discerns, "St Paul could say that the 'pillars' were shaking the churches of Galatia through their uncontrolled disciples" (*Galatians*, 87). Paul will pursue these relations in v. 10 and in detail in chap. 2.

8-9 Paul gets down to "brass tacks" as regards the troublers by pronouncing a curse upon them or anyone else—including himself and angels—who would dare bring "another gospel." "Here Paul is breathing fire. His zeal is so fervent that he almost begins to curse the angels themselves" (Luther, quoted by George, *Galatians*, 97-98)! To modern sensitivities, the language of these verses would be highly offensive. However, Paul is not to be judged by the standards of the political correctness which so preoccupies our generation, especially when "the truth of the gospel" (2:5, 14) was on the line.

Angels are likely singled out because of their role in the mediation of the law (Deut 33:2 (LXX); Acts 7:53; Heb 2:1; cf. Gal 3:19-20). But even the exalted status of angels would not exempt them from cursing if they preached another gospel. As Dunn notes, a standard feature of Jewish apocalypses is angelic messengers who place a heavenly stamp of approval on a message to be delivered. Paul would thus be implying that in comparison with such awe-inspiring beings, the people to whom the Galatians were listening were far less weighty in authority (*Galatians*, 45). Moreover, it is not irrelevant that later, in 2 Cor 11:13-15, Paul will call this same basic group no less than imitators of Satan, who disguises himself as an "angel of light."

---

[30] See Ciampa, *Scripture*, 79-83.

[31] See Cummins, *Paul*, 101. Cummins adds that the activity of the agitators is said to include "compelling" the Galatians to be circumcised (6:12). This, he says, is reminiscent of the efforts of Antiochus IV to "compel" (*anagkazō*) the Maccabean martyrs to forsake the fundamental expressions of their Torah-obedience. "Ironically, from Paul's standpoint, the Agitators' compulsion toward circumcision (and Torah-obedience) was but a replication of the very persecution (for Christ) that it sought to avoid" (ibid., 102). Cf. the comments on 4:29.

Paul's "curse" (*anathema*) is equivalent to the same term in the Hebrew Bible (*ḥērem*), which means a "devoted thing" or a "sacred ban" set apart for divine destruction (e.g., Lev 27:28-29; Deut 7:26; 13:17; 30:7; Josh 6:17-18; 7:1, 11-13).[32] Deut 21:23 likewise sheds light on Paul's reference to the curse. In this verse, a different word than *ḥērem* is used (*qillah*). Here, the person who hangs on a tree is regarded as an apostate from the covenant and is for that reason a "devoted thing," "God's curse" (*qillath Elohim*).

From Paul's perspective, those who "pervert the gospel of Christ" ought to be regarded as such apostates, only from the new covenant. They should receive the same treatment as that meted out to Christ by their non-Christian Jewish compatriots when they nailed him to a Roman cross (= the tree of Deut 21:22-23. 1QS 2:5-17 contains a passage not dissimilar to Paul's own imprecation, though it goes on at much more length.). In their case, however, the curse is that of the new covenant. Paul picks up on the language of the Torah, but his application is within the framework of his gospel. So ironically, the curse of the gospel is the eschatological curse of the law imposed on those who prefer it over the Christ of Paul's proclamation.[33]

Verse 9 reiterates the point for the sake of emphasis by recalling what Paul said previously. Whether "as we have already said" refers back to v. 8 or to Paul's original mission to the churches of Galatia is an open question. What is important is that these people received the only authorized gospel from Paul and, therefore, from God the Father and the Lord Jesus Christ (1:1, 3). In Paul, "receive" (*paralambanō*), along with "deliver" or "pass on" (*paradidōmi*), is technical terminology for receiving and passing on the apostolic tradition. Actually, the terms did not originate with Paul, because he takes them over from Judaism (*paralambanō* = *qibbēl*; *paradidōmi* = *masar*), where they referred to the reception and transmission of Jewish tradition (e.g., Gal 1:12; 1 Cor 11:2, 23; 15:1, 3; Phil 4:9; cf. Mark 7:4; Acts 7:53). In the present passage, the implication is that "the gospel of Christ" has superseded the Torah, especially as interpreted by rabbinic teaching. The divine tradition has now assumed a new shape.

10 The rhetorical question of v. 10 is best viewed as the climax of the paragraph begun with v. 6 rather than the start of a new paragraph or even a transition between the two (accounting for the con-

---

[32] On the covenant context of cursing, see Morland, *Rhetoric*, 33-97.
[33] Cf. Ciampa, *Scripture*, 83-88; Morland, *Rhetoric*, 142-79.

junction "for" at the head of the sentence). If anyone has charged Paul with being a "man-pleaser" (cf. *Pss. Sol.* 4:7, 8, 19; Eph 6:6; Col 3:22), then his tone in these verses should be proof enough that he is not. He is decidedly not "all things to all men" (1 Cor 9:22) in the sense that his detractors would have the Galatians believe. As he maintains elsewhere, "We are not trying to please men but God, who tests our hearts" (1 Thess 2:4). From the Jewish/Judaizing perspective, the charge of people-pleasing would have been leveled because superficially it would have appeared that Paul has dispensed with the law only in order to be a successful missionary.

Paul thus denies that he is attempting (the present tense as denoting attempted action) to "persuade" or "please" certain people. The verb "persuade" (*peithō*) was current in the ancient world and bore the negative connotation of persuasion with an improper end in view (Betz, *Galatians*, 54-55). But more to the point, Cummins proposes that *peithō* has reference to the efforts of the Maccabean martyrs (in 2 and 4 Maccabees) to persuade one another to remain faithful in the face of their tormentors' efforts to persuade them otherwise—"this being a means of convincing the latter of the superiority of the Jewish way of life." Paul, however, is convinced that the agitators' demand for circumcision and Torah observance is a persuasion (*peismonē*) which does not come from God who calls the Galatian converts to obey (*peithō*) the truth (5:7-8). Paul seeks only to persuade people concerning justification and reconciliation as effected by the death and resurrection of Christ (2 Cor 5:9, 11). "In essence, whereas the Agitators stand in the Maccabean tradition of persuading men and God of their zeal for the cause of Judaism, Paul's mission is devoted to persuading men and God of his commitment to the cause of Christ" (*Paul*, 113).

Similarly, the verb translated "please" (*areskō*) in v. 10:b, c can have shades of "accommodating oneself" to the desires of others, or, in the current vernacular, "kissing up" to people. It is true that "please" in v. 10a has two objects: "men" and "God." But in the case of God, the verb must assume a different significance than as applied to human beings. Apart from 1 Thess 2:4, the most appropriate parallel is 2 Cor 5:9: "So we make it our goal to please him, whether we are at home in the body or away from it."

The "men" to whom Paul was supposedly pandering take in a wide variety of individuals. Writing as he does in vv. 6-9, he certainly was not seeking to curry the favor of Christian Gentiles in general, let alone that of the Galatians. Likewise, he could not be fairly accused of seeking to "persuade" or "please" the Judaizers. They recognized Jesus as the Messiah, but there was no real comprehension on their part that he had brought an end to the law. Consequently, Paul, as the "servant of Christ," incurs their wrath when it appears that he has lessened the covenant obligations of the people of God. Moreover, in his endeavor to please God rather than human beings, he is implying that his antagonists are not pleasing to God, just as he was not while he was a "zealot" for the law and "traditions of the fathers" (1:13-14; Phil 3:6).

These "men" comprise more than the above mentioned groups. In light of v. 1, which makes the first mention of "men," the mother church in Jerusalem and the apostles in particular must be included. This identification would make sense given that Paul was alleged to have received his commission and marching orders from Jerusalem. However, some explanation is required because the main target in his crosshairs in vv. 6-9 is the Judaizers and their false gospel. In a word, as Paul writes Galatians, Jerusalem is too closely aligned with the circumcision party, as will become evident in chap. 2, where Paul will effectively assert that he is more consistent with gospel principles than the "pillar" apostles. Thus, in pronouncing a divine imprecation on the "Torah-gospel" of the Judaizers, Paul is at the same time calling into question the involvement of "men" such as James and Peter with "the believers who belonged to the party of the Pharisees" (Acts 15:5).

Paul is emphatic that if he were still pleasing men, he would not and could not be the servant of Christ, who preeminently was exposed to the hatred of the Jewish establishment with its zealotry for the law, the land, the temple and the national life. He regularly announces that he is a "servant (slave) of Christ" (Rom 1:1; Phil 1:1; Titus 1:1).[34] But here he may be suggesting as well that he is a "suffering servant," as he does in Rom 15:21 and Acts 13:47, where he applies the Servant songs of Isa 52:15 and Isa 49:6 respectively to his own ministry (see below on v. 15). Paul was marked out for such suffering on the Damascus Road (Acts 9:15-16).

---

[34] Cf. Cummins, *Paul*, 210-11; Dodd, *"I,"* 148-51. That it is duty of a servant/slave to please his master, is treated in detail by Tsang, *Slaves*, 63-74. The slave metaphor, as Tsang shows, is rooted not only the Greco-Roman world of Paul's day but also in the OT.

Section Notes

6 Martyn raises the possibility that the Judaizers may have rooted their conception of the "good news" in the LXX of Ps 67:12 (Hebrew 68:12): "The Lord gives the word [that is, the Law]; great is the company of those who bore the tidings" (*hoi euangelizomenoi*). He notes that in the midrash (commentary) on the Psalms the text is interpreted in such a way as to combine the several elements: "The Law itself constitutes the glad tidings; the evangelists who conveyed the tidings of the Law are numerous; and they brought the nomistic tidings to the Gentiles." In a similar way, the Teachers may have told the Galatians that they were bringing the glad tidings of the covenantal law to the nations (*Galatians*, 134). In any event, what certainly molded the expectations of the other missionaries was a literal reading of such passages such as Isa 2:1-4 and Mic 4:1-4, according to which the nations were to make their "eschatological pilgrimage" to Jerusalem to submit to none other than the law. From their perspective, what could be clearer?

6 Wright indicates that "good news" was also used in the Greco-Roman world with reference to the accession of a new emperor and in imperial decrees (see further Martyn, *Galatians*, 127-28; Dickson, "Gospel," 214-15; Schnelle, *Paul*, 405-6; O'Brien, *Gospel*, 78-79). Thus, there is a twofold background to Paul's use of *euangelion*. If this association was in Paul's mind, he may be viewed as staking a claim for the kingship of Christ as over against that of the Roman emperor. "If and when YHWH set up his own king as the true ruler, his true earthly representative, all other kingdoms would be confronted with their rightful overlord" (*Paul*, 44). See also ibid., 56-57, 88-89, 149; id., "Gospel and Theology," 227-29, 232-33; id., "Paul's Gospel." See further on 1:22.

8 Arnold informs us that the language of cursing in Galatians finds parallels in the Anatolian inscriptions. He considers that this theme of cursing may have been prompted simply and only by Paul's citation of Deuteronomy; but it does raise the question of why this passage was brought into the discussion in the first place. Did Paul's opponents raise this passage with the Galatians because it combined the theme of cursing with the theme of law observance? On the part of the Jewish Christian missionaries, this would have been a brilliant contextualization given the fact that a fear of being cursed was an integral part of the Anatolian culture. Numerous curse tablets, he says, can be cited to illustrate this feature of the belief-structure of these people. Paul, however, appears to turn the tables on his opponents by magnifying the crucifixion of Jesus as effective for taking the curse that properly belonged to all people because of their failure to observe the law (3:13). He then takes it a step further by wishing that anyone who teaches something contrary to this good news of utter and complete redemption in Christ would come under a curse (1:8-9) ("Folk Belief," 447).

PAUL'S AUTOBIOGRAPHY AS PARADIGM (1:11-2:21)

The purpose of the long section of 1:11-2:21 has been debated for some time. Frequently it is titled "Paul's defense of his apostleship" or "Paul's defense of his gospel." Yet this reading fails to perceive that Paul is essentially on the offensive, not the defensive. He is in fact asserting authority, not answering allegations (Schütz, *Anatomy*, 114-58). This division of the letter reaches its climax when Paul confronts none other than Peter in Antioch and administers to him a stinging rebuke, a sure sign that his authority is to be recognized on a par with that of Cephas, one of the "pillars" of Jerusalem. Moreover, if his authority is equal, it is also one that he maintains independently of the mother church.

But the major component of this unusual passage in Paul's letters is "Pauline autobiography;" that is, Paul writes about himself principally to present an example to his converts and to provide contrastive models between his ministry and that of his rivals.[35] As Gaventa puts it, "Paul presents himself as an example of the working of the gospel" ("Autobiography," 313). The gist of this "autobiography as paradigm" is actually stated later, in 4:12: "I plead with you, brothers, become like me, for I became like you." As Gaventa explains, "become like me" means that the Galatians are to imitate Paul "by rejecting all that threatens to remove them from an exclusive relationship to the gospel." Correspondingly, "for I became like you" means that "one reason for their imitation of Paul is that Paul has already rejected his zeal for the Law and the tradition."[36] Such is Paul's "biography of reversal" (Schütz, *Anatomy*, 133).

---

[35] Schütz, *Anatomy*, 128-58; Lyons, *Autobiography*; Dodd, *"I;"* Hubbard, *Creation*, 191-99; de Boer, *Imitation*. Fiore shows that Paul's promotion of himself as an example falls into line with Greco-Roman precedents ("Paul," 228-37). Such self-exemplification, therefore, would probably not have come as a surprise to his Galatian readers or have been offensive to them.

[36] Gaventa, "Autobiography," 321. Cf. Dunn, "Paul's Conversion," 88-90. Hays writes that Paul's desire for the Galatians to imitate him may seem immodest to modern readers. However, in the ancient world it was commonplace. Philosophers and moral teachers were expected to provide a model for others. But most notably, in most of Paul's imitation passages he urges his readers to conform to Christ's example of self-sacrificial suffering for the sake of others, as exemplified by his own conduct (*Galatians*, 293).

In short, when Paul came to Christ he ceased to be a "zealot" for the "traditions of the fathers." The Galatians, on the other hand, having come to Christ, want to become such zealots as Paul was! Paul thus presents himself as an exemplar who has arrived at "the conviction that there is only one gospel and that it requires *the abandonment of all prior commitments, conventions, and value systems*. Zeal for tradition, maintenance of the law, ethnic and social barriers, and observance of feast days are alike insofar as they threaten to undermine the exclusive claim of the gospel" (Gaventa, "Autobiography," 319, italics mine). Another way to put it is that Paul's zeal has now been redirected, from the law to love of Christ and his people.[37]

> From his own account it is clear that in his former way of life as a zealous Jew—not least as expressed in his persecution of the church—Paul stood firmly in the tradition of the Maccabean model of Judaism. However, God's dramatic disclosure of Jesus as the Son of God had resulted in a radical reconfiguration of Paul's person and vocation: from latter-day Maccabean to a Christian apostle now completely conformed to the martyred and exalted Messiah Jesus. This transformation provided a stark counter-example for those of his Galatian converts now under the influence of Agitators' promulgation of matters Jewish, and was the fundamental standpoint from which Paul was prepared to critique even the apostle Peter whose recent conduct (in Antioch) also threatened to undermine conformity to Christ.[38]

---

[37] See at length Cummins, *Paul*, 120-37, 148-49. Cummins appropriately terms Paul an "ironic Maccabean figure," by which he means that "Paul stands in the tradition of zeal as represented by the leading figures in the Maccabean revolt, but with a zeal which is now dramatically redeployed in the service of his commitment to the martyred and risen Messiah Jesus" (ibid., 95, n. 2).

[38] Cummins, *Paul*, 126. Cummins adds later: "Thus, rather than the Gentile embracing the Maccabees' God, here we have the zealous Jew transformed by God in virtue of his encounter with one whom he now recognizes as the representative and redeemer of those he had being persecuting: the martyred but now exalted Messiah/Son of God. No longer a Maccabean-inspired servant of Judaism, Paul now embarks upon a prophetic ministry to Jew and Gentile alike, ready to suffer and die for Messiah Jesus and his people. Immediate confirmation of his transformation and its effect is provided by the plots against him by antagonistic Jews both in Damascus and then Jerusalem (Acts 9.23-30). Such opposition will continue throughout his ministry, not least in Antioch" (ibid., 149).

GALATIANS CHAPTER ONE

A. The Divine Origin of Paul's Gospel (1:11-12)

In his introduction, Paul has arrested the attention of his audience by raising several of the letter's leading concerns. Now, as a kind of preface to his autobiographical narrative, Paul states a thesis. It comes by way of a blunt assertion that the origin of his gospel, unlike that of his detractors, is "from above," and not "from below."

11-12 As his transition into the narrative portion of the letter, Paul address his "brothers" (and "sisters") (*adelphoi*). This term of endearment, like "neighbor" (Luke 10:29-37), has undergone a redefinition. At one time, the title would have been restricted to the Jewish people, but now it is applied universally to all who believe in Christ. These verses reiterate vv. 1-4 for the sake of emphasis. If previously Paul had said that his apostleship is not "from" or "through" human beings, then here he stresses that the gospel preached by him is "not to any degree human" (*kata anthrōpon*) in origin. He did not receive it from humans, and he was not taught by them as though he needed to sit at anyone's feet. Therefore, his motivation in preaching has nothing to do with pleasing people. The reference is again to the "pillars" in Jerusalem.

But even though these verses are transitional, they are at the same time a kind of superscription to what follows. Matera is right to stress that this theme of the origin of the gospel is foundational to everything Paul will say in the letter. "Because the gospel originates with God, what seemed utterly impossible has taken place: God has accepted the Gentiles into the commonwealth of Israel on the basis of faith rather than on the basis of the works of the law.... Since Paul's law-free gospel originates with God, the Galatians should refuse all efforts by others to make them adopt the works of the law" (*Galatians*, 55). It is just this basic proposition that Paul will illustrate by his own life, when he turned from the law to Christ.

This superhuman origin of his gospel is something that Paul "makes known" to his "brothers." The verb "make known" (NIV: "I want you to know") (*gnōrizō*), along with its Hebrew equivalents, is used of divine revelation (Dan 2:23, 28-30, 45; 5:7-8, 15-17; 7:16 [Theodotian]; 1QpHab 7:4-5; 1QH 4:27-28; 7:27; 1 Cor 15:1; Eph 1:9; 3:3-5, 10; 6:19; Col 1:27). Paul did not receive (by way of a chain of human tradition) anything from others, but as apostle *he* reveals the gospel of Christ to the nations (see 1 Cor

15:1, where *gnōrizō* is used identically). Quite explicitly, then, Paul claims to be an organ of divine revelation and, by implication, denies this to his antagonists. Below, in 1:15, he will range himself with Isaiah and Jeremiah as a prophet (of the new covenant). Paul had previously made the gospel known to the Galatians, but now he reasserts or "rereveals," with the same authority the divine origin of what was communicated to them on his original missionary journey.

No doubt because of assertions to the contrary, Paul is compelled once more to deny that his gospel is human in origin or in mediation (*ou kata anthrōpon*). Furthermore, he was not "taught" this gospel. In a manner remarkably dissimilar to his training as a young rabbinical student, whereby he was taught both Torah and interpretive tradition "line upon line and precept upon precept," his proclamation and mission to the nations came "straight down from above" by virtue of his vision of the risen Christ on the Damascus Road.

Thus, his denial is reinforced by the positive assertion that he received his gospel "by revelation of Jesus Christ." "By revelation" (*di' apokalupseōs*) is the antithesis to the claim that Paul's gospel owes its origin to any "human" (*kata anthrōpon*) agency or intervention (v. 11). The phrase "revelation of Jesus Christ" could mean either that Christ is the revealer or that he is the one revealed. But since both things are actually true, there is no need to distinguish formally between them. It comes as no surprise that the word "revelation" (*apokalupsis*) is associated with divine disclosure and guidance, as in 2:2 (also 1 Cor 14:6, 26; 2 Cor 12:1, 7), and eschatological events (Rom 2:5; 8:19; 1 Cor 1:7; 2 Thess 1:7). Here, the clear reference is to the Damascus Road, where the risen Christ was disclosed to Paul and from whom he received his commission to go to the Gentiles. This revelation had confronted Paul with the inescapable reality of the Crucified One. "From beyond the age of evil and death the living Christ appeared to him; and because of this undeniable, absolutely authoritative experience, Paul had no choice but to believe that the claim of the Nazarene's followers was, after all, true" (Williams, *Galatians*, 44).

According to Acts 9:17; 26:16, Jesus "appeared" in his christophany to Paul for this very purpose. On that occasion, God was pleased to reveal his son "in" (and consequently "through") Paul (Gal 1:15). Paul has seen no mere angel but the Lord Jesus himself. To describe his experience as an "apocalypse," says Dunn, not only underlines its heavenly authority but also implies that it has "eschatological significance as the key that unlocked the mystery of God's purpose for his creation, the keystone of the whole arch of human history" (*Galatians*, 53). Not only is Paul's message eschatological, that is, the announcement of the fulfillment of the Scriptures, he himself is an eschatological person. "The Age to Come had been inaugurated. Saul himself was summoned to be its agent. He was to declare to the pagan world that YHWH, the God of Israel, was the one true God of the whole world, and that in Jesus of Nazareth he had overcome evil and was creating a new world in which justice and peace would reign supreme" (Wright, *Paul*, 37). No wonder, he can say elsewhere (1 Cor 9:16): "Woe to me if I do not preach the gospel" (RSV), because with his presence and in his proclamation the new creation arrives.

"Revelation," especially of the "mystery," is an important word in Paul's theological vocabulary.[39] When the Son of God was revealed to Paul on the way to Damascus, simultaneously he received insight into the "mystery of Christ," that is, how it is that God has now reconciled Jew and Gentile in one body in order to render to King Jesus the obedience of faith (Rom 16:25-26; Eph 2:11-22; Col 1:25-28). It is this very insight he wishes others to appreciate (Eph 3:1-6; Col 2:2)—and not least the Galatians. If they understood the nature of Christ's revelation to Paul, they would not be seeking to follow the Judaizers' lead in reerecting the "dividing wall of hostility" (Eph 2:14 [RSV]) between nations (cf. Gal 2:18).

B. Paul's Former Life in Judaism (1:13-14)

If vv. 11-12 are a kind of thesis Paul seeks to defend throughout the first major section of the letter, he now commences the first part of his "autobiography as paradigm" by recounting his conduct prior to his encounter with the risen Christ. If anything characterized Saul of Tarsus, it was "zeal for the law." And Paul, the apostle and author of this epistle, apparently thought it necessary to embark on his narrative at this point. "His readers needed to be reminded that he knew Judaism from inside, and indeed was a prime exponent of it. He knew therefore what were its attractions and appealing strengths" (Dunn, *Galatians*, 55).

13 Paul's autobiographical narrative commences with a reminder to the Galatians that they have heard it before, maybe from Paul himself, or perhaps because his enemies tried to use his former

---

[39] Bockmuehl, *Revelation*; Carson, "Mystery."

zealotry as a weapon against him, with the charge of either hypocrisy or overreaction to his erstwhile conduct. The sum and total of his pre-Christian existence is summed up by "my previous way of life in Judaism." The one Greek noun translated "previous way of life" (*anastrophē*) corresponds to the Hebrew verb "walk" (*halak*), "The word which more than any other characterizes the Jewish understanding of the obligations laid upon the devout" (Dunn, *Galatians*, 56).[40] From this verb was to develop the concept of *halakah*, teaching that governed the Israelite's walk with God. The plural of this noun, *halakoth*, designates the "rulings" of the various rabbinic teachers.[41] Over against Paul's former "Jewish walk," the Galatian letter will inform us that there is a "Christian walk," one that corresponds to "walking by the Spirit" (5:16, 25), who engenders unity, peace and harmony in the new creation (cf. *anastrophē* in 1 Tim 4:12; Heb 13:7; 1 Pet 1:15; 2:12).

Paul's former "walk" was in "Judaism." The name "Judaism" was apparently coined by the author of 2 Maccabees (2:21; 8:1; 14:38; cf. 4 Macc 4:26) in conscious reaction to "Hellenism," also a word of his coinage (4:13). In brief, "Judaism" is "'the Jewish way of belief and life' as contrasted to the way of life in Hellenism" (Hansen, *Galatians*, 43). In a day when the Jewish people were so hard-pressed to maintain their distinctive ethnic and covenantal identity, "Judaism," remarks one Jewish scholar, demarcated "a sort of fenced-off area in which Jewish lives are led."[42] Moreover, Cummins points out that the LXX usages of *Ioudaismos* pertain to the martyr's zeal and self-sacrifice on behalf of Judaism, a point well worth weighing given Paul's present train of thought. He adds that the incorporative phrase "in Judaism" conveys the all-embracive commitment involved on the part of the martyr and may

---

[40] See Gen 5:22; 17:1; Exod 16:4; Deut 8:6; 1 Kgs 6:12; Ps 101:6; Prov 20:7; Dan 9:10; Luke 1:6; cf. *T. Ash.* 6:3; 2 Macc 6:23. Cummins (*Paul*, 121) shows that *anastrophē* is applied to the exemplary way of life of the martyr Eleazar (2 Macc 6:23; cf. Tob 4:14). The synonymous term *agōgē*, "conduct" or "manner of life," occurs at 2 Macc 4:16; 6:8; 11:24. Less to the point but perhaps lurking in the background is *anastrophē* as the nurture and training of a young man in the Greco-Roman world (Malina/Neyrey, *Portraits*, 27-28).

[41] See Schürer, *History*, 2.339-46. Tomson defines *halakah* as "a system of consciously guided practical conduct, in which all human acts and functions have a specific significance" (*Paul*, 221).

[42] Amir, "*IOUDAISMOS*," 39. On the terms "Jew" and "Judaism," see further Dunn, "Judaism," 232-35; id., "Who Did Paul," 179-85; id., *Jesus Remembered*, 260-65; Ciampa, *Scripture*, 106-8; Harvey, *Israel*.

be taken as analogous to "in the law" (Rom 3:19; Phil 3:6) (*Paul*, 121).

The equivalent of "Judaism" appears in verbal form in 2:14: "Live as a Jew," which in that context means to avoid such intimate contact with Gentiles as table fellowship. Hengel adds that "Judaism" means "both political and genetic associations with the Jewish nation and exclusive belief in the one God of Israel, together with observance of the Torah given by him" (*Judaism*, 1.1-2). As a religious, ethnic and sociological unit, this "Judaism" was composed of "four pillars:" (1) monotheism; (2) election; (3) covenant focused in Torah; and (4) land focused in temple. "Characteristic of early Judaism was the sense of Israel's distinctiveness and privilege as the people chosen by God and marked out from the other nations by this covenant relation and by the Torah practice of those loyal to this covenant (and thus to God)."[43]

With the passage of time, particularly given the Syrian and Roman conquests of Palestine, "Judaism" became synonymous with "zeal for the law" and an implacable nationalism that was prepared to deal harshly with even an apparent usurpation of power over the law and the temple. For this reason, Paul's subsequent struggle against circumcision and the law was not least a "betrayal of Judaism" in the eyes of his Judaistic opponents because of its "ethnic political consequences" (Hengel, *Judaism*, 1.307-8). As the argument of Galatians develops, it will become apparent that "Judaism" is now passé and has been superseded by another entity, namely, "the church of God" as centered in the person of Jesus Christ. In practical terms, this means that "Paul believes that observance of the Torah is neither necessary nor sufficient to make or keep one a member of the people of God. The people of God are no longer under the Mosaic covenant in Paul's view, rather they are under the new covenant which is grounded in the earlier Abrahamic one." When Paul ended his career as a persecutor, he came to see "a fundamental distinction between being a Torah-true Jew and a Jewish follower of Jesus Christ" (Witherington, *Grace*, 98, 104).

According to his own testimony, Paul's career in Judaism entailed no less than brutality: "How intensely (*kath' huperbolēn*) I persecuted the church of God and tried to destroy it." He uses here the vocabulary of zeal with verbs in the Greek imperfect tense, denoting past progressive action ("I used to persecute") and, in the

---

[43] Dunn, *Partings*, 28. On monotheism and election, see further Wright, *Perspective*, 83-129.

case of the second, attempted action ("I tried to destroy"). (1) "Persecute" (*diōkō*). The verb is used notably in 1 Macc 2:47; 3:5 to describe the Maccabees' pursuit of "the sons of arrogance" and "the lawless," including apostate Jews (Cummins, *Paul*, 121-22). (2) "Destroy" or "annihilate" (*portheō*). As Hengel informs us, the verb has a very harsh ring and denotes violent action (*Pre-Christian Paul*, 71-72). In Josephus, *J. W.* 4.534, it denotes the burning of the villages and towns of Idumaea by Simon bar Giora and is used synonymously with "lay waste" (*lumaiomai*). The latter verb is used by Luke in Acts 8:3 to describe Saul's persecuting activity: "Saul began to *destroy* the church. Going from house to house, he dragged off men and women and put them in prison."

That Paul's image as a persecutor of the church made an indelible impression emerges from the assessment of him by the churches of Judea: "The man who formerly persecuted us is now preaching the faith he once tried to destroy" (1:23). Moreover, according to Acts 9:21, all who heard the newly converted Paul preach "were astonished and said, 'Is not this the man who devastated those in Jerusalem who call on this name...'." Paul's persecuting campaign did not flinch at the use of violence, a picture certainly confirmed by the portrait of him in Acts 8:1-3; 9:1-2; 22:4; 26:9. As George remarks, Paul could put on his résumé that he had zealously persecuted the church (Phil 3:6) (*Galatians*, 115). It may be that his ire was especially aroused by Stephen's speech (Acts 7), in which this Hellenistic Jewish believer had the audacity to charge that his contemporaries were as guilty of idolatry as their fathers in the wilderness, particularly as regarded the temple, a "house made with hands," that is, a pagan temple or an idol.[44] Saul, then, perceived the new faith as a dire threat to everything he held dear in "Judaism," not only theologically but sociologically as well.[45]

Any suggestion that the boundaries between Israel and the nations had been eradicated and the law decentralized could not be tolerated—let alone the idea of a crucified Messiah. But the road to Damascus changed all that, and years later he could still lament the

---

[44] See Dunn, *Partings*, 64-67; Kilgallen, *Speech*, 90-98. As an important qualification, both Bryan (*Jesus*, 230) and Franklin (*Christ*, 105-6) are correct that the temple is not portrayed as inherently idolatrous. Rather, the complaint is against an attitude that assigned permanence and finality to the temple.

[45] Paul's targets may have been mainly Hellenistic Jewish believers, but, as Schnelle cautions, persecution of one segment of the church would certainly have impacted the other segments (*Paul*, 84-85).

fact that he formerly blasphemed, persecuted and insulted not only the church but the Lord Jesus himself (1 Tim 1:13 = Acts 9:4; 22:7; 26:14; cf. 1 Cor 15:9). Not only so, he could later summarize his whole pre-Christian experience as "loss" and "excrement" (*skubala*) (Phil 3:7-8). The latter term is particularly scathing, because as a Pharisee Paul was preeminently concerned with purity. But now he reduces the entirety of his "former life in Judaism" to one of the most *impure* items on the list!

The object of his rage was "the church of God." Such was the radicalness of Paul's conversion that the noxious heresy he once tried to decimate he now recognizes to be nothing other than the assembly of Yahweh, not simply a breakaway movement from Judaism instigated by the carpenter of Galilee. The irony of the situation is such that "the very actions aimed at preserving the purity of the assembly of Israel had actually been directed against that assembly itself" (Dunn, *Galatians*, 58)!

14 Coordinate with Paul's zealot-like persecution of the church was his "advance" or "progress" in Judaism. So precocious was he that he outstripped a great many of his contemporaries, presumably in learning, devotion, realization of the Pharisaic ideals of Torah observance, influence and jealousy for the God of Israel. The Jewish factor is further stressed by the mention of Paul's race.[46] "Race" (the word is obscured by NIV) also occurs in 2 Cor 11:26; Phil 3:5, where it refers to the people of Israel. Once more, he uses the imperfect tense of the verb, "advance," to call attention to his constant progress in the ways of Israel. The springboard of his advancement was his "excessive" (*perissoterōs*) zeal which resulted in such an intense (*kath' huperbolēn*) persecution of the disciples of Jesus (v. 13), as it were, a devastation "above and beyond the call of duty."

Some commentators wish to restrict "zeal" to "ardent observation of the Torah," in conformity to what was expected of a first-century Jew. Certainly it does mean this much. But the very mention of zeal calls to mind the war for independence against the Syrians some two hundred years before Paul wrote Galatians. The war was spearheaded by an aged priest named Mattathias who issued the summons: "Let every one who is zealous for the law and supports the covenant come out with me" (1 Macc 2:27)! Mattathias himself was but a throwback to Phinehas (Num 25:10-13, remembered by 1 Macc 2:26, 54; 4 Macc 18:12; Sir 45:23-24),

---

[46] A biblical theology of race is developed by J. D. Hays, *People*.

whose own zeal for Yahweh set the pattern for all subsequent defenders of covenant purity (Num 25:11-15; Ps 106:30-31).[47] For good reason, Wright can say that zeal for a first-century Jew was something he did with a knife (*Paul*, 27)![48] From that point onward, "zeal for the law" became the order of the day for all loyalist Jews.[49]

Such zeal had become all the more relevant since the Roman takeover of Palestine and the resurgence of "zealot" activities which would eventually erupt in another war not many years after Paul's mission (in the first quarter of the second century AD, a final uprising would take place under Bar Kochba, who likewise modeled himself on zealot precedents). Saul of Tarsus, then, would have agreed with one of his forebears: "I am full of zeal against all evil-doers and men of falsehood" (1QH 14:14; cf. 1QS 9:22), and with one who was later to say: "Everyone who sheds the blood of godless men is like one who offers a sacrifice" (*Num. R.* 21:3, on Num 25:13). Paul's agenda as a "zealot" is well summarized by Wright: (1) he was zealous for Israel's God and for the Torah; (2) he intended that he and others should keep the Torah so wholeheartedly in the present that they would be marked out as those who would be vindicated on the great coming day of the Lord when he finally acted to redeem his people; (3) he intended to hasten this day by forcing other Jews to keep the Torah in his way, using violence if and when necessary (*Paul*, 35).

His almost unrivaled zeal was spurred by "the traditions of the fathers." This phrase finds its rootage in such pre-Christian Jewish texts as Sir 8:9; 1 Macc 2:19-22; 2 Macc 6:1; 3 Macc 1:3, 23; 4 Macc 16:16; 18:5; *1 Enoch* 52:9; Josephus, *Ant.* 11.140; 13.297, 408; 19.349; Philo, *Spec. Laws* 2.253.[50] The same idea comes over into the gospels as the "tradition of the elders" or the "traditions of men" (Matt 15:2-3, 6; Mark 7:3, 5, 8-9, 13). Acts 22:3 is notably parallel to our text: "I am a Jew, born in Tarsus in Cilicia, but brought up in this city at the feet of Gamaliel, *educated strictly according to our ancestral law, being zealous for God*, just as all of you are today" (NRSV). "The traditions of the fathers" are nor-

---

[47] See Garlington, *Obedience*, 114-21.

[48] See further Donaldson, "Zealot;" Fairchild, "Associations;" Witherington, *Grace*, 101-4; Schnelle, *Paul*, 66-69, 83-86; Cummins, *Paul*, 122.

[49] See Hengel, *Zealots*, esp. 146-312; Cummins, *Paul*, 54-72; Donaldson, *ISBE* (2nd ed.), 4.1175-79; Udoh, "Views," 216-18; Brown, *Death*, 1.686-93 (along with other revolutionary movements, pp. 679-93).

[50] See further Schlier, *Galater*, 51-52.

mally classified according to two central components. (1) The teachings and practices developed in the Pharisaic schools of Second Temple Judaism, which later were codified in the Mishnah, Talmud(s), Jewish commentaries (*midrashim*) and devotional literature (*haggadah*). (2) The interpretations of a more popular nature that arose in the synagogues of Paul's day, which were to become the Aramaic paraphrases of the OT (*targumim*).[51]

All in all, many of these "traditions" came to be regarded as on a par with the written Scriptures, so much so that Jesus could castigate the Pharisees for allowing their tradition to nullify the Word of God (Mark 7:8-13). When Paul was so obsessed by these traditions, he was unable to distinguish practically between the teaching and practices of the fathers and the actual word from Yahweh's mouth (Deut 8:3). If we ask why Paul describes so graphically his zeal for the law and devotion to Judaism, the answer resides in "Pauline autobiography." If he, "the chief of sinners" (1 Tim 1:13—note the context) was converted so drastically from the path of dedication to the law and zealous persecution of the church, then the Galatians can and must turn from the "other gospel" and "other Christ" of the Judaizers back to the One who called them in grace.

C. Paul's Conversion/Calling and Its Immediate Results (1:15-17)

In his "autobiography as paradigm," Paul has spoken thus far of the divine origin of his gospel (1:11-12) and has given a quick summary of his former life in Judaism (1:13-14). Now he comes on to speak of the sovereign purpose of God which turned him from a ravager of the church into what he *should* have been as the Lord's servant. As a member of Israel, he should have been a light to the nations. That purpose had been frustrated by his zeal for the paternal traditions, but now it has been realized by his conversion to Christ and his commission to preach him among the Gentiles. These verses also validate Paul's claims to an apostleship independent of Jerusalem, because it was God who was pleased to separate him, and immediately after his call he did not confer with anyone but bypassed Jerusalem altogether.

15 Paul's brilliant career in Judaism, as capped by his attempted decimation of the church, came to an abrupt halt when he encountered the living Christ on the Damascus road. In spite of his savage

---

[51] See Evans, *Writings*, 97-148.

assault on God's Anointed, God was, nevertheless, pleased to call Saul of Tarsus to his service. The verb "pleased" (*eudokeō*), which in the Greek Bible gives voice to divine decision (Ps 39:14; 67:17 [LXX]; Luke 12:32; 1 Cor 1:21; Col 1:9), speaks of God's sovereign purpose in counteracting Saul's attack on his church. He had no intentions of reversing his course, believing that he was doing God service (John 16:2 is directly relevant). But on the way to Damascus his actual destiny was revealed when he was soundly converted to Christ and began to go in precisely the opposite direction. The related noun "good pleasure" (*eudokia*) likewise has the sovereign design in view (e.g., Matt 11:26; Luke 2:14; 10:21; Phil 2:13). In the Psalms, Yahweh's good pleasure has as its object none other than the chosen people (e.g., Ps 44:3; 68:16; 85:1; 142:11; 144:4).[52] The Lord's pleasure, then, is tantamount to "grace," or, in Paul's own phrase, "the election of grace" (Rom 11:5). That Paul, as apostle, is the recipient of electing grace is confirmed by his echoes of Jer 1:5 and Isa 49:1 in this verse, according to which he was separated from his mother's womb.

It was on the Damascus Road that God's good pleasure was expressed by his "call" of the erstwhile persecutor. Paul uses a verb of Israel's election and calling (*kaleō*), when he speaks of himself as being called. Note how in Rom 1:1 he terms himself a "called apostle" (*klētos apostolos*), along with the Roman Christians, who are also the "called" of God (Rom 1:6-7). The implication is that Paul the Christian still identifies himself as an elect Israelite, but an Israelite in whom the ideal of Israel's calling has been realized. What is implicit in the present verse is explicitly affirmed in Rom 11:1: "I am an Israelite." In both the present context and that of Romans 9-11, Paul can maintain his identity as a "true Israelite," but one who now reaches out to the Gentiles and invites them to embrace the privileges of the chosen people, preeminently the Messiah himself (Rom 9:4-5).

Paul's calling in time and space, however, was preceded by an eternal purpose. It is true that his historical commissioning as apostle is called a "separation" (cf. Acts 13:2), with a possible glance backward to his "separated" status as a Pharisee.[53] Nevertheless, the outstanding factor here is that before he was ever called in time and space he was "separated" in another sense, from his mother's

---

[52] On Israel's election see, Rowley, *Election*; Sohn, *Election*; Wright, *Perspective*, 108-110.

[53] Dunn, *Galatians*, 63. Cf. Bruce, *Galatians*, 92; Schlier, *Galater*, 53. On "separate" or "set apart," see Betz, *Galatians*, 70, n. 134; Mußner, *Galaterbrief*, 82-83.

womb. In so saying, he alludes to Jer 1:5 and Isa 49:1 (as does the author of 1QH 9:30). In the broader context of Isa 49:1, it is surely significant that the Servant, who, like Jeremiah, was also called from the womb, is also given a commission to restore the tribes of Jacob and be a light to the ends of the earth (Isa 49:6).[54]

By his echo of these texts (and possibly other prophetic calls such as Isaiah 6 and Ezekiel 1, with parallels in *1 Enoch*), Paul claims, no less, to be an organ of revelation on a par with the Prophets. This assertion has implications for Gal 1:11, where Paul makes the gospel known in a prophetic manner to the nations. It is not to be overlooked that Jer 1:5 states emphatically that the Lord appointed Jeremiah to be a "prophet to the nations," who has been set "over nations and kingdoms" (1:10). Paul thus fulfills the role of Jeremiah in his preaching of Christ. Not only so, he is a "servant of Yahweh" too. And this is not the only place where he describes himself in such terms. In Rom 15:21, he likewise quotes Isa 49:6 in reference to his ministry; and according to Acts 13:47, he does the same with Isa 52:15 (Acts 18:9 similarly reflects Isa 43:5).[55] As Dunn discerns, in assuming this servant-role, Paul never would have conceived of himself as an apostate from Israel, but rather as Israel's eschatological apostle who, in his preaching to the Gentiles, was fulfilling Israel's obligation to shine as a light to the nations.[56] I would add that Paul's identification as the servant, alongside Jesus, accounts for his enormous suffering (Acts 9:15-16; 2 Cor 11:23-29; Gal 6:17).

Witherington comments that Paul's present role as apostle is actually a return to what he should have been as a faithful servant. Because his "former life in Judaism" had been at such variance with God's purposes in Christ, it was incumbent on him finally to take up what God wanted for him all along. Therefore, Paul was not, as alleged, an opportunist, a flatterer or fickle. To this I would add that Paul's assumption of his proper role marks him out as a true Israelite, who, as the people *in toto*, should have been a light

---

[54] See Dunn, "Apostate or Apostle," 259-60.
[55] See Dunn, *Jesus and Spirit*, 113; Wagner, "Isaiah," 130-32; Kerrigan, "Echoes," 217.
[56] Dunn, "Apostate or Apostle," 263-64. Later he concludes: "The gospel was a fulfilment of Israel's own hopes, an extension of God's covenant love for Israel, an extension of Israel itself. So too Paul's apostleship was part of God's purpose for Israel. Paul could never have accepted that his apostleship to the Gentiles constituted apostasy from Israel. Quite the contrary, he was apostle to the Gentiles precisely as apostle *for* Israel, apostle *of* Israel" (ibid., 269).

to the nations. He came to realize that he existed for the nations, and not the nations for him (4 Ezra 6:55-59). His election/calling thus fulfills the reason of Israel's election/calling. From this point onward, the apostle is so identified with the nations/Gentiles that he can call himself an "apostle of the Gentiles" (Rom 11:13; cf. Rom 1:1, 5, 13; 15:16, 18; Eph 3:1, 8; Col 1:23; 1 Thess 2:16; 1 Tim 2:8; 3:16; 2 Tim 4:17; cf. also Acts 9:15; 22:15, 21; 26:17-18, 20; 28:28).

As in Gal 2:9; Rom 1:5; 12:3; 15:15, Paul reasserts that his calling was "through his grace." In spite of what his antagonists may think, he has been the recipient of grace. If God's grace is his covenant love as now (re)focused in the new covenant, Paul is the steward of such grace, which has enabled him to preach the "unsearchable riches of Christ" (Eph 3:8) to the nations.[57] As one called and separated, he is sent to those outside the Mosaic covenant, who in the eyes of Judaism had no claim to grace.

16 The purpose of God's good pleasure in separating and calling the apostle was to reveal his Son. There is an ambiguity in Paul's language. The Greek literally reads "to reveal his son in me" (*en emoi*). The meaning could be an internal revelation made within Paul's psyche, or "in" could be taken in the instrumental sense of "by means of me."

A stronger case can be made for the former, for three at least reasons. (1) The latter reading would make the second clause of v. 16 redundant.

(2) An emphasis on Paul's inward transformation would account for the radical change of attitude on his part. If his commission was to turn people "from darkness to light and from the dominion of Satan to God" (Acts 26:18 [NASB]), then he himself had to experience the light of the new creation flooding into his own "heart of darkness" (2 Cor 4:6). Henceforth, he could no longer regard Christ, as he once did, "according to the flesh" (2 Cor 5:16), that is, from the vantage point of a (Jewish) person still influenced by the values of the old creation. And if Christ was "revealed in" Paul, he continues to "live in" him (2:20), the flip side of his being in Christ (3:26, 28). In addition to this internal experience of Christ, Paul elsewhere can speak of seeing Christ or of Christ appearing to him (e.g., 1 Cor 11:1; 15:8), with the external phenomena complementing the internal revelation.

---

[57] See O'Brien, *Gospel*, 12-17.

(3) An internal manifestation of Christ fits well into Paul's present train of thought. The revelation/commission granted to him was entirely supernatural, meaning he had no contact with "flesh and blood" in the process of becoming a light to the nations. The occurrence of the very phrase "flesh and blood" in Matt 16:17 is both enlightening and ironic, because Jesus clarifies to the original twelve apostles that Peter's confession of him as the Christ has its origin not in a human revelation but in the good pleasure of the heavenly Father. In view of all of this, Cummins can aptly comment that "in me" means "in my person," that is, the complete reconfiguration of Paul's entire self. "The exalted Son of God is now constitutive of his entire life, an existence which Paul elsewhere describes as "Christ in me" (*Paul*, 123).[58] Cf. Phil 1:30, where "in me" is repeated for emphasis.

The purpose of this revelation to the apostle was that he might proclaim the Son of God "among the nations." "Among the nations" needs little explanation, except to say that with Paul's preaching the promise to Abraham begins to be fulfilled: "In you all the families of the earth will be blessed" (Gen 12:3; 18:18; 22:18; 26:4; 28:14 [NASB]). His conversion/calling is thus a pivotal event in salvation history.

The sonship of Christ is a very large and very complex aspect of NT theology and Pauline theology in particular. In the present setting, it is Jesus' messianic status as Israel's king that is in view. He is the Son of God who fulfills the promises to Israel and becomes the king not only of Israel but of the whole world. This means that at heart Paul's gospel is a royal announcement (Wright, *Paul*, 53-55, 57). As a Pharisee, Paul would have expected one kind of king, but the historical realization of the promises to the fathers has taught him otherwise. This is why he begins with the image of a Messiah who has given this community its distinctive identity (recalling that one of Paul's prime purposes is to affirm the new constituency of the people of God). On the one hand, as the

---

[58] Cummins proposes that *en emoi* echoes 2 Macc 7:37-38: "I, like my brothers, give up body and life for the laws of our fathers, appealing to God to show mercy soon to our nation and by afflictions and plagues to make you confess that he alone is God, and *through me* (*en emoi*) and my brothers to bring to an end the wrath of the Almighty which has justly fallen on our whole nation." In this light, Paul would mean to invoke himself in "a martyr-like role as one whose faithfulness is a means of participating in divine redemption: God in Christ...in him" (*Paul*, 124). The link might be strengthened by the consideration that the martyred son conceives of his self-sacrifice as the means of a Gentile confessing the God of Israel.

Anointed, he is the fulfillment of Israel's hope and Israel's law (1 Sam 7:14; Ps 2:8; cf. 1QSa 2:11-12; 4QFlor 1:10-13; 4QpsDan A^a; 4Q246; 4Q521).

On the other hand, it is he, contrary to the teaching of the Judaizers, who has received all just as they are without distinction (cf. Rom 3:22; 10:12; 15:7). By virtue of the work of God's Son, "our peace," there are no longer two "old men" divided by a "wall of hostility" but one "new man" reconciled in one body through the cross (Eph 2:14-16). Stated otherwise, there is now a "third race," the "church of God" which stands over against Jew and Gentile (1 Cor 10:32). Yet it is the cessation of hostilities between Jew and Gentile that has such profound implications for the life of the church as the people of the new creation. Paul thus stresses that the Christ of his proclamation is of a different stripe altogether than the Messiah of his opponents' preaching. Their "other Jesus" (2 Cor 11:4) engenders only the evils of the old chaotic existence (Gal 5:12, 15, 19-21, 26).

That Paul's commission came directly from the risen Christ is confirmed by his immediate reaction to the christophany: "Immediately, I did not consult with flesh and blood." The verb "consult" or "confer" (*prosanatithēmi*) would seem to mean the same here as it does in 2:6, namely, "to add something to someone by giving him instructions or information." Dunn's further nuancing, "consult in order to be given a skilled or authoritative interpretation," also makes sense in this context. The practical thrust of the verb is that Paul did not have to resort to any other person to be told what the "revelation of Jesus Christ" meant. His understanding of the gospel was given him directly by Christ and did not require clarification, ratification or confirmation by human beings ("flesh and blood"), in particular the likes of Peter and James.

17 Verse 17a relates the second immediate result of Paul's conversion/calling: "Nor did I go up to Jerusalem to see those who were apostles before I was." Paul does not specify precisely who these "apostles before me" were, but judging from 1:18-2:13, he certainly has in view Peter and James and those of the Twelve who were still in Jerusalem. Whatever their precise identity, the heart of Paul's argument is twofold: (1) his acknowledgment that his predecessors in the apostolate are to be recognized as speaking authoritatively on behalf of Christ; (2) notwithstanding their preeminence, he did not consult them to shed any additional light on the revelation of Christ to him. He consistently maintains his independence of them.

The positive counterpart of both negative immediate effects of Paul's conversion is stated by v. 17b: "I went into Arabia and later returned to Damascus." Where precisely Paul went and why he went there are matters of dispute. Matera explains that while "Arabia" can denote the area east of Jerusalem, it usually refers to "the vast desert peninsula between Iraq and the Persian Gulf on the east, the Indian Ocean on the south, and the Red Sea on the west" (*Galatians*, 61). Most scholars opt for Arabia as being the kingdom of Nabatea, especially given its proximity to Damascus. But Longenecker confirms that the Nabatean kingdom of Arabia was "a rather large and somewhat amorphous geographical entity in Paul's day" (*Galatians*, 34). Jervis writes to the same effect: the boundaries of this kingdom were somewhat fluid during the Middle Nabatean period (30 BC-AD 70) but seem to have included what today is Sinai, the Negev, the east side of the Jordan Valley rift, much of Jordan, and some of Saudi Arabia (*Galatians*, 46).[59] That Paul visited Nabatea would seem to be confirmed by 2 Cor 11:32, which mentions King Aretas, who would be the Nabatean king Aretas IV.

At the very least, then, the datum of importance is that Paul was nowhere near Jerusalem when he was called to go to the Gentiles, nor for three years afterwards. In point of fact, *he deliberately gave Jerusalem as wide a berth as possible*. This fact is all the more striking considering that Jerusalem was the Holy City.[60] Jerusalem, according to Ezek 5:5; 38:12, was the "center of the nations, with countries round about her," whose inhabitants "dwell at the center of the earth" (as reflected in *Jub.* 8:12, 19; *1 Enoch* 26:1; *Sib. Or.* 5:250).[61] Preeminently, Jerusalem had its temple—"the holiest temple in the world" (2 Macc 5:15). The temple was the organizing center of Jewish life and a theological symbol of tremendous emotive power. Moreover, the geographical complex of Jerusalem and temple had a significance all its own (in 11QTemple 45-47, Jerusalem is but an extension of the temple). The Holy City

---

[59] On Arabia, see further Millar, *Near East*, 387-436.

[60] On Jerusalem, see Walker, *Holy City*; Hess/Wenham (eds.), *Zion*.

[61] See further Bauckham, "James," 417-27; Scott, *"Imago Mundi,"* 368-73. Scott shows how the concept of Jerusalem as the "navel of the earth" makes contact with the Table of Nations in Genesis 10 and evidences the "Israel-centric" perspective that is characteristic of the Table of Nations tradition (ibid., 369). He further demonstrates that Ezekiel 38-39 and Isa 66:18-21 (and later sources) draw upon the Table of Nations as a paradigm for the eschatological future (ibid., 369-73). Scott then argues that Paul envisaged his mission geographically in terms of the original pattern of Genesis 10 (ibid., 374-81). See at length his *Paul*.

was located in the highlands of Israel, with Mount Zion as its highest point and the temple as the most imposing building in the land (see Josephus, *Ant.* 15.412 [11.5]; *Ep. Arist.* 83-84). In view of all this, for Paul to skirt Jerusalem and then return directly to Damascus was tantamount to saying that the new faith has been decentralized from the Holy City and that the temple is now outmoded. Consequently, the original apostles had no advantage over him by way of status or of the authority and legitimacy of his gospel.

If the place of Paul's temporary residence is not precisely clear, then its purpose is not stated explicitly either. Numerous scholars have suggested that he began to fulfill his mission to preach the Son of God "among the Gentiles." Such, of course, is a distinct possibility, especially if the demographics of the region made it a field ripe for harvest. Others maintain, rightly I think, that there is an additional factor, namely, Paul went to Arabia to study, meditate, pray and prepare himself for the work to which he had been called. But why Arabia in particular? I would suggest that Paul means for us to think as much in theological as in geographical terms. A clue is provided by 4:25: Mount Sinai is in Arabia, making Arabia the place of the giving of the law. There is nothing to preclude the possibility that Paul may have journeyed as far as the Sinai Peninsula and that Mount Sinai, in his thinking, is part of "Arabia," especially given the amorphous character of the region. It is impossible to be certain, but Paul may well have gone to Mount Sinai to contemplate the law in the light of Christ. What better place to confirm that his Torah-zeal had been wrongheaded and to conclude that Christ is indeed the end of the law (Rom 10:4; Gal 3:23-25)? The symbolism of the situation invites consideration.

Section Note

17 Wright has proposed that we are to understand the trip to Arabia in light of the "zeal for the law" motif of 1:13-14, as it takes its place within the broad context of the "theology of zeal" in Second Temple Judaism ("Paul, Arabia"). As a persecutor of the church, Paul would have modeled himself on such examples of zeal in the OT as Phinehas and Elijah by committing violence against those he perceived to the heirs of the compromised Jews of Numbers 25 and the Baal worshippers of 1 Kings 18. Elijah especially attracted his attention, because after playing the role of "a man of zeal" (1 Kgs 18:20-40; 19:14), the prophet then journeys to "Horeb, the mountain of God" (1 Kgs 19:8) and eventually returns by way of the wilderness of Damascus (1 Kgs 19:15). Likewise, when Paul was stopped in his tracks by the Damascus revelation, he did what Elijah

did: he went off to Mount Sinai and afterward returned to Damascus. Given this sequence of events, "Whatever still, small voice he may have heard, it was certainly not underwriting the kind of zeal in which he had been indulging up until then. His zeal was now to be redirected.... He was to become the herald of the new king" (ibid., 687). Hand in hand with Paul's "new job description," that is, as a servant rather than a zealot, went his newfound conviction that the true and loyal people of God are not, after all, defined by their allegiance to the "works of the Torah" (ibid., 688). Wright concedes that the parallels between Paul and Elijah are not exact. Nevertheless, they are suggestive enough to warrant serious consideration.

With a certain adjustment, Wright's suggestion is quite attractive. In a manner reminiscent of Elijah, Paul, the former "zealot," ceases from his violence, travels to Mount Sinai and then returns to Damascus, fully convinced that Gentiles *as* Gentiles are acceptable to God (see also Ciampa, *Scripture*, 121-23. Ciampa suggests as well that there are parallels between Paul and Moses in Paul's eventual arrival in Jerusalem (*Scripture*, 119-20.) The adjustment is that given Elijah's time and circumstances, his zeal was altogether right and justifiable, and we do not receive the impression from 1 Kings that Elijah needed in principle to break off his "zealot-like" activities (especially in view of Deuteronomy 13). Paul's zeal, by contrast, was far from justifiable because he had wrongly identified the followers of Jesus with the renegades of Numbers 25 and 1 Kings 18. It was something from which he was obliged to cease and desist immediately.

D. Paul's First Visit to Jerusalem (1:18-20)

If vv. 16b-17 related the immediate results of Paul's conversion and calling, then vv. 18-20 begin to detail the more long-term effects of his experience (continuing up to 2:14).

18-19 Verse 18 begins with "then," the first in a series of three such "thens" (along with 1:21; 2:1), marking the three major divisions in Paul's relations with Jerusalem. In 1:18; 2:1, the adverb seems to bear the connotation of "only then," or "it was not until then." Thus, it was only "after three years" that Paul went up to Jerusalem. In keeping with the inclusive method of time-reckoning in the ancient world, it has to be recognized that "after three years" may mean only "in the third year" rather than "three full years later." Added to this, it is uncertain if he means the third year from his conversion or the third year after the sojourn in Arabia. But one way or the other, it was some time before the apostle returned to Jerusalem after embarking for Damascus on his persecuting campaign. It should be obvious, then, that Paul did not *"immediately* confer with flesh and blood." For Paul, the facts speak for themselves. He could not be beholden to Jerusalem if he was away from there for some three years and once he went up again stayed only fifteen days.

The trip referred to here fits easily enough into Acts 9:23-30, although there is quite a lot of variation between the two accounts. Yet the Acts narrative does not imply any indebtedness on Paul's part to the Jerusalem apostles. Its stated purpose was "to visit Cephas." Paul may have preferred the Aramaic form Cephas because it symbolized Peter's commitment to take the gospel to the Jews, just as his own switch of name from Saul to Paul may have symbolized his commitment to the Gentiles. The precise meaning of "visit" (NIV: "get acquainted with") (*historeō*) is debatable. Since Paul would have been eager to meet Peter, a translation such as "to become acquainted with" or "to get to know" would convey the sense well enough. But there seems to be something else involved as well, that is, "to visit for the purpose of gathering information."[62] There would have been at least three pieces of information he would have wished to garner: (1) personal knowledge of Peter himself; (2) confirmation that he and Peter were in accord as regards the gospel and that there was a unity of witness between them; (3) details of the life and ministry of Jesus. Some try to weaken the sense of "visit" to avoid any implications of Paul's apostleship being compromised. However, his apostleship is not necessarily compromised at all and, in all probability, Paul's knowledge of the historical Jesus was to some extent informed by Peter (possibly, e.g., Acts 20:35; 1 Cor 11:23-26). C. H. Dodd is credited with the quip that Paul surely did not spend two weeks talking to Peter about the weather!

The verb "to get to know" thus served Paul's purpose well, by putting the emphasis on the development of a personal relationship with Peter. Certainly the implication of the next clause, "and I stayed with him fifteen days," must be that the "getting to know" was fairly extensive, especially as followed by the firm denial that during this fortnight he saw any of the other apostles (v. 19). It is true, that the "fifteen days" are set over against the "three years" of the previous period; but even so, "The point is that it was long enough to get to know Peter well, but not long enough to be thoroughly instructed in his new faith" (Dunn, *Galatians*, 73-74). Paul definitely "was not taught" in the sense that he denies in v. 12. Longenecker rightly comments: "To learn about the details of Je-

---

[62] See Dunn, *Jesus, Paul*, 112-13, 126-28; Kilpatrick, "*HISTORESAI KEPHAN*."

sus' earthly life from Peter and to be subordinate to or dependent on Peter for his apostleship and Gentile mission are clearly quite different matters. Paul is willing to acknowledge the former, but he is adamant in his rejection of the latter" (*Galatians*, 38).

That Paul's brief stay in Jerusalem was not a defining moment of his apostleship is confirmed by another fact: "I saw none of the other apostles—only James, the Lord's brother" (v. 19). He specifies that James is the "brother of the Lord." This, of course, was a well-known fact. Perhaps Paul mentions it because: (1) by the use of this honorific title, he shows his respect and regard for this leading figure in the mother church; (2) as the Lord's brother, James would have possessed information about the historical Jesus not readily accessible to others. It is true that the verb of v. 19 ("see") is not the same as that of v. 18. Nevertheless, we can safely assume that Paul did not talk to James about the weather either! Part of his purpose was to learn about Jesus and not to be indoctrinated by the apostles. It is also true that James was such a dominant personality in the Jerusalem church that a visit was inevitable, not simply as a matter of courtesy, but more importantly to confirm that he and James were in essential agreement as regards the gospel. Paul thus implies that he is theologically closer to James than his opponents, a point that should have made an impression on the Galatians.

Whether Paul actually names James an apostle is a matter of dispute. In strictly grammatical terms, this would appear to be the case.[63] If James was an apostle, it certainly would have enhanced his prestige and the awe in which the Galatian churches probably held him. That James would have been the thirteenth or even fourteenth apostle (if Matthias is included, Acts 1:26) is not really a problem since the number is symbolic in any event and seems to have been fluid (cf. 1 Thess 2:6). Others than the Twelve could be called "apostles" because they did apostolic work. What is important is that if the Judaizers appealed to James as a source of authority, then Paul can inform them that he was received by the Lord's brother as an equal in the work without James holding any sway over him. And the point would have been all the more impactful if James was an apostle.

20 Such was the crucial importance of these facts that he feels compelled to add: "I assure you before God that what I am writing you is no lie." The Galatians had only Paul's word for his account

---

[63] See Lightfoot, *Galatians*, 84-85; Longenecker, *Galatians*, 38; Witherington, *Grace*, 120; Fung, *Galatians*, 77-78.

of the Jerusalem trip, and his version was probably under attack by the opponents. So, he takes what effectively is an oath (see also Rom 1:9; 9:1-3; 1 Cor 15:31; 2 Cor 1:23; 2:17; 4:2; 11:10-11, 31; Gal 1:20; Phil 1:8; 1 Thess 2:5, 10; 1 Tim 2:7). It is notable that Paul uses the oath formula only to testify to the divine origin of his apostleship, mission and gospel.[64] As he stands in the presence of the Father who called him to be an apostle, he gives his readers the most solemn assurance possible that his account of the Jerusalem trip is the unvarnished truth. The language is strong, but no stronger than that encountered thus far. Paul is sensitive to the fact that if the Galatians do not believe his version of events, they will inevitably endanger their souls by their rejection of his gospel. "By calling God as his witness, Paul wishes to tell the Galatians once again (cf. 1:6) that adherence to the Teachers' message involves them in defection from God" (Martyn, *Galatians*, 174).

E. The Aftermath of the Jerusalem Visit (1:21-24)

Having stated the facts about his first visit to Jerusalem, Paul now moves on to the next phase of his personal history. But since this period had relatively little bearing on his present concerns, he passes over it with some haste. Despite some fourteen years of life and ministry, the only thing that interested Paul was that during this interval he had been far away from Judea and the Jerusalem leadership.

21 After the stay in Jerusalem, Paul "then" departed to the realms of Syria and Cilicia (consonant with Acts 9:30; 11:25-26). Here is the second in the series of three "thens," marking his relations with Jerusalem. Once more, Paul's personal history refutes the allegations of his detractors: he went far from Jerusalem after he had been there only fifteen days. The length of this trip is not stated, and it is possible that Paul passes over a great deal of time, including missionary activity, with a simple summary statement. What he wishes to impress upon the Galatians is that his stay in Jerusalem was brief and that he gave preference to Gentile locations. If we bring Acts 11:25-26 into the picture, Paul appears to have settled

---

[64] See Garlington, "Oath-Taking," 168-69 (= *Essays*, 76). Paul's willingness to go on oath may reflect the Roman practice of swearing outside of court in order both to settle before going to trial and to assure an opposing party that one was indeed prepared to stand before a court of inquiry (Sampley, "Before God"). It is more likely, though, that Paul moves within the sphere of Hebrew/covenantal jurisprudence (Garlington, "Oath-Taking," 141-51 [= *Essays*, 75-76]).

for a while in Antioch of Syria and thus identified with a dominantly Gentile church.

22 That Paul's involvement in Palestine was minimal is confirmed by the further datum that he remained "unknown by face to the churches of Judea" (KJV). At first glance, it might appear unlikely that *Saul the persecutor* (1:13) could have been unknown to Judean Christians, especially in view of Acts 8:3. However, Witherington (*Grace*, 124-25) calls attention to several germane points. (1) Neither Acts 8:3 nor Gal 1:13 suggests that Saul ever persecuted any house groups outside of Jerusalem itself. (2) There may have been an expansion of the church into Judea from the time of the persecution until Paul's departure to Syria and Cilicia, so that Paul would have in fact been unknown in Judea. Note that Acts 1:8 does speak of the movement of the gospel from Jerusalem to "all Judea." (3) Verse 23 seems to relate the report about Paul by the Jerusalem church to these other churches, meaning that their acquaintance with Paul was secondhand. But in addition to these suggestions of Witherington, there is another possibility as well, namely, that the main object of Paul's wrath could have been the Greek-speaking Hellenists, as represented by the likes of Stephen, especially in his polemic against the abuse of the temple. Thus, it could be that these particular targets allured him away from Palestine to places like Damascus.

The churches of Judea were "in Christ." "In Christ" is perhaps the most clearly identifiable Pauline phrase (occurring about eighty times in his letters) and represents the actual showcase of his theology.[65] The concept of being in Christ contains at least three dimensions.

(1) The *historical*. To be in Christ is to belong to that era of world history inaugurated with his coming. This is the complex of new covenant/new creation as contrasted with what has gone before. Paul thinks of Christ as "the new realm God is now establishing in the world." Thus, "While the churches are geographically located in Judea, they are more importantly located in Christ" (Martyn, *Galatians*, 176). In the main, Paul contrasts the "in

---

[65] A definitive work in English on union with Christ is yet to be written. For the time-being, see Dunn, *Theology of Paul,* 390-412; Schnelle, *Paul,* 481-82; Ridderbos, *Paul,* 57-64; Moo, *Romans,* 391-95; Gaffin, *Resurrection,* 50-58, 130-34; Wedderburn, "Observations." Albert Schweitzer termed the "in Christ experience" Paul's "Christ-mysticism" (*Mysticism,* 3, et passim). Sanders, however, rightly felt uncomfortable with this nomenclature, preferring rather to speak of Paul's participationist soteriology (*Paul,* 463-72, 502-8).

Christ" experience with the period of the Mosaic law and covenant. In Galatians itself, "in Christ" is tantamount to the age of the Spirit as over against the age of the "flesh" (3:1-3). It is in Christ that all previous distinctions have been obliterated (Gal 3:26, 28). "In Christ" is the answer to not only being "in the law" (Rom 2:12; 3:19), but also to being "in Adam" (1 Cor 15:22; cf. Rom 5:12-6:6).

(2) The *personal*. To be "in Christ" is to know him and the power of his resurrection (Phil 3:10), to "live in" him (Gal 2:20), be a member of his body (Rom 12:4-5; 1 Cor 6:15; Eph 1:23; 4:13; 5:30) and to be conformed to his image (Rom 8:29).[66]

(3) The *messianic*. Wright suggests with a good deal of plausibility that the Greek word *Christos* is to be taken specifically as "Messiah" (*Climax*, chaps. 2 and 3). This being so, Paul's use of "in Christ," "body of Christ," etc., is to be understood in terms of membership within the royal family, the "Messiah-people." Says Wright: "Israel's king sums up his people in himself; what is true of him is true of them" ("Paul's Gospel," 166).

In each of its three dimensions, "in Christ" marks the difference between Paul's pre-Christian condition "in Judaism" (1:13-14) and the freedom in which he now luxuriates (2:4, 17). Existence "in Christ" has made it possible for Gentiles to inherit the blessing of Abraham (3:14) and has rendered insignificant the old distinctions between "circumcised" and "uncircumcised." Correspondingly, as pertains to all three, there is an implied criticism of the opponents. (1) The *historical*. The Judaizers want to live in the old and new ages simultaneously. They are glad to have Jesus as Messiah, but their conception of the Messiah is one linked to the past. Their Christ is one who would serve the Torah and uphold its perpetuity into the present time. For Paul, however, to have one foot in both ages is a impossibility, because his Messiah has now obliterated the distinctions between Israel and the nations. (2) The *personal*. The Jewish Christian missionaries certainly conceived of themselves as in some sense joined to the Messiah. In their estimation, they were "Christians." Yet Paul has a different assessment of them. As "false brothers smuggled in to spy out our freedom in Christ" (2:4), they could not have been actual members of his body, who know the power of his resurrection. Whatever their claims, Paul knows that they are not "in Christ" in any meaningful sense. (3) The *messianic*. Akin to the previous point, such people are simply not part of the royal family, just because their concep-

---

[66] See Ridderbos, *Paul*, 57-64.

tion of the king is skewed and faulty. In point of fact, the Jesus of Paul's preaching would have been repugnant to his adversaries, a Messiah who admits the uncircumcised and unclean into his household and assembly.

The question arises whether Paul, by repeatedly evoking "in Christ" in his letters, has replaced one bounded system (Judaism) with another (Christianity). The answer is yes. "Just as Paul had previously been 'in Judaism' so now he and Christian congregations were 'in Christ' as a distinct and distinguishable bounded social entity" (Witherington, *Grace*, 125). Christ, therefore, is the new "boundary marker" of the Christian community. This is why the two main rites of the Christian church, baptism and Lord's supper, symbolize union with him.

In principle, what pertains to Judaism pertains as well to imperial Rome and its demand of Emperor worship. With the appearance of the volumes edited by Horsley,[67] students of the NT have become increasingly aware that the Emperor cult permeated every aspect of life in the Mediterranean basin. As Wright explains:

> The evidence now available, including that from epigraphy and archaeology, appears to show that the cult of Caesar, so far from being one new religion among many in the Roman world, had already by the time of Paul's missionary activity become not only the dominant cult in a large part of the empire, certainly in the parts where Paul was active, but was actually the means (as opposed to overt large-scale military presence) whereby the Romans managed to control and govern such huge areas as came under their sway. The emperor's far-off presence was made ubiquitous by the standard means of statues and coins (the latter being the principal mass medium of the ancient world), reflecting his image throughout his domains; he was the great benefactor, through whom the great blessings of justice and peace, and a host of lesser ones besides, were showered outwards upon the grateful populace—who in turn worshipped him, honored him, and paid him taxes.[68]

In this light, Wright challenges us to approach what has been called Paul's "theology," and to find in it not simply a few social

---

[67] Horsley (ed.), *Paul and Empire, Paul and Politics, Paul and Roman Imperial Order*.

[68] Wright, "Paul's Gospel," 161. See further Wright, *Perspective*, 59-79.

or political "implications," but rather a major challenge to precisely that imperial cult and ideology which was part of the air Paul and his converts breathed. Paul's missionary work must be conceived not simply in terms of a traveling evangelist offering people a new religious experience but of an ambassador for a king-in-waiting, establishing cells of people loyal to this new king, and ordering their lives according to his story, his symbols and his praxis, and their minds according to this truth. Practically, he says, this means that Paul, in announcing the gospel, was more like a royal herald than a religious preacher or theological teacher (ibid., 161-2, 65).

In sum, within Paul's "autobiography as paradigm," the phrase "in Christ" give voice to his conviction that Jesus the Christ has supplanted every rival system of belief and commitment. There is no Lord but Jesus, and there is no empire of lasting significance except his. Given that Galatians addresses subjects of Rome influenced by Jewish teachers, Paul challenges any system of thought, Roman or Jewish, that presents itself under the guise of empire. Like John the Seer (Rev 11:5), Paul proclaims in effect that "The kingdom of the world has become the kingdom of our Lord and of his Christ, and he shall reign for ever and ever" (RSV).

23-24 Verse 23 is the epitome of the entire first chapter of Galatians: the persecutor has become a proclaimer. In Paul's words, "The only thing they kept hearing was that 'Our former persecutor now preaches the faith which once he tried to destroy'" (Dunn's translation). Paul's zeal has now been redirected to Christ; and the most astonishing thing of all is that his "new zeal" is nothing other than love directed toward those who were the former objects of his hatred. One can only begin to imagine how astonished the churches of Judea must have been at this news!

It is from this newfound stance of being "in Christ" that Paul began to preach "the faith." This is the first usage of the word which as much as any other characterizes the theology of Galatians (employed some twenty-two times). "Faith" translates the Greek *pistis*, which is the equivalent of the Hebrew word for faith, *'emunah*. In the OT, *'emunah* is always two-sided: faith (trust) and faithfulness (perseverance). These two components are so closely connected that frequently the best translation of *'emunah* (and *pistis*) is "faith(fulness)."[69] In Galatians, Paul presupposes this meaning of faith as derived from his OT/Jewish heritage. What is distinctive to him is faith's new object—Christ. The faith and obedience due to Yahweh in the Mosaic covenant has now been refocused on Jesus the Messiah. From now on, faith is specifically *faith in Jesus Christ* (see below on 2:16), and with his coming faith has become universalized; it no longer assumes a nationalistic bias, as fixed on the Torah of Israel (as in, e.g., Sir 32:24-33:3; *2 Apoc. Bar.* 48:22-24).

It is significant that the first occurrence of faith in Galatians has the definite article. "The faith" is thus equivalent to "Christianity." The bulk of the letter will argue precisely that "the faith" has now displaced the Torah, so that the two have become totally incompatible. Therefore, the basic choice placed before the Galatians boils down to *Christ or the Torah*. For Paul, "'faith' had become so characteristic of the new movement to which he now belonged, that it could function as an identity marker, an identification which was sufficiently distinct to denote and define the movement itself" (Dunn, *Galatians*, 84).

The bottom line to the whole Jerusalem episode is doxology: "They kept on glorifying God because of me" (v. 24, echoing 1:5). Rather than a threat to the Judean churches, Paul is perceived to be a friend, implying that his message and sympathies were one with theirs. If this point is established, a great deal of wind will be taken out of the Judaizers' sails. A number of commentators accept that Paul's words echo Isa 49:3: "You are my servant, Israel, in whom I will be glorified" (RSV). If true, then Paul's status as servant of Yahweh (see above on 1:10, 15) would be confirmed even further and his mission endowed with all the more credibility. As Cummins expresses it, Paul is:

> The exemplary (suffering) servant of the Messiah-conformed Israel in which God is truly glorified. Such recognition from those amongst whom Paul had not even ministered clearly constitutes a thinly veiled polemic against his errant Galatian converts, who are now in danger of glorifying that which Paul has rejected in and through his conformity to the crucified Christ (Gal. 6.12-13) (*Paul*, 128-29).

---

[69] See Garlington, *Obedience*, 10-13 (note esp. Perry, "*'emunah*"). For literature on faith in Paul, see ibid., 2, nn. 5, 6, to which I would add Barth, *EDNT*, 3.91-97; Spicq, *TLNT*, 3.110-16; Schnelle, *Paul*, 521-27.

To "glorify" God is to praise him for the display of his attributes. In the case of Saul the persecutor, the divine attribute most conspicuously displayed is that of long-suffering mercy. According to Exod 33:19; 34:6, God's very essence is depicted in these terms, as 1 Tim 1:12-14 confirms. In Paul's case, the God of Israel maintained covenant faithfulness even to an erring sheep (*à la* Ps 119:176) who was fiercely determined to obliterate his latter-day people.

Section Note

15 For all the talk these days about Paul's "commissioning" rather than "conversion," the apostle was "converted" in strict terms, that is, he was "turned around" from the course of zealotry to that of the bondservice to the Lord Jesus Christ, even with all its reproach and self-sacrifice. See the important discussions of Witherington, *Grace*, 107-115, and O'Brien, "Was Paul Converted." Both rightly stress that calling/commissioning accompany conversion, but conversion itself is primary and foremost. To the same effect are Matera, *Galatians*, 62-63; Barrett, *Freedom*, 110-11, n. 7. On Paul's conversion/calling and its consequences, see further Dunn, *Jesus, Paul*, 89-107; id., "Paul's Conversion;" id., "Apostate or Apostle;" Schnelle, *Paul*, 87-102; Wright, *Paul*, 35-37; O'Brien, *Gospel*, 1-21; Kim, *Origin*; Longenecker (ed.), *Road*; Murphy-O'Connor, *Paul*, 71-101; Peace, *Conversion*, 17-101; Ashton, *Religion*, 73-104.

GALATIANS CHAPTER TWO

F. Paul's Second Visit to Jerusalem (2:1-10)

As Paul moves into this segment of the letter, he passes over a sizable portion of his life in silence. He does so both because these years had elapsed far away from Jerusalem and because his concern is to recount only those incidents that had a direct bearing on his relations with the other apostles and the mother church. The episode recalled in 2:1-10 is particularly important because it signaled a critical juncture in the history of the early church, when Paul chose to make Titus a test case with regard to circumcision and Gentile admission into the newly created assembly of Christ.

1 Chapter two begins with the third in the sequence of three "thens," bearing, in this case, the connotation of "only then." The interval of Paul's absence from Jerusalem was no less than fourteen years. Again it is not clear whether Paul begins his calculation from the Damascus Road or from the first visit to Jerusalem. Either way, he was once more away from the Holy City for well over a decade (on the inclusive method of time-reckoning) and possibly for as much as seventeen years. This being so, he could hardly be accused of leaning on Jerusalem for authorization, support or theological instruction.

Paul was in the company of both Barnabas and Titus. Barnabas was a person highly respected in the early Palestinian church.[1] In spite of his subsequent behavior in Antioch, the witness of Barnabas would carry significant weight with the Galatians and certainly in Jerusalem. The mention of him here would confirm that he and Paul were actually at one in their stance on Gentile freedom from the law in Christ. It is true that Barnabas would later play the "hypocrite;" but even so, he, as Peter, is represented by Paul as being only temporarily inconsistent with his real convictions. In contrast to Barnabas, Titus was an uncircumcised Gentile, previously unknown to the churches of Judea and perhaps converted directly from paganism by Paul. It is in the person of Titus that Paul makes his gospel to the nations present by "a piece of its fruit" (Martyn, *Galatians*, 190).

Titus is thus a crucial figure at this pivotal point of the history of primitive Christianity. It would stand to reason that Paul pur-

---

[1] On Titus, see Barrett, *Essays*, 118-31; Bauckham, "Barnabas."

posely took along this prototype of the Galatians themselves to provoke a confrontation with the Judaizers, and in such a showdown to use Titus as a test case to confirm that he and Jerusalem were in accord. Hansen remarks: "Paul's inclusion of Titus on his team boldly expressed his conviction that it was not necessary for Greek Christians to change their ethnic identity by becoming Jews in order to be included in the church. The presence of Titus forced the conference to resolve the issue of discrimination against Gentile Christians" (*Galatians*, 54). Hansen further comments that Paul's company, comprised of the Jewish Barnabas and the Greek Titus, was a living illustration of the new freedom in Christ. "His team was a microcosmic expression of the power of the gospel to break down the barriers that had separated Jews and Gentiles and to create a new unity in Christ—a unity that transcends the ethnic, cultural and social divisions in the world" (ibid.).

2 Paul went up to Jerusalem "in response to a revelation" (possibly the "revelation" of Agabus, Acts 11:28). As in his previous movements (1:12), he stresses the divine mandate of his mission. "He went at heaven's behest, not at Jerusalem's, nor even Antioch's" (Dunn, *Galatians*, 91). Hence, Paul's version of events and his own "revelations" to the Galatians (see on 1:11) may be relied on. His commission truly is from God the Father and the Lord Jesus Christ. Cummins is correct that Paul's language indicates that the nature and intent of his visit was "in accordance with" (*kata apokalupsin*) the origin and subsequent outworking of God's disclosure of his Son in him (1:11-12). "It was this which governed Paul's position in relation to all that transpired during this visit, not least any *kata anthrōpon* ["human"] attempts to undermine the truth of the gospel" (*Paul*, 130).

Once in the capital city, Paul set before the apostles the gospel he was accustomed to preaching among the Gentiles. The verb "set before" (*anatithēmi*) has an ring of confidence about it. It does mean to "submit for someone's consideration." However, there is no idea that the one making the submission is inferior in status to those giving their consideration. Certainly we do not receive the impression that Paul approached the "pillars" as an underling requesting an imprimatur to be placed upon his apostleship and gospel. On the contrary, as v. 9 makes very clear, Paul was received as an equal when it was perceived that he indeed had been the recipient of "grace." This is why he is bold enough to describe his peers as "those who were of repute" (RSV), or, as NIV renders aptly: "Those who seemed to be leaders."

GALATIANS CHAPTER TWO

The word (participle) here means "to be recognized as being something" and, consequently, to be influential. Paul's phrasing is subtle. He does acknowledge that Peter and the others are worthy of recognition and thus shows due respect for them. At the same time, he seeks to distance himself somewhat from them. To say that they are "reputed to be something" implies that some people are holding them in too high regard, not recognizing that their current friendliness towards the circumcisers is ill-advised.[2] It is not until Acts 15, apparently, that the Jerusalem "pillars" break definitively with "the believers who belonged to the party of the Pharisees" (Acts 15:5). Until then, Paul is content with the knowledge that "God's *eschatological* vocation is the only authorization to be acknowledged among human beings" (Martyn, *Galatians*, 192).

Paul's interview with the Jerusalem contingent was "in private," perhaps because of the volatility of the subject matter. Maybe he mentions this because the meeting was not a matter of common knowledge, and its very occurrence could have been suppressed by his enemies. On the surface, it might seem odd that Paul, so many years into a settled and mature outreach to the Gentiles, would deem it necessary to touch base with Jerusalem. However, the clue is provided by Acts 15:1. Up to the "apostolic conference," the troublers were insisting: "Unless you are circumcised, according to the custom taught by Moses, you cannot be saved."[3] It was the vociferous and persistent onslaught of this group that forced the issue for Paul. Wherever he went, they were sure to follow (cf. 2 Cor 10:13-18; Phil 3:2), even as late as the letter to Titus (1:10).

The encounter was thus necessary to prevent potential disaster: "Lest somehow (*mē pōs*) I was running or had run in vain."[4] "Run" is the familiar athletic metaphor used by Paul elsewhere (Gal 5:7; 1

---

[2] Cummins summarizes the interpretations of Paul's designations of the Jerusalem apostles in 2:2, 6, 9 as follows: (a) honorific; (b) dismissive; (c) rhetorically nuanced; (d) simply a way of indicating that one must judge not according to appearance but reality. He sees elements of truth in all of them: "In emulating God-in-Christ the apostles are (a) worthy of their esteem; but to the degree that they ever become misaligned with that which is 'of man' rather than 'of God in Christ', then (b) their repute is undermined accordingly. It is this which accounts for (c) the rhetorical variability of the designations, and (d) provides the wider frame of reference within which to differentiate correctly between what is 'false' and what is 'real'" (*Paul*, 133).

[3] On the "conference," see Witherington, *Grace*, 13-20; Schnelle, *Paul*, 121-32.

[4] The present and aorist tenses of "run" are written from the perspective of Paul's trip to Jerusalem: at that point in time he "was running" and "had run."

Cor 9:24-26; Phil 2:6; 2 Tim 2:4-5; 4:7), signifying disciplined exertion towards a goal.[5] There may be as well an oblique reference to 1:13, Paul's "manner of life" or his "walk" (*anastrophē*) in the traditions of the fathers. "Running" would thus be an intensification of "walking" (Ps 119:32; Rom 9:16). As Paul had once "walked" in Judaism, now he "runs" in Christ. In 4:11 he repeats his fear of laboring in vain, but with the ultimate hope that his work is not actually futile. See the comments on that verse.

It was in the midst of this race that Paul became genuinely anxious about the outcome of his session with the other apostles. His fear was for Christianity as a whole and the very character of the gospel. The nascent church might have been fundamentally divided from the outset had it not been established that he and Jerusalem were in agreement. All his endeavors on behalf of *universal Jew/Gentile equality in Christ* ("the obedience of faith *among all the nations*" [Rom 1:5; 16:26]) would have been in vain if the Judaizers had won the day. Had word gotten out that the vote went against him, the opponents could have capitalized on the situation and would have had in their hands a weighty club indeed. If they could claim Peter, James and the others, the Gentile outreach could have been placed in dire jeopardy, with the result that the face of Christianity itself might have been forever altered. Wright's observations on the new people of God as a community of love have equal applicability here:

> This life of *agape* [love] serves...as a critique from within of the Pharisaic Judaism in which Paul had grown up. Notoriously and obviously, his appeal for the Jew-plus-Gentile united family in Christ cuts against all attempts to make Christianity a sub-branch of Judaism. Here we find some of his sharpest polemic; this, indeed, is why it is so sharp at precisely this point. He sees all too clearly that if the church splits into Jewish Christian and Gentile Christian factions, perhaps with some Gentile Christians joining the Jewish Christians by undergoing circumcision, this will mean that the principalities and powers are still after all ruling the world; that they have not after all been defeated by Christ on the cross; that there is no such thing as a renewed humanity, and that he has all along been whistling in the dark in pretending that there is (*Paul*, 147).

---

[5] The running metaphor is akin to the *agōn* (striving) motif in Paul (see Cummins, *Paul*, 130).

Martyn quite rightly adds that a negative stance on the part of Jerusalem would leave Antioch (Paul) with only two alternatives: "To abandon its circumcision-free mission to the Gentiles, or to maintain that mission at the price of a rift with Jerusalem that would have produced two churches, one drawn from Jews and a second drawn to an increasing extent from Gentiles" (*Galatians*, 193).[6] For Paul, this was simply unthinkable because Christ, on the cross, demolished the enmity between Jew and Gentile (Eph 2:14-22); and the "word of the cross" (1 Cor 1:18) is in the process of creating a new beginning, a new history. "Indeed, he would run 'in vain' if the Galatians acceptance of the gospel and their faith in Christ were not sufficient for their eschatological redemption" (Betz, *Galatians*, 88). That Paul had legitimate fears for his Galatian readers is evident from 3:4 and especially 4:11, where again he voices his trepidation that his labors may have been "in vain." Proof positive is that the Galatians "were running well" at one time (5:2), but now they are in danger of abandoning the distinctively Christian race altogether.

3 Paul's resolve to hold the line on Gentile freedom is now related as the central issue of the meeting: "Yet not even Titus, who was with me, was compelled to be circumcised, even though he was a Greek." The sentence begins with "but," or better, "nevertheless" (*all'*). The force of the conjunction is that in spite of Paul's initial apprehensions, the Gentile Titus was not forced to undergo the knife once they had reached Jerusalem.

Titus grabbed everyone's attention just because he was a "Greek." "Titus was so obviously a Greek and not a Jew; if Paul could successfully defend his position in relation to Titus he could sustain it for all Greeks" (Dunn, *Galatians*, 95). Titus is thus the paradigm for all "Greeks" who come to Christ just as they are (cf. John 12:20 and, ironically, John 7:35). From the Jewish perspective, the whole of the civilized pagan world was epitomized by the word "Greek" (2 Macc 4:36; 11:2; 4 Macc 18:20). Paul himself regularly employs the phrase "Jew and Greek" (Rom 1:16; 2:9-10; 3:9; 10:12; 1 Cor 1:22, 24; 10:32; 12:13; Gal 3:28; Col 3:11). A similar way of distinguishing the two groups is "circumcision" and "uncircumcision" (Rom 3:30; Gal 5:6; cf. Gal 2:9).

---

[6] See also Burton, *Galatians*, 73; Bruce, *Galatians*, 111; Longenecker, *Galatians*, 49; Fung, *Galatians*, 90; Hansen, *Galatians*, 55-56.

The issue is thus focused precisely in terms of ethnicity as typified by circumcision, "The great point of contention in the entire controversy between Paul and his opponents" (Ridderbos, *Galatians*, 82). This is why circumcision is a leading motif in the letter (2:7-9, 12; 5:2-3, 6, 11; 6:12-13, 15; cf. 3:28). As the opponents saw things, the fact that Titus was a Greek surely would have compelled circumcision. But for Paul just the opposite was the case, now that Christ has removed the requirement of circumcision in the flesh and has himself circumcised/baptized his followers in the Spirit (Col 2:11-15, in fulfillment of Deut 10:16; 30:6; Jer 4:4). The latter-day church of God is not the prolongation of ethnic Israel.

Circumcision was such a fundamental tenet of the Jewish faith that it was taken as axiomatic.[7] One fact that emerges from the notices taken of the Jews in Greco-Roman literature is that although other ancient peoples practiced circumcision, Israel preeminently was known as "the circumcised."[8] Tacitus succinctly summarizes the pagan point of view: "They have introduced the practice of circumcision to show that they are different from others" (*Histories* 5.5.2; cf. Juvenal, *Satire* 14.98-106). This notice comes in the context of heavy criticism of the Jews, whose practices, according to Tacitus, are "sinister and revolting." These people, he says, engage in "wickedness" and are no less than "wretches!"

Nevertheless, in spite of pagan misunderstanding and misrepresentation, circumcision signified one's inclusion in the Abrahamic covenant (as furthered by the Sinai covenant). According to Gen 17:11, circumcision was the "sign" of the covenant with Abraham (also *Jub.* 15:28-29; Rom 4:11; cf. Josephus, *J. W.* 2.17.9 [454]). As the covenant sign, circumcision functioned as *the* foremost badge of covenant membership. Its neglect is excoriated in no uncertain terms by Gen 17:13b-14: "So shall my covenant be in your flesh an *everlasting covenant. Any uncircumcised male who is*

---

[7] Philo assigns four reasons why circumcision was instituted among the Jews. Among them is that the practice "assimilates the circumcised member to the heart. For as both are framed to serve for generation, thought being generated by the spirit force in the heart, living creatures by the reproductive organ, the earliest men held that the unseen and superior element to which the concepts of the mind owe their existence should have assimilated to it the visible and apparent, the natural parent of the things perceived by sense" (*Spec. Laws* 1.1-2. Quote from 1.1.6.).

[8] See Dunn, *Galatians*, 95-96; George, *Galatians*, 142-44. The pagan sources are conveniently assembled in Stern, *Authors* (see 3.114 for references to circumcision).

not circumcised in the flesh of his foreskin shall be cut off from his people; he has broken my covenant."

From the Maccabean period onward, the rite became more and more a sign of one's identification with and fidelity to the Jewish people, particularly in times of crisis. This conviction comes strongly to the fore in a text such as *Jub.* 15:25, 28-29. In this passage, the writer actually merges the Abrahamic and Sinai covenants, the "sign" of the former functioning as that of the latter as well (which was actually the sabbath, Exod 31:12-17). His theology of circumcision is predicated on Abraham's own example: "And Abraham circumcised his son on the eighth day. He was the first one circumcised according to the covenant which was ordained forever" (*Jub.* 16:26). For "the sons of Israel" (*Jub.* 3:15; 7:9, 13, 23) and "the generation of Jacob" (*Jub.* 5:2) to become as "the uncircumcised" was for them to throw off their entire heritage as Jews. In terms of Gen 17:14 (*Jub.* 15:25), such were to be cut off from the people; they have broken the covenant. *Jub.* 15:33-34 places in the mouth of Abraham a prophecy of Israel's refusal to perform circumcision, including this imprecation: "And there is therefore for them no forgiveness or pardon so that they might be pardoned and forgiven from all of the sins of this eternal error."[9]

This would have been precisely the attitude of the law teachers: circumcision was not only a badge of identity, it was of the essence of fidelity to God. Their outlook can be further illustrated by another historical incident. Josephus relates the story of Izates, king of Adiabene, who about this very time attempted to become a proselyte to Judaism without being circumcised. However, a rigorous rabbi named Eleazar strongly reproved the king in these terms: "In your ignorance, O king, you are guilty of the greatest offense against the law and thereby against God. For you ought not merely to read the law but also, and even more, to do what is commanded in it. How long will you continue to be uncircumcised? If you have not yet read the law concerning this matter, read it now, so that you may know what an impiety it is that you commit" (*Ant.* 20.44-

---

[9] See further F. Watson, *Paul*, 231-32. deSilva (*Introduction*, 503) further points to Philo's pronouncements on circumcision. For Philo, the rite has a profound moral and ethical significance, as do all the laws (*Migr. Abr.* 89). Specifically, circumcision is a symbol for the removal of the pleasures and passions of the flesh (*Migr. Abr.* 92; *Spec. Laws* 1.305; *Quaest. in Gen.* 3.48, 52). See Borgen, "Circumcision," 38-40.

45).[10] In a similar vein, Trypho the Jew expresses to Justin his amazement at the Christian way of life:

> But this is what we are most at a loss about: that you professing to be pious, and supposing yourselves better than others, are not in any particular separated from them, and do not alter your mode of living from the nations, in that you observe no festivals or sabbaths, and *do not have the rite of circumcision.*[11]

In light of all this, Paul's declaration that "even Titus was not compelled to be circumcised" takes on a special potency. Not even the leaders in Jerusalem, for all their standing and influence, could withstand the force of Paul's argumentation and would not accede to the Judaizers' demand that this Gentile be circumcised. This is Paul's real point to the Galatians: he and the original disciples of Jesus agreed as to the essence of the gospel for the nations. Jerusalem thus verified his conviction that circumcision is of no avail and means nothing (5:6; 6:15). The emotional impact of such a pronouncement may elude us, but in the setting of predestruction Judaism the people of God paid a terrible price to preserve this most prominent boundary marker of the covenant (1 Macc 1:60-61). Nevertheless, Paul was insistent that Titus—and all Greeks—must

---

[10] Hays notes that in the same passage another Jew actually advised the king against circumcision (*Galatians*, 22). Yet as far as the sources go, this would have been the exception rather than the rule. As quoted by Hays, Fredriksen's take on the Gentiles being saved eschatologically apart from becoming Jews is a bit too idealistic (= "Judaism," 247), at least for Paul's day. Borgen points out that Philo (*Migr. Abr.* 86-93) criticized other Jews for ignoring the external observance of circumcision, though they understood the ethical side well enough ("Circumcision," 39). For Hays and Fredriksen, there is the additional problem of Acts 15:1, 5; 21:21.

[11] Justin, *Dialogue with Trypho*, 10 (quoted by Garland, "Defense," 167). On circumcision, see the extensive essay of Derouchie, "Circumcision," along with Witherington, *Grace*, 455-58; Barclay, *Obeying*, 45-60; Segal, *Paul*, 187-223; Nolland, "Proselytes;" McKnight, *Light*, 79-82. O. Betz (*TRE*, 5.718-19) shows how some rabbinic sources actually equate "the blood of the covenant" (Exod 24:8) with "the blood of circumcision." *m. Ned.* 3:11 goes even further by making circumcision the reason for creation (!): "Great is circumcision, for if it were not for that, the Holy One, blessed be he, would not have created the world, since it says, 'thus says the Lord: but for my covenant day and night, I should not have set forth the ordinances of heaven and earth' (Jer 33:25)." On circumcision in tannaitic authors, see further Hoffman, *Covenant*, in conjunction with Derouchie, "Circumcision." Derouchie shows that the Prophets use "foreskin" language to denote hostility to the God of Israel.

not be compelled to submit to circumcision. Otherwise, "the truth of the gospel" (2:5, 14) would be jeopardized for all time.

4-5 These verses are one rather long sentence whose syntax is not altogether coherent. They are actually an incomplete sentence (anacoluthon). But as Luther discerned, "Anyone who is inflamed while speaking cannot at the same time observe the grammatical rules" (quoted by Dunn, *Galatians*, 97). The options in translation basically boil down to two. (1) NIV, which seeks to smooth out the sentence with a parenthetical insertion: "[This matter arose] because some false brothers had infiltrated our ranks to spy on the freedom we have in Christ Jesus and to make us slaves." (2) Martyn's paraphrase: "But, because of the False Brothers...we found it necessary to fight for the truth of the gospel."[12] Either way, Paul's drift is clear enough. On the occasion when it was decided that Titus would not have to be circumcised, there were "false brothers" present who sought to sway the judgment in their favor; but to them Paul would not submit.

Reading between the lines, it would appear that these "false brothers" brought considerable pressure to bear on the apostles and expected that they might actually get somewhere with them. This is suggested by the fact that even sometime later in Antioch "the people from James" were able to intimidate Cephas, Barnabas and "the rest of the Jews" (2:12-13). Their influence in the infant church is not to be minimized. The group is best identified with "some of the believers who belonged to the party of the Pharisees," who made their way to Antioch and demanded circumcision of the Gentiles in order for them to be saved (Acts 15:1-5). This is indeed ironic, given that Paul too was once a Pharisee; but his "former life in Judaism" would have given him all the more insight into what makes such people "tick."

---

[12] An alternate understanding of the syntax of v. 4 is proposed by W. Walker ("Why Paul Went"). According to Walker, the two prepositional phrases "according to revelation" (v. 2) and "because of the false brothers secretly brought in" (v. 4) are syntactically parallel and linked to the verb "went up" (v. 2). Together they indicate the twofold reason for Paul's trip to Jerusalem: he went up *in accordance with* a revelation and *because of* the false brothers. This is attractive in that it removes some of the syntactical difficulties, but even Walker admits there are problems with it. No least, I would say, because even his translation requires an elliptical element and that v. 3 intervenes between vv. 2 and 4. Furthermore, this interpretation requires that the false brothers had been "slipped in" sometime before Paul arrived in Jerusalem, whereas it certainly seems that it was a specific meeting in the capital city that was invaded by the opponents.

These "brothers" were "false" simply because their exclusivistic theology and practice were at variance with the gospel. In addition, their claims to apostleship and a Gentile mission were altogether bogus: "For such men are *false apostles*, deceitful workmen, masquerading as apostles of Christ. And no wonder, for Satan himself masquerades as an angel of light. It is not surprising, then, if his servants masquerade as servants of righteousness" (2 Cor 11:13-15a). For Paul, these interlopers were satanically deceptive through and through. They were, quite simply, *"men who do evil,"* "mutilators of the flesh" (Phil 3:2)![13]

According to Paul's vivid image, these "false brothers" were "smuggled in" (*pareisaktous*). NIV omits this word. It is a rare military term, meaning "secretly brought in" (NASB) or "secretly smuggled in."[14] Strictly speaking, it is a verbal adjective and is passive in voice. It is true that this is a metaphor and we cannot read too much into the passive. Nevertheless, Paul may be suggesting that this group was invited to the meeting by James and the others, with the further implication that although he objected to their presence, they were admitted anyway. If so, James, Peter and company unwittingly played into the hands of the circumcision party by allowing their participation. However hesitant the apostles may have been, it was as though they had smuggled the circumcisers in.

The other side of the coin is that there was a concerted effort on the part of the false brothers to crash the meeting: they "infiltrated our ranks" or "sneaked in." Their purpose was "to spy out our freedom which we have in Christ Jesus, that they might bring us into bondage" (RSV). By the use of another espionage metaphor (NIV: "spy on"), Paul intimates that his opponents were acting in a strategic military manner for the very purpose of sabotaging his law-free gospel to the Gentiles (Ciampa, *Scripture*, 137-43). From Paul's perspective, the design of the false brothers was nothing less than enslaving him and his Gentile converts (see Tsang, *Slaves*, 81-87). Since the object of their "reconnoitering mission" was "our freedom," they sought to obtain an "intelligence report" so that they could know better how to take "our freedom" away. They wanted to know exactly what Paul was teaching the Gentiles so

---

[13] In 2 Cor 10:13-14, Paul depicts this same basic group in terms of a racing metaphor. Paul refuses to boast beyond his limits, but rather keeps within the "lane" (*kanōn*) allotted to him, one that took him as far as Corinth. The implication is that his detractors there were not even assigned a lane and are running without being sent.

[14] See Betz, *Galatians*, 90, n. 305; Witherington, *Grace*, 136.

that they could devise appropriate counterarguments. As Guthrie puts it, "They were acting like intelligence-agents building up a case against slackness over Jewish ritual requirements" (*Galatians*, 80).

We can assume that these people applied all their learning and cleverness to the cause of Gentile submission to the yoke of the Torah. Given their set of assumptions, they must have made a very plausible case indeed. Yet Paul worked with a different set of assumptions, and for him the opponents' campaign could have no other end than to "make us slaves" or "reduce us to abject slavery" (Lightfoot). Their aim was none other than to divest the church of its "inalienable possession" (Ridderbos) by bringing it under the domain of the law. A significant parallel is 2 Cor 11:20, where Paul is compelled to upbraid the Corinthians because they were too willing to be enslaved by these "false apostles" (= "false brothers").

The motif of bondage to the law was introduced in chap. 1 and will be reasserted prominently in 3:23-25; 4:1-11; 5:1-12, marking Paul's main concern in Galatians as the fight for the freedom Christ died to procure.[15] So ironically, the Torah was the emblem of Israel's release from Egypt, "the house of bondage."[16] Moreover, only two hundred years before this letter, the war of liberation from Israel's Syrian captors was nothing other than a fight on behalf of the law. Many "freedom fighters" died that the nation might enjoy deliverance from its pagan oppressors. But now Paul declares that life under the law is a new form of slavery in comparison to the liberty bestowed on the new people by the Lord who is the Spirit (2 Cor 3:17). This is why he emphasizes that our freedom is "in Christ Jesus." Union with Christ means deliverance from sin and the burden of the law (Acts 13:39; Rom 6:7, 18; cf. Matt 11:28-30; Acts 15:10), not enslavement to the values of the old creation (Gal 4:3, 9) (see my *Defense*, esp. 119-34).

To be sure, the Judaizers did not conceive of themselves as "slave merchants." "Expressed in their own terms, the concerns of this group's members would be quite other: to ensure that the new movement within Judaism remained true to the principles and practices of the covenant clearly laid down in the Torah...reinforced by the Maccabean crisis, and promoted particularly by the Pharisees" (Dunn, *Galatians*, 99). As far as they were

---

[15] "Freedom" (*eleutheria*) occurs four times (2:4; 5:1, 13); "free" (*eleutheros*) six times (3:28; 4:22, 23, 26, 30, 31); the verb "free" once (5:1).

[16] See Ciampa, *Scripture*, 140-42; Keesmaat, *Paul*, 186, 193-99.

concerned, they were about the business of liberating Gentiles from the slavery of paganism. But Paul saw things quite differently. In time, Peter would come to the same settled conviction. Speaking of the Torah, he questions the Jerusalem assembly: "Now then, why do you try to test God by putting on the necks of the disciples a yoke that neither we nor our fathers have been able to bear" (Acts 15:10)?

In spite of the unwelcomed presence of the Judaizers, Paul is emphatic: "We did not give in to them for a moment, so that the truth of the gospel might remain with you." Paul was not adverse to submission to legitimate authority (Acts 23:5; Rom 13:1, 5; 1 Cor 16:16; Eph 5:21-24; Col 3:18, 20, 22). But in the case of his opponents, he steadfastly refused to acknowledge that they had any meaningful authority because they had perverted the gospel (1:7) and were really out of step with the heartfelt convictions of the Jerusalem apostles, in spite of the latter's ambivalence at this point in time.

At stake was "the truth of the gospel." "Truth" in this setting certainly means "that which is actual and factual" as opposed to the propaganda of the "*false* brothers" (cf. 4:16-17; 5:7). Yet there is an additional element. In its biblical setting, "truth," along with its adjectival form "true," corresponds to "faithfulness" in the OT (Hebrew '*emunah*) (e.g., John 1:17; Col 1:5; 2 Thess 2:12-13). "Faithfulness" in turn has particular reference to God's reliability respecting his covenant (e.g., Exod 33:19-34:9; Deut 32:4). "The truth of the gospel" is thus God's covenant faithfulness embodied in the gospel preached by Paul. And because this gospel announces release from captivity (see on 1:6), it alone can insure the freedom for which Christ died and to which we have been called (5:1-12, 13). "The truth of the gospel" is a circumcision-free gospel; anything else is "another gospel" by definition. Paul, then, withstood the opposition that this truth might "remain" with the Galatians; that is, that it might never be wrenched from them, as the Judaizers were pulling out all the stops to do.

6 In terms of its structure, v. 6 is one of the most difficult sentences in the letter (another incomplete sentence). Paul begins by writing, "from those who were of repute…," but then does not finish. NIV handles it as well as could be expected: "As for those who seemed to be important—whatever they were makes no difference to me; God does not judge by external appearance—those men added nothing to my message."[17] Paul's language is frankly dismissive. However, it is, as Dunn observes, the kind of reputation the "pillars" had among others that Paul treats so dismissively (*Galatians*, 102). He is not denigrating their actual status, but the way it had been commercialized by some, most notably the Judaizers. He is able to take exception to the consensus because "God shows no partiality" (RSV), or, literally translated, "God does not receive the face of a person" (see Hubbard, *Creation*, 197-98). This was a well-known dictum in the OT and Judaism (Lev 19:15; Deut 1:17; 10:17; 16:19; 1 Sam 16:7; 2 Chr 14:7; Job 13:10; Prov 18:5; Mal 2:9; Sir 35:12-13; *Jub.* 5:16; *Pss. Sol.* 2:18; *1 Enoch* 63:8; cf. Rom 2:11; Jas 2:1-7; 1 Pet 1:17).[18] It is interesting that Paul says that what they were "formerly" (*pote*) did not matter to him, implying that in the course of events their overinflated status in the eyes of many had diminished.

The most telling point of all is that "those men added nothing to my message." On the contrary, "those of repute" contributed nothing to his authority or to the content of his message; and certainly they made no modifications in his circumcision-free and law-free gospel, requiring that "Gentile Christians be circumcised and live a nomistic lifestyle in accordance with the Jewish Torah" (Longenecker, *Galatians*, 54). Nor did they place any restrictions on his field of labors. The momentous significance of this agreement between Paul and Jerusalem is not to be underestimated. The decision reached here was one of the most important ever made in the history of the church. "On the outcome of the Jerusalem consultation hung the whole future of the infant faith: whether Paul's mission would become an independent movement, or whether it would remain in fellowship with the Judean churches..." (Dunn, *Galatians*, 105).

7-10 The final verses of this paragraph are one complex sentence. Verses 7 and 9 constitute the main thought by stating that when the Jerusalem apostles recognized Paul's apostleship and message, they extended to Paul and Barnabas the right hand of fellowship. This is the real point of this paragraph. Verse 8 comes in between as a parenthetical insertion confirming that same God commis-

---

[17] Judging by the last clause of the verse, the elliptical element of the first clause is not so hard to reconstruct. It would be something to the effect that "from those who were of repute I received no further instruction." Perhaps implicit as well is a denial that Paul's apostleship received some sort of imprimatur from Jerusalem.

[18] See Faber, "*Prosōpolēmpsia*."

sioned both Peter and Paul. Verse 10 voices the mutual agreement of both groups that the poor should be remembered.

Not only did the other apostles not add anything to Paul's authority and message, "on the contrary" (*alla tounantion*: a strong reversal of what was just said), when they "came to see the fact" (*idontes*) that Paul had been entrusted with "the gospel of the uncircumcision" (v. 7) and "came to recognize" (*gnontes*) the grace given to him (v. 8), they gladly admitted Paul into their circle and received him as an equal. Jerusalem's recognition of Paul was apparently brought about by Paul's own attitude toward them and the circumcision of Titus. His steadfastness convinced them that he had been entrusted with "the gospel of the circumcision." "Entrusted" (*pepisteumai*) is a strong term. Historically, it corresponds to Israel's guardianship of the law (Sir 1:15; Rom 3:3).

By being entrusted with this gospel, Paul claims to be on a par with those who, in times past, were appointed guardians of the Word of God (cf. 1 Cor 11:17; 1 Thess 2:4; 1 Tim 1:11; Titus 1:3). Likewise, the fact that Paul was given "grace" (cf. Rom 1:5; 12:3; 15:15) testifies once more to the reality that his gospel is the embodiment and revelation of God's covenantal favor to his latter-day people and that the apostle himself has been enabled to look beyond the traditions of Israel to the true character of the person and work of the Messiah.

Such a perception of "grace" stands at the heart of the Paul's controversy with the rival teachers and, consequently, at the core of Galatians. As Martyn observes, the dispute did not center around whether there would be a Gentile mission or not, but rather around the fundamental character of that mission and thus the "truth of the gospel," that is, whether God's deed in Christ is entirely devoid of prior requirements, such as circumcision, etc. (*Galatians*, 203-4). In a word, Paul would have nothing to do with Christ *plus something else*, because, as Hendriksen puts it accurately: "A supplemented Christ is a supplanted Christ" (*Galatians*, 112).

In between vv. 7 and 9, Paul affirms that his calling and that of Peter have the same divine origin (v. 8). Paul writes that the same God who was at work in Peter was "at work" in himself as well.[19] Martyn comments that rather than referring to God, and specifically to God's action, merely by means of a passive verb, "I had

---

[19] Hays points to 1 Cor 12:6, 11 as the best parallel to v. 8. It is here that Paul likewise uses the verb "work" (*energeō*) in speaking of the functioning of the members of Christ's body (*Galatians*, 226).

been entrusted," Paul identifies God by a substantive participle. It is a pattern, he notes, that Paul frequently employs in Galatians:

The one who called you	1:6
The one who singled me out	1:15
The one who called me	1:15
The one who was at work	2:8
The one who supplies the Spirit	3:5
The one who works miracles	3:5
The one who called you	5:8

"By this means, Paul emphasizes the crux of the meeting: the issue was not that of devising a set of humanly conceived plans, but rather a matter of perceiving God's identity, by learning what God is actually doing. God is the actor; the church's task is to see what God is doing and to follow in his way" (*Galatians*, 202). Moreover, once Peter and the others came to perceive Paul's office, the outcome of their meeting was "a *confession* oriented to God's activity" and "an *acknowledgment* of God's evangelical action in the world, an acknowledgment doubtless gained in God's enabling presence" (ibid., 203, italics his) as granted by the Spirit. When the right hand of fellowship was extended to Paul and Barnabas by James, Peter and John, there was a recognition that indeed there was a common participation (*koinōnia*) in God's work. "God's eschatological people is bound together by the integrity of God's eschatological activity through them" (ibid., 205).

There was thus no qualitative difference between Peter and Paul, only divergent spheres of labor. The question arises as to whether their respective ministries were divided along geographical or demographical lines. In all probability it was both; and Peter and Paul simply continued on as they had for quite a few years now. That Paul was sent to the "uncircumcision" and Peter to the "circumcision" is not to be taken in absolute terms, however, as witnessed by the fact that Paul's practice was to begin his preaching in local synagogues (e.g., Acts 13:14-43) and that it was Peter who took the message to the Gentile Cornelius (Acts 10).

James, Cephas and John are called by Paul "pillars." The most frequent reference to "pillars" in the LXX is to the supports of the tabernacle and later of the temple. Notable are the twin pillars in front of Solomon's temple (1 Kgs 7:15-22; 2 Chr 3:15-17), named Jachin and Boaz, which may have had covenantal significance (2 Kgs 23:3; 2 Chr 34:31). Furthermore, it is possible that the Jerusalem church understood "pillars" eschatologically, that is, James,

Cephas and John were probably regarded by the Jerusalem church as "the pillars of the eschatological temple of God's people, that is, as the main support on which their own community was built..." (Dunn, *Galatians*, 109-10).[20]

Some Jews, at least, expected a new temple to be raised in the age to come, as based on Ezekiel 40-48 (e.g., *Jub.* 1:17-28; *1 Enoch* 90:28-29; 11QTemple; *T. Benj.* 9:2; *2 Apoc. Bar.* 32:3-4);[21] and the NT announces that this new temple has been erected as the body of Christ (Mark 14:58; John 2:19; Acts 6:14; 1 Cor 3:16-17; 2 Cor 6:16; Eph 2:19-21; Heb 3:6; 10:21; 1 Pet 2:5).[22] The significance of "pillar" as applied to the Jerusalem leaders is explained by Witherington:

> In other words, calling these three men pillars was no small honor rating. It meant they were holding up and holding together the people of God being now renewed and restored in Christ. It invested in these men an enormous importance and implied they had tremendous power and authority (*Grace*, 143).

This being so, how bold—and to some how impudent—Paul must have appeared when he told the Galatians: "whatever they were makes no difference to me!"

At the same time, Paul's "honor rating" of them increases the significance of their gesture: they "gave me and Barnabas the right hand of fellowship," not as superiors to an inferior but as equals in a common cause. "Fellowship" (*koinōnia*) in Paul signifies sharing something in common with someone (from *koinos*, "common") and consequently entails community.[23] Paul himself was thus invited into the ranks of the "eschatological pillars." This is the high

---

[20] See also Witherington, *Grace*, 143; Martyn, *Galatians*, 205; Longenecker, *Galatians*, 57; Ciampa, *Scripture*, 149-51; Bauckham, "James," 441-50; Barrett, "Apostles." Bauckham ("James," 443) and Cummins (*Paul*, 134) have demonstrated that underlying the pillar metaphor is the designation of the temple in Isa 54:11-12 (see on 4:27). The oracle as a whole functions to assure Israel of God's Zion-focused everlasting covenant with his righteous people (Isa 54:9-17). For Paul, of course, things have changed, and Zion is now understood in terms of God's Christ-focused covenant (see on 4:21-31).

[21] See McKelvey, *Temple*, 9-41; Gärtner, *Temple*, 16-46; Sanders, *Jesus*, 77-90; Bryan, *Jesus*, 189-206; Beale, *Temple*, 154-66; Tan, *Traditions*, 23-51.

[22] See Hafemann, "Spirit," 183-88.

[23] O'Brien, *DPL*, 293-95; Banks, *Community*.

point and the real point of the one long sentence constituting this paragraph.

Cummins points out that the expression "give the right hand" (*didonai dexian*) figures prominently in 1 and 2 Maccabees. It betokens an official compact involving the giving and receiving of pledges of friendship and/or terms of peace. Within the Maccabean framework, this was bound up with efforts to live according to the Torah-based way of life, and thereby attain the truly lasting peace of the covenant. For Paul, however, this compact is defined as one of distinctively Christian "fellowship." For this reason, "Fellowship is itself defined most fundamentally in terms of a common life conformed to the crucified and risen Christ, and common cause in the outworking of divine reconciliation thus effected" (*Paul*, 132).

The only requirement made of Paul was that he remember the poor. Lührmann suggests that "remember" evokes the theme of remembering Zion (Psalm 137 and frequently in Zechariah) (*Galatians*, 41). This would make sense, given that the church is the eschatological Zion, the people of Christ's new creation reign. Paul hastens to add that he was only too eager to do this very thing. The verb he uses, *spoudazō*, is a "zeal" word, meaning "be zealous" or more generally "make every effort." Here we have a unique indication that Paul the apostle was as zealous for the gospel as Saul the Pharisee was for the traditions of his fathers (1:14). But now his zeal has been redirected in the paths of love for the very people he formerly tried to wipe off the face of the earth. Here is none other than the marvel of grace, the complete transformation of mind, heart, will and personality into precisely the opposite of what they had been. If the first Christians had known the words of William Cowper, no doubt they would have applied them to the conversion of Saul of Tarsus: "God moves in a mysterious way his wonders to perform!"

Underlying this request is the theology of the poor in both Testaments.[24] The Torah made provision for the welfare of the poor (e.g., Deut 24:10-22; cf. Ruth 2:1-7).[25] The OT more broadly takes the side of the poor and identifies them as the true people of Yahweh. They are the oppressed (Ezek 18:12) who are persecuted by the wicked (1 Sam 2:7-8 [cf. Luke 1:48, 52]; Ps 10:2, 9; 12:5;

---

[24] See Hauck/Bammel, *TDNT*, 6.888-915; Croft, *Individual*, 49-72; Kraus, *Theology*, 150-54; Keck, "Poor;" Ridderbos, *Kingdom*, 185-192; Dunn, *Call*, 32-61; Hoppe, *Poor*; Blomberg, *Poverty*, 33-110; Roth, *Blind*, 112-41; Schmidt, *Hostility*; Bammel, "Poor;" Bassler, *God*.

[25] See Brin, *Studies*, 74-89.

14:6; 72:4, 14; Isa 3:14-15; 32:7; Dan 4:27; Amos 8:4-6). Yet it is they who trust the Lord (Isa 14:32) and form the flock of the messianic king (Ps 72:1-4, 12-14; Zech 11:7, 11; cf. Ezekiel 34).[26]

Paul thus acknowledges that the poor in Jerusalem (and elsewhere) constitute the true people, and his later letters reveal that he did indeed make good on his promise of taking up a collection, mainly from Gentile churches (Rom 15:25-29; 1 Cor 16:3-4; 2 Corinthians 8-9; cf. Acts 24:17). In Rom 15:25-29, Paul intimates that the collection is the means by which Gentile Christians, who have shared in Israel's blessings, make their "eschatological pilgrimage" to Zion (as foretold by the Prophets) to contribute to their Jewish brethren. From this perspective, the collection was with a view to the fulfillment of Isa 60:5-7: "The wealth on the seas will be brought to you, to you the riches of the nations will come" (v. 5). In its own way, this is a strong intimation of the interdependence of Jew and Gentile in the common body of Christ: both constitute God's latter-day new covenant people.[27]

Section Notes

1 The relation of Paul's second trip to Jerusalem to the accounts in Acts will always be debated. The two main options are to dovetail Gal 2:1-10 with either Acts 11:27-30 or Acts 15, although the possibility exists that it does not correspond to either but to a journey unmentioned by Acts. A good case can be made for Acts 11:27-30. This is so mainly because a meaningful sequence of events can be reconstructed in Paul's relations with Jerusalem and with Peter in particular.

(1) On Pentecost, Peter announces that the promise is "for you and your children and for all who are far off—for all whom the Lord our God will call" (Acts 2:39). Here Peter declares that both Jew ("you and your children") and Gentile ("all that are far off") are to be the recipients of "the promise," that is, the promised Holy Spirit (Isa 4:2-6; 11:1-2; 32:15; 42:1; 44:3; 59:21; 61:1; cf. 63:11; Ezek 36:26-27; 37:14; 39:29; Joel 2:28-29; Acts 1:4; 2:14-21, 33, 38; Rom 5:5; Gal 3:14; Eph 1:13) who comes as the fulfillment of the prophetic hope for the glorious future (new creation).

(2) Nevertheless, his preaching on this occasion did not fully impact his own insight into God's purposes. According to Acts 10:9-16, Peter still needed to be taught that no human being is "common or unclean." It

---

[26] The theme is likewise picked up by intertestamental literature. See Ciampa, *Scripture*, 152-54; Garlington, *Obedience*, 170, n. 42.

[27] On the collection, see McKnight, *DPL*, 143-47 (with other literature); Lüdemann, *Paul*, 77-81; Nickle, *Collection*; Hurtado, "Collection;" Downs, "Collection;" W. D. Davies, *Gospel*, 195-208; Georgi, *Poor*; Joubert, *Paul*.

was only after this vision on the rooftop of Simon the tanner's house that he was prepared to take the gospel to Cornelius and his family.

(3) The immediate aftermath of Peter's preaching to the Gentiles was that he was able to withstand the criticisms of the circumcision party by informing them that the same gift of the Spirit was given to them as it was to "us when we believed in the Lord Jesus Christ" (Acts 11:17 [RSV]). His account was so compelling that even the circumcision party had to concede: "Then to the Gentiles also God has granted repentance unto life" (Acts 11:18).

(4) Shortly thereafter, Paul and Barnabas journey to Jerusalem and engaged in the confrontation related in Gal 2:1-10. During this encounter, Peter apparently stands firms in his convictions about Gentile equality in the church, or at least no wavering on his part is recorded.

(5) Next, comes the incident at Antioch, when Peter withdraws from the Gentiles, signifying in effect that they are not really acceptable as they are. Paul, accordingly, rebukes Peter and the other Jews for their "hypocrisy."

(6) Finally, after all this, the apostles convene in Jerusalem and announce that Gentiles are not to be burdened with circumcision and Torah observance, with Peter and James taking the lead (Acts 15:6-21). At last, the circumcision party is seen in its true colors by all, and the apostles unite by distancing themselves from this group.

This reconstruction hardly resolves all the chronological questions pertaining to Galatians in relation to Acts, but it does present a consistent sequence of events from Antioch to Jerusalem, back to Antioch, and finally to Jerusalem again. The problems of Pauline chronology are taken up by Lüdemann, *Paul*; Murphy-O'Connor, *Paul*, 1-31; Riesner, *Period*; Hengel/Schwemer, *Paul*; Hengel, "Stance."

2 Cummins (*Paul*, 131) proposes that the *agōn* motif, so prominent in 2 and 4 Maccabees, provides the backdrop to the present passage. Paul, the athlete-martyr, visited Jerusalem in order that his fellow apostles might vindicate his much afflicted ministry in service of the martyred and exalted Jesus. Cummins construes the contentious situation in Jerusalem as a Christian version of a typical Maccabean crisis, with the roles radically reversed. Paul, according to Cummins, thus again appears as something of a martyr figure, and this becomes all the more evident from his ensuing account of the opposition he met while in Jerusalem. Certain "false brethren" infiltrated the private meeting to "spy out" the freedom which those in Christ shared together. Paul construes this action as an attack on the truth of the gospel and an attempt to enslave.

"Thus Paul, ardent apostle to the Gentiles, zealously defends the truth of the gospel—that is, God's covenant faithfulness in Christ which is now under threat—and resists all attempts to enslave those whom he represents." However, his Jewish Christian opponents, who may have seen themselves in the tradition of Judas Maccabeus and those who "secretly entered" enemy territory to enlist any who remain in Judaism (2

Macc 8:1), are aligning themselves with all that is opposed to God in Christ. Their attempt to compel the Gentile Christian Titus to be circumcised is reminiscent of both Antiochus IV's efforts to compel the Maccabean martyrs to forsake their Torah food laws, and the Maccabees' enforced circumcision of apostate Jews (ibid.; cf. pp. 157-58). Paul now regards both forms of coercion as equally antithetic to the gospel of Christ. In essence, Paul's stance was that God's covenant faithfulness was now manifest not *via* a Jewish way of life, as lived and died for during the Maccabean period, but through a new way of life "in Christ Jesus," in conformity to the martyred and risen Messiah Jesus.

3 The question is frequently raised as to why Titus was not circumcised and Timothy was (Acts 16:3). However, the matter is easily resolved. For one thing, Timothy was half-Jewish and circumcision would not have been inappropriate, especially for his mission. But mainly, there was no intimidation brought to bear in the case of Timothy, and his circumcision was not necessary in order to enter the people of God. Paul, rather, acted on the freedom he himself had in Christ to become a "Jew" for the sake of gospel proclamation (see Cousar, *Galatians*, 40).

9 Aus has proposed that three "pillars" of James, Peter and John were modeled on the three patriarchs, Abraham, Isaac and Jacob and were deliberately regarded by the Jerusalem church as an analog to these great figures in the history of Israel ("Pillars"). According to Aus, Paul simply could not accept such an overblown veneration of the apostles. It may be that Aus is right and wrong at the same time: right in that these men probably were favored too highly in some quarters of the primitive church, and wrong in that Paul does not deny to them the status of pillars, as would seem to be confirmed by Eph 2:20, where he uses a similar architectural image to depict all the apostles as the foundation of the church.

G. The Incident at Antioch (2:11-14)

The famous incident at Antioch forms the bridge from autobiography to salvation history. As contrasted especially with Peter, Paul demonstrates in a real life setting what it means for Gentiles to be equals in Christ, thus underscoring that a "judaizing" lifestyle is not necessary in order to please the Lord of the new covenant. The episode grows out of the Jerusalem consultation and forms a juxtaposition to it. If Peter and the others had agreed with Paul respecting "the truth of the gospel," in Antioch Peter, Barnabas and the other Jews seemed to have reversed their original conviction. Paul thus deemed it necessary to preserve this truth even at the expense of confronting Cephas and running the risk of disrupting relations with Jerusalem. Bligh is correct that all through the autobiographical portion of the letter Paul is setting the scene for this climactic dispute at Antioch. Bligh also plausibly suggests that Paul pens this section of the letter to counteract propaganda on the part of the Judaizers that placed Peter in a favorable light and portrayed him unsympathetically.[28]

Before proceeding, it is necessary to stress that the row over table fellowship went far beyond the sociological concerns embedded in the phrase "live as a Jew" (v. 14). As we shall see, salvation itself was at stake, inasmuch as "this situation presented a theological challenge to the very core of the gospel itself." That is to say, individuals would be obliged to become "practicing Jews *in order the secure their salvific relationship to God*" (Rapa, *Meaning*, 127, italics his). Peter's temporary defection, then, carried with it definite "gospel-damaging implications" (ibid., 128).

11 Verse 11 begins with "but," not the strongly adversative Greek conjunction *alla* but the softer *de*. However, this entire section stands in very pointed contrast to the harmonious relations between Paul and Jerusalem at the end of the last section. Among other things, Paul's subsequent dealings with Jerusalem confirm his attitude toward the apostles. They indeed did not at this point fully grasp the dimensions and implications of the gospel, as evidenced by the behavior of Peter and the other Jews under pressure from "the people from James."

Just why Peter journeyed to Antioch is not clear. It could be that he was pursuing the division of labor agreed on earlier in Jerusalem, since there was a large Jewish colony in the city.[29] It is equally possible, to use an athletic metaphor, that Peter was send as an "advance scout" to prepare the way for the visit of the people of James. If so, in keeping with the espionage imagery of 2:4, the circumcision party may have been using Peter as a kind of "spy" to confirm their suspicious about the church in Antioch. In any event, "When Cephas came to Antioch I opposed him to his face," writes Paul, "because he stood condemned" (RSV). The grammatical construction joins the main verb, "was" (*ēn*), in the imperfect tense, with the perfect participle (*ketegnōsmenos*) and reads like a pluperfect, thus heightening the idea of a past existing state. Peter had no excuses: he "was convicted of wrong" or "was guilty."

---

[28] Bligh, *Galatians*, 173, 175.
[29] Josephus, *J. W.* 7.43.45. See Schürer, *History*, 3.1, 13-14; Cummins, *Paul*, 138-55; Bockmuehl, *Law*, 52-61.

Peter was not so much self-condemned as condemned before the bar of God's judgment, not only for undermining the agreement arrived at in Jerusalem (2:1-10), but more in particular for exhibiting infidelity to the gospel itself (see on v. 14). "Peter's actions are on trial before the assembly of the faithful and in the presence of God, and Paul is saying that he is already condemned before the divine tribunal" (Witherington, *Grace*, 151). Cummins has demonstrated that there is an underlying judicial setting to the incident at Antioch (*Paul*, 180-82, 186-87). In this courtroom of God and his people, Peter's actions were such, Cummins maintains, that repentance and reconciliation were required to avert eschatological judgment itself (ibid., 186). If he is right, then the stakes in Antioch were very high indeed.[30] Peter's temporary defection on this occasion could even be viewed as tantamount to another denial of Christ (Matt 26:69-75 and pars.).

The question arises whether Peter violated the exact terms of the Jerusalem consultation. Strictly speaking, the answer is no. As Witherington rightly discerns, that accord consisted of three factors: (1) no circumcision for Gentiles; (2) two distinct spheres of ministry, involving Jews and Gentiles respectively; (3) Paul was to remember the poor (ibid., 153). Peter did not appear to contravene any of these stipulations as such. Nevertheless, even though there may not have been a formal beach of the agreement, Peter certainly did run afoul of the spirit and intention of the Jerusalem meeting. Given the backdrop of the meal in Pharisaic tradition (see below on v. 12), he did turn coat and act in a manner radically inconsistent with the ideals of the agreement, namely, that Jews and Gentiles are equal in Christ and that Gentiles do not have to become "observant Jews" in order to be acceptable to Christ.

Paul would have none of what was effectively a double standard, one for the circumcised and one for the uncircumcised. It is very telling that what Paul actually criticizes Peter for is his *inconsistency of lifestyle*: he, a Jew who chose to "live as a Gentile," has now reverted to a "Judaizing" way of life. Paul perceived such a flip-flop as sending confusing signals to all who looked on. As Betz remarks, the issue at stake was Cephas' "shifting attitude with regard to the Jewish dietary and purity laws" (*Galatians*, 107), an

---

[30] Cummins also suggests that Paul's verdict is ironic in that it may draw on the language of the synagogue law court in pronouncing Peter "condemned." In particular, Peter might have been condemned by such a court for eating with Gentiles, thus incurring the punishment of Deut 25:1-4: the forty stripes. But in Paul's courtroom, Peter is "condemned" for just the opposite reason (*Paul*, 187).

attitude first fixed on the housetop of Simon the tanner (Acts 10:9-16) and confirmed by Peter's visit to Cornelius (Acts 10:17-11:48).

The Aramaic form of Peter's name, Cephas, is used to underscore his connection with the Palestinian church and perhaps as well his undesirable liaison with the Judaizers. Paul "withstood him to his face" (cf. the kindred idiom in Deut 7:24; 9:2; 11:25; Josh 1:5). If, in v. 6, Paul insisted that "God does not receive the face of a person," that is, show partiality, here he proves it by himself being no respecter of "faces" or persons. "The abruptness and forthrightness of Paul's language indicate a depth of feeling and outrage which the rest of his account makes no effort to conceal" (Dunn, *Galatians*, 117).

12 The reason for Peter's condemnation is stated in no uncertain terms. What Paul will call "hypocrisy" in v. 13 is here related as Peter's glaringly inconsistent behavior: "Before certain men came from James, he used to eat with the Gentiles. But when they arrived, he began to draw back and separate himself from the Gentiles because he was afraid of those who belonged to the circumcision group." Up to a certain point, writes Paul, Peter "used to eat" (Greek imperfect tense) with Gentiles, that is, he was in the habit of eating with them prior to the arrival of the people from James, at least from the time of Acts 10 (see Acts 11:3). This is confirmed by v. 14: "If you a Jew live like a Gentile and not like a Jew...." The fact that Peter probably ate Gentile (unclean) food as well (contrary to Leviticus 11 and Deuteronomy 14) would have horrified the delegation from James all the more.[31] The fear of eating with Gentiles was perhaps engendered by the association of unclean food with Israel in exile. According to Hos 9:3: "They will not remain in the LORD's land; Ephraim will return to Egypt and eat unclean food in Assyria." The situation was exacerbated by the fact that in the ancient world generally food and wine were normally dedicated to idols.[32] At least some Jewish attitudes toward eating with Gentiles and Gentile food are reflected in *Jub.* 22:16; Tob 1:10-13; Add Esth 14:17; Jdt 10:5; 12:1-20; 2 Macc 6-7; 3 Macc 3:4, 7; 4 Macc 6:15, 17; *Jos. Asen.* 7:1; *Ep. Arist.* 142;

---

[31] On unclean food and Peter's eating of it, see McKnight, *Galatians*, 101-2; Jervis, *Galatians*, 65-66; Sanders, *Jewish Law*, 23-28; id., "Association."

[32] Hays (*Galatians*, 233) adds that while eating with Gentiles was not technically forbidden by the law, many Jews would have preferred to separate themselves as much as possible out of a general sense that Gentiles were unclean and distasteful. He then cites Tacitus (*Histories*, 5.5.1-2), who complains that the Jews are misanthropic people who "eat separately" from others.

Josephus, *Ant.* 4.137; cf. Dan 1:8-16. See the second section note to this verse.

Just how long Peter was in Antioch before these people arrived is not stated, although it was certainly long enough that Peter had established a pattern of behavior and a reputation that could be termed "live like a Gentile" (2:14), long enough as well for the Jerusalem authorities to have found out about it and sent their delegation to interrogate Peter on the matter.

As to the identity of the interloping group, it will not do to weaken the sense of "the men from James" to something like "certain people who *purported* to be from James," as though James himself had nothing to do with the arrival of this group. On the contrary, the real impact of this subsection of Paul's autobiography hinges on James' desire to have a report of what was going on in Antioch, even after he and the other apostles came to recognize the legitimacy of Paul's gospel to the nations. It is possible, even probable, that this group did not represent James with full integrity. Nevertheless, James was the moving force behind the delegation. If, in Jerusalem, it was actually James who "smuggled" the troublemakers into the meeting (2:4), then it would follow that it was he who had sent these men on a recognizance mission to "check out" the church in Antioch.[33]

It may be very well that the "false brothers" inferred something from the division of labors between Paul and Peter agreed on in Jerusalem, namely, that Peter's mission to the circumcised entailed a strict separation of Jewish believers from Gentiles in regard to food and purity.[34] As they saw things, they were simply being consistent with the Jerusalem accord. If so, we can believe that James' own motives were not malicious. Yet he must have been under considerable pressure from the circumcision party, and Peter conveniently played right into the hands of those who wanted to return as negative as report as possible to James. Paul's reaction is predictable, because at this point in time he could see something James could not, namely, that the Lord's brother was too closely

---

[33] One of the odd twists of history is that the arrival of these "Judaizers," as we call them, in Antioch is not without precedent. Josephus relates that every city in Syria had both Jews and "*Judaizers*" (*ioudaizontas*) (*J. W.* 2.18.2 [462-63]), that is, those who retained their Jewish identity in the face of violent onslaught. From Paul's perspective, therefore, these Christian Judaizers may represent a throwback to days gone by.

[34] Their outlook was the same as the author of 4QMMT (C7): "We have separated ourselves from the multitude of the people [and all their impurity]."

aligned with the "circumcision group" and was running the risk of splitting the infant church down the middle.

Peter's withdrawal is related by the verbs "retreat" (NIV: "draw back") (*hupostellō*) and "separate" (*aphorizō*). The former word is a military term. It speaks of a strategy; that is, the move was deliberately calculated on Peter's part. Like a battleship taking zigzag evasive maneuvers against a submarine, Peter seems to have plotted his withdrawal from the Gentile brothers and sisters. The tense of the verb likewise suggests that Peter did not all at once stop eating with the uncircumcised, but rather he gradually *began to separate himself* (Greek inceptive imperfect tense) upon the arrival of the people from James. Thus, he deliberately plotted a strategy and apparently began to make excuses for his shift in eating habits. The latter word originates in Jewish discussions about ritual purity and separation from persons and objects considered to be unclean (cf. Acts 10:14 = Ezek 4:14).[35] The same verb is used by Paul of his apostolic call (1:15; Rom 1:1; cf. Acts 13:2), maybe with a glance at his "separated" life as a Pharisee. Pharisee-like separation is definitely being hinted at here (the very word "Pharisee" in its Hebrew form, probably stems from the verb *parash*, "separate"). In any event, the real seriousness of Peter's "retreat" is highlighted by 2:18-19: the re-erection of the barriers which once stood between Jew and Gentile.

Peter withdrew because he feared "those of the circumcision." Their identity is obvious enough from the parallel references in Acts 15:1, 5: these are the "believers of the party of the Pharisees," or, as we call them, the "Judaizers." Peter's fear can be assessed variously. It may have been quite innocent: Peter was concerned that if word got out that he had mingled with Gentiles and had "apostatized" from Judaism (cf. Acts 21:21), it would prove to be a stumbling block for the Jews whom he wanted to evangelize.

Additionally, however, there may have been a self-centered dimension to his withdrawal. The men from James were powerful and influential members of the Palestinian church and could wield considerable influence in Judea. As far as Peter was concerned, his reputation was on the line. "In Paul's terms," according to Betz, "Cephas 'feared' the 'political' consequences of losing his position of power. Peter chose the position of power and denied his theological convictions" (*Galatians*, 109). That his was not an unwarranted fear is illustrated by Acts 21:20-26, according to which

---

[35] See Poorthuis/Schwartz (eds.), *Purity*; Newton, *Purity*; Booth, *Jesus*, 117-54; Bryan, *Jesus*, 130-56; Holmén, *Jesus*, 221-33.

there were myriads of Jewish Christians who were still zealous for the law, even at that late date. In this regard, the Peter of Galatians 2 is not out of character with the Peter of the Gospel passion narratives, who, impelled by fear, denied his Lord three times, even with an oath. Perhaps Peter remembered all too well the criticism brought against Jesus for eating with "sinners" (Mark 2:16; Luke 15:2; 19:1-10) and that aimed at himself by the very group who now have managed to intimidate him (Acts 11:3: "You went into the house of uncircumcised men and ate with them"). Not accidentally, in 2:15 Paul relates the common Jewish equation of "Gentiles" with "sinners." Peter was thus under the gun not to sully the purity of the covenant as understood by these Jewish Christian missionaries. From this vantage point, "Peter did not act on the basis of his own theological convictions, but irrationally out of fear" (Betz, *Galatians*, 109).

There may be another reason for his fear lurking in the background. Longenecker (following Jewett, "Agitators") proposes that the Judaizers themselves were motivated by fear of the zealot movement in Palestine, a movement which threatened to ransack the nascent church if it continued to receive Gentiles apart from "the works of the law." As Longenecker observes, the "theology of zeal" current at this time sought to purge Israel of all foreign elements in hope that God would bring in the messianic age (*Galatians*, xciii). Therefore:

> Jewish Christians in Judea were stimulated by Zealot pressure into a nomistic campaign among their fellow Christians in the late forties and early fifties. Their goal was to avert the suspicion that they were in communion with lawless Gentiles. It appears that the Judean Christians convinced themselves that circumcision of Gentile Christians would thwart Zealot reprisals (Jewett, "Agitators," 205).[36]

If this reconstruction is correct, Peter would have been motivated by the same fears as the circumcisers themselves. It is worth pointing out that Antioch was the city from which the Hellenistic onslaught against the Jewish people originated (under king Antiochus IV Epiphanes) some two centuries earlier. Thus, the very mention of the city would have been like red lights flashing before the eyes of the Judaizers. Moreover, on this occasion Peter proba-

---

[36] See further Witherington, *Grace*, 155-56; Hansen, *Galatians*, 63.

bly told himself that a completely law-free church would have driven a wedge between the Jerusalem congregations, now under pressure from the zealots, and Gentile churches such as Antioch. Given such a scenario, remarks Longenecker, Peter believed he was acting in the best interest of the church at Antioch: his fears were theologically motivated. "Cephas was, in fact, attempting to avert a break between the Jerusalem church and the community of believers at Antioch, even though Paul interpreted his action as doing just the opposite."[37]

The central issue is that of table fellowship. In the ancient world generally, hospitality was a given, virtually a sacred obligation. In Jewish life, the meal had a kind of "sacramental character:" "the meal beginning with the host speaking a blessing over the bread and then passing it to the others at the table so that all in eating of the bread might share in the blessing spoken over it" (Dunn, *Galatians*, 118). Tomson rightly stresses that the importance of table fellowship is not to be underestimated: "Eating together is a basic expression of social belonging rooted in earliest childhood experience" (*Paul*, 222). And, of course, the kind of food served was all-important: it had to be "clean" according to the law of Moses. The dietary laws were thus a very important species of *halakah*: the faithful Jew's sanctification consisted in adherence to these demands. "It is an elementary concept in Judaism that it matters what you eat" (ibid., 221).

Peter, then, did a complete about-face from his own "former life in Judaism" by eating the "food of the Gentiles" (Dan 1:8-16; Tob 1:10-13; Jdt 10:5; 12:1-20). There is evidence that as a general rule Jews of this period discouraged mixed table fellowship because it was feared that eating with Gentiles would result in idolatry.[38] This being so, in the eyes of the circumcision party Peter was guilty of the most radical and intolerable breach of the Torah that one could imagine—idolatry. For them, the very doctrine of God was at stake (note, ironically, Peter's former attitude as reflected in Acts 10:28).

The point is underscored by the fact that in Pharisaic tradition in particular, unless one could be accepted at the meal table one was not qualified for entrance into the kingdom of God, which the table itself portrayed. Feasting and wine in biblical imagery are symbols of the eschatological age (Isa 25:6-8; Jer 31:10-12; Amos 9:12-15). The metaphor of the banquet subsequently is found in

---

[37] Longenecker, *Galatians*, 74; cf. Dunn, *Galatians*, 125-26.
[38] See Esler, *Galatians*, 93-116; id., *Community*, 71-109; Tomson, *Paul*, 230-36.

Jewish literature (4 Ezra 2:38; *1 Enoch* 10:19; 62:14; *2 Apoc. Bar.* 29:5-8; 1QSa 2:11-23; *Gen. Rab.* 62:2; *b. San.* 153a). Within the Gospels, the bliss of the messianic age is symbolized as a great meal (e.g., Matt 8:11; Luke 14:15; John 2:1-11). This image is used to portray the present realization of the kingdom of God (Mark 14:22-25; 1 Cor 11:23-26) as well as the future consummation when the believer will sit at table with the risen Christ and share in his kingdom (Mark 14:25; Luke 22:30; Rev 19:9).

McKnight has shown that Jesus' own practice of table fellowship was meant to make a point, namely, that he has come to restructure the social fabric of Israel. As he notes, table fellowship, in the first century context, represented a particular vision for Israel and God's will concerning Israel: one did not eat with persons whose view of Israel were incompatible with one's own. "For Jews of the first century…inclusion in a meal setting symbolized acceptance of another person, including that person's social status, moral practices, and attitude toward Israel's covenant God" (*Vision*, 45). The meal, then, was an "acted parable," not only of social relationships but of ultimate salvation itself. Thus, by eating with "sinners," Jesus declares that the kingdom of God as inaugurated by him is of a different sort than expected by so many of his peers. In short, an alternative program was advocated for the people of God in their historical existence as well as another understanding of Israel's nature and purpose as a people.[39] From now on, the kingdom of God would be constituted of those who hitherto had been entirely unacceptable.[40]

What the Jesus of the Gospels began to do, Paul the apostle continues in his churches as all their members partake of one common meal: all without distinction are invited to the messianic banquet of Jesus the Messiah. Therefore, the issue at stake in Galatia was nothing less than participation in the age to come or ultimate salvation, especially considering that table fellowship could symbolize the end of exile, restoration, forgiveness and social acceptance (McKnight, *Vision*, 44, citing 2 Kgs 25:27-30). This is particularly so if, as in Corinth, the Lord's Supper in Antioch was celebrated in the context of a communal meal.[41]

---

[39] See Borg, *Conflict*, 97-109.

[40] Cf. Wright, *Jesus*, 149. Nanos similarly concludes that what the "men from James" objected to was the acceptance of (uncircumcised) Gentiles as social equals, in his words, "Righteoused ones of God on the same terms as the Jewish participants" ("What Was at Stake," 316).

[41] See Cummins, *Paul*, 169-73.

As long as Peter ate with these uncircumcised and non-kosher brothers and sisters, he bore witness that they were acceptable just as they were. However, when he withdrew, he left a contradictory example and said in effect that they are not acceptable after all and, therefore, are not the subjects of Messiah's reign. For all intents and purposes, Peter seemed to be in agreement with the "believers of the party of the Pharisees:" "Unless you are circumcised, according to the custom taught by Moses, you cannot be saved" (Acts 15:5). Barrett explains that the Judaizers do not say that Gentile cannot be saved at all, but rather they can be saved only under the proper conditions. "The Judaeans simply affirm the familiar proposition: the Jews are the elect people of God, and male Jews are circumcised" (*Acts*, 2.699). No wonder, Paul cuts loose with both barrels!

Cummins stresses that Peter's withdrawal was a failure to be faithful to Christ and his latter-day community. "At its worst, his withdrawal under pressure constitutes a failure to remain unwavering in his commitment to the truth of the gospel, and as such could be construed as 'trampling' upon the saints and the Son of God" (*Paul*, 175). That this necessarily entails dissociation from both is implied in Paul's ensuing reference to the fact that Peter "separated himself." This is ironic because Paul conceived of his own life's work as being "set apart" by the God who revealed his Son in him (Gal 1:15-16; 2:20; Rom 1:1).

> He laboured to ensure that his converts remained unaffected by that which would undermine their nascent faith including those whose Torah-based conception of God's elect people caused them to insist that Gentile followers of Christ must adopt circumcision and strict Torah-observance. However, it is with such that Peter is now in danger of aligning himself in Antioch. Thus, whereas Peter may have conceived of his removal from mixed table fellowship as a necessary act of separation/purity, Paul considers it to be a fundamental confusion of categories, and as a movement in the direction of exclusion from God's Son and his people (ibid., 176).

13 Peter's withdrawal is termed by Paul "hypocrisy." "The rest of the Jews also played the hypocrite with him, so that even Barnabas was carried away with their hypocrisy." In the Greek context, the verb used here (*hupokrinomai*) means "to be a play actor," that is, "To pretend to be something one is not" or "to deceive deliberately." Many commentators press this meaning, and it does make a certain kind of sense in the present setting. Matera, for example, maintains: "Paul intimates that Peter and the other Jewish Christians no longer believed in the validity of the dietary legislation but pretended to do so because they feared those associated with James" (*Galatians*, 86).

Nevertheless, another dimension of "hypocrisy"—one really more to the point—stems from the Jewish context, in which the "hypocrite" was the one inconsistent with biblical principles (e.g., Matthew 23; cf. Rom 12:9 ["unhypocritical love" = consistent love]), so much so that he actually became an enemy of God, one led astray (Garland, *Intention*, 96-117). In fact, one can be so inconsistent with the truth that one runs the risk of becoming defiant toward God and an apostate.[42] As McKnight informs us, "hypocrite" carries with it the notions of wickedness, opposition to God and his truth, and even heresy. "Peter was not simply 'acting' here; he was not simply 'deceiving through pretense.' Instead, he was *morally* wrong because he was *theologically* wrong" (*Galatians*, 106). Garland's contention that the hypocrisy of Matthew 23 signals the failure of the leaders of Israel, who radically subverted the will of God (*Intention*, 117), is clearly applicable to the incident in Antioch, because certainly that is what happened when Peter, Barnabas and the other Jewish Christians abandoned Paul for the sake of keeping the peace with the circumcisers. Garland's work is especially relevant in that he shows that Matthew 23 was directed to the Christian church as *a warning to church leaders* against the kind of hypocrisy evidenced among the Pharisees (ibid., 117-18).[43]

This Jewish context suggests that the intent of Peter, Barnabas and the others, was not to hoodwink anyone. Rather, their "hypocrisy" consisted in their failure to "run a straight course with regard to the truth of the gospel" (v. 14). Their conduct was discordant with what they had done before. Paul, then, assessed Peter's behavior as being inconsistent with both his normal lifestyle and the intent of the Jerusalem agreement.[44] Paul is certainly not insinuat-

---

[42] Garland shows that in Diaspora Judaism the Greek *hupokritēs* can be equivalent to the Hebrew *hanaph*, "apostate" (*Intention*, 96-97, n. 20).

[43] Cf. Davies/Allison, *Matthew*, 3.262-63.

[44] Udoh ("Views," 233) is right that Paul's logic in opposing Peter was impeccable: Peter's refusal of table fellowship in Antioch meant that, inconsistent with the Jerusalem agreement, Gentiles could not in fact accepted into the messianic community without being required to observe the Law. Peter was for this reason building up once again the barriers that had been torn down (2:18).

ing that these brothers had gone so far as to become apostates and enemies of God. Nevertheless, their about-face was decidedly at variance with God's will, and if they were to become consistent with their behavior on this particular occasion, then the long-lasting effects of their actions would be devastating for the newly formed assembly of Jesus the Messiah.

The conduct of Barnabas was especially grievous: "*Even Barnabas* was carried away"—not at all what would have been expected of this "son of encouragement." It was Barnabas who had first introduced Paul to the Jerusalem church (Acts 9:27) and had accompanied him on his pioneering mission to the Galatians (Acts 14). A segment of the Galatian churches anyway must have been as shocked and saddened as Paul himself upon hearing of this temporary defection on Barnabas' part. Whereas Barnabas and Paul once withstood the circumcisers together, Paul now had to stand alone.

14 Paul's response to the situation was uninhibited: "When I saw that they were not acting in line with the truth of the gospel, I said to Peter in front of them all, 'You are a Jew, yet you live like a Gentile and not like a Jew. How is it, then, that you force Gentiles to follow Jewish customs'?" His charge against Peter, in front of the entire assembly, was essentially one: he was not "straightforward about the truth of the gospel" (NASB), as demonstrated by his inconsistency of life respecting the law and Gentile freedom from it. He had become "all things to all men" in a wholly illegitimate sense.

The verb of v. 14a (*orthopodeō*, from which the English "orthopedics" is derived) means "to walk straight" or "to go straight toward a goal." Peter and the others had thus deviated from the ideal course of Jew/Gentile relations in Christ. "The truth of the gospel" pertains to Jew and Gentile united in Christ. But the "crooked path" of Peter and the other Jewish Christians was in danger of permanently disrupting that unity. Paul would not allow an *apartheid* to gain a toehold in the churches under his oversight. Segregation and rigid separationism are not the Christian "walk" (see on 1:13; 2:2; cf. Gal 5:25; Eph 4:1, 17; Col 1:10; 2:6; Rom 13:13). Garland's contemporization is much to the point:

> If there had been a church bus at Antioch, the Gentiles would always have had to move to the back. In the church building, one might find a Gentile water fountain and a Jewish water fountain; and the Gentiles

would have had to sit in a special Gentile balcony section. Signs in various areas of the church might warn, "Jews Only, No Gentiles Allowed," and the bulletin logo might announce "Separate but Equal in Christ." In practice, however, the Gentile Christians were considered to be unfit for full equality. The compulsion was subtle but real. If Gentiles wanted to eat the Lord's Supper with Cephas and the other Jewish Christians, they would have to do something to make themselves fit. They would have to become Jews, submit to circumcision and abide by Jewish dietary regulations. The truth of the gospel, as far as Paul was concerned, does not mix with this kind of compulsion ("Defense," 170-71).

Peter's basic problem, according to Paul, was that he flip-flopped as regards his day-in and day-out mode of living. His "hypocrisy" (inconsistency) is further underscored: the one who once lived as a Gentile has suddenly reverted to living as Jew. While he "lived like a Gentile," Cephas did not feel conscience-bound to follow the Torah, with all its restrictions and prohibitions, as a rule of duty, chief among which would have been regulations concerning circumcision, diet, purity and special days. At one time, he did indeed "live like a Jew," that is, he maintained his Jewish distinctiveness from pagans in all regards (cf. Philo, *Legat.* 159, 170, 256). Yet Paul knew full well that this was a thing of the past. Dunn is correct to qualify that "live like a Gentile" does not necessarily mean a total abandonment of Jewish ways (*Galatians*, 127-28). But at least Peter had become cognizant that a life honoring to God no longer required strict Torah observance, particularly as embellished by Pharisaic *halakah*.

The precise nuance of the phrase "the truth of the gospel" has been assessed variously by the commentators (see Betz, *Galatians*, 92). However, Cummins is right that none of them has taken sufficient account of the biblical conception of "truth" (*alētheia*) as messianically recast by Paul. With respect to the Jewish background, the LXX regularly employs *alētheia* as the Greek dress for the Hebrew *'emunah*, meaning "faith(fulness)" (see on 1:23; 2:5, 16), and not least, Cummins remarks, in relation to God's own faithfulness and the reciprocal faithfulness of those in covenant relationship with him (*Paul*, 183). It is this which was catastrophically overthrown by the attack of Antiochus IV on Israel's temple-focused and Torah-based way of life and which could only be restored by errant Israel returning to God's "truth;" that is, "By reciprocating the love and faithfulness so characteristic of God himself and of his covenant relationship with his people" (ibid.).

But with the turning of the ages, the "truth" is now pointedly that of the *gospel*. "For Paul the truth of the gospel centres upon God's love and faithfulness as now manifested in Messiah Jesus and his followers" (ibid.). From Paul's vantage point, therefore, the central issue in Antioch was fidelity to God's "truth" as embodied eschatologically in the good news of Christ. Therefore, Peter, Barnabas, and the "rest of the Jews" were perilously close to proving unfaithful to the new covenant and its Lord, the one who came preaching peace to those who are "far off" (Gentiles) and those who are "near" (Jews) (Eph 2:17).

> It is this "truth of the gospel" which Peter's conduct has undermined. In his regression towards matters Jewish he has completely misconstrued the advantages of being a Jew by failing to conform his life to the outworking of God's truth—his covenant faithfulness—in Jesus the Messiah and his people (ibid., 184).

It was bad enough that Peter capitulated to the circumcisers as regards his personal practice, but it was worse still that he "tried to compel" (Greek conative present tense) Gentiles to "judaize" (*Ioudaizein*) (NIV: "Follow Jewish customs;" NASB: "Live like Jews"). "To judaize" obviously enough means to live a life in accordance with the Torah (cf. Josephus, *J. W.* 2.18.2 [462-63]). But if we can judge by 1:14, "judaize" or "live like Jews," would have entailed not only Torah observance, but also the "traditions of the Fathers," which encompassed various theological traditions and attempts to apply the law to everyday life (later to become the *halakoth*, the rabbinic "rulings" pertaining to observance of Torah). In the Gospels, the "traditions of the Fathers" are labeled the "traditions of the elders" or the "traditions of men" (Matt 15:2-3, 6; Mark 7:3, 5, 8-9, 13).

By his actions, Peter was effectively attempting to force his Gentile brothers and sisters into the mold of the law (and accompanying traditions), with the implication that otherwise they would not be acceptable to Jerusalem—or to God. As Betz observes, Peter had explicitly or implicitly made a demand on Gentiles to become partakers of the Torah covenant. In effect, he had done the same as the "false brothers" at Jerusalem (*Galatians*, 112. The same word "compel" [*anankazō*] occurs in 2:3.). "Peter, in effect, was destroying the gospel of Jesus Christ by demanding that the converts at Galatia become Jews. In such a situation, there was no gospel because the work of Christ had been eliminated" (McKnight, *Galatians*, 107). In short, Paul's objection was that Jewish laws and customs had been made *a necessary part of the gospel*.

Paul does not tell us whether Peter accepted his reproof and changed his practice. Perhaps he is silent because Peter, on that occasion at least, was not prepared to give in. But the longer-lasting effects are plain enough, because by the time of Acts 15, Peter, in conscious opposition to the circumcision party, is an outspoken champion of Gentile freedom. In fact, in Acts 15 Peter and James both speak spontaneously, as if they had been prepared by the incident in Antioch.

Section Notes

11-14 Cummins takes the narrative substructure of the incident at Antioch to be the Maccabean martyr stories. Paul, according to Cummins, "Emerges as one standing in ironic relation to the Maccabean tradition as he now responds to Peter's movement in the direction of a rigorous Judaism by faithfully defending the truth of the gospel, namely, the outworking of God's grace in the martyred and exalted Jesus, Messiah and Son of God, and in the eschatological people of God together conformed to him" (*Paul*, 161). The story line of Gal 2:11-21 as a whole, he maintains, represents a christological reworking of the Maccabean narrative as, for example, exemplified in the story of the martyrs Eleazar (2 Macc 6:18-31) and the Jewish mother and her seven sons (2 Macc 7:1-42). From this it is concluded that, for Paul, fundamentally table fellowship is not a question of adherence to Torah food laws but of the new community's (Jew + Gentile) communal involvement with their eschatological redeemer in the already inaugurated messianic kingdom of God. It is this which Peter is forsaking as he withdraws from mixed table fellowship. "By capitulating to those pressing for strict adherence to a Jewish way of life (who may themselves have come under the constraints of a Maccabean-inspired zeal), Peter fails to remain faithful to his martyr-exemplar Christ, and indeed also undermines the faithfulness of others. Hence, Paul responds by defending the truth of the gospel. In this contest Paul stands Daniel-like, but now in the cause of Christ rather than Judaism, and again demonstrates himself faithful to the martyred and exalted Messiah disclosed in him" (ibid., 161-62).

From the Judaizing point of view, Peter's withdrawal from table fellowship could be construed as loyalty to all that the martyrs exemplified and for which they died, especially given that the issue in 2 Maccabees 6 and 7 was *the refusal of the faithful to eat pork* (see Garlington, *Obedience*, 148-55). However, says Cummins, Paul's Christ-governed perspective viewed matters differently. "Peter's withdrawal represented a failure of faith which threatened the truth of the gospel and so had to be countered by Paul's own [ironic, I would say] martyr-like stance. Its immediate consequence was already evident: Gentiles were being persuaded to displace Christ with an unnecessary, divisive and potentially apostate commitment to a Judaism which Paul himself had left behind. Indeed, at risk was inclusive commensality with the now exalted eschatological redeemer within the already inaugurated kingdom of God. In essence, this was an assault on the grace of God as revealed in the crucified and risen Jesus, and in those living in him" (*Paul*, 188).

12 On table fellowship, see further Esler, *Galatians*, 93-116; George, *Galatians*, 172-73; Dunn, *Jesus, Paul*, 137-48; id., *Christ and Spirit*, 1.96-111; id., *Jesus Remembered*, 599-606; McKnight, *Vision*, 41-49; Borg, *Conflict*, 93-112; Bartchy, *DJG*, 796-900; Smith, *ABD*, 6.302-4; Udoh, "Views," 231-33. Trends of interpretation are summarized by Nanos, "What Was at Stake," 292-300. The precise character of the table fellowship in Antioch is a complicated matter, including its relationship to the Lord's Supper (see Cummins, *Paul*, 164-73). Cummins summarizes the various positions (ibid., 164-66) and opts for the view that idol meat may have been placed on the tables in Antioch. In any event, he thinks that the disruption of the fellowship had less to do with the food being eaten than with the Gentile company being kept (ibid., 165). My own inclination is that the menu was the primary stumbling block to the men from James.

12 The extent to which Jews would have engaged in social intercourse with Gentiles, including participation in meals, has been debated back and forth between Dunn (*Jesus, Paul*, 129-82), Esler (*Galatians*, 91-116; *Community*, 71-89), Sanders ("Association") and Nanos ("What Was at Stake"). Dunn, Sanders and Nanos are essentially on the same page in maintaining that Jews and Gentiles associated with one another in varying degrees, while Esler argues against any commensalism between observant Jews and Gentiles in the first century. The debate is summarized by T. L. Carter, *Paul*, 94-95. His conclusion is balanced: "On the basis of the evidence available, it is not possible to draw definitive conclusions as to the nature of the table fellowship at Antioch. Esler is right to argue that Jewish food laws did reinforce Jewish isolationism, but such social boundaries were constantly subject to erosion as a result of pressure to conform to the surrounding Gentile world" (ibid., 95). Bockmuehl (*Law*, 58) surmises that an observant Jew could have held one of four positions regarding eating with Gentiles: (1) refuse all table fellowship and refuse to enter a Gentile house; (2) invite Gentiles to their house and prepare a Jewish meal; (3) take their own food to a Gentile's house; (4) dine with Gentiles on the understanding that the food was neither prohibited by the Torah nor tainted with idolatry.

12 Schnelle is of the view that the issue was one of purity. For the opponents, purity was determined by the Torah, whereas for Paul purity consists in a sanctification of life, including such important matters as abstaining from immorality. It was a matter of how each party understood its own foundational structure. For Paul, the basis for the demand for purity is not the law but the separation from the power of sin as accomplished in baptism (*Paul*, 134-35). He is right as regards the difference of foundational structure between Paul and the Judaizers, but to make purity the heart of the Antioch incident is probably wide of the mark.

H. Summary and Transition (2:15-21)

At first glance, the concluding verses of chap. 2 appear to be disjointed from "Paul's autobiography as paradigm." However, on closer examination it is apparent that Paul does not in fact leave off talking about himself. Repeatedly in this coda to first major segment of the letter, he refers to himself, along with other like-minded Jewish Christians, either in the first person singular or plural or by means of the reflexive pronoun. The convictions at which he arrived about the vindication (justification) of the people of God were forged on the anvil of his own experience, as he made the painful transition from zealot persecutor of the church to proclaimer of the gospel. But not only does the paragraph bring to a close what has gone before, it also forms a transition into chaps. 3-4, in which Paul will expound in detail the salvation-historical grounding of his Christian certitude that Christ has ended the law, fulfilled the promise to Abraham and procured the gift of the Spirit for the reconstituted people of the new covenant.

It is Paul's own experience of grace that represents the climax of the story of Israel. As Lührmann quite rightly observes, these verses contain the theological essence of what Paul's conversion meant to him (*Galatians*, 46). He and all believers have come into the inheritance promised to the patriarchs, as ensured by the giving of the law, whose function was to place a hedge around Israel until the coming of her King. And now that the King has come, the true seed of Abraham are those who have simply put their trust in Jesus. In all this, as Martyn writes, Paul's argument is more than a response to the opponents; it is also a "repreaching of the gospel" (*Galatians*, 247).

Betz maintains that 2:15-21 is the *propositio* (proposition) of the letter, which, in his words, "Sums up the *naratio's* [narrative's] material content" and "sets up the arguments to be discussed later in the *probatio* [proof]" (*Galatians*, 114). A number of interpreters who invoke Betz focus narrowly on vv. 16-17 and take *the theme* of Galatians to be justification by faith. A certain case can be made for this, because the ensuing chapters mention justification four times (3:8, 11, 24; 5:4). Nevertheless, 2:15-21 is more inclusive than justification, and as one keeps reading it becomes apparent that in terms of the sheer volume of ideas the real center of gravity of the letter's "theological" segment is the onset of the new age, the identity of the seed of Abraham, the gift of the Spirit and liberation from the bondage of the law. In a nutshell, *Paul's concern is with the new age of the Spirit as inaugurated "in Christ" apart from the law*. Justification is a vital ingredient of the whole, but still essentially a subspecies of Paul's thought.[45]

15 Paul is very much concerned to emphasize that he and like-minded Jewish believers are "Jews by birth." The Greek noun translated "by birth" (*phusei*) appears in Rom 11:21, 24 in the sense of Israel being the "natural" branches, while the Gentiles are the "unnatural" (*para phusin*) branches. The Jews are marked out as the aboriginal people, by virtue of physical descent from Abraham, whereas the Gentiles are latecomers to the covenant. Jewishness, in other words, is determined by "nature" or birth. The same connotations are present in this verse. Paul speaks as any Jew of the period would have: there are Jews "by birth" as opposed to "sinners of the Gentiles" (literal translation). Birth and lineage separate Jew from Gentile, and the covenant with Israel distinguishes "saint" from "sinner."[46]

For the first time in the letter, Paul uses the first person plural to denote Jewish Christians. In this particular case, he probably includes Peter and Barnabas (and, in principle, James), notwithstanding their wavering in Antioch. He draws on the experience of Jewish believers, those who had been nurtured in Judaism and taught the word of God. The impact of vv. 15-16 is just this: *even we* (*kai hēmeis*) know that justification is not by "works of the law" but by "faith in Jesus Christ." In v. 16b, it is stated just this way: "*Even*

---

[45] The literature is enormous, but good starting points (representing various stances) are: Schnelle, *Paul*, 454-77; Martyn, *Galatians*, 264-75; Hays, "Justification;" Howard, *Crisis*, 46-65; Smiles, *Gospel*, 133-46; Wright, *Paul*, 113-33; Gorman, *Cruciformity*, 122-46; McGrath, *Studies*, 355-480; id., *DPL*, 517-23; Seifrid, *Justification*; id., *Christ*; Schlatter, *Theology*, 228-41; Wintle, "Justification;" Garlington, *Essays*, 285-99; Segal, *Paul*, 174-83.

[46] For a more detailed exposition of vv. 15-16, see my *Defense*, 29-58. The thesis of that study is that Paul plays on and challenges the traditional Jewish distinction between "saints" and "sinners." This is in keeping with phenomenon of role reversal in Galatians, especially in 3:10-13 and 4:21-31.

we have believed..." (literal translation). By identifying himself and his associates as thoroughly Jewish believers, Paul disavows that the people from James are the legitimate heirs of Israel's hope. He would have us think very much in terms of "them and us." One might paraphrase vv. 15-16: "As distinct from *them*, the Judaizers and their followers, *we*, notwithstanding our Jewish heritage, know that a person is not justified from works of Torah but by faith in Christ; *even we*, who share the same historic biblical values as our opponents, have trusted in Christ for justification." This confirms again the inconsistency of Peter and Barnabas in withdrawing from the Gentiles.

"Gentile sinners" is a phrase that would have resonated in Jewish ears.[47] As Dunn points out (*Galatians*, 133), in Jewish thought "sinners" meant preeminently "those whose lawless conduct marked them out as outside the covenant, destined for destruction and so not to be consorted with" (1 Sam 15:18; 24:28; Ps 1:1; 9:15-17; 37:34-36; 58:10; Prov 12:12-13; Sir 7:16; 9:11; 41:5-11). As such, the term was synonymous with "Gentiles," who by definition were outside the covenant or "lawless" (Ps 9:15-17; 1 Macc 1:34; 2:44, 48; Tob 13:6; *Jub.* 23:23-24; 24:28 [cf. *Jub.* 22:16: "Do not eat with them"]; *Pss. Sol.* 1:1; 2:1-2; 17:22-25; 4 Ezra 3:28-36; 4:23; cf. Matt 5:47; Luke 6:33). Still more striking, he notes, is the way in which the same term was used among the various Jewish factions. Members of one group would call themselves the "righteous," while outsiders were "sinners" (1 Macc 1:34; 2:44, 48; *1 Enoch* 5:4-7; 82:4-5; 1QH 2:8-12; 1QpHab 4:4-8; *Pss. Sol.* 4:8; 13:6-12). Synonymous with "sinners" were also terms like "lawless" (*anomoi* and *paranomoi*) and "ungodly" (*asebeis*).[48]

By invoking such phraseology, Paul, for rhetorical purposes, reckons himself among the company of the rank-and-file Jew who looked upon the rest of the world as outside the realm of God's covenant righteousness and, by definition, "sinful." "He looked out...from that perspective at the rest of humankind, echoing the dismissive attitude of the faithful member of the covenant people towards the non-Jews—'Gentile sinners'."[49] The "Gentile sinner,"

---

[47] The phrase is literally "sinners from the Gentiles." The preposition "from" (*ek*) is used in its "partisan" sense of "belonging to." See below on v. 16.

[48] On "lawless" and "ungodly," see respectively my *Obedience*, 91-102; 53-55, 84-86.

[49] Dunn, *Galatians*, 133. On the "sinners," see Dunn, *Jesus, Paul*, 71-77, 150-51; id., *Partings*, 102-7; id., *Jesus Remembered*, 526-32; Betz, *Galatians*, 115; Gar-

from such a vantage point, was without hope (cf. Eph 2:12).[50] In so writing, Paul is probably adopting the very words of the Jerusalem delegation, who were summoning the word "sinners" to pressure the Galatians into becoming *really* "righteous" by coming under the yoke of the Torah, and in particular by practicing the dietary restrictions commanded by Moses. Paul, then, with a touch of irony, gives his readers a glimpse of what these teachers really think of them. They are not acceptable as they are, but rather must conform to rigid notions of what righteousness is all about.

16 Verse 16 continues the sentence begun in v. 15 with the participle "knowing." NASB translates quite literally: "We are Jews by nature and not sinners from among the Gentiles; nevertheless knowing that a man is not justified by the works of the Law but through faith in Christ Jesus." NIV, by contrast, renders the participle as a finite verb and provides a somewhat smoother reading: "We who are Jews by birth and not 'Gentile sinners' know that a man is not justified by observing the law, but by faith in Jesus Christ."[51] Either way, Paul's point is that God's method of vindicating/justifying his latter-day people is matter well-known to every Jewish believer. According to Witherington, "He assumes it is the proper and normal view of Jewish Christians, in light of what they know and believe about the work of Christ" (*Grace*, 173). If the Teachers in Galatia purport to represent the Jewish position on justification, Paul informs his readers that such is not the case. He and his company ("all the brothers with me," 1:2) have truly experienced God's justifying deed in Christ—and that apart from "the works of the law." In principle, this group includes James, Barnabas and Peter. The latter two may have wavered briefly in Antioch, but in their right mind they would have been compelled to bear witness to the veracity of Paul's claim.

What is well-known to Paul and the others is that a person is not justified "from the works of the law" (literal translation) but through faith in Jesus Christ. Each element of the proposition of v. 16a, "justified," "works of the law," and "faith in Jesus Christ" has become the object of intensive controversy in modern study. Hays

---

lington, *Obedience*, 49-55, 95-98; Pancaro, *Law*, 30-44, 119; and at length Winninge, *Sinners*.

[50] Betz cites 2 Macc 6:12-17, which states the Jewish position with regard to the sinfulness of Jews in contrast to Gentiles. The sins of the nations are punished with a view to destruction, while Jewish sinners are merely disciplined (*Galatians*, 115, n. 27).

[51] On the construction, see Longenecker, *Galatians*, 83.

is correct that Paul uses theological shorthand, and each phrase has to be unpacked carefully (*Galatians*, 236).

"Justified"

The characteristic Pauline verb articulating the justification of the people of God is *dikaioō*, translated traditionally as "justify" (Rom 2:13; 3:4, 20, 24, 26, 28, 30; 4:2, 5; 5:1; 6:7; 8:30, 33; 1 Cor 6:11; Gal 2:16, 17; 3:8, 11, 24; 5:4; Titus 3:7). The usage of this verb in the Greek OT, the matrix of Paul's own employment of it, is complex, especially when compared with the various Hebrew words underlying it. *Dikaioō* (like any other word) assumes different shades of meaning according to context. But because of its occurrence in juridical settings, meanings like "justify," "vindicate," "acquit" stand out and provide a forensic framework within which to place Paul's doctrine of justification.

Yet Paul's teaching on justification is more comprehensive than the verb *dikaioō*, because the idea of justification is linked to the concept of the righteousness of God in the OT.[52] Strictly speaking, there is no independent doctrine of justification which is detachable from righteousness as a generic category. This means that the semantic range of *dikaioō* is broadened by its relation to the Hebrew/covenantal concept of the "righteousness of God" (*dikaiosunē theou*). God's righteousness in the OT finds two points of contact with justification in Paul.

(1) There is the forensic/juridical setting of the Mosaic covenantal courtroom. The person who is vindicated and thus acquitted of all charges is declared to be "righteous" (Hebrew $ts^e ddiq$ = Greek *dikaios*) and then treated as such. Yet it is vital to remember that even in these instances in the LXX where *dikaioō* is strongly forensic, Ziesler reminds us that it is forensic in the *Hebrew* sense, that is, the verb signifies "restoration of the community or covenant relationship, and thus cannot be separated from the ethical altogether. The restoration is not merely to a standing, but to an existence in the relationship." As a result, "righteousness" in this scenario has reference to a vindicated *existence* conferred on a per-

---

[52] Treatments of righteousness language are provided by Burton, *Galatians*, 460-68; Esler, *Galatians*, 161-64; Ziesler, *Righteousness*, 52-127; Reumann, *Righteousness*, 12-22; Kertelge, *Rechtfertigung*, 15-45; Klaiber, *Gerecht*, 13-70; Przybylski, *Righteousness*, 8-76; Hill, *Words*, 82-120; Stuhlmacher, *Gerechtigkeit*, 102-84; G. N. Davies, *Faith*, passim; Schreiner, *Paul*, 189-217; Seifrid, "Righteousness Language;" Onesti/Brauch, *DPL*, 827-32; Wright, "Righteousness;" Garlington, "Righteousness."

son by a gracious God. "What this means is that men live together in freedom, possessing their civil rights in a good society. *It is not just a vindicated status, but a vindicated life*" (*Righteousness*, 20, 25, italics mine).[53] As Rapa states it precisely:

> The importance of this observation for the proper interpretation of Galatians 2:16 cannot be overstated. When Paul speaks of being "justified" here, he has in mind *both* the relational forensic category of acquittal for sins *and* the consequent ethical "right" behavior pattern of God's people. The one who is "righteous" or "justified" is at the same time in right relationship to God, and, *as a necessary component of that relationship,* is living an ethical lifestyle as based upon the character of God. This, Paul affirms, comes about "not by the works of the law," but rather through "faith in" or "the faithfulness of" Jesus Christ. Relational approval before God and its consequent (and necessarily attendant) ethical lifestyle is for Paul not a matter of "works of the law," as Peter's actions implied and the Judaizers must have taught. On the contrary, this circumstance can only come about through the agency determined by God. That agency is trust in God and his promises, as now…most notably bound up in the person and work of Jesus Christ (*Meaning*, 134, italics his).

To this I would add the voices of Crossan and Reed:

> Faith does not mean intellectual consent to a proposition, but vital commitment to a program. Obviously, one could summarize a program in a proposition, but faith can never be reduced to factual assent rather than total dedication. Faith (*pistis*) is not just a partial mindset, but a total lifestyle commitment. The crucial aspect of faith as commitment is that it is always an interactive process, a bilateral contract, a two-way street. Faith is covenantal and presumes faithfulness from both parties with, of course, all appropriate differences and distinctions.[54]

---

[53] See also Gorman, *Cruciformity*, 142-43; Rapa, *Meaning*, 132-34.

[54] Crossan/Reed, *Paul*, 385-86. Likewise Hays: the verb "justify" "points not merely to a forensic declaration of acquittal from guilt but also to God's ultimate action of powerfully setting right all that has gone wrong" (*Galatians*, 237). At the end of the day, justification entails "rectification" (ibid., 238). Cf. Bruce, "Curse," 34.

Therefore, the one of whom "justification" is predicated is regarded as "righteous," that is, committed to the covenant and the God of the covenant in a household relationship. Likewise, Käsemann writes that in the OT and Judaism generally *dikaiosunē* has in view the relations of community members: "Originally signifying trustworthiness in regard to the community, it came to mean the rehabilitated standing of a member of the community who had been acquitted of an offense against it" ("Righteousness," 172). Reumann concurs that righteousness/justice/justification terminology in the Hebrew scriptures is "action-oriented," not just "status" or "being" language, and "binds together forensic, ethical and other aspects in such a way that some sort of more unified ancient Near Eastern view can readily be presupposed" (*Righteousness*, 16). In brief, it is the righteous person who is recognized in his true character and thus vindicated against all charges). Just how such a conception of "justification" can square with Paul's declaration that God justifies the *ungodly* (Rom 4:5) will be clarified below.

(2) The other point of contact between righteousness in the OT and Paul is the outlook on Israel's future as evidenced in the Prophets and several of the Psalms. The Prophets characteristically contemplate Israel's removal into Babylonian captivity because of her idolatry. Yet one day the nation is to return to her land when Yahweh acts in power to deliver her from bondage. At the time of this new exodus, the remnant of the people will enjoy the definitive forgiveness of sins, the restoration of the broken covenant, the glorious new creation and vindication as those faithful to the Lord. It is Yahweh who vindicates the faithful from the charges of their enemies, who assume that he is unable to deliver his people and suppose that their faith in him is in vain.[55] It is he who exonerates them, when in the "eschatological courtroom" he judges their oppressors (Isa 10:5-19; Hab 2:2-20) and brings them back to the land from which they will never be uprooted again (cf. Wright, *Paul*, 33-34).

It is in this context of promised deliverance that God is said to act righteously on behalf of his own. Especially striking is that in a number of key passages the terms "righteousness" and "salvation" (or "be justified") are placed in synonymous parallelism, e.g., Isa 45:8; 45:21-25; 46:13; 51:5–6, 8; 56:1; 59:17; 61:10; 62:1-2; 63:1; Ps 24:6; 51:14; 71:15–16; 98:1-3, 8-9 (LXX 97:2-3, 8-9); 4 Ezra

---

[55] It is just in this vein that the Servant of the Lord is confident that Yahweh will vindicate him from every charge of wrongdoing (Isa 50:7-8a).

8:36, 39–40; CD 20:20; 1QS 11:11–15; *1 Enoch* 99:10. Noteworthy as well are Ps 35:27-28 (LXX 34:27-28); 72:1-4 (LXX 71:1-4, 7); 85:11-13 (LXX 84:12-14); 96:13 (LXX 95:13); 103:6; Isa 9:7 (LXX 9:6); 11:1-2, 5; 45:8, 22-25; 51:5-6; 53:10-11; 61:11; Jer 23:5-6; Mal 4:2 (LXX 3:20).[56]

Several comments are in order. First, "righteousness" and "salvation" are synonymous, at least virtually so. The logic behind this is not difficult to discern. Righteousness by definition is God's fidelity to his people within the covenant bond. As Wright expresses it, the phrase "the righteousness of God" (*dikaiosunē theou*) to a reader of the LXX would have one obvious meaning: "God's own faithfulness to his promises, to the covenant."[57] It is especially in Isaiah 40-55 that God's righteousness is that aspect of his character which compels him to save Israel, despite the nation's perversity and lostness. "God has made promises; Israel can trust those promises. God's righteousness is thus cognate with his trustworthiness on the one hand, and Israel's salvation on the other." He further notes that at the heart of the picture in Isaiah is the figure of the suffering servant through whom God's righteous purpose is finally accomplished (*Paul*, 96). Psalm 98 is likewise explicit that the revelation of God's righteousness to the nations is commensurate with the fact that he has remembered his lovingkindness and faithfulness to the house of Israel. Therefore, he demonstrates his fidelity when he springs into action to deliver Israel from her bondage (note that Psalm 98 is echoed in Rom 1:16-17, which likewise places in parallel "righteousness" and "salvation"). Thus, a formal definition of the Greek phrase *dikaiosunē theou* could be stated as: "God's faithfulness to his covenant with Israel, as a result of which he saves her from her exile in Babylon" (ibid., 96-97). Ps 98:2 and 103:6 sum it all up: "The Lord has made known his victory, he has revealed his vindication in the sight of the nations;" "The Lord works vindication and justice for all who are oppressed." In both texts, "vindication" is literally "righteousness."

Second, the return of Israel from exile *is* Israel's justification. Isa 45:25 in the LXX actually uses the verb *dikaioō*, translated "justified" by NASB. It is true that the Hebrew of the passage can be fairly be rendered "found righteous" (as NIV). Yet the net effect

---

[56] See the further assemblage of passages by Gundry, "Nonimputation," 36-38.

[57] I have propounded this understanding of righteousness in *Defense*, 66-97, and "New Perspective Reading," 63-68.

is the same: the people who return from exile are the vindicated ones whose righteousness is now made evident.

Third, the Hebrew of Isa 62:1-2 speaks of Israel's ("her") righteousness and salvation. However, the LXX has "my," referring to God, instead of "her." This may be accounted for by the textual tradition followed by the LXX at this point. Be that as it may, on the theological level there is no problem, because the blazing demonstration of Israel's righteousness and salvation is made possible only by the prior revelation of the Lord's righteousness/salvation.

These two interrelated branches of righteousness in the OT, of which Paul was heir, combine to inform us that justification, in his thought, is the vindication of the righteous, that is, faithful people of God. In eschatological perspective, believers in Christ have been exonerated in the final assize and have been admitted into the privileges, responsibilities and fellowship of the covenant. Given the parallel of "righteousness" and "salvation" in the Psalms and Prophets, and given especially the backdrop of captivity and return from exile, *dikaioō* in Paul means to "vindicate as the people of God" (when they return from exile). Historically, when the Lord caused Israel to return to the land, he vindicated the faithful remnant against the accusations of their enemies that they had rightly been taken into captivity, and that because of them Yahweh's name had been blasphemed among the nations (Isa 52:5; Rom 2:24). Their vindication corresponds to the advent of a righteous king, the outpouring of the Spirit and the renewal of the covenant, resulting in peace and prosperity (Isaiah 32).[58] In Paul, all this is transposed into the "higher octave" of what God has done in Christ at the turning of the ages—his own "eschatological courtroom." The actual enemy of believers is not Babylon but Satan. He is the strong man who held them in the bondage of sin (Matt 12:29; Luke 11:21-22); he is "the accuser of our brothers, who accuses them before our God day and night" (Rev 12:10; cf. Rom 8:33-34a).

It is this cluster of ideas that is embodied by *dikaioō*. If God's righteousness is "his intervention in a saving act on behalf of his people," then the passive voice of the verb means "to be an object of the saving righteousness of God (so as to be well-pleasing to him at the judgment)" (Motyer, "Righteousness," 48). When God

---

[58] Against the backdrop of a passage like Isaiah 32, Gorman's definition of justification represents a variation of the one proposed by me, but still one very much in keeping with it: "To be justified is to be restored to right covenant relations now, with certain hope of acquittal on the future day of judgment.... (*Apostle*, 201).

in Christ intervenes to save his covenant partners, he plants them again in the newly created land, the new heavens and earth, never to be removed. This is "salvation" in the pregnant sense of the term: deliverance from evil and the bestowal of "peace" on a redeemed people.

In short, justification in Paul signals deliverance from exile and freedom from bondage (again one of the key motifs of Galatians). One of the clearest indications is the relationship of Rom 6:7 and 18. In the former verse, *dikaioō* is literally translated "justified from sin." As such, it forms a parallelism with the verb "liberated from sin" (*eleutheroō*) in 6:18. The parallel is best preserved by rendering 6:7 as "freed from sin." Therefore, when Paul writes of justification, he characteristically has in mind the new exodus on which the latter-day people of God have embarked. Moreover, this saving righteousness is cosmic in its dimensions. At the end of the day, "the righteousness of God" is actively directed at the rescue of the creation. God's righteousness is his relation-restoring love.[59]

Within the setting of Paul's mission to the nations, justification functions to delineate just who are the latter-day people of God. In the eschatological new exodus which has been brought to pass in Christ, *it is Gentiles who are as much the vindicated people as Jews*, and this quite irrespective of Torah-loyalty, inclusive of circumcision and the other traditional badges of Jewish self-identity. Therefore, justification is very much a covenantal term, speaking to the issue of the identity of the people of God (see Dumbrell, "Justification").

It is here that the perspective of Rom 3:21-26 is directly parallel to the outlook of Galatians. According to that passage, in his righteousness (as defined above), God has acted in Christ to remove the sin-barrier that stood between himself and an apostate humanity *in toto* (Rom 1:18-3:20). Jew and Greek alike are now the object of the saving fidelity of the God of Israel. Since all have sinned and fall short of the glory of God (Rom 3:23), all are now freely justified by his grace through the redemption which is in Christ Jesus. The covenant with Israel always envisaged a worldwide family. But Israel, clinging to her own special status as the covenant bearer, has betrayed the purpose for which that covenant was made. "It is as though the postman were to imagine that all the letters in his bag were intended for him" (Wright, *Paul*, 108)!

---

[59] Käsemann, "Righteousness;" Onesti/Brauch, *DPL*, 836-37; Barth, *Justification*, 17, 74-82.

An important corollary is that the *center of gravity* of Paul's thought on justification is more the corporate body of Christ than the individual believer. As W. D. Davies writes:

> That there was such a personal dimension need not be denied, but it existed within and not separated from a communal and, indeed, a cosmic dimension. Paul's doctrine of justification by faith was not solely and not primarily oriented towards the individual but to the interpretation of the people of God. The justified man was "in Christ", which is a communal concept. And, necessarily because it was eschatological, the doctrine moved towards the salvation of the world, a new creation ("Paul," 715-16).

Davies further points out that in both Galatians and Romans the discussion of justification by faith is immediately followed by that of the constitution of the people of God (ibid., 716; cf. Cousar, *Galatians*, 56-58). In the present context of Gal 2:16-17, *dikaioō* has to do specifically with the vindication/restoration of Jews who have believed in Christ. No longer do they anticipate being vindicated at the last judgment by virtue of their loyalty to the God of Israel and his law; but rather eschatological vindication has taken place at the cross of Christ (v. 20), and "works of the law" are no longer relevant—this is a matter of common and well-established knowledge.

Finally, if it be asked, How can God justify the ungodly while being consistent with the practice of the Hebrew courtroom to acquit only the righteous? The answer quite simply is that those who were formerly ungodly in Adam have been made righteous in Christ. Here the perspective Phil 3:9 is much to the point. Paul speaks of a "righteousness from God" (*dikaiosunē ek theou*). It is God's own righteousness, defined as "covenant fidelity," that entails *the gift of righteousness*. In his own righteousness, God enables us to become what he is—righteous (2 Cor 5:21). His loyalty to his people consists in his conforming them to himself, so that he and they may live in uninterrupted covenant fellowship. God's righteousness has provided Christ as the propitiation for sins (Rom 3:21-26). In Adam all are guilty, but God has removed their guilt by means of Christ and thus can vindicate them as his faithful people. In these actions are embodied God's covenant faithfulness.

Without constructing a full-blown *ordo salutis* (order of salvation), there is a logical process whereby God is able to justify sinners. By the work of the Spirit we are united with Christ and become God's righteousness in him; and on that basis God the judge pronounces us righteous and entitled to the full privileges of covenant membership. After all is said and done, Luther was right that the righteousness God requires is the righteousness he provides in Christ.

"Works of the Law"

As much debated as justification/righteousness is Paul's famous phrase "(the) works of the law."[60] Stated simply, "the works of the law" have reference to "the obligations laid upon the Israelites by virtue of their membership of Israel," whose purpose was "to show covenant members how to live within the covenant" (Dunn, *Galatians*, 135-36). These are *covenant works*—"those regulations prescribed by the law which any good Jew would simply take for granted to describe what a good Jew did" (Dunn, *Jesus, Paul*, 194).[61] For this reason, "It would be virtually impossible to conceive of participation in God's covenant, and so in God's covenant righteousness, apart from these observances, these works of the law" (ibid., 193). As such, the phrase articulates the whole duty (and privilege) of the Jew living under the Mosaic covenant. Martyn, then, wisely cautions us that the word "works" can be misleading: "The expression simply summarizes the grand and complex activity of the Jew, who faithfully walks with God along the path God has opened up for him in the law" (*Galatians*, 261).

From one vantage point, "works of the law" encompassed the entirety of the Mosaic legislation, with no exceptions. From another, by Paul's day the phrase had taken on more specific connotations. Within the historical climate of Second Temple Judaism, especially from the time of the Maccabean revolt, key elements of the law had become the acid tests of loyalty to Judaism, now dubbed the "boundary markers" of Jewish self-identification (as

---

[60] On the various interpretations of the phrase, see Schreiner, *DPL*, 975-79; Schnelle, *Paul*, 280-81. As is so of all the categories in this section of chap. 2, research on the law has been both extensive and intensive. Accessible recent sources are Rapa, *Meaning*; Dunn, *Theology of Paul*, 128-61; id., (ed.), *Paul and the Mosaic Law*; Schnelle, *Paul*, 506-21, all with extensive references.

[61] Schlier shows that "works of the law" in some literature appear as "works of the commandments," or in rabbinic traditions simply as "works." These "works" constitute the "law of the Lord" as over against the "law of Beliar" (*Galater*, 91-92). This would tend to confirm that when Paul uses the word "works" by itself, he employs it as shorthand for the longer phrase "works of the law."

placed in vogue by Dunn, *Jesus, Paul*, e.g., 192, 194).[62] These were circumcision, food laws, purity laws, sabbath observance and temple worship. These hardly exhausted the Jew's obligations under the law, but they did focus attention on crucial elements of his walk. This is so because it was precisely these components of the Torah which had come under attack during the Seleucid persecution of the Jews in the second century BC. Because of pagan "zeal against the law," "zeal for the (works of the) law" became the byword of the loyalists to the Jewish cause (1 Macc 2:26-27).

In brief, writes Hays, "'works of the law' refer primarily to practices commanded by the law (circumcision, dietary laws, sabbath observance) that distinctively mark Jewish ethnic identity; *these symbolize comprehensive obedience to the law's covenant obligations.*"[63] As Hays is careful to state, works of the law are not confined to the "boundary markers." Rather, it is the "boundary markers" which in the historical setting served to focus the faithful Israelite's commitment to the entire revealed will of God.[64] These were the "litmus paper" tests of fidelity. Accordingly, Witherington can say that by his use of the phrase Paul opposes "obedience to the Mosaic Law and seeking to be part of the community that relates to God on the basis of the Mosaic covenant." This is objectionable because "the Mosaic Law and obedience to it is not, in Paul's view, how one got into Christ, how one stays in Christ, or how one goes on in Christ. It is no longer what defines and delimits who the people of God are and how they ought to live and behave."[65]

In arriving at such a conception of "works of the law," recent scholarship has concentrated on the historical setting in which these words assume their significance. Apart from the general at-

---

[62] See at length Christiansen, *Covenant*.

[63] Hays, "Notes," 2185 (italics mine). Cf. Hays, *Galatians*, 238-39, 251; Dunn, *Theology of Paul*, 354-59; Ziesler, *Galatians*, 25-26; Garland, "Defense," 168. According to Sanders, "There is...something which is common to circumcision, Sabbath, and food laws, and which sets them off from other laws; they created a social distinction between Jews and other races in the Greco-Roman world" (*Paul, the Law*, 102).

[64] This being so, the thunder is taken out of Das' attempt to impute to Dunn a notion of works of the law that would restrict the scope of the phrase to the boundary markers (*Paul*, 155-60). Das' criticisms are set in the context of his endeavor to argue that, for Paul, the law must be kept perfectly (see the section note to 3:10-13).

[65] Witherington, *Grace*, 172. To the same effect are McKnight, *Galatians*, 119-21; Hansen, *Galatians*, 69-70; Ziesler, *Galatians*, 26.

mosphere of zeal for the law and the desire on the part of Israelites to maintain their distinctive covenant identity, especially noteworthy is the occurrence of strikingly similar phrases in the DSS (1QS 5:21, 23; 6:18; 4QFlor 1:7; cf. 1QH 1:26; 4:31; CD 13:11).[66]

4QMMT is particularly intriguing because its very title is, as normally translated, "*Some of the Works of the Torah*" (*miqsat maasē ha-torah*). This writing has been called a "halakic letter," in which a representative of the sect apparently airs his grievances about "the state of the nation" to the religious/political establishment in Jerusalem.[67] The letter contains an exhortation for its readers to follow the example of the godly kings of Israel and a warning that they will incur the curses of Deuteronomy if they do not reconsider their own beliefs and practices *vis-à-vis* the demands of the law. If the readers do mend their ways, it will be "reckoned to them as righteousness" (see below on 3:6). It is in this setting that "works of the Torah" articulates the community's own standard of covenant life. The members of the sect thus define themselves in relation to other Jews by their distinctive "walk" (*halakah*) in the ways of Yahweh.

In the present context of Galatians 2, the phrase "works of the law" serves to pinpoint the dispute with the Judaizers. By his inconsistency, Peter had effectively sent the message that Gentiles must submit to the law in order to be acceptable to God. Paul counters this false impression by the emphatic assertion that "we know" that works of the law have become irrelevant as far as justification is concerned. At one time, the Jewish faithful directed their faith toward Yahweh, believing that he would vindicate those

---

[66] See Rapa, *Meaning*, 53-56. Winger's attempt to eliminate 4QFlor 1:7 from consideration is not at all convincing (*Law*, 135). Not only Vermes' translation of the passage (quoted by Winger) but that of Martinez renders: "And he commanded to build for himself a temple of man, to offer him in it, before him, the works of the law" (*Scrolls*, 136). Here, "the works of the law" are tantamount to the community's sacrifice as placed upon the altar of the temple. The application to Paul is hardly speculative, as Winger claims, but indicates that the sect's covenantal duty was regarded in sacrificial terms, an idea very much relevant to Paul. Moreover, contra Winger, this is not the only occurrence of the phrase *maasē ha-torah* in the Scrolls (as cited above). The subsequent publication of 4QMMT (unavailable to Winger) simply nails down the case.

[67] On 4QMMT, see Dunn, *Theology of Paul*, 357-58; id., "4QMMT;" Ciampa, *Scripture*, 186-91; Pate, *Communities*, 47-48, 58-61; Das, *Paul and the Jews*, 41, n. 61; Abegg, "4QMMT;" Kampen/Bernstein (eds.), *4QMMT*; Rapa, *Meaning*, 54; Schnelle, *Paul*, 281-82 (n. 56). The entire text with commentary is in Qimron/Strugnell (eds.), *Discoveries*.

who maintained their allegiance to him, as that allegiance was expressed by remaining within the Torah.

Crucial here is an appreciation of the centrality of the Torah in Israel's self-consciousness of being the chosen people. It is the book of Deuteronomy which gives the classic statement of the role of the Torah in the life of the people. The heart of the book (chaps. 5-28) consists of a restatement of the covenant made at Sinai. Deut 29:1 sums up the whole of that block of material: "These are the words of the covenant which the Lord commanded Moses to make with the sons of Israel in the land of Moab, besides the covenant which He had made with them at Horeb" (NASB). Throughout the book the emphasis of covenant life is sustained and reinforced in numerous restatements of the promise (and warnings): "This do and live" (Deut 4:1, 10, 40; 5:29-33; 6:1-2, 18, 24; 7:12-13). This promise does not originate in Deuteronomy, because Lev 18:5 had already said: "So you shall keep My statutes and My judgments, by which a man may live if he does them; I am the Lord" (NASB).

But with the turning of the ages, as Paul will clarify especially in 3:23-25, the law has served its purpose in salvation history, namely, to lead Israel to Christ. From this point onward, to cling to the Torah is nothing less than idolatry (4:8-9), because such zeal for the law obscures one's view of the Christ and the actual nature of his work, making the law, rather than Christ, the "Jewish gateway to salvation."

> This is why faith in Christ and "works of the law" are opposites: one cannot opt for Christ's system *and* Moses' system at the same time because they are mutually exclusive options for salvation. Either one believes in Christ or one chooses to commit oneself to the law. One cannot live under both systems without destroying one or the other's integrity (Mcknight, *Galatians*, 122).

Paul, then, asserts that justification is not "from works of the law" (*ex ergōn nomou*). Even excellent scholars like Betz and Mcknight translate this phrase as: "on the basis of works of the Torah." Betz's particular rationale is that Paul's Greek phrase is a "theological abbreviation" for the longer proposition that the works of the law form the "basis" of salvation in the Jewish schema. The problem, however, is twofold. One, a certain amount of presuppositional work goes into this reading, that is, presuppositions regarding the character of first-century Judaism and Paul's response to it. Two, such a paraphrase is linguistically unnecessary. I would argue that Paul's Greek is not an abbreviation for something longer, but a replete statement that makes perfectly good sense as it stands.

In point of fact, Paul uses prepositions very carefully. Characteristically, we find *dia* ("through"), *en* ("in") and *ek* ("from"). The first speaks of means: one is justified by the instrumentality of faith in Christ. The second denotes locality or sphere: Paul avows that justification is to not be located or found within the parameters of the ancient covenant people. Inherent in the third is the notion of source or origin. But in this vicinity of the letter it takes on the nuance of belonging: to be "from" a realm means to belong to it. This is the "partisan" use of *ek*.[68] Consequently, by the use of this preposition, Paul asserts that justification is not to be had by belonging to the old community as walled about by the Torah ("the works of the law").[69] This usage of *ek* is paralleled by the following verses. 2:15 speaks of "sinners from the Gentiles." These are sinners who are identified with Gentiles. 3:12 is Paul's assertion that the law is "not of faith," meaning that the law and faith do not belong to the same phase of salvation history.[70] In 3:18, the promise to Abraham cannot be *ek nomou*, or by retention of membership in that state of affairs that postdated the promise. Likewise, according to 3:21, if the law could make alive, then righteousness would be "from the law" (*ek nomou*), that is, righteousness would come by way of individuals assuming their place within the confines of the Torah. And even without *ek*, he can use the genitive case to the same effect in 3:20: Moses the mediator is not "of one," that is, Moses does not belong to the unified people of God; he is not "one of them." See the commentary on the respective verses.

Therefore, "those of faith" (*hoi ek pisteōs*)—they who belong to the company of faith (3:7, 9)—seek to be justified "in Christ"

---

[68] See BDAG, 296: "In these cases the idea belonging, the partisan use, often completely overshadows that of origin." The lexicon translates *hoi ex nomou* in Rom 4:14 as "partisans of the law." Likewise, Rom 9:6: *hoi ex Israēl* are "Israelites." Cf. Rom 2:8; 16:10. Schnelle points out that *ek* occurs twenty times in 2:16-3:24, with the comment that a life that can stand justified before God cannot result *from* works of the law (*Paul*, 279). I have explored this element of Paul's syntax in the forthcoming article, "Partisan *Ek*."

[69] The notion of belonging is likewise present in Rom 3:30 (*ex ergōn nomou*); 4:14 (*hoi ek nomou*); 4:16 (*tō ek nomou*) 10:5 (*hē dikaiosunē ek nomou*). To the same effect is *dikaiosunēn tēn ek nomou* of Phil 3:9.

[70] Not dissimilar is the phrase "the men from (*apo*) James" (2:12). Those who came from James belonged to the same community as James (at that point in time).

(2:17), in the realm and era of Christ-faith (*ek pisteōs Christou*) (2:16c) and through the instrumentality of trust in him (*dia pisteōs Iēsou Christou*) (2:16a).[71] Paul's convictions stand in sharp relief to those of his opponents, who are "from the circumcision" (*ek peritomēs*) (2:12) and "from works of the law" (*ex ergōn nomou*) (3:10; cf. Rom 4:14). These are they who remain within and belong to the community of the Mosaic covenant; they are "in the law" (3:11; 5:4; cf. Rom 2:12; 3:19; Phil 3:6) and desire to be "under the law" (4:21; cf. 3:23; 4:4; 5:18; 1 Cor 9:20).[72] It is they who seek to be justified *ex ergōn nomou* and *en nomō* (3:11; 5:4).[73] For variations on the theme, see Phil 3:5, 9.

"Faith in Jesus Christ"

"Works of the Torah" have given way to "faith in Jesus Christ." The Greek phrase traditionally translated "faith in Jesus Christ" (*pistis Iēsou Christou*) has itself been the subject of a great deal of investigation in recent times. The growing consensus is that Paul has in view the covenant faithfulness of Christ himself (taking the genitive case of *Iēsou Christou* to be subjective genitive) (see the first section note to this verse). This reading is attractive in many ways; and it is undoubtedly true that the NT does represent Jesus as the man of faith, especially in the Gospel temptation narratives and the Letter to the Hebrews (see the first section note to v. 16). Nevertheless, it is doubtful that this single phrase in Paul could

---

[71] Note in 2:16 the way Paul sticks with *ek*: three times as he denies justification from the law and one has affirms justification from faith in Christ. But, as in Rom 3:30, he also pens *dia* as an alternative way of affirming the role of faith.

[72] Cosgrove confirms that Paul characteristically construes "justify" (*dikaioō*) with prepositions indicating locality, not evidential basis ("Justification," esp. 654-61). Cosgrove then rightly remarks: "The question never becomes whether one can be justified *on the basis of* the law or works but remains always whether one can be justified in the sphere of the law" (ibid., 662). The only possible exception to the rule is Phil 3:9: the righteousness "based on faith" (*epi tē pistei*). Yet it is noteworthy that faith is construed with the noun "righteousness," not the verb *dikaioō*. For righteousness to be based on faith is a way of saying that Paul's newfound conformity to Christ has faith in him as its foundation. Such a faith-based righteousness stands in stark opposition to Paul's former righteousness "according to the law" (*kata nomon*, 3:5), "in the law" (*en nomō*, 3:6) and "from the law" (*ek nomou*, 3:9). Even here, Paul has moved from the realm of law to that of (Christic-) faith.

[73] In the extant letters, Paul never construes the verb *dikaioō* with *dia* plus *nomou*. At least once (Gal 2:21), he conceives of a righteousness that might come *dia nomou*. This stands to reason given texts such as Lev 18:5; Deut 4:1, 10, 40; 5:29-33; 6:1-2, 18, 24; 7:12-13.

bear that much semantic freight.[74] Moreover, the particular phraseology *ek pisteōs Christou* (2:16c), as set in contrast to *ex ergōn nomou*, is an instance of Paul's "partisan" use of the preposition *ek*. "From faith in Jesus Christ" entails our participation in the faith-community, with Jesus as the object of our faith.

Without championing the traditional translation for the sake of tradition, Paul's language is best taken as our faith which is directed *specifically and exclusively* to Jesus Christ (cf. Mußner, *Galaterbrief*, 171). In grammatical categories, the genitive case could be called adjectival genitive, that is, that part of the phrase literally translated "of Jesus Christ" defines in some manner the character of the "faith" which is placed in him. Hultgren appropriately renders the whole phrase as "Christic faith" ("Formulation," 257, 259-60). That is to say, the faith which was once directed to the God of Israel now finds its object in Jesus the Christ.

It is surely significant that Paul nowhere provides a formal definition of faith, simply because he presupposes the meaning to be found in the OT and Jewish tradition. What is distinctive about his teaching on faith is its *christological focus*. With the advent of Jesus the Messiah, the only legitimate faith is that which finds its repose in him, the one who is "the end of the law" (Rom 10:4). At one time, faith assumed a nationalistic bias and was meaningless apart from the devotion of the believing Israelite to the Torah, the expression of God's covenant will for his people. But now that the "dividing wall of hostility" (Eph 2:15) has come down in Christ, faith latches specifically onto this one who has accepted all the nations without distinction (Rom 1:1-7; 15:7; Eph 2:17; Acts 2:39). This reading that Christ both defines faith and is the object of faith is confirmed by the second clause of v. 16: "Even we have believed in Christ Jesus" (the first two clauses of the verse could be looked upon as a kind of synonymous parallelism), and v. 20b: Paul lives by "faith in the Son of God" (*tou huiou tou theou* is clearly objective genitive).

As a working definition of faith, McKnight's is as good as any: faith is "the initial and continual response of trust in, and obedience to, Christ by a person for the purpose of acceptance with God" (*Galatians*, 121). The Greek word for "faith" in the NT (*pistis*) corresponds to the Hebrew word for "faith" in the OT (*'emunah*), which always signifies faith in and faithfulness to God.

---

[74] For defenses of the traditional reading of *pistis Iēsou Christou*, see Dunn, "*PISTIS CHRISTOU*;" Cranfield, "Question;" Silva, "Faith;" T. L. Carter, *Paul*, 98, n. 55.

As the godly Israelite was to trust in Yahweh for life and salvation, the Christian has directed his faith(fulness) to Christ. Faith as such is not redefined; in essence, its OT meaning is preserved. But Paul has in view a faith which is detached from Jewish "covenantal nomism," meaning that one "gets in" the people of God by faith alone; and once in, one "stays in" the covenant relationship by virtue of the same faith, which is no longer attached to the "works of Torah." Henceforth, according to v. 16d, "from works of the law no flesh shall be justified." Therefore, the Reformation stress on "faith alone" (*sola fide*) captures the heart of Paul's missionary theology.

The sum of this crucial and pivotal statement of v. 16a, with all its complications and disputed components, is that Jewish Christians ("even we") are fully convinced that with the onset of the eschaton, Christ, not the law, is the "gateway to salvation." Faith is to be specifically directed to him, the Lord (*kurios*) of the new covenant, and such trust has displaced commitment to the Torah as the emblem of faithfulness to Yahweh. The only conclusion could be that "a person is not justified by (from) works of the law *but only* (*ean mē*) through faith in Jesus Christ."

The remainder of v. 16 is a buttressing and further unpacking of the complex proposition of its first clause. Paul restates emphatically that "even we have believed in Christ Jesus in order to be justified by faith in Christ and not from works of the law" (my translation). In light of everything said above, his meaning is clear enough. Yet to substantiate his claim, Paul feels compelled to add: "Because from works of the law no flesh will be justified." These words (as those of Rom 3:20) are an echo of Ps 143:2: "And do not enter into judgment with Your servant, For in Your sight no man living is righteous" (NASB). As George informs us, Psalm 143 is a prayer to God for deliverance from the enemy. As he notes, the rescue envisioned there depends entirely on God's faithfulness and righteousness (which, as we recall, are virtually one and the same): "For your name's sake, O LORD, preserve my life; in your righteousness, bring me out of trouble." (v. 11). George appropriately concludes: "Thus rather than merely snatching a proof text to support his predetermined conclusion, Paul had in mind the motif of unilateral rescue and divine deliverance that pervades the entire Psalm" (*Galatians*, 191). In light of the above discussion of justification and righteousness, Paul's citation of this text is entirely understandable, because justification by definition entails Israel's deliverance from her enemies. Psalm 143 thus recalls the deliverance from exile motif associated with God's righteousness when he intervenes on the behalf of his oppressed people.[75]

The verse alluded to by Paul, comments Anderson, is rather unique in a lament: instead of hinting at his own righteousness and protesting innocence,[76] the Psalmist recognizes that all humans are sinful in the sight of God (*Psalms*, 2.926). In humility and with a sense of realism, David confesses that in his heart of hearts he is no better than his enemies. For this reason, he pleads with God not to "enter into judgment" with him. This means, according to Anderson: "Do not subject me to a strict examination in which my human insignificance and sinfulness would become painfully obvious; rather judge between your servant and his persecutors.... If the standard were certain absolute principles, then no one would be righteous before God" (ibid., 926-27). David shrinks from such an examination because "no one living is righteous before you."[77]

In the Psalms, righteousness is, on the one side, measured just in terms of one's commitment to the covenant bond as expressed by the observance of the law (Kraus, *Theology*, 154-62). In this regard, David can say: "The Lord has rewarded me according to my righteousness; According to the cleanness of my hands He has recompensed me" (Ps 18:20 [NASB]); and "I have done justice

---

[75] It is in just this regard that Paul echoes Psalm 143 (LXX Psalm 142) in Rom 3:3-7. Coming close to Käsemann's conception of righteousness as "salvation-creating power," Hays explains that *dikaiosunē* has to do with God's covenant fidelity as manifested in his saving activity (*Conversion*, 50-60). In the Prophets, this saving activity is consistently Israel's deliverance from exile.

[76] See in detail Kwakkel, *Righteousness*.

[77] Weiser adds: "As he faces God in prayer his sinfulness dawns on him; at the same time he comes to realize that God would be quite justified in 'entering into judgment with him'. He visualizes his sinfulness within the larger context of the universal sinfulness of mankind and so recognizes its ultimate seriousness as a failure before God that is inherent in man's nature and therefore cannot be overcome by his own efforts.... And when he bases his petition that God may not enter into judgment with him on the argument that no man living is righteous before him, then this statement is not meant as an excuse which by pointing to the others who are subject to the same condemnation seeks to reduce his own guilt and responsibility. On the contrary, he discerns in the fact that all men are in bondage to sin and are unable to free themselves from it by their own efforts (cf. vv. 8, 10) the utter seriousness and power of sin; he realizes that this is his own personal situation in which but one way is left open to him: to give himself wholly up to the grace of God. This is why he does not even make the slightest attempt, which we frequently encounter elsewhere, to protest his innocence and look for a legal claim that might justify his petition. As he utters his petition, which includes the confession of sin, he comes before God as a suppliant, not as one who makes demands on him" (*Psalms*, 819).

and righteousness; Do not leave me to my oppressors" (Ps 119:121 [NASB]). But the other side of the coin is highlighted by Ps 143:2: left to themselves and unaided by grace, the righteous could never stand in judgment before the God of the universe. "If *no one* could claim to be sinless or just before God, that included members of the covenant people" (Dunn, *Galatians*, 140).

The appropriateness of Psalm 143 to make this point goes without saying, especially as compared with Paul's employment of David's penitential confession, Ps 32:1-2, in Rom 4:7-8. By underscoring the factor of human sinfulness, he stresses that justification hinges on divine enabling; one must be possessed of a righteousness that comes from God, because, in the words of Isa 64:6, our righteousness is nothing but filthy rags (note especially the context here: God's sovereign power is exercised in a new exodus to deliver Israel from captivity). The law by itself cannot provide what it demands; not that the law is deficient, but it has become "weak through the flesh" (Rom 8:3), that is, human idolatry and inability. Thus it is that the Lord himself—the Lord Jesus Christ—must become the righteousness of his people (2 Cor 5:21 = Isa 61:10; Jer 23:6; 33:16).

Given that Paul in this letter constantly has his eye on his opponents, and given that he is more than prepared to call into question their profession of being "true brothers" and possessors of the Spirit, it is not unlikely that implicit in his evocation of Psalm 143 is a denial that the circumcisers have been aided by the grace necessary to stand before God in judgment. What is here more or less subliminal, comes to the surface later. According to 3:10-13, the rival teachers are nothing but apostates; in 4:21-31 they are the children of the flesh; and in chaps. 5-6 they engender only the "works of the flesh" and create an atmosphere of "biting and devouring." If anyone should not enter into judgment with God, it is certainly they.

It must be said that in terms of historical realism no right-minded Jew of Paul's day would have denied the verities of sin and the necessity of a righteousness which comes from God, as sufficiently illustrated by the penitential prayer tradition and the Qumran scrolls (e.g., 1QS 11:1-3, 5, 11-12, 13-15; 1QH 4:30-33; 7:30-31; 13:17).[78] So, to understand Paul's evocation of Psalm 143,

---

[78] On the penitential prayer tradition, see Werline, *Prayer*; Newman, *Praying*; Boda, *Praying* (as summarized in his "Praying"). A bibliography of penitential prayer can be accessed online at http://divinity.mcmaster.ca/boda/prayer/index.html.

we must take notice of his whole train of thought, as this comes to the fore in his adaptation, not exact quotation, of the Psalm (more momentarily). His concern is not for justification in the abstract but specifically a justification of "flesh" that would come from "works of the law." However cognizant the Jew would have been of sin and the need of divine righteousness, he would have been just as quick to insist that the law, God's preeminent means of grace, was given to rectify the multitude of evils caused by Adam's sin. But not so for Paul. According to his teaching elsewhere, the law works wrath (Rom 4:15) and increases the trespass (Rom 5:20), so that the Mosaic period as a whole could be summarized as an era of condemnation (2 Corinthians 3). The law was never intended to be the sphere of eschatological justification; it was, rather, a pointer to Christ (3:23-24).

Paul thus counters the notion that the law was given to reverse the curse. In pressing law observance on Gentile Christians, the Judaizers thought that it was the law itself, under God, which provided righteousness and life. God, to be sure, is the ultimate source of both; but the channel of blessing is the Torah (e.g., Sir 17:11; 45:5; Bar 3:9; 4:1; cf. 4 Ezra 7:127-31; 14:22, 29, 30, 34; *Pss. Sol.* 14:2-3; Ps.-Philo 23.10, all building on Lev 18:5; Deut 4:1, 10, 40; 5:29-33; 6:1-2, 18, 24; 7:12-13). There was no thought of a Christ who bestows his own righteousness on the people—and certainly not apart from the law. For them, Jesus the Messiah was but a servant of the Torah, not its goal and reason for existence.

It is in this theological and pastoral climate that Paul is bold enough to modify the actual wording of Ps 143:2. Where the Psalmist said: "No *living being* will be justified *before you*," Paul rephrases: "*From works of the law* no *flesh* will be justified." There are two obvious differences between the original wording of the Psalm and Paul's reworking of it. One is the insertion of "works of the law" and the deletion of "before you." "Works of the law" articulated the Israelite's responsibilities within the covenant and served to set the standard of his commitment to Yahweh. It was by remaining within the parameters of the Torah that one could be assured of a favorable verdict at the last judgment.

The other alteration is the substitution of "flesh" for "living being." "Flesh" (Hebrew *basar*; Greek *sarx*) is common enough in the OT and LXX as a designation of the human being, especially from the vantage point of the finitude, weakness and corruptibility of the human race (e.g., Gen 6:12; Isa 31:3; cf. Sir 31:1; 1QH 15:21). But "flesh" in Galatians mainly bears connotations of the old creation in which the Judaizers live and to which they wish to compel the Galatians to return (see on 3:1). Both components together, "works of the law" and "flesh," are an index to the Jewish/Judaistic position on justification. It is just "flesh" that will, according to such an ideology, be justified "from works of the law." It is to this end that Paul's rivals want to make "a good showing in the flesh" (6:11).

It is over against these taken-for-granted points of orthodoxy on the part of his Jewish rivals that Paul avows: "no flesh" can be justified/vindicated "from works of the law."

> In speaking of "all flesh" Paul has in view primarily and precisely those who think their acceptability to God and standing before God does depend on their physical descent from Abraham, their national identity as Jews. It is precisely this attitude, which puts too much stress on fleshly relationships and fleshly rites, precisely this attitude which Paul excoriates in his parting shot in 6.12-13—"they want to make a good showing in the flesh...they want to glory in your flesh" (Dunn, *Jesus, Paul*, 199).

Dunn further observes that with Psalm 143 more sharply defined in terms of physical and national identification, the addition of "from works of the law" is merely a further clarification of "flesh," because the works of the law in this letter, as epitomized by circumcision and the like, are primarily acts of the flesh (ibid., 199-200). Flesh, for this reason, was high on the Judaizers' agenda. T. L. Carter adds that Paul's substitution of "flesh" for "living being" anticipates the eschatological distinction between flesh and Spirit that he will draw at the end of the letter. Sinfulness is not defined in terms of Gentiles who disregard the Jewish law; instead, Paul's use of "flesh" defines sin in terms of universal participation in the present evil age (1:4). "Those whose existence is determined by flesh rather than by Spirit are [on] the wrong side of the eschatological boundary and so cannot be justified by works of Jewish Torah" (*Paul*, 101). All this being said, it has to be remembered that "flesh" preeminently in Galatians is *circumcision*. In his concluding summary of the letter, Paul identifies his opponents just as "those who want to make a good showing in the flesh" and to "glory in your flesh" (RSV) (6:12, 13). Unlike Paul (1 Cor 7:18-19), for them circumcision is still one of the commandments of God.

It is by means of his reworked version of Ps 143:2 that Paul both nails down his premise of v. 16a and paves the way for 3:10-

13, in which he will audaciously assert that the Jewish teachers and their committed followers are under the curse of the law just because of their (idolatrous) attachment to the flesh = law. In v. 16, Paul thus redraws the boundaries that serve to demarcate the people of God. Carter is right to the extent that he recognizes that, according to Paul, the Jewish people themselves [and the Jewish Christian missionaries] are on the outside. In thinking that the key to a right relation to God is a matter of observing the law, they are "simply trying the wrong door." This, as he continues, is a radical position indeed: "The law and its observance were central to the Jewish symbolic universe, fundamental to their identification of themselves as having been elected to be God's covenant people" (ibid., 101).

17-18 Verse 17 enters the picture with its continued stress on the experience of those Jewish Christians who have come to faith in Christ. Paul now poses a rhetorical question, intended, presumably, to ward off an objection from the Judaizers' side: "But if, while seeking to be justified in Christ, we ourselves have also been found sinners, is Christ then a minister of sin?" (NASB).[79] Commentators such as Witherington and Martyn are probably correct that "seeking" has reference to ultimate justification in the final judgment (see on 5:5). Paul has already embraced Christ as the justifier of those who place their trust in him and continues to exercise faith in this Christ as the one whose righteousness alone will suffice in the last day. In his own phrase, Paul renders to Jesus "the obedience of faith" (Rom 1:5; 16:26).

By the emphatic pronoun "we ourselves," Paul includes not only "all the brothers with me" (1:2) but Peter, James and Barnabas, who in their right mind would have been compelled to agree with Paul. In stark contrast, the opponents, who have been using Peter, James and Barnabas, think that a justification, present or ultimate, which bypasses the Torah turns a person into a "Gentile sinner" (v. 15), thus making Christ a "minister of sin" (*harmatias diakonos*), a probable reverse allusion to Isa 53:11 (see the section note to this verse).[80]

---

[79] Cummins suggests that the verb "found" (*huriskō*) has covenantal associations. To "be found" a "sinner," or apostate, stands in contrast with those where were "found" to be faithful during the Seleucid persecution of the Jews (*Paul*, 208-9).

[80] Hays suggests that *diakonos* is also an allusion to the table fellowship row of vv. 11-14; that is, Christ has been turned into a "table-waiter of sin" (*Galatians*, 241). Dunn proposes that the noun may be an ironic reference to Jesus' own table

This comes as no surprise given that the circumcision party, if anything, would have sought adamantly to preserve the separated status of the people of God, and particularly the integrity of the Messiah. Accordingly, "sin" means what it does in so many places in Scripture and Jewish literature—apostasy.[81] "Sinners," or "Gentile sinners," accordingly, are those inimical to God's covenant (see on 2:15). So, from the Judaizers' point of view, to seek to be justified in *Paul's Christ* meant the abandonment of God's age-old standard of righteousness, which for them was nothing short of forsaking the covenant and becoming as pagans. To them, the conclusion was inevitable: *Paul's Jesus* is nothing but a "promoter of apostasy"—a scandalous idea to those who believed that the Messiah was to be "sin"-less (*Pss. Sol.* 17:36; *T. Jud.* 24:1). Proof positive was Paul's willingness to allow Jews and uncircumcised Gentiles to partake of the same (non-kosher) food!

Paul's comeback is introduced by his customary "absolutely not" (*mē genoito*)! Witherington points out that Paul is particularly prone to use this expression when it is suggested that freedom from the law will encourage people to sin (*Grace*, 186). This emphatic disclaimer is followed in v. 18 by a response to the accusation brought against him: "If I rebuild what I destroyed, I prove that I am a lawbreaker."

The imagery of "tearing down" what was "put up" probably alludes to Israel as the people protected by a wall (Isa 5:2, 5; *Ep. Arist.* 139; Eph 2:14). In Jeremiah, the related idioms of "building" and "planting" mean to establish a new community. Note in particular the return from exile setting of this expression (Jer 31:27-30). Paul has been responsible for the building of the new covenant community (1 Cor 3:10-15), the eschatological temple of God (Eph 2:11-3:6), which of necessity entailed the "tearing down" of the old community. Because of this plan of God for the fullness of time (Eph 1:10; 1 Cor 10:11), his reply to the opponents entails a role reversal. It is precisely in rebuilding the things that he "tore down" or "dismantled" (*kataluō*), that is, a Torah observant lifestyle characteristic of the old Israel, that he would become a "transgressor," that is, a "violator of the law" or effectively "apostate" (*parabatēs*), not the other way around.

Cummins (*Paul*, 214-15) maintains that although the noun *parabatēs* does not appear in the LXX, it assumes, nonetheless,

---

fellowship with "sinners" and his self-description as a *diakonos* (Mark 10:45) (*Galatians*, 141).

[81] As documented throughout Garlington, *Obedience*; id., *Faith*, 89-94.

overtones of Torah violation by virtue of its connection with the cognate verb *parabainō*, which is used of the Maccabean martyrs, who preferred death rather than "transgress" the covenant, not least the food laws (2 Macc 7:2; 4 Macc 9:1; 13:15; 16:24).[82] The irony, therefore, is that "transgression" has now been redefined: what once was covenant loyalty is now seen to be defection from Christ.[83] Were Paul to insist on the segregated status of the ancient people as insured by the law (e.g., Num 23:9; *Ep. Arist.* 139-42; *Jub.* 22:16), *then* he would transgress with respect to God's eschatological purpose in Christ, *then* he would be found unfaithful to the one who was destined to be the end of the law (Rom 10:4; Gal 3:23-26) (see further on 3:10-13).[84] Bluntly put, to rebuild the law is to betray Christ (Smiles, *Gospel*, 159-62). "Transgressor" thus assumes a new meaning in light of the Christ-event. Martyn writes: "The result of this sentence is a radical redefinition of transgression, and especially a radically altered view of the relation between transgression and Law observance" (*Galatians*, 256). The term used to mean one who forsook the law; but now it means to embrace the law as being a necessary complement to the "in Christ" experience.

19-21 Verse 19 comes into play as additional confirmation of the previous verse. If Paul has demolished the law, it is because in his experience he had died to it; indeed, it was the law itself that brought about his demise.[85] The law, as it were, became the in-

---

[82] Paul himself uses *parabatēs* in Rom 2:25-27 to denote violation of the law. Likewise, he employs the cognate noun *parabasis*, "transgression," with reference to the breaking of the law in Rom 3:23; 4:15; Gal 3:19. Of relevance to our present verse is the appearance of *parabasis* in Rom 5:14 as a designation of Adam's apostasy/idolatry.

[83] Lambrecht ("Paul's Reasoning," 64) points to Rom 2:23, 25, 27; 4:15; Gal 3:19, where *parabainō* and *parabatēs* mean "transgressing the law." This again underscores the irony of the present usage: Paul has in mind a transgression of God's new initiative in Christ (ibid., 66). See also Hays, *Galatians*, 242; Segal, *Paul*, 202-3.

[84] According to Cummins, from Paul's vantage point, Peter's actions in Antioch constituted an even more profound problem: "Peter is in danger of returning to an Israel whose constant Torah transgression attests to the fact that Israel serves, rather than solves, the worldwide problem of Adamic sin, which has in fact now been dealt with in Messiah Jesus" (*Paul*, 215. See further ibid., 219-225; cf. Garlington, *Faith*, 82-84.). In this light, the Messiah came in order to deliver Israel-in-Adam (Cummins, *Paul*, 225-28).

[85] The various modern interpretations are summarized by Cummins, *Paul*, 217-18. The view taken here most closely corresponds to his (ii): The law had a provi-

strument of its own cessation in his experience: "I *through* the law died to the law." To "die" in this metaphorical sense means to leave one realm and take up residence in another (Rom 6:6, 10-11; 7:4). The parallel is Rom 7:7-13. The logic of that passage is that even though the law per se is not sin, it was by the law's instrumentality that Paul came to recognize his own idolatry, that is, his violation of the tenth commandment, which, in his own words, is tantamount to idolatry (Col 3:5).[86]

Because of the deathblow administered by the law, Paul became convinced that the Torah could not insure life, as he formerly thought, simply because he was not the faithful person he imagined himself to be. The words of Ps 143:2 must have come crashing in upon him: "Do not enter into judgment with your servant, for in your sight no man living is righteous." At this point in time, Paul became profoundly aware that his righteousness must come from none other than the Son of God, who loved him and gave himself for him.

Carter clearly sees that the law's sentence upon Paul as a transgressor has eschatological significance:

> In thus dying through the law, he also dies to the law in order to live for God. This statement is developed in the claim that he has been crucified with Christ: as Christ died under the law, so Paul has been crucified with Christ, so that he no longer lives, but Christ lives in him. *It is by dying through the law as a transgressor of the law that Paul participates in the eschatological life of Christ.*... As he has done in verses 15-16, Paul thus places himself firmly outside the ethnic boundary of the law, but inside the eschatological boundary between the righteous and the wicked instigated by the coming of Christ (1:4). Indeed, by saying that he died through the law so that he might live to God, Paul suggests that it is only by being placed outside the law as a transgressor that it is possible to share in the life of Christ. Within the social context of Galatians, this claim has an important double function. Firstly, Paul thereby identifies himself with his Galatian converts and signals that those who are outside the law nevertheless participate

---

sional role in preparing for and pointing towards the advent of Christ.

[86] Hays proposes that since the law played an active role in the death of Jesus, Paul's death to the law came about through his being crucified with Christ (*Galatians*, 243). This is plausible enough on its own terms, but Hays is too quick to dismiss Romans 7 from consideration.

in the eschatological life of the age to come—a point he reinforces by asking on what basis they received the eschatological Spirit in 3:6. Secondly, by saying that he died to the law to live to God, Paul implies that those who are not outside the law do not share in the eschatological life, and this is a claim that he develops in 3:7-14 (*Paul*, 109-10, italics mine).

We see, then, in Paul the example of one who was placed under the discipline of the law, who was "shut up to sin" (Gal 3:22), in order that he might find Christ. He applies the macrocosm of this salvation-historical principle to the microcosm of his own experience. More specifically, his is the prophetic language of death and resurrection, as applied to Israel's exile and restoration (see on 1:1). The curses of Deuteronomy were brought home to him when the law forced him to confront his idolatry; but then in finding Christ, the blessings of resurrection life—as it were, return from exile—were secured by the Lord who bore the curses of the covenant in his own person and then rose to procure the new creation. As Ciampa comments (*Scripture*, 209):

> It is suggested here that the best background for this idea [i.e., Paul's death to the law] is found in two ideas: the understanding, based above all on Deuteronomic theology, that Israel's death (exile) occurred through the execution of the curses of the Mosaic covenant and law upon the sinful people of God; and the identification of Christ with his people (or, with the believer). In the final part of this verse [Gal 2:19], and all of the following, Paul makes it clear that his participation in this exile-restoration, death-and (resurrection-) life schema is by means of identification with Christ in his crucifixion and resurrection.

And if Paul died "to the law," he is no longer "of the law" (*ek nomou*), "of works of the law" (*ex ergōn nomou*) or "in the law" (*en nomō*), but rather "in Christ" (*en Christō*) and "of faith in Jesus Christ" (*ek pisteōs Iēsou Christou*). It was only when he left the arena of the law that he came alive to God: "Through the Law I died to the Law, *so that I might live to God*" (NASB). This implies that while he thought he was alive by virtue of his possession of the Torah, he was actually dead with regard to God—a powerful irony indeed. Again the parallel is Rom 7:7-13.

Hays points to 4 Macc 16:24-25:

> By these words the mother of the seven encouraged and persuaded each of her sons to die *rather than violate God's commandment*. They knew also that those who die for the sake of God *live to God*, as do Abraham and Isaac and Jacob and all the patriarchs.

Then comments Hays:

> Unlike the Maccabean martyrs, Paul has died not *for* the Law but *to* it, and he claims thereby to have found life before God. This new life includes, of course, the fellowship of Jews and Gentiles together in a single worshiping congregation gathered in the name of Jesus. Those who are calling for a retreat from this radical new form of community are simply, in Paul's view, living on the wrong side of the cross, in the old age (*Galatians*, 243).

In addition to this obvious irony, Gal 2:19 can be read as Paul's response to the Jewish conviction that fidelity to the law is automatically to possess life. Perhaps adapting Ben Sira's phrase "the law of life" (Sir 17:11; 45:5), the author of Baruch commends to his readers "the commandments of life" (Bar 3:9; 4:1; cf. 4 Ezra 14:30; *Pss. Sol.* 14:2). They are called "the laws of life" because, when they are followed, they insure life. These commandments are no less than the very embodiment of Israel's wisdom: "All who hold her fast will live, and those who forsake her will die" (4:1). Paul may have Bar 3:9; 4:1 in mind when in Rom 7:10 he writes of "the commandment which was unto life." These Jewish texts have as their point of departure the OT pronouncements: "This do and live" (Deut 4:1, 10, 40; 5:29-33; 6:1-2, 18, 24; 7:12-13), and "You shall therefore keep my statutes and my ordinances, by doing which a man shall live" (Lev 18:5). But now a complete reversal of perspectives has unfolded: Paul has died to the law that he might live to God. He implies that the Judaizers are still as he used to be: they are alive to the law but dead to God!

> The astonishment caused by the first part of the sentence proves to be only a prelude to the shocking amazement occasioned by the last clause. Paul says that the purpose of his being separated by death from the realm of the Law is that he might exist as one who is alive in the realm of God. One can scarcely think of a statement more thoroughly foreign to the theology of

the Teachers (and to Jewish and Jewish-Christian theology in general). It is not an exercise in mere fantasy to imagine that, as Paul's messenger finished reading v 18, the Teachers jumped to their feet, loudly charging Paul with blasphemy (Martyn, *Galatians*, 257)!

Paul's death to the law is patterned after none other than Jesus' own death to "sin," that is, the old creation and Adamic existence, and present life which he lives "to God" (Rom 6:10). (Throughout Romans 5-8, "law" and "sin" serve as synonyms of the old order of things.) Note the emphatic "I" (*egō*) at the beginning of v. 19, corresponding to the "we" and "even we" of the previous verses. Paul is the voice of all those Jewish Christians who have died to the law. In his case, the law has revealed sin and increased the trespass: *he is an Israelite in whom the law has achieved its overall redemptive purpose*. Therefore, those Galatians who are being seduced by the Judaizers must remember that all believers have been crucified with Christ (Rom 6:5-6). In this regard, comments Gorman, "The believer's faith conforms to Christ's faith. Specifically, the believer's faith is cruciform because Christ's faith(fulness) was expressed on the cross" (*Cruciformity*, 141). And in conforming to Christ, they must also *imitate the apostle*, recalling that they too once died to the law through the body of Christ (Rom 7:4). After all, the theme of 1:11-2:21 is *Paul's autobiography as paradigm*.

Verse 20 adds that Paul's death to the law corresponds to his crucifixion "with Christ."[87] The verb "to be crucified with" (*susstauroō*) underlines the factor of participation. He is now identified with the outcast one of Israel ("sinner"), the reprobate of Deut 21:23, who endured "the death of the cross" (Phil 2:8).[88] Once more there is a powerful irony: Paul's identification with the one crucified "outside the camp" (Heb 13:13) brought his actual apostasy from God to an end. Christ, then, far from being an agent of sin is precisely the opposite. The verb is in the Greek perfect tense, denoting an action which began in the past and still continues in its effects. When he first believed, Paul was nailed to Christ's cross. Yet that was only the beginning of the story. His entire walk in the flesh is now one of cruciform existence, in which he is treated as one deserving death "outside the camp." It is in his

---

[87] In the English translations, the words, "I have been crucified with Christ," are found in v. 20, while in editions of the Greek NT they form the final clause of v. 19.

[88] On Paul's identification with Christ's crucifixion, see Martyn's extended note (*Galatians*, 277-80).

person that the sufferings of Christ will be filled to the full (Acts 9:16; Phil 3:10; Col 1:24).

And yet the crucifixion of Christ also entails his resurrection. If Paul has been crucified with Christ, then he has also been raised with him: "I no longer live, but Christ lives in me." "That old I," says Martyn, "has not been merely renewed. Having been crucified with Christ, it has been replaced by the risen Christ himself" (*Galatians*, 258). That death and resurrection are inextricably intertwined is forcefully illustrated by Phil 3:10-11: "I want to know Christ and the power of his resurrection and the fellowship of sharing in his sufferings, becoming like him in his death, and so, somehow, to attain to the resurrection from the dead." It is just this pattern of crucifixion-resurrection that sets the stage for life in the Spirit (see on 5:22-23).

The repeated emphatic "I" in v. 20 bears, in the parlance of psychology, the connotations of "ego" (a transliteration of the Greek word for "I"). Paul's former "I" had found its identity in Judaism as one of its leading lights. His very reason for existence was to maintain the God-instituted boundaries between his people and the Gentiles. But now it is no longer Paul's ego which controls the direction of his life and his allegiances but rather Christ who has become his actual life. Christ is henceforth the captain of Paul's soul and the master of his fate. Paul lives because Christ is in him by the Spirit (cf. Rom 8:10; 2 Cor 13:5; Eph 3:7; Col 1:27). The Spirit for him has become the Spirit of Christ, with the result that his sufferings are intended to be the complement of those of his Lord. The one who died as an outlaw demolished the distinctions between peoples and taught the apostle what life truly is. Like Peter (Acts 10:9-16), Paul had to learn to call no person common or unclean. "It was this Christ who was now the focus of Paul's life—the Jewish Messiah who was also for the out-law, the non-Jew" (Dunn, *Galatians*, 145).

Invoking his principal doctrine of union with Christ (see on 1:22), Paul can say that his whole existence "in the flesh" is now by "faith in the Son of God." Faith is not simply the apostle's initial response to the Christ of the cross but a continual trusting in and clinging to him (the Hebrew root for "faith," *'aman*, means to "lean on" the God of Israel). For this reason, even in Paul's hour of sharpest pain, the exalted Jesus assures him that his grace is sufficient for him (2 Cor 12:9). "Flesh," in this setting, bears two connotations: (1) Paul as a vulnerable human being subject to the vicissitudes of this age; (2) Paul as a descendant of Abraham, a "Hebrew born of Hebrews" (Phil 3:5).

The second is really more to the point. Paul was born a Jew, and a Jew he remained; but his Jewishness has now found its authentic moorings in him who is the climax of Israel's story. No longer is his faith exercised in zeal for the law but for the Christ who revealed himself on the Damascus Road and commissioned the apostle to preach him among the nations. Witherington doubts that "flesh" means Jewishness because Paul is presenting himself as a paradigm for all Christians, including Gentiles (*Grace*, 191, n. 69). But more precisely, he is addressing Gentiles who are under pressure to become Jewish; and his relief of the pressure is an affirmation that he and other Jewish Christians have found authentic existence in Christ apart from the law. If the law is not necessary for them, but only faith in the Son of God, then it is not vital for Gentiles either.

It is none other than the "Son of God," with all the connotations of kingship and exaltation borne by the phrase, who "loved" Paul and "gave himself" for him on the cross. The idea was unthinkable to Paul's contemporaries, but for him the cross was not an afterthought or a mistake, an embarrassment to be explained away or ignored; rather, the cross is the locus of the love of Christ. This affirmation of Christ's self-deliverance to the cross corresponds to the identical statement of 1:4. These words speak of the intention of Christ to go to the cross as integral to the eternal purpose of God. It is for this reason that Paul boasts in the cross, by which he has been crucified to the world (that is, the old creation) and the world to him (6:14).

Hubbard points out that Paul often speaks of the sacrificial death of Christ, but nowhere else is this described as "for me." Paul is usually more inclusive, *à la* Gal 1:3-4; 1 Cor 15:3; 1 Thess 5:10 (*Creation*, 128). He furthermore calls attention to the fact that Paul's "dying" formulas are often linked with love (Rom 5:8; 8:32, 35; 2 Cor 5:14). In the present setting, these data are all the more striking.

> Paul perceived God's action in Christ not only as the death of the messiah for Israel, and as the reconciliation of the world, but also as an action with a direct bearing on Saul of Tarsus. He understood it as a sacrifice of love "for me" which demanded an appropriate response. It was because Paul saw Christ's death not only in its abstract corporate significance, but also in its concrete personal relevance that he was willing, following the example of his Lord, to "spend and be spent" on behalf of his churches (cf. 2 Cor. 8.9 with 12.15). It was

> Christ's death "for us all" which focused Paul's attention on the world, but it was Christ's death "for me" that set his feet on the road: "for the love of Christ compels us" (ibid.).

Yet, by way of balance, Christ's death for Paul was not limited to Paul, because it is none other than the cross that most profoundly impacts the controversy over table fellowship.

> Paul proclaims that God has chosen to set things right in the world through the cross and through bringing into being a new people in which the old barrier between Jew and Gentile is broken down and made irrelevant. The cross cuts away all the systems of distinction by which we set ourselves apart from others, including the distinction between Jew and Gentile. Thus, when Peter refuses to eat with Gentiles, he is living as though the cross were of no effect. Those who have been crucified with Christ will no longer separate themselves from one another but will gather around one table. (Hays, *Galatians*, 245)

Verse 21 is intended to head off another objection from the Judaizing camp, namely, that Paul's gospel nullifies the grace of God: "I do not set aside the grace of God, for if righteousness could be gained through the law, Christ died for nothing!" As Burton proposes, "grace" was such a favorite term for Paul that the opponents perhaps took it up in order to charge that he was really making of no account of the grace of God to Israel (*Galatians*, 149). "Nullify" (NIV, NASB: "set aside") (*atheteō*) is a juridical verb applied to the rendering inoperative or making void of a covenant or agreement (1 Macc 11:36; 2 Macc 13:25; Gal 3:5). The term is just what one would expect, because "grace" is God's covenant love for Israel. Thus, in nullifying the grace of God, as the charge goes, Paul is accused of making shipwreck the covenant relationship itself. The charge is at least intelligible, given that for the opponents the Torah *is* "God's gracious gift par excellence."[89]

---

[89] Martyn, *Galatians*, 59-60. Likewise, Longenecker, *Galatians*, 94. Shauf ("Galatians 2.20," 97-98) asserts that "grace" is never used by Paul as tantamount to Torah, and that the present verse reflects not a charge brought against Paul but his accusation of the opponents: it is they who nullify God's grace by their insistence on the law. He makes a certain point, because, in point of fact, this is the case as regards the circumcisers, inasmuch as they make the locus of God's grace the Torah rather than Christ. But given that "grace" is Yahweh's covenant devotion

However, this is precisely what Paul does not do, because "if righteousness is through the law, then Christ died for no purpose." His vocabulary shifts from "grace" to "righteousness," because "righteousness" is the outcome of "grace." If God's grace is his self-giving to his people in his election and sustenance of them, then Israel's expected response was righteousness, her fidelity to the terms of the covenant relationship established at Sinai. Righteousness thus speaks of Israel's obligations and privileges under the law. This being so, Paul's logic is clear enough: if the old state of affairs simply continues into this era, then the death of Christ is to "no purpose" (*dōrean*), just because the Sinai covenant has made every provision for salvation and life, and God's people might as well continue under that covenant. As ever, Paul argues from history and eschatology.

Martyn appropriately juxtaposes the respective outlooks of the opponents and Paul:

Opponents	**Paul**
God makes things right through the Law	God makes things right through Christ's death

He then adds:

> If the first were true, then the second would not be true, and the conclusion would be that Christ's death happened as an inconsequential event, rather than as God's effective enactment of rectification. Here Paul provides the antinomy that will prove to be fundamental to the entire letter: God's making things right by Christ's cross rather than by the Law (*Galatians*, 260).

"So," Dunn contributes, "any retreat back into a Judaism, or Jewish Christianity, which insisted that Jew and Gentile should eat separately was to render invalid the whole gospel—as indeed also Israel's own election (Rom. xi.5-6)" (*Galatians*, 148)! Paul's underlying assumption, obviously not shared by the Judaizers, is that Christ's death was designed specifically to usher in the new age by setting aside the Torah in its existing form. By contrast, for the rival missionaries, *Christ actually did die for no reason*. At best,

---

to Israel, it still makes sense that the law-teachers themselves would identify the Mosaic legislation with "God's gracious gift par excellence."

the cross was a tragic mistake, either to be ignored or explained away, and certainly not intended to provide the occasion for boasting (6:14).

Paul's own logic is developed at length in Eph 2:11-22 (and even more elaborately by the Letter to the Hebrews). If we ask, How could Paul reason in such a presuppositional manner? The answer is twofold. (1) He is still appealing to the experience of Jewish Christians, who know that justification comes by way of Christ alone. The implication is that the Judaizers are not Jewish *Christians*; they are still "false brothers" (2:4). In 3:1-6, Paul will likewise appeal to the experience of the Galatians, who received the Spirit not by "works of the law" but by "the hearing of faith." (2) Paul knew from his conversations with Peter and James (1:18-19) that Jesus had in fact begun to break down the boundaries between Israel and the nations by his disregard of the purity traditions (Mark 1:40-44; 7:1-8), the dietary laws (Mark 7:14-23) and sabbath observance (John 5:2-18), not to mention his establishment of table fellowship with those considered to be beyond the pale of God's grace. Most strikingly, it is he who presaged the destruction of the temple and the whole sacrificial cultus (Matthew 24 and pars.).

Section Notes

15-21 Cummins ably analyzes the argument of 2:15-21 in light of the Maccabean tradition (*Paul*, 229-30). Paul's line of argumentation, says Cummins, gives theological breadth and depth to what was at stake in his stance against Peter's withdrawal from table fellowship in Antioch. He systematically subverts the position of those Jewish Christians who, in the tradition of the Maccabees, equated life among the people of God with a Torah-focused Judaism. Remonstrating against such a view, Paul first takes issue with that very Jewish polemic so characteristic of the Maccabean period; that is, there is no longer a Jew-Gentile (sinner) divide because vindication as the (afflicted) covenant people of God is not a function of adherence to "works of the law" but of corporate conformity to the faithful Messiah Jesus. In advocating this radical claim, Paul clearly comes under considerable opposition. Indeed, in the view of his adversaries, it means that he and all other such Jewish Christians are "sinners" found to be outside the people of God. Indeed, a further and even more extreme inference is that Paul's Messiah is a servant of sin.

Paul recoils at the very idea, and presses his counterclaim. Indeed, now the profound and paradoxical aspect to his role as one who stands in ironic relation to the Maccabean tradition emerges all the more clearly. He will not, as the Maccabees did, and Peter and others now risk doing, rebuild Judaism—a Judaism which was dismantled when he encountered, believed in, and became conformed to Christ. Paul's rationale is twofold.

First, Israel's ultimate enemy is not found in the form of Gentile sinners or even Jewish apostates but deeply within itself. That is to say, Israel, no less than the Gentiles, is in Adam. Hence, it is not Paul but rather his Jewish Christian opponents who could be designated servants of "sin" or Adamic apostasy.

Second, this scenario is all the more incredible since it is precisely in and through Christ that they have been rescued from that very condition towards which they are in danger of returning. Here the paradox is at its most profound. It is the Jesus whom Israel rejected due to sin's abuse of Torah within the nation who, in taking Israel's sin upon himself, proved to be Israel's representative, martyred and now exalted Messiah. He is the eschatological redeemer who rescued Israel from an affliction which lay within, and even now he enables Israel to live a risen and exalted life as the people of God. A gracious God has ultimately manifested his love and covenant faithfulness in the self-sacrifice of his Son; through him, and those in him (Jew and Gentile), he has reconciled Israel and thence the whole world.

16 Hays' ground-breaking study of the narrative substructure of Galatians is well known to students of this letter. See particularly his *Faith* (appendices 1 and 2 of which reprint the debate between Hays and Dunn) and throughout *Galatians*. Hays maintains that underlying the epistolary format of Galatians is a Jesus-narrative, specifically that of Jesus' covenant faithfulness, as embodied in Paul's unique phrase "faith of Jesus Christ" (*pistis Iēsou Christou*). Hays sets "rectification through the faithfulness of Jesus Christ" over against the individualism of historic Protestantism, which, for him, celebrates the subjective faith-experience of individuals as though religious experience were an end in itself. In pointed contrast, Hays insists that a careful reading of Galatians shows that the letter is "a powerful attack on such self-referential accounts of salvation." "From start to finish," he avers, "Paul proclaims that *God* has acted to set the world right and to rescue us from slavery to human religious programs" (*Galatians*, 195, italics his). Among others who have taken up the cause are: Hooker, "*PISTIS CHRISTOU*;" B. W. Longenecker, "Defining," 79-89; id., *Triumph*, 95-107; Cummins, *Paul*, 198-206; Foster, "Contribution;" Choi, "*PISTIS*;" Campbell, "Story," 120-23. Essential bibliographies are provided by Bruce (*Galatians*, 138-39) and Longenecker (*Galatians*, 87). More comprehensive listings are provided by Wallis, *Faith*; Rapa, *Meaning*, 178, n. 57. I would call attention to the debates (including Hays' contribution) contained in Johnson/Hay (eds.), *Pauline Theology IV*, 33-92.

My objection is hardly to the idea of Christ's covenant faithfulness. Indeed, the notion of Jesus as the man of faith(fulness) is very much present in Paul and other portions of the NT. Rather, the problem is the imposition of a great deal of semantic freight onto the single phrase *pistis*

Iēsou Christou, especially when parallel usages of this type of genitive case can be cited in favor of a more traditional reading (see Dunn's linguistic analysis in *"PISTIS CHRISTOU"*).[90] Hays' exegesis is especially strained when it comes to his messianic reading of Hab 2:4. It is true that the LXX places a messianic construction on Habakkuk's "the righteous one" (*ho dikaios*), an interpretation that plays readily into the hands of the author of Hebrews (Heb 10:37-38). However, in both Gal 3:11 and Rom 1:17, Paul consciously avoids the LXX of Hab 2:4, especially its first clause. In context, at least as far as the MT is concerned, the "righteous one" continues to place his faith in Yahweh, in hopes of deliverance from exile. In Paul, this becomes the believer in Jesus who eschatologically experiences the new exodus of redemption.

All that said, there is still an undeniable Jesus-narrative to be found in this letter. Yet, as Gorman has demonstrated so aptly (*Apostle*, 192-222; *Cruciformity*, passim), the story in question is mainly that of *the cross*. To be sure, for Gorman the story of the cross is an aspect of Jesus' covenant faithfulness; and, not surprisingly, Gorman is entirely sympathetic with Hays' reading of *pistis Iēsou Christou*. But the point here is to say that it is the cross that ought particularly to be played up, given the internal evidence of Galatians itself. For Paul, the story of the Messiah *is* the story of the cross, not, as the other missionaries would have it, a "blasphemous contradiction of terms" (Bruce). For them, Messiah's story is one of triumphalism and unqualified glory, not the self-giving of Jesus on the cross of shame and degradation.

16 Cummins helpfully places the focus on righteousness as God's faithfulness to the covenant with Israel in its historical setting (*Paul*, 195). In Second Temple Judaism, he notes, the ever-present concern of God's faithfulness to his covenant promises to Israel is a dominant motif. This is particularly true in reference to times of crisis such as the tensions attending the return from the Babylonian exile, the Maccabean revolt and the Roman destruction of Jerusalem. A recurrent theme is that despite all appearances God will not forsake Israel but, after disciplining and delaying to allow time for repentance, he will act to inaugurate a glorious new Israel-centered kingdom. In the interim, his people must themselves be righteous; that is, even in the midst of suffering, they must remain faithful members of the covenant community and retain their righteousness by remaining obedient to the law and all that comprises the Jewish way of life, assured that their divine vindication will ensue.

Cummins continues that just such an understanding was evident notably in the instances of Maccabean martyrdom. It was God's sovereign rule and covenantal faithfulness which came under attack when "truth was cast down to the ground" during the Maccabean crisis (Dan 8:12). God's truth could only be restored when Israel reciprocated his covenant

---

[90] The same applies to Wright's singular view that *pistis* is Christ's faithfulness to the divine plan for Israel.

love and faithfulness, even if this entailed suffering and martyrdom. In this way, the nation would atone for sin, experience divine deliverance and enjoy lasting vindication—the most potent symbol of this ultimate end being the Danielic vision of the exalted "one like a son of man" (Dan 7:13). Indeed, the eschatological realization of God's righteousness/truth also figured prominently in those texts and traditions indebted to Daniel's human-like figure. Thus, God would rescue his afflicted people and initiate a kingdom characterized by peace and truth (4Q246); and, notwithstanding Israel's devastation by those devoid of truth/righteousness, God's covenant faithfulness would eventually be realized through Israel's eschatological redeemer (4 Ezra 6:55-9; 11-13). Likewise, other texts in the Maccabean tradition also shared this vision, notably 4 Maccabees with its martyr figures who lived in accordance "with the truth," and thus gained the "immortal victory" whereby they "lived to God" (4 Macc 6:16-18; 7:3, 19; 16:25).

This milieu of righteousness has a direct bearing on the Galatian crisis and the scenario that was unfolding in Antioch. The Maccabean martyrs' steadfast adherence to food laws, circumcision, sabbath observance, and suchlike, was regarded as both a witness to and assurance of their eventual vindication as God's true people. In Galatia, the opponents were seeking to persuade Paul's converts to adopt circumcision and Jewish calendric practices, indeed, all "works of the law" which represented a move towards a Jewish pattern of life. For Paul, however, the ultimate vindication of God's righteous people found its rootage in their faith(fulness) directed toward Jesus of Nazareth.

16 Without negating the definition of "works of the law" as proposed above, Cummins provides a helpful balance in one's overall assessment of the function of the phrase in Paul (*Paul*, 197-98). Paul's critique of the "works of the law," he rightly observes, was not that the Torah was bad, nor that the desire to obey it was misguided, nor even that a lifestyle of Torah obedience was necessarily without any value. On the other hand, as some proponents of the new perspective have suggested, neither was it simply a matter that such practices raised a barrier between Jews and Gentiles by the maintenance of an Israel-focused "nationalist righteousness."

Although these last two considerations do indeed represent part of Paul's concern, they were but symptomatic of, and only served to perpetuate, a much more deep-seated problem. For Paul, the (re)adoption of the "works of the law," and of a life "in Judaism," involved putting oneself "under the law." From its usage in Galatians and Romans, this phrase is shorthand for more than simply Israel's Torah-based way of life. Rather, by virtue of its conceptual alignment with cognate expressions such as "under a curse" (Gal 3:10), "under the elemental spirits of the universe" (Gal 4:3), and "under sin" (Rom 3:9; 7:14), and its direct contrast with "under grace" (Rom 6:14, 15), it takes on much darker overtones. Paul makes no bones about it: the law is an enslaving power (see Das, *Paul and the Jews*, 151-55).

From Paul's God-in-Christ standpoint, life "under [the curse of] the law" meant that Israel was both bound by but unable to obey the Torah and thus incurred its condemnation rather than its blessing, and this was attributable to the fact that Israel (no less than the Gentiles) was given over to the old age/sphere of Adamic sin. Thus, to pursue the "works of the law" was to exacerbate this most fundamental problem—and indeed to undermine its only solution: justification through faith in Jesus Christ.

Such an appraisal of the "dark side" of "works of the law" is in accord with the line of exposition pursued in this commentary. Paul relegates, no less, the law to the period of the old creation with its manifold problems of sin, apostasy and Adamic existence resulting in chaos (it is to be noted that Dunn's discussion of the law takes place just under the rubric of "Humankind under Indictment," *Theology of Paul*, 79-161). My only qualification is that Israel's inability to keep the law is to be defined in terms of idolatry, not a failure to keep the law perfectly. Idolatry/apostasy was always the nation's shortfall; and now, with the advent of the gospel of Christ, its idolatry, so ironically, has taken the form of its very allegiance to the Torah to the rejection of Christ (see on 3:10-13; 4:8-10).

Contrary to Sanders (and Hays), Paul does move from plight to solution (Thielman, *Plight*; id., *Paul*, 160-88), and Cummins is precisely right that to pursue the "works of the law" is to exacerbate the fundamental problem of the "curse of the law" and to undermine its only solution: justification through faith in Jesus Christ. Unwarranted devotion to the works of the law obscures the purpose (teleology) of the law: to pave the way for Christ (Gal 3:23-26; Rom 10:4).

17 T. L. Carter (*Paul*, 105) quite plausibly suggests that the language of v. 17 evokes Isa 53:11, according to which the righteous Servant of Yahweh makes many righteous (Hebrew *yatsdiq tsadiq*). "Galatians 2:17 is thus linked to Isaiah 53:11 by the twin concepts of Christ as the servant who justifies. In Isaiah 53:11, the righteous servant justifies many and puts them right with God. In Galatians 2:17, because those who seek justification in Christ are found to be sinners, in effect, Paul's opponents claim that Paul reverses the role ascribed to Christ in Isaiah 53:11. Their argument is that, if Christ as the servant makes people sinners instead of putting them right with God, Christ must be the servant of sin, rather than the righteous servant of the Lord. It is no wonder that Paul denies the charge with an emphatic *mē genoito*"—"let it never be!"

GALATIANS CHAPTER THREE

THE ARGUMENT FROM SCRIPTURE AND SALVATION HISTORY (3:1-4:31)

The first two chapters of the letter have been chiefly a narrative, setting forth the most relevant events of the course of Paul's life, both as a "zealot" for the law and afterward as an apostle of Christ. In Paul's "autobiography as paradigm," everything hinged on the proposition that his conversion to Christ entailed a break with the law and a new vision of God's purposes for the nations. From this point onward, every former loyalty and allegiance had to be set aside for the sake of knowing Christ and the power of his resurrection (Phil 3:4-11). If Paul is still zealous in any sense, his zeal has now been rechanneled in the direction of love and service of those who had been the objects of his persecuting rage. As he enters now into the main theological phase of his epistle, he does so with a keen awareness of the crisis in Galatia. The implication of the preceding section is that Paul saw the incident at Antioch and the situation in Galatia as crucial test cases of the validity of his gospel to the Gentiles. "Consequently," remarks Dunn, "The stand Paul took there [Antioch], on the basis of the common ground of faith in Jesus Christ and the common gospel of his self-giving on the cross, was equally applicable to the Galatian believers" (*Galatians*, 150-51).

Chapters 3-4 are frequently reckoned as the *probatio* section of the letter, that is, the "proof" or arguments in support. However, the classification tends to be artificial, because from the outset Paul has been engaging in various arguments. In 2:15-21, he appealed, as part of his proof, to the experience of Jewish believers. Now he turns to the whole church and appeals to their experience of the Spirit. In a nutshell, they received the Spirit not in the old era of the "flesh" (= "works of the law"), but in the new, eschatological age by "the hearing of faith." It is important to insist, however that Paul grounds his argument not in subjective impressions but in the OT Prophets, especially Isaiah, who identify the true seed as those upon whom the Spirit will rest (for references, see on 2:1).

This watershed experience should have been enough to convince anyone of the character of Paul's gospel. But because of the "spell" cast over them by the Judaizers (3:1), he must start from square one again and make the gift of the Spirit the foundation of an elaborate argument derived from salvation history. "This is his first point in an argument which uses appeal to experience and personal relationship, exposition of salvation-history, exegesis of Scripture and theological logic set out in a sequence of interlocking strips like a well-made page of papyrus" (Dunn, *Galatians*, 151). It is none other than the stress of the opening verses of "the argument from salvation history" that are recalled in what follows (3:8, 14, 27; 4:5-7, 29; 5:1, 5, 7-8, 16-18, 21-22, 25; 6:8).[1] The Spirit occupies the forefront in the argument of the letter and provides the decisive clue as to the problem in Galatia.[2] In plain terms, *Who possesses the Spirit: is it the law-people or the faith-in-Christ-people?* That is the question!

A. The Spirit and the Gospel (3:1-5)

Having narrated the most relevant elements of his experience up to the present moment, Paul is able at last to embark on the main section of his biblical/theological arguments to the Galatians. In turning to address them directly, he plays his main "trump card" (Dunn), namely, their own experience of the Holy Spirit when they first believed. The crux of 3:1-5, therefore, is that "the Spirit renders the law obsolete" (Hubbard, *Creation*, 201). The appeal to experience is one to which Paul will return more than once as he pens the remainder of this letter.

If the language of this opening salvo of chap. 3 seems harsh, it is nonetheless true that Paul's use of such "frank speech" (*parrēsia*) is hardly unprecedented in his and the Galatians' environment. Sampley ("Paul," 293-99) has demonstrated that the practice runs through a whole corpus of Greco-Roman literature, and that, most strikingly, it is "frank speech" that *most clearly distinguishes a friend from a flatterer* (ibid., 294). All the more relevant, then, is the piercing question of 4:16: "Have I then become your enemy by telling you the truth (RSV)?"[3]

---

[1] Thatcher's study of the "Plot" of 3:1-18 is a useful corrective to scholars such as Sanders and Beker, to the effect that Paul's argument is either inconsistent or exhibits a prooftexting methodology. Paul's approach, rather, is a history of redemption.

[2] Fee notes that from 3:2 onward "Spirit" (*pneuma*) occurs sixteen or seventeen times (3:2, 3, 5, 14; 4:6, 29; 5:5, 16, 17, 18, 22, 25; 6:1, 8) and "spiritual" (*pneumatikoi*) once (6:1) (*Presence*, 369).

[3] See further Sampley, "Paul," 299-304; Fitzgerald, "Paul."

GALATIANS CHAPTER THREE

1 Verse one commences with the first in a series of disconcerting questions: "You foolish Galatians! Who has bewitched you? Before your very eyes Jesus Christ was clearly portrayed as crucified." It is frequently suggested that this kind of stinging rebuke was common in contemporary diatribe, and that readers in South Galatia particularly would be sensitive to such a rhetorical device. Yet Paul's language is far from merely rhetorical: he was genuinely baffled at the apparent determination of these people to abandon his gospel "so quickly" (1:3 = Exod 32:8; Deut 9:16). For this reason, he upbraids them in the same terms that Jesus reproved the disciples in Luke 24:25 by calling them "foolish" (*anoētoi*). The meaning is not so much "stupid" as "undiscerning." Or, as McKnight explains, Paul's point is that they were illogical in committing themselves to his gospel and thereafter succumbing to the Judaizers' "Moses-gospel." How could they be fooled after learning about the crucifixion of Christ (*Galatians*, 136)? The term appears again in v. 3 (Rom 1:14). Witherington notes that in first-century Mediterranean culture a "fool" was not simply a moral failure but one who disrespected social boundaries, with the effect that one brought shame upon oneself (the same is true today).[4] By way of application, writes Witherington, "The issue here in part is violation of community boundaries, and in Paul's view to enter the community bounded by the Mosaic Law is to exit the community bounded by allegiance to Christ. In short, Paul sees apostasy looming on the horizon and he will marshal all his arsenal of arguments to prevent it" (*Grace*, 201).

The extent of his frustration with them is brought to the fore by: "Who bewitched you!"[5] Paul's exclamation may be understood in various ways.[6] (1) It is possible that the expression is metaphorical and idiomatic, akin to the English "whatever possessed you!" (2) The rival teachers, according to Paul, actually have placed a spell, or cast an "evil eye," on the Galatians.[7] (3) Paul is aligning

---

[4] On shame and honor, see Jewett, "Paul."

[5] The manuscript tradition followed by the KJV inserts the words: "That you should not obey the truth." Most textual critics believe that this insertion took place under the influence of 5:17. George comments: "While the textual evidence suggests that the phrase does not belong in 3:1, its meaning is certainly congruent with the context there. The Galatians' lack of ability to distinguish truth from error was the result of their willful blindness. They had become 'fascinated' by the false teachers because they did not obey the truth as it was originally proclaimed to them by Paul and Barnabas" (*Galatians*, 207-8, n. 7).

[6] See further Eastman, "Evil Eye," 69-70, n. 2.

[7] See B. W. Longenecker, *Triumph*, 150-57; Neyrey, "Bewitched;" id., *Paul*, 181-

the law teachers with the Devil and locating them within the "present evil age" (1:3; 2 Cor 11:13-15a). (4) As Eastman argues ("Evil Eye"), there is here an intertextual echo the curses of the covenant in Deuteronomy 28, especially vv. 53-57. According to Deut 28:56, the siege of the Israelite towns will be so terrible that even the most tender and compassionate of persons will possess an evil eye, that is, an unwillingness to share food with others. The LXX of the verse actually employs the same verb, "bewitch," that Paul uses here in 3:1 (*baskanō*), in connection with "eye" (literally, "bewitch with her eye"). This reading makes a great deal of sense and serves to highlight the irony of the Galatian situation. The Judaizers sought to deliver their converts *from* the curse of the law, but instead they have delivered them *to* this very curse. All in all, a combination of (3) and (4) best suits the present train of thought and Paul's take on the curse in relation to his opponents. Whatever we say, the Galatians were being seduced by the rhetoric of the agitators (cf. 2 Cor 11:3).

Paul's question is appropriate in light of the manner in which Christ was preached to them. It is true that verb translated by NIV as "clearly portrayed as crucified" (*prographō*) could rendered literally as "write beforehand," referring either to a previous communication from Paul to the Galatians or possibly predictions of the death of Christ in the OT.[8] Alternately, it could mean "display or proclaim publicly," with the graphic nature of Paul's portrayal of Christ's crucifixion in view. Along these lines, it has been suggested that Paul used visual aids (icons) or even put on a theatrical presentation (a "passion play"). It is generally agreed that the second translation is correct, so that Paul is understood to be reminding the readers of the vividness of his verbal (not visual) presentation of the crucifixion. Davis argues the very interesting case that Paul's portrayal of Christ went beyond the verbal to embrace his very person. That is to say, his own body, the public display of his sufferings for Christ, was "God's theater." Christ's crucifixion, in other words, was replicated in Paul's own crucifixion experience

---

206. Neyrey's particular argument is summarized and critiqued by T. L. Carter, *Paul*, 80-86. Eastman ("Evil Eye," 76-78) includes a discussion of the verb *baskanō*.

[8] Hays, for example, proposes with some plausibility that the translation "write beforehand" refers not to the Gospel passion narratives, which had not been written at this time, but to the lament Psalms interpreted as prefigurations of Christ's crucifixion (*Galatians*, 250-51). One might think specifically of Psalms 18 and 22 as well as the Servant Songs of Isaiah, most notably Isaiah 53. Conceivably, *prographô* may contain elements of "write beforehand" and " display graphically."

with Christ (2:20) ("*Proegraphē*," 206-12). As linked with 2:20, this makes a good deal of sense and certainly would be consonant with 6:17: the "marks" (*stigmata*) of Christ on Paul's body.

Martyn further notes that the verb thus understood can bear one of two accents: "to proclaim publicly" or "to proclaim by providing a vivid portrait." Here we see a combination of the two (*Galatians*, 283). The usage amounts to: the "crucified Christ was so vividly represented to the Galatians that they could see him on the cross with their own eyes." Paul's preaching bore all "the clearness of a public proclamation on a bulletin-board" (Burton, *Galatians*, 143). This is one of the few glimpses we get into Paul's actual delivery in preaching. It must have been very passionate and must have made a corresponding impression on his listeners, probably bringing tears to the eyes of all who heard. Paul's bewilderment and grief, then, are all the more magnified. How could those who were so moved by the preaching of the cross now be prepared to abandon the cross in favor of an alternative, the law? The cross, not the Torah, is the demonstration of God's love! As Paul was later to remind the Romans: "God demonstrates his own love for us in this: While we were still sinners, Christ died for us" (Rom 5:8).

If anything, it was the preaching of Christ *crucified* (= 1 Cor 1:18-2:5) that radically distinguished Paul from the circumcision party. It seems as though the latter had convinced the Galatians that Christ's crucifixion was of little, if any, significance, whereas for the former it was, and is, of paramount importance. According to 2:19, Paul, as a Jewish believer, has been crucified with Christ; and it is in just these terms that he appeals to the Galatians' initial reception of Christ as *the crucified one*, who was regarded by his own countrymen as being as bad as a Gentile. Yet, to borrow the words of Peter, "To you who believe he is precious" (1 Pet 2:7). If only the Galatians would call to mind that it was the will of the Lord to bruise him (1 Pet 2:24 = Isa 53:5, 10), their love affair with the law would end and they would have a renewed vision of and love for the one "who gave himself for our sins to rescue us from the present evil age" (1:3). In point of fact, it is *only* the cross that can deal with the curse, especially as it comes to expression in the "evil eye."

> Christ crucified is presented here not merely as the antidote to the evil eye, but as the antidote to the curse of which the evil eye is but one manifestation.... Christ on the cross absorbs the harmful power of the curse. In this

way, Christ opens the way for both the reception and the ongoing presence of the Spirit, who lead the Galatians from vulnerable childhood to maturity... (Eastman, "Evil Eye," 72).

2 Paul wants to know one thing only:[9] Did they receive the Spirit "from works of the law" (*ex ergōn nomou*) or "from the hearing of faith" (*ex akoēs pisteōs*)? These respective phrases "from works of the law" and "from the hearing of faith" have frequently been understood as though they were in the Greek dative case, that is, "*by* works of the law" and "*by* the hearing of faith." However, the preposition again is "from" (*ek*), with stress placed on origin but also embracing its "partisan" sense (see on 2:16). Thus, Paul points to "the hearing of faith" rather than "works of the law" as the matrix of the Galatians' experience of the Spirit. It is those who thus experience the Spirit who form the "faith-party" (*hoi ek pisteōs*, v. 7). The particular phrase, "the hearing of faith," is open to interpretation. It possibly echoes Isa 53:1: "Who has believed our report" (*akoē*)? If so, then the Gentile Galatians have in fact responded to Isaiah's "report" concerning the Servant of Yahweh. But there is another possibility: given that in the OT hearing is tantamount to faith, Paul's meaning can be captured by rendering: "the *response* of faith," that is, the response which is faith. Consequently, "the *hearing* of faith" and "the *obedience* of faith" (Rom 1:5; 16:26) would depict the same activity: believing reception of the gospel. In this case, faith would be depicted as right hearing. It is not easy to decide between these alternatives; but perhaps we do not have to. Frequently in Paul there is an element of deliberate ambiguity, which turns out to be an advantage rather than a handicap in interpreting key phrases of his.[10]

Receiving the Spirit in the NT is practically technical terminology for conversion and the commencement of discipleship (Rom 8:15; 1 Cor 2:12; 2 Cor 11:4; Gal 3:14). The same is true of baptism in the Spirit (Rom 6:3-4; 1 Cor 12:13; Col 2:12). Dunn observes that "for Paul and the first Christians this [receiving the Spirit] was the decisive and determinative element in the event or process of conversion and initiation; hence the nearest thing to a

---

[9] The aorist infinitive (*mathein*) probably has a bit of dramatic force: I want to know (learn) *right now*....

[10] One such phrase is the "obedience of faith" (*hupakoē pisteōs*) of Rom 1:5; 16:26, entailing both the obedience that consists in faith and the obedience that grows out of faith. See my *Faith*, 10-31.

definition of 'Christian' in the NT."[11] For Paul to assert that the Galatians received the Spirit was a declaration they had been united with the eschatological people, on whom the Spirit was to be poured in the Messianic age (Isa 4:2-6; 11:1-2; 32:15; 42:1; 44:3; 59:21; 61:1; cf. 63:11; Ezek 36:26-27; 37:14; 39:29; Joel 2:28-29).[12] The fact that they—mainly Gentiles—were "drenched" in the Spirit (1 Cor 12:13) "from the hearing of faith" rather than "from works of the law" is proof positive that God has fulfilled the promise of the Spirit to his ancient people irrespective of socio-theological distinctives and devotion to the Torah. "For Paul, the indisputable fact that they have the Spirit is proof that they are God's people, and his argument is that the law had nothing to do with it. It therefore cannot be a necessary condition for being the people of God" (Ziesler, *Galatians*, 32). Or, as Dunn, puts it, "Since God had thus united them to his eschatological people, on whom the Spirit had been poured...nothing more than that common participation in the Spirit was necessary for them formally to be recognized as part of that people" (*Galatians*, 153-54).

3 Paul's astonishment is such that he again calls his readers "foolish." By means of another rhetorical question, he asks: "Having begun by the Spirit, are you now being perfected by the flesh" (NASB)? The verse exudes the language of eschatology. The operative words of v. 3b are the eschatological verbs "begin" (*enarchomai*) and "perfect" (*epiteleō*). The participle "having begun" marks the inception of the Galatians' Christianity "in the Spirit" at the turning of the ages,[13] and "being perfected" is eschatological in the forward-looking sense inasmuch as it contemplates the consummation of the process of perfection begun with the advent of Christ and the Spirit, when the final victory will be won and the

---

[11] Dunn, *Galatians*, 153. See also Dunn, *Theology of Paul*, 419-25; Lull, *Spirit*, 53-95.

[12] Dunn (*Galatians*, 154) points to passages in Jewish literature which reflect similar claims to experience of the Spirit (1QS 4:21; CD 2:12; 1QH 12:12; 14:13; 16:12; *Odes Sol.* 6:2; 11:2) and yet retain the traditional Jewish hostility to the nations (CD 11:15; 1Qsa 1:21; 1QM 16:1; 1QHab 5:3-4; *Odes Sol.* 10:5; 29:8). For Paul, the reception of the Spirit *ipso facto* unites Jew and Gentile and precludes xenophobia.

[13] In 3b, "now" (*nun*) in all probability, is to be construed with "having begun" rather than with what follows. The reason for thinking so is that "now" in Paul is characteristically eschatological, signifying the onset of the new age (e.g., Rom 3:31; 5:10; 6:22; 7:6, 17; 8:1). Thus, the Galatians have begun *now*, in the era of the end-time manifestation of God's "grace" (5:5; cf. John 1:17).

people of God are sanctified fully (note as well the terminology of beginning and perfection in Phil 1:6 and Heb 6:10). The problem, however, is that the readers want to be perfected "in the flesh."

"Flesh" in this place, by way of contrast with "Spirit," is not "human effort" (NIV); it is, rather, the *era* of the flesh, that is, the old covenant/old creation as superintended by the law of Moses (Barclay, *Obeying*, 202-15). As observed above, the old aeon can be called "flesh" because the Torah ministered largely to that dimension of human nature, making "flesh" high on the Judaizers' agenda. This is so particularly as regards circumcision, "the covenant in the flesh" (Gen 17:13; Sir 44:20). In this respect, 6:12-13, the good showing "in the flesh," summarizes the entire message of the opponents. Thus, the question of v. 3 is pointedly historical in thrust. No wonder, the Galatians are "foolish." Their quest for perfection is anachronistic: they are going in the wrong direction; they want to reverse the plan of the ages! Theirs is "a futile attempt to swim against the current of salvation history!"[14]

4-5 Expressing his fear that the Galatians may have "experienced" so many things "in vain," Paul again appeals to something very well-known by them; that is, it is God who, in this "now" time, keeps on supplying them with the Spirit.[15] The continual stream of the Spirit finds its source in the age of the Spirit, not the age of the flesh. In a manner resembling Heb 2:3-4, there is the appeal is to the powerful working of the Spirit as exemplified by the working of "powers." These "powers" (*dunameis*) are the extension of the same "powers" that attended Jesus' preaching of the kingdom and the coming of the kingdom "in power" to the disciples at Pentecost (e.g., Matt 14:2; Mark 6:2; Acts 2:22; cf. 1 Cor 12:10; Col 1:29; 2 Thess 2:9). These are "the powers of the age to come" (Heb 6:5). In fact, the parallel with Hebrews is suggestive to the extent that both the Galatians and the Hebrews were running the same risk of falling away after experiencing the eschatological arrival of "the Holy Spirit of the promise" (Eph 1:13). They were in danger of

---

[14] Thielman, *Theology*, 268. Lurking in the background is perhaps also the notion of the Spirit as divine power, as contrasted with the weakness of the law (4:9; 5:16-26).

[15] The verb *paschō* here can also mean "suffer;" and it is not unlikely that the Galatians' "experience" of the Spirit entailed a certain amount of suffering, including persecution at the hands of the Judaizers (see on 4:29). In 2 Cor 11:21-12:10, Paul intertwines his own sufferings with the "signs and wonders and mighty works" that attended his ministry. See the footnote to 6:17.

repeating the wilderness apostasy of Israel (see Wilson, "Apostasy").

Paul's point "is to remind the Galatians of a range of experiences which should have been enough to demonstrate that they were indeed recipients of the eschatological Spirit and that the way they had come into these experiences remained the pattern for life in the Spirit" (Dunn, *Galatians*, 156-57). Given the importance of a Spirit-filled experience, Paul does not hesitate to repeat the main question: is "it by the works of the Law, or by hearing with faith" (NASB)? Obviously, it was the latter.

> Paul evidently could refer the Galatians not only to their beginning experience of the Spirit, but also to what had been their characteristic experience since then—as an experience of engracing and empowering which had been independent of any works of the law and had come to them solely as they heard and responded with faith to the message preached (ibid., 158).

George is quite right that Paul's opponents would have abhorred his antithesis between the gift of the Spirit and the works of the law, particularly as far as circumcision is concerned. "For them the granting of the Spirit was merely a preliminary initiation into the Christian faith, one that remained vacuous and incomplete until it was perfected by receiving the sign of physical incorporation into the people of Israel" (*Galatians*, 213). Fee likewise can say:

> For the agitators, the gift of the Spirit apparently meant the need to be "completed" by adhering to Torah, especially by submitting to circumcision. After all, this was common Jewish expectation, derived from Jer 31:31-34 and Ezek 11:19-20; 36:26-27, that the gift of the eschatological Spirit would lead people to obey the Law. For Paul, the gift of the Spirit, along with the death and resurrection of Christ, meant the end of the time of Torah. The old covenant had failed precisely because it was not accompanied by the Spirit. Thus the advent of Christ and the Spirit meant an end to the old covenant; the new covenant, ratified through the death of Christ, had been instituted through the gift of the Spirit, who thereby replaced Torah (*Presence*, 369).

Section Note

1-5 The issue of the Spirit is posed somewhat differently but essentially in accord with my assessment by scholars like Cosgrove and Hafemann. Cosgrove contends that the core concern of Galatians is whether believers can promote their ongoing experience of the Spirit by doing the law (*Cross*, 2. See the whole discussion of pp. 1-86.). Hafemann similarly maintains that the controversy addressed by 3:2b is a disagreement over the relationship between keeping the law and experiencing life in the Spirit. The answers to the rhetorical questions in 3:2b and 5, based on the Galatians' own experience, are meant to settle the argument: the source of the Galatians' continuing life in the Spirit is the same as their initial reception of the Spirit ("Exile," 340, n. 29).

With the question, Who possesses the Spirit? I have attempted to focus the issue on the Spirit as the latter-day identity marker of Christians of the Pauline stripe as over against the Judaizing variety. Hafemann comes close to this in his recognition that "it is this common-ground experience of the Spirit as *the ultimate content of the Abrahamic promise*, not the penultimate status of sonship *per se*, that provides the foundation of Paul's polemic in Galatians 3-4" ("Exile," 350-51, italics his). The reason, he says, is immediately evident: *the presence of the Spirit is the mark of the new age of the new creation under the new covenant*. Paul's focus on the status of Abraham's heirs in 3:26-29 and 4:1-7 is, therefore, not for its own sake. Paul introduces the issue of status-transfer for Jews and Gentiles in order to raise the issue of inheritance (cf. 3:29; 4:5, 7), which in turn points to the eschatological transition from "the present evil age" (1:4) to the age of "realized heirship."

Hence, for the Galatians to move back to the Sinai covenant now would be to deny that Christ and faith in him were the foundation for the reception of the Spirit as the fulfillment of the promise and covenant with Abraham. "To live like a Jew" (2:14) as a requirement for continuing on with Christ is to import life "under the Law" into the new age of the Spirit. From Paul's perspective, to accept such a requirement would imply a radical denial of the need for and the eschatological significance of the death of Christ, both anthropologically, as that which frees one from the power of sin, and historically, as that which brings about the turn of the ages (1:4; 2:19-21; 3:13; 4:5; 5:2; 6:14) (ibid., 351, italics mine).[16]

---

[16] Incidentally, Hafemann is correct that Galatians is not *about* "getting in" and "staying in." Nevertheless, I would offer the rejoinder that the letter has a bearing on the question: one "gets in" by faith alone and "stays in" by means of a continual dependence on and walk in the Spirit.

B. Faithful Abraham (3:6-9)

Paul now commences an elaborate exposition of Scripture, which is prolonged until the end of chap. 4. It comes as no surprise that a mainstay of his argument is his appeal to Abraham, the redoubtable father of the Jewish people, who was reckoned righteous "from the hearing of faith," not "from works of the law." In both Galatians and Romans, it is *the story of Abraham* that reveals so much of Paul's intentions and the inner workings of his thought.[17]

It is in Abraham's actual footsteps that the Galatians ought to walk, not those of the law teachers who were using the patriarch to argue their case for a law-observant church. It is just in this regard that we are not to overlook the immediate reason why Paul appeals to Abraham's faith. As is evident especially from vv. 7-9, Abraham was the outstanding pre-Mosaic recipient of the "gospel." In this capacity, he is the exemplar *par excellence* of those who receive the Spirit by virtue of the hearing of faith, not Torah-works. Abraham thus belongs to "us," the "faith-people," not to "them," the "works-of-the-law-people." In principle, Abraham was part of the new creation that has come to fruition in Christ and the Spirit, not the old and outmoded age that has now passed away with the fullness of time.

6 The conjunction "thus" which begins v. 6 is intended to place Abraham in the category of those who are justified "from" the "hearing of faith" as opposed to "works of the law." Perhaps "thus," "just as," or "accordingly" (*kathōs*) is shorthand for the longer introductory formula, "thus it is written," because immediately Paul quotes Gen 15:6. But it is more likely that the conjunction is to be paraphrased something like this: "Thus it is in the case of Abraham" or "things were the same with Abraham" (Martyn) (cf. NIV's "consider Abraham"). In the vernacular, we would say: "It's like this with Abraham." Stanley, then, is right that *kathōs* introduces Abraham as an example to be followed, as one who exhibited the kind of "hearing of faith" that Paul implicitly commends at the end of v. 5 (*Arguing*, 121, n, 21). In any event, the appeal to Abraham is natural enough, given that the Israelites were the "seed" of Abraham (Ps 105:6; Isa 41:8) and that he is the "father" of the race (Genesis 12-24; Isa 51:2; Matt 3:9). Moreover, in

---

[17] See Stockhausen, "Principles," 158-63. The Abraham narrative of Genesis is traced out in detail by F. Watson, *Paul*, 167-269.

Jewish tradition, Abraham was considered the epitome of fidelity to God in times of testing (Sir 44:19; 1 Macc 2:50-52; *T. Levi* 9:1-14; *T. Benj.* 10:4; *T. Abr.* 17:2; *Jub.* 23:10; 51:1-2; 16:20; 17:17-18; 23:10; CD 3:2-4; 16:1, 5-6; *2 Apoc. Bar.* 57:1-3; Philo *Abr.* 275-76; *m. Kidd.* 4; 14). He was the first convert from paganism to the true God (Josh 24:2-3; *Jub.* 11:16-17; 12; *Apocalypse of Abraham* 1-8; Philo, *Abr.* 60-88; Josephus, *Ant.* 1.154-57; Pseudo-Philo, *Bib. Ant.* 23:5).[18] For these reasons, descent from Abraham was a matter of some pride (*Pss. Sol.* 9:17; 3 Macc 6:3). In all probability, Paul's specific appeal to Abraham stems from the Judaizers' arguments based on sonship to Abraham.

Given the specific connotations of "works of the law," Paul (as in Romans 4) argues two points: (1) Abraham, contrary to Jewish tradition (Sir 44:20; *2 Apoc. Bar.* 57:2; CD 3:2),[19] did not live in the era of the law and, therefore, could not have been considered a member of the Mosaic covenant by virtue of law-keeping. (2) In light of vv. 2-3, Paul places Abraham in the era of the Spirit, even though he lived millennia before the actual turning of the ages. Because of the eschatological situation, he can claim Abraham for his camp rather than that of the Judaizers. No doubt, Paul refers to Abraham in the first place because of the way the opponents put him forward as their champion, given especially the tradition that Abraham kept the law before Sinai. But as is frequently the case, Paul turns the tables. For him, a straight line can be drawn from Abraham to the age of the Spirit, with the period of the law forming a "great parenthesis" between the patriarch and the Messiah. *Abraham belongs to the "now time" not the "then time."*[20]

From one perspective, Paul's appeal to Gen 15:6 is obvious. This is the one passage where righteousness is said to be reckoned

---

[18] On the pre-Pauline Abraham traditions, see Calvert-Koyzis, *Paul*, 6-84; id., "Abraham," 225-35; Hansen, *Abraham*, 175-99; F. Watson, *Paul*, 167-269; Siker, *Jews*, 17-27; Nickelsburg, "Abraham;" Longenecker, *Galatians*, 110-11; G. N. Davies, *Faith*, 144-47; Eisenbaum, "Paul," 134-35. The Abrahamic covenant in the Hebrew Scriptures has come in for frequent treatment. Williamson, *Abraham*, provides extensive literature.

[19] See further Str-B, 3.204-6.

[20] Longenecker ("Illustrations," 191) relates that throughout Galatians Paul seems to be interacting with a typically Jewish understanding, as expressed most clearly in the Talmud, that truth comes in two stages: first in an elemental form and then in a developed form. I surmise that Paul would have agreed, but with the proviso that the revelation in Christ represents the most developed form of truth. Therefore, since the Torah is not God's final word, Abraham is logically aligned with Paul's law-free proclamation, as opposed to the law-bound message of the opponents.

to the patriarch before his circumcision and well before the giving of the law on Sinai. Jewish tradition tended to link this verse with Abraham's subsequent trial of faith, Genesis 22, culminating in the declaration of 22:12: "For now I know that you fear God, seeing you have not withheld your son, your only son, from me" (see Sir 44:19-21; 1 Macc 2:52; *Jub.* 17:15-18; *m. 'abot* 5:3; cf. Jas 2:23). The comparison was right and proper because Genesis 15 itself represented one of the trials of Abraham's faith. Abraham's pilgrimage begins in Genesis 12 (as confirmed by Heb 11:8). But by the time of Genesis 15 his faith is beginning to wane. Thus, the Lord buttresses his promise by appealing to the stars of heaven as being the number of his descendants.

From another perspective, Paul's use of Gen 15:6 is remarkable within the historical context in which he writes. The standard Jewish appeal to Abraham, as noted above, was his keeping of the law, along with his sacrifice of Isaac (Genesis 22) and his resistance of idolatry. For intertestamental authors the tested and true Abraham was a reflection and legitimization of themselves, that is, of those faithful to the Torah in the midst of an apostate generation. In this setting, Paul's appeal to Gen 15:6 is unique. To be sure, this passage, as well as Genesis 22, bears witness to a time of testing in Abraham's life, when he was tempted to disbelieve God's word of promise. Yet it is for this very reason that it suits Paul's purposes so well. When the patriarch believed the Lord, he was shut up to faith alone in his word apart from even the "work" of sacrificing his son, and certainly before his circumcision.

Paul thus appeals to an incident years before the offering of Isaac to establish that "faith alone" was the operative principle of God's covenant with him. If later Abraham was obedient, as Gen 22:18 states, it was an obedience which was the outgrowth of such a faith. To be sure, Judaism itself affirmed the "obedience of faith" (Rom 1:5; 16:26) in this sense (Garlington, *Obedience*); but Gen 15:6 places it beyond doubt that Abraham could not have been justified "from works of the Torah" (v. 2), coming, as it does, before the episode customarily appealed to by Jewish apologists.

Gen 15:6 states that "it was reckoned to him as righteousness." The idiom "to reckon to" (Greek *logizomai eis* = Hebrew *hashab l^e*) means "to consider something to be true" or "to regard as" (e.g., Rom 9:8). According to Von Rad, the Hebrew verb denotes "a process of thought which results in a value-judgment, but in which this value-judgment is related not to the speaker but to the value of an object."[21] That is to say, a thing is considered to be thus and so simply because it is.[22] Therefore, when he continued to believe, Abraham was considered by God to be a faithful, covenant keeping person. The only other place in the OT where the exact phrase is used is Ps 106:31, which declares that righteousness was reckoned to Phinehas when he acted with righteous zeal toward those who defiled the covenant (Numbers 25).[23]

It should be clarified that the issue between Paul and the opponents was not faith in Jesus as such—that much they held in common. "It was," rather, "what followed from faith, the ongoing demands of the covenant law on the covenant member which were at issue" (Dunn, *Galatians*, 162). But if Abraham had simply to believe, then his spiritual posterity need do no more than that; and if he could be considered a faithful covenant-keeper apart from circumcision and the Torah, then so can his seed.

> Paul's rhetorical move here will be not to follow the Jewish approach of interpreting Abraham's faith in light of his later faithfulness in regard to Isaac and submission to circumcision, but rather to focus on what was true about Abraham at and from the beginning of his walk with God, which is to say what was true about his life that Paul could readily parallel in the lives of the Galatians (Witherington, *Grace*, 225).

7 In view of the way Abraham was actually declared to be a covenant keeper, Paul writes: "Understand, then, that the faith-people are the sons of Abraham" (my translation). It is because Abraham really belongs to the era of the Spirit that Paul can claim that "those of faith" and *they alone* are Abraham's true sons and daughters. In keeping with the way Paul uses the preposition *ek* in Galatians (see on 2:16), "those of faith" (*hoi ek pisteōs*) are the people who belong to the new community of faith identified with Jesus the crucified Messiah. In contrast to them are "those from the circumcision" (*tous ek peritomēs*) (2:12) and "those of works the

---

[21] Von Rad, "Faith," 125-26. See especially Lev 7:11-18; 17:1-9; Num 18:25-32, and my comments in my "Rejoinder" to John Piper (= *Defense*, 167-97), as contra the reading of these texts by Carson, "Vindication," 58-59. On the idiom, *logizomai eis*, see further Heiland, *Anrechnung*, passim; id., *TDNT*, 4.284-86, 289-92.

[22] See further Abegg, "4QMMT;" Garlington, *Essays*, 377-81; id., "Rejoinder" (= *Defense*, 167-97).

[23] But note 1 Macc 2:52 and especially 4QMMT C31-32. See Abegg, "4QMMT;" Garlington, "Rejoinder" (= *Defense*, 167-97).

law" (*hosoi ex ergōn nomou*) (3:10; cf. Rom 4:14). These are the individuals who insist on clinging to the community of the old creation as regulated by the Torah. Hays is right that in both cases *ek* serves to suggest that the object of the preposition is the source of being or key identity marker for the people in question. They are the "faith people" or the "circumcision people" (*Galatians*, 256). In so formulating these phrases, Paul seeks to shift the focus of covenant identity away from preoccupation with the law and back to Christic faith as characterizing God's people. As ironic as it is, the "sons of Abraham" no longer have to be Jewish!

8 That Abraham, in principle, belongs to the company of faith who occupy the age of the Spirit is confirmed by the statement that the Scriptures themselves foresaw the justification of the Gentiles and thus preached the gospel beforehand to the patriarch. Paul's personification of Scripture as a preacher of the gospel is indicative of his high view of the sacred text as the expression of God's will. "Paul sees the Scriptures as alive, active, speaking, even locking people up under sin (Gal. 3.22). Paul is able to say this because he identifies what Scriptures says with what God says.... Scripture is seen as a written transcript of the living divine Word that comes directly from the mind and mouth of God, and so can be personified as it is here" (Witherington, *Grace*, 227). This gospel preaching took the form of the basic promise made to Abraham: "In you shall all the nations be blessed" (Gen 12:3; 18:18; 22:17-18; 26:4; 28:14; Ps 71:17 [LXX]; Sir 44:21 [LXX]; Acts 3:25).

The gospel was thus universalistic from the beginning. This has implications for the controversy in Galatia, inasmuch as the law, while it still stood, was an impediment to the fulfillment of the Abrahamic blessing. "Blessed" in general means to receive grace and peace and to be sustained and prospered in them. Specifically, *the* blessing (of Abraham) Paul has in view is that of *sonship to God through Christ by virtue of the gift of the Spirit as the believer is now identified as the true seed of Abraham* (3:26-29).[24]

9 Verse 9 reiterates the basic point of v. 7 by drawing a conclusion: "So, then, those who are of faith are blessed with faithful Abraham" (my translation). These people alone are the fulfillment of Gen 12:3. As Dunn notes, the link provided by the first Scripture (Gen 15:6), that is, promise, seed, faith, when added to the

---

[24] On the linkage of the blessing and the Spirit, see particularly Witherington, *Grace*, 228-29; Williams, "Justification," 97-98.

link provided by the second text (Gen 12:3), that is, promise, blessing, Gentiles, points clearly to the conclusion that the blessing of Abraham came to the faith of Abraham and thus to those who share that faith (*Galatians*, 166). Furthermore, the present tense "are blessed" is deliberate: "It is not simply that the way had now become open for Gentiles of faith to share the promised blessing in the future; it is rather they were *already* sharing that blessing" (ibid., 166-67).

It is striking that Paul speaks of "faithful (*pistos*) Abraham" (the most natural translation) rather than of "Abraham who had faith" or "believing Abraham" (the majority rendering). Of course, Abraham was characterized by his faith, but it was a faith against all odds; Abraham was "faithful" in the comprehensive sense. The combination of Gen 12:3; Gen 15:6; and Gen 22:1-14 suggests as much, as drawn out by Rom 4:18-22:

> In hope *he believed against hope*, that he should become the father of many nations; as he had been told, "So shall your descendants be." *He did not weaken in faith* when he considered his own body, which was as good as dead because he was about a hundred years old, or when he considered the barrenness of Sarah's womb. *No distrust made him waver* concerning the promise of God, but *he grew strong in his faith* as he gave glory to God, *fully convinced* that God was able to do what he had promised. *That is why his faith was "reckoned to him as righteousness"* (RSV).

The polemical impact of the verse is that fidelity to God does not depend on law observance. This, in turn, implies that the Judaizers and their followers cannot be the sons of Abraham, because they refuse to walk "in his footsteps" (Rom 4:12). By the nature of the case, then, their program of converting the nations to the law in order to become the seed of Abraham is illegitimate and contradicts the very example of the patriarch himself, who was believing and faithful before circumcision and the advent of the Torah onto the stage of human history. Martyn is right that the Judaizers would have paraphrased Gen 12:3 to read: "Those who faithfully observe the law are blessed with faithfully observant Abraham" (*Galatians*, 302). For Paul, however, "Abraham who in Judaism is the prototype of 'righteousness through obedience to the Torah' now has become the prototype of the 'men of faith'" (Betz, *Galatians*, 143).

GALATIANS CHAPTER THREE

C. The Curse of the Law (3:10-14)[25]

As Paul, in 3:10-14, turns directly to the "curse of the law," the "curse" is placed conspicuously in contrast to the "blessing" of Abraham (below, in vv. 13-14, the order is reversed: the curse of the law turns into the blessing of Abraham). In this schema, "blessing" belongs to the eras of Abraham and the Spirit, while the age of the Torah is epitomized as "curse."[26] So far, it has been intimated that the Judaizers are under the curse because they have, for all practical purposes, self-consciously chosen to remain in the age of the law, thus opposing God's eschatological designs in Christ. As Betz puts it, the logic behind Paul's words is simply that exclusion from blessing equals curse; and the "men of the Torah" are excluded from blessing because they regard the observance of the law as a condition for salvation (*Galatians*, 144). But while these ideas are present from the outset of the letter, they are, more or less, subliminal. It is Paul's use of the OT in 3:10-13 which elevates his underlying intentions from mere impressions to an articulated tactic in his dealings with his antagonists.

10 As Paul begins to unfold his agenda, v. 10a is connected with the foregoing verses by means of its first "for" (*gar*). The conjunction is causal strictly speaking: those who are "of works of the law" (*ex ergōn nomou*) or, according to v. 11, "in the law" (*en nomō*), are not "blessed with Abraham." These are individuals whose identity is derived from the law and who are "under the curse" (*hupo kataran*) because of *their involvement with the Torah*. To support this proposition, Deut 27:26 is introduced by the "for" of the second clause. "cursed is everyone who does not abide in everything written in the book of the law, to do them" (my translation).[27] Yet it is just the quotation of this text to support the propo-

---

[25] For a more detailed treatment of the passage see my "Role Reversal," 95-106 (= *Essays*, 222-232); and Wisdom, *Blessing*, 43-62, 154-82; Bruce, "Curse." Paul's citation techniques of the OT texts are detailed by Stanley, *Paul*, 238-48.

[26] In this letter, to be "under the curse" (*hupo kataran*) is synonymous with being in the old age. It is equivalent to "under sin" (*hupo hamartian*) (3:22), "under law" (*hupo nomon*) (3:23), "under guardians and stewards" (*hupo epitropous kai oikonomous*) (4:2) and "under the elements of the world" (*hupo ta stoicheia tou kosmou*) (4:3). See further Belleville, "Under Law."

[27] As Paul quotes it, the LXX (not the Hebrew text) contains the adjective "all:" "Cursed is everyone who does not abide by *all things* written in the book of the law, to perform them" (NASB). *If* there is any emphasis on "all" (only in the LXX), it is qualitative, not quantitative. Israel was not free to pick and choose

sition of the first clause that has occasioned problems going as far back as Luther's day. It was Luther who first observed that the two sentences of Paul and Moses seem to be contrary. For Paul, those who do the law are cursed, but Moses says that the curse falls on those who do *not* do the words of the law.[28] My contention is that the problem is resolved in terms of the ideology of role reversal inherent in vv. 10-13. It is just because the Judaizers and their followers champion the Torah that they fall under its curse as apostates from the eschatological purposes of God in Christ. The "law people" are cursed by none other than the Torah itself, the very law to which they are unswervingly loyal and to which they look as the paradigm of Jesus' messiahship and God's will for his covenant partners.[29] See on v. 13.

Deut 27:26, as all the passages quoted in vv. 10-13, is concerned with fidelity to God's covenant as opposed to idolatry and apostasy.[30] Paul advances an adapted version of the LXX, according to which the operative word of the verse is "remain," that is, in the law, as complemented by "do" (the latter is parallel to and defined by the former). The Hebrew, however, as reflected by NASB, reads "confirm the words of this law." The Israelite was to "uphold" or "support" "the words of this law," which were given to regulate the relationship between Yahweh and his people. In so doing, one would honor one's prior faith-commitment to Yahweh. The same note of allegiance to (or renewal of) the covenant is sounded in, e.g., 2 Kgs 23:3, 24. By way of further illustration, 1 Sam 15:11, 13; Jer 35:15, 16 present us with a study in contrast: as over against those who have broken faith with the Lord, there are

---

from the variety of the commandments: each one had its peculiar importance. It is in this sense that Paul can write in Gal 5:3 that everyone who receives circumcision is bound to keep *the whole law*. Comments Witherington: "For Paul the Law is a package deal, and one cannot separate out one portion of its commandments from another. All must be obeyed if one is under the Law" (*Grace*, 353).

[28] Cited by Stanley, "Curse," 481; id., *Arguing*, 124, n. 25.

[29] One cannot help but wonder if in nomenclature "those who are of works of the law" corresponds to similar phrases in the DSS, namely, "the people of the community" (1QS 5:1) and "the people of the law" (4QS 1:1). If so, the identity of the group is the more readily discernible: they are the people devoted to the standards of the covenant.

[30] The quotation of these OT texts forms a chiasmus (on which, see Thomson, *Chiasmus*; Jeremias, "Chiasmus"):

A Curse (Deut 27:26)
  B Life (Hab 2:4)
  B Life (Lev 18:5)
A Curse (Deut 21:23)

individuals who have "upheld" the Torah. At heart, then, the point of Deut 27:26 is: "Cursed be anyone who is fundamentally disloyal to the law—anyone who does not, by his actions, show that he is on the side of the law and anxious to 'make the law stand'" (Bligh, *Galatians*, 257).

11 Having confronted his opponents with a text threatening apostasy with the wrath of God, in v. 11 Paul turns to the other side of the coin, to a prophetic passage calling to mind Yahweh's vindication of his faithful people, who are "blessed" rather than "cursed." Hab 2:4 is introduced as providing the reason why it is obvious (*dēlon*) that "in the law no one is justified before God." "In the law" is the functional equivalent of "those who are of works of the law" in the previous verse. Accordingly, for Paul it is evident that those who remain "in the law," the Judaizers and those like them, cannot be "justified before God," simply because, in the words of Hab 2:4, "the righteous shall live by faith," the implication being that these people do not belong to the company of the righteous who will live by virtue of their faith(fulness).

Hab 2:4 represents an outstanding instance of God's intervention to save his people (his "righteousness"). In context, the prophet is confronted with the impending invasion of the holy land by the Chaldeans. The fact that a nation far more sinful than Israel should be the instrument of her judgment occasions a crisis of faith on Habakkuk's part. In the face of his pleas, God answers that in time he will punish the Chaldeans for their iniquity. In the meantime, however, the righteous of Israel will "live," that is, by their fidelity to the covenant they will survive the enemy invasion and return to their own land. Such is the original meaning of "the righteous will live by his faith(fulness)." The focus is not on how one becomes righteous; but rather, the righteousness of the covenant is presupposed. And Yahweh's assurance to the prophet is just that the righteous person will live through the judgment and ultimately be vindicated ("justified") by his faith(fulness). The basic and really simple point, then, is that in the original setting it is the faith(fulness) of the righteous Israelite which will ensure his deliverance: when the judgment falls, it is reliance on the Lord himself which will see him through.[31]

---

[31] However, the irony of Paul's usage of this text should not go unnoticed. A famous illustration is provided by 1QHab 8:1-3: "Interpreted, this [that is, Hab 2:4] concerns all who observe the Law in the House of Judah, whom God will deliver from the House of Judgment because of their suffering [or "toil"—probably a

Again, Paul quite consciously draws on a passage from the Jewish Scriptures that speaks directly to the issue of perseverance versus apostasy. In this particular case, he chooses one which has as its life setting a crisis of faith in the history of Israel. As was to become the order of the day during the Greek and Roman periods, the preexilic people of God are forced to decide for Yahweh, despite a pagan presence pummeling them with brute violence. In view of such a daunting prospect, Habakkuk ponders the question later to be raised by Jewish Apocalyptic: Is Yahweh able to deliver his people and bring just retribution on their enemies?[32] The answer is that in spite of all, those who continue to trust in him will, by virtue of that faith(fulness), survive the devastation. Accordingly, the return of the faithful remnant to the land will be their "justification," that is, their vindication as the righteous people of God.

12 Here, Paul returns to the books of Moses, again to support a thesis. This time the thesis is: "the law is not of faith;" rather "the one who does them will live in them." The link with Hab 2:4 is provided by "life," as signaled by "will live" in both verses. The choice of words, "the law is not of faith," is certainly terse, but is explicable given Paul's propensity for prepositions of origin ("from") and sphere ("in") (*ek* and *en*). To say that the law is "not of faith" is to affirm that the law and faith belong to distinctly different historical realms: the former does not occupy the same turf in the salvation-historical continuum as the latter.

The two components of Lev 18:5 are "do" and "live." "Do" is clarified by the immediate context, inasmuch as it stands in parallel

---

reference to the toil of obedience to the law] and because of their faith in the Teacher of Righteousness." As expected, deliverance is bound up with law-obedience. Paul, however, has detached faith(fulness) from its specifically Mosaic setting: faith(fulness) is still required, but its specific object is Christ, not the Torah. For him Hab 2:4 proves that the righteousness of God is now revealed apart from the "works of the law." Comments Schnelle: "In contrast to the pious of Qumran, for whom faith and the observance of the Torah are an organic unity, Paul sharply distinguishes between them. Whereas only the doers of the law attain to salvation according to the understanding of Qumran and within Judaism generally, salvation for Paul is something that transcends Torah observance and is entirely a matter of faith" (*Paul*, 288).

[32] Hays (*Conversion*, 140-42) is correct that Habakkuk comes in the setting of apocalyptic/eschatological blessings and that Paul announces the arrival of these blessings in Galatians. However, unlike the LXX and Hebrews, Paul does not read Hab 2:4 as a messianic text. For him (and the MT of Habakkuk), the "righteous one" is the covenant loyalist.

to "keeping" the commandments and "walking" in them. The point is hardly that of earning anything (with the unspoken assumption that no one actually can earn life by keeping the law). It is, instead, perseverance in the standards set by Yahweh's covenant, as opposed to giving heed to the "statutes" of the Egyptians and the Canaanites. When one "does" the law, one acknowledges that Yahweh is one's God and that his will alone determines the norms of covenantal life, in contrast to the licentious deities of the outside world, who permit the "abominations" prohibited by Lev 18:6-30. To "do the law," in short, is to be "obedient," that is, to remain faithful to the God who called his people out of bondage.

"Live" is likewise qualified by the covenant setting. On this basis, it is arguable that the life in question is not eschatological or eternal as such. On one level, the life of Lev 18:5 is physical and earthly, even though such a life is a happy one, in which a person enjoys God's bounty of health, children, friends and prosperity (cf. Lev 26:3-13; Deut 28:1-14; 30:11-20; Neh 9:29; Ezek 20:11). "Live," then, does mean primarily "to go on living" in the land as a result of obedience to the law. Even so, we must reckon with the fact that in certain strands of Jewish interpretation the eschatological dimension is very much present. For example, 1QS 4:6-8 makes "everlasting blessing and eternal joy in life without end" the extension of "long life" and "fruitfulness" here and now (cf. Dan 12:2; Wis 2:23 [passim]; 2 Macc 7:9; 4 Macc 15:3; 17:12). Conversely, reserved for those who follow "the spirit of falsehood" (the apostates) are a multitude of plagues now and "everlasting damnation," "eternal torment" and "endless disgrace" hereafter (1QS 4:12-14). Likewise, *Tg. Ps.-J.* and *Tg. Onq.* to Lev 18:5 both posit everlasting life as the reward of doing the Torah (cf. Luke 10:25). Indeed, such an eschatological slant on the life of Lev 18:5 would have played readily into Paul's hands, as he transposes the life of the Torah into eternal life in Christ (see the second section note to this verse) It is on this note that Galatians virtually commences (1:2): Jesus' resurrection inaugurates the eternal messianic age, corresponding, as it does, to the oracles concerning the captivity and restoration of Israel, the nation's own death and resurrection (e.g., Isa 26:19; Ezek 37:1-14; Hos 6:1-2).

In brief, Lev 18:5 is the OT's classic statement of "covenantal nomism." The verse is "a typical expression of what Israel saw as its obligation and promise under the covenant;" it is an expression of how first-century Jews would have understood righteousness, that is, "life within the covenant, 'covenantal nomism,' the pattern of religion and life which marked out the righteous, the people of the covenant" (Dunn, *Romans*, 2.601). Therefore, one continues to live within the covenant relationship by compliance with its terms, that is, by "doing the law" or perseverance. It is life as the outcome of law observance which doubtlessly gave rise to the expressions "the law of life" (Sir 17:11; 45:5) and "the commandments of life" (Bar 3:9; 4:1; cf. *Pss. Sol.* 14:2; 1QS 4:6-8; *Ep. Arist.* 127; 4 Ezra 14:30; Philo, *Cong.* 86-87). These commandments are no less than the very embodiment of Israel's wisdom: "All who hold her fast will live, and those who forsake her will die" (Bar 4:1).[33]

Virtually every commentator recognizes that Paul, in some way or the other, plays off believing and doing in v. 12. But in what sense are the two set in opposition? The majority of scholars assume that they are mutually exclusive by the nature of the case: "faith" by definition excludes "works," and vice versa. However, in historical perspective, any dichotomy between believing and doing in the Jewish schema is simply off base: Judaism was and is as much a "faith system" as Christianity. The inseparability of faith and obedience in the Hebrew Bible is still intact, but in Paul both have been refocused on Jesus, the crucified Messiah.

It is true that v. 12 poses a problem for this reading. Its proposition, "the law is not of faith," is buttressed by the words of Lev 18:5: "The one who does them will live in them." On the usual interpretation, Paul is taken to mean that "the law has nothing to do with faith" in this sense: whereas the law required performance, the gospel enjoins only faith. As the argument goes, anyone who would be justified "on the basis of works" must reckon seriously with what the Torah itself says: "The one who *does* them will live in them." However, this more or less traditional interpretation falters for two reasons. (1) "Doing the law," according to the context of Lev 18:5, is not "achievement" but the exercise of faith within the parameters of the covenant. (2) Neither the OT nor later Jewish theology recognize a distinction between doing and believing: they are the two sides of the same coin (see Yinger, *Paul*, 19-140).

Therefore, the resolution of the problem must be sought along the lines of the historical character of Paul's argument. His is not a topical discussion of faith and works but an epochal delineation of the respective places of law and faith in salvation history. We are to think of two historical eras, meaning that the law, the period of the "disciplinarian" cannot arise "from faith" (*ek pisteōs*), the period of maturity (3:23-25), simply because of the chronological impossibility of the procedure (again, 3:1-5). Even if, for the sake

---
[33] See Cosgrove, *Cross*, 90-91.

of argument, "of faith" encapsulates a "faith-principle," the faith in question is specifically "faith in Jesus Christ" (2:16) and "the faith" which have now come to displace the era of the "disciplinarian" (3:23-25), which possessed its own kind of "faith-principle." Still, What is the precise relationship of the two clauses of v. 12?

If our analysis is correct that the law and (Christian) faith belong to distinct historical eras, then we may answer by paraphrasing v. 12: "The law and faith may occupy separate historical compartments ("the law is not of faith"), *nevertheless* (*all'* [cf. 2:3]), the Torah's own standard of fidelity remains intact" ("the one who does them will live in them"). Now, however, the call for faithfulness has been projected into the present eschatological context, whereby "doing the law" is redefined as faith(fulness) directed to *the Christ of Paul's gospel*. In his letters, we need not look far to find a parallel. According to Rom 2:13, it is the "doers of the law" who will be justified in eschatological judgment. Here likewise Paul alludes to Lev 18:5 and applies this word of Moses to the present eschatological setting: it is "in Christ," as the remainder of Romans will clarify, that one becomes a "doer of the law."[34]

As regards the Judaizers, this principle of life as a result of adherence to the Torah does not apply, because they have failed to observe the law in its overall salvific design, that is, to lead Israel to Christ (3:23-25). In short, they live in the wrong age and will not relinquish the law in favor of a law-free gospel as procured by the death of the Messiah "on the tree." Herein resides their apostasy.

13 Christ redeemed us from the curse of the law. The verb "redeemed" (*exagorazō*) is chosen because of its biblical associations with the liberation of slaves. Two acts of liberation in the OT particularly stand out. One is the exodus from Egypt, "the house of bondage." The other is new exodus from Babylon, as anticipated by the Prophets. The typological potential of this concept is exploited by the NT generally, and not least by Paul.

However, in Galatians, Paul is driving at something very specific, namely, the "new bondage" is that of the Torah. The motif emerges clearly enough from the ensuing train of thought: (1)

---

[34] See my *Faith*, 44-71 The expression "the doers of the law," as modeled on Lev 18:5 and Deut 4:1, 10, 40; 5:29-33; 6:1-2, 18, 24; 7:12-13, crops up in 1 Macc 2:67, where it designates loyalist Jews who would be vindicated against the Gentiles by divine justice. Significant also are 1QpHab 7:11; 8:1; 12:4-5. See my, *Faith*, 67-71.

3:23-25 likens life under the law to the constraints imposed by a "disciplinarian;" (2) 4:4 has in view the redemption of "those under the law," an especially novel idea, since, in historical perspective, "those under the law" would have been free from (Egyptian) bondage by the nature of the case (cf. John 8:33); (3) 4:8-9 equates devotion to the Sinai covenant with the bondage of pagan idolatry. The Messiah is treated by Israel as an outcast and thus brings the curses of Deuteronomy to a climax; but in the process, he liberates his new people from the "bondage" which still curses the Judaizers and potentially their admirers. In particular, it is Jewish Christians who have been redeemed (on "us," see the section note to vv. 13-14). But if Jewish believers had to be redeemed from the law, then Gentiles must not be brought under it either, otherwise the death of Christ was for nothing.

In supporting his proposition, Paul cites a final text, Deut 21:23.[35] According to that passage, the curse is the death penalty meted out to the reprobate son, who would not "obey the voice of his parents." Deuteronomy 21 is composed of a set of disparate laws relating to murder, war and family affairs. While there appears to be no unifying element to the chapter as such, vv. 18-23 form a fairly well-defined pericope: the death of the son (vv. 18-21) and his subsequent treatment (vv. 22-23).

That the son is "stubborn" and "rebellious" is instructive in itself, because these are terms characteristic of Israel's resistance of and apostasy from Yahweh's lordship in the wilderness and afterwards. Thus, while the son's behavior was in the first instance confined to a household, its implicit threat would be against the security and continuity of the covenant community at large. His deportment is all the more grievous because of its specific nature, that is, disobedience to parents, which, according to Deut 27:16, *ipso facto* incurs Yahweh's curse. He is further characterized as "a glutton and a drunkard," an index to the kind of life led by one who has rejected not only his parents but Yahweh as his God (cf. Prov 23:20). In light of Matt 11:19; Luke 7:34, "glutton and drunkard" may have become a stereotyped idiom for "apostate" by the first century. But be that as it may, "glutton and drunkard" is juxtaposed to "obey," which throughout the OT and Jewish literature uniformly signals covenant fidelity.

---

[35] Bruce points out that Deut 21:23 is connected to Deut 27:26 by means of the device named *gezerah shawah* ("equal category"), which depends on the presence of a common term in the two texts brought together ("Curse," 30).

GALATIANS CHAPTER THREE

After the evil had been purged from Israel by the death of this man (v. 21), the corpse was to be hanged on a tree or wooden post as an example to others (cf. Num 25:4; Josh 10:26-27; 2 Sam 21:6-9). This is not crucifixion as such, simply because the person was affixed to the tree after death. Moreover, the body was to be buried on the same day as the capital punishment, not left to suffer the further degradation of being consumed by scavengers. Even so, the hanged man was nothing less than the "curse" or "repudiation" of God, whose severity of punishment was reserved for individuals who had cursed God and in turn must incur his curse (cf. Job 2:9). The issue was not that of infringing this or that peculiarity of the Torah, but rather the repudiation of Yahweh himself, along with his chosen people. This is why the hanged man suffered a formal and terminal separation from the community of God's people.

It is in just this role that Paul casts Christ. Here is *the ultimate role reversal—the cursing of the Messiah by the Torah.*[36] By definition, the Davidic king was the representative of Yahweh and the embodiment of his righteousness. Yet as startling as it must have been, Paul consigns his Messiah to the curse that befell the apostate of Deut 21:23.[37] The Messiah is treated by Israel as an outcast and thus brings the curses of Deuteronomy to a climax; but in the process, he liberates his new people from the "bondage" which still curses the Judaizers.[38] In his own words in 2 Cor 5:21: "He made Him who knew no sin to be sin on our behalf, so that we might become the righteousness of God in Him" (NASB).

That the notion of the Messiah bearing the curse was scandalous in the extreme is illustrated vividly by Trypho's rejoinder to Justin:

---

[36] See further Morland, *Rhetoric*, 182-233; McLean, *Christ*, 113-40. Hahn would appear to be correct in connecting the cross with the binding (*Aqedah*) of Isaac in Genesis 22 by way of typology ("Covenant," 96-97). See on 3:15, 16.

[37] Bruce maintains that Paul omits the words "by God" after "cursed" (in the LXX) because he wanted to avoid the suggestion that Christ on the cross by God, an idea, he thinks, that would be difficult to square with Christ's endurance of the cross as his supreme act of obedience to God. But this does not work for at least two reasons. For one, the omission of "by God" could be because it was so obvious from Deut 21:23 that the individual was "the curse *of God*" (Hebrew text). Two, there is the *prima facie* meaning of this verse: Christ "became a curse for us." Whose curse would he have become other than God's?

[38] Given the background of covenant curse assumed by Paul, it is very plausible to think that Paul is claiming that "those of works of the law" are cursed like Israel, which is still in exile, because they are not "in Christ," who exhausted the curse and ushered in the age of blessing and restoration, in spite of B. W. Longenecker's doubts, (*Triumph*, 137-39). See the second section note to 1:1.

> Sir, these and suchlike passages of Scripture compel us to await One who is great and glorious, and takes over the everlasting kingdom from the Ancient of Days as Son of man. But this your so-called Christ is without honor and glory so that he has even fallen into the uttermost curse that is in the Law of God, for he was crucified (*Dialogue with Trypho*, 31-32, quoted by Garland, "Defense," 176).

Yet Garland's observation says it all *vis-à-vis* Paul's Christian convictions as forged on the Damascus Road: "Paul has made a theological about-face and now saw that curse in an utterly new light. It was a sign of God's love and of Jesus giving himself for him (2:20), and not only for him but for all, Jews and Gentiles alike" (ibid.).

In summarizing the significance of Gal 3:10-13, the key to its meaning resides in the phenomenon of role reversal, whereby, in light of the Christ-event and the presence of the eschatological Spirit, fidelity to the God of Israel has been redefined. At one time, to cling tenaciously to the law was the indispensable element of fidelity to God. However, given that Jesus the Messiah, for Paul, has abrogated the Torah, and considering that the Galatian believers received the Spirit by "the hearing of faith," not "works of the law," Zealot-like devotion to the law is now considered by the apostle to be the sin of sins—apostasy, consisting in infidelity to the salvific plan of God for "the ends of the ages" (1 Cor 10:11).

The passage contains two pivotal words: "life" and "curse." "Life" is the reward of the righteous Israelite's faith(fulness). In the first instance, this life is continued blessing in the land, including health, prosperity, family and friends, etc. In the larger perspective, however, life is expanded to include "eternal life," particularly as Paul regards "life" to be the extension to others of the resurrection life of Christ. Correspondingly, "curse" is to be defined as the death penalty reserved for the renegade to the covenant. Such a one was not permitted to live in the land, the place of God's blessing, and could not, therefore, attain to the life of the age to come. The curse was, most pointedly, "the curse of the law," that is, "The curse of the Law is the curse which the Law brings and which, in this sense, the Law itself is" (Betz, *Galatians*, 149). Both life and cursing (death) combine to form a complex whole, and both carry clear covenantal overtones: "'life' is the chief blessing of the covenant, as death is its chief curse" (Wright, *Climax*, 149). Both are developed with respect to the opponents in

Galatia: they must bear the curse of exclusion from the bliss of the age to come.[39]

As regards Paul's invocation of the cursing passages in particular, Deut 21:23; 27:26 correspond to his own curse of Gal 1:8-9, which could be rendered: "Cursed be any man who is fundamentally disloyal to the gospel" (Bligh, *Galatians*, 257). There is, one might say, not only "the curse of the law," but as well "the curse of the gospel," a curse pronounced against those who would revert to the law. So ironically, the curse of the gospel is the eschatological curse of the law imposed on those who prefer it over the Christ of Paul's proclamation.[40] But the Judaizers are not only cursed by Paul's gospel as apostates, they are, as it were, "ministers of sin" (2:17). They not only reject this gospel, but actively promote defection from it to their "other gospel." They, in other words, are in the same class as an angel who might conceivably preach such a gospel and who are for that reason anathema.

It is just role reversal resulting from the eschatological situation that opens an avenue of understanding to the problem posed by Luther, that is, whereas Gal 3:10a pronounces a curse upon anyone who would attempt to live by the Torah, the biblical text to which Paul appeals, Deut 27:26, affirms just the opposite: the curse falls not on those who do the Law, but on those who *fail* to do it (Gal 3:10b). My explanation is that there is an irony involved in Paul's assertion and its biblical support. That is to say, in their very keeping of the law the opponents have not kept it, because

---

[39] Hays justifiably rejects the notion that Paul, in writing of the curse, is asserting the unfulfillability of the Law. That is to say, those who try to keep the Law are under a curse because they are bound to fall short of perfect obedience and thus incur God's wrath. Normally, I would add, this reading is defended by the evocation of a "suppressed premise," namely, the law required perfect obedience, but no one can actually do such a thing. However, comments Hays: "This is such a ridiculous caricature of Judaism...that it could hardly have been taken seriously as a persuasive argument in Paul's time. If Paul had made such claims, the rival Missionaries could easily have refuted him by pointing out that the Law makes ample provision for forgiveness of transgressions through repentance, through the sacrificial system, and through the solemn annual celebration of the Day of Atonement. In fact, however, Paul does not say that it is impossible to obey the Law, although this supposition has been read into the text by many generations of Christian interpreters" (*Galatians*, 257).

[40] Paul's "curse" (*anathema*) is equivalent to the Hebrew *hērem*, sacred cursing (e.g., Lev 27:28-29; Deut 7:26; 30:7; Josh 6:17-18; 7:1, 11-13). From his perspective, those who "pervert the gospel of Christ" (1:7) ought to receive the same treatment as that meted out to Christ by their non-Christian Jewish compatriots. In their case, however, the curse is that of the new covenant. Paul picks up on the language of the Torah, but his application is within the framework of his gospel.

they have not "upheld" it in its eschatological design to point Israel to Jesus of Nazareth as the one who has done away with the barriers of separation between nations.[41] Their "infidelity" thus consists in their retention of a Torah which *ipso facto* was nationalistically restrictive.

To state it yet another way, it is because the opponents retain their identity as Jews of the Mosaic stripe that they have failed to "do the law;" it is because they are "in the law" and "of works of the law" that they are condemned by the Torah's curse. Therefore, given Paul's set of assumptions, Deut 27:26 can be placed in service because doing the law is now tantamount to not doing the law. Since the turning of the ages, to live by the law is a failure to keep the law! In a word, the opponents are apostates in a newly (re)defined eschatological sense.

Calvert-Koyzis is correct, then, to pose the issue in these terms: Who is the true monotheist? Of course, belief in the one God was at the core of everything that Judaism and the Judaizers stood for. Yet given their determination to bring Gentiles under the law, the opponents have effectively abandoned their biblical monotheism.

> Abraham's faith was in the promises of God that eventually included the Gentiles. The Judaizers have lost their fidelity to God because they have not really believed in the God of Abraham. In their zeal to inculcate the badges of Jewish nationalism, the Judaizers no longer show their faithfulness to the God through whom Gentiles were eventually included in the people of God through Christ. In this new eschatological age, the Judaizers have locked themselves into the old ways that deny true fidelity to the God of Abraham who fulfilled his promise through the inclusion of the Gentiles into the people of God as Gentiles (*Paul*, 98-99).

In other words, those who view the law as the paradigm of the new age are the antipode of Abraham, who was the first anti-idolater and monotheist.

---

[41] T. L. Carter (*Paul*, 113) finds this explanation unconvincing because, as he writes, Deut 27:26 defines transgression in terms of non-observance of the requirements of Torah. I can only reiterate that because of the eschatological situation, observance of Torah has become non-observance in the intended sense of Deuteronomy, namely, infidelity. Carter has failed to appreciate the irony of the situation.

Paul has radically revised what it meant to be a descendant of Abraham. Rather than Abraham exemplifying the ideal Jew who believed in the one God and obeyed the law, particularly circumcision, the descendant of Abraham who is now 'in Christ' is justified by his faith in Christ and identified by the Spirit and the fruits thereof. Obedience to the law is now actually a form of idolatry that God's people are to reject for faith in the one God. Paul uses the Abraham traditions for his own ends, providing a new definition of the people of God who are guided not by law, but by the Spirit, and whose faith rests in the one God through whom the promise of Abraham that he would be a blessing to all the nations is brought to fruition in Jesus Christ. The foundational boundary marker for the people of God in Christ is monotheistic faith and the true monotheists are those who reject the law as necessary for membership in God's people just as Abraham rejected idolatry (ibid., 113-14).[42]

14 Verse 14 contains two purpose clauses, both stemming from the proposition that Christ redeemed us from the curse of the law. With these clauses, Paul summarizes in reverse order the argument of 3:1-5 and 3:6-23.

If Christ redeemed "us," that is, Jewish believers, from the curse of the law (v. 13), it was in order that such a blessing "might come to the Gentiles in Christ Jesus." In so saying, Paul concedes that those Jews who now believe in Christ the Messiah were at one time in an apostate condition before God, as born into the world in Adam without the presence of the indwelling Spirit. The law's curse thus threatened them with death (exile). Historically, because of their privileged position in salvation history, it was necessary that believers among the ancient people be redeemed first in order that the benefits of Christ's work might be extended to the nations. This is in accordance with the prophetic outlook for the restoration of Israel and the inclusion of the Gentiles into the kingdom of God (cf. Rom 1:16; Acts 13:46a; and see the section note to vv. 13-14.) And if Jews needed to be liberated from the law's curse, then the Gentile Galatians certainly should resist the pressure to be brought under it!

Longenecker observes that "to the Gentiles" receives the emphasis in Paul's sentence, because the inclusion of the Gentiles is

---

[42] The opening segment of her book (pp. 6-84) is devoted to the portrait of Abraham in Jewish literature as the first convert to monotheism.

the chief point of the Galatian letter. Furthermore, "in Christ Jesus" is Paul's whole gospel in a nutshell, which is not so much argued as presupposed. "Positively," he continues, "'being in Christ' is the connection between Abraham and Gentile Christians; conversely, it is the reality that absolutely negates the Judaizers' attempt to relate Gentile Christians to Abraham by means of Torah observance" (*Galatians*, 123).[43]

"The blessing of Abraham," as stated previously, is that of sonship to God through Christ by virtue of the gift of the Spirit as the believer is now identified as the true seed of Abraham. The phrase is drawn from Gen 28:3-4:

> May God Almighty bless you and make you fruitful and increase your numbers until you become a community of peoples. May he give you and your descendants the blessing given to Abraham, so that you may take possession of the land where you now live as an alien, the land God gave to Abraham.

This blessing is theirs "in Christ Jesus." This is not a proposition the Judaizers would have denied as such; but for them Christ was the servant of the Torah and could not possibly bring the blessing of Abraham to the nations apart from the yoke of the law. For them the blessing could come only through the law as ministered by the Christ.

The second part of the parallelism, introduced by the second purpose clause, states the same objective in different words: "The blessing of Abraham" is rephrased as "The promise of the Spirit."[44] As Ridderbos comments, "The gift of the Spirit is now designated as the content of the promise to Abraham. It is the guarantee or pledge of the perfected redemption which Abraham was promised" (*Galatians*, 128). The Spirit is thereby "*the ultimate content of the Abrahamic promise*" (Hafemann, "Exile," 350, italics his).

That the Spirit was indeed promised is evident from Isa 4:2-6; 11:1-2; 32:15; 42:1; 44:3; 61:1; 63:11; Ezek 36:26-27; 37:14; 39:29; Joel 2:28-29; cf. Acts 1:4; 2:14-21, 33, 38; Rom 5:5; Eph 1:13.[45] The coming of the Spirit is the fulfillment of the long-awaited hope for the age to come. This hope included the expecta-

---

[43] In Galatians, "in Christ" occurs also in 1:22; 2:4, 17; 3:26, 28; 5:6, 10.

[44] The two purpose (*hina*) clauses of v. 14 are coordinate and equal rather than the second being subordinated to the first.

[45] Promise is a leading motif in Galatians (3:16, 17, 18, 21, 22, 29; 4:23, 28).

tion that the Spirit would be poured out "on all flesh," so that his presence signals the arrival of the new age and, therefore, the fulfillment of the Abrahamic blessing for all nations. An especially noteworthy text is Isa 44:3, because of the way it brings together "Spirit" and "blessing."

> For I will pour water on the thirsty land,
>   and streams on the dry ground;
> I will pour my *Spirit* upon your descendants,
>   and my *blessing* on your offspring. (RSV)

In the setting of Isaiah, the "descendants" (*sperma* = "seed") would have been the Israelites, Abraham's physical progeny, who returned from exile. But as ever, Paul transposes matters into the eschatological present, so that the "seed" are now *all* who believe.

Now that the Spirit has come, Paul can make his presence tantamount to the blessing of Abraham for at least two reasons: (1) it is none other than the Spirit, according to Gal 4:5-7, who has secured our adoption as sons and daughters to God, which is another way of saying that we are Abraham's offspring; (2) the reception of the Spirit is equivalent to our being reckoned righteous, as Abraham was (3:6 = Gen 15:6).

> How has God fulfilled the promise to Abraham? The answer is "through the Spirit." Through the Spirit Abraham has gained innumerable children among the Gentiles. The Gentiles have become Abraham's descendants through the Spirit which they have received on the basis of faith of Jesus Christ in whom they believe (Matera, *Galatians*, 125).

It is "we," Jew and Gentile, who have received the promise of the spirit. Dunn comments that the first person plural confirms that Paul takes "all the nations" of v. 8 seriously—"not just Jews, not just Gentiles, but all who have actually received the Spirit, Jews and Gentiles" (*Galatians*, 179). The polemical edge of this is not to be missed. "The effect of Paul's argument," states T. L. Carter, "Again is to identify as righteous those Gentiles outside the law who have received the eschatological Spirit, while his opponents, who adhere to the ethnic boundary of the law, are placed under its curse" (*Paul*, 114).

All this is "through faith." Again, the opponents would not have denied the necessity of faith in Jesus the Messiah. But for Paul faith is always faith alone in Christ, a faith which bypasses the Torah altogether. This well-known character of faith is implied by the presence of definite article (literally, "the faith"). Such faith is so axiomatic in Paul's preaching that in 3:23 he can speak of the coming of "the faith."

Section Notes

10-13 In reaction to the New Perspective, a number of scholars have insisted that Paul's theology demands perfect obedience to the law if one would be saved by it, especially in a passage such as Gal 3:10-13. To one degree or the other, the position is represented by Das, *Paul*, 145-70; id., *Paul and Jews*, 142-48; Gathercole, *Boasting*; Seifrid, "Righteousness Language," 434-38; Schreiner, *Law*. In fairness, none of these scholars would deny that there is an element of ethnic exclusivity about the law, to which Paul objects (e.g., Das, *Paul and Jews*, 149-51). Additionally, it is true that some proponents of the New Perspective have failed to recognize that the law that distinguishes the Jewish people from other nations also places a burden of obedience on them (as conceded in my review of Gathercole [*Defense*, 199-221]). However, it is just the character of the obedience required that forms the crux of the issue: is it sinless perfection or perseverance as complemented by covenantal works? The above exposition has endeavored to argue for the latter. The Judaizers, and Jews generally, would be saved by the law because of their fidelity to it, expecting to be vindicated (justified) in the last judgment just for their steadfastness in the commandments.

Scholars antagonistic to the New Perspective like to fasten on the language of "perfection" in Scripture and Jewish literature, which is interpreted in the quantitative sense of sinlessness, not in its actual *qualitative* sense of "covenant wholeness." The distinction is important. In a document such as 1QS 1:7-8; 3:9b-12, to "walk in perfection in all God's ways" is hardly sinless perfection, but rather a wholehearted commitment to honor the entirety of the Lord's revealed will. Otherwise put, perfection is simply a David-like desire to seek God and follow his commandments with all one's heart (Ps 119:2, 10, 34, 69, 145). See my *Essays*, 361 (= *Defense*, 85). The exposition of Gal 3:10-13 submitted above seeks to root the curse of the law in apostasy, not a lack of "perfection" in the commonly assumed understanding.

10 That the LXX chose "remain" (*emmenō*) for the Hebrew *yaqim* ("uphold") is understandable, given that the verb "has the meaning of remaining within a specified territory" (Schlier, *Galater*, 132). Its selection may reflect the climate in which portions of the translation took place, that is, the necessity of persevering in "the holy covenant" (1 Macc 1:15) in the face of the Hellenistic onslaught. Elsewhere, *emmenō* likewise means "persevere in" (Sir 2:10; 6:20; 11:21 [in parallel to *pisteuō*, "believe"]; 1 Macc 10:26, 27; Philo, *Cong.* 125; Josephus, *Ag. Ap.* 2.257; cf. Num

23:19). See also BDAG, 322-23. Wevers confirms that although *menō* plus *en* does not display the transitive nature of the Hebrew construction of Deut 27:26, the Greek rendering "to abide by" or "persist in" is not far removed from the sense of the original "cause to stand," "establish," "uphold" (*Notes*, 425). Furthermore, in other crucial passages in Deuteronomy, the kindred *menō en*, as it reproduces *debaq b^e* ("cleave to"), denotes dedication to Yahweh and continuance in his ways (e.g., 11:22; 13:4; 30:20; cf. Josh 22:5; 23:8-11).

In these verses, the phrase stands in parallel with the synonymous expressions "keeping the commandments" and "loving Yahweh." Thus, it comes as no surprise that the idea of "remaining"/"abiding"/"cleaving" is taken up by later Jewish literature. Ben Sira, for example, more than once correlates cleaving to God with obedience (e.g., Sir 11:22; 13:4; 30:20). To "cleave" (*debaq*) to God entails dispositions such as love, fear and faith, virtues commended by the scribe throughout his book. The usage carries over into the NT in such passages as John 15:1-11, according to which the disciples must "abide in" (*menō en*) Christ.

12 Gathercole's essay on Lev 18:5 ("Torah") marshals numerous texts to demonstrate that in Jewish interpretation "life" goes beyond the original scope of Leviticus to include the age to come. His findings serve as a corrective to those scholars who would restrict life to the Deuteronomic lengthening of days in the land. In fact, this exegetical tradition forms a transition into Paul's application of Lev 18:5 to eternal life in Christ in Gal 3:12.

On the cautionary side, Gathercole's argument requires qualification in several areas. (1) The promissory and regulatory functions of the Torah are not to be played off against one another (as in his treatment of Bar 4:1), as though both dimensions cannot coexist. (2) As in his *Boasting*, Gathercole posits that there is a "frequent tension" in Jewish literature that salvation is based both on Torah-obedience and God's gracious election. At this point, we need to be informed by Yinger's study (*Paul*), which rightly concludes that there is no actual tension between grace/election and obedience: both exist quite harmoniously side by side. The tension is only in the minds of Western (systematic) theologians. (3) Gathercole maintains that Paul is in dialogue with a Judaism that thought in terms of obedience, final judgment and eternal life, not a Judaism merely organized around sin, repentance, forgiveness, exile and restoration. True enough. But the danger here is one of falsely bifurcating categories that actually overlap to a considerable degree. In particular, obedience resulting in eternal life is focused precisely on the return from exile, when the definitive forgiveness of sins would take place (Jer 31:34). In any event, obedience, in Jewish thinking, is not tantamount to "earning salvation" or "legalism," but rather the fulfillment of covenant responsibilities, which is tantamount to faithfulness to the God of the covenant.

13 In time, crucifixion came to be regarded in some circles as fulfilling Deut 21:22-23. Especially striking is 11QTemple 64:6-13, a halakic interpretation of Deut 21:22-23, which explicitly equates crucifixion with Yahweh's curse against *traitors to Israel*. In a similar vein, 4QpNah 5-8 possibly alludes to Deut 21:22-23 in its notice that "the lion of wrath" (Alexander Jannaeus) introduced into Palestine the practice of hanging "living men, which was never done before in Israel." Fitzmyer ("Crucifixion," 498-507; "Paul," 607-9), in agreement with Yadin (*Scroll*, 1.373-79), accepts the linkage of the two passages from the Scrolls and concludes that crucifixion was in fact favored by some Jews as a means of execution of criminals—and both passages seek to justify this method of capital punishment by an application of Deut 21:22-23. See also Wilcox, "Tree," 88-90; O. Betz, "Jesus," 81-85; Zias/Charlesworth, "Crucifixion," 277-79; Bruce, "Curse," 31.

Scholars such as Das (*Paul and Jews*, 47) and Fredriksen ("Judaism," 250) maintain that there is nothing in Deut 21:23 that automatically compels the conclusion that one who hangs on a tree is under God's curse. Das in particular cites 2 Sam 21:12 (the case of Saul and Jonathan) and Josephus *Ant.* 13.14.2.380 (the crucifixion of the eight hundred Pharisees crucified by Alexander Jannaeus) as evidence that Jews did not regard the tree as such as God's curse. Fair enough, especially given the divergent contexts in which the tree/crucifixion is found. But apart from the neglect of the passages cited in the previous paragraph, Deut 21:23 itself is not ambiguous: the recalcitrant "glutton and drunkard" bears the curse of capital punishment because of his apostasy and then is subjected to the emblem of that curse—attachment to a tree.

13-14 The scope "us" in v. 13 has always been disputed. It can be taken inclusively, so as to embrace Gentiles, or exclusively, with Paul's sights set on redeemed Jews. The line of interpretation pursued here is that the reference is exclusive: believing Israel is first redeemed in order that this redemption might be extended to the Gentiles. Above, reference was made to two key passages. The well-known Rom 1:16 speaks in terms of a priority: "To the Jew first and also to the Greek;" and according to Acts 13:46a, it is Paul who says, "It was necessary that the word of God should be spoken first to you" (RSV). It was Donaldson ("Curse") who originally argued that there are two steps between "cross" and "Gentiles:" "Christ through the cross redeemed Israel from the curse of the law so that the blessing of Abraham might come to the Gentiles in Christ Jesus" (ibid., 97). Donaldson schematically lays this pattern out as follows (ibid., 98):

a) *Israel's plight*
- under the curse of the law
- confined under the law
- under law as slaves of the elemental spirits

b) *Christ identifies with Israel's plight*
- he became a curse for us
- faith/Christ came
- born under the law

c) *In order to redeem Israel from this plight*
- Christ redeemed us
- now that faith has come we are no longer under a pedagogue
- to redeem those under the law

d) *With the result that Gentiles share in salvation on equal terms with Jews*
- so that the blessing of Abraham might come to the Gentiles in Christ Jesus, so that we (Jews and Gentiles) might receive the promise of the Spirit through faith
- for in Christ Jesus you are all (Jews and Gentiles) sons of God through faith
- so that we (Jews and Gentiles) might receive adoption as sons

Donaldson buttresses his argument by reference to a pattern, of which, he says, Paul was demonstrably aware, one that corresponds exactly to the pattern of vv. 13-14, namely, "The strand of eschatological expectation that anticipated a massive turning of the Gentiles to Yahweh as a consequence of the end-time redemption of Israel" (ibid., 98-99). He notes that the expectation of the participation of the Gentiles in eschatological salvation is one aspect of a rich and deep-rooted pattern of eschatological hope. The pattern goes back as far as Isaiah and other prophets and is replicated in Jewish literature (notably Tob 14:5-7; *Sib. Or.* 3:701).

Against the dark background of Israel's present plight—dispersion among the nations, oppression by foreign powers, unfaithfulness to the covenant within Israel—a glorious future is depicted for Israel "on that day." Israel's enemies will be overthrown (e.g., Isa 24:23; 29:8; Joel 3:9-21; Mic 4:11-13; Zech 14:12-15; *Pss. Sol.* 17:24, 32; *2 Apoc. Bar.* 72:1-6), Jerusalem will be restored and glorified (e.g., Isa 2:2-4/Mic 4:1-3; Isa 60:1-22; Jer 31:23, 38-40; Ezek 17:22-24, 40-48; Zech 8:1-23; 14:10-11, 20-21; *1 Enoch* 90:28-29; *Jub.* 1:15-17; Bar 5:1-4; *2 Apoc. Bar.* 4:2-4), the scattered exiles will be gathered to Zion (e.g., Jer 31:1-25; Ezek 20:33-44; Isaiah 35; Zech 8:7-8, 20-23; Bar 4:36-37; 5:5-9; *Pss. Sol.* 11:1-3; 17:50; *Jub.* 1:15-17; *Tg. Jer.* 31:23; *Tg. Isa.* 4:3; 6:13), Yahweh and/or his anointed will be enthroned in universal sovereignty (e.g., Isa 24:23; 52:7; Ezek 17:22-24; 20:33, 40; 34:11-16, 23-31; 43:7; Mic 4:6-7; 5:2-4; Zech 14:8-11; *Jub.* 1:28; *Pss. Sol.* 17:23-51), and his people will enjoy untold blessings (e.g., Isa 25:6-10a; 30:23; 35:5-6; 61:6; Jer 31:12; Joel 2:26; Amos 9:13-15; *1 Enoch* 90:32-38; *Pss. Sol.* 17:28-31; *Sib. Or.* 111:702-9, 741-60).

The Gentiles frequently appear in this picture. Sometimes their role is depicted in negative terms: judgment by Yahweh and servitude to Israel (e.g., Isa 18:7; 60:1-22; 66:18-21; Hag 2:21-22; *Pss. Sol.* 17:32-34; *2 Apoc. Bar.* 72:1-6; *Tg. Isa.* 25:6-10). But just as often, the Gentiles are depicted positively as sharing with Israel in eschatological blessing. They forsake their false gods and turn to Yahweh, they join in the eschatological procession to Zion, and they participate in the final banquet (e.g., Isa 2:2-3/Mic 4:1-2; Isa 25:6-10a; 56:6-8; Zech 8:20-23; Tob 13:11; *1 Enoch* 90:30, 33; *Sib. Or.* 111:710-23, 772-76; LXX Isa 54:15; LXX Amos 9:12). See Schnabel, "Israel," 39-42; id., *Mission*, 67-173. The important thing to observe is that in this eschatological scenario, the inclusion of the Gentiles in salvation is one by-product of Yahweh's final deliverance of Israel. There is, then, a striking formal similarity between this picture and the sequence of salvation in Gal 3:13-14, which Donaldson proceeds to demonstrate in more detail (ibid., 100-7).

This same pattern of Israel's release from exile and consequent Gentile salvation is also taken up by Wright, *Climax*, 137-56. To reduce his argument to its essence, three elements are envisaged. (1) The expectation of eschatological pilgrimage: Israel's restoration leads to Gentile salvation. (2) Christ as Israel's representative undergoes the curses of the covenant (exile) and his resurrection is Israel's restoration; (3) The Gentile mission based on Christ's work. In my view, this reading of Gal 3:13-14 is entirely satisfying and entirely in accord with the prophetic expectation of Israel's redemption ("us," v. 13) as the basis for Gentile inclusion in the people of God ("we," v. 14).[46]

D. The Law and the Promise (3:15-18)

The argument of these verses is apparently intended to take up and answer a piece of logic on the part of the opponents. That logic was to the effect that an earlier revelation is to be modified by a later one.[47] The Judaizers firmly believed in the promise to Abraham and its ultimate realization. However, they likewise believed that the universality of the Abrahamic covenant had to be qualified by the Torah, thus rendering the Gentiles Torah-keepers before they could lay claim to sonship to Abraham. Paul here argues the other way around: it is the earlier revelation (covenant) that takes priority over the later. Once the bond with the patriarch was set in place, it could not be effectively nullified by a subsequent administration.

---

[46] Donaldson subsequently changed his mind (*Paul*, 191-94), arguing now that Paul did not in fact envision the redemption of Israel as having taken place. But he was right the first time.

[47] See Longenecker, *Galatians*, xcv-xcvi.

15 Paul still acknowledges the Christian character of his readers by addressing them as "brothers." He has not given up on them yet, even though they may be confused Christians. He speaks to them "in a human manner" (*kata anthrōpon*).[48] NASB renders: "I speak in terms of human relations," while NIV has: "Let me take an example from everyday life." The example cited from everyday life is that of a will or a covenant (*diathēkē*). It is disputed whether the reference is to a last will and testament in the Greco-Roman environment or to a Hebrew covenant made between human beings. On the one side, Paul does argue pervasively from the OT; yet, on the other, he uses familiar Hellenistic legal terms: "ratify" (*kuroō*), "nullify" (*atheteō*) and "add a codicil" (*epidiatassomai*). The problem with the latter suggestion is that Greek and Roman law did make provision for a testament to be changed at any time.[49] This leads some scholars to suggest that the reference could be to a Jewish institution called the *mattenat bari*, which could not be altered (see Kuula, *Law*, 97, n. 2). There are difficulties in both directions, which has led to an acute exegetical impasse.[50]

But all in all, the strongest argument can be made for *diathēkē* in the sense of covenant, and specifically God's covenant with Abraham. Hahn's study of this verse proceeds from the basis that, in the Near Eastern context, self-malediction or self-curse is of the essence of the covenant making process ("Covenant," 85). In the Bible itself, the most famous example is that of Gen 15:17-21, where Yahweh invokes self-cursing on himself if he does not bring to pass his promises to Abraham.[51] Such being the case, Paul's statement that "no one annuls or supplements even a human *diathēkē* once it is ratified" makes excellent sense, especially as this reading of *diathēkē* coheres with the "covenant logic" of 3:6-18 (ibid., 86). It could be added that *diathēkē* elsewhere in Paul is "covenant," a fact not to be dismissed lightly.[52]

Hahn then recalls that in Genesis there are two distinct covenant-making episodes in the life of Abraham, 15:17-21 and 17:1-27. Moreover, in addition to these incidents, Paul, like other first-

---

[48] See also Rom 3:5; 6:19; 1 Cor 9:8.

[49] See Betz, *Galatians*, 155; Hahn, "Covenant," 81-82.

[50] See Kuula, *Law*, 97-98; Hahn, "Covenant," 81-83.

[51] See Kline, *Oath*, 39-49; Hillers, *Covenant*, 102-6; Williamson, *Abraham*, 121-44; Clements, *Abraham*.

[52] It is likewise relevant the LXX normally renders the Hebrew word for "covenant," *berith*, by *diathēkē*.

century Jews, would have recognized another episode in the Abraham narrative as the ratification of the covenant, namely, the divine oath at the *Aqedah* ("binding") of Isaac (Gen 22:15-18).[53] Drawing upon various texts from the OT, Second Temple Judaism and the NT, Hahn demonstrates that "oath" and "covenant" were considered to be equivalent terms: oath is covenant and covenant is oath (Gen 17:7 and 26:3). Then, quoting T. D. Alexander, Hahn relates: "Following the successful outcome of his testing of Abraham, God confirms with an oath in 22:16-18 what he had earlier promised. *It is this oath which ratifies or establishes the covenant*" (ibid., 90, italics his).[54] Therefore, argues Hahn, Paul must have in mind the covenant ratification of Genesis 22, particularly as it is only 22:16-18 that contains all three elements of the promise to Abraham: (1) ratification by God with a solemn oath; (2) the specification of Abraham and his seed as the beneficiaries of the oath; (3) blessing of the Gentiles. Hahn buttresses his argument with allusions to the *Aqedah* in the nearby context, mainly the connection of the cross to the *Aqedah* in terms of an Isaac typology on Paul's part (ibid., 92-94).

In my estimation, Hahn's data provide the best reading of *diathēkē* as over against the alternatives. But the heart of the matter is simply stated: God established his covenant with Abraham in an irrevocable manner, so that it could never be annulled or allow for add-ons. Paul's logic thus runs counter to that of the law teachers in Galatia, who were arguing precisely that the Mosaic covenant had supplemented the prior covenant with Abraham.[55]

16 Paul states what was obvious to any Jew: the promises were spoken to Abraham and his seed. The word "promise" does not occur in Genesis, but the concept is implied in the Abraham story.

---

[53] The *Aqedah* occupied Second Temple and rabbinic authors to a considerable extent. See Swetnam, *Jesus*, 23-85; Brown, *Death*, 2.1435-44.

[54] Hahn points further to the equivalence of oath and covenant in Gen 21:22-34; 26:26-33; 31:43-54 as corresponding to Gen 22:16-18.

[55] "Paul sees the historical priority of the Abrahamic covenant *vis-à-vis* the Mosaic covenant as revealing the theological *primacy* of God's sworn obligation to bless all nations, over and against Israel's sworn obligation to keep the Sinaitic Torah (v. 17). In other words, Paul argues that since the Mosaic covenant is *subsequent* to the Abrahamic, God's purpose in binding Israel at Sinai to keep the Law (i.e., as Abraham's seed) must be legally *subordinated* to his purpose in binding himself at the Aqedah to bless all the nations (i.e., through Abraham's seed). What God promised to Abraham was not negated by what happened at Sinai" (Hahn, "Covenant," 98).

GALATIANS CHAPTER THREE

Dunn is right that "promise" summarizes the various passages where God says "I will give" (*Galatians*, 183). "Promises" is in the plural because of the multifaceted dimension of what lay in store for the patriarch. McKnight (*Galatians*, 168) lists eight separate promises: (1) offspring; (2) blessing for Abraham; (3) a great name; (4) blessings or cursing, depending on how one treated Abraham; (5) occupancy of the promised land; (6) blessing of Gentiles; (7) God being God to his people; (8) kings descending from Abraham. To the list must be added the gift of the Spirit. Since God fulfills his pledge through the operation of his Spirit, the promise of many descendants is simultaneously the promise of the Spirit, who is the means by which sons of Abraham would be created out of people who had been enslaved.

These promises did not terminate on Abraham alone, because his "seed" also were to inherit everything assured to him in the covenant (Gen 12:7; 13:15; 15:18; 17:8; 24:7).[56] Martyn calls attention to the fact that Paul leaves out two of Genesis 17's major motifs: God's assurance that Abraham and his seed with inherit the land of Canaan and the definition of the covenant as the rite of circumcision to be observed in every generation. "For Paul God's covenantal promise to Abraham consists of only one thing, God's assurance that he will one day bless the Gentiles in Abraham (*Galatians*, 339). Martyn is correct that such a move was certain to have elicited sharp criticism from the Teachers.

Verse 16b plays on the singular "seed" as opposed to the plural "seeds:" "He does not say, 'And to seeds,' as referring to many, but rather to one, 'And to your seed,' that is, Christ" (NASB). In a manner apparently unique to ancient Judaism, Paul identifies Abraham's seed with the Messiah. He is bold enough to claim that Christ was ultimately in view when God made a covenant with Abraham. By virtue of the incarnation, Christ became the fulfillment of what was promised to the patriarch. "Paul wanted to show that the greater fulfillment of the promise is not biological but Christological" (George, *Galatians*, 247). It is well-known that the Greek word *sperma* (Hebrew *zera'*) is a collective noun and is rightly translated as "descendants" (the targums usually render the Hebrew "seed" by the Aramaic "sons"). For this reason, Paul has often been charged with exegetical slight of hand when he plays on the singular of the term.

---

[56] As especially evident in the LXX, the terms "seed" and "covenant" are frequently correlated in Gen 17:1-11 (see Betz, *Galatians*, 156).

But several factors must be taken into account. *First*, "seed," in the first instance, did refer to an individual, Isaac and thereafter to Abraham's more remote descendants. Hahn rightly maintains that it is not coincidental that the narrative of Genesis 22 stresses three times that Isaac is the *one* or *only* son of Abraham (vv. 2, 12, 16), pointedly excluding Ishmael and any other progeny ("Covenant," 96). The connection with Isaac is only strengthened by Paul's connection of the cross with the *Aqedah*, the "binding" or sacrifice of Isaac. His Isaac typology is here fully operative (ibid., 96-97). By these means, then, it is possible to draw a direct line from Isaac to Christ, the latter being the eschatological Isaac or seed of Abraham. *Second*, Paul is simply pointing out that the singular word "seed," rather than "children" or "descendants," is appropriate because Israel had always believed that the ultimate messianic blessing would come through a single individual. *Third*, it is precisely the collective character of the noun that serves Paul's purposes so well (cf. Rom 4:13-18). Abraham's seed *is* Christ, though not Christ as a private person. Rather, Christ is the representative head of a people (cf. Rom 5:12-19).

V. 16 thus paves the way for vv. 26 and 29, where the apostle declares that *all*, Gentile as well as Jew, are the sons of God and the seed of Abraham through faith in Christ Jesus. "The intention is not to deny that Abraham's seed is multitudinous in number, but to affirm that Christ's preeminence as that 'seed' carries with it the implication that all 'in Christ' are equally Abraham's seed" (Dunn, *Galatians*, 185). An important corollary is that "Christ is the 'seed' because, and insofar as, the promised single family of Abraham is brought into being in and through him and him alone. It therefore finds its identity in him. He is its incorporation" (Wright, *Climax*, 166). The oneness of the seed, that is, Christ, thus insures the oneness of the body of Christ, a oneness which was in danger of being destroyed by the opponents in Galatia.

17 Paul's point is that the law, which came so long after the Abrahamic covenant, does not invalidate the promise.[57] Since the covenant with Abraham is irrevocable, the law cannot introduce any changes in God's arrangement with the patriarch. Therefore, "The promise stands firm and the mode of relating to God is faith rather than works of the law" (McKnight, *Galatians*, 167). It was necessary to insist on this because the Judaizers had qualified the former

---

[57] The figure 430 is based on Exod 12:40 (as is Josephus, *Ant.* 2.318). The number 400 in Gen 15:13; Acts 7:6; Josephus, *Ant.* 2.204 is rounded.

revelation to Abraham in light of the later revelation to Moses, thereby constricting the promise to those who submitted to circumcision and the Mosaic regulations. But the promise was that Abraham would have a universal seed, and as long as the law stood, that promise was incapable of fulfillment. For all practical purposes, then, Paul's opponents had nullified the previously ratified covenant by their demand of law observance on the part of the Gentiles. We recall as well that Jewish tradition had Abraham keeping the law before its inception on Mount Sinai (see above on 3:6). But Paul, as Betz rightly notes, turns the traditional Jewish view upside down: "Instead of attributing to Abraham a foreknowledge of the Torah, Paul deprives the Sinai Torah of any significance" (*Galatians*, 159).

18 This contrary-to-fact conditional sentence is supportive of the previous statement and serves to summarize the argument of vv. 15-17. "Because the inheritance was something God gave to Abraham by speaking a promise to him, the source of that inheritance cannot be the later-arriving law" (Martyn, *Galatians*, 342). Consequently, continued membership in the community of the "later-arriving law" cannot insure the fulfillment of said promise; such is an exercise in futility. Here, Paul clearly sets promise over against law, that is, the entire Mosaic system. In light of v. 21a, the contrast cannot be absolute. Indeed, the giving of the law, it could be argued, was to the end that the promise be realized after all (v. 19b). But the Judaizers' mistake was that of retaining the law after it had served its purpose, thereby making it the *sine qua non* receiving the inheritance. For all practical purposes, the law, for them, was the source of the inheritance (*ek nomou*), since it could be had by no other means.

As ever in this letter, Paul reasons historically and eschatologically: the promise was prior to law and, therefore, takes precedent over it. The inheritance cannot be "from the law," because it was the salvation-historical function of the promise to Abraham, not the Torah, to vouch it safe to latter-day people. Once more, Paul's logic is seen to be 180 degrees away from that of his opponents. Bluntly put, for him Abraham takes precedent over Moses.[58] In point of fact, *Paul is dispensing with Moses altogether.*

This "inheritance" (*klēronomia*) is all of what was "graciously given" (*kecharistai*) to Abraham (see on v. 16), centering on an

---

[58] As further intimated by the word order of 18b: "To Abraham" is placed forward in the emphatic position.

innumerable seed, including uncircumcised Gentiles, and the gift of the Spirit. "In a word, the inheritance is the church-creating Spirit of Christ" (Martyn, *Galatians*, 343). Ultimately, the inheritance entails a new heavens and earth (Isa 65:17), when the "hope of righteousness" (Gal 5:5) is realized.

E. Why the Law (3:19-25)?

So far, Paul has given strong reasons for the Galatians to resist the pressure to submit to the law. But, in thus arguing, the question arises: Why was the law given at all? The Judaizers probably reasoned that Paul has proven too much. From their vantage point, it would have appeared as if he was denying that the law had any purpose at all and, indeed, was asserting that the law was actually contrary to the realization of the promise to Abraham. Paul thus counters their objections by arguing that the Torah had a very definite, though limited, place in the salvation-historical purposes of God.

19 From the foregoing discussion arises the inevitable question, "Why then the law?" Paul's answer is: "It was added because of transgressions until the Seed to whom the promise referred had come." The disputed part of the verse is the statement that the law was added "because of transgressions." This has been understood variously: (1) to restrain transgressions; (2) to identify transgressions; (3) to multiply transgressions or increase the awareness of sins, thus showing humanity its need of a savior (Rom 3:20; 4:15; 5:20); (4) to turn sin into transgression, that is, the law makes it clear that every sin is a sin against God; (5) positively, to provide a way of dealing with transgressions, namely, in the sacrificial system.[59]

All in all, the most satisfactory interpretation is the one that best comports with the words "until the seed should come" and with the proposition of v. 24 that the law was a disciplinarian to bring Israel to Christ. John Brown puts his finger on the issue by remarking that the law was given because of Israel's propensity to idolatry. The Torah was thus "an order of things admirably adapted to preserve them a distinct and peculiar people." The effect of placing the people under the law was "to preserve the revelation of mercy through the Messiah, of which they were the depositaries..." (*Galatians*, 150). Paul, therefore, views the law christologi-

---

[59] See further Hays, *Galatians*, 266; Kuula, *Law*, 135-39.

cally and eschatologically, as designed to restrain the idolatry of Israel until such time as the seed, that is, Christ, should appear. Perhaps "transgressions" (or "trespasses") was chosen instead of "sins" because of the former word's association with the fall of Adam, which was tantamount to an act of idolatry (Rom 5:14, 15, 16, 17, 18). That the noun is in the plural does not detract from the Adamic reference, simply because all infractions of the divine will are ultimately traced back to idolatry (as per Rom 1:18-31).

Over against his opponents, who held to the eternity of the law,[60] for Paul the law had a beginning ("was added") and an end ("until the seed should come"). The law was an important parenthesis between the Abrahamic covenant and the fulfillment of the promises to Abraham in Christ—but a parenthesis nonetheless, a temporary means of God's dealings with the chosen people.

The law was ordained through angels by the hand of an intermediary. That angels were involved in the giving of the law is evident from the LXX of Deut 32:2 and Ps 67:18 (see also *Jub.* 1:27-2:1; CD 5:18; Acts 7:38, 53; Heb 2:2; Josephus, *Ant.* 15.5.3.136; Philo, *Som.* 1.143). The intermediary is, no doubt, Moses, through whose instrumentality the law was ordained (Lev 26:46). The combination of angels and Moses the mediator suggests there is a deliberate contrast with both the Abrahamic covenant, which was spoken by God himself, and the new covenant, which, if we may draw upon Heb 1:2; 2:b, was communicated directly in the Son of God. The Torah, on the other hand, was not given by the one God directly but only through subordinate angelic beings (Betz, *Galatians*, 168, 169-70). Without denigrating the law as such, Paul nonetheless implies that the Mosaic economy is inferior to that of the "administration suitable to the fullness of the times" in Christ (Eph 1:10 [NASB]). "The law is not on the same par with the covenant of promise not only because it was chronologically limited but also because it was handed down by angels with a man acting as a go-between" (George, *Galatians*, 256).

20 This is probably the most difficult sentence in the letter to interpret. Paul writes literally: "The mediator is not of one, but God is one." Commentators tend to reason in terms of the notion of a mediator generally. That is to say, a mediator entails at least one other individual than the principal parties of an agreement. NEB

---

[60] For example, *Bar* 4:1; *2 Apoc. Bar.* 77:15; *1 Enoch* 99:2; Wis 18:4; *Jub.* 1:27; 3:31; 6:17; Josephus, *Ag. Ap.* 2.277; Philo, *Vit. Mos.* 2.3, 14. See further W. D. Davies, *Torah*; Banks, "Role;" Garland, "Defense," 178-79.

approximates this sense by rendering: "An intermediary is not needed for one party acting alone." It is thought that this argues for the inferiority of the law to the Abrahamic promise (as fulfilled in the new covenant), because the issue is one of immediacy and intimacy, lacking in the former and present in the latter. According to Longenecker, "Its point has to do with the inferiority of the Law because of its indirect introduction into the people's existence" (*Galatians*, 142). Witherington agrees "that the Law was given through a mediator certainly suggests a certain separation or distance between the Holy God and the people God has chosen. Intimacy such as Abraham experienced comes only through faith and by grace" (*Grace*, 259).

The problem with this tack is that it fails to perceive the specific point at which Paul is driving. Rather than *a* mediator, Paul has in mind *the* mediator of the old covenant—Moses (v. 19).[61] As Tsang says, Moses goes unnamed not because he is unimportant, but because he is well known (*Slaves*, 108). Once this is understood, the problems of v. 20 mainly disappear. As Wright calls to mind, throughout this context Paul places a premium on the *unity* of the one family of God.[62] Consequently, "one" comprehends *the unified people as now comprised of all nations*—and it is for just this reason that *Moses the mediator* cannot be "of one" or "belong to one" simply because he mediated on behalf of Israel alone, excluding the nations.[63] Moses, therefore, represents a people separated to itself (Num 23:9; 4QMMT C7) rather than one united with the rest of humanity in Christ.[64]

---

[61] Hays (*Galatians*, 267) points to Philo's *Life of Moses* 2.166, where Moses is given the title of "mediator and reconciler."

[62] Wright, *Climax*, 163-64; *Perspective*, 113-14. In eschatological perspective, a passage such as Jer 31:1 probably ran through Paul's mind: "At that time I will be the God of all the families of Israel and they shall be my people," not to mention Gen 12:3: "I will bless those who bless you, and him who curses you I will curse; and by you all the families of the earth shall be blessed."

[63] "Of one" is tantamount to "belonging to one." The same preposition "of" (*ek*) in 3:9-12 consistently designates those who trace their origin and identity to either the period of the law or the period of faith. One may belong to one or the other, but not both at the same time.

[64] In this light, Num 23:9 is striking indeed:
"For from the top of the mountains I see him,
  from the hills I behold him;
  lo, a people dwelling alone,
  and not reckoning itself among the nations!" (RSV).
So is 4QMMT C7: "We have separated ourselves from the multitude of the people [and all their impurity]."

Over against the division implied by the mediatorship of Moses, Paul places the oneness or the unity of God, no doubt alluding to the *Shema* of Deut 6:4 (as he does in Rom 3:30 and 1 Cor 8:6). The theological impact of the contrast is easy enough to understand. Reading Gal 3:20 similarly to Rom 3:30, Wright's conclusion follows inevitably: "Monotheism demands as its corollary a single united family; the Torah, unable to produce this, cannot therefore be the final and permanent expression of the will of the One God" (*Climax*, 170). Consequently, "Paul is saying that Moses, to whom the Galatians are being tempted to look for membership in the true people of God, is not the one through whom that single family is brought about" (ibid., 169).

It must have appeared to Paul's antagonists that his preaching actually repudiated the *Shema*, just because this confession of the pious Israelite articulated loyalty to the true God as opposed to the idolatry of the nations. To the Jewish mind, to do away with the law was *ipso facto* to deny the oneness of Israel's God and open the floodgates to all sorts of pagan corruptions (*Ep. Arist.* 139-42). But Paul reasons the other way around: the law represents a fracturing of the human race and must go in order to restore the original unity of mankind (cf. Eph 2:11-22). The gospel, therefore, preserves the unity of God as surely as the Torah, but it has the incalculable added benefit of bringing the nations together. In fact, it not unreasonable to suppose that the unity of God is better exhibited by Paul's gospel, just because a united people is the mirror image of the God who is one.

By way of confirmation, Hays notes that the oneness of God in v. 20 is to be connected with the singularity of the seed in v. and the oneness of the people of God in v. 28, with the comment:

> The deficiency of the law, therefore, may be related to its divisive character, its inability to bring Jews and Gentiles together into a single new people. The oneness of God can be rightly reflected only in a community unified by the fulfillment of God's promise in Christ (*Galatians*, 267-68).

21 In view of such an apparently negative appraisal of the law, that is, negative to Paul's opponents and possibly the Galatians, another question arises, "Is the law against the promises of God?"[65] The

---

[65] Here is an actual piece of "Pauline rhetoric." As in Romans 6-7 and 9-11, Paul engages his opponents in the synagogue style of debate. As Jeremias explains with regard to Romans: "We see in these objections a piece of living missionary

question is natural enough given the light in which Paul has cast the Torah and its mediator. His reply is the familiar "absolutely not" (*mē genoito*). He denies the antithesis that many would infer from the previous verse by stating: "For if a law had been given that could impart life, then righteousness would certainly have come by the law."

In denying that the law could impart life, Paul apparently drives a wedge between the biblical/Jewish association of life and Torah (Lev 18:5; Deut 6:24; 30:15-20; Prov 3:1-2; 6:23; Sir 17:11 ["the law of life"]; Bar 3:9; 4:1; *Pss. Sol.* 14:2). As Dunn observes, the solution is to be found in the verb "impart life" (*zōopoieō*) (literally, "make alive"). The verb almost always describes a work exclusive to God or his Spirit (2 Kgs 5:7; Neh 9:6; Job 36:6; Ps 71:20; John 6:21, 63; Rom 4:17; 8:11; 1 Cor 15:22, 45; 2 Cor 3:6; 1 Pet 3:8).

> The point is, then, that it was not the law's function to "make alive"; that is a power which only God can exercise. The implication is clear: to exalt the law, in effect, to the status of an angelic power, as though it could fulfil the divine role of making alive, is a mistake. That is not the role intended for the law by God—the passive of "give" indicating God as the giver (Dunn, *Galatians*, 193).

Of particular note is the occurrence of *zōopoieō* in connection with resurrection in 1 Cor 15:22, 45, where "make alive" effectively means to raise from the dead. In thought, we are taken back to Ezekiel 37 and all the prophetic passages that depict Israel's return from exile as a resurrection from the dead (Gowan, *Theology*). Such connotations are probably attached to *zōopoieō* here as well. The work of resurrection that attends release from exile and the enjoyment eternal life is that of God's life-giving Spirit, not Israel's law. Paul will argue in vv. 23-25 that the law's intention was bring Israel to Christ and to that whole state of affairs he elsewhere denominates a "new creation" (2 Cor 5:17). Therefore, the

---

endeavor. He preaches before Jews. At first they listen to him. But soon comes a point where they cannot let him continue. He is interrupted. Objections and protests come from all sides. We are witnesses of the discussion" ("Gedankenführung," 270). Ridderbos adds that Paul provides us with a clear illustration of how he "argued" (*dialegomai*) in the synagogues of the Diaspora (Acts 17:2, 17; 18:4, 19; 19:8, 9) (*Romeinen*, 12). In this letter too, in repreaching his gospel to the Galatians Paul interacts with his opponents in the manner to which he and they were accustomed.

law itself can never make alive but only point to the life-giver, the one who is our righteousness (Isa 61:10; Jer 23:6; 33:16; 2 Cor 5:21).

If such was the intended the role of the law, then "righteousness would certainly have come *from* (*ek*) the law." As noted before (on 2:16 and 3:7), the preposition *ek* marks belonging to a realm or sphere (the "partisan" usage). Thus, a righteousness "from the law" is one that comes by way of participation in law-community, where the Torah holds sway. For the Judaizers, that simply stood to reason. For them, righteousness was most decidedly "of the law of God" (*T. Dan* 6:11).[66] Yet Paul is thinking eschatologically, as eschatology has a bearing on both christology and pneumatology. One's standing in the new covenant is a reality made possible by the life-giving work of Christ and the Spirit.[67] Such standing in God's new covenant could not possibly come by the law, because, according to v. 12, "the law is not of faith," that is, the law and Christian faith belong to completely separate historical eras, and the law was never designed to take the place assigned to the Spirit.

In once again invoking the eschatological dimension of the law, Paul implies that his detractors in Galatia have aligned themselves with the wrong age. For this reason, "The mistake of Paul's Jewish-Christian opponents was to assume in effect that righteousness, acceptance by God and sustaining them within the relationship with God, came 'from the law' rather than from the life-giving Spirit" (Dunn, *Galatians*, 193-94). In spite of what they might have claimed, the Jewish Christian missionaries made the law usurp the place of the Spirit in the long-term purposes of God.

It is just here that the discrepancy between the apostle and the Jewish teachers is most evident. For the latter, law and life go together, because the one is inconceivable apart from the other. They

---

[66] There is every reason to believe that Paul's rivals would have endorsed fully the outlook of their forebears, who said that Israel was to "walk in *obedience* to the law" (CD 7:7), that is, "To observe *the whole law* of the Lord" (*T. Judah* 26:1; *T. Gad* 3:1; *T. Asher* 6:3), to "walk in perfection in *all His ways*" (CD 2:16), "*Obeying all His instructions*" (CD 7.5; cf. 1QS 1.3-5), "To act according to *the exact tenor of the Law*" (CD 4:8), and to "Cling to the covenant of the fathers" (1QS 2:9; 1 Macc 2:50). In short, Israel was to observe 'The righteousness of the law of God' (*T. Dan* 6:11) and live "The life of righteousness" by walking in "The ways of truth and righteousness" (4 Macc 13:24; Tob 1:3). It was as true of first-century Judaism as of the Maccabean martyrs: "We should truly bring shame upon our ancestors if we did not live in obedience to the Law and take Moses as our counselor" (4 Macc 9:2).

[67] On the connection of life and Spirit, see Hubbard, *Creation*, 116-22, 125-26.

would not have though in terms of "either/or," but "both/and." If life is to be had by clinging to and upholding the law (Lev 18:5; Deut 4:1, 10, 40; 5:29-33; 6:1-2, 18, 24; 7:12-13; 27:26; 30:15-20), then the parameters set by the law must be the arena and source of righteousness. This particularly so as life is the outcome of righteousness, as encapsulated in the command: "This do and live." But Paul's reasoning is to the opposite effect: the law was not given for the purpose of making alive; therefore, righteousness cannot of the law. This take on the law is only to be expected by this time. Given its temporal function in salvation history, the Torah was meant to be a signpost to Christ and the Spirit, the actual life-givers. It was a means to an end rather than an end in itself. Otherwise stated, the life proffered by the law was existence in the land, but not the ultimate reality of a new heavens and new earth (see above on v. 12). Paul, then, as ever, is thinking eschatologically—beyond Israel in the land—with his sights set on the "latter days" and the actual procurement of the promise to Abraham, the inheritance.

Moreover, it is not to be overlooked that although "this do and live" functioned as the working principle of the Mosaic covenant, the nation by and large did not "do" and consequently did not "live." Rather, they suffered the pain of exile because of disobedience (idolatry). Rom 8:3 simply nails down the point: "The law is weak through the flesh." Israel thus provides an object-lesson to the world: it is only in Christ that one can be a "doer of the law" and thus live (Rom 2:6-13).[68] At the end of the day, the law, for all its invaluable and indispensable service in salvation history, remains "Christotelic" (Enns, *Inspiration*, 154). As regards righteousness, Christ is the goal (*telos*) of the law (Rom 10:4).

22 Rather than there being a life-giving law, "the Scripture" (*hē graphē*) has shut up all things under sin. Since "the Scripture" is practically tantamount to "the law," Paul invites his readers to hear what the Torah itself says. The verb "shut up" (*sugkleiō*) means to confine, imprison or lock up. In light of the following verse, which assigns a confining function to the law, "the Scripture" is probably best taken as a synonym for "the law." The law's role, therefore, was one of imprisoning the entire (old) creation—"all things"— under the power, sway and condemnation of sin, so that the promise might be realized *solely by faith in Christ* (*ek pisteōs Christou*) (cf. Rom 11:32). As Witherington suggests, it is possible to take this statement apocalyptically: "Paul would mean that all of the

---

[68] See my *Faith*, 44-71.

created order, including humans, was under the power of sin and feeling the effects of the fall" (*Grace*, 260).

Various commentators propose that Paul has in view the knowledge of sin that is revealed or at least intensified by the law, as though such knowledge was lacking beforehand (e.g., Longenecker, *Galatians*, 144-45). However, Kuula is right that the plain meaning of the text is that "the Scripture" plays a *confining*, not revelatory, role (*Law*, 161). That is to say, its function was to detain the old creation, of which Israel was part and parcel, in a state of condemnation until such time as God would deal with sin in Christ. Bluntly put, the law itself provided no way out of the human predicament and no ultimate salvation. Its design was but to pave the way for the one who make an end of sin. The equivalent thought is expressed in Rom 3:25: sin was not finally atoned for until the display of God's righteousness by means of the blood of Christ. As Ebeling so insightfully comments, instead of a protective fence for Israel, Paul turns the law into the opposite:

> The Jewish understanding of the Torah uses the metaphor of a fence to express this idea. The Torah is for Israel a protective fence. It prevents contact with everything unclean, which is kept outside, and it restrains the desire to break out and overstep the salutary boundary. It would almost be possible to say that Paul takes a polemical stance toward this image of the Torah as a beneficent fence by radicalizing it and thus transforming it into its opposite. It is not the law but the sin preceding the law that must be first taken into account. And it is no longer a protective fence but a prison from which there is no escape. Within this transformed metaphor the law does not have the function of partially breaking through the walls of sin, making a breach in them to open a way of escape. On the contrary, the law has the function of an additional attendant, a prison guard who makes those who live in the custody of sin fully aware of where they are (*Truth*, 194).

Paul thus views the period of the law as one of confinement (bondage) under the power of sin (cf. Rom 3:9), awaiting the liberation of the people of God which was to take place when the promise was given by faith (cf. again v. 19, according to which the law was added to provide a hedge for idolatrous Israel). By imprisoning the old world "under sin," God meant to preclude every other means of salvation than the fulfillment of the promise *in Christ*. Martyn puts it eloquently:

> In short, when the Law seemed to be collusion with Sin, imprisoning the whole of creation under Sin's power, it actually served the purpose of God. It did that, however, only by its role as a jailer. It shut every door that might seem to lead from the human orb to the possession of God's promise, and in *that way* it played its part in God's plan to make his own entry into the human orb. And the intention behind both imprisonment and divine entry was God's determination to give the promise—thus making things right—by the faith of Christ (*Galatians*, 361, italics his).

23 Verse 23 continues and amplifies the thought of the previous verse. If v. 22 stated that "the Scripture" shut up "all things," the entirety of the old creation, under the power of sin, the present verse maintains that those who were anticipating the realization of the promise ("we") were themselves subject to the law's imprisoning role, with a view to the coming of faith in its eschatological manifestation. The climax of Israel's history has transpired in the case of Paul and all likeminded Jewish Christians: in them the law has achieved its overall salvation-historical goal.[69] This imprisonment was in effect until the coming of "the faith." The reference is to the faith just mentioned in v. 22, that is, belief in Christ. The law, therefore, is terminated once it has served its purpose of pointing Israel to Christ. Underlying Paul's thought is the apocalyptic conception of the two ages (cf. 1:4), as indicated by the verbs "coming" and "to be revealed."

24-25 Paul draws a conclusion from vv. 22 and 23: the law was a disciplinarian whose activities had Christ in view. In so doing, he draws on an personage well-known in the Greco-Roman world: the

---

[69] Witherington rightly observes that we are to pay careful attention to the use of pronouns throughout Paul's arguments in chaps. 3-4. "In the 'we' passages Paul is describing the situation of those under the Law, namely Jews, which of course included Paul before his conversion to Christ. In the 'you' passages Paul is directly addressing the Galatians, who were apparently overwhelmingly Gentile in terms of ethnic extraction. Paul is indeed arguing that salvation brought by Christ came to the Jews first, but also that it came to them so that they might fulfill their proper role of being a light to the Gentiles" (*Grace*, 267).

paidagōgos.[70] This "disciplinarian" or "custodian" was a slave who had charge of a youthful male at least into late adolescence. He was not so much a teacher (despite the English derivation of "pedagogue") as one who led a youth to and from school and saw to his care, protection and discipline. For many youths, their experience of the pedagogue could be decidedly unpleasant, and most were glad to be rid of such taskmasters. This pointedly negative connotation of *paidagōgos* is not to be dismissed, especially as the disciplinary role of the law corresponds to its confining function in vv. 22-23. From this perspective, the law is something Israel should have been glad to dispense with.

Nevertheless, there is another side to the Paul's image that is not to be jettisoned. The pedagogue did serve a useful purpose; and by drawing on the metaphor of the disciplinarian, Paul casts the law in just this light.

> Israel was like a child growing up in an evil world: the law gave it the protection it needed from idolatry and the lower moral standards prevalent in the Gentile world; the law thus involved a degree of restriction for Israel and separation from the rest of the world; but it was a temporary role, since the child would grow up, and when that happened there would be no need of the custodial slave and the restrictive rules which separated the growing youth from the rest of the world could be removed (Dunn, *Galatians*, 199).

Paul is careful to specify that the law acted in this capacity until Christ appeared (*eis Christon*), and once he does, it passes off the scene. In the words of Rom 10:4, Christ is the end of the law. The apostle once more denies the eternity of the Torah. The ultimate aim of the law's tutelage was that we might be justified by (from) faith. The law could not achieve this end; "it was only a holding operation until the conditions typified in the case of Abraham (promise before law) could be realized in eschatological fulness with the coming of Christ" (Dunn, *Galatians*, 199). In writing of the law as "our custodian" that "we" might be justified by faith in Christ (*ek pisteōs*), Paul still thinks in terms of his own coming to

---

[70] See, among many, Witherington, *Grace*, 262-67; Longenecker, *Galatians*, 146-48; Lull, "Pedagogue;" Kuula, *Law*, 176-79; Young, "*PAIDAGOGOS*;" id., "Figure;" Gordon, "*PAIDAGOGOS*;" Tsang, *Slaves*, 110-12. See ibid., 105-16, for a detailed treatment of the slavery metaphor of 3:23-26.

Christ. In him and other like-minded Jewish believers the law has achieved its goal.

Verse 25 states the reality that now obtains for the people of God since the coming of Christ: "Now that faith has come, we are no longer under the supervision of the law." "Here Paul delivers the *coup de grâce* to the Judaizers' argument for Gentile Christians to live a lifestyle governed by the Mosaic law" (Longenecker, *Galatians*, 149). By "faith" is meant trust in Jesus Christ apart from the necessity of law observance—faith alone.

F. The Sons of God and the Seed of Abraham (3:26-29)

Paul has now clarified the role of the law: its purpose was to act as a fence around and a guardian over Israel until the coming of Christ. Its passing away in the fullness of time now signifies that all the Galatians are God's sons because the Torah no longer poses a barrier between Jew and Gentile. With law observance no longer a necessity, every believer in Christ is the seed of Abraham and an heir according to promise.

26 The conjunction "for" that begins v. 26 indicates that the following assertion is as much the basis of the argument just completed as its conclusion (Dunn, *Galatians*, 201). That is to say, universal sonship to God was the object in view as Paul penned the words of vv. 21-25. The fact that sonship is no longer restricted to Israel is proof positive that the law has passed off the scene. The phrase "sons of God" is a very familiar one from the OT and Jewish literature.[71] In short, Israel, and Israel only, was the son(s) of God (Exod 4:22-23; Deut 14:1; Isa 43:6; Jer 31:9; Hos 1:10; 11:1; *Jub.* 1:24-25; Sir 36:17; Wis 2:13-18; 5:5; 3 Macc 6:28; 4 Ezra 6:55-59; cf. Sir 4:10; 51:10; 2 Macc 7:34). Paul's startling pronouncement, then, is that "you *all*" (cf. Rom 1:7) are God's sons (and daughters) simply by virtue of faith in Christ. The Torah no longer plays a role in defining and delineating the family of God. Paul's repeated "faith in Christ Jesus" may seem redundant to modern readers, but the apostle will not let go of this formula, because "As 'faith' has replaced the law as the distinctive mark of the 'sons of God', so 'Christ Jesus' has replaced ethnic Israel as the social context of this sonship" (Dunn, *Galatians*, 202).

---

[71] On the whole subject of sonship, see Byrne, *Sons*.

27 Paul now explains how the Galatians became the sons of God, as indicated by the "for" which begins the sentence. They were able to exercise faith in Christ and thus become God's children because of their baptism into Christ by the Holy Spirit. The phrase "baptized into Christ" is a metaphor which originates with John the Baptist's proclamation that the Coming One would baptize in the Holy Spirit and fire (Matt 3:11). Jesus thereafter adapts the concept by applying it to his death (Luke 12:49-50). Paul then uses it of the Spirit's incorporation of believers into Christ (Rom 6:3; 1 Cor 12:13; Col 2:12). Dunn explains that this metaphor is drawn from the ritual act of baptism but is not identical with it. "We may assume that the two moments (ritual act and metaphor) were regularly experienced as one—hence the vitality of the metaphor, and the force of the subsequent theology of sacrament (a spiritual reality in, with and under the physical action)" (*Galatians*, 203). Paul once more appeals to his readers' experience of the Spirit: if they became the sons of God by virtue of Spirit-baptism (in the age of the Spirit [3:3]), it could not have been by "works of the law," and such works could never now define their relationship to and standing before God.

In the second clause, the metaphor changes to that of putting on clothes. The notion of changing clothes was familiar enough for taking on certain characteristics or virtues. But in several passages in the OT the change of clothes stands for the experience of God's salvation (2 Chr 6:41; Job 29:14; Ps 132:16; Isa 52:1; 61:10; Zech 3:3-5), a meaning altogether pertinent to the present context and the other places where Paul draws on the image (see at length, Kim, *Clothing*). Isa 52:1 and 61:10 are particularly striking because of the setting of return from exile in this portion of the prophecy. Because of their endowment with the Spirit, believers have been clothed with the "garments of salvation" and the "robe of righteousness" (Isa 61:10); they have been delivered from the bondage of exile, as it were, and have entered into the blessings of a new creation. This clothing image, as Hays observes, is one of Paul's ways of speaking of union with Christ (2:20). In such a union, those who are "in Christ" share in his divine sonship and take on his character (*Galatians*, 272).

The verb "put on" (NIV: "Have clothed yourselves") "signifies an act of the will—a responding to Christ and a commitment to Christ whereby the life and character (that is, the Spirit) of Jesus is received (henceforth to be manifested in a new way of life), and whereby participation in the *kainē ktisis* [new creation] (6.15), in the new humanity of Christ is granted (3.29)" (Dunn, *Baptism*,

110). Paul thus calls to mind "the personality transformations which the coming of the Spirit had wrought among the Galatians during his ministry" (Dunn, *Galatians*, 205). Elsewhere in Paul "put on" occurs in ethical contexts (Rom 13:14; Eph 4:24; Col 3:10) with a view to eschatological completion (Rom 13:11-14; 2 Cor 5:3).

28 In a manner resembling 1 Cor 12:13, the great practical implication of baptism into Christ is now drawn out; that is, the work of the Spirit has united all believers without distinction in the body of Christ. Paul hereby breaks down the barriers that used to separate individuals and groups. The most obvious divide was between Jew and Gentile (the two "old men" of Eph 2:15). To say "neither Jew nor Greek" means one faith in Christ characterizes both divisions of humanity, without the law imposing between them to make them distinct from each other. From now on, there is neither Jew nor Greek but the church of God (1 Cor 10:32).

A second barrier that existed in ancient society was that of slave and free, particularly as regards economic and social status. Slaves, of course, were entirely at the disposal of their masters, and their lives were not their own to do with as they pleased. But in Christ their lives have become meaningful because they are hid with Christ in God (Col 3:3). A third division was between male and female. Before the advent of Christianity, women did not enjoy true equality in either Greco-Roman or Jewish society.[72] But Paul's statement is a declaration that in Christ they are no longer disadvantaged or considered to be inferior in the sight of God, particularly as regards circumcision (see the section note to this verse).

Paul's choice of contrasts covers the full range of the most profound distinctions within human society: racial/cultural, social/economic, sexual/gender. "Our saying assumes that these distinctions are *not determinative* of whether one can be in the people of God and what one's status will be once in the body of Christ. What ultimately matters in Paul's view is not creation but the new creation" (Witherington, *Grace*, 271). Paul's language, as Dunn adds, "Implies a radically reshaped social world as viewed from a Christian perspective" (*Galatians*, 207). All such differences have been forever banished, "for you are all one in Christ Jesus." Without using the "body language" of his other letters, Paul assumes that the Christian community is in fact one body consisting of

---

[72] Cf. Josephus, *Ag. Ap.* 2.24. See further Schnelle, *Paul*, 291-92.

many members, all of whom are distinct but equal (Rom 12:4-5; 1 Cor 6:15-17; 10:17; 12:12-20; Col 3:15).[73] Paul's manifesto of equality in Christ stands in radical contrast to the outlook of his adversaries, who, no doubt, would have endorsed all the distinctions which the apostle repudiates.

29 This segment of the argument concludes with a recapitulating description of believers: all who belong to Christ are the seed of Abraham and heirs in accordance with the promise made to the patriarch. The identity of the seed of Abraham was of utmost importance to the Judaizers, because "seed" was synonymous with the objects of God's approval. For them, no one could claim descent from the patriarch who was uncircumcised and non-observant with regard to the Torah. But Paul's assessment of the seed was radically distinct from that of the other missionaries. Being an heir of the promise (see above on v. 16) depended on being in Christ, the very Christ who has obliterated the distinctions between Jew/Gentile, slave/free, male/female—a Christ quite different to that of the opponents. All of the great blessings promised to the progenitor of the Jewish nation are the possession of faith alone. For the Galatians, as Martyn comments, there are no outstanding conditions to be met; their redemption consists of their already belonging to Christ (*Galatians*, 377). Accordingly, "Those believers in Galatia who had been told that they could not share in the blessing of Abraham without sharing in Abraham's seed by means of circumcision could be reassured that their share in that inheritance was already secure" (Dunn, *Galatians*, 208).

In redefining and reshaping Abraham's seed, Paul uses a peculiar turn of phrase: "If you are *of Christ*." Hartman speaks to the issue by informing us that Paul's genitive case "of Christ" (*Christou*) is common in Greek and indicates not only possession but also membership of a group, kinship or close fellowship. He fur-

---

[73] Hays is quite right to counsel that there is an Already/Not Yet tension inherent in Paul's declaration of equality in Christ. The key to understanding his thought on this question, says Hays, is to recognize that Paul sees the church as an alternative community that prefigures the new creation in the midst of a world that continues to resist God's justice. Thus, Paul is not calling for a revolution in which slaves rise up and demand freedom; rather, in this verse he is declaring that God has created a new community in which the baptized already share equality. Yet, because the present socio-political realities of this world are soon to pass away, Paul elsewhere counsels his converts to remain in the social station in which they found themselves at the time of their conversion (1 Cor 7:17-24, 29-31). This not a matter of "social conservatism," but one of "eschatological patience," as we eagerly await God's coming new order (*Galatians*, 272-73).

ther notes that the usage can be illustrated by a phenomenon in many religions, in which a god is represented as the lord of his adherents, inasmuch as he reigns over them and takes them under his protection (e.g., Isa 44:5). "This is how in Gal 3.29 the Galatians belong to Christ: he determines their identity and their life-conditions" (*Name*, 57-58). This is called by Hartman "Christ-communion."[74] It is such "Christ-communion" that has turned the erstwhile pagan Galatians, as well as "Jews by birth" (2:15), into the "seed of Abraham."

Section Note

28 T. Martin ("Covenant") proposes that the pairs of antitheses in 3:28—Jew/Gentile, slave/free, male/female—are rooted in the covenant of circumcision, that is, the Abrahamic covenant of Gen 17:9-14, which precisely makes such distinctions. Martin argues that the verse does not proclaim an absolute abolition of these distinctions but only their irrelevance for entrance into the Christian community: participation in baptism and full membership in the new people hinge solely on faith in Christ. The antithesis male/female particularly attracts his attention. "In response to the Agitators' insistence on the distinctions in the Covenant of Circumcision, Paul simply denies that these distinctions have any relevance for determining candidates for Christian baptism and entry into the Christian community. Whereas not everyone in the Jewish community is circumcised, everyone in the Christian community is baptized. Thus, *baptism into Christ provides for a unity that cannot be realized in a circumcised community*" (ibid., 124, italics mine).

Based on Martin's analysis, I would offer the following observations. (1) The focus of Gal 3:28 is precisely on the constitution and, therefore, the unity of the new covenant community. The point is not to say that no distinctions whatsoever exist between Jew/Gentile, slave/free, male/female throughout the course of this age. It is, rather, that such differences no longer have a bearing on the identity and constituency of the latter-day people of God. This is particularly so as regards male/female. Martin, then, is quite right that the covenant of circumcision distinguishes be-

---

[74] Hartman, *Name*, 56. As background, Hartman cites the OT and Jewish concepts of the covenant between God and his people (ibid., 58, n. 17). A typical feature occurs in Exod 19:5: "You shall be my possession among all peoples" (cf. Deut 29:12). The same holds true for the new covenant: "At that time I will be the God of all the families of Israel and they shall be my people" (Jer 31:1). See also Jer 32:38; Deut 27:9; *1 Enoch* 1:8 ("they will belong to God"). In addition, from Qumran: 1Q22 13:9 ("you bought us to be an eternal people to you"); 1Q22 2:1 ("today you will be a people to God, your God"); 1Q34bis 3:2:5 ("you have elected for you a people at the time of your pleasure"). Cf. 1QS 4:18-23; *Jub.* 1:22-25.

tween men and women just along these lines, whereas the new covenant does not. Martin quotes Stephen Clark to this effect:

> In this context, the phrase "neither male nor female" takes on a special significance, because women could not be circumcised. Circumcision was a sign of the covenant of Israel and was only open to the male.... The woman [according to Paul], then, comes into the covenant relation of God's people through her own faith and baptism, and is fully part of the covenant relationship with God.... The free circumcised male was the only full Israelite. It is against this background that we have to understand "neither male nor female" (ibid., 118, n. 26, 119).

(2) By way of qualification, Martin too quickly dismisses any allusion to Gen 1:27: "Male and female he created them." It is true, as Martin says, that the pair can stand on its own apart from the Genesis creation account. However, given that much of this letter is taken up, explicitly or implicitly, with the theme of new creation, an echo of Gen 1:27 would be much to Paul's purpose. The point would be that in Christ the ontological equality of man and woman, which was widely doubted in the ancient world (not to mention the modern), is restored in the new creation/new covenant complex. Note especially in Gen 1:26-27 the interplay of singular and plural and male and female in the depiction of the human being as the image of God: "Then God said, 'Let us make *man* [singular] in our image, after our likeness; and let *them* [plural] have dominion over the fish of the sea, and over the birds of the air, and over the cattle, and over all the earth, and over every creeping thing that creeps upon the earth.' So God created *man* [singular] in his own image, in the image of God he created *him* [singular]; *male and female* he created *them*" [plural] (RSV).

(3) If the Abrahamic covenant is preeminently the covenant of circumcision, then one is cautioned against drawing facile parallels between it and the new covenant. It is obviously true from Galatians that the Abrahamic covenant is fulfilled and finds its reason for being in Christ. Nevertheless, since the very distinctions—Jew/Gentile, slave/free, male/female—repudiated by Paul as regards covenant standing are grounded in the Abrahamic covenant, it can never provide the paradigm for one's inclusion in the new covenant community. This datum has a direct bearing on the issues of baptism and church membership. Given that an element of diversity rather than a simple equation characterizes Paul's delineation of the two covenants, it follows that inclusion in the body of Christ hinges on individual faith and not on a previous family relationship. All who entered the Abrahamic and Mosaic covenants did so precisely by circumcision; yet it is circumcision that Paul now declares to be irrelevant.

GALATIANS CHAPTER FOUR

G. Heirs and Sons of God (4:1-7)

Once more, Paul juxtaposes the condition of his readers before and after coming to Christ. This subsection of the argument is essentially a recapitulation of 3:23-29. However, there is a difference in emphasis. What is stressed at this point is the contrast of the Galatians' previous condition of slavery with their present status of sonship.

1-2 By way of illustration, Paul states what was familiar enough to anyone living in the Greco-Roman world of his day: as long as the heir of the estate is a child, he is no different than a slave, even though he is potentially master of all. Apparently, Paul was thinking of *patria potestas* in Roman law, whereby the head of a household exercised absolute power over all persons and property in a family unit.[1] A person under *patria potestas*, even though the heir of the entire property, legally was not differentiated from a slave. The common denominator of the two is that the minor and the slave equally lacked the capacity of self-determination. "The situation envisaged," writes Dunn, "is an ironic reversal of the claim made in iii.28: 'in Christ' means an equality of *liberty* for slave and free; 'under the law' means an equality of *restriction* for slave and heir under age" (*Galatians*, 210).

In terms of *patria potestas*, the father appoints "guardians" and "trustees" for the children who are to inherit the estate after his death.[2] During this period of time in which the heir is a minor, he is potentially the legal owner of the inheritance, but for the time-being he is prevented from disposing of it at will. But when the time set by the father elapses, the child becomes an adult and assumes the right to do with the property whatever he pleases.[3] With

---

[1] See Nicholas, "*Patria Potestas*." The one who exercised *patria potestas* was the *Pater Familias*, who held almost absolute sway over the household. See L. M. White, "Paul," 457-64.

[2] See Betz, *Galatians*, 203-4; Walters, "Paul," 62; Tsang, *Slaves*, 123-24. Tsang, ibid., 116-31, takes up the slave metaphor inherent in this passage.

[3] Betz relates that the time for the end of the child's tutelage was set by Roman law, not the father. But then he notes that there are examples from provincial legal practice in which the testator does set the term of the guardianship, raising the possibility that Paul was more acquainted the provincial practice than the standards of Roman law (*Galatians*, 204). However, it is equally possible that we

this illustration, Paul has in mind the eschatological time set by God for the maturation of his people. Since the coming of Christ, they are no longer babes but full-grown adults and are treated as such. Why, then, would the Galatians want to revert to a condition in which they are treated not as grown-ups but as minors? Why, as Israel in the wilderness, would they want to embrace the slavery of Egypt? See the section note to vv. 1-7.

3 Here, Paul completes his analogy—and what an analogy it proves to be. "The sentence comprising vv. 3-5 is nothing less than the theological center of the entire letter. It contains nearly all of the letter's major motifs, and it relates them to one another in such a way as to state what we may call the good news of Paul's letter to the Galatians" (Martyn, *Galatians*, 388).

"We" has reference to Jewish Christians who have now come out from under the bondage of the law. These are the same people who have come to recognize that justification is by faith in Christ and not from works of the law ("even we," according to 2:16b). The force of Paul's logic is that if "we" have been liberated from the law, then surely it is foolish in the extreme for the largely Gentile Galatians to want to be enslaved to that from which their Jewish brethren have been freed. According to vv. 8 and 9 of this chapter, life under the law is no better than the pagan idolatry in which the readers were once enmeshed.

The enslavement of this period of childhood was under "the elements of the world" (*ta stoicheia tou kosmou*), occurring also in Gal 4:9; Col 2:8, 20). The precise meaning of "elements" is a matter of long-standing dispute.[4] Scholars reckon that in ancient sources the word could denote several things at the same time: (1) the "elemental substances" of which the cosmos is composed: earth, air, fire and water (Empedocles); (2) the heavenly bodies or supramundane powers which influence or even determine human destiny; (3) the "elementary forms" of religion (now superseded by the coming of faith in Christ).

Given the present train of thought, it would not be out of line to suggest that each of these elements of "the elements" have a bearing on interpretation. There were the supernatural powers that were deemed to have existed in Greco-Roman paganism, those

---

have here a compressed way of writing, which is not uncommon in Paul. That is to say, in appointing guardians and trustees, the father effectively sets the time of *their* auspices.

[4] See the survey of Calvert-Koyzis, *Paul*, 104-10.

entities called by 4:8 "beings that are by nature no gods" (also 1 Cor 2:8; 8:5-6; 10:20-21).[5] But then as well, Paul, like the writer of Hebrews (Heb 5:12), looks upon the Mosaic revelation as a period of "elements," of "ABCs," during which Israel was being taught the rudiments of the service of God.[6] Thus, it would appear that Paul views the "elements" as at least two dimensional in their makeup. Remembering that it is in this very context that he dares to identify the Torah with pagan idolatry (vv. 8-11), it makes sense to think that for him (2) and (3) are more or less the same thing (as appears to be the case also in Col 2:8, 20). Yet additionally, it is worth passing on that Hays (following Martyn) thinks that a reference to "natural elements" (1) would be in keeping with the mission of the law teachers. For them, the Torah provided the true understanding of the natural world and the heavenly bodies and thus regulated the calendar of religious activities (*Galatians*, 283). See further on v. 10.

This prior phase of salvation history can be called "the elements of *the world*" because "world" connotes "old creation," the cosmos before and outside of Christ (Bandstra, *Law*, 173). Adams is quite right that "world" is the "crucified world" of 6:14, the "present evil age" of 1:4. "It is no neutral entity; it is the sphere of opposition and hostility to God" (*Constructing*, 230). "World," then, underscores the solidarity of Israel and its Torah with the rest of humanity—a rather startling proposition to a first-century Jew! This is why Paul can make the equally startling assertion that the Torah is no better than pagan religion (4:8-9)! For this reason, Gentiles should not cave in to the pressure to embrace attitudes and practices which even Jewish Christians now recognize to be outmoded.

Thus, in rather conspicuous contrast to his antagonists, for Paul the antidote to ravages of the old creation is not the law but the Spirit.[7]

---

[5] In fairness, I would pass along Stanton's caveat that a link between *stoicheia* as a term and the demonic is hard to establish until much later than Paul's time ("Law," 114).

[6] See Belleville, "Under Law," 67-68; Bayes, *Weakness*, 126-29 (see p. 127, n. 2, for further literature). Heb 5:12 uses the extended phrase: "The elements of the beginning of the oracles of God" (*ta stoicheia tēs archēs tōn logiōn tou theou*).

[7] Paul thus denies what was to become the standard view of rabbinic Judaism, namely, that the Torah holds in check the "evil inclination." See the section note to 5:13. For him, the law avails nothing; the Spirit is "all in all."

> In short, in Paul's view the only adequate remedy for the human predicament...is a "new creation" in which the obstacles to human freedom—sin, the flesh and death—are deprived of their power. It is for this reason that the Spirit is not at the periphery but at the center of the new historical epoch (Lull, *Spirit*, 104).

4-5[8] The advent of "the fullness of the time" is equivalent to both a child's coming of age, in the analogy of 4:2, and the "coming of faith," in 3:23-25. The imagery of "fullness" is that of a container being steadily filled until it is full. "The implication is of a set purpose of God having been brought to fruition over a period and its eschatological climax enacted at the time appointed by him" (Dunn, *Galatians*, 213-14). The notion of fullness in the NT generally has to do with the "eschatological measure:" the purpose of "fulfilling" is to reach this complete measure of God's purpose (Jeremias, *Theology*, 84). If the very purpose of Israel's history was to point her to Christ, then that purpose has been achieved by his advent, death and resurrection. God has "filled up" his long anticipated design of salvation by sending forth his Son. Here once more is Paul's apocalyptic frame of reference. "God is conceived as having a cosmic timetable and an appointed day to break into humanity's history of misery to bring the promised redemption."[9]

The "time" which has been fulfilled also comes to the fore in Mark 1:15, where it designates the period of preparation for the gospel, during which salvation history was running its course in anticipation of the kingdom God. That epoch has now given way to the time of the Son of God.[10] "The measure of time assigned by God for the fulfillment of the promise of the kingdom has been 'filled up,' and so come to its end. If it has reached its limit, there is no further waiting" (Beasley-Murray, *Jesus*, 73).

---

[8] Vv. 4-5 are a chiasmus:
A God sent his Son
   B Born under the law
   B To redeem those under the law
A That we might receive adoption as sons.

[9] Hays, *Galatians*, 283. Hays passes along other texts: Dan 8:19; 11:35; 1QpHab 7:2; Luke 21:24; Acts 1:7; 3:21; Eph 1:10.

[10] The resemblance to Mark 1:15 is a further indication that underling Galatians is a Jesus-narrative derived from the Gospels. In this instance, Mark's story and Paul's story respectively coincide just at the fulfillment of the age of preparation and the onset of the new age.

Paul's denomination of Christ as the "Son" makes particular sense in the immediate context. From 3:6 onwards, there has been an interplay between "seed," "heirs," "children" and "sons," including the interconnection of "sons of Abraham" and "sons of God." Since the Galatian believers share in Christ's sonship, they are as well the sons of Abraham. In Jewish thinking, there could be no higher privilege than being Abraham's offspring. Paul grants this much to those who imitate the example of the patriarch's faith. But he goes them one better: sonship to God in Christ places them in a position of unprecedented privilege. How, then, could these people think to treat their sonship to God so lightly by reverting to a time before the sending of his Son and the full manifestation of grace and truth in him (John 1:17)?

Yet there is another dimension to Christ's sonship than his salvation-historical function as the Messiah of Israel, because God "sent forth" his Son. It is true that sending can be predicated of human messengers (e.g., Judg 6:8; Jer 7:25; Ezek 2:3; Hag 1:12). But given Paul's high christology, the sending of the Son implies his preexistence in the very form of God, as one equal with God, in whom the whole fullness of deity dwells (Phil 2:6; Col 2:9; cf. John 1:1, 18). The same point is made in Rom 8:3: the incarnation marks not only the sending of the Son of God but the advent of God the Son.

To say that Christ was born of a woman describes both the effect and the process of his sending. "Born of a woman" is a Hebrew expression for the human being (Job 14:1; 15:14; 25:4; 1QS 11:21; 1QH 13:14; 18:12-13; Matt 11:11). From this vantage point, Paul asserts that Jesus identified with humanity and partook of the human condition, or, in the words of Rom 8:3, he came bearing the "likeness of sinful flesh." Paul's Last Adam christology is here implicit: he is the man who retraces the course of Adam through the "likeness of sinful flesh" to death in order that by his exaltation he might bring to a climax God's purpose for creating humankind, that is, to place all things under his feet (Ps 8:6; Heb 2:5-9). This is the effect of his sending. Yet the process of his entry into the world is noteworthy too. The "woman" in question, Mary, is the "eschatological Eve," the one who gives birth to the seed destined the crush the head of the serpent (Gen 3:15).

That Jesus was "born under the law" is expected in view of the way the argument from 3:19 has been impelled by the category "under the law." By this phrase, Paul underscores Jesus' Jewishness. The one destined to redeem "those under the law" (v. 5a), that is, Jews, was by birth a Jew himself, one "under the law" (a similar point is made in Rom 1:3, with the notice that Jesus was "born of the seed of David according to the flesh"). If the Judaizers were to any degree pressing for Jesus' Jewishness, Paul grants that he did indeed live during the period of the Torah. Yet anyone familiar with the gospel story should have known that at his crucifixion he died to "sin" (Rom 6:10), that is, the era of the old creation, and by his resurrection rose in newness of life to a new age.[11] The Galatians, therefore, must follow his example by leaving the old age behind and entering fully into the freedom and blessings of a new creation. Like the writer of this letter, they too must die to the law in order to live to God (2:19).

The intention of Jesus' birth of a woman, under the law, is stated by the two purpose clauses of v. 5. In the first, the death of Christ is represented as the redemption of believing Israelites ("those under the law"). The thought of redemption is repeated from 3:13, with renewed stress on the liberation of slaves, the slavery in question being to *the law*, "the elements of the world." Once again, the implication is that if even Jews needed to be freed from the law, Gentiles certainly have no business accommodating themselves to that state of affairs—they would only have to be delivered from it anyway!

The second purpose clause states the reason why historically Jewish believers have been redeemed, that is, in order that all Christians might receive the adoption as sons and daughters. The "we" of this clause is best understood as referring to all who have received the Holy Spirit as the Spirit of sonship (Rom 8:15). In a manner not dissimilar to Rom 1:16, Paul speaks of a sequence of events: something is first done on behalf of Israel in order to make possible the dissemination of God's grace to the nations. Ideally speaking, Israel's very identity was to be found in this historical process. It is just by virtue of the work of the Servant who was sent to the "lost sheep of the house Israel" (Matt 15:24) that the ancient people were intended eschatologically to be the light to the nations (Isa 42:6; 49:6; 51:4; 60:3).

In Christian theology and preaching, adoption is frequently likened to the Greco-Roman or even the modern practice of accepting an individual child into a household, with all the rights and

---

[11] That there is an underlying Jesus-narrative in Galatians has been demonstrated by Hays, *Faith*; Dunn, *Theology of Galatians*, 41-46. See further the essays in B. W. Longenecker (ed.), *Dynamics*, esp. the contribution of D. A. Campbell (pp. 97-124). But Gorman comes closest to Paul's actually narrative in Galatians: the story is that of *the cross* (*Apostle*, 183-226; id., *Cruciformity*, passim).

privileges pertaining thereto. But while there are decidedly rights and privileges attached to sonship to God, Paul moves within the OT/Jewish sphere of thought, according to which sonship (*huiothesia*) was one of the distinctive marks of Israelite identity (Rom 9:4). Within this universe of discourse, the stress falls not so much on the individual as on the corporate makeup of the people of God. Israel was adopted as God's son at Mount Sinai, thus marking the birth of a nation.[12] Paul stands squarely within this tradition; yet he is bold enough to announce that "we"—both Jew and Gentile—have been adopted into God's new covenant family and formed into a new Israel. All of this has transpired not because of circumcision and allegiance to the Torah but because of faith alone in Christ and the gift of his Spirit.[13]

6 Paul now states the corollary of adoption: sonship means possession of the Spirit, who enables the believer to call upon God as Father (as in Rom 8:15-16). The order of sonship followed by the gift of the Spirit may seem curious at first. However, Longenecker is no doubt right that sonship and receiving the Spirit are so intimately related that they can be spoken of in either order (*Galatians*, 173). In point of fact, adoption and the receiving of the Spirit are coincident in time. Hays takes it a step further. Without downplaying the reception of the Spirit as essential to conversion/initiation, he correctly comments that Paul here is not describing the history of the individual believer, but rather he is narrating God's redemptive invasion of an enslaved world. The sending of the son must come first and afterwards the Spirit can be sent to those who are adopted by virtue of his liberating death (*Galatian*, 285).

It is just the latter-day children of God, the possessors of the Spirit, who have an awareness of God's fatherhood as modeled on Jesus' own experience of invoking God as *Abba* (e.g., Luke 10:21; 22:42).[14] To address God as *Abba* is a peculiar blessing of the new

---

[12] Scott, *Adoption*; Hafemann, "Exile," 329-37; Keesmaat, *Paul*, 165-57; Wilson, "Apostasy," 560. Walters ("Paul") provides a useful overview of adoption and inheritance in the Greco-Roman world, Romans and Galatians. Walters' data are impressive enough to lead us to believe that an allusion to Roman adoptive practices may lurk in the background of Paul's use of *huiothesia*. However, he has done nothing to shift the paradigm away from Scott's biblical/Jewish framework of the concept.

[13] See Hafemann, "Exile," 350-51.

[14] See Jeremias, *Theology*, 61-68; id., *Prayers*, 11-65; Dunn, *Jesus and Spirit*, 11-40; Stein, *Method*, 80-87.

covenant, as underscored by the fact that there appear to be no real Jewish precedents for the practice (Witherington, *Christology*, 216-21). The Galatians thus occupy a place of unparalleled privilege, which they must not despise by retreating into the age of the Torah, in which such an intimate relation to God did not exist. Paul yet again appeals to the experience of the Galatians: at their conversion, God sent the Spirit of his Son into their hearts (in fulfillment of Ezek 36:26-27; Joel 2:28 = Acts 2:17-21; Rom 5:5). Their awareness of the fatherhood of God was the result of "having begun in the Spirit" (3:3), not of their more recent infatuation with the Torah. Paul's syntax is clear that it the Spirit who cries out to God on behalf of the believer, though the other side of the coin is evident in Rom 8:15: the believer calls upon God the Father as energized by the Spirit.

7 The conclusion of the matter is that the Galatians are no longer slaves but sons and heirs. Just as Paul brought his self-defense to a close with a personal testimony of his own experience of Christ's sonship (2:20), so now he addresses each person in the congregations (with the singular "you") in terms of his own sonship to God in Christ. Paul can tell his readers that they are "no longer" slaves because, in point of fact, the Gentiles among them once were just that when they were in bondage to beings that are "no gods" (v. 8). Similarly, the Jewish division of the church was in bondage as well, to the law. The reminder was necessary because these people were on the brink of collapsing into the slavery of the Torah. It would be a stark denial of their privileged status as sons to return to a condition in which they were no better off than the lowliest slave in the household. And if they are sons, they are, by the nature of the case, heirs also.

Their inheritance is that which was promised to Abraham in its totality (see on 3:16). God himself is the great benefactor, because they are "heirs of God," and, according to Rom 8:17, "joint heirs with Christ" of the entire created universe (cf. Heb 1:2; 2:5-9). All this is "through God." By virtue of a new creation and a new exodus, God has formed them into a new family by bestowing on them sonship and enduing them with the Spirit of his unique Son. He has done everything sovereignly, graciously and, so strikingly, in a manner altogether unthinkable to the Judaizers—apart from the law (cf. Rom 3:21)!

GALATIANS CHAPTER FOUR

Section Notes

1-7 Scott (*Adoption*, 121-86), Hafemann ("Exile") and Keesmaat (*Paul*, 155-73) have demonstrated that lying behind 4:1-7 is the motif of Israel in bondage. As the son of God, the nation is kept in a period of slavery until the exodus ("the time set by the father," v. 2). As Keesmaat in particular concludes: "Not only does Paul's terminology in 4.1-7…support the exodus as the interpretative context for these images; the story Paul tells is a movement from slavery to sonship, with the temptation to go back into slavery. God has made God's self known to them in this new liberating event, as God did so long ago in the first liberating event. Such a revelation, especially when linked with the desire to return to slavery, parallels the exodus narrative. As such it provides a comparison which calls the Galatians to recognize their God and continue to participate in this new exodus event, lest they be judged not worthy of the inheritance" (*Paul*, 173).

Thus, Paul's emphasis here, comments Hafemann, is not existential but eschatological and ties into the overall pattern of Israel's return from exile in the letter. The parallels between 3:10, 22, 23 and 4:1-5, Hafemann argues, point to Paul's own summary of the flow of biblical history in which, from the time of her sin with the golden calf onward, Israel lived under the judgment of God proclaimed in the law (that is, "the curse of the law" of 3:10) because of her transgressions against the covenant as detailed by that same law (3:19). Furthermore, as the Deuteronomic backdrop to 3:10 makes clear, the curse of the law climaxed in Israel's eventual exile. The law's purpose was "to shut (Israel) up to the faith which was later to be revealed" (3:23b), at the time when Christ would redeem (Israel) from the law's curse (3:13). In other words, in the terms of 4:1-5, the purpose of the law was to teach Israel that "under the law" she was still a sinful "child" awaiting her inheritance of redemption. Read in this light, Paul's reflections on the function of the law and its curse are part of an extensive post-biblical tradition in which Israel's rebellious nature is stressed as evidence of the need for a restoration of the people through a renewed, eschatological manifestation of the power of God ("Exile," 345-46).

4 Jesus' birth "of a woman" opens a possible insight into Paul's missionary theology. If Mary can be identified as the "eschatological Eve," then it should be recalled that the original Eve was "the mother of *all* living" (Gen 3:20). Mary, therefore, as this eschatological woman, marks the beginning of a new humanity composed of *all* who belong to Christ. With the birth of Jesus, the first man of the new creation, the biblical story comes full circle with a return to the time when the Jew/Gentile divide did not exist.

6 The phrase "the Spirit of his Son" gives voice to a uniquely intimate relationship between the second and third persons of the Trinity. The salvation-historical basis of this relationship is the resurrection of Christ. According to Paul's teaching elsewhere, Christ became "Son of God in power" by virtue of the Spirit raising him from the dead (Rom 1:4). At this juncture, the Last Adam "became life-giving Spirit" (1 Cor 15:45). From the resurrection onward, he exists *as* life-giving Spirit. Ontologically and functionally there is such an identification of Jesus and the Spirit that Paul can say "the Lord is the Spirit" (2 Cor 3:17) (see Gaffin, *Resurrection*, 78-97). Acts 16:7 comes close to Gal 4:6 with its phrase "the Spirit of Jesus." The usage is especially conspicuous in that "the Spirit of Jesus" takes the place of "the Spirit of Yahweh" in the OT (see Stählin, "*Pneuma Iēsou*").

H. Don't Become Slaves Again (4:8-11)

In his exhortations to the Galatians not to abandon Christ in favor of the Torah, Paul has laid great stress on sonship and in particular on the freedom enjoyed by grown-up sons and daughters in the household of God's new covenant. Consistent with that line of reasoning, he now comes to stress in rather shocking terms that life under the law is no better than his readers' former bondage to idols. The one form of idolatry is as bad as the other! They might as well have never left paganism! "In short," comments Martyn, "Gentile observance of the Law is equivalent to Gentile ignorance of God;" and, according to Kuula, "Observance of the law is simply equated with idolatry."[15] Wilson proposes that Paul has in mind passages such as Exod 14:10-12 (cf. Exod 16:3; 17:3) Num 14:2-4 (cf. Num 11:4-6, 18); Neh 9:17, Israel's desire to return to Egypt. As he remarks: "Of course, neither the Galatians nor the Israelites desired to return to *slavery*; they simply wanted the benefits of their former situation without the costs of their present one. For Paul, however, this was tantamount to forsaking the service of God for the service of another" ("Apostasy," 561). Wilson further calls to mind 2 Chron 12:5, 8; Jer 5:19; Josh 24:14-20, according to which the Lord taunts his people for their wanton desire to forsake him for the service of other masters. For Paul, such references would have immediate applicability:

---

[15] Martyn, *Galatians*, 410; Kuula, *Law*, 126. See also Wright, *Paul*, 144. I have treated the Torah = idolatry motif of Romans 1:18-2:29 in *Faith*, 32-43. See also Dunn's powerful development of "the effects of sin—misdirected religion" (*Theology of Paul*, 114-19).

The Galatians are obviously faced with a similar choice: "Whom shall you serve?" As recently converted pagans, they know the "bondage" of servitude to "beings that are not gods" (4.8). Moreover, they have come to know God—rather, to be known by him in an Exodus-like redemption (4.9a with 4.1-7). Their present defection or "return" to the *stoicheia*...then is doubly astonishing: it represents a *relapse* to the slave-service of former times—to a period when they neither knew God nor were known by him! This is as ridiculous as the Israelites wanting to return to Egypt after having been liberated from slavery by coming to know the one true God. "Would that we were in Egypt; we want to go back."[16]

8 Here is one the clearest indications that those to whom the argument is addressed were mostly Gentiles who were being induced to adopt a Torah-lifestyle (covenantal nomism) as the token of their sonship. They are characterized by their former ignorance of the God of Israel (*à la* Ps 79:6; Jer 10:25; Jdt 9:7; 2 Macc 1:27; Eph 2:12; 2 Thess 1:8). Knowledge of God is a recognizably OT attribute of his people. Israel's great privilege was to acknowledge and thus render obedience to the God of the covenant (Deut 4:39; Ps 9:10; 46:10; Isa 43:10; Hos 8:2; Mic 6:5; Wis 2:13). The knowledge of God was a prized commodity to which the nation was to aspire (Prov 2:5; 9:10; Jer 31:34; Dan 11:32). If the people failed to know God, they were, accordingly, rebuked (Isa 1:3; Hos 4:6; 5:4; 6:6).[17] The verb "to know" does not mean, in the everyday sense, "to acquire knowledge about," but "to experience." In reminding the Galatians that they did not know God, Paul maintains that they had "no experience of his covenantal grace, and did not

---

[16] Wilson, "Apostasy," 563. Cf. Keesmaat, *Paul*, 173. Picking up Barclay's observation that God's people are freed in order to serve him (*Obeying*, 109, n. 7), Wilson further proposes that the genius of the exodus experience was not about the manumission of slaves but the *change of masters*. "Exodus liberation, then, was understood as a new form of enslavement" (ibid., 566). The upshot is rather obvious. The Galatians were liberated by Christ in order to serve him; but like Israel of old, now they want to retreat to the service of the old master. Given that they were largely Gentiles, the parallel may not be exact, but it is certainly striking enough to have arrested their attention.

[17] These prophetic passages are instances of the covenant lawsuit (*rib*) motif, as modeled on Deuteronomy 32. As illustrated especially by Isa 1:3, God's people should have known him, but because they have not, the Lord takes them to task for being worse than animals, who know their master!

realize that he was the only God—hence the gods they worshipped were 'no gods'" (Dunn, *Galatians*, 224, citing Isa 37:19; Jer 2:11; 5:7; 16:20; Wis 12:27; 1 Cor 8:4-6).

But in becoming the sons of God and possessing the "Spirit of his Son," Paul's readers have come to experience God in the intimacy of a family relationship. In their knowledge of God, these former pagan idolaters have assumed, no less, the identity of Israel. Their erstwhile ignorance of the true God and their service of man-made deities were no less than slavery, because far from delivering them from their sins and giving them an authentic reason for existence, their "gods" simply reinforced the propensities of their own hearts, thus enslaving them to a life lived solely for the sake of self-gratification and self-aggrandizement (see the converse in 2 Cor 5:15). Added to this is the fact that Paul conceives of pagan religion as under the dominance of demonic powers (1 Cor 10:20-21), making life outside Christ a veritable servitude to Satan.[18]

9 The antithesis of the Galatians' former ignorance of God is stated in both the active and passive voices. At their conversion, they came to know God and entered into that relationship which typified Israel's covenant identity. The other side of the coin is that they came to be known by God. This dimension of the knowledge of God likewise reflects the special relation of Israel to Yahweh, with God's knowledge of the people being tantamount to his election of them (Gen 18:19; Hos 5:3; 13:5; Amos 3:2; cf. Rom 8:29). The adjustment from the active to the passive voice is important because it underscores that one's acknowledgment of God is made possible only through the divine initiative. "It is a two-way relationship, of acknowledgment and obligation; but the personal knowing of God is made possible only by God's knowing the person."[19] It was important that the Galatians be reminded of what happened at their conversion, because they had already begun to experience knowing God and being known by him quite apart from the law; and as the next part of the verse will confirm, any return to the law would result in a forfeiture of the knowledge of God.

In light of what transpired when the readers came to know God, the questions naturally arises: How can they turn back to "the weak and poor elements?" Why do they want to become slaves all

---

[18] See Howard, *Crisis*, 66-82.
[19] Dunn, *Galatians*, 225. Hays adds: "The Galatians have entered a new world not because of some epistemological advance of their own, but because God, in elective love, has 'known' them" (*Galatians*, 287).

over again to that which is so decidedly inferior to what they have experienced in Christ by the Spirit? No doubt, Paul's opponents would have been stunned by the claim that service of Torah is entails the same servitude as devotion to the Anatolian deities, which, in Paul's own words, are "by nature are no gods." Nevertheless, for Paul the claim stands, because from the vantage point of real liberty in Christ, the law represents a retrogression to a state of immaturity, under the tutelage of the disciplinarian (3:23-24). Compared to what he has come to enjoy in Christ, life under the law could be nothing but bondage. This consideration gains in strength when the Spirit is brought into the picture. One of the questions looming large in Galatians is: Who really has the Spirit? For Paul the answer is clear: "Where the Spirit of the Lord is, there is *liberty*" (2 Cor 3:17), the climactic statement of an entire chapter addressing the same concern as this segment of Galatians. Those who possess the Spirit ("born after the Spirit," 4:29) must be free, even as their mother is free (4:21-31).

The verb "turn back" (various forms of *strephō*) has a significance all its own, as it is an OT term for apostasy from Yahweh (e.g., Num 14:43; 1 Sam 15:11; 1 Kgs 9:6; Ps 78:41; Jer 3:19). It is in this sense that Paul employs the verb, and in so doing he is adamant that a return to the traditional Jewish understanding of the covenant as defined by the law is no less than apostasy from the God whom the Galatians had come to know in Christ (cf. again 1:6, as reflective of Exod 32:8; Deut 9:16). If they should consummate their defection to the Torah, they would cease to experience the covenant grace of God. Everything gained by their knowledge of God would be lost.

> Paul was convinced that Gentiles who believed in the gospel of Christ and received the Spirit of God's Son had thereby come to experience and share in what the choice of Abraham and of Israel had been all about. In seeking to grasp Israel's privilege more firmly the judaizing Gentiles were in danger of losing that very promise and blessing in which they already shared (Dunn, *Galatians*, 225).

The present tense of the verb, however, indicates that the apostasy was only in process and could still be averted. No wonder, all of Paul's passion and persuasive abilities are given full rein in this epistle.

These "elements" or "ABCs," that is, the Torah with its myriad of restrictions for the immature, are called "weak" mainly because they are ineffectual in contrast to the powers that have been unleashed with turning of the ages and the advent of the Spirit (cf. Heb 6:5-6 with its same conjunction of the Spirit and "the powers of the age to come"). Even if we allow the perspective of Rom 8:3 that the law is weak "through the flesh," it remains true that only God can do what the law could not. Additionally, since Paul has just identified the law with idolatry, he likely here alludes to the idol-parodies of the OT, in which the images are denounced as impotent in comparison to the might of the living God (Ps 115:3-8; 135:15-18; Isa 40:18-20; 44:9-17; 46:5-7; Jer 10:1-16; Hab 2:18-19).

Ironically enough, Paul's depiction of the Torah recalls the Jewish portrait of the futility of Gentile idolatry in Wis 13:18-19 ("For health he appeals to a thing that is weak; for life he prays to a thing that is dead...he asks strength of a thing whose hands have no strength"), which itself reflects the OT idol-parodies.[20] The Galatians ought to pay particular attention to this point, because according to Psalm 115:18, *all who trust in idols become like them*.[21] For this reason, Paul can say elsewhere that the law—the new idol, as it were—weakens, not strengthens, its devotees (Rom 14:1-2; 15:1; 1 Cor 8:7, 9-12; 9:22)!

Besides being "weak," the "elements" are "poor," because life under the law was an impoverishment as compared to the riches of grace and truth to be had in Christ. Once one has embraced the "substance" of fulfillment, what has preceded is as insubstantial as a "shadow" (Col 2:17). The "elements of the world" can never satisfy, simply because the fullness of deity dwells in Christ, and in him we have come to fullness of life (Col 2:9-10). Therefore, like the Colossians, the Galatians are not to be made a prey of by the traditions of human beings (Col 2:8). Paul feels particularly compelled to press for the richness of the "in Christ" experience because of the growing doubts in the minds of his readers.

---

[20] See Roth, "For Life." Romans 1, in its depiction of idols and idolaters, is likewise modeled on passages from the Wisdom of Solomon. See the parallels as adduced (in English) by Metzger, *Introduction*, 159, and (in Greek) by Sanday/Headlam, *Romans*, 51-52. See further deSilva, *Apocrypha*, 150-51; Garlington, *Obedience*, 68, n. 13; id., *Faith*, 35.

[21] This is what accounts for the language of Isa 6:10, quoted a number of times in the NT: those who worship idols become as blind and deaf as they. See Beale, "Taunt."

> The implication here may be that the experience of God's acceptance and of the Spirit which still gripped Paul so powerfully was already fading for many of his converts; or that the well-developed system of centuries-old Judaism made the still undeveloped ritual and liturgy of the churches seem bare and less satisfying (Dunn, *Galatians*, 226-27).

Hays is probably right that this verse is "the most stunning sentence in this entire confrontational letter," and that "Paul could hardly have said anything more calculated to arouse the outrage of the Missionaries." But it was all in the endeavor "to jolt the Galatians out of the hypnotic spell of the Law-gospel" (*Galatians*, 287).

10 Paul laments that some of the "weak and poor elements" have especially attracted the Galatians' attention: "Days, months, seasons and years." By "days" he would certainly have in mind the sabbath and perhaps even the day of atonement, if the Judaizers were going so far as to press for its observance. The sabbath, as the sign of the Mosaic covenant (Exod 31:12-17), was one of the most prominent of the boundary markers which served to distinguish Israel from the nations. Violation of the sabbath ranked along with disregard of the food laws as the two chief marks of covenant disloyalty (Josephus, *Ant.* 11.346). The elaborated traditions of sabbath-keeping attested in Second Temple literature indicate the importance of the sabbath as a condition of covenant righteousness in the Jewish consciousness of the period (e.g., *Jub.* 2:17-33; CD 10:14-11:18; cf. Mark 2:23-3:5). "Months" would have reference to the offerings at the beginning of each month (the new moon), according to Num 10:10; 28:11-15. The "seasons" or "special times" are likely the "appointed feasts" of Israel, as enjoined by Leviticus 23 and 25. As far as "years" go, one thinks of the sabbatical year (Lev 25:1-7) and the year of Jubilee (Lev 25:8-24).[22]

---

[22] Hays asks why Paul speaks so generically here and not specifically of "festivals, new moons or sabbaths," as he does in Col 2:16. The answer is that he may be alluding to the biblical creation story, which says that the lights were placed in the dome of the sky on the fourth day of creation "for signs and for seasons and for days and years" (Gen 1:14 [NRSV]). If this text no longer provides a warrant, as it did in Judaism, for observing special times and seasons, it can only be for the same reason that there is no longer "male and female" in Christ: the new creation has broken in. Furthermore, writes Hays, by using these generic terms rather than the specific terminology of the Jewish liturgical calendar, Paul facilitates his provocative linking of the Law with the *stoicheia*. When one strips away the specific terminology of the Jewish festivals, Paul suggests, one sees that they are in essence just another kind of nature religion! He is saying, in effect, "You used to be

Each of these observances was held to be of the essence of Torah-obedience, and any infraction would have been looked upon as willful disdain of the requirements of the covenant. But from the vantage point of the age of the Spirit, what could be "weaker" or "poorer" than "days, months, seasons and years?!" These are only the shadows of preparation—Christ is the substance of fulfillment (Col 2:17). Unless the Galatians come to recognize this, they will lapse into the same kind of observance of religious holidays as formerly when they celebrated the special days of the Roman calendar in veneration of the emperor (see Tsang, *Slaves*, 118 and the first section note to vv. 8-11). Paul's thrust is clear: *the Jewish calendar is nothing but paganism revisited!* Calvert-Koyzis is right: "In equating observance of the law with paganism, Paul makes the law the ultimate taboo for a child of Abraham" (*Paul*, 110). See the second section note to vv. 8-11 below.

Hays calls to mind that the Galatians were probably being pressured to adopt a pattern of life in keeping with fixed calendrical observances. The observances of the Jewish liturgical calendar were calibrated to the motions of the sun and moon (sabbath, new-moon festivals, the Day of Atonement, Passover and other festivals). Jewish sources from the Second Temple period show that there was heated controversy between advocates of lunar and solar calendrical systems over the proper way of keeping times and seasons. For example, *Jubilees*, a text championing the solar calendar, insists that "the Lord set the sun as a great sign upon the earth for days, sabbaths, months, feast (days), years, sabbaths of years, jubilees, and for all the (appointed) times of the years" (*Jub.* 2:9). See also *1 Enoch* 82:7-9.

> Thus it is quite likely that the Missionaries would have impressed on the Galatians the importance not only of being circumcised but also of keeping the sabbaths and feasts at the proper astronomically determined times. If so, it would make sense for Paul to assert that the Galatians' newfound interest in observing Jewish festivals was leading them back into bondage under the power of the astral elements.[23]

---

in slavery to the cosmic elements; if you come under the Law, you will be back under the control of these same cosmic forces" (*Galatians*, 288).

[23] Hays, *Galatians*, 288. See also Schnelle, *Paul*, 274. The Qumran community disparagingly referred to the Jewish festivals in Jerusalem as "the feasts of *the Gentiles*," because they were observed according to the Roman lunar calendar.

11 The section ends on a note of heartfelt concern. Because these people have advanced so far and so quickly in becoming observant Jews, Paul can only fear that his labors on their behalf have all been in vain. The present tense of the verb "fear" indicates that their defection from the gospel has begun but that the final outcome is still undetermined. The perfect tense "have labored" refers to Paul's past ministry among them and its continuing result. But at this point in time it appears that there might not be any lasting effect—which is why Paul fears for them. But he has not given up on them yet, as is obvious from the following paragraph, in which he appeals to them in the tenderest terms as both his "brothers" (v. 12) and his "children" (v. 19). In fact, as Wagner informs us ("Isaiah," 132-33), Paul's fear of having run in vain, here and in 2:2, is an echo of the Servant of Yahweh, who likewise laments, "I have labored in vain, I have spent my strength for nothing and vanity" (Isa 49:4a) (RSV). But even so, ultimately his confidence remains unshaken: "Yet surely my right is with the Lord, and my recompense with my God" (49:4b). This is to be matched with Isa 65:23 (LXX): "My chosen ones will not labor in vain, nor will they bear children for a curse." Wagner, then, can write: "The note of hopeful expectation expressed here and in Isa. 49:4, where the Servant entrusts his labours to God and looks to God alone for vindication, finds its echo in Paul's untiring labours on behalf of his 'children'" (ibid., 132). Or, in Paul's own words elsewhere, "your labor is not in vain in the Lord" (1 Cor 15:58).

Section Notes

8-11 Witherington proposes that Paul's parallel between Torah observance and pagan idolatry finds its precise point of correspondence in the emperor cult of the first-century Greco-Roman world (*Grace*, 298-99). If the Jewish calendar was replete with special occasions, the Roman calendar was too: months, seasons and years were allocated to special recognition and celebration, all in the service of the worship of the emperor. "Paul is drawing an analogy between going back to observing the calendrical feasts and days of the Emperor cult with going forward and accepting the calendrical observances enunciated in the Mosaic covenant. He wishes his converts to do neither, and so he throws odium on what the audience is contemplating doing by suggesting it would be similar to committing apostasy, it would be similar to going back to Emperor worship" (ibid., 298). That the imperial cult pervaded every aspect of life in this period is demonstrated by White, *Apostle*, chaps. 4, 5, 7; Horsley (ed.), *Paul and Empire*; id., (ed.), *Paul and Politics*; W. Carter, *Matthew*;

Kraybill, *Cult*; Witulski, *Adressaten*, 128-75; Wright, *Perspective*, 59-79. Cf. Storkey, *Jesus*, passim.

On a related point, Witherington (following Barclay) suggests that Judaism, with its fixed set of rituals, sacrifices, temple, etc., would have appealed to former pagans just because it filled the social void left by their departure from their former religion, with its own elaborate cultus (*Grace*, 361-62). By assuming the status of proselytes, the Galatians could hope "to identify themselves with the local synagogues and thus hold at least a more understandable and recognizable place in society" (Barclay, *Obeying*, 60).

8-11 As evident from the quotation above, Calvert-Koyzis proposes that Paul's admonition against lapsing into idolatry recalls the Abraham traditions of the intertestamental period. According to these sources, Abraham was the "archetypal anti-idolater," who resisted the seductions of pagan worship. This being so, "Paul makes the law the ultimate taboo for a child of Abraham by equating observance of the law with idolatry. The opponents of Paul, presumably Jewish Christians, had been compelling the Gentile Christians in Galatia to live like Jews by adding the concept of law to the gospel. However, in his letter to the Galatians, Paul has used the Abraham traditions for his own purposes. Now that the Christians in Galatians are also children of Abraham by virtue of being 'in Christ', the idolatry which they are to avoid is obedience to the law." This is the thesis of her *Paul*, as distilled in "Abraham" (quote from ibid., 236-37).

8 According to one translation, Paul writes that pagan deities are "by nature" (*phusei*) no gods, meaning that these gods do not exist "in reality." Alternatively, Paul's Greek could be translated "in nature," signifying that the Galatians' deities were nothing more than "natural things," belonging to the created realm that can be perceived by the senses. Either way, Paul's basic point is matched by 1 Cor 8:4-6, which maintains that "no idol exists in the world, and that there exists no god except the 'One'" (translation by Betz). Betz can appropriately comment: "These 'so-called gods' do exist and have power, but only to the extent that they are being worshipped. In other words, Paul does not deny that these 'so-called gods' exist, but their 'existence' consists merely of the superstitious imaginations and projections of the worshippers" (*Galatians*, 215).

9 Because the law weakens rather than strengthens its adherents, Paul admonishes the "strong" in faith in the Roman congregations (Rom 15:1) not to cause the "weak" to "stumble" (Rom 14:21). The English "stumble" translates *skandalizō*, the standard verb in the Greek Bible for apostasy. Certain (Jewish) believers had indeed been weakened because of their continuing praxis of the Torah. For this reason, the others, by flaunting their liberty, must not push them over the edge back into Judaism and thus into apostasy from Christ.

GALATIANS CHAPTER FOUR

I. A Personal Appeal (4:12-20)

From the outset of his "argument from Scripture and salvation history," Paul has engaged the Galatians with a number of pointed observations from the OT, according to his distinctive reading and application of these texts. He has one remaining argument from the Scriptures, in vv. 21-31. But before proceeding, he pauses for a personal aside, one that very tenderly recalls the emotional bond between him and his readers. The mood of this paragraph serves to counterbalance the more severe tone of his earlier rebuke of them as "foolish" (3:1, 3) and "bewitched" (3:1).

12 Commencing Paul's personal appeal is a plea for his brothers and sisters to become as he is, because he became as they. This means not simply to put themselves in Paul's place, but to imitate what he became when he encountered Jesus on the Damascus Road. At that time, he died to the law (2:19), ceased to be a zealot for the traditions of the fathers (1:14) and began to live as the Galatians before they came under the spell of the Judaizers (3:1). It is in this sense that Paul became like them. In his words elsewhere, he became as one "outside the law" (1 Cor 9:21). In becoming like Paul, in turn, they likewise would die to the law and return to their law-free condition before the arrival of the Teachers from Jerusalem. Instead of observing such "elements of the world" as days, months, seasons and years, they need to recognize that the blessings of being Abraham's sons do not depend on Torah observance and Jewish self-identity, only on faith in Christ. Paul can address them as "brothers" because they became and still were members of God's new family just as they found themselves, simply by believing reception of *his* gospel, a gospel which makes *no distinction* between Jew and Gentile in the plan of salvation (Rom 1:16; 2:11; 3:22; 10:12).

Somewhat abruptly, he exclaims that the Galatians did him "no harm" (as explicated by vv. 13-14). His mind moves rapidly from their original acceptance of his law-free gospel to their reception of him personally.[24] As he writes, however, the atmosphere has changed from affection to animosity by the presence of the oppo-

---

[24] That the Galatians did Paul no harm may allude to the fact that so frequently he was done harm, verbally and physically, by those who reacted so violently to his preaching (Acts 13:45, 50; 14:2-5, 19-22; 17:5-9; 18:5-6; 19:28-41; 21:11, 27-36; 22:22-23; 23:12-15, 20-21; Rom 15:31; 2 Cor 11:23-26; Gal 6:17; 2 Tim 4:14). Hays adds that the text echoes Hellenistic ideas about friendship, in that it was a commonplace maxim that friends do not harm friends (*Galatians*, 293).

nents, whose "other gospel" has engendered nothing but "biting and devouring" (5:15) among Paul's friends and their growing dissatisfaction with him.

13-14 That Paul's brothers did him "no harm" is clarified by the state in which he arrived among them, when he preached the gospel to them earlier (*to proteron*).[25] Had they intended him any hurt, certainly they could have taken full advantage of the debilitated condition in which he came upon the scene. He informs them that he might have gone elsewhere to evangelize, but it was because of the "weakness in my flesh" that he diverted to Galatia. The phrase denotes some illness, ailment or other untoward physical condition, possibly Paul's "thorn in the flesh" of 2 Cor 12:7. It is tempting to link Paul's "weakness in my flesh" with the "marks" or "stripes" that he bears in his flesh (6:17; cf. 2 Cor 11:24-25). These correspond to Jesus' own "marks" resulting from his scourging preceding the crucifixion (see on 6:17). Perhaps a hint in this direction is that the Galatians received Paul *as Christ Jesus*. Judging from the account in Acts, Paul was so mistreated in his evangelistic efforts that he must have arrived in Anatolia in such a battered and bruised condition that it would have been shocking to most sensibilities. But whatever the "weakness of my flesh" was precisely, it was in such a bodily state that was used in the providence of God to bring the gospel to these people for the first time. His infirmity turned out for their salvation, and initially they were more than glad to view his presence among them in just this light.

If Paul's physical condition remains a mystery, his reception by the Galatians is not. His problem was a genuine trial to them, but they did not "despise" him or "spit out" (literal translations). "Despise" is a strong word that connotes an angry repudiation of someone (e.g., Isa 53:3; Matt 6:24; Luke 18:9; Rom 14:3, 10), and especially the treatment received by Jesus himself during the passion (Luke 23:11; Acts 4:11). "Spit out" can mean simply to "react disdainfully," or it may allude to the ancient practice of spitting as a defense mechanism against sickness or the warding off of evil spirits (the two were often associated). All in all, Paul's state of being and appearance were such that they normally would have

---

[25] The Greek *to proteron*, "earlier," "formerly," "beforehand," must refer to Paul's initial visit to Galatia. Martyn's contention that Paul, in this letter, repreaches the gospel would be confirmed by his recollection of that earlier occasion on which he first "preached the gospel" (*euēngelisamēn*) to them. Since by now they have virtually forgotten it, Paul deems it necessary to repreach it.

evoked contempt and revulsion, if not out-and-out fright, on the part of onlookers. Such was his condition that it formed a "trial" or "temptation" (*peirasmon*) for the Galatians.[26] As Bruce explains, "They might have been tempted to treat both himself and his message with contempt and loathing" (*Galatians*, 209).

But far from reacting as others might have, the Galatians welcomed the apostle as an angel (or messenger) of God. "The contrast is the apposite one: instead of regarding Paul as a tool or victim of demonic powers, they had realized that he came with God's message, that is, as one sent from God" (Dunn, *Galatians*, 234).[27] And not merely as an angel, Paul was received as Christ Jesus himself. Paul echoes the genius of commissioning: the one sent is as the sender. He was selected and fully appointed by the risen Christ to take the gospel to the nations (see on 1:15); and there was a time when the readers had no doubts about it. Now, however, all that has changed, and many in Galatia were willing to believe that the circumcisers, not Paul, were the authentic agents of Christ. What a reversal of their original convictions! They should have known that it was just Paul's sufferings that served to validate his gospel and apostleship (see the section note to vv. 13-14). No wonder, Paul is, as it were, in the pangs of childbirth until Christ is formed in their midst (4:20)!

15 In recalling the Galatians' uncommonly warm welcome of him, Paul now asks, "Where, then, is your blessedness?" The word normally translated "blessedness" (*makarismos*) is ambiguous. (1) Blessing could be what they received when they embraced his gospel, that is, the blessing of being God's sons through Christ ("the blessing of Abraham," 3:14). (2) The term could designate a blessed or happy frame of mind (NIV: "joy"). (3) Hays proposes that *makarismos* is not a state of blessedness but the pronouncement of blessing, as in Rom 4:6, 9, the only other place where Paul uses the word. Paul, then, would be asking his friends what happened to the word of blessing they once pronounced on him (*Galatians*, 294). Hays is probably right, although we should not overlook that in Galatians there is a "theology of blessing." The recipi-

---

[26] There are variant readings in the manuscripts. One, *ton peirasmon humōn*, would be "the trial which you experienced." Another, *ton peirasmon mou*, would be "the trial which I caused" (Bruce, *Galatians*, 209).

[27] The Galatians' benevolent reception of Paul stands out all the more in view of the fact that shared suffering, in that climate, was a token of friendship (Fredrickson, "Paul," 178). All the more poignant, then, is the cry of 4:16: "Have I then become your enemy by telling you the truth (RSV)?"

ents of the letter were in danger of losing their sonship in Christ, and their state of mind was anything but happy or joyful. Judging from 5:15, 19-21, 26, the exclusivistic theology of the Judaizers was bearing its evil fruit in a life of strife, discontent and an inability to cope with the impulses of the flesh. Life under the law is anything but joyous (cf. Matt 11:28; Acts 15:10). How very different is their present disposition as compared to the time when they would have pulled out their very eyes and given them to Paul.[28] Back then, they were willing to help him in any way they could, proof positive of their "blessedness," or, if Hays is correct, "pronouncement of blessing" on Paul.

16 One question follows another. If Paul came to them in a supreme act of friendship and was received by them as a friend, has he all of a sudden become their enemy by telling them the truth?! The "truth" is at least threefold: (1) Paul's law-free gospel of "no distinction" between Jew and Gentile, which brought such wrath upon his head by those enamored of the law; (2) his warnings to the Galatians that, in their foolishness, they could lose everything that has been procured in Christ; (3) his characterization of the circumcisers as false brothers and apostates with regard to God's purposes in Christ. All three in combination were sufficient for at least a faction of the Galatian churches to regard Paul as an enemy—and most certainly they did so under the influence of the other teachers, who likely called Paul their enemy without mincing words. Reading between the lines, we may deduce that the Galatians did indeed have an enemy; but it was the enemy within, their current mentors, not Paul.

Hays suggests that the other missionaries perhaps have persuaded the Galatians that Paul has betrayed them by preaching a watered-down gospel that lacked the full benefit of circumcision and Torah observance. "If so, Paul now challenges their motives for alienating the affections of the Galatians away from him. He, Paul, tells the truth, whereas they are manipulators and flatterers who are preventing the Galatians from living in the truth (5:7)" (*Galatians*, 295).

17 That Paul eyes the rival missionaries as the Galatians' enemies is evident from the way he abruptly reintroduces them simply as

---

[28] It is often deduced that Paul's "weakness of the flesh" was an eye problem. However, Hays (following Betz) shows that "tearing out the eyes" was a proverbial expression, like our colloquialism "cut off the right arm" (*Galatians*, 294).

"they." His complaint is that "they" are "zealous" for his friends. The verb "be zealous" (*zēloō*) bears a variety of meanings, both positive and negative (BDAG, 427). But given that this verb, along with the cognate noun "zealot," played such a conspicuous role in the history of Judaism (see on 1:14), it is likely that it here takes on specific connotations. That is to say, the Judaizers' zeal for the Gentile Galatians meant pulling out all the stops to bring them into conformity to Moses. As Dunn explains:

> The claim made for and by Galatian Gentiles to full participation in the covenant of Israel, without regard for the distinctive 'works of the law', would be precisely the challenge which would arouse Phinehas-like zeal—a challenge met, in the case of the other missionaries, by the attempt to eliminate such a breach of covenant boundaries by fully incorporating the Gentile converts in question (*Galatians*, 237).

Not surprisingly, Paul views such zeal as wasted in a bad cause: the Judaizers' efforts are "for no good." Comments Witherington: "Like the zeal Paul himself had previously exhibited, this zeal also is not according to knowledge and not going in a proper direction, it is to no good end" (*Grace*, 313).

The most accurate insight into the motives and tactics of the opponents is that they wanted to shut the Galatians out (NASB: "exclude you"). From one perspective, the Teachers were trying to shut these people *in* by confining them within the walls of the Torah. However, Paul's reference is to the new covenant community as constituted by Jesus the Messiah (Matt 16:18: "*my* church"). From this vantage point, the Judaizers were endeavoring, no less, to exclude the Galatians *from* the latter-day people of God by confining them within the "prison house" of the law (3:22), with its requirements of circumcision, etc. Quite unwittingly, this, in principle, is what Peter was doing when he withdrew from the Gentiles upon the arrival of the men from James (2:11-14). On that occasion, Hays appropriately comments, the Jewish Christians withdrew from fellowship with Gentile Christians, thus shutting them out in order to put pressure on them to "Judaize." This is why "Paul looks at the Galatian situation with psychological realism and sees that the exclusivity of the Jewish-Christian Missionaries makes their religious 'club' seem highly desirable to those who are on the outside" (*Galatians*, 295). Yet, I would add, to become an insider of this "club" necessarily meant that one had to become an outsider as regards "the truth of the gospel" and the recently reformed messianic community. Circumcision *into* Moses meant nothing other than exit *from* Christ.

If the design of the Jewish missionaries was to withdraw the Galatians from the Pauline communities, it was in order that they might receive a corresponding show of zeal from these newly constituted "honorary Jews." In every regard, their hope was that they and their protégés would share beliefs and values derived from the Torah, so that, apart from anything else, each could participate fully in table fellowship without compromise. Correspondingly, their zeal for one another would result in their "zealous" (violent) treatment of all others who refused to conform to their standards of belief and conduct (thus giving rise to the attitudes decried by Paul in 5:15, 19-21, 26; 2 Cor 11:20).

18 Paul qualifies that zeal is a double-sided virtue, "Highly desirable, but easily prone to excess" (Dunn, *Galatians*, 239). Zeal in itself is not objectionable. Indeed, zeal has its upside, because elsewhere he exhorts Christians not to "flag in zeal" (*spoudē*), but to be "burning in the Spirit" (Rom 12:11; cf. Acts 18:25), as he himself continued to be zealous for his churches (2 Cor 11:2). According to this very letter, Paul's erstwhile zeal for the traditions of the fathers has now been rechanneled in the direction of love for those whom he formerly despised and attempted to decimate. So, Paul can affirm here that it is always good to be "courted zealously (*zēlousthai*) in a good cause" (*en kalō*). Paul is the one doing the courting, and not only, he says, when he is present with them, but also in the present epistle. The Judaizers, by contrast, are courting the Galatians, but to no good end. They were headed down the wrong road in their zeal both for Moses and those proclaiming Moses, a road very familiar to Paul since he had once trod it. Rather, the "good cause" is the "good news" of Paul's proclamation, for which they ought to be aflame even when Paul is not there to prod them.

We recall that underlying human zeal is the divine jealousy of God for his people (e.g., Exod 20:5; 34:14; Deut 4:24; 5:9). Thus, Paul's zealous courting of the Galatians is modeled on Yahweh's husbandly jealousy for his "wife," Israel. Yet Paul's yearning over the Galatians was not peculiar to them. To the same effect, he writes to the Corinthians: "I feel a *divine jealousy* (*theou zēlō*) for you, for I betrothed you to Christ to present you as a pure bride to her one husband" (2 Cor 11:2) (RSV).

19 The very fact that Paul can address these recalcitrant Christians as "my children" is an index to his heart. They may be in revolt against him, but he still is their parent in the gospel. On several occasions, Paul can depict his relation to his converts under the imagery of a father (1 Cor 4:14, 17; 2 Cor 6:13; 12:14; Phil 2:22; 1 Thess 2:11). But in one instance he switches genders and likens himself to a wet nurse (1 Thess 2:7). In the present verse too, he assumes the female role—a woman in labor—in order to intensify the sense of his feelings toward his "children." Paul might have thought that his labor pains were at an end on his first visit when he brought them to birth in Christ. But now he has to endure agony all over again until Christ is finally formed within them.

At first sight, the second half of v. 19 seems to contradict the first half, or at least Paul appears to be mixing his metaphors: he is in labor, but Christ is being formed in the Galatians, as though they were giving birth to Christ. It has been thought by some that the seeming incongruity of the two parts of the verse is due to Paul letting his emotions get out of hand and so failing to be consistent with his imagery. However, far from being merely an emotional appeal from a man whose argumentative powers have temporarily escaped him, Gal 4:19 occupies a pivotal place in the paragraph of 4:12-20 (and really of the whole letter). So speaks Gaventa, who has shown convincingly that quite contrary to being an emotional outburst, Paul employs a conventional metaphor—a woman in the throes of childbirth—to identify his apostolic work with the apocalyptic expectation of a new world order. That is to say, the goal of Paul's ministry is no less than the new creation being formed within the communities of believers in Galatia ("Maternity").

Gaventa fastens on the verb "be in the pains of childbirth" (*ōdinō*), along with cognate noun "travail" or "birth pains" (*ōdin*). These words appear in the LXX in apocalyptic contexts having to do with a coming cataclysm, as being like the anguish of a woman giving birth (Isa 13:6, 8; Jer 6:24; Mic 4:10 [all three depicting Israel's removal into exile]; cf. Isa 54:1). In other literature, the association of birth pains and tribulation occurs as well. *1 Enoch* 62:4 depicts the "labor pains" that will come, at the last judgment, upon the rulers of this age (cf. *2 Apoc. Bar.* 56:6; 4 Ezra 4:42). In a distinct but related manner, 1QH 3:7-10 describes the birth of the Dead Sea community in just the same terms, as coming into existence through "belly pangs" and "grievous pains." In all these texts, there is the association of the anguish of childbirth with the passing of an old order and the coming of a new. The NT takes up the same imagery in apocalyptic passages such as Matt 24:8; Mark

13:8; Rom 8:22; Rev 12:2; 1 Thess 5:3, all occupied with the end of the age as transpiring through labor pains.

Gaventa concludes that the same association is at work here in Gal 4:19 too. "Paul's anguish, his travail, is not simply a personal matter or a literary convention having to do with friendship or rebirth but reflects the anguish of the whole created order as it awaits the fulfillment of God's action in Jesus Christ" (ibid., 194). At stake, she writes, are not the birth pangs of an individual apostle but those of the cosmos itself. "Paul's labor is that of an individual who knows that the world has been invaded by a new reality: a crucified Lord who confronts and overturns the world" (ibid.).

For Christ to be "formed" within the Galatians, then, is not simply for them to develop spiritually or morally. Rather, "The formation of Christ among the Galatians is simultaneously their crucifixion with Christ. It means that the eclipse of the old occurs among them" (ibid.).

> The letter reflects Paul's convictions that the Galatians were called, that they had heard the gospel, and that they responded in faith. But he also believes that they are in danger of turning again, of converting back to their earlier views. For that reason he speaks of his own labor with them and the need of Christ to be formed (ibid.).

This is precisely the thrust of 2 Cor 5:17: "So if anyone is in Christ, there is a new creation: everything old has passed away; see, everything has become new" (NRSV). The burden of Paul's appeal to the Corinthian churches is that they, like the Galatians, leave behind the "old things" of the Mosaic covenant as promoted by his opponents and embrace the "new things" that have arrived in Christ (see Hubbard, *Creation*, 133-87). In this regard, one senses more than a touch of irony in Paul's use of the birth pangs metaphor as compared to 1QH 3:7-10. That community so devoted to the Torah likened its origin to labor pains. Paul, on the other hand, is also in the throes of childbirth—but to bring forth a community free from the law!

Eisenbaum has underscored how telling this last observation is. The essence of the "new perspective" on Paul, she notes, is that the apostle followed monotheism to its logical conclusion (as in the use of the *Shema* in Rom 3:29). "Believing in the divine impartiality of God, and as a result of his experience of the risen Christ, Paul was led to abandon the idea of Israel's uniqueness in the pursuit of theological and anthropological universalism. Jews 'by birth' no longer hold the privileges they once held.... As one scholar puts it, Paul renders 'all genealogies irrelevant'" ("Paul," 142, quoting H. Eilberg-Schwartz). Especially striking in this present context, she observes that there is evidence that men could claim powers of reproduction through the dissemination of religious instruction. Again citing Eilberg-Schwartz:

> Rabbis fathered "children" through the teaching of Torah. As the learning of Torah emerged as the paradigmatic religious act in the rabbinic community, it absorbed the symbolic capital which had earlier been invested in procreation. Concerns about reproduction and lineage were symbolically extended from the human body to the Torah knowledge itself (ibid., 143-44).

Eisenbaum appropriately concludes: "Paul's description of Abraham's procreative act of faith mirrors his self-understanding as apostle to the Gentiles. Paul creates Abrahamic descendants not through biological reproduction but through his preaching and teaching. He is a verbal progenitor, struggling to 'form' Christ in his gentile 'children'" (ibid., 144).

It needs to be clarified that it is not only Paul's preaching but his person which is in view when he portrays himself as a woman giving birth. Fridrichsen explains that when Paul (in Rom 1:1) refers to himself as a "called apostle," he characterizes himself as an "eschatological person:" "He is a man who has been appointed to a proper place and a peculiar task in the series of events to be accomplished in the final days of this world" (*Apostle*, 3). As Christ's apostle, the new creation dawns in the life of individuals by virtue of *his very presence*. No wonder, he can tell the Corinthians, "Woe to me if I do not preach the gospel" (1 Cor 9:16) (RSV)!

In sum, Christ, as the bringer of the new creation, is being formed "within" the Galatian communities (not "in" them as a fetus in their "womb," as though they could give birth to Christ). It is Paul's person and preaching, not that of his detractors, which is bringing this about. Therefore, he is willing to suffer no less than the agony of childbirth *until* Christ is finally fully formed in their midst. Some commentators propose that underlying Paul's determination to bear with the Galatians is his Already/Not Yet soteriology, whereby salvation is set forth as a "work in progress" that will be consummated on the Day of Christ. However, it is more likely that he has in view the congealment of convictions on the part of the communities that it is his gospel, not the "gospel" of the other "apostles," which is the implement of the new world order. As a good pastor, Paul is willing to endure whatever is necessary until the end-time manifestation of Christ is stabilized in Galatia.

20 The section ends on a note of perplexity and concern. Paul's wish to be present with the Galatians is entirely understandable. If he were there, he would hope to change the tone he has necessarily had to assume with them in this letter. Paul literally writes that he wants to change his voice, which perhaps means that he desires to *ex*change this written communication for actual speaking. Personal encounters are always more effective than letters, and it is to his regret that he was unable to be with them. If he is at his wits' end with them, it is for good reason. If it was through his ministry that the new creation arrived in Galatia, no wonder he is perplexed that so many do not have to eyes to see it. They prefer an alternative vision of the kingdom of God.

Section Note

13-14 Hafemann ("Exile," 354-56; id., "Weakness") shows that Paul's appeal to his suffering and to the response his sickness evoked from the Galatians is not an aside in his argument but an essential aspect of his polemic. Both demonstrate that the new age of the inheritance of the Spirit has in fact dawned and that the Galatians' previous experience of God's covenant blessing was legitimate (cf. 4:14-15 with 3:1-5). From Paul's perspective, nothing else can adequately explain either his own suffering (4:13-14; cf. 1:10; 5:11; 6:17) and willingness to live like a Gentile (4:12; cf. 1 Cor 9:21), or the loving response of the Galatians in return (4:14; cf. 5:6, 13-23; 6:15). Conversely, the Judaizers' exclusion of the Galatians until they conform to the practices of the Sinai covenant reveals the impurity of their motives (4:17-18; cf. 2:13; 6:12). As a result, if the Galatians were to follow them, they would be denying the reality of their previous "blessing" (4:15a; cf. 3:1-5).

Drawing on the work of E. Baasland, Hafemann points to the conceptual link between Paul's suffering in 4:14 and the OT "curse" tradition based on the connection between sin and suffering/persecution. The most convincing evidence of this is found in the *arur* (curse) catalogue of Deut 27:15-26; 28:15-19. Against this backdrop, the polemical significance of Paul's statement in 4:14 becomes readily apparent. Paul's reference in Gal 3:10 to Deut 27:26 (28:15) as an essential part of his dispute with the Judaizers points to the likely inference that they were probably using this same tradition against Paul, arguing from his suffering that he was the one who was still under the curse of the law (cf. his fivefold punishment as a transgressor by the synagogue in accordance with Deut 25:1-3 [2 Cor 11:24]). Thus, Paul's suffering had posed a "temptation" to the Galatians (4:14a). But in contrast to Paul's opponents, the Galatians' earlier acceptance of him in spite of his suffering indicated their former approval of his gospel and of his apostleship, to which Paul now calls them back. Paul insists that his sufferings are not the result of a curse, but they show that he belongs to Christ, who redeemed him from that very curse (3:13; 4:5).

Finally, Hafemann observes that Paul's argument in Galatians 4 follows the same structure and content exhibited in 2 Cor 2:14-4:6, where Paul is fighting a similar challenge against his apostleship and the nature of his gospel. In both cases, Paul supports the legitimacy of his apostleship by pointing to the mediatorial role played by his suffering in the preaching of the Gospel (cf. 2 Cor 2:14-17 with Gal 4:13) and then turns to the past response of his readers as evidence not only of his own legitimacy, but also of their past experience of the Spirit and blessing (cf. 2 Cor 3:1-3 with Gal 4:14-15). And in both cases, Paul subsequently offers an argument from Scripture in order to fortify the appeal from his own personal experience and that of his readers (cf. 2 Cor 3:4-18 with 4:21-20, esp. 3:14-15 with 4:21-25). In Gal 4:12-30, Paul is thus establishing the same twofold argument he employed elsewhere when the gospel was on the line. A comparison with 2 Cor 3:4-4:6 also makes it clear that Paul's foundational argument for the truth of the gospel and for the legitimacy of his own apostleship derives from the Scriptures themselves as they testify to the essential difference between the nature of the old and new covenants (cf. 2 Cor 3:6, 14 with 4:24).

J. The Story of Hagar and Sarah (4:21-31)[29]

Paul may be perplexed about his "children," but he is not ready to give up the fight yet. In one final appeal to the Scriptures, he calls upon all of his creative dexterity as "a teacher of the nations in faith and truth" (1 Tim 2:7). Seeing that so much of the argument thus far has been derived from the promises to Abraham, we are not surprised that for one last time Paul returns to the Abraham narrative of Genesis. What follows is not so much a independent argument as an illustration or additional documentation of the point already made. In the ensuing paragraph, Paul will demonstrate how the initial fulfillment of these promises foreshadowed their eschatological realization now occurring through his ministry (see the important and insightful essay of Jobes, "Jerusalem," as

---

[29] For a listing of recent literature devoted to the passage, see De Boer, "Quotation," 372, n. 8.

summarized in the second section note to these verses). By this means, he reintroduces and elaborates the key motif of freedom.

It is very likely that Paul pursues the story of Sarah/Isaac and Hagar/Ishmael because the opponents had taken up these materials in order to prove their case (Barrett, *Essays*, 154-70). And as Barrett says elsewhere, "Paul was obliged to follow them point to point because he could not afford to let it appear that his opponents had the Old Testament—the Bible—on their side" (*Freedom*, 44). See the first section note to these verses. Indeed, a face value reading of the narrative would tend to support the Judaizers' position simply because it was the Gentile slave girl and her son who were expelled from the Abrahamic community (Barrett, *Essays*, 162). It is quite believable that they would have argued that the Galatians could not be heirs of Abraham as long as they remained in their uncircumcised state and kept aloof from the Torah. But by virtue of the phenomenon of role reversal (see on 3:10-13),[30] Paul is able to turn the tables and, no doubt to the deep chagrin of the circumcisers, maintain that they are the neo-pagans who ought to be turfed out of the Christian camp![31]

Hays cites *Jub.* 16:17-18 as an illustration of the Judaizers' interpretation of Genesis 16, one that gave a place of special prominence to Abraham's physical descendants through Isaac. And not only so, the author declares that Isaac's offspring would not be counted among the nations, but rather they would become the special possession of the Lord (= Exod 19:5-6). Hays then offers the comment that if this is what the Galatians had been told about the Genesis narrative, then "Paul is executing a bold counter-reading,

---

[30] A. Davis is of the view that Paul is employing an ancient allegorical device whereby an author would draw upon two modes of argumentation in order to startle the reader and act as markers leading to the Hebrew Scriptures for deeper spiritual interpretations (from the summary of her "Allegorically Speaking," 161). According to Davis, Paul, in keeping with this method, generates contradictory statements concerning the narrative of Hagar and Sarah. I would submit, however, that Andrew Perriman, as quoted by Davis, is closer to the truth. Paul's so-called "historical contradiction," according to Perriman, is "neither an accident nor an embarrassment but an important aspect of his argumentative strategy" (ibid., 167). Yet I would venture to add that even "historical contradiction" is not the most appropriate way of analyzing Paul's strategy, but rather role reversal in light of the eschatological situation.

[31] Several scholars connect the Hagar-Sarah allegory with the closing appeals and exhortations that began with 4:12 ("become like me") extending through 4:20. As George explains, the appeal begun at 4:12 continues into the story of Hagar and Sarah, coming to a crescendo with the command of 4:30: "Get rid of the slave woman and her son," that is, expel the Judaizers from your midst (*Galatians*, 333). See further Longenecker, *Galatians*, 199; Hansen, *Abraham*, 141-54.

reversing the polarity of the story by claiming that that it is the uncircumcised Gentiles converts who correspond to Isaac, the child of the promise" (*Galatians*, 301).

The whole passage is constructed in terms of opposites: the two sons of Abraham, representing flesh and Spirit respectively, are born of two women who stand for two covenants. The one covenant, as symbolized by the Egyptian slave, has now become passé, while the other, as typified by the mother of the Jewish race, is the eschatological form of God's speaking in Christ (cf. Heb 1:2).[32] In reminding us of the "apocalyptic antinomies" of Galatians, Das writes that here "a new pair of opposites comes into existence as the elements of the invading world do battle against the elements of this present age. The old world is waging its last stand." This explains the new and striking pairs of opposites in 4:21-31 associated with the two Jerusalems, the one below and the one above. One child is born in slavery and the other in freedom. One is in the flesh; the other is in the Spirit. The new creation in the Spirit is at war with the world of the flesh (*Paul and Jews*, 36).

The question arises, How can Paul treat Genesis 16-21 as he does? A frequent answer is that his methodology resides in a combination of allegory and typology (see, e.g., Fung, *Galatians*, 217-20). Allegorical exegesis of the OT and other literature, whereby a secondary referent was given to a text, was common enough in Paul's day.[33] The Galatians likely would have been familiar with the practice and would have found it, if well-constructed, convincing.[34] If the method was being applied to the text by the other

---

[32] Martyn connects 4:21-31 with the foregoing appeal in 4:12-20. In the latter passage, Paul lamented the labor pains he had to endure in order for Christ to be formed in the Galatians' midst (v. 19). He then notes that the word "child" (*teknon*) occurs four times in the Hagar-Sarah story, where it designates the offspring of both mothers, identified respectively as the children of the present Jerusalem and those of the heavenly Jerusalem. Martyn concludes that the two groups, representing the two covenants, are to be identified with the followers of the law-observant mission of the Teachers and those of the law-free gospel of Paul (*Issues*, 191-208). Witherington further clarifies that Paul's allegory has to do not with non-Christian Judaism and Christianity, but rather with two distinct visions of Christianity: the Pauline type or that of the other missionaries. "The argument here is an in-house one involving polemics against Judaizing Christians" (*Grace*, 331-32, quote from p. 332).

[33] Even Greek authors, in particular Homer, were allegorized to serve as vehicles for higher philosophical truths, or to alter the *prima facie* meaning of a writing if it was thought to be embarrassing in some regard.

[34] On allegory, see Longenecker, *Galatians*, 209-10; id., *Exegesis*, 30-33; Witherington, *Grace*, 321-28, 330; id., *Paul Quest*, 258-61. Witherington explains that

evangelists, then Paul will do the same and go them one better by showing how the history can be turned to his advantage as well: "Paul is perhaps engaging here in the time-honored rhetorical practice of stealing another's thunder by taking his best argument and using it to support one's own case."[35]

A typological approach to the story takes its *prima facie* meaning seriously as history. In typology, there is a true correspondence between persons and events in the OT and those contemporaneous with a NT writer.[36] In the present case, the OT narrative has placed in motion a series of events that has now reached its high point in Paul's law-free gospel to the nations. The realities that have transpired through his ministry were enacted beforehand in the case of Abraham's two sons.[37] In regard to typology, Paul is seen not to be placing a construction on the OT text but as perceiving what was inherent in the narrative as read in the light of Christ and the new covenant.[38]

No doubt, it will always be debated whether Paul moves within the realm of allegory or typology, or both. In any event, it is worth noting that the verb of v. 24 (*allēgoreō*) is a late word that need mean nothing more than "to speak with another meaning." And, in light of Jobes' study, Paul's handling of the OT is far from an arbitrary imposition of an assumed meaning onto the text. Writes Jobes ("Jerusalem," 317-18): "He is simply preparing his

---

"it is of the essence of allegory that the interpretation offered is not literally true about the subjects *within* the story, but rather it is true of persons outside the story, either members of the audience or those the audience knows about" (ibid., 323). This would certainly fit in the case of the Galatians and the Judaizers. Furthermore, Witherington has drawn some relevant parallels between Paul's handling of Genesis 21 and that of Philo (*Grace*, 324-25).

[35] Witherington, *Grace*, 328. See also Longenecker, *Exegesis*, 110-13; id., "Illustrations," 190-97, and the first section note to 4:21-31.

[36] This means that typology is not a species of allegory (as per A. Davis, "Allegorically Speaking," 165). Contra Davis, typology is not a method of saying one thing but meaning another. Rather, typology ties into the notion of *sensus plenior*, a "fuller meaning" to the OT text that becomes apparently only from the perspective added by the NT, and in particular the "Christotelic" reading of the Hebrew Scriptures. See LaSor, "*Sensus Plenior;*" Moo, "Problem."

[37] On typology, see Foulkes, *Acts*; Ellis, *Use*, 126-35; id., *Old Testament*, 105-9, 141-57; Goppelt, *Typos*; France, *Jesus*, 38-43; Snodgrass, "Use;" Witherington, *Paul Quest*, 255-58.

[38] On Paul's approach to the Scriptures, see, among many, Ellis, *Use*; Hays, *Echoes*; Koch, *Schrift*; Longenecker, *Exegesis*, 88-116; Evans/Sanders (eds.), *Paul*; Witherington, *Paul Quest*, 230-62; and with some reservation, Stanley, *Paul and Arguing*.

readers to understand that his exposition of Sarah and Hagar goes beyond the traditional historical understanding of these women. He is transforming the story of Sarah and Hagar from narrative history to (realized) prophetic proclamation just as Isaiah did" (that is, in Isaiah's treatment of the barrenness theme). Lincoln adds: "Paul serves up a cake, the basic ingredients of which are typological but which has some allegorical icing. What saves his allegorizing from becoming capricious is his deep concern with the history of salvation and his attempts even here to see Hagar, Sinai and Jerusalem in relation to the on-going process of God's redemptive activity" (*Paradise*, 14). De Boer likewise evaluates Paul's methodology as a combination of allegory and typology, with his use of Isa 54:1 being "both profoundly *christological* and *apocalyptic* (De Boer, "Quotation," 372, italics his).

Whichever route we take, Longenecker's summary of Paul's take on the Genesis story is well worth weighing. After a survey of the Hagar-Sarah story in Jewish authors (*Galatians*, 200-6), Longenecker proposes four points of significance for understanding Paul's own treatment of it.

> (1) Paul's Jewish heritage, which was not averse to highlighting the contrasts and conflicts of the story; (2) tendencies within the various streams of Judaism generally to contemporize the persons and places of the biblical narrative for their own purposes, whether such contemporizations be understood as allegorical or typological treatments; (3) the Judaizers' contemporization of the story, with the polemics of their usage probably directed against Paul; and (4) Paul's own *ad hominem* use, with his polemics directed against the Judaizers (ibid., 206).

Apart from such biblical/salvation-historical considerations, the sociological setting of these verses calls for some comment. S. Elliott has broken important ground by focusing on the Anatolian cult of the Great Mother as providing a possible explanation for Paul's presentation of the Hagar-Sarah story (*Cutting*, as summarized in her "Mother"). Although Paul's analogy is thoroughly Jewish, she contends that in a masterful way of contextualizing his argument, Paul developed this analogy because it would communicate so powerfully to his Anatolian readers. In brief, just as Jews under the old covenant live in slavery to a mother (Hagar) corresponding to a mountain (Sinai), in a similar fashion the Galatians also lived in slavery to a mother (the Anatolian Mother Goddess) who corresponded to a mountain. The solution, then, is for the Galatians to reject both mountain mothers and live in the freedom that Christ provides.

Her explanation does provide a plausible solution to the question of why Paul emphasizes a mountain analogy as well as why he can expect such a Jewish mode of argumentation to be grasped by Gentiles. She contends that Paul constructs his argument in such a way that the Galatian Gentiles would infer a comparison between their own Mother Goddess, whom they could even speak of as "Mountain Mother." The end result is a subtle but rhetorically powerful appeal to the Galatians to reject the teaching of the Jewish Christian missionaries, simply because their advocacy of the law is another form of slavery—just to a different Mountain Mother! If she is right, then Paul's employment of the Hagar/Mount Sinai image is even more startling than we have imagined: the one Mountain Mother is no better than the other!

21 After his tender, mother-like appeal, Paul now resumes a stronger tone, addressed directly to that segment of the church that is quite prepared to commit itself to a nomistic way of life. Those who wish to be under the regime of the law ought to "hear" the law in the biblical sense of hearing, that is, to "obey" its dictates (possibly an echo of the *Shema*, Deut 6:4). What he is building up to is v. 30 and the law's demand that the slave woman and her son, that is, the Judaizers, be given their walking papers from the Galatian congregations. "Law" is here used in a twofold sense: the "commandment and statutes" regulating the covenant made with Israel, and the Torah more broadly defined as Scripture.

22 The basic premise is stated by Paul's customary appeal to Scripture ("as it is written"): Abraham had two sons (Gen 16:15; 21:2). But his point is not that the patriarch had more than one child (in fact, he had many sons, Gen 25:1-6) but that their respective mothers were a slave and a free woman. It is of interest that in the LXX Hagar is called a slave girl (*paidiskē*) more than once, but Sarah is never called "free."[39] This means that the "emphasis on her free status, crucial for Paul's reading, is brought to the story by Paul himself" (Hays, *Echoes*, 113). Not that he has read something into the text, but rather he calls attention to what was obvious enough from the Genesis narrative.

---

[39] On the noun *paidiskē*, see Tsang, *Slaves*, 95-96.

In any event, it is just the disparity of slavery and freedom that forms the climax of this passage in vv. 30-31, as it spills over into 5:1, 13. But even before he comes to that point, Paul is already implicitly engaged in role reversal. As Martyn notes, the contrast between slave and free played a role in the Teachers' reading of Genesis 16-21. According to them, "The Law-observant descendants of Abraham through Sarah—the Isaacs—are free people, whereas Law-less Gentiles, descendants through Hagar—the Ishmaels—are slaves" (*Galatians*, 434). By the time Paul is through, it will be just the other way around! Paul's subliminal message is that those who rely on the flesh, descent from Abraham as signified by circumcision, are slaves, not free.

It is often noted that while the slave girl, Hagar, is mentioned by name, the free woman, Sarah, is not. This may be because Paul is more interested in what Sarah represents—freedom—than in her as a historical person. But there is another reason, namely, that *Paul* is playing her role and speaking with her voice, particularly in v. 30. If we ask, Whom does Sarah represent, or better, Who represents Sarah in this story? the answer is the "woman" who was in labor pains with the Galatians—Paul! "If the agitators are to be cast out," confirms Witherington, "then the original spiritual mother of the Galatians is to be once more embraced.... The voice of Sarah is now also the voice of Paul" (*Grace*, 325).

23 The two sons are further juxtaposed by the manner of their birth—a crucial point. On the one hand, Ishmael was born "according to the flesh."[40] NIV is justified in translating "in the ordinary way," that is, by means of normal human reproduction. Yet usually (though not exclusively) "according to the flesh" in Paul has a negative ring about it, especially when set over against "according to the Spirit" or, in the present case, "through promise." The negative connotation of "flesh" would seem to have two points of reference. The one is Abraham's attempt, as urged on by Sarah (Gen 16:1-2), to bring about God's extraordinary promise by ordinary means. The other is that the agitators were appealing to their fleshly descent from Abraham, with whom the covenant was sealed by circumcision, to validate their claims as the people of

---

[40] Paul uses the perfect tense of the verb "be born" (*gegennētai*) because he has in mind not simply the past historical facts of the births of Ishmael's and Isaac, but also the continuing result of those births in the persons of the opponents, who are now the "latter-day Ishmaelites," and that segment of the Galatian churches which is "like Isaac children of the promise." See the exposition below.

God and, consequently, their missionary message. The cutting edge of Paul's observation is that the opponents were attempting to generate churches in the same manner that Abraham begot Ishmael.

> The Teachers and others active in the Law-observant mission to the Gentiles are begetting churches by the (impotent) power of the flesh. Circumcising the flesh, that is to say, as though that were the potent antidote to the power of the flesh, they are engaged in a human, religious exercise that no more involves the power of God than did the arrangement (via Hagar) by which Abraham and Sarah got Ishmael (Martyn, *Galatians*, 435-36).

By contrast to Ishmael, Isaac was born of the free woman through promise. Isaac's birth from the barren Sarah was wholly extraordinary, by the power of God (or the Spirit, 4:29), and could never have occurred "the ordinary way."[41] We might have expected Paul to have written "according to promise" to counterbalance "according to the flesh." Instead, he says "through promise," stressing (as in 3:18) the instrumentality of the promise, with God's word effecting what was promised. Again, there is something beneath the surface here. The promise of the seed was made with respect to Isaac, not Ishmael. Therefore, the latter-day "Ishmaelites," the Judaizers, cannot be the recipients of the Abrahamic promise, even though "according to the flesh" they can trace their origins back to the father of the race.[42]

24 Here Paul states his methodology. According to NIV, the story of the two women can "be taken figuratively." Alternatively, NASB renders the verb (*allēgoreō*) as "allegorically speaking."[43] If

---

[41] Martyn argues that Paul's Greek phrases "according to the flesh" and "through promise" mean respectively "by the power of the flesh" and "by the power of the promises." The latter expression is matched by v. 29: "The one born of the power of the Spirit" (*Galatians*, 435).

[42] The equation Judaizers = Ishmael would have been particularly offensive if 1QM 2:13's attitude toward the latter was more widespread; that is, Ishmael was the progenitor of the "sons of darkness."

[43] After a perusal of the verb *allēgoreō* and the cognate noun *allēgoria*, Di Mattei concludes that the participle employed by Paul must mean "spoken allegorically," as opposed to "interpreted allegorically" ("Allegory," 107). Di Mattei complains that the latter definition, as exemplified by Dunn, Longenecker and others, fails to do justice to the linguistic data and represents an intrusion of "hermeneutical

the latter rendering is more nearly correct, then Paul is seen to place an allegorical interpretation on the OT text. The verb occurs only here in biblical Greek, but frequently in Philo, who famously subjected the OT to allegorical readings.[44] The basic assumption of the allegorical approach is that the text has another referent than its primary historical one. Allegorizing an historical text, says Witherington, is a way of contemporizing it by giving it a secondary referent (not a "deeper meaning") (*Grace*, 330). But Paul is to be distinguished from Philo (and later allegorizers) in that his handling of the Scriptures here is more in line with typology than allegory.[45] That is to say, the historical facts as presented by the Genesis narrative foreshadowed the events of Paul's day, namely, his law-free mission to the Gentiles and the counterattack of the Judaizers (note v. 29).

Whether allegorically or typologically (or both), the two women stand for two covenants. If a covenant may be defined as a "familial bond of commitment," then Paul envisages God as entering into this family bond on two distinct occasions. It is tempting to think in terms of the "old covenant" and "new covenant" distinction in the NT (Luke 22:20; 1 Cor 11:25; 2 Cor 3:6; Heb 8:6-13). However, in the present case our assessment of these covenants has to be more nuanced. Most likely, Paul has in mind the Mosaic administration as over against the Abrahamic covenant, as it flows into and finds its fulfillment in the new covenant in Christ. As Hays puts it, "The contrast is drawn between the old covenant at Sinai and the older covenant with Abraham, that turns out in Paul's rereading to find its true meaning in Christ."[46] We might, then, speak of the Abrahamic covenant/new covenant complex.

---

prejudices" into the interpretive process. Yet his own approach is not problem-free. For one, his data do allow for some instances of *allēgoreō* as "interpret allegorically" in Hellenistic and Jewish authors, opening up the possibility that Paul may be using it in this sense too. But mainly, Di Mattei's own "hermeneutical prejudices" effective turn the text of Genesis into an allegory as originally intended rather than serious history. Whatever we say about Paul's handling of the story, he did take it at face value as history.

[44] See Dunn, *Galatians*, 247-48; Di Mattei, "Allegory," 106, n. 18; A. Davis, "Allegorically Speaking," 163-64; Tsang, *Slaves*, 89-91.

[45] It is arguable that Paul's approach is much more typological than allegorical when his reading of Genesis is compared to a *real* allegory, namely, that of Philo. Philo (*Cher.* 8-9; *Sob.* 7-9) takes Abraham's two sons to be a symbolical portrayal of how the soul (Abraham) must transcend the realm of sense perception and sophistry (Hagar/Ishmael) and ascend to a higher knowledge of wisdom and virtue (Sarah/Isaac).

[46] Hays, *Echoes*, 114; id. *Galatians*, 302.

Therefore, writes Jobes, there is not a straight line through history connecting the Galatian Christians with the Sinai covenant and the Sinai covenant with the Abrahamic: "This is precisely what the Judaizers were implicitly arguing when they insisted on circumcision for Christians" ("Jerusalem," 317). Paul views the Mosaic period as a kind of "parenthesis" between Abraham and Christ.[47]

As Paul descends to particulars, he zeroes in, first of all, on the one covenant which is "from Mount Sinai," "bearing children for slavery" (NASB). Since Sinai is not called by name in the Genesis account, we must assume that Paul reads it in light of what the other teachers are presently saying about the Sinaitic covenantal law.[48] "When Paul says that the Hagar covenant is from Mount Sinai, he shows that he is working out his interpretation *from* present developments *to* the Genesis stories" (Martyn, *Galatians*, 436). That Paul should make Hagar—an Egyptian no less—stand for Sinai is a remarkable instance of role reversal, and no doubt would have been like pouring salt into an open wound as far as the opponents were concerned. Then he adds insult to injury by the assertion that Hagar/Mount Sinai is currently bearing children for slavery. If "like begets like," then a slave woman can do no other than reproduce slaves.

Of course, Hagar and Mount Sinai are really the Judaizers, who are currently making slaves of the Galatians, which is why Paul pulls no punches in informing them what precisely they are letting themselves in for. If Paul could speak of himself as a mother to his converts (v. 19), then he also could conceive of his rivals as mothers, only they are Hagar-like mothers who give birth to slaves by bringing them under the dominion of Mount Sinai.[49] In an ironic twist, some of the Galatian Christians, by embracing Moses, were returning to Egypt instead of pressing on to the promised land. This is all the more ironic as the law was given in the context of Israel's liberation from Egypt (see on 2:5). As Hays reminds us, "The Sinai Torah was given precisely as the covenant

---

[47] It is for this reason that Paul purposely does not complete the Sarah-side of the parallel construction of the two women, because he does not want us to gain the impression that there is a rigorous parity between Hagar and Sarah.

[48] It is possible to draw a loose connection between Hagar and Sinai from the biblical materials (Gen 21:10-21, 31; Num 10:11-12; 12:16). See Martyn, *Galatians*, 437, n. 129.

[49] Martyn proposes that the phrase "bearing children" is a metaphor for gaining converts (*Galatians*, 451-54). Hays picks up on this suggestion and adds that Hagar represents the covenant proclaimed by the Jewish Christian missionaries, whose work provoked Paul to write the letter (*Galatians*, 302).

sealing God's liberation of Israel from slavery in Egypt" (*Echoes*, 115).

25 The first clause of this verse informs (or reminds) the audience that, geographically speaking, Hagar = Mount Sinai is in Arabia.[50] Some commentators suggest that Paul mentions this because Arabia is the land of Hagar's descendants through Ishmael.[51] If this was in his mind, his point would seem to be that the law actually came from Hagar's territory, another way of consigning the law to the old creation and aligning it with the "elements" of pagan religion (4:9). Be that as it may, Ridderbos is right that since the location of this mountain is outside the pale of the promised land, the whole era of the law lies outside the domain of fulfillment (*Galatians*, 177). Hagar = Sinai "corresponds to" (or "stands in line with") the present Jerusalem,[52] because the Holy City itself is in bondage with its children (inhabitants). Both are slave mothers and both produce offspring in their own image. The law teachers could have accepted a certain identification of Sinai with Jerusalem because, of course, it was the law given on Sinai that led eventually to the establishment of the capital city with its temple worship. But we can imagine that their breath was taken away by Paul's characterization of both Sinai and Jerusalem as citadels of slavery! The "slavery" or "bondage" is the same as throughout Galatians, that is, the Torah as opposed to the freedom of Paul's gospel.

---

[50] Di Mattei points out that in targumic tradition an identification was also made between Hagar and Arabia ("Allegory," 112). Di Mattei also argues that Paul has in mind the *name* of Hagar because of the presence of the neuter definite article (*to*) before "Hagar," thus supporting, he maintains, an allegorical reading of our passage. He is probably right about this exegetical datum; but even so, a name can hardly be disassociated from a person. The historicity of the Genesis narrative remains intact.

[51] According to Gen 25:6, 18, Hagar and Ishmael were expelled to "the land of the East," the region later to be known as Arabia.

[52] The verb *sustoicheō*, translated "corresponds to," means to "place in the same column." As George points out (*Galatians*, 342), throughout this passage Paul was establishing two columns of implied correspondences and complementary antitheses:

Hagar	Sarah
Ishmael, the son of slavery	Isaac, the son of freedom
Birth "according to the flesh"	Birth "through the promise"
Old Covenant	New Covenant
Mount Sinai	[Mount Zion]
Present Jerusalem	Heavenly Jerusalem

Moreover, Kahl reminds us that the land of Israel was literally in bondage to the Romans, with everything implied thereby.[53] But instead of promoting the violent overthrow of the Romans, as the Zealots were soon to do, Paul advocates a nonviolent subversion of the Roman law and a messianic/apocalyptic reinterpretation of the Jewish law by having Jews and Gentiles, circumcised and uncircumcised, eat together at one table and serve each other in one universal community. For him, this is how the worldwide kingdom of God replaces Caesar's empire; how "we," as citizens of the Jerusalem above, can become free despite the present Jerusalem's slavery ("Hagar," 231).

In addition to everything else, when Paul coins the phrase "the Now Jerusalem," he aligns the city with "the present evil age" (1:4), the era of the "flesh" (3:3) and the period of "the elements of the world" (4:3, 9). And as if all this were not enough, Paul says no less than that Jerusalem, the mother of the Jews, *is* Hagar, the mother of the Arabs! By invoking once again the motif of role reversal, whereby Jews are turned into Gentiles, Paul continues to build up to the climactic demand of v. 30 that the neo-pagans be expelled from the community of the "new Israel" (6:16).

The mention of Jerusalem has a particular bearing on the opponents, because Jerusalem was the place of their origin, as "the people from James" (2:12). Witherington is right to remind us that these people did not see themselves as a separate entity from Judaism but rather as a movement within it. Their allegiance was to the present Jerusalem and their Jewish heritage, not just to the Jerusalem church (*Grace*, 334). In taking their gospel to the nations, they sought to promote the greater glory of Zion by the eschatological pilgrimage of the nations to the capital city (Isa 2:2-4; 56:6-7; 66:18-21; Mic 4:1-4; Zech 2:11; 14:16-19). For Paul, however, this covenantally nomistic path was not a viable option because "it is a failure to grasp the radical implications of the Gospel, in particular of Christ's death and resurrection, and the implications of the new eschatological situation of Christians" (ibid., 334). The bottom line for Paul, then, is regardless of how his rivals conceive of themselves and their mission, they really belong to the "Now Jerusalem" enmeshed in its slavery, its idolatrous attachment to the Torah (4:8-10). The sooner the Galatians wake up and realize this, the better off they will be.

---

[53] Kahl, "Hagar," 229-32. Hays adds that a contemporary observer would have to look no farther than the Fortress of Antonia, where Roman troops were stationed immediately adjacent to the temple (*Galatians*, 304).

26 On the other side of the equation stands "the Above Jerusalem." The notion of a heavenly Jerusalem is familiar from Jewish apocalyptic thought, according to which there was "an ideal form of Jerusalem in the purpose of God, waiting, as it were, in heaven to be revealed at the end time, when God's purpose would be completely fulfilled" (Dunn, *Galatians*, 253). This expectation was apparently based on Exod 25:9, 40, where Moses was told to construct the tabernacle in accordance with the pattern shown him on Sinai (see also Wis 9:8; Heb 8:5). This is intriguing in itself because it is on Sinai, the very place of the giving of the law, that an intimation is given of a higher reality than the law, a dimension that can be described as "above" rather than "below" (or "now"). This apocalyptic vision of a heavenly city of God (e.g., Isa 65:17-25; *2 Apoc. Bar.* 4:2-7; 4 Ezra 7:26; 8:52; 10:25-27; 13:36; *2 Enoch* 55:2) is taken up by the NT (Hebrews 8-10; 11:10, 16; 12:22-23; Rev 3:12; 21:1-3, 10-11, 22-27).[54]

What is distinctive about Paul's "Above Jerusalem" is that it is not merely on the way but is present already, with the revelation of Christ in Galatia. His Jerusalem is the new order of salvation, the powers of the age to come (Heb 6:5) that have been unleashed with the presence of the Holy Spirit. Stated otherwise, this is the city where Christ rules (Eph 1:20; 2:6; 4:10; Phil 3:20) and from which he dispatches his Spirit to produce in his people the new birth. In this sense, heaven has come down to earth in anticipation of the consummation of all things. (In a reversal of metaphors, Paul can declare that believers have been elevated to heaven and made to sit at Christ's right hand [Eph 2:6; Col 3:1].) "The heavenly Jerusalem is…to be viewed as *the new age depicted in spatial terms* and the anticipation of the full life of this new age is now present in the church."[55] Ultimately, the heavenly Jerusalem is the new heavens and earth, the finalized kingdom of God over which Christ is to reign, the origin and dwelling place of believers.

Such a city, corresponding to the age of fulfillment, can be nothing but "free," that is, not bound to the Torah as the present Jerusalem. If the Judaizers and their devotees have a mother—Hagar/Mount Sinai/present Jerusalem—who generates slaves, then Paul and those like him have a mother too—Sarah/Above Jerusalem—who gives birth to free people. Without mentioning Sarah by

---

[54] See further Longenecker, *Galatians*, 214; Lincoln, *Paradise*, 18-22; Gorman, *Apostle*, 213.
[55] Lincoln, *Paradise*, 25, italics mine; and De Boer, "Quotation," 373, 380.

name, Paul's allegory/typology is completed by an oblique reference to her (the "free woman" of v. 22): she is the emblem of the freedom embodied by the heavenly Jerusalem. This is *our* mother.[56] When we recall that Paul is probably casting himself in a Sarah-like role, it would follow that he is making an implicit claim to the Galatians: it is through his gospel, and his alone, that Christ from the "Above Jerusalem" is pouring out his Spirit to give birth to people of God (cf. on v. 19).

Paul's conception of the heavenly and free Jerusalem means that the focus of salvation history has shifted from the earthly to the heavenly realm. As De Boer can comment, these two realities are engaged in an apocalyptic struggle. However, the outcome of the struggle is not in doubt, as the quotation from Isa 54:1 with its eschatological promise make so plain ("Quotation," 377). For Paul, the hope of Israel lies not in Jerusalem but in Jesus Christ, "The one who fulfils all that Jerusalem dimly foreshadowed in regard to the presence of God with his people" (Lincoln, *Paradise*, 30). The name Jerusalem is retained and the significance of that name for the fulfillment of God's promises to Israel still stands in the background. Nevertheless, what God has accomplished in Christ has radically altered the meaning of Jerusalem. "The old category has been reinterpreted so that no longer in view is a restored national capital which will be the geographical centre for the ingathering of the nations in the Messianic era but Jerusalem can now designate instead the focal point of the heavenly existence of the new age" (ibid.).

Lincoln further observes that the Prophets, and in particular Isaiah, saw the final salvation in terms of a "centripetal" movement in which all the nations would be gathered to a renewed and glorified Jerusalem (Isa 2:2-4; 56:6-7; 66:18-21; Mic 4:1-4; Zech 2:11; 14:16-19). "For Paul this prophetic motif is being fulfilled, for those Gentiles who are children of promise do come to a Jerusalem glorified by the presence of God but because of Christ's exaltation this Jerusalem is not on earth but has become the focal point of the heavenly dimension" (ibid., 32). I might add that the expectation of a new Jerusalem arose out of the anticipated destruction of Zion, at the time of Israel's deportation to Babylon. For Paul, these prophecies of the rebuilding of the city have come to pass with the apoca-

---

[56] That Paul should call a city "our mother" is only to be expected in view of the imagery of "mother Zion" as attested from his Jewish heritage (Ps 87:5; Isa 1:26; 51:18; 54:1; 66:7-11; Jer 50:1; Hos 4:5; 4 Ezra 10:7; *2 Apoc. Bar.* 3:1; 10:16).

lyptic descent of the heavenly Jerusalem. The people of God have returned from exile.[57]

This readjustment of perspectives on Jerusalem has decided implications for the way in which the Galatians should regard the "mother church" in that city. The "false brothers" were probably claiming that the Jerusalem assembly, in sponsoring their law-observant mission, was properly mothering the Gentiles. No doubt, such claims were exaggerated, if not out-and-out false. But Paul's way of dealing with their allegations is to place the present Jerusalem in its true light.[58] Hopefully, in time the readers of this letter would come to see that Jerusalem in the most meaningful sense—the "true" Jerusalem—is "above," not "below." As Lincoln states so ably:

> But as it took time for the first generation of Jewish Christians to recognize the implications of Christ's death and resurrection for their attitude to the temple and its worship, so it took time for the implications of what had happened in Christ to be seen with regard to the role of Jerusalem. It was Paul, the apostle to the Gentiles, who saw most clearly what was at stake. He was convinced that believers need not look to the law-observing church of Jerusalem as their mother-church. Their true mother and the guarantor of their freedom is instead the heavenly Jerusalem. Christ, the church's Lord, is in heaven and therefore the church is inextricably bound up with the heavenly order and cannot be dependent on any earthly city, whether it be Jerusalem, Antioch or Rome. No earthly centre is to be regarded any longer as the official headquarters of the church.

---

[57] The hope for a new and glorified Jerusalem is evident from passages such as Isaiah 2; 54:10-14; 60-62; Ezekiel 40-48; Zechariah 12-14. Yet these visions of the future are cast very much in terms of Israel's national hopes which center around the earthly Jerusalem (for references in Jewish literature, see Lincoln, *Paradise*, 19). In Paul, the expectations of this renewed mother city are transposed into the "Above Jerusalem," which is now the seat of the glory of God in Christ.

[58] Martyn has argued that "Jerusalem" is used here in the same sense as in 1:17-18; 2:1, that is, as a metonym for the law-observant Jewish Christian church located there, not the non-Christian Jewish community (*Galatians*, 440, 458-66; *Issues*, 25-36; cf. De Boer, "Quotation," 381; Mußner, *Galaterbrief*, 325). The problem with absolutizing this distinction is that in 2:1-10 Paul acknowledges the calling and status of the apostles and affirms that he and they were on friendly terms. Thus, it does not really ring true that he should, in 4:21-31, classify them as the carnal seed of the bondwoman. Contra Martyn and De Boer, the persecuting zeal of the opponents (4:29) should not be traced back to Jerusalem assembly.

Rather the church is thrown on to its relation to the heavenly realm and its glorified Lord for its rule (*Paradise*, 31).

27 As per Paul's normal practice in argumentation, he draws on a biblical text for confirmation and/or illustration. The passage chosen this time is Isa 54:1.[59]

> Sing, O barren one, who did not bear;
>   break forth into singing and cry aloud,
>   you who have not been in travail!
> For the children of the desolate one will be more
>   than the children of her that is married, says the LORD. (RSV)

The quotation is especially appropriate as it comes at the beginning of a sermon in which the Lord comforts the exiles by reassuring them that once again he would take them for his wife (54:4-8) and that a new beginning would soon commence, like that following the flood (54:9-10). At the time of the restoration, the new Jerusalem will be rebuilt of precious stones (54:11-12), an echo of Solomon's dedication of the temple (1 Chr 29:2), which itself echoes Gen 2:10-14. For the time-being, the city is desolate, like a deserted wife (Isa 50:1; 64:10) who is childless. Yet when the exiles return, she will be overflowing with inhabitants; the abandoned one will become the fruitful mother-city (Isa 1:26). The image of the barren woman naturally links up with Sarah. Implicitly, the prophet echoes Gen 11:30 ("Sarah was barren and she had no child"). But the link is made explicit in Isa 51:2: "Look to Abraham your father and Sarah who bore you." The city, as Sarah herself, will be one day the "mother of nations" (Gen 17:16). For Paul, the promise of Isa 54:1 has direct applicability to the controversy with the opponents:

> To the False Brothers the circumcision-free mission is a Godless enterprise and, for that reason, barren. In reality, says Paul, the circumcision-free mission, enjoying the blessing of God, is vastly more fecund than the Law-observant mission that is an extension of the pre-

---

[59] De Boer points out that the step from Genesis narrative regarding Sarah to Isa 54:1 is not a great one, for several reasons. (1) Following Jobes, he notes that there are considerable verbal similarities between Gen 11:30 and Isa 54:1 (see the second section note to 4:21-31). (2) Outside of Genesis, Sarah is mentioned by name only in Isa 51:2. (3) Given Isa 51:2, it is possible that Isaiah intended to make an allusion to Sarah and her barrenness in 54:1.

sent and earthly Jerusalem church (Martyn, *Galatians*, 443).

The restored Jerusalem, therefore, represents the fulfillment of the promise that Sarah's (and Abraham's) offspring would be as numerous as the stars (Gen 15:5; 17:16; Isa 51:2). All of this would be suggestive to Paul of a new, heavenly Jerusalem. For him, Isa 54:1 has come to pass with the appearance of the "Above Jerusalem" now at the "ends of the ages" (1 Cor 10:11). Paul's claim, therefore, is that in his mission and preaching the exiles have returned to inhabit their glorified city. Israel's hoped for restoration has transpired eschatologically with the influx of the Gentiles into the new covenant community. Di Mattei comments: "The Gentiles are thus seen as the heirs of the New Jerusalem because, according to Paul's reading of Isaiah, that is exactly what the prophet speaks of at every turn of the page: the Nations shall be justified and assembled in the end of days" ("Allegory," 116, citing Isa 2:2-3; 14:2; 25:5-7; 51:5; 52:15; 54:3; 55:4-5). To this De Boer adds: "The Isaian text is thus brought by Paul into the service of christologically determined apocalyptic eschatology: the promise contained in Isa 54.1 has come to pass, as his application of the text to the Galatians in the next verse bears out: 'you, brethren, like Isaac, are children of promise like Isaac'" ("Quotation," 378).

Isa 54:1 was also the subject of attention in Jewish literature, the point being made that Jerusalem was left desolate because her children had turned away from the law (see Dunn, *Galatians*, 255). The law teachers might well have made hay of this tradition by pressing that Jerusalem's bareness was due precisely to an abandonment of the Torah. Yet, needless to say, Paul views the problem the other way around: it is adherence to the law that is the cause of Jerusalem's present problems. The tragedy is that the rank and file of Paul's fellow Jews remain banished in exile just because of their zeal for the Torah and the traditions.[60]

---

[60] See Hafemann, "Exile," 356-67. By way of extreme irony in predicting the overthrow of Jerusalem and the temple, Jesus declares that those who are with child are cursed rather than blessed (Matt 24:19 and pars.). Evans is right that this is a deliberate allusion to Isa 54:1. According to Evans, "Here is an example of the hermeneutics of prophetic criticism, hermeneutics which Jesus employed in assessing Israel's assumptions and interpretation of its sacred tradition" ("Predictions," 118). The irony consists in the fact that in Isaiah's vision the restored Jerusalem, formerly barren and deserted, was to be overflowing with inhabitants at the time of the return from exile. But now with the destruction of the second temple, the Jerusalem teeming with "children" is once again going to be desolate and laid low (Matt 23:3: "Behold, your house is forsaken and desolate" [RSV]). The "Be-

28 Paul's commentary on Abraham's two sons, which began in v. 22, developed into an exposition of their respective mothers (vv. 23-27). Here he returns to the principal subject with his declaration: "Now you, brothers, like Isaac, are children of promise." The "you" is comprehensive of all the Galatian believers, but the focus is on the Gentile portion of the churches. Just as they were, uncircumcised and non-kosher, they betoken the fulfillment of the promise that Abraham and Sarah would have countless descendants. To be sure, Jewish tradition took it for granted that the line of covenant promise ran through Sarah rather than Hagar and Isaac rather than Ishmael. But Paul's boldness resides in the way he fastens on Isaac's character as a child of promise (as in Rom 9:7-9) rather than his ethnic identity and his circumcision as a member of the Abrahamic community. In the same qualitative manner, the readers of this epistle are the promised children by virtue of divine intervention, not submission to the law. Their "birth," in its own way, is just as miraculous as that of Isaac.

29 But if the Galatians really are the Isaac-like children of God, "born after the Spirit," then they must count on rough treatment from the Ishmael-like sons of Hagar. The formula "just as then/so also now" is a further indication that Paul is moving within the realm of typology: an incident in the camp of Abraham gives expression to events playing themselves out in Paul's day. The reference is to Gen 21:9, which speaks of Ishmael "playing" with Isaac. In itself, the term "play" is neutral and can refer to innocent fun. But the verb can also assume darker overtones: "play" in the sense of "make fun," "scorn" or "mock" (thus NIV and NASB), and perhaps even some form of physical harassment is not to be ruled out. Sarah's reaction (Gen 21:10) tends to support this more negative reading. Gen 16:12 confirms Ishmael's quarrelsome character, which possibly was in Paul's mind as he ascribes to the other

---

low Jerusalem" suffers the fate of the original temple—barrenness—while the "Above Jerusalem" of Paul is filled to overflowing. The irony is intensified by Jesus' counsel for Christians to flee from the midst of the city (Mark 13:14; Luke 21:21). This echoes Jeremiah's warning for the people to flee from the midst of Babylon (Jer 51:6; cf. 50:8; 51:45. See Evans, "Predictions," 115.). In other words, Jerusalem has become another Babylon, quite in keeping with Paul's sympathies in Galatians 4.

teachers an Ishmaelian disposition. Later Jewish expositions of the passage are to this effect.[61]

Whatever precisely was involved in this "play," Paul interprets it as the persecution of Isaac by Ishmael. The verb "persecute" (*diōkō*) is in the imperfect tense, as though Ishmael customarily persecuted Isaac. But this persecution is not simply ancient history—it is still going on, as the opponents have in their crosshairs recalcitrant members of the Galatian congregations. Paul considers that he is also a target of theirs (5:11; cf. 6:12).[62] Lincoln plausibly suggests that what Paul has in mind is Ishmael mocking Isaac's claim to the inheritance. If this is so, then the Judaizers are cast in the role of Abraham's first son by mocking and jeering at the claims of the "latter-day Isaacs," the uncircumcised Galatians, to be heirs by faith alone (*Paradise*, 27).[63] Such a characterization of the opponents would have been especially offensive to them, as they themselves probably assumed the voice of Sarah in her demand to put the foreigners out of the Abrahamic community.

The struggle between the two offspring of Abraham is depicted as a conflict between flesh and Spirit. Again Paul makes a typological identification: the persecutors, like Ishmael, are born in accordance with the flesh, the persecuted, like Isaac, are born in accordance with Spirit. The first flesh/Spirit antithesis in the letter appears in 3:3, where Paul distinguishes between the age of the flesh, the old creation, and the age of the Spirit, the new creation. 4:23, accordingly, depicts the birth of Ishmael as being "according to the flesh," as over against the birth of Isaac "through promise." In 5:16-26, flesh and Spirit are juxtaposed once more, this time in

---

[61] Bruce, *Galatians*, 223-24. Hays wants to see Paul as tying into these exegetical traditions that interpreted Ishmael's "playing" with Isaac as some sort of malicious activity, which allowed him to place negative spin on Ishmael (*Galatians*, 305). However, the specific rabbinic sources are too late to assume that this tradition was current in Paul's lifetime.

[62] Kahl notes that "persecute" is the term used of the law-based pre-Damascus Paul himself in 1:13-14, 23 ("Hagar," 222, n. 6). The opponents are thus like the "old Paul" in their concerted effort to eliminate all opposition to their gospel of circumcision.

[63] In light of 2 Cor 11:20, an element of physical intimidation cannot be ruled out of the "persecuting" activities of the opponents: "For you put up with it when someone makes slaves of you, or preys upon you, or takes advantage of you, or puts on airs, or gives you a slap in the face" (NRSV). It is just in this context that Paul refers to those who come bringing "another Jesus," "another Spirit" and "another gospel" (11:4). His depiction of these preachers tallies precisely with the "other gospel" of the Galatian interlopers (1:6-9), who have effectively foisted "another Jesus" and "another Spirit" on the congregations founded by the apostle.

a dominantly ethical context. In every case, flesh and Spirit (promise) stand for historical entities, either the old age which has terminated with Christ or the new era which marks its inception from his advent.[64] In the present verse, flesh describes those who are born by natural generation and take their stand on their fleshly descent from Abraham. They still belong to the era of the law, the old creation and "the present evil age" with its "elements." Spirit, by contrast, is the mode of birth of Isaac-like people, who have been begotten through the power of God's Spirit (cf. John 3:6, 8) and belong to the age of the Spirit or the heavenly Jerusalem.

30 Paul now directly assumes the role of Sarah and speaks in her voice (from Gen 21:10), as he demands that the slave girl and her son, that is, the Judaizers and their followers, be thrown out of the Christian assemblies in Galatia: *they* can never inherit the promise with the children of the free woman. This is just the focal point of the Hagar-Sarah allegory/typology—the imperative to expel the bondswoman and her son. This is the climax to which Paul has been building from v. 21. If the troublers were appealing to Genesis 21 and labeling Paul's gospel "Ishmaelian," then Paul turns the tables and throws the passage back into their faces. His "logic of reversal" (Hays, *Echoes*, 120) throughout this whole passage finds its practical application just here. As combined with 5:1, this ultimatum to get rid of the troublers represents the reason why Galatians was written.[65]

Sarah originally said: "That slave woman's son will never share in the inheritance with my son Isaac." Di Mattei shows that Paul's Greek, "the son of the slave girl" (or "handmaiden") (*ho huios tēs paidiskēs*), is not as startling as it might appear. Already in Ps

---

[64] See Russell, *Conflict*. "Paul does not draw a distinction between 'flesh' as a moral category and 'flesh' as denoting ethnic identity, as least when that ethnic identity is seen to have determinative significance for participation in covenant blessings" (Dunn, *Galatians*, 257).

[65] Cummins proposes another historical irony in Paul's demand to oust the agitators from the new covenant community. He notes that the Maccabean crisis was viewed as the outworking of the Deuteronomic curse upon Israel's apostasy. "Envisaged at its worst, it involved Israel's enemies (both Gentiles and Jewish apostates) seeking to eradicate all memory of Israel from the land by handing it over to alien residents (1 Macc. 3.34b-36; 12.53-13.6, 20). The required remedy was the destruction of the enemy, not least those from within (1 Macc. 3.1-9; 7.21-4), and a renewed covenant commitment by Israel" (*Paul*, 105, n. 42). If such a linkage is accepted, Paul is seen once again to classify the opponents as "Fifth Columnists" within the camp of the new Israel, who need to be shown the door for the sake maintaining the integrity of the community.

85:16; 115:15; Wis 9:4-5, the phrase functions as a "Jewish covenantal self-designation." Hence, the conclusion: "The expression *ho huios tēs paidiskēs* may therefore have been in use in the Judaism of Paul's day to designate the children of Jerusalem, the children of the covenant which Yahweh had made to the flesh and blood seed of Abraham."[66] If so, then Paul is seen to be engaging once again in radical role reversal: now "the son of the slave girl" is just the opposite of its original usage: a "Jewish covenantal self-designation" has been turned into a designation of fleshly bondage.[67]

Moreover, Paul feels the freedom to modify Sarah's original words regarding Isaac to suit his purposes at hand: "My son Isaac" is changed to "the son of the free woman." In so doing, he stresses the freedom of Sarah as the mother of Isaac and sounds yet again the note of liberty that has resounded throughout this entire passage. But even with Paul's alteration of Sarah's words, it is Scripture speaking; and the Galatians are obliged to heed the biblical injunction to purge the camp of its adversaries. "If for the sake of the truth of the gospel the apostle can and must pronounce a curse on the Teachers (1:8-9), then the Galatian churches' adherence to the truth of the gospel requires them to expel from their congregations the Teachers..." (Martyn, *Galatians*, 446).

31 The inevitable conclusion is that we are not children of the slave but of the free woman. In so saying, Paul brings the argument full circle from where it began in v. 22. Actually, this is the summary and conclusion of the entirety of 3:1-4:30 and provides the answer to the central question of this long section: Who are the true members of Abraham's family? The argument has been sustained and detailed, but necessary because "somehow the Galatians had become confused, 'bewitched,' about their own spiritual identity despite the fact that the Spirit had been abundantly poured upon them when they were first converted to Christ" (George, *Galatians*, 348). By desiring circumcision they are indeed seeking to be a child of Abraham, but to be a child of Abraham *with Hagar*, thus a brother of Ishmael and disqualified for the inheritance.

As an expression of his ultimate (though temporarily shaken) confidence in them, Paul can address them warmly as "brothers"

---

[66] Di Mattei, "Allegory," 114, citing further 1QH 7:26; 1QS 11:16; 4Q381 fr. 33; 4Q381 fr.15.

[67] On the slave metaphor of this verse, see the extensive treatment of Tsang, *Slaves*, 87-104.

and shift to the first person plural "we," so as to reckon them among the inhabitants of the free, heavenly Jerusalem (cf. Heb 10:39). Because this is so, it makes no sense for them to continue acting like slave children.

All this said, Witherington ably epitomizes Paul's argument of 4:21-31:

> In a *tour de force* argument Paul has identified the agitators in Galatia with Hagar, and himself with Sarah. Each is on the way to producing children, the former for slavery, the latter for freedom. Paul takes the high ground of identifying himself and his Gentile converts as the true heirs of the promises to Abraham, and suggests that the agitators, even in spite of their Jewishness, are the real Ishmaelites giving birth to slaves. Paul believes that the story of Isaac is being revisited in the experience of the Galatians, "his children" just as the story of Sarah has been revisited in the experience of Paul (cf. 4.18-20). His exhortation to them in essence is to become what they already are... (*Grace*, 339).

Section Notes

21-31 Longenecker ("Illustrations," 191-92) relates that throughout Galatians Paul seems to be interacting with a typically Jewish understanding, as expressed most clearly in the Talmud, that truth comes in two stages: first in an elemental form and then in a developed form. More particularly, in Galatians he seems to be countering the Judaizers' application of this Jewish understanding to the effect that Paul's message is an elemental form of the gospel proclamation while theirs is the developed form. According to Longenecker, the Judaizers' argument seems to have run along the following lines: (1) that while Paul directed his Galatian converts to Genesis 15:6 in support of his emphasis on faith, they must realize that the developed form of God's covenant with Abraham appears in Genesis 17:4-14 with its requirement of circumcision emphatically stated in vv. 10-14; (2) that while Paul spoke only of Abraham and his faith, the full development of Israel's religious legislation came with Moses; (3) that while Paul spoke of the promises of the gospel, the promises were actually made to Abraham and his "seed," which means the Jewish nation, and (4) that while Paul assured his converts that they were the children of Abraham, the question must be raised as to which of Abraham's children they represent, for Abraham had two sons: the first being Ishmael the son of the handmaid Hagar, and the second being Isaac who was born later to the true wife Sarah.

In explicating their position, the Judaizers undoubtedly claimed that Paul's preaching represented an "Ishmaelian" gospel. Their argument probably was that while Ishmael was indeed the first son of Abraham, it was only Isaac who was the true son. Thus, it is only as Paul's converts are related to Isaac and the Jewish nation, not to Ishmael, the non-Jewish son, that they can legitimately be called "children of Abraham."

In response, writes Longenecker, Paul sets out in allegorical fashion two contrasting lines of salvation history: (1) the line of Hagar and Ishmael, which has to do with slavery and the natural process of procreation, and (2) the line of Sarah and Isaac, which has to do with freedom and promise. But Paul's contemporization of the Hagar-Sarah story does not stop there. He makes matters even more explicit by introducing two further dualities (one incomplete, but implied): Mount Sinai and the present city of Jerusalem, on the one hand, contrasted with "the Jerusalem that is above"—the eschatological Mount Zion being understood as equivalent, though it is not expressed.

Paul's allegorical treatment of the Hagar-Sarah story, says Longenecker, has a decidedly polemical thrust. He maintains that in *ad hominem* fashion Paul is asserting that he too can set up an allegorical understanding of the Hagar/Sarah story, in contradistinction to how the Judaizers were reading the story, and that his version best represents the intent of God. In effect, he responds that it is not his message but theirs that is Ishmaelian; it is Hagar, who has contact with Mount Sinai, who should be associated with the present city of Jerusalem. This explains the bondage of Jerusalem and her emissaries. Furthermore, it is Sarah, Isaac and the spiritual Jerusalem who are involved in the promises of God and are linked with Paul and his Gentile converts (the "we" of v. 31) as being the true children of promise in association with them.

21-31 Jobes' study of this passage is sufficiently important to warrant a distillation of its contents, along with modifications and applications of my own. Connecting with Hays' *Echoes*, Jobes approaches Paul's use of Isa 54:1 with a hermeneutic of "intertextuality." Simply defined, intertextuality pertains to the way in which one text of Scripture reflects or echoes earlier ones. This phenomenon is also called "metalepsis." The genius of intertextuality resides as much in what is *not* said as in what is actually stated. As Hays puts it, "When a literary echo links the text in which it occurs to an earlier text, the figurative effect of the echo can lie in the unstated or suppressed…points of resonance between the two texts" (*Echoes*, 20). As applied to Paul's use of Isa 54:1, the apostle takes as his point of departure Isaiah's metaphorical linkage of Abraham and Sarah with an eschatologically restored Jerusalem. But what occupied his attention is not Isa 54:1 by itself, but rather "the whole rippling pool of promise found in the latter chapters of that prophetic book" (*Echoes*, 120).[68] In

---

[68] Quite noticeably, Isa 54:1 follows upon 53:2-12. "The suffering of the Lord's servant is followed immediately in Isaiah by the call of the barren one to rejoice. Paul's citation of Isa 54:1 sets up waves of resonance with Isaiah's proclamation of the suffering servant and Jerusalem's future that ripple through the *probatio* of

other words, this text, like all others, is to be understood in the light of its broader context (see Beale [ed.], *Doctrine*, 137-309). What may appear to be "missing links" in Paul's employment of Isa 54:1 are supplied by its setting.

The theme of barrenness is first found in the OT in Gen 11:30: "Sarah was barren and she had no child." The issue of barrenness reappears in the narratives of Isaac and Rebecca (Gen 25:21) and Jacob and Rachel (Gen 30:1). See also 1 Sam 1:2, 6 (cf. 2 Kgs 4:14). In all these instances, Jobes remarks, barrenness is presented as a fact in the lives of great people in Israel's past. In every case, barrenness was overcome by God, and the barren woman produced a son who became a hero in Israel's history ("Jerusalem," 306-7). Isaiah, however, totally transformed the theme of barrenness, from the story of the birth of a child to the story of a birth of a people. Following Mary Callaway, Jobes maintains that Isaiah uses the theme of barrenness not to speak of God's past faithfulness to his people, but to proclaim a future manifestation of his power.

In his transformation from narrative to prophetic proclamation, Isaiah employs the story of Sarah both implicitly and explicitly. Implicitly, Isa 54:1 echoes Gen 11:30. Explicitly, the prophet refers to Sarah not as the mother of Isaac but as the mother of "those who pursue righteousness and seek the Lord" (Isa 51:2). "Isaiah's transformation associates Sarah's barrenness with the miraculous birth of a people whose heart is after God, instead of with the birth of an individual son to an individual woman" (ibid., 307-8). It is Isaiah's development of the barren woman theme that enables Paul to apply the prophet's original proclamation to ethnic Israel of release from exile to all who "pursue righteousness and seek the Lord" (irrespective of circumcision).

Isaiah's transformation also provides for Paul the association of Sarah's barrenness with a city, specifically Jerusalem. In Isaiah's lifetime, it was customary to personify a capital city as a female, whose inhabitants were her "children." During times of war, when a nation was conquered and its people exiled, the city was considered to be a barren woman rejected by her husband. By reason of having no husband and no son, the barren woman was considered as good as dead. "Thus the plight of the barren woman portrayed the worst situation a people could find itself in. To continue in exile under foreign subjugation did indeed mean death to a national and ethnic entity. This was precisely the historical situation of Jerusalem to which Isaiah spoke his proclamation of 54:1" (ibid., 308).

Isaiah prophecies against Jerusalem. Its people are called an "evil seed" in 1:14 because they have "forsaken the Lord and provoked the Holy One of Israel." The unfaithfulness of the people has invoked the curses of the covenant. For them the covenant has become a covenant of death, and the people who expect covenant blessing hope in a lie (28:15). The plight of the barren and rejected Jerusalem is further described in Isa 64:10: "The city of your holiness has become desolate, Zion has become

---

Gal 3:1-4:31" (Jobes, "Jerusalem," 313).

a wilderness, Jerusalem, a curse" (Jobes' translation). Jerusalem is cursed because of the sins of the people, whom the city, by metonymy, represents. Because the nation has forsaken its covenant with the Lord, he has forsaken it.

However, unlike other peoples who lost their national identity when conquered and exiled, Isaiah proclaims the good news that Israel will return to its land and be restored. Jerusalem, the barren woman, considered as good as dead, will live again with her many children. What God did for Sarah in the past, he will do in the future for the barren Jerusalem. Isaiah announces to Jerusalem that after she has been judged for her infidelity, she will be called "city of righteousness, the faithful *mother-city* (*mētropolis*) of Zion" (1:26).

Isaiah thus presents two images of a personified female Jerusalem: the one a barren and rejected woman, and the other a faithful mother. "Isaiah reminds Israel that just as Yahweh intervened to transform Sarah from a barren woman as good as dead to a fruitful mother of many children, so he will transform a Jerusalem destroyed by sin into a city with a thriving population of righteous seed. Isaiah's proclamation draws a continuity between Jerusalem in exile and Jerusalem in glory" ("Jerusalem," 310-11). As such, Isaiah provides a canonical basis for Paul later to distinguish and separate the two. When the apostle refers to the "Now Jerusalem" (Gal 4:25) and the "Above Jerusalem" (4:26), he is echoing Isaiah's portrayal of the two Jerusalems. In Galatians, these two Jerusalems represent, by metonymy, the two sides of Paul's antithesis between the states of being "of the law" and "of faith" (3:2, 5, 12, 23-25).

In transforming narrative history into prophetic proclamation, Isaiah introduces the Holy Spirit as defining the future seed of the faithful mother-city Jerusalem. See in particular Isa 44:1-3; 59:21. By contrast, the seed of the barren and rejected Jerusalem are banished to exile as those who have "framed counsel, not by me, and *covenants not by my Spirit*, to add sins to sins" (30:1). "Isaiah speaks of a seed of Abraham who are apart from God's Spirit and who suffer judgment. Just as Isaiah speaks of two Jerusalems, he speaks of two seeds, one who inherits covenant blessings, the other covenant curses. Isaiah merges the concepts of seed, inheritance, and covenant with the operation of the Holy Spirit as he prophetically transforms the theme of barrenness. The seed of the patriarchs whose mother-city is the redeemed Jerusalem is transformed in Isaiah to be, without the mention of circumcision, those who pursue righteousness and seek the Lord, those to whom the Holy Spirit is given" ("Jerusalem," 311).

The prophet thus provides a canonical development of a theme that is obviously well-suited to Paul's argument in Galatians as he defines who precisely the seed are and are not. The true seed of Abraham and sons of God are those who simply believe in Jesus apart from circumcision (3:7, 16, 18, 19, 29; 4:1, 5-7, 22, 31); they inhabit the heavenly Jerusalem. On the other hand, those who seek to be Abraham's seed from works of the law inhabit the barren and cursed Jerusalem; they are still in exile.

In sum, it is by identifying the barren woman with the restored city of Jerusalem and her ability now to give birth that Isaiah's proclamation provides Paul with a basis to employ Isa 54:1 in his polemic against the Judaizers. The barren woman, in other words, is Sarah, who though childless throughout most of her life, has at last mothered many children by means of Paul's gospel. Of course, Sarah did give birth to Isaac, but Isaac, in Paul's typology, is but the "first installment" on God's promise to provide Abraham with a worldwide progeny.

Cosgrove has drawn the same implication from Paul's treatment of Sarah. He maintains that, typologically speaking, Sarah remained barren throughout history until the coming of her "seed," that is, Christ, through whom many other children have been begotten. Therefore: "If Isa 51:1, in speaking of Sarah-Jerusalem, implies that her barrenness extends until the eschatological time of fulfillment, *then the law has given Sarah no children*. And with this point Paul reinforces in the strongest possible terms the repeated accent in Galatians that *life* (the Spirit, realization of the promise, access to the inheritance, the blessing of Abraham) is not to be found in the Torah" ("Sarah," 231, italics his). Martyn makes a similar point. In noting how Paul applies Isa 54:1 to his controversy with the opponents, he writes that to the false brothers the circumcision-free mission of Paul is a godless enterprise and, for that reason, barren. But Paul rejoins that, in reality, it is his circumcision-free mission that is vastly more fruitful than that of the law-observant mission of his rivals (*Galatians*, 443).

All this sets the stage for the birth motif of Gal 4:27. Whereas the "Now Jerusalem," the city of the law, remains barren and cursed, the "Above Jerusalem" has at last given birth. For Paul's argument to make sense, it must be that the barren one of Isa 54:1 has in fact given birth. We have defined the heavenly Jerusalem as the age to come depicted in spatial terms (see on v. 26). "Jerusalem" is the new order of salvation, the powers of the age to come that have been unleashed with the presence of the Holy Spirit. This is the city where Christ rules and from which he dispatches his Spirit to produce in his people the new birth. Isaiah's Jerusalem, therefore, has become fruitful by virtue of the work of the Spirit, who is operative through Paul's ministry, as he is the "mother" of the Galatians, the one who has begotten them in the gospel (see on 4:12, 22). Paul thus intertwines the metaphors of Jerusalem giving birth, by the Spirit, with that of his own "motherhood." Jobes, however, has introduced another important factor into the equation, namely, the resurrection of Christ as birth.

Perhaps she has overstated the case by maintaining that Paul's use of Isa 54:1 would not support the argument of Gal 4:21-31 unless he construed the resurrection of Christ to be the miraculous birth which would transform the barren Jerusalem into the fruitful mother-city (Isa 1:26). Nevertheless, she is correct that Paul can associate resurrection with birth (Rom 1:4 [= Ps 2:8]; Col 1:18). The Isaianic backdrop of this identification is Isa 26:17-19, which depicts Israel's restoration as a woman in childbirth and as a resurrection from the dead. And hand in hand with these metaphors goes that of the breath of God, which is his Spirit. Accordingly, Jerusalem gives birth when Jesus is raised from the dead: "When Jesus arose from death, all of the elect seed of Abraham were also born.... Because Jesus Christ has been raised from the dead, Isaiah's vision of a rejoicing Jerusalem and of a transformed seed of Abraham who inherits the promise has consequently been realized" ("Jerusalem," 316).

Jobes then draws out the application of Christ's resurrection to Paul's relationship to contemporary Israel. Since the only way to be a child of both mother Jerusalem and mother Sarah is found in Christ's resurrection, the Mosaic law from Sinai has in fact given Sarah no children, neither has it caused the barren one of Isa 54:1 to rejoice. The Jews who reject Christ's resurrection are of the same standing as Ishmael, who was a circumcised son of Abraham, but not a son of Sarah, and who, therefore, gained no part in the inheritance. Ishmael's mother, Hagar, is, therefore, an apt representation of the relationship of the Mosaic covenant to the Abrahamic covenant, not an arbitrary allegorical assignment.

Paul thus concludes that the Jews of the "Now Jerusalem," who have rejected the resurrection of Jesus, are indeed akin to Ishmael, and therefore can be rightly described as children of Ishmael's mother, Hagar (Gal 4:23). In principle, what Jobes says of non-Christian Jews applies to the circumcision party as well. It would appear that they accepted Jesus' resurrection, but for all practical purposes they are the inhabitants of the earthly, barren and cursed Jerusalem. Because they have made Jesus merely a servant of the Torah, they remain in exile; they are no better than circumcised Ishmael for all their profession of Jesus as the risen Messiah.

The bottom line is that by proclaiming Isa 54:1 in the light of Christ's resurrection, Paul has shown the Galatian Christians from Scripture (the law itself) that by desiring circumcision they are indeed seeking to be a child of Abraham, but to be a child of Abraham *with Hagar*, thus a brother of Ishmael and disqualified for the inheritance. The aversion to this thought sets the Galatians up for the transition to application in Gal 4:28-31 and the punch line of Paul's argument: "But you, brothers, are like Isaac, children of promise;" therefore, get rid of the idea of being circumcised!

All this raises the question of hermeneutics, that is, Paul's exegetical methods as opposed to those of the rival missionaries. Says Jobes: "Paul's grievance against the Judaizers is...a grievance about their use of Scripture. Like many of our own generation who attempt to apply the OT directly to contemporary situations, the Judaizers had lifted Genesis 21 from its redemptive-historical location and had argued directly from there to circumcision of the Galatian Christians. Specifically, they had attempted to apply Genesis 21 to the Galatian church without considering the intervening revelation of Isaiah that had transformed the Genesis material and, most importantly, without reference to the resurrection of Jesus Christ. Paul was therefore correcting an errant hermeneutic. The radical reversal effected in Gal 4:21-31 pivots on the resurrection of Jesus Christ and indicates that the resurrection has far-reaching hermeneutical implications. Beware of the one who attempts to apply Scripture apart from that great historical and hermeneutical fact" ("Jerusalem," 318)!

GALATIANS CHAPTER FIVE

FREEDOM IN THE SPIRIT (5:1-6:18)

Galatians has a number of leading motifs, but the most outstanding is freedom (2:4-5; 3:23-29; 4:1-11, 21-31; 5:1-12, 13). In fact, Paul's whole reason for writing can be summed up in the cry of 5:1: "It is for freedom that Christ has set us free!" This "Declaration of Christian Independence" comes at a crucial juncture and turning point in the epistle—and for good reason. "Like a lawyer pleading for a client in danger of being found guilty of a capital crime, he must have seen this as the critical moment. If he could not convince his Galatian audiences now he might never have another chance; his work with them, and their freedom in Christ might be lost irretrievably" (Dunn, *Galatians*, 260).

However, it is not only freedom *from* something—the law—that engages Paul's attention as he brings his entire *tour de force* argument to a close.[1] Rather, freedom is *to* something as well, because freedom is *in the Spirit*, who enables the believer to bear the "fruit of the Spirit" (5:22-23) and live a life well pleasing to God, a reversal of the chaos that used to characterize existence outside of Christ. "Where Paul speaks of freedom from specific ethical norms [the law] he never means freedom as liberation [absolutely speaking] but always freedom as ethical obligation" (Cosgrove, *Cross*, 161).[2] The tragedy of the Galatian situation was that instead of the freedom of the Spirit engendering the fruit of peace, harmony and Christlikeness, there reigned biting, devouring, suspicion and the various other "works of the flesh" (5:19-21). All this dotted the Galatian landscape because of a preoccupation with the law, which could do no other than produce bondage and the bitter existence of the slave children under its domain (4:21-31). Christian liberty, therefore, is one of the most important corollaries of our deliverance from the "present evil age." It is for such liberty that Christ died and rose again (see on 1:1).

---

[1] To reiterate from the Introduction, the most succinct commentary on Galatians is 2 Cor 3:17: "Now the Lord is the Spirit, and *where the Spirit of the Lord is, there is freedom*" (that is, from the law).

[2] On life in the Spirit/Christian obedience in Galatians, esp. chaps. 5-6, see Fee, *Presence*, 420-71; Barclay, *Obeying*, 106-215; Dunn, *Theology of Galatians*, 101-20; Barrett, *Freedom*, 32-90; Cosgrove, *Cross*, 147-94; B. W. Longenecker, *Triumph*, 69-88; Kuula, *Law*, 37-45; Schnelle, *Paul*, 295-96.

At first glance, 5:1-6:18 appears to be a disparate collection of ethical maxims and exhortations with no organic connection to what has preceded.[3] This is a conclusion to be resisted, because the thrust of all the arguments in the letter has been in the direction of these concluding exhortations and forming a basis for them. The paraenesis (exhortation) of this final segment of Galatians is the target at which Paul has been aiming from chapter one, verse one. Witherington informs us that there are two major themes in chaps. 5-6: the continuation of arguments against circumcision and the law, and a positive assessment of how Christians should live since they are not to submit to the Mosaic law. The two arguments are deliberately presented in this sequence—in order to make a crucial and telling point. "Paul will stress that the Spirit and the pattern or Law of Christ, not the Mosaic Law and circumcision, will provide guidance and empowerment necessary to live a life pleasing to God" (*Grace*, 359). In a nutshell, Paul bluntly denies that the law can hold the flesh in check. In so doing, he takes issue with what was to become the standard rabbinic view that the Torah could control the "evil inclination."

Fee confirms that the most basic contrast throughout these chapters is between life in the Spirit lived out by faith and life lived on the basis of Torah observance.[4] This is what makes this portion of the letter "a crucial part of the *argument* of Galatians, not simply a collection of paraenesis added at the end, after the theological argument is in place. The ethical result of the life of the Spirit is part of the essential argument of the letter, since this is the burning question, 'How do believers *live*'?" In answering the ques-

---

[3] Paul's employment ethical maxims would come as no surprise to his readers, given that they lived in a "persuasive world" in which exhortation often took the form of maxim (Ramsaran, "Paul").

[4] Hafemann has shown that there was a distinct element of continuity between Paul and the Qumran community as regards the role of the Spirit in the eschatological age: both Paul and Qumran, he says, were convinced that obedience to the law was made possible under the new covenant by the power of the Spirit ("Spirit," 180-83). In all probability, the opponents in Galatia would have maintained a similar theology of the Spirit. What Hafemann does not stress, however, is that the law, for Paul, is now the "law of Christ," which has jettisoned many of the distinctives held dear by the circumcisers. In principle, Paul and his Jewish contemporaries could agree on the necessity of the Spirit to obey the law, but the central dispute revolved around the precise content and character of the law. Is this a law designed to keep in place a sacred fence around the people of God, or one that liberates them from the Mosaic strictures and treats them like grown-up sons and daughters? In Galatians 5, Paul's key concern is for *eleutheria*—freedom.

tion, Paul provides a reply to the Judaizers who themselves were asking, If Torah observance is eliminated altogether, then what about obedience?[5] Gorman poses the questions similarly:

> *Is Paul's gospel of cross, faith, and Spirit capable of enabling people to keep the covenant into which they have supposedly been incorporated?* Or, on the other hand, *Is the Law necessary after all to counteract the twin realities of sin and the flesh?* These last two chapters constitute Paul's emphatic yes to the first question and no to the second. They present an overview of life in the Spirit as a life lived according to the cross. It is a life, paradoxically, of both radical freedom and radical "slavery"—not freedom from responsibility, and not slavery to the Law, but the freedom of death to the "flesh" and cruciform love for others in the Spirit. Ironically, such a life in fact fulfills the Law (*Apostle*, 215, italics his).

A. The Call to Freedom (5:1-6)

Longenecker is surely right that these verses are directly relevant to all that Paul has said in chaps. 1-4. "They give expression to Paul's deepest concerns about his Galatian converts and epitomize his attitude toward the entire Galatian controversy. All that Paul has argued for and exhorted previously in Galatians comes to focus here" (*Galatians*, 221). His "call to freedom" begins with the ringing declaration that Christ has set us free. Thereafter his tone becomes very severe indeed, but only to the end that he might shock these people into an awareness of their perilous condition.

1 Commentators are divided as to whether 5:1 should be connected with 4:21-31 as its conclusion, or whether it begins a new section. I have opted for the latter, although the verse may be looked upon as a transition from the salvation-historical segment of the letter to the exhortations of chaps. 5-6. In any event, this summons to freedom is, in its own right, the high water mark of the epistle: "'Freedom' is the central theological concept which sums the Christian's situation before God as well as in this world. It is the basic concept underlying Paul's argument throughout the letter" (Betz, *Gala-*

---

[5] Fee, *Presence*, 385, 421, 422. See also Fee, *Exegesis*, 154-72. The other missionaries certainly would have been agreement with *Ep. Arist.* 139-42, according to which the food laws in particular were meant to guard Israel from all kinds of pagan immorality.

tians, 255). Hays agrees that Gal 5:1 encapsulates the message of the letter in a single powerful slogan (*Galatians*, 306). Freedom represents a return to the Garden of Eden before the onset of the bondage of sin—a veritable new creation (see ibid., 256-57). It is well to remember that the new creation is the age of the Spirit. If a crucial question in Galatians is, Who really possesses the Spirit? then Paul's answer is that we who are free from the law have experienced the Spirit of God. For this reason, he can sum up his entire discussion of the new covenant in 2 Corinthians 3 with the words: "Where the Spirit of the Lord is, there is freedom" (v. 17).

In English, "for freedom Christ has set us free" seems redundant. But this is a fairly typical biblical way of speaking so as to emphasize an idea. It is as though Paul were saying, "freedom is the very design of the work of Christ—this and none other!" The notion of liberation finds its ultimate point of contact in the OT with the release of Israel from bondage (see on 2:4-5; 4:24). Yet again Paul announces that the people of God have returned from exile with the death and resurrection of Christ, who himself endured the curses of the covenant and then rose to procure the blessings of a renewed covenant in the "above Jerusalem" (4:26). By his whole work, Christ has brought the covenant to its climax (see on 1:1 and the section note to 1:3).

Therefore, to embrace the law is like returning to Egypt or Babylon; in the words of 3:3, it is going in the wrong direction! Rom 6:18 articulates the same point of view. According to that verse, we have been liberated from "sin," that is, the old creation as headed by the first Adam, and have now become "slaves of righteousness" (note how "*liberated* from sin" in v. 18 is paralleled by "*justified* from sin" in v. 7).[6] This verse thus merges Gal 5:1 and 13. According to both epistles, we have been *liberated* from sin and the law in order to bear the fruit of the Spirit; but the same emancipation is called *slavery* of another sort. As paradoxical as it may appear, true freedom is to be found in bondservice to the principles of the new creation.[7]

In view of such realities, Paul can only exclaim, "Stand firm!" The cry, writes Dunn, is almost like a military commander rallying wavering troops. As he notes, the imagery of standing was a favor-

---

[6] The parallel of "justified" (*dikaioō*) and "liberated" (*eleutheroō*) in Rom 6:7 and 18 suggests that justification has as its design deliverance from the bondage of sin in the comprehensive sense, as the whole of Romans 6 makes clear.

[7] There may be a tie-in with Lev 25:55, according to which the slaves liberated in the year of Jubilee were nonetheless the Lord's servants.

ite of Paul—that of taking a firm stand and holding strongly to it. "What Paul calls for is a corresponding firmness of resolve on the part of his readers; their firmness of purpose should reflect the assured character of the divine grace in which they already stood" (*Galatians*, 262). But standing firm is not enough, they must be resolved not to be subject again to a yoke of slavery. "Again" (as in 4:9) refers to their previous bondage to "the elements of the world," which for them was originally paganism but now is the law. The verb of this clause is in the middle voice, which entails volition on the part of the readers. Moreover, whenever the present imperative is construed with the negative (*mē*), the effect is: "Stop letting yourselves be entangled in a yoke of slavery."

The metaphor of the yoke, in some instances, can bear a positive sense, as in the submission of a disciple to a master (Sir 51:26; Matt 11:29-30). In this regard, it is very possible that the phrase "the yoke of the law" was already current in Paul's day as an expression of submission to and compliance with the requirements of the Torah.[8] If so, then the "yoke of slavery" is an oblique reference to "the yoke of the law," but in such a way as to turn a positive metaphor into a negative one, especially in light of the Maccabean associations of this term (see the section note to this verse). From the opposite viewpoint, Barclay demonstrates from texts that the "fence" provided by the law was considered to be one of its glories (note esp. Josephus, *Ag. Ap.* 2.174). In terms of its purpose and function "fence" is the functional equivalent of "yoke." This leads Barclay to comment that "Paul's claim that this 'protective custody' had come to an end could therefore be interpreted by the agitators as both dangerous and irresponsible" (*Obeying*, 107).

Once again, the Torah is consigned to the period of slavery, along with sin, death and "the present evil age." As Peter himself was finally to see, the law was "a yoke which neither our fathers nor we have been able to bear" (Acts 15:10) (NASB). The irony of Paul's language is intensified by the fact that during the Maccabean crisis Israel struggled to liberate itself from "the yoke of the Gentiles" (1 Macc 13:41). Dunn's observation here is much to the point: the situation, he says, has now been reversed, with Jews attempting to bring Gentiles into subservience to them. For Paul, this will never do. "The gospel of Messiah Jesus was not about Gen-

---

[8] See Bruce, *Galatians*, 226; Longenecker, *Galatians*, 224-25. Barclay (*Obeying*, 63, n. 76) points out that "yoke of the Torah" has its roots in the OT conception of the yoke of God (Jer 2:20; 5:5; Ps 2:3). Ben Sira interpreted this as the yoke of wisdom (Sir 51:25).

tiles' having to submit to Jewish customs which obliterated their distinctiveness as Gentiles...but about freedom from such distinctions for both Jew and Gentile" (*Galatians*, 263).

2 Equally as abrupt as v. 1, this sentence begins with "behold" (NASB; NIV: "Mark my words!"), reflecting a Hebrew expression, *hinneh*, which is frequently the equivalent of an exclamation point. Because Paul wants to grab the audience's attention and have them pay special attention to what follows, his words take the form of a solemn affidavit—"I, Paul, say to you." By using the emphatic personal pronoun (*egō*) along with his name, he would remind them (from 1:1) that he is the one commissioned by Christ to take the gospel to Galatia. He thus wields the "big stick" of apostolic authority (cf. 1 Cor 4:21). But at the same time, they should recall that Paul was their "mother" (4:19) who cared deeply for their welfare.

His warning has specific reference to circumcision (mentioned four times in this paragraph). His language implies that the readers had not yet undergone the knife, but they were giving it serious consideration. From 4:10 it is evident that they had begun to celebrate the distinctive days of the Jewish calendar. That was enough of an imposition on their freedom. But the issue of circumcision was the decisive one, because until they were circumcised their identity as Gentiles would remain distinct. However, more than freedom was at stake, because according to Acts 15:1, the very message of the Judaizers was: "*Unless you are circumcised...you cannot be saved.*" For them, circumcision was no less than the way into the community of the saved, and without it there could be no acceptance before God. Paul, then, is barely restrained in his emotions. He knows that if he could only stop his "children" before they reached the point of circumcision, he could still save the day for "the truth of the gospel" (2:5, 14).

Paul will draw out the logical consequences of circumcision in the next verse, but for the moment he is adamant that if these people are circumcised Christ will do them no good. The issue is stated starkly in black and white terms because circumcision was the way into the Mosaic covenant *in toto* (v. 3), which for both Jews and Judaizing Christians was the gateway to salvation. Thus, the alternatives for Paul were *either* Christ *or* the law. And if it is the law, Christ will benefit them nothing because his entire work has been rendered redundant. If the Torah provided everything, then Jesus' life of righteousness and his sacrificial death for sin would have been unnecessary. The future tense of the verb, "Christ *will be of no value* (*ouden ōphelēsei*) to you at all," has an eschatological as well as a present reference. That is to say, in the last judgment, Christ will not be their savior if they opt for the law in the place of him.[9]

The imposition of circumcision and a nomistic lifestyle on Gentile believers to complement their faith takes us back to the central issue of Galatians: Does righteousness come from the law or from faith in Christ alone? Paul is so resolute because for Gentiles to embrace the Jewish Torah is to make Christianity law-centered rather than Christ-centered. The present verse finds its direct analogue in 2:21: if justification is through the law, then Christ died to no purpose. Betz pinpoints the crux of the matter: if Christ alone, for the Galatians, were insufficient, "They would deny their status as 'believers in Christ,' and thereby their 'justification by faith' which would save them in the eschatological judgment. They would deprive themselves from [*sic*] all the redemptive benefits which the name Christ includes" (*Galatians*, 259).

In the final analysis, two competing concepts of the covenant were at stake. Witherington explains:

> In Paul's view, God only has one covenant, one agreement about the relationship between himself and his people, at a time. To submit to the Mosaic covenant is to imply clearly that the covenant inaugurated by Christ is null and void. It is also to suggest that Christ's death did not accomplish what Paul says it did accomplish—exhaust the oath curse of the Law covenant and so bring to an end the reign of the Law covenant over God's people. Thus, the Galatians are confronted with a choice between two covenants and thus two manners of living faithfully before God (*Grace*, 367).

3 The solemn affidavit of the previous verse now becomes a more formalized oath formula ("I testify..."),[10] in which he draws out the logical corollary of circumcision: debt to the entire law. His testi-

---

[9] The attempt of Gundry Volf to dismiss any reference here to future judgment misses the connection of 5:2 with 5:5 and 6:7-9 (*Paul*, 209). To be sure, going back under the law means a forfeiture of liberty at the present time, as she states. Nevertheless, the present and the future are linked as Paul envisages both an Already and a Not Yet of salvation.

[10] Paul testifies "again," which is best taken as a reference to v. 2. In both vv. 2 and 3, for the sake of emphasis he says the same thing twice in slightly different ways.

mony is directed toward every person who is "getting himself circumcised" (middle voice). The present tense could indicate that some actually were undergoing the rite, or it could express attempted or intended action. Either way, circumcision of necessity entails obligation to the whole law (literally, "You are a debtor...").[11] His reasoning is obvious enough: "For Paul the Law is a package deal, and one cannot separate out one portion of its commandments from another. All must be obeyed if one is under the law" (Witherington, *Grace*, 353).[12] One was not, in other words, free to pick and choose from among the commandments. What is in view is the typical Jewish mindset which understood "doing the [whole] law" (Lev 18:5; Deut 4:1, 10, 40; 5:29-33; 6:1-2, 18, 24; 7:12-13) as the obligation and privilege of those within the covenant.

> It is this total way of life to which Paul refers here. He reminds his would-be Gentile Judaizers that what was being demanded of them was not simply a matter of a single act of circumcision, but a whole way of life, a complete assimilation and absorption of any distinctively Gentile identity into the status of Jewish proselyte (Dunn, *Galatians*, 267).[13]

Likewise Hays:

> He is telling the Galatians that if they choose to be circumcised, they are crossing a guarded border into an occupied territory where the Law rules. The Law is a total way of life, a religious system that makes a total demand on one's life. To come under the Law (3:23; 4:4-5, 21) is to enter a sphere where the Law is sovereign. One cannot then pick and choose which commandments to follow; it is a total package. One must ei-

---

[11] There is an intentional play on words between vv. 2 and 3: Christ will not benefit them (*ōphelēsei*), but, instead, they will be debtors (*opheiletēs*).

[12] "...the Mosaic Law is seen as a cohesive whole—obedience to any part of it is part of obedience to the whole, and transgression of any part of it, is transgression of the whole" (Witherington, *Grace*, 368; cf. Longenecker, *Galatians*, 227).

[13] The stress thus falls not on a legalistic pursuit of perfection in the law but a commitment to the whole of what the Torah required of its adherents. Dunn seeks to redress the balance in the present much misunderstood passage. "No Jew that we know of thought of the Jewish way of life as a *perfect* life, without sin or failure. Rather, it was a *total* way of life which, through the cult, its sacrifices and atonement, provided a means of dealing with sin and failure" (*Galatians*, 266).

ther get in or get out. (Here we no doubt hear an echo of Paul the rigorous Pharisee, who well understood the comprehensive demand of the Law during his earlier period of surpassing zeal for the traditions of his ancestors.) (*Galatians*, 312).

A Gentile who commences his observance of the law, remarks Martyn, "Sets out on a path that has no terminus.... Face-to-face with the plural law [as Martyn terms it], he becomes a permanent debtor (*opheiletēs*), whose bill is always due" (*Galatians*, 470-71). Perhaps Paul presses this point because his opponents had introduced a program of "gradualism" into the Galatian churches, whereby only selected commandments were made obligatory at first. This would be a strategy of incrementalism. If so, then Paul seeks to underscore their inconsistency with what the Torah itself demands.

The letter to the Galatians is filled with ironies, and in the case of circumcision we find one of the most remarkable ironies of all. From one vantage point, some of the Gentile believers were intent on entering the Mosaic community through the normal gate, circumcision. But from Paul's outlook the rite was having the opposite effect as regards their standing in Christ. "From his perspective, circumcision of Gentile Christians was not a ritual of entrance but of exit.... Although Jews still practiced circumcision as an entrance ritual, Paul sees it as a ritual of exit, apostasy, when practiced by the followers of Jesus" (Neyrey, *Paul*, 89). This is why, in the next verse, Paul minces no words in warning that all who head down the path initiated by circumcision will be severed from Christ.

4 Paul is worried not about circumcision as an isolated act or as a thing in itself, but rather what it will lead to: the endeavor to be justified "in the law." The most emphatic element of the verse is placed forward into the first clause: "You have been severed from Christ" (NASB). The verb translated "severed" (*katargeō*) frequently means to make ineffective or nullify (BDAG, 525). In the present cast, it signifies the dissolution of a relationship, namely, the Galatians' former (covenant) relationship to Christ. But commentators point out that the verb can mean "cut off." If this usage was in Paul's mind at all, then there would be a deliberate play on circumcision: those who "cut" the flesh are "cut off" from Christ. A formal commitment to the Torah through circumcision is equivalent to ending the relationship with the Christ of Paul's gospel. At heart, then, two competing conceptions of the Messiah are at stake. There is Paul's Messiah, who has received all without distinction (Rom 1:1-7; 2:11; 3:22; 10:12; 15:7), and there is the Messiah of the Judaizers, who "forced Jesus back into the role of a purely Jewish messiah rather than that of last Adam and Lord of all" (Dunn, *Galatians*, 268). One is obliged to decide.

Those who are estranged from Christ are just those who are seeking to be "justified in the law" (an echo of 2:16; 3:11). The present tense again denotes either action in progress or attempted action (NIV: "You who are trying to be justified").[14] What is important is that a portion of the Galatians are on the verge of making the Torah, not Christ, the arena in which they would seek to be justified before God (both now and in the day of judgment). The most fitting commentary on the present verse is again 2:21: if justification is through the law, then Christ died to no purpose (see on 5:2). Paul and those like him have come down solidly on the side of *solus Christus*.

If those who want to be justified in the law have severed their relationship with Christ, they have, by the nature of the case, "fallen away from grace." The verb "fall away" (*ekpiptō*) is used of a withering flower falling from its stem to the ground (Jas 1:11; 1 Pet 1:24) or of a ship failing to hold its course (Acts 27:26, 29). "God's grace in Christ...is like the stem which supports the flower and through which the life-sustaining sustenance flows. Or like the channel which leads to safety between the rocks of disaster, a course from which they were in danger of being driven by dangerous currents and cross winds" (Dunn, *Galatians*, 268-69).

To understand this verse, it is necessary to reckon with the *historical* nature of Paul's argumentation throughout Galatians. "Grace" stands for the present *era* in which God's latter-day covenant love has been manifested in Christ (as in John 1:17), just as "Spirit" in 3:3 stands for the *age* of the Spirit, the new covenant and the new creation. As Hays puts, it grace is conceived as a location, a sphere from which the Galatians will exile themselves if they persist in their course of action (*Galatians*, 313). Consequently, if the readers opted for the law in the place of Christ, they would abandon the eschatological *epoch* of God's final disclosure

---

[14] The present tense of the second clause, "You are attempting to be justified" (*dikaiousthe*) contrasts with the aorist of the first clause, "You have been severed" (*katērgēthēte*) and that of the third clause, "You have fallen away from grace" (*exepesate*). "Even the beginning of such an attempt (present tense) marks a decisive breach with Christ (aorist tense); to go down that road is to have turned one's back on Christ" (Dunn, *Galatians*, 267).

of himself in his Son and, not least, they would forfeit *the freedom of grace*. Gal 3:3 continues to be paradigmatic: one must not retreat into the age of the "flesh" and so forsake the time of the "Spirit." To do so is to apostatize from Christ. Says Witherington:

> Paul could hardly have made any clearer that a person who chooses to submit to the Law who seeks final justification by being "in the Law" (or we can translate "by means of the Law"), has in effect committed apostasy, has fallen from grace, has even severed themselves from relationship with Christ. For Paul there is no room for compromise on this issue.[15]

5 In contrast to those who are being allured by the law as the realm of their justification, "we" (emphatic position in the verse) "by the Spirit" and "from faith" are awaiting the hope of righteousness.[16] The "we," consistent with Paul's usage throughout the letter, probably has reference to "we Jewish Christians." In a manner akin to 2:16b and 4:3, the point is that if *even we* await the hope of righteousness by the Spirit, from faith, then how much less should Gentiles expect to receive their ultimate vindication by allegiance to the Mosaic law. "Faith," as everywhere in Paul, means trust in Jesus alone as over against Jesus plus something else, normally circumcision and law observance.

"By the Spirit" reminds us that we live in the age of the Spirit and are enabled by him to persevere through the wilderness of this world, as Jesus himself was (Luke 4:1). It is in this sense that we are "led by the Spirit" (Rom 8:14). Both faith and the Spirit are set forth as eschatological realities in contrast to the law, now obsolete, that can do nothing to effect our standing with God. "The latter not only fails to provide righteousness now, but offers no hope for the future; life in the Spirit, however, includes living a life of genuine righteousness now…and having absolute certainty about its final outcome" (Fee, *Presence*, 419).

The verb "await" (*apekdechomai*) is always used by Paul of future eschatological expectation (Rom 8:19, 23, 25; 1 Cor 1:7; Phil 3:20). Paul, then, anticipates a time when the believer's pre-

---

[15] Witherington, *Grace*, 369. Adams likewise affirms that to assimilate to Judaism is to alienate oneself from the new creation (*Constructing*, 228).

[16] Paul's sentence begins with the conjunction "for" (*gar*). But as Longenecker explains, the conjunction does not signify cause or inference, but rather it serves to introduce a series of abbreviated statements of significant theological importance (*Galatians*, 229).

sent possession of righteousness will be brought to its crowning conclusion at the end of this age. "Righteousness," as normally in the Bible, designates a standing in a relationship—that of the covenant—as well as one's commitment to the relationship as embodied in the "fruit" of perseverance (Gal 5:22-23; Luke 8:15). In Paul's soteriology, the believer is made acceptable by the gracious gift of God's sacrifice of his Son, who is received by faith, and thereafter he is caused by the same grace to render to king Jesus the "obedience of faith" for his name's sake (Rom 1:5; 16:26) (see the section note to v. 4). "Righteousness has both a present and a future dimension; it speaks of a people who have achieved a very positive identity in the present but who know that their race is not yet run and that a bright future awaits them" (Esler, *Galatians*, 175). In Paul's words elsewhere: "Continue to work out your salvation with fear and trembling, for it is God who works in you to will and to act according to his good purpose" (Phil 2:12-13); and "he who began a good work in you will carry it on to completion until the day of Christ Jesus" (Phil 1:6).[17]

All in all, Paul speaks here of "the full realization of the new character now in Christ begun" (Ziesler, *Righteousness*, 179), our perfect conformity to the image of Christ, which coincides with our vindication as God's faithful people in the day of judgment.[18] In justification, as in every other dimension of soteriology, there is a Not Yet as well as an Already (Matt 12:36-37; Rom 2:13; cf. 5:9-10). "Clearly expressed here is the 'future tense' of justification—to be justified/counted acceptable to God, not simply as an initial act (conversion), but as a sustained relationship with God culminating in the favourable verdict of the final judgement" (Dunn, *Galatians*, 271).[19] Fee agrees: "Our present justification/righteousness based on the work of Christ and the Spirit is what will be realized—*provided that we continue in faith and the Spirit and do not return to slavery, which promises no eschatological reward, only death*" (*Presence*, 419, italics mine).

---

[17] Cf. 1 Sam 26:23: "The Lord rewards every man for his righteousness and his faithfulness."

[18] Kertelge is not convinced that the hope of righteousness has anything to do with judgment as such, only with the eschatological expectation of the consummation of salvation (*Rechtfertigung*, 148-49). However, the events of the end-time are always represented as a complex, with judgment occupying an integral place in the complex as the final confirmation that we have been participants in salvation, as epitomized by righteousness.

[19] See also Betz, *Galatians*, 262; Yinger, *Paul*, 143-289; Garlington, *Faith*, 44-71; contra Fung, *Galatians*, 232-35.

It is the expectation of righteousness that forms the Christian's hope. "Hope" (*elpis*) is one of the great words in Paul (e.g., Rom 4:18; 5:2, 4, 5; 8:20, 24, 25; 12:12; 15:13; 1 Cor 13:13; 15:19; Col 1:27; 1 Thess 1:3; Titus 1:2; 2:13; 3:7). By definition, hope is faith directed toward the future; it is the anticipation of the consummation of the ages. For this reason, hope impels the Christian life and spurs us on to perseverance in view of the goal to be attained in the last day. Hope, then, is like love (v. 6) in that it energizes our lives. Because this is so, Fee can speak of the heart of Paul's gospel as "eschatological hope through faith in Christ, as lived out in the present by the power of the Spirit in a life of loving servanthood" (*Exegesis*, 159). From one angle, the eschaton has been realized in our present hope, but, from another, our present hope is an index to the events of the eschaton. As an integral ingredient of faith, hope preeminently signifies the hoped-for reality of the heavenly Jerusalem.[20]

Thus, the waiting and patience that accompany hope, along with the groaning of the Christian, have a specific object. Hope is not the vague possibility of a better life in some indefinite future but the glory of the age to come, the redemption of the body, the adoption as sons and daughters and cosmic peace. All these expectations can be summarized as "righteousness," because from God's standpoint righteousness is his commitment to restore the creation to its pristine condition (Käsemann, "Righteousness").

6 That one day our righteousness is going to be completed and fully realized in Christ and by the Spirit (apart from the law) is now confirmed in slightly different words: it is not circumcision or uncircumcision that matter, but "faith working through love." The operative principle of God's ultimate vindication of his people is not the Torah with its boundary markers of Jewish identity but a

---

[20] See Schreiner, *Paul*, 271-305; Beker, *Paul*, 146-48. Paul seems to distinguish between hope and the promise and does not normally use the promise for the hope of the Christian or as the content of the Christian hope (except for 2 Cor 6:14-7:1). The promise usually refers to the OT promises, which are confirmed by Christ (Rom 4:16; 2 Cor 1:19-20). Thus, the Gentiles have received in Christ the promised Spirit (Gal 3:14; cf. Gal 3:22; Eph 1:14). The promise and the hope refer to different objects, as the terminological shift from promise (Romans 4) to hope (Romans 5) in Romans shows. Whereas the object of the promise is the Christ-event, the object of Christian hope is directed to those glories that the Christ-event has opened up for the future (Rom 8:18-30; cf. Col 1:27: "Christ in you, the hope of glory").

faith (in Christ alone) impelled by love.[21] This is what really counts, not circumcision! How shocking such a declaration must have sounded to those who had set their eyes and hopes on Isa 52:1; Ezek 44:9, both foretelling a time when no uncircumcised person would enter the assembly of Israel. Moreover, as Derouchie's study inform us, the Hebrew Bible employed precisely the word "foreskin" (Greek *akrobustia*, normally translated, as in this verse, "uncircumcision") to articulate opposition to the God of Israel and his purposes ("Circumcision," esp. 190-202). On the surface, it would appear that Paul has the effrontery, not to say the out-and-out gall, to reverse the prophets willy nilly, even given that the very concept of Israel for him has undergone redefinition (6:16). How could the Prophets say one thing and Paul another?

The answer resides in the character of "eschatological circumcision." It was Moses who originally demanded that Israel circumcise the foreskins of their hearts (Deut 10:16), as repeated by Jeremiah (4:4).[22] But since an idolatrous and apostate was unable to comply, this requirement would be performed by Lord himself at the time of return from exile (Deut 30:6). And now that the definitive return from exile has taken place in Christ, the "true Jew" is the one characterized by inward, not outward, circumcision (Rom 2:25-29). What counts is not the removal of foreskins, but the renewal and regeneration of the inward person. This is why Paul can write in Col 2:11-13:

> In him also you were circumcised with a circumcision made without hands, by putting off the body of flesh in the circumcision of Christ; and you were buried with him in baptism, in which you were also raised with him through faith in the working of God, who raised him from the dead. And you, who were dead in trespasses and the uncircumcision of your flesh, God made alive together with him, having forgiven us all our trespasses… (RSV).

Here, it is Christ the circumciser who has cleansed the hearts of his people by the impartation (baptism) of the Spirit. This is in accord with John the Baptist's promise that the Coming One would

---

[21] See Dunn, "Circumcision nor Uncircumcision." The present statement invites comparison with 1 Thess 1:3, where Paul commends his readers' "work of faith and labor of love and steadfastness of hope in our Lord Jesus Christ" (cf. the same triad in 1 Cor 13:13).

[22] See Derouchie, "Circumcision," 196-200.

baptize with "Spirit-and-fire" (Matt 3:11; Luke 3:16), as affirmed further by the apostle in 1 Cor 12:13. Therefore, Paul concurs with his forebears Isaiah and Ezekiel that, in the latter days, no uncircumcised person will enter the assembly of Israel. Only, this "eschatological circumcision" has rendered obsolete the "circumcision of the flesh." Since the new "Israel of God" now walks by another "rule" (Gal 6:16) than "Israel according to the flesh" (1 Cor 10:18), the cutting of human flesh has given way to the removal of the filth of the inward person. The "true Jew," from now on, is the one described in the following terms:

> For a person is not a Jew who is one outwardly, nor is true circumcision something external and physical. Rather, a person is a Jew who is one inwardly, and real circumcision is a matter of the heart—it is spiritual and not literal. Such a person receives praise not from others but from God (Rom 2:28-29) (NRSV).

These realities, not law observance as encapsulated by circumcision, are what characterize existence "in Christ Jesus." Below, in v. 14, Paul will state what was a perfectly acceptable dictum to Judaism and Judaizers, namely, that love fulfills the law. What is radical, however, is that he negates circumcision as a necessary means of expressing one's love (and faith) to the God of Israel (as also in 6:15; Col 3:11). In 1 Cor 7:19, a passage very much like our own, he explicitly sets the rite in opposition to the "commandments of God!" Being "in Christ Jesus," therefore, entails a fundamental reappraisal of what constitutes acceptability to God. The circumcision/non-circumcision distinction between Jews and Gentiles has been eradicated altogether. Henceforth, the only thing necessary for Gentiles, or Jews for that matter, was God's gift of the Spirit through faith. Christlikeness as engendered by the Spirit is the new "boundary marker" of the people of God. Circumcision has been rendered entirely obsolete.[23]

The verb translated "has any value" by NIV and "means anything" by NASB is a "power" word (see Spicq, *Agapè*, 2.168-72). Quite literally, it could be rendered: neither circumcision nor uncircumcision "are powerful" (or "avail") for anything. At issue are

---

[23] Religious symbols and practice, remarks Betz, make sense only if they correspond to and are integrated with the doctrinal presuppositions of a particular religion. "This applies to the Galatian problem insofar as Paul separates Gentile Christianity from Judaism and establishes it *de facto* as a new religion" (*Galatians*, 263).

two rival sources of power which result in qualitatively different outlooks on life in the covenant community. The one is the law and the other is an activist faith with love as its energizing agent.[24] The former is impotent to justify and effect any change in one's life, while the latter is God's own power (through the Spirit) exercised in a new creation (cf. 3:5).

> What are set in contrast are two conflicting sources of power—rite and status, which are not merely rite and status, but which give significance to everything else, which provide a basis for the whole life before God, which determine and characterize mind-set and community. On the one hand a community and mind-set determined by a rite which divided humanity into two thus sharply distinct classes ("the circumcision" and "the uncircumcision..."). On the other a mind-set and community characterized by the openness of faith and the spontaneity of love. Paul affirms that the coming of Christ and of being "in Christ" has radically reduced the power of the first and has shown that effective power to change life and community to the righteousness for which God looks lies in the latter (Dunn, *Galatians*, 271).

The Christian life, therefore, is one of dynamic activism, because "in Christ" is an empowering relationship to Christ, which expresses itself in love. As Dunn underscores, Paul understood "in Christ" as a new and living relationship active in well-doing (cf. Rom 2:7, 10). He understood justification as a "sustained relationship with God through Christ, which produced the righteousness looked for and acknowledged by God (love)." Such an understanding should not be perceived as a threat to *sola fide*, for "it is precisely that complete reliance on and openness to God's grace which comes to expression in love" (*Galatians*, 272. See the section note to this verse.). To this Furnish adds:

> Paul's preaching of love does not just stand alongside his emphasis on justification by faith but is vitally related to it. To believe in Christ means to belong to him, and to belong to him means to share in his death and in the power of his resurrection. Thereby one's whole life is radically reoriented from sin to righteousness as he is

---

[24] The participle *energoumenē* is in the middle voice: "Faith *working itself out* through love."

freed from bondage to himself and placed under the truly liberating dominion of God's grace.[25]

That Paul should single out love as the focal point of faith is understandable in light of the argument of chaps. 5-6 as a whole. According to his portrait, his opponents were stimulating the Galatians to "bite and devour one another" (5:15). In spite of their claims, the Teachers do not really "abide in all things written in the book of the law," because they have neglected the principal part—love. Over against them, "the whole law" for Paul "is fulfilled in one word, 'You shall love your neighbor as yourself'" (5:14).[26]

In our verse, love is particularly set in opposition to circumcision because of the latter's function as one of the acid tests of loyalty to the God of Israel. For the apostle, however, what matters in the new creation is faith working through love (5:6; cf. 6:15) and Christians serving one another through love (5:13). For this reason, love heads the list of the fruit of the Spirit (5:20). If one walks by the Spirit (5:25), instead of being conceited and provoking others (5:26), one will bear the brother's burden and so fulfill the law of Christ (6:1-2). Even this sketch of the love motif in this part of the letter informs us that the theology of love was vital to Paul because, *the lovelessness of the Judaizers was the product of their exclusivistic theology.*[27]

If we ask, What is love anyway? the answer, in general terms, is seeking the highest good of others as defined by the law of Christ (6:2).[28] But the very phrase "law of Christ" points us to Christ himself, the great exemplar of love, the one who was willing to assume the position of the lowliest slave in the household in order to minister to others and finally give his life as a ransom for many (Mark 10:35; John 13:3-16). As Paul puts it so concretely in this letter, Christ's love was exhibited when he "gave himself" on the cross (2:20). Martyn is surely right that this faith-energized love is not a romantic feeling but "the concrete pattern of life, established and incited by Christ's faithful, dying love for us. Under the sign of the cross (5:24) this loving pattern of life is continued

---

[25] Furnish, *Love Command*, 92. See further ibid., 91-131; Furnish, *Theology*, 181-206; Gorman, *Cruciformity*, 155-267.

[26] See further Martyn, *Galatians*, 503-18.

[27] See further Garlington, *Faith*, 64-67; id., "Burden Bearing," 153-58.

[28] Cf. Schneider, *EDNT*, 1.10-11.

in the community in which each member is the servant of the other, bearing the other's burdens."[29]

Section Notes

1 Cummins appropriately points to Acts 15:10: "Now therefore why do you make trial of God by putting a yoke upon the neck of the disciples which neither our fathers nor we have been able to bear" (RSV)? He observes that the distinctive term "yoke" (*zugos*) is used figuratively in the LXX to denote the oppression of Israel, not least during the Maccabean period when the final removal of the "yoke" of Seleucid rule and the commencement of the Hasmonean dynasty is the cause of national celebration (1 Macc 13:41; cf. 8:18). "The implication is clear: the unnecessary imposition of circumcision and Torah observance upon the Gentile converts denotes a Jewish nationalism which is itself a function of the same enslavement Israel itself had experienced at the hands of its enemies, freedom from which is to be found only through God in Messiah Jesus" (*Paul*, 158).

2 Witherington (*Grace*, 366) proposes that there may be more beneath the surface as regards circumcision. He notes that a close examination of Ancient Near East covenanting procedures, including those followed by the Israelites, shows that the sign of a covenant was often connected with the oath curse that went with the covenant and symbolized the curses that applied if one did not obey the covenant stipulations. In the case of the Mosaic covenant, the cutting off of the flesh was a symbol that God would cut off a person and perhaps also his descendants from the community of believers, indeed perhaps even cut them off from the land of the living, if the covenant was not kept. This is what it meant to experience the anathema or oath curse, the judgment of God on covenant breakers. The symbolism was particularly apt, since the sign pertained to the organ of generation and symbolized the cutting off of one's life if one did not keep the covenant. If all this was in the mind of the Judaizers, no wonder Paul is up in arms! And so ironically, Paul reasons that it is just by circumcision that the troublers have cut themselves off from the new covenant (cf. 5:12)!

4 In view of v. 5, Paul has in mind just as much future justification as present. Barrett proposes: "Justification…is a beginning, and a process; and it leads to a consummation at the future judgement, when God's initial gracious verdict on the sinner is—or, it may be, is not—confirmed" (*Freedom*, 65). Witherington adds: "This lattermost possibility Paul emphasizes here, but he believes that the one who submits to the Law has already in this act cut themselves [*sic*] off from Christ…. His point is that

---

[29] Martyn, *Galatians*, 474; cf. Wright, *Paul*, 145-48.

it is neither necessary nor beneficial to keep the Law if the goal is justification before God or at the final judgment" (*Grace*, 369). Both scholars have in view the peril of apostasy. Barrett, more broadly, is alert to the possibility of falling away before the final judgment, in which case God's gracious verdict is not confirmed. Witherington zeros in on the specific historical issue in Galatia; that is, the apostasy of the readers would consist in their embracing the law of Moses in preference to Christ alone. In this regard, the Torah is symbolic of any alternative to Christ as the gateway to salvation.

McKnight's conclusion respecting perseverance in Hebrews is equally applicable to Galatians. Paul contemplates what Mcknight calls the "phenomenological-true believer" (I prefer "confessing believer"): his warnings against apostasy and encouragements to fidelity are directed to people who genuinely believe for a time, but who will, nonetheless, forsake Christ, *if theirs is not a persevering faith*. As McKnight puts it, those who finally apostatize are believers in every observable sense; even so, they can stop believing and forfeit eternal salvation ("Warning Passages," 24). Hence, what Christian theology calls "true" or "saving" faith is none other than *persevering* faith. Given that "salvation" (in Paul and Hebrews) is dominantly future-eschatological, it is best to speak not of "losing" salvation but of failing to enter into the salvation which is yet to be (ibid., 58).

6 Fitzmyer asks: "Paul certainly does not mean that human beings can be justified by love alone; *but can they be without it?*" As he continues, Paul's "last word" in Galatians (6:11-18) sums up the meaning of the cross without any explicit reference to righteousness/justification, or even to faith. This leads Fitzmyer to conclude: "To me, at least, it shows that 'the cross' can be expressed without such recourse and that it has other aspects significant for human existence and salvation than merely justification by grace through faith" ("Basis," 209). George (*Galatians*, 362) and Fung (*Galatians*, 230) quote Günter Bornkamm to the effect that such an understanding of the relation of faith and love is a species of synergism (*Paul*, 153). Bornkamm, in turn, quotes Luther: "Works based on faith are done through love, but man is not justified *by* love" (ibid., italics mine).

One may agree. But still, Fitzmyer's question persists: Can one be justified *without* love? And the sequence of vv. 4-6—justification, hope of righteousness, faith working through love—compels the conclusion, no. It is only those who bear the fruit of the Spirit, preeminently love, against whom there is no law (5:22-23). In short, it is love that fulfills the law (5:14). If faith does not work *through love*, there will be no completion and realization of righteousness in the last day (5:6). At this point in time, righteousness remains a hope to be laid hold of by a faith which is inseparable from love. No love, no true faith. It is none other than faith working through love that makes one a "doer of the law" (Rom 2:13) (see Garlington, *Faith*, 64-67). Barrett finely says: "There is no conflict between faith and love; faith expresses itself in love. Anything that does not work itself out in love, though it may conceivably be verbal orthodoxy, is not faith in Paul's sense of the term" (*Freedom*, 71).

B. Run the Race (5:7-12)

Paul continues his make-or-break argument to the Galatians. In vv. 1-6, he summoned them to freedom, warned them of the pitfalls of circumcision and placed before them the prospect of future righteousness. Now he calls upon them, in the words of Heb 12:1, to run the race set before them and not be hindered from obeying the truth by those who really do not have their best interests at heart. The paragraph is punctuated by a series of brief sentences ("snorts of indignation" [Dunn]) in which he hopes to jar them loose from their attachment to the law and the law teachers.

7 Paul laments that at one time the readers were "running well." In so saying, he draws on one of his favorite metaphors as taken from the athletic contests (1 Cor 9:24-27; Phil 3:14; 2 Tim 4:7; Acts 20:24). We recall from 1:13 that "walk" is a term indicative of the Jew's devotion to and perseverance in the covenant. Paul then "baptizes" the term and applies it to the believer's perseverance in Christ. "Running" says essentially the same thing as "walking," but serves to intensify the idea. David gives voice to this in his exclamation, "I will *run* in the way of your commandments" (Ps 119:32). It is significant that Paul can use such a metaphor all the while insisting that justification and the Christian life are a matter of faith from beginning to end. He can do so because "faith working through love" requires all the concentration and self-discipline of an Olympic runner.

Naturally, the question arises, "Who cut in on you?" As Rogers/Rogers indicate: "The word suggests a breaking into or obstruction of the Galatian Christians in the course of following the truth. The picture is that of the runner who has allowed his progress to be blocked or who is still running, but on the wrong course" (*Key*, 430). The question is rhetorical (as in 3:1) because Paul knows very well who has "cut in." The verb here probably alludes to the "cutting" of circumcision, in which case "the missionaries have 'cut in' on them by demanding to cut the flesh of their foreskins" (Hays, *Galatians*, 315).

Frequently, questions in the Bible are intended to make people think rather than acquire information (e.g., Gen 3:11; 4:9; 1 Kgs 19:13). Paul wants them to consider just what kind of persons have been a hindrance to them. In light of 3:1 ("who has bewitched you?") and 2 Cor 11:13-15, Paul may be implying that more sinister forces are at work behind the human troublemakers in Galatia (cf. 1 Thess 2:18). "Who?" then, becomes a very pertinent inquiry. The main verb of the sentence is rightly rendered as "cut in" by NIV, in keeping with the metaphor of a race. The bogus apostles, as it were, have cut in on the believers in Galatia and have jeopardized their ability to cross the finishline, because cutting in, or crossing lanes, frequently has the effect of making a runner stumble. And one must cross the finishline—including Paul (1 Cor 9:27).

The effect of the agitators' interference is that the Galatians were in the process of not obeying the truth, that is, "the truth of the [circumcision-free] gospel" (2:5, 14). The verb means essentially "be persuaded" (the idea is repeated in vv. 8, 10). Paul thought of acceptance of the gospel as a matter of mind and intellect as distinct from faith as a "leap into the dark." It is an experience which must engage one's full mental capacities. It is to this end that Paul has brought out his whole arsenal of arguments in the letter, that he might *convince* the readers of the veracity of his preaching of Christ. Nevertheless, persuasion is meant to result in obedience (hence, the legitimacy of translating the verb as "obey"). The truth is not only to be believed but to be obeyed as well. Since truth is a package deal—not only commitment to Christ in faith but the obedience of faith resulting from union with him—one must ever be in submission to the truth. It is for this reason that John can speak of "doing the truth" (1 John 1:6), and Paul himself can later coin the phrase "the truth which accords with godliness" (Titus 1:1 [RSV]).

8 Baldly stated, "That kind of persuasion does not come from the one who calls you." The "persuasion" in question refers to the other teachers' conception of what sonship to Abraham and acceptability to God entails. In depicting God as the one who calls them, Paul returns to the verb (*kaleō*) that bespeaks Israel's election and calling (see on 1:15). This calling, in the OT, is unfolded along two related yet distinct lines.[30] The one is that Israel was the called people in that its national existence commenced with the summons (election) of Yahweh at Mount Sinai. Later prophetic preaching can presuppose this as a foundational factor in the national self-consciousness (e.g., Isa 41:9 [calling is paralleled by

---

[30] See Garlington, *Obedience*, 238-39.

election]; 42:6; 43:1; 45:3; 48:12; 51:2).[31] The other is the prophetic demand for Israel to turn from idolatry and back to the covenant (Isa 50:2; 65:12; 66:4; Jer 7:13).

In applying the concept of calling to believers in Jesus the Christ (cf. Rom 1:6-7; 9:24), Paul confers upon them a distinction which was supposed to characterize the ancient people but in his day by and large did not. That is to say, the nations have responded to the call of Paul's gospel with faith's obedience, while Israel, who has heard the call (Rom 10:18), is a "disobedient and contrary people" (Rom 10:21). Among the nations, it is the Galatians who have complied with the prophetic challenge to turn from idols and embrace Yahweh's covenant; they are the new Israel, God's possession, a kingdom of priests and a holy nation (Exod 19:6; Gal 6:16; Eph 1:14; 1 Pet 2:9); it is they, according to the Isaiah passages cited just above, who have returned from exile in response to the divine call. Yet, as inexplicable as it may seem, the very same people were in the process of renouncing God's call to freedom and new covenant life and were bent on returning to the idol of the Torah. *That* persuasion is certainly not from God, only the Judaizers.[32]

9 With a change of metaphor (probably quoting a current proverb, as in 1 Cor 5:6), Paul further expresses his concern over the insidious nature of the law teachers' influence. Their presence and message are like a little leaven that permeates a whole lump of dough. There is here not only the well-known fact that only a tiny portion of yeast causes bread to rise (Matt 13:33; Luke 13:20), but also the negative connotation of "leaven" as symbolizing something corrupting and undesirable (Betz, *Galatians*, 266). Given that the circumcision party was composed of former Pharisees (Acts 15:5), Paul may be in touch with the warning of Jesus that his disciples were to beware precisely "the leaven of the Pharisees" (Matt 16:6, 11; Mark 8:15; Luke 12:1). Be that as it may, by experience he knew that a minimal exposure to false teaching goes a long way— too long! Even flirtation with the circumcision-gospel of the troublers, if taken to its logical conclusion, would have at least a twofold effect.

---

[31] Such consciousness is evidenced by 1QM 3:2; 4:10-11, wherein the Qumran community names itself the "called of God" (cf. 1QM 2:7; 14:5; 1QSa 1:27; 2:2, 11; CD 2:11; 4:3-4).

[32] Paul perhaps uses "persuasion" (*peismonē*) in the sense of the "empty rhetoric" of the opponents (see Betz, *Galatians*, 265).

For one, the readers would abandon Christ for the sake of the law and thus fall under the curse of the gospel (1:8, 9; 3:10-13); they would do no less than forfeit eternal life. For another, the church would forever be bifurcated into Jewish and Gentile factions, thus creating chaos in the place of order and peace. That such factionalism had already begun to rear its ugly head is evident from this very context (5:15, 19-21, 26; 6:1-5). And Galatia was not the only place where Paul was confronted with the problem. He felt obliged to admonish the Roman congregations also to take note of those (Jewish) teachers who were creating "dissensions" and "stumbling blocks" (Rom 16:17).

These two words in tandem are the "double whammy" to the church: "dissensions" (*dichostasiai*) are particularly heinous because of their devastating effects on the harmony of the assemblies (cf. 1 Cor 1:10-17); and the "stumbling blocks" (*ta skandala*) are no less than "enticements to apostasy" (BDAG, 926). Those who create such enticements, in both Rome and Galatia, have as their hidden agenda the seduction of people away from Christ and after themselves. There is, in point of fact, a cause and effect relationship between divisions in the church and the potential of apostasy. Were the church to disintegrate as a result of its internal strife, the only real alternative would be the abandonment of Christianity altogether (Garlington, *Faith*, 22-23).

10 Paul has had to speak frankly and boldly for his friends' own good, particularly as the fundamental issue before them was no less than apostasy from Christ. But here he moderates his tone and expresses his ultimate confidence in them (note how the writer of Hebrews [6:1-12] does the very same). This is not simply rhetoric but Paul's confidence "in the Lord" that the Galatians will finally do the right thing by expelling the Judaizers (4:30) and renewing their love to Christ. By the phrase "in the Lord," he expresses his optimism that these people really are Christians, notwithstanding their temporary distraction by the troublers. Stemming from such assurance, Paul was sure that his readers would take "no other view" than his convictions respecting Christ and "the truth of the gospel."

On the other hand, the one causing all the trouble (see on 1:7) will bear his judgment. The judgment in question is that of the "curse of the law" which has become the "curse of the gospel" (see on 1:8-9; 3:13). Reasoning from vv. 2-6, and indeed from this entire context, it would follow that Paul denies to the agitators a faith which works through love (v. 6). Consequently, they possess no righteousness that will be consummated in the eschatological courtroom (v. 5), and on that day Christ will do them no good (v. 2). Why Paul speaks of "the troubler" in the singular is uncertain, unless he has in mind a prominent "ringleader" among the circumcising group. By adding "whoever he is," he is perhaps indicating that he does not know this individual personally or by name. He is not interested in personalities but issues.[33]

11 If the opposition group is comprised of "troublemakers," then Paul will relate that he too has been on the receiving end of their trouble. There is a long-standing debate as to his precise point of reference and the reason why he even raises the matter.[34] Borgen ("Circumcision") and Hays (*Galatians*, 316) propose that the troublemakers were telling the Galatians that Paul really did preach circumcision on certain occasions, but withheld this information from them for fear of offending them (as a "man pleaser"). Hays in particular adds that grist for this rumor mill could been provided by Paul's circumcision of Timothy (Acts 16:1-3).

Alternatively, I would propose that he raises the point in order to demonstrate that the opponents really are what he says they are, because their troublemaking was not confined to the Galatians, but extended to him as well.[35] And rather than think that these "troublers" were accusing Paul of preaching circumcision in other locales, the intention is that Paul, at one point in time, did indeed "preach" the necessity of circumcision for any who would attach themselves to the house of Israel (cf. Jdt 14:10). If so, then the complete thought would be: "If I am still preaching circumcision, as I once did...."[36] In this case, the verb "preach" (*kērussō*) does not bear the technical sense of Christian proclamation, the kerygma, but the more generalized meaning of "proclaim" or "declare." Perhaps he chose the term because his opponents had made circumcision precisely an integral element of their "preaching," their "kerygma." In his pre-Christian days, Paul would have consented to such "preaching," but after the Damascus Road, the con-

---

[33] Betz adds that it was customary in the ancient world not to name an opponent, so as not to give free publicity to the opposition (*Galatians*, 267-68).

[34] See Dunn, *Galatians*, 278-80.

[35] As observed previously, "troubler" possibly recalls Achar, the "troubler of Israel" (1 Chr 2:7). See on 1:7.

[36] An apparent obstacle to this line of interpretation is that Paul's conditional sentence is not contrary to fact but realistic (with present tenses). However, if the sentence is elliptical, as I propose, the difficulty is alleviated.

tent of his kerygma became Christ only and him crucified (1 Cor 1:23; 2:2). It is just Paul's distinctively Christian "preaching," a proclamation which precluded circumcision, that invited persecution from the circumcision party as well as from non-Christian Judaism. If he were still insisting on circumcision for proselytes to join the people of God, then his enemies would not be enemies; they would have nothing but affection and accolades for him. But as it is, he continues to be harassed by them.[37]

He does not specify what form this persecution took, whether physical or verbal abuse, or both. But perhaps the most telling factor is derived from Paul's mention of the persecution of Isaac by Ishmael in 4:29, that is, Ishmael's mocking of Isaac's claim to the inheritance. It is in this regard that the persecution is still going on, with the Judaizers in particular being cast in the role of Abraham's first son by jeering at the claims of the latter-day Isaacs (the Galatians) to be heirs by faith alone. It is in the same sense that the troublers persecute Paul as well, and indeed preeminently Paul because of his unwavering stand for Gentile freedom. For them, if anyone is to be denied the status of son of Abraham and heir of the inheritance, surely it is Paul, the arch heretic and apostate![38]

Among other reasons, circumcision is so objectionable because it nullifies (literally, "abolishes") the "offense" of the cross. "Offense," in Greek, is "stumbling block" (*skandalon*). Originally, the stumbling block is something that proves to be a trap, a source of embarrassment and offense or a provocation that arouses resentment and resistance (see Betz, *Galatians*, 269). In this more general sense, the term appears in the NT (along with the cognate verb

---

[37] 5:11 is to be compared with 6:12. In both cases, circumcision and persecution are linked. The question often arises as to why Paul, in his days as a Pharisee, persecuted the church. Donaldson proposes that it was because Christ was being presented as a rival boundary marker for the people of Israel (*Paul*, 78). Or, as I would say, the law is no longer the *sine qua non* of final salvation. This is true, because for Paul Christ, his cross and the Spirit are the "boundary markers" of the new covenant. It is to be stressed that the cross of Christ demarcates the new people of God as much as he and his Spirit. It is none other than the "scandal of the cross" (5:11) that aroused the persecuting zeal of Saul the Pharisee, and now the apostle Paul finds himself on the receiving end of the hatred of the cross. Cf. Schnelle, *Paul*, 85-86.

[38] See Hengel, *Judaism*, 2.204, n. 305; Gaston, "Paul," 53-57; Dunn, *Unity*, 241; id., *Word*, 44-64. An interesting sidelight is provided by Paul's mention of receiving the forty stripes less one (2 Cor 11:24). According to Jewish practice, each lash was accompanied by a passage from the Torah warning against apostasy. We remember that the penultimate word in Galatians is that Paul bears in his body the "marks" (*stigmata*) of Jesus (6:17).

"stumble" [*skandalizō*]) as an "impediment" to faith or action (Matt 5:29; 16:23; 18:7; Rom 14:13; 16:17; 1 John 2:10; Rev 2:14).

More specifically, though, the vocabulary of being "scandalized" pertains to unbelief and apostasy as respects Jesus the Christ (e.g., Matt 13:21, 57; 15:12; 18:6, 7; 24:10; John 6:61; Rom 9:33; 11:9; 1 Cor 1:23). In this regard, Jesus fulfills the role of Yahweh, who declared himself to be the "rock of offense" to Israel, on which many would stumble, fall, be broken and snared (Isa 8:14-15). Besides marking the end of the Jew/Gentile divide in human history (Eph 2:14-16), Jesus' cross was preeminently the stumbling block to the people of Israel because the notion of a crucified Messiah was "a blasphemous contradiction in terms" (Bruce, *Galatians*, 166). It was the cross that placed Jesus in the position of the reprobate of Deut 21:18-23 (see on 3:13). It was for just this reason that the circumcisers were ashamed of the cross and refused to endure persecution for its sake (6:12).

Paul's language is not to be evacuated of its force: the cross is deliberately calculated to offend that portion of humanity that will not look to it as God's judgment against and remedy for its sin (Rom 3:25-26; Col 1:20; 2:14). "It is precisely the fact that the cross is an offense that makes 'the theology of the cross' such a powerful critical principle in Christian theology and such a weighty counterbalance to all pride of position, nationhood or lifestyle" (Dunn, *Galatians*, 282). Betz speaks to the same effect: "The Christian message presents the unbeliever with a central and indispensable element of 'provocation' and 'alienation.' Without this element, the Christian message has lost its integrity and identity, that is, its truth" (*Galatians*, 270). See especially Rom 11:9. But for Paul and all Christians, the cross, with all its offense, is glorious (6:14) and attractive: it is God's only provision for the forgiveness of sins and marks the central point of salvation history (see the introduction to 1:1-5). For Paul: no cross, no gospel.

12 A section replete with blunt assertions now concludes with a *cutting* remark indeed (pun irresistible)! Paul wishes, no less, that the circumcisers, "those who are unsettling you,"[39] would do a

---

[39] Bruce (*Galatians*, 238) notes that Paul's participle here is also used by Luke in Acts 17:16 and 21:38. The latter is especially interesting as Paul is accused of being "the Egyptian" who fomented an uprising against Rome consisting of 4,000 *sicarii* (dagger men).

proper job on themselves.[40] Since they are so concerned with the removal of foreskins, they should go all the way and excise the whole apparatus! Some think Paul is resorting to black humor as a vehicle of sarcasm;[41] and it is indeed possible that he is having a chuckle up his sleeve at the opponents' expense. But it is fair to say that his mood is fundamentally serious, especially where final judgment looms on the horizon (vv. 2-6). Alternatively, it is believed that the present verse is simply an emotional outburst, which Paul might have thought better of he had been in a calmer frame of mind. But this fails to do justice to the text for reasons to be explained momentarily. To be sure, the apparent harshness or even coarseness of Paul's language can be ameliorated by the times in which he lived.[42] But more to the point, by wearing his heart on his sleeve, he shows how passionately he cares for his "children" and how much he deplores the tactics of those teachers who were infecting them with their "other gospel."

Although this verse (and letter) certainly bristles with emotion, a serious and even dispassionate theological proposition underlies Paul's choice of words. According to Lev 21:20 and Deut 23:1, no man whose sexual organs had been mutilated was allowed to enter the assembly of the Lord. Barrett takes up this datum and explains: "Circumcision (so its advocates urged) was a necessary qualification for membership of the people of God; castration was a disqualification. So that…Paul would be saying: 'I wish those people who want to qualify you for membership would disqualify themselves" (*Freedom*, 70). Neyrey adds that mutilation or castration meant that one's line of descendants is literally "cut off" from the covenant of Israel, a "profound curse" (*Paul*, 192). Yet Paul's real concern is not with the assembly of Israel but the assembly of Christ. He takes a Mosaic principle and ironically applies it to the new covenant community. As Neyrey continues, "Mutilation symbolically suggests Paul's desire that these heretics be cut off from the church, made shameful, and rendered permanently unclean. Permanent removal from the holy body, then, is the ritual described in 5:12" (ibid.). Dunn speaks similarly: "Paul expresses the wish that a rite understood as one of dedication and commitment to

---

[40] If any aspect of Galatians qualifies as "rhetorical," this is it. The construction, *ophelon* with the future indicative, expresses an obtainable wish, although its realization is inconceivable (Rogers/Rogers, *Key*, 430).

[41] Betz points out that jokes about eunuchs were commonplace in Greek diatribe (*Galatians*, 270).

[42] See Dunn, *Galatians*, 283-84.

Yahweh might become one which excluded from the presence of Yahweh (in the worshipping assembly)" (*Galatians*, 283).

All these assessments of Paul's intentions accord with the imperative of 4:30 that the law teachers be ousted from the authentic Abrahamic camp—only he wants the troublers to *disqualify themselves* and not wait to be shown the door![43] "What Paul is really referring to here is the agitators inflicting the oath, curse upon themselves, and so cutting themselves out of the covenant community rather than cutting off the Galatians from the Christian community" (Witherington, *Grace*, 374).

The role reversal motif once more arises in Paul's treatment of the Judaizers. If they were to castrate themselves, they would become like the members of the cult of Cybele, localized in Galatia, a form of paganism thoroughly despised by Jews (as it was, they were already disliked by the Romans, who considered circumcision to be a form of castration)![44] George is correct that Paul's readers could not have missed his allusion: "The Judaizers who made so much of circumcision were really no better guides to the spiritual life than the pagan priests who castrated themselves in service to an idolatrous religion" (*Galatians*, 372).[45] In thought, Paul recapitulates 4:8-11.

C. The Responsibilities of Freedom in the Spirit (5:13-6:10)

One might think that the thrust of Paul's appeal to the Galatians is all but complete. Yet such is not the case, because one vital dimension of his argument remains outstanding—the obligations of freedom in the Spirit. Paul was well aware that freedom is a "heady mixture." "The removal of old constraints can easily lead to a

---

[43] Dunn comments that Paul's swipe at the opponents has the further force of a *reductio ad absurdum*: "One slice with the knife = acceptability to God; another slice with the knife = total unacceptability to God. The ridiculousness of such distinctions makes the requirement of the one (circumcision) as much the prohibition of the other (the castrated) equally ridiculous in God's sight" (*Galatians*, 284).

[44] See Das, *Paul and Jews*, 20-21; T. Martin, "Whose Flesh;" and esp. S. Elliott, "Mother," 671-76. In a posting to "Corpus Paulinum" (corpus-paul@lists.ibiblio.org), Elliott reaffirms: "I find it hard to envision Paul being able to speak of castration in the Anatolian context with a ritual connection in circumcision without it evoking an association with the Galli's ritual castration. Even if 5:12 were the only such allusion, the association would be unavoidable given their presence. With the other allusions, this functions fairly neatly as a last 'zinger'."

[45] In accord are Martyn, *Galatians*, 478; Dunn, *Galatians*, 283.

wider breakdown of discipline.... Liberty once gained might easily become the occasion for the license of self-indulgence" (Dunn, *Galatians*, 285). Given that so much of this letter has been taken up with championing a law-free gospel, Paul now feels it incumbent on himself to clarify how liberation from the law cannot and must not devolve into license.[46] Just because a Christian possesses the Spirit does not mean that he is lawless. As Paul expresses it elsewhere, he is not without law toward God but is "under Christ's law" (*ennomos Christou*) (1 Cor 9:21). See on 6:2.

Indeed, it is "the law of Christ" (6:2), with its call for the service of others, that gives concrete and practical expression to the inward endowment with God's Spirit. "A theology of freedom, particularly freedom from the law, which did not explain how that theology translated into daily living would have been a theology of irresponsibility" (Dunn, *Galatians*, 285). It is not necessary to assume the existence of a libertine or antinomian circle in the Galatian churches. Paul simply knew from experience that his teaching could be distorted to the extent that it was no longer recognizable as his own (cf. Rom 6:1-2).

The point was all the more necessary to impress upon former pagans just because of the environment of hedonism and the abandonment of restraints in which they lived. The Judaizers sought to counter the degenerative tendencies of the Greco-Roman milieu by imposing the law. Paul agrees that the baser propensities of human nature must be held in check and that individuals must cultivate an ethical standard commensurate with their calling as believers. The difference is that Paul, quite out of character with his former Jewish convictions, remonstrates that only the Spirit can produce the fruit befitting those who call upon the name of Christ as Lord. The Torah is absolutely powerless to generate new creation life. Of the essence of understanding this portion of the letter is a recognition that Paul's concern from beginning to end is, as Fee rightly discerns, with the Christian life in community, not with the interior life of the individual Christian. The fruit of the Spirit engenders love, joy and peace within the community, not in the first instance within the believer's own heart (*Exegesis*, 161). This is not to

---

[46] Thomson takes 5:13-6:2 to be an elaborate chiasmus. The central element occurs in 5:21b: Paul's warning against the indulgence of the works of the flesh (*Chiasmus*, 116-51). His suggestion is attractive, but it artificially ends the unit of thought short of 6:10. Barclay's somewhat more complicated structuring of 5:25-6:10 is perhaps closer to the mark (*Obeying*, 149-50).

brush the individual aside, but it is to recognize that individuals are saved in order to be members of a body.

(1) Freedom Means Love (5:13-15)

13 As Paul turns directly to the theme of the responsibilities of liberty in the Spirit, he reiterates from v. 1 the all-important call to freedom.[47] He places the plural pronoun "you" in the emphatic position to stress that the recipients of his letter find their self-identity precisely in their birth of the "free woman," not the slave (4:31). Accordingly, he calls them "brothers" once more because he is sure of the genuineness of their faith, notwithstanding their momentary attraction to the covenantal nomism of the law teachers. But having asserted again the central thesis of this letter—freedom—he turns to the other side of the coin: they are not to use their liberty as an opportunity or pretext for the flesh. The noun here (*aphormē*) is literally a military staging area or base of operations. As Hays explains, the Galatians have been caught up in a cosmic conflict, and they must take care not to let the territory won for them by Christ become a staging ground for a counterattack by the hostile power of the flesh (*Galatians*, 321). In this elimination of the "headquarters" of the flesh, we recall that freedom is not only *from* the old enslavement but *to* a new responsibility. "The freedom of God has both aspects, otherwise it is not God's freedom" (Dunn, *Galatians*, 287).

"Flesh" in Paul has numerous connotations.[48] But three aspects especially stand out. The one is the human condition in its weakness, vulnerability and belongingness to this world, with all that is implied. Another is captured in part by NIV's translation of "flesh" as "sinful nature," because the flesh has become the "headquarters" of sin (Rom 7:14-25). In particular, flesh can stand for sin because of the egocentricity of fallen humanity.[49] This dimension

---

[47] The conjunction "for" (*gar*) points to the continuity of what follows with what has preceded.

[48] See Dunn, *Theology of Paul*, 62-70; Erickson, *DPL*, 303-6; Jewett, *Terms*, 49-166; Sand, *EDNT*, 3.230-33; Spicq, *TLNT*, 3.235-41. Hays is right that in Galatians Paul plays artfully on the ambiguity of "flesh" (*Galatians*, 321).

[49] By extension, flesh in this sense can stand for "everything aside from God in which one places his final trust" (Jewett, *Terms*, 103). Käsemann similarly states that "existence is 'flesh' in so far as it has given itself over to the world of flesh, serves that world and allows itself to be determined by it" (quoted by T. L. Carter, *Paul*, 119).

was certainly in Paul's mind here, because the antithesis of indulging the flesh is the service of one another.

A third use of the term is especially prominent in Galatians, that is, flesh as a synonym of the old creation, the era of the Torah.[50] To be sure, writing in this ethical context, Paul wants his readers to flee the service of the sinful ego—in all its ramifications—for the sake of helping others. But the historical connotation of "flesh" is never out of sight. That is to say, those who choose to remain on the wrong side of the eschatological divide cannot help but serve self and give rein to the impulses of the flesh in the negatively ethical sense (see the section note to this verse).[51] According to T. L. Carter, "Paul thus employs the term *sarx* [flesh] precisely because it sums up human existence in this age, as opposed to the life of the age to come, which is characterised by *pneuma* [Spirit]. By identifying sins as 'works of the flesh', Paul brands as sinful the natural behaviour of all humanity apart from the Spirit" (*Paul*, 119).[52]

The antidote to the indulgence of the flesh is the loving service of others. If, according to v. 6, faith works "through love," then v. 13 clarifies specifically what Paul means: it is "through love" that one embraces a new kind of servitude (the verb *douleuō*), that of ministry to other people (with a possible glance at Mark 9:35; 10:42-44). Barrett is right that "The opposite of flesh is love...love that looks away from the self and its wishes, even its real needs, to the neighbor, and spends its resources on his needs" (*Freedom*, 72-73). Dunn likewise confirms: "The expression of true (or Christian) freedom is not self-indulgence but subordination of mere self-assertiveness to meeting the needs of others" (*Galatians*, 288). We can take it a step further and say that the *only way* to preserve Christian freedom is to exercise love: "Christian freedom is freedom to love and therefore freedom to serve" (George, *Galatians*, 378).

---

[50] See on 3:3; 4:29 and Fee, *Presence*, 430-31; Jewett, *Terms*, 95-101.

[51] Fee appropriately observes that to live "according to the flesh" is "to live in keeping with the values and desires of life in the present age that stand in absolute contradiction to God and his ways. Hence the ultimate contrasts in Paul are eschatological: life 'according to the flesh,' lived according to the present age that has been condemned through the cross and is passing away, or life 'according to the Spirit,' lived in keeping with the values and norms of the coming age inaugurated by Christ through his death and resurrection and empowered by the eschatological Spirit" (*Presence*, 431).

[52] Barclay likewise maintains that flesh designates what is human, in contrast to the divine activity displayed on the cross and in the Spirit (*Obeying*, 178-215).

As paradoxical as it is, therefore, freedom from the law—the old slavery (4:8, 9, 25)—is willing bondage to righteousness (Rom 6:16-18), and true liberty can be found only in such bondage. Such a notion would have had a shock effect on Paul's reading audience, simply because slavery was the very antithesis of freedom.[53] From Paul's perspective, however, "freedom and slavery are not simply mutually exclusive terms; they stand in the closest possible relationship to one another and can only be adequately defined in terms of object and goal: what we are slave *to* and what we are free *for*" (George, *Galatians*, 378). Paul will provide a concrete example of this "loving slavery" in 6:1-5, but the principle applies in all sorts of situations. It is just by their servitude to others that the Galatians would become, like Paul himself (Rom 1:1, etc.), slaves of the Lord Jesus Christ.

14 The Galatians are to serve one another through love because it is none other than love that fulfills the law in its entirety.[54] As observed on 4:4, the verb "fulfill" (*plēroō*) and its cognates in the NT bear distinctively salvation-historical overtones, as they signal the "eschatological measure," the completion of the eternal plan of salvation in Christ (e.g., Matt 5:17; Mark 1:15).[55] The law of Moses, even with all its minute restrictions for children, was intended to create a community of love. This is the substance of the Mosaic legislation and its intention; the "whole law," in all its ramifications, was designed to do none other than generate such a people. Jesus, accordingly, could assume it to be axiomatic that love to God and neighbor is the summary of the entire Torah (Matt 22:34-40).

This being so, Paul's reasoning is that the law attains its original reason for existence in the eschatological assemblies of Christ

---

[53] Hays writes that Paul's image of mutual slavery would have sounded strange and even offensive to Greek ears. The ideal of Hellenistic philosophy, especially Stoicism, was to attain to a position of autonomous detachment (*Galatians*, 321-22). On ancient slavery as the backdrop to Paul's slave imagery in Galatians, see D. Martin, *Slavery*, 1-49; M. J. Harris, *Slave*, 25-45; Tsang, *Slaves*, 21-62; D. J. Williams, *Metaphors*, 111-40; Harrill, "Paul," 575-85; Balch, "Paul," 271-73, 280-82; Witherington, *Paul Quest*, 194-202.

[54] The possibility of summing up the law in a single formulation was not new to Paul. See Dunn, *Galatians*, 289.

[55] Hays notes that the phrase "fulfill the law" is distinctively of Christian coinage, with no precedents in Jewish texts (*Galatians*, 322).

when through love its members become the slaves of others.[56] He was especially compelled to press this point because his opponents had forgotten that love lies at the very heart of the Torah. The Judaizers would not have put it in so many words, but for them the law was, for all practical purposes, fulfilled by a "sanctified hatred" towards all who would not conform to their conception of covenantal fidelity. As former Pharisees, the circumcision party brought the baggage of their sectarian attitudes over into the Gentile mission. It is surely to the point that Bickerman can characterize Pharisaism as "a belligerent movement that knew how to hate."[57]

"Fulfilling the law" and "doing the law" are not to be thought of as distinct activities (in spite of Betz's lengthy defense of the distinction, *Galatians*, 275-76).[58] Rather, the demand of the Torah to do and live (Lev 18:5; Deut 4:1, 10, 40; 5:29-33; 6:1-2, 18, 24; 7:12-13) is commensurate with the love that the Israelite was to display toward God (Deut 5:10; 6:5; 7:9; 10:12; 11:13; 13:3; 30:6) and his people (Lev 19:18). When through love the law was "done," the result was the realization of the ideal of covenant relationships. However, the history of Israel demonstrates that the ideal was rarely attained, especially in the first-century context in which each of the various Jewish enclaves was vying for the titles "true elect" and "true remnant" to the exclusion all other Jews (M. A. Elliott, *Survivors*).

Paul thus claims that the Christian church, as the end-time community, has realized the very reason the law was given through Moses, even though the church is not under the Torah but rather the law of Christ (see the section note to this verse). It is in this vein that Jesus defined his followers: "A new commandment I give to you, that you love one another, even as I have loved you, that you also love one another. By this all men will know that you are my disciples, if you have love for one another" (John 13:34-35). It was, of course, Jesus himself who preeminently fulfilled the law

---

[56] See Fee, *Presence*, 815-16. The English "is fulfilled" is an accommodation of Paul's Greek perfect tense (*peplērōtai*). In all likelihood, he is using the perfect in its normal sense of a past action whose consequences extend into the present.

[57] Bickerman, *Ezra*, 103. See further Garlington, "Burden Bearing," 154-55 (= *Essays*, 252-54).

[58] That fulfilling the law is commensurate with doing the law follows from a comparison of the present verse with Rom 2:13, where the "doers of the law" are just those who realize the ideal set before Adam in the Garden (see Garlington, *Faith*, 56-60). Contra Westerholm, as cited by Longenecker, *Galatians*, 242, and George, *Galatians*, 383.

by taking on the form of a servant and in love gave himself as a ransom for many (see Longenecker, *Galatians*, 243). This last mentioned consideration should confirm that love never operates in the abstract, nor is it to be extracted from ethical norms ("all you need is love"). Rather, as we will see below, love is the implementation of the law of Christ with regard to the members of his body. Jesus' own self-sacrificial love is to be replicated in the church.

The "one word" that fulfills the law is Lev 19:18.[59] Hays writes that Paul can draw on a text such as this because the law has now become a witness to the gospel, and from his new vantage point as a Christian he can see something in the Torah he never could before (*Galatians*, 322). In its original setting, the "neighbor" of this verse is the fellow Israelite. But Lev 19:34 (Deut 10:19) clarifies that it was not only one's compatriot who was to be loved but also the stranger who sojourned among the nation. Thus, the law required love to be shown toward all people. With the passage of time, however, the scope of "neighbor" was constricted by at least some Jewish groups to their own membership (e.g., CD 9:2-8). In such a context, the radical character of the parable of the Good Samaritan stands out like a sore thumb. The neighbor, in Jesus' teaching, is actually those who were considered to be reprobates by the rank and file of the "righteous" of Israel!

Paul likewise expands the range of "neighbor," so as to include uncircumcised and non-kosher Gentiles just as they were (also Gal 6:10 is very much in the spirit of Lev 19:34). The problem with the rival teachers is that they would (and could) not love anyone unlike themselves. Their assumption was that God hated everyone outside his covenant with Israel, and, therefore, God's enemies were their enemies too. In this light, Jesus appears as a very radical figure in the history of Judaism, because his kingdom requires precisely that we love our enemies, so that we may be like our heavenly Father (Matt 5:43-48). Paul followed suit. Whereas the various Jewish enclaves believed that the law was fulfilled when they maintained themselves as a people separated from their hated enemies, for Paul just the opposite was true: the fulfillment of the law is commensurate with the obliteration of sectarian distinctions and the reception of all without distinction.[60]

---

[59] Paul's citation of Lev 19:18 may well stem from Jesus' own quotation of it, in combination with Deut 6:4-5, as his summary of the purpose of the law (Matt 22:34-40; Mark 12:28-34).

[60] Hays relates that later rabbinic sources reflect various debates about how to sum up the law under a small number of commandments or fundamental princi-

15 The alternative to love which fulfills the law is the animal-like behavior of biting, devouring and consuming (cf. 1 Cor 15:32).[61] Witherington notes that this verse describes a progression: "First the animal bites the prey, then it tears at the flesh of the victim, then finally it consumes its prey" (*Grace*, 384). If the Galatians do not love one another from the heart, they will surely lapse into the chaos of the old creation, in which self only reigns. In fact, the present tenses of the verse probably imply that "dogfights" were already under way in the churches. These were nothing but the bitter fruits of slavery engendered by the latter-day Ishmaelites, the children of bondage. Paul was aware of the Jewish factionalism of the Second Temple period, with all its sectarian disputes and acrid recriminations.[62] And not only our verse but Romans 14-15 bear witness to his fear that the Christian assemblies might end up as sharply divided and bitterly embroiled in infighting as any of the Jewish groups.

Section Note

14 Witherington is surely right that Paul is not here rebuilding what the whole letter has labored to demolish. Rather, "He is arguing that if the Galatians continue to follow his advice and the leading of the Spirit, the essential aims of the Law will be already fulfilled paradoxically without submitting to circumcision and the Mosaic covenant" (*Grace*, 381). He goes on to remark that when Paul speaks of Christians fulfilling the law (Gal 5:14; Rom 8:4; 13:8-10), he is not prescribing obedience to the Mosaic standards as such, but "describing the correspondence between Christian behavior and what the Law demands or describing how what has happened in the lives of Christians by means of the Spirit's work amounts to a fulfillment of the Law in believers…. To fulfill the Law

---

ples. But these texts differ from Gal 5:14 in one crucial way: the rabbis never entertained the idea that their summarizing categories could replace specific commandments or relieve one of the necessity of obeying such commands as circumcision, food laws and the sabbath (*Galatians*, 323).

[61] Betz points out that comparison of bad conduct with the behavior of wild animals was commonplace in Greek diatribe literature (*Galatians*, 277). Additionally, Paul may have had in mind the wild beasts as they symbolize the chaos of the old creation (cf. 1 Cor 15:32) (Garlington, *Essays*, 89-91). Even more to the point perhaps, Cummins calls to mind the "bestial" conduct of Israel's oppressors in Daniel 7 and the *Animal Apocalypse* of *1 Enoch* 85-90 (*Paul*, 105, n. 40). Such an allusion would certainly be in keeping with the tendency of this letter to redefine Paul's Torah-true antagonists as the enemies and troublers of the new Israel brought into being by his gospel.

[62] See Dunn, *Jesus Remembered*, 265-86.

implies to satisfy completely its essential requirements, and such fulfillment can only transpire among fallen human beings in the eschatological age among those guided and empowered by the eschatological gift of the Spirit..." (ibid., 382).

(2) Spirit Versus Flesh (5:16-26)

In presenting the alternatives of Spirit versus flesh, Paul ties into the biblical teaching concerning the "two ways," either that of obedience to God or of apostasy (see Bligh, *Galatians*, 447-56). At the same time, his list of virtues and vices is not unlike those of the moral philosophers of his day (Engberg-Pederson, "Paul"). Paul's methodology, then, may be looked upon as a kind of "double whammy" in driving home the necessity of Spirit-obedience as the displacement of flesh-disobedience.

16 If v. 13 exhorted the believers in Galatia not to use their freedom as an opportunity for the flesh, then the present verse informs them that walking by the Spirit is the way to avoid fulfilling the flesh's desires.[63] The typical OT metaphor of walking (e.g., Exod 18:20; Deut 13:4-5; Ps 86:11; Isa 33:15) is taken up again to describe Christian deportment (see on 1:13; 2:2; cf. Gal 5:25; Eph 4:1, 17; Col 1:10; 2:6; Rom 13:13).[64] Paul deliberately uses the covenantal language of the Hebrew Bible to impact on those familiar with the Jewish lifestyle. Moreover, anyone conversant with the Scriptures would know that walking was specifically in God's laws or statutes (e.g., Exod 16:4; Lev 18:4; Jer 44:23; Ezek 5:6-7).

Therefore, by speaking of a walk "by the Spirit," Paul poses an alternative understanding of how the people of God should conduct themselves, not according to the Torah but by looking to the Spirit for empowerment.[65] "Ethical life," remarks Fee, "is still a matter of

---

[63] The verse begins with "but I say," a common formula in Paul for introducing a new division of a letter and calling particular attention to what is to follow.

[64] George (*Galatians*, 386) points out that in chap. 5 Paul uses four distinct verbs to designate the Spirit-controlled life of the believer, all of which are more or less equivalent in meaning: walk in the Spirit (v. 16), be led by the Spirit (v. 18), live by the Spirit (v. 25a), keep in step with the Spirit (v. 25b).

[65] Betz notes that the phrase "by the Spirit" expresses origin as well as the quality of that way of life (*Galatians*, 278). Fee also addresses the dative case of "Spirit" (*pneumati*) and concludes that it may be either instrumental ("walk by means of, that is, empowered by, the Spirit") or locative of sphere ("walk in the sphere of the Spirit"). Fee rightly argues that there is an overlap in Paul's syntax that is not to be confined by rigid grammatical categories. Hence, "Even though one is to walk by means of the Spirit, one does so because one is also to walk in the sphere

'walking in the ways of God,' but for Paul this is empowered for God's new covenant people by God's empowering presence in the person of the Holy Spirit" (*Presence*, 430).

> After all, Paul's point in all of this must not be lost sight of: in a world in which Torah observance no longer obtains, the Spirit is sufficient and adequate to accomplish God's purposes in and among his people. Spirit people march to a different drummer, and the Spirit empowers them to live in such a way that their lives evidence that fact; their behavior is of a decidedly different character from that of their former way of life. Just as with the "works of Torah," the time for the "works of the flesh" belongs to the past. Spirit people, by walking in the Spirit by whom they began life in Christ, will thereby not walk in the ways of their pagan past (ibid., 433-34).

Betz likewise confirms that the imperative "walk by the Spirit" "sums up the Apostle's paraenesis, and therefore defines Paul's concept of the Christian life" (*Galatians*, 277).

By using the active voice of the verb, Paul stresses an activism on the part of the believer (the balance is struck in v. 18 with the passive "led by the Spirit").[66] Paul envisions "a life-style and decision-making which constantly referred back to that inward fact or consciousness of the Spirit's presence, and which sought to bring it to expression in daily life" (Dunn, *Galatians*, 296). Or, according to Hansen, "His command speaks of a way of living in which all aspects of life are directed and transformed by the Spirit" (*Galatians*, 168). Surprisingly, it is normally overlooked by commentators that the Spirit works in conjunction with the Word: to walk by the Spirit entails and demands attention to the Word of God, whereby the Third Person of the Trinity imparts the ability to crucify the flesh with its passions and desires (5:24). By pressing upon the readers the reality of the Spirit, Paul reminds them (from 3:3) that they should continue as they began: perfection in the

---

of the Spirit, that is, in the arena of the Spirit's present life and activity" (*Presence*, 430).

[66] According to Fee, in the present verse Paul speaks by way of imperative, not by way of a passive indicative (as in v. 18). "Life in the Spirit is not passive submission to the Spirit to do a supernatural work in one's life; rather, it requires conscious effort, so that the indwelling Spirit may accomplish his ends in one's life" (*Presence*, 433).

Spirit is to be had by a persevering walk in the Spirit, not by a return to the age of the flesh.

If Christians consistently walk by the Spirit, they will not "perfect the desire of the flesh" (my translation). Paul's language takes the form of a promise respecting the non-fulfillment of the flesh's desire.[67] The verb of this clause, here translated by me "perfect" (*teleō*), is related to that of 3:3b (*epiteleō*). If there is a perfection in the Spirit, then there is also a perverse kind of "perfection" of the flesh. Unless the flesh-driven impulse is held in check, this "desire of the flesh" (1 John 2:16) will attain its logical end in the eschatological destruction of the individual (cf. Jas 1:14-15). This is why those who practice "the works of the flesh" will not inherit the kingdom of God (5:21). The antipode of this "damnation history" is found in the consummation of the righteousness that we are currently anticipating (5:5).

Paul's way of putting things, remarks Witherington, "Emphasizes that living life in the Spirit does not prevent one from having fleshly desires, but it does give one the power to avoid acting on these desires and so bringing them to completion" (*Grace*, 393). The singular "desire (*epithumia*) of the flesh" is a way of epitomizing all the impulses of the sinful nature as a unitary principle of appetite gone out of control (as its appearance in Jas 1:14-15 and 1 John 2:16). (The various manifestations of "desire" will be enumerated in vv. 19-21.) Just because the power of the flesh resides in its appeal to the weakness of human nature, the power of the Spirit must counterbalance the flesh's allurements and enable one to be a "survivor" in the wilderness of this world. Otherwise put, by the Spirit "we are more than conquerors through him who loved us" (Rom 8:37).

17 The necessity of walking by the Spirit is now reinforced by the reality of the warfare constantly waged between the flesh and the Spirit throughout this "present evil age." What follows, Dunn remarks, is "one of the most realistic and psychologically insightful observations made by Paul" (*Galatians*, 297). In brief, Paul's point is that if our lives are not directed and transformed by the Spirit, the flesh will win the war! Literally translated, Paul says, "the flesh desires against the Spirit, and the Spirit desires against the flesh"

---

[67] Burton comments that Paul's Greek (*ou mē telesēte*) "is equivalent to an emphatic promissory future…expressing, not a command, but a strong assurance that if they walk by the Spirit they will not, in fact, fulfill the flesh-lust" (*Galatians*, 299).

(as rendered adequately by NIV and NASB). Flesh (defined as the sinful ego) and the Holy Spirit are set forth as two personages with wills, desires and purposes of their own, each being in conflict with the other. Both inhabit the believer, making him both flesh and Spirit at the same time. Paul depicts an inward contradiction of an individual pulled in two directions.

As a distillation of what he will say at more length in Rom 7:14-25, he has in view the condition of one who lives in two worlds at the same time—in the overlap of the Already and the Not Yet—and feels simultaneously the influence of both ages.[68] We have made a beginning in the Spirit, but the "present evil age" is still with us and beckons us back into the paths of idolatry. Consequently, there is a tension that characterizes Christian existence this side of the resurrection (cf. Rom 8:18-25 and throughout 2 Corinthians).

> Paul uses the symbolism [that is, of flesh] here, not because he regards the flesh as inherently evil, but because it accurately symbolises the ambiguous status of those who have entered into the eschatological era through receiving the Spirit, but who still have to live "in the flesh" in the present evil age. By opposing the flesh to the eschatological Spirit, Paul adapts the tension between the good inside and evil outside symbolised by the flesh, and applies it to the eschatological tension between present and future experienced by members of the community. It is this tension which finds expression in his combination of the indicative and imperative in Galatians 5:16-6:8 (T. L. Carter, *Paul*, 121).

No wonder, endurance is required as we eagerly await the hope of righteousness (Gal 5:5; Rom 8:24-25)—"let us not grow weary in well-doing" (6:9). To be sure, in principle the believer has left the flesh behind in that he has died to "sin" (Rom 6:11), that is, the old creation headed by the first Adam and dominated by "the god of this world." Nevertheless, sin and the flesh hang on and continue to proffer their numerous attractions.[69] "Here the real-

---

[68] See Garlington, *Faith*, 110-43 (= *Essays*, 169-211); Dunn, "Rom. 7,14-25;" id., *Romans*, 1.387-99, 403-12.

[69] The warfare of Gal 5:17 is rooted in "apocalyptic war," wherein two cosmic orders vie for dominance. See Martyn, *Galatians*, 524-36. Thus, in his own person the believer is the microcosm of cosmic forces in competition.

ity is clear: 'in the flesh' is an inescapable aspect of the human condition, so that believers too cannot escape it as long as this mortal life continues" (Dunn, *Galatians*, 298). To this George adds: "There is no spiritual technique or second blessing that can propel the believer onto a higher plane of Christian living where this battle must no longer be fought" (*Galatians*, 387-88).

If the desires of flesh and Spirit "are in conflict with each other,"[70] the result is that the Christian is prevented from doing the things that he wants to do.[71] Paul's language cuts in two directions at the same time: the flesh opposes the Spirit when we want to follow the Spirit, and the Spirit checks the flesh when we want to succumb to the flesh.[72] Or, as Burton asks, "Does the man choose evil, the Spirit opposes him; does he choose good, the flesh hinders him" (*Galatians*, 302). However, by analogy with Rom 7:14-25, Paul's main focus is on the believer's frustrated desire to do the will of God wholly and completely.[73] Of course, the believer *wants* to do the bidding of the Spirit (as parallel to Paul's "willing I" and his delight in the law of God in Rom 7:14-25).

His point is not that we only seldom perform the will of God and fail to attain to any measures of victory, nor that flesh and Spirit are equal powers in the conflict.[74] It is, rather, that we fall

---

[70] The verb here (*antikeimai*) means to "be in opposition to." As such it voices one of the "apocalyptic antinomies" of Galatians. See Martyn, *Issues*, 111-23; id., *Galatians*, 570-74.

[71] A *hina* clause normally expresses purpose, though at times it indicates results. Either makes sense here. Either flesh and Spirit purpose to keep the individual from accomplishing the desires of the other, or this is the result of their warfare. The practical effect is the same either way.

[72] See Longenecker, *Galatians*, 246; Betz, *Galatians*, 280-81.

[73] It is frequently denied that Romans 7 and the present text are related because, as the argument goes, there is no mention of the Spirit in the former passage. However, this is to overlook the obvious. Rom 7:6 makes explicit mention of the "newness of Spirit" as over against the "oldness of the letter" (*gramma*), which is the law. The verse sets forth a paradigm of old versus new and thus sets the stage for the discussion of 7:14-25, which plays precisely on the warfare of these two competing entities. Moreover, in 7:14, Paul calls the law "spiritual," which everywhere in his letters refers to the Holy Spirit. Specifically, the law is derived from the Spirit and is the expression of God's will as conveyed through the Spirit. I would agree with Hubbard that Romans often provides the best commentary on Galatians (*Creation*, 221).

[74] "In the battle between the forces of flesh and Spirit there is no stalemate, but the Spirit takes the lead, overwhelms, and thus defeats evil" (Betz, *Galatians*, 281). This in itself is a sufficient answer to Fee's allegation that our reading of this text leaves the believer in a helpless situation (*Presence*, 435-36). Fung is likewise wide of the mark with the claim that Gal 5:17 envisages a different situa-

short of the ideals of the new creation as articulated by the *spiritual* law of God (Rom 7:14). It is in this relative, not absolute, sense that Paul can exclaim in Rom 7:19: "For what I do is not the good I want to do; no, the evil I do not want to do—this I keep on doing." If, climactically, he cries out "wretched person that I am" (Rom 7:24), it is his longing for the full freedom of Christ to be realized when he is finally adopted as God's son (Rom 8:23). And so it is with every Christian. This is why, again, "There must be that inward resolution and determined discipline to side with the Spirit *against oneself* in what is an ongoing and inescapable warfare, so long as the flesh continues to be a factor (that is, for the duration of this earthly life)."[75]

18 If one is obliged actively to walk by the Spirit, here the other side of the coin is stated: the Spirit himself takes the lead in the enablement of the believer to engage in the conflict with the flesh. If it is possible to be "led" by various illicit desires (1 Cor 12:2; 2 Tim 3:6), then the Spirit acts as an inner compulsion to restrain the uprisings of the flesh and empower us not to surrender to the baser appetites of human nature. The leading of the Spirit is not guidance in decision-making, but the impartation of ability to persevere in the flesh/Spirit conflict, just as Jesus himself was led by the Spirit through the wilderness (Luke 4:1) and so remained faithful to his Father. The tie-in to the wilderness is all the more appropriate in light of Beale's study of the background of Galatians 5. Beale appeals to texts such as Isa 57:16-18, where the "Spirit coming down

---

tion from Rom 7:14-25. According to Fung, whereas the latter passage describes an unequal conflict, here the battle between flesh and Spirit stands under the promise of victory (*Galatians*, 250). However, this reading fails to reckon with the very pronounced presence of victory in Rom 7:25: it is God who will most decidedly deliver Paul from his body of death, in the resurrection (cf. 1 Cor 15:57). Additionally, our verse does speak of the believer's victory over the flesh, but it does so in the context of constant struggle and the reality that the flesh will, in this life, frustrate our desire for complete conformity to the ways of the Spirit.

[75] Dunn, *Galatians*, 299-300, italics his. Cf. Schlier, *Galater*, 250. Barclay posits that this reading of v. 17 sets up an inconsistency with v. 16, Paul's confidence that if one walks by the Spirit, one will not "perfect" the flesh (*Obeying*, 113). In reply, v. 17, on our interpretation, is intended to complement the perspective of the preceding verse by providing a very good reason indeed to "walk by the Spirit!" Walking by the Spirit becomes all the more imperative in view of the battle lines drawn between himself and the flesh. Besides, the flesh does not "continually," that is, at *every* juncture, defeat the Spirit's wishes, but enough of the time that believers cannot attain to the degree of obedience that they desire—which, at the end of the day, is full conformity to Christ. Anything short of this will not do.

from God" occurs in connection with the leading of Israel through the wilderness back to the land. In like manner, Isa 63:13 speaks of God's leading of Israel through the Red Sea in direct conjunction with the "Holy Spirit" placed in the midst of the nation. Paul thus places the leading of the Spirit into an eschatological framework, with the Galatians as the latter-day Spirit-led people. As Beale remarks: "The Galatians are those who have begun to participate in the fulfillment of Isaiah's prophecies of new Exodus and new creation, which is probably one reason Paul calls them 'the Israel of God' in 6:16" ("Background," 13-14).

With this salvation-historical background in place, its is evident enough that the "leading of the Spirit" is not to be understood mystically, but as the Spirit enabling us to persevere through our own wilderness as we are granted the ability to understand and apply the Word of God. We recall that it was just by his citation of God's Word that the Lord defeated the Devil in the desert, and it was David who hid the Word in his heart that he might not sin (Ps 119:11).

It is true that the passive voice of "led" balances the active voice of "walk" in v. 16. (This usage is often called the "divine passive:" God is the one leading his people.) But as Fee reminds us, in Galatians 5, one is urged to "walk by the Spirit" or "live by the Spirit" by deliberately conforming one's life to the Spirit. "If such a person is also described as being 'led by the Spirit,' that does not mean passively; it means to rise up and follow the Spirit by walking in obedience to the Spirit's desire" (*Presence*, 433).

It is only those who experience the Spirit's leading who are "not under the law." This description of the Spirit-people is directed at those who were buying into the proposition that the Torah provided both the standard of their daily walk and the wherewithal to comply with that standard. Hence, Paul's overriding concern, especially in this latter portion of the letter, is to show that a "walk" determined by the Spirit was what the readers needed, not the continued tutelage of the law.[76] There are, to be sure, "rules" to the Christian life, but these for Paul are embedded in the "law of Christ" (6:2), not the law of Moses. Fee can justly say that "believers who walk by the Spirit do so because they are following where the Spirit leads; and the Spirit leads in 'the law of Christ,' in ways that both reflect and pattern after Christ himself.... This is why

---

[76] Commentators point out that Paul uses the verbal form (*agō*) of the noun of 3:24-25, the "disciplinarian" (*paidagōgos*) whose function it was to lead Israel to Christ.

Torah observance is totally irrelevant; for the one led by the Spirit in 'the law of Christ' the *aim* of the Torah has been fulfilled" (*Presence*, 438). But even with the objective principles provided by Christ's law, what is preeminently needed is the Spirit to write the law on the heart (Jer 31:33-34; 2 Cor 3:3) and impart the desire to comply with God's will (Rom 7:16). This is what happens when the Spirit baptizes into Christ (1 Cor 12:13).

In telling the Galatians that Spirit-led people are not "not under the law," Paul is making two closely related points. The one is that they do not live in the age of the law, before the outpouring of the Spirit, the time of bondage. In this sense, they are not "under the authority" of the Mosaic economy. Historically speaking, Spirit and law occupy different turf in salvation history (again 3:3, 12). Indeed, the advent of the Spirit is proof positive that the era of the Torah has passed away forever. Or, in practical terms, the Spirit does not lead one in the way of the Torah, only in the path of the law of Christ. Those who devote themselves to law observance do not, in point of fact, possess the Spirit. The other is that they are not under the "curse of the law" (3:13), or, in the words of v. 23, *against* them there is no law. Should they choose to go back to the period of the Torah's hegemony, then they would violate God's salvific purpose for the ends of the ages in Christ (see on 3:10-13), because only Christ and the Spirit can do what the law could not (Rom 8:1-8. See on 5:2, 4.). As Paul puts it to the Corinthians, the "letter" (the law) kills, but the Spirit makes alive (2 Cor 3:6). It is in this twofold sense that the believer is "not under law but under grace" (Rom 6:14).

19-21 For almost the remainder of chap. 5, Paul writes in more detail about the various manifestations of flesh and Spirit respectively in the ongoing battle between the two. As he catalogues the particular vices pertaining to the flesh, he would have us recognize them as the concrete ways in which the "desire of the flesh" (v. 16) comes to expression in real life. In providing this list of unseemly practices and attitudes, Paul falls in line with other ancient writers, who likewise denounced unethical behavior (as did Jesus, Mark 7:21-22).[77] Certainly the Judaism of his day would have condemned such practices as idolatry, sorcery, sexual immorality and

---

[77] See Betz, Longenecker, *Galatians*, 249-52; *Galatians*, 281-82; Witherington, *Grace*, 403-5. Arnold points out that not only such things as sexual impropriety and witchcraft were strictly forbidden by the Anatolian deities, but also acts of anger, hatred and violence ("Folk Belief," 441).

drunkenness, particularly in light of a text like *T. Jud.* 23:1-5, which cites licentiousness, witchcraft and idolatry as the reasons for Israel's exile. That the fleshly works on Paul's list are unoriginal is seen from the fact that each finds a counterpart in the OT.[78]

Yet it is just the areas of agreement between Paul and his Jewish counterparts that makes his particular treatment of these matters all the more startling. By calling all these vices "the works of the flesh," he deliberately echoes his own phrase "the works of the law" (2:16; 3:2, 5, 10), incumbent on those who are "under the law" (v. 18). In other words, the works of the law really are the works of the flesh, and vice versa! No doubt, the Judaizers would have been scandalized to the core by such an identification of "works of the flesh" and "works of the law." But in spite of what must have been vociferous protests from their quarters, Paul reiterates in different words the point of v. 6: circumcision avails for nothing, what matters, and what works in defeating the flesh, is "faith working through love," as one walks "by the Spirit" (v. 16). Paul's linkage of law with flesh, as outrageous as it must have seemed to his enemies, was intended to jolt the readers into a recognition of the direction in which their thinking was moving. If, under the influence of the other teachers, they wanted to win the war against the flesh, they had better be informed that they were going about it the wrong way. The law only weakens them in the struggle (see on 4:9); only the Spirit can cause them to be victorious. Additionally, assuming the yoke of the Torah would deprive them of their blood-bought freedom in Christ.

Paul is certain that these works of the flesh are "obvious." Indeed, he assumes that any reader of this epistle—including his opponents—would agree that all such "works" are deplorable. Yet his list is not simply replete with generalities, because the bulk of the items pertain specifically to the Galatian situation. Things such as "hatred, discord, jealousy, fits of rage, selfish ambition, dissensions, factions and envy" had apparently become characteristic of these congregations as a result of the exclusivistic theology of the circumcisers. It is because of the predominance of such dispositions that "flesh" throughout this entire context assumes, for the most part, the connotation of hatred and its attendant attitudes. This is the old way of living, when "we lived in malice and envy, being hated and hating one another" (Titus 3:3). The situation was rapidly becoming chaotic, and Paul had to address these issues

---

[78] See the catalogue of Bayes, *Weakness*, 169, nn. 1, 2.

head-on in order to bring his brothers and sisters back into the peace of the new creation (1:3; 6:16).

Structurally, Paul's list of fleshly works may be compared to a sandwich. The two outer slices of "bread," comprised respectively of "sexual immorality," "impurity" and "debauchery" (v. 19b) and "drunkenness" and "orgies" (v. 21a) catalogue sins that everyone in Galatia would have abominated as totally unacceptable behavior. But it is the "meat" of the sandwich (v. 20) that contains the bite. Under the influence of their recent mentors, these new Christians had become obtuse to the sins that actually destroy the church: the "works of the flesh" *as hatred and its attendant attitudes*. It is the seriousness of these in particular that Paul was compelled to bring to the attention of his readers.[79] It is the practice of none other than these that will prohibit one from inheriting the kingdom of God (v. 21b). The point needed particularly to be driven home, inasmuch as the "meat" of the sandwich is the product of a "righteous indignation" whose effect is often the abuse of others. This is why Paul pens 6:1-5: even those who fall must be restored in "a spirit of gentleness." Paul would have us beware of any variety of "sanctified hatred."

The first "slice of bread" of Paul's "sandwich" is headed by *sexual immorality*, just because of the widespread laxness of attitudes toward sex in the Greco-Roman world, especially given that cult prostitution was integral to so much of the religion of the day. The phrase may well have reminded the Galatians of their former worship of the Anatolian Mother Goddess. From a biblical perspective, illicit sex is condemned for at least two reasons. One is that the sexual capacities of human beings make them Godlike in their ability to produce after their own kind. Accordingly, the image of God is the most distorted in unlawful sexual relations. Two, marriage was intended to be an image of the covenant relation between God and his people (and among the members of the Godhead). For this reason, idolatry is likened to adultery in the Hebrew Scriptures (e.g., Jer 3:1-4:4; Hosea 1-3) and Jewish literature.[80]

Impurity was a word familiar from the OT, indicating ritual uncleanness. But here it assumes a more general moral sense and

---

[79] Dunn likewise observes that there is a strategy to the order of Paul's catalogue (see the section note to vv. 19-21): "By 'topping and tailing' his list with items which he could be sure his Galatian audiences would echo warmly, his hope no doubt was that the items in the heart of the list directed more at them themselves would strike home with greater impact" (*Galatians*, 306).

[80] See Ortlund, *Whoredom*; Garlington, *Obedience*, 190.

relates mainly to sexual matters. The reference would be to all kinds of unseemly practices deemed despicable by morally minded people.

Debauchery has to do with both sexual excess (Wis 14:26; Rom 13:13; 1 Pet 4:3) and sexual perversion (2 Pet 2:7). Sometimes it is associated with "wanton violence" or "outrageous acts" (LSJ, 255) and would denote, from this angle, sexual violence, as associated with the baser levels of society in both the ancient and the modern world. Dunn justly remarks that rejection of God regularly and inevitably results in the sexual appetite's becoming one of the desires of the flesh which dominate existence and relationships and, if left unchecked, can lead all too quickly to dehumanizing excesses (Rom 1:21-27). "In nothing did early Christianity so thoroughly revolutionize the ethical standards of the pagan world as in regard to sexual relationships" (*Galatians*, 304, quoting G. S. Duncan).

Idolatry is a term of Christian coinage (1 Cor 5:10-11; 6:9; 10:7, 14; Col 3:5), but, of course, it was none other than Judaism that distinguished itself by its worship of the one true God (Deut 6:4) as over against the multiple deities of the pagan Pantheon;[81] and attacks on idolatry were common among Jewish authors (e.g., Wisdom 12-15; *Sib. Or.* 3:8-45). Idolatry has many ramifications, but at heart it is the projection of one's own psyche onto a supposed god, and by the act of prostrating oneself before an image, the worshipper hoped to manipulate the god represented by the idol. In the final analysis, idolatry is the service of self. No doubt, Paul's Galatian converts from paganism would have heartily agreed, as would the circumcision party. But we recall from 4:8-10 that the Torah is now an idol. If the readers should complete their "conversion" to the law, they would be no better off than when they did obeisance to objects of wood and stone.

Witchcraft (or *sorcery*) is derived from the word for "drug" (*pharmakon*). Because drugs were so often employed in occult practices, the two became associated in the popular mind. This kind of "magic" was a regular feature of Hellenistic religion and pop culture, but was strictly forbidden by the law of Moses (Exod 22:18; Lev 19:26, 31; 20:6; Deut 18:9-14). It has to be qualified that the Galatians, as inhabitants of Anatolia, would have been accustomed to such a prohibition against witchcraft, as evidenced by

---

[81] See Dunn, *Partings*, 19-21.

the propitiatory inscriptions.[82] This was one vice that all would have denounced, Jews and religious Anatolians.

All of the above items would have evoked disgust from any Jewish or God-fearing person; and, in all likelihood, none of them was actually being indulged by the members of the Galatian assemblies. Such corruptions would have been the furthest thing from the minds of any one of them. However, the central section of his catalogue—the "meat of the sandwich"—hits closer to home and is intended to alert the Galatians to sins they really are guilty of and need to rectify at once. Later, Paul would have to admonish the Corinthians precisely along these lines (2 Cor 12:2).

We are not surprised, then, to read of *hatred*, because it is the fountainhead of all the other problems enumerated through the end of v. 20. NASB more literally renders this noun (in the plural) as "outbursts of anger." Dunn most adequately renders as "hostile feelings and actions." The term gives voice to antagonistic feelings and/or actions across a divide. The only other occurrences of the word in the NT have to do with enmity between God and humanity (Rom 8:7; Jas 4:4), between individuals (Luke 23:12) and, most strikingly, between Jews and Gentiles (Eph 2:14, 16).

Paul's object in using this word is altogether plain. The troublers, for all their self-perceived good intentions, are actually stirring up enmity toward Gentiles *as* Gentiles, thus creating class divisions and re-erecting the ethnic hostilities that colored Jewish and non-Jewish relations before the abolition of the "dividing wall of hostility" (Eph 2:14). This should be all the proof the Galatians needed to convince them that in following the agitators they were, in point of fact, fulfilling the "desire of the flesh." If their definition of "flesh" needed expanding beyond matters sensual, then Paul informs them of the wider ranging significance of the term.

Discord is a natural companion to hostile feelings and actions. Once emotions and words get out of hand, a party spirit, factionalism and church splits soon follow suit—a veritable return to chaos.

---

[82] Arnold points to an inscription illustrating the use of witchcraft by one person against another, one that came under the judgment of the gods. The situation involved a certain Iucundus, who went mad. A rumor spread that his mother-in-law had used witchcraft against him and had put curses in the temple of the gods. As a consequence of her misdeed, the woman and her son were punished. The gods then order the curses to be removed from the temple, and the grandsons of the woman propitiated the gods. "This account is especially significant for interpreting Galatians insofar as it provides us with a concrete illustration of the use of witchcraft in central Anatolia" ("Folk Belief," 442).

Closely associated with *discord* is *jealousy*. The word is literally "zeal" (*zēlos*), which can have both a positive and a negative sense. Here the latter is obviously in view and denotes "envy" of various sorts as the result of one enclave boasting over against another. In context, this jealousy would have reference to resentment on the part of some groups against other groups who were laying claim to being the true people of God. In this regard, the Galatian Christians were simply replicating the sectarianism of the Judaism of this time frame. And we are not to forget that "zeal" in this letter has to do with fervent devotion to the Torah, including, if necessary, violence in order to purify and maintain the standards of the covenant community (see on 1:14 and 4:18). While zeal can be a good thing, it is well to remember that it is a double-sided virtue, highly desirable but easily prone to excess.

Fits of rage take this ugly scenario a step further and speak of the total abandonment of restraint on the part of those who are "zealous" for their peculiar conception of God's people and his will for them. The gratification of the flesh finds its absolute low point in these kinds of outbursts. Those who indulge in them (the "revilers" of 1 Cor 6:10) will not inherit the kingdom of God.

Selfish ambitions, in this setting, are not far removed from "factious ambitions." This is the self-assertiveness of one faction of the church vaunting itself as the most loyal to the will of God. Perhaps Paul remembered his own "selfish ambition," when he boasted in his standing as a Pharisee, the strictest sect of mainstream Judaism (Acts 26:5; Phil 3:5-6; cf. Gal 1:14).

Dissensions are another way of making the same basic point (see on 5:9). These are so heinous because of the way they impact on the unity of the Spirit and the bond of peace (Eph 4:3).

Factions are yet another synonymous expression of the divisive effects of giving the flesh full reign. This word (*hairesis*) is the one from which "heresy" was later to be derived. In the NT itself, the term means simply a party or a sect (e.g., Acts 5:17). But it is significant that the circumcising group is designated precisely "the *party* of the Pharisees" (Acts 15:5). It was just these people who were creating the dissensions in Galatia: a faction was creating "factions" after its own image. And it is down this road that Paul did not want the Gentile Christians to head—the assembly of Jesus the Messiah was not meant to be a throwback to the divisiveness of then contemporary Judaism.

> The implication again is clear, that Paul saw these as dangers particularly confronting the Galatian churches.

> His concern, we may say, was that the factionalism which disfigured late second-Temple Judaism might be imported into the new movement by the activities of the other missionaries. Since that factionalism was characteristically exclusive and judgemental of other Jews, discounting them as "sinners" and as those whose actions effectively put themselves outside the covenant people.... Paul had every reason to resist such censorious factionalism in his own churches (Dunn, *Galatians*, 305).

Where self-assertive ambition resulting in factions raises its head, then *envy* of others is sure to follow. In general terms, the attitude in question is "the grudging spirit that cannot bear to contemplate someone else's prosperity" (Bruce, *Galatians*, 306). But as all the terms in this central section of the works of the flesh, envy has a particular bearing on the Galatian situation. Some among the community may be making unjustified claims to being God's *real* people, but others are responding with an unjustifiable jealousy.

Paul piles on the "second slice of bread" in his return to practices that would have been deplored by everyone. *Drunkenness* and *orgies* naturally went together in the pagan environment of Paul's day. The former term is actually in the plural and has to do not simply with drinking too much but with regular drinking bouts, the *symposia* in private homes and especially at the major feasts in pagan temples. The latter word actually means "excessive feasting," as used most notably of a festal procession in honor of Dionysus (or Bacchus), the god of drink. As Longenecker points out, the reference is not just to drunken revelry but to carousing and/or orgies such as accompany bouts of drinking and the festivals honoring the gods (*Galatians*, 257). The stories of the gluttonous and drunken Roman feasts, always accompanied by sex, are infamous. Paul could have added to his list, but it was sufficient to end his enumeration with "and the like." Betz is right that "Evil occurs in innumerable forms, and only some examples are provided in the list" (*Galatians*, 284). The readers could easily fill in the blanks.

Without any break in the syntactical structure of vv. 19-21, Paul adds that those who "practice" (*prassō*) the items on his vice-list will by no means inherit the eschatological kingdom of God. It is just in these terms that he also admonished the Corinthians (1 Cor 5:9-10). "The warning here must be taken quite seriously. Paul is telling his Galatian Christian converts that if they behave in these sorts of ways they will find themselves on the outside looking in, without inheritance when the Dominion [the kingdom of God] comes in fullness to earth" (Witherington, *Grace*, 407).[83] In advance of the Day of Christ, Paul warns the readers, even as he did earlier (probably on his first visit to them), that the quality of one's life does matter in the judgment.

In this regard, Paul and James are on the same page, particularly as the latter asks the question whether a faith without works can save (Jas 2:14). The answer is plainly no. Because there is a future phase of the kingdom's coming, one must be sure that one's life, measured as a whole, is a "good thing" (2 Cor 5:10). Paul certainly does not have in mind sinless perfection or anything approaching it, but rather righteousness as responsible covenant behavior as befits those who name the name of Christ. Phrased otherwise, one must walk by the Spirit (v. 16). But the examples of malfeasance catalogued in vv. 19-21, particularly the incipient factionalism of the Galatian churches, are the very antithesis of the Spirit.

That Paul can speak of the age to come as an inheritance ties into the biblical-theological argumentation of chaps. 3-4 of the letter. The notion of inheritance was basic to Jewish self-identity. Israel knew itself to be the people who stood to inherit the promises made to Abraham, most prominently perpetual descendants and the land (see on 3:16). By reintroducing the theme of inheritance (from 3:18) in this context, Paul seeks yet again to underscore the fact that the inheritance of the Abrahamic promises depends on the Spirit and not on the flesh, with flesh defined as the whole Torah embraced by the act of circumcision (5:3). The decisive event of salvation history has already occurred with the turning of the ages in Christ. Therefore, the Galatians need do no more than persevere in the new covenant ratified by Christ's blood— "and the conduct of those who will enter into the full inheritance in the end is conduct motivated and enabled by the Spirit, not conduct determined by desires of the flesh or by activities on the level of the flesh" (Dunn, *Galatians*, 307).

22-23 Paul now turns to the other side of the coin in his delineation of the fruit of the Spirit.[84] Fruit is a natural enough biblical meta-

---

[83] In 1QS 4:12-14, there is an eschatological warning following a list of vices.

[84] The singular "fruit" may represent the unifying nature of these qualities as opposed to the divisive effects of the works of the flesh (Betz, *Galatians*, 286; Witherington, *Grace*, 408). Alternatively, the singular may designate a comprehensive principle, corresponding to the singular "desire of the flesh" in 5:16.

phor for the consequences of one's life, whether good or evil (e.g., Prov 1:31; Jer 17:10; Amos 6:12; Matt 3:8).[85] In point of fact, each Greek term employed by Paul is already present in the LXX.[86] Hellenistic writers were also familiar with the figure (Betz, *Galatians*, 286-87).

Yet the imagery of fruit in Paul's depiction of life in the Spirit goes beyond generalities and ties in specifically with his theology of the new creation. We first encounter fruit in the Genesis creation account and later in the flood narrative (itself a new beginning) (Gen 1:11, 12, 22, 28, 29; 3:2, 3, 6, 12; 8:17; 9:1, 7). Later, the fruitfulness of the land features prominently in the prophecies respecting Israel's return from exile (Isa 4:2; 11:1-5; 27:5b-6; 29:17; 32:15-18; 44:2-4; 51:3; 57:18; 60:21; 61:1; 65:21; Jer 23:3; 31:5; Ezek 17:23; 34:27; 36:8, 11, 30; 47:12; Amos 9:14; Joel 2:22; Zech 8:12). In the prophetic vision, Palestine was to be made like the Garden of Eden before Adam's fall, a veritable new creation.[87]

Beale's study of the prophetic backdrop of these verses ("Background") has demonstrated that Isaiah 32 and 57, especially in the LXX, are especially prominent in their depiction of the restoration of Israel as a time of fruitfulness (see the other passages cited immediately above). But the prosperity goes beyond material abundance to include ethical and spiritual qualities. According Isa 32:16-18:

Then justice will dwell in the wilderness,
  and righteousness abide in the fruitful field.
And the effect of righteousness will be peace,
  and the result of righteousness, quietness and trust for ever.
My people will abide in a peaceful habitation,
  in secure dwellings, and in quiet resting places. (RSV)

---

[85] Deidun attempts to find in "fruit" the image of the "inner dynamics of the Spirit" along with the "passivity" of the Christian: "The 'fruit' is not the product of the Christian's labouring, but the effect of another's activity" (*Morality*, 81). Indeed, he is right that the fruit is produced in us by the Spirit. Nevertheless, the fruit bearing process is not passivity, but entails faith actively "working through love" as the believer "walks by the Spirit" (see on 5:6, 16). See again Fee, *Presence*, 433. We might say that the Spirit is never more in control than when we are in control.

[86] See Bayes, *Weakness*, 169, n. 4.

[87] One of the central promises of the Abrahamic covenant is fruitfulness in terms of the patriarch's descendants (Gen 17:6; 28:3; 35:11; 47:27; 48:4; Exod 1:7). This too carries over into Galatians, because these Gentile believers are the actualization of Abraham's seed.

All this is the result of the outpouring of the Spirit from on high (v. 15). Likewise, Isa 57:15-18 contains the assurance:

For thus says the high and lofty One
  who inhabits eternity, whose name is Holy:
"I dwell in the high and holy place,
  and also with him who is of a contrite and humble spirit,
  to revive the spirit of the humble,
  and to revive the heart of the contrite.
For I will not contend for ever,
  nor will I always be angry;
  for from me proceeds the spirit,
  and I have made the breath of life.
I have seen his ways, but I will heal him;
  I will lead him and requite him with comfort,
  creating for his mourners the fruit of the lips. (RSV)

Against this backdrop, a remarkable phenomenon of the NT is that the land all but drops out of sight and becomes symbolic (typological) for other realities: the land now stands for the new heavens and earth, and the fruitfulness of the land comes to typify the lives of Christians (e.g., John 15:8; Phil 1:11). Thus, in speaking of "the fruit of the Spirit," Paul announces that the new creation has arrived in Galatia. His audience has entered that new creation not by virtue of Torah observance, which pertains to the age of the flesh, but because of the descent of the Spirit upon them in Pentecostal blessing. It is they, uncircumcised as they are, who fulfill the imagery of the productive land; they are the new Israel which has returned from exile; they are the fruitful vine the old Israel failed to be (John 15:2-8, in contrast to Isa 5:1-6; Jer 8:13; Hos 9:10; 14:6-7; Hab 3:17).[88]

Beale further roots the Christian life of 5:22-25 in the resurrection of the end-time Israel. Phrases such as "the fruit of the Spirit," "living by the Spirit" and "walking by the Spirit" are best understood as "resurrection living." It is Ezek 37:3-14 that links resurrection directly with Spirit, and the LXX of Isa 57:15-19 assigns to the Spirit the giving of resurrection life. Therefore, Gal 5:22-25 is like Isa 57:15-19 in not only combining "Spirit" and "fruit," along

---

[88] Beale shows that in certain strains of Jewish literature eschatological Israel is expected to be spiritually fruitful ("Background," 16-20). But, I would add, for Paul the radical difference is that his mainly Gentile readers are bearing fruit apart from a commitment to the Torah, thereby constituting an Israel (6:16) that would have been unrecognizable to Paul's ancestors and many of his contemporaries.

with the mention of "joy," "peace" and "patience," but also in making the Spirit the source of resurrection life. Such resurrection existence finds a precedent in Gal 2:19-20, which sets the pattern of crucifixion-resurrection, whereby the believer's experience is identified with Christ's own death and resurrection ("Background," 20-22).

It is to be stressed that these pictures of resurrection and fruitful living stand in the sharpest contrast to the chaos so disturbingly depicted by "the works of the flesh." If the bulk of those works was hatred and its attendant phenomena, mainly discord and strife, then the fruit of the Spirit, commencing with love, finds its unifying factor in a community at rest and enjoying the benefits of mutual understanding, support and encouragement. As far as the order of the "fruit" is concerned, Dunn can remark that in contrast to the list of vices, where the "sting" comes in the middle, in the catalogue of virtues the points where Paul was seeking to exert the most pressure come at the beginning and the end (*Galatians*, 311).

The fountainhead of all the fruit enumerated here is *love*, simply because the Christian walk commences with the love of God being poured into our hearts by the Holy Spirit (Rom 5:5). If love is seeking the highest good of others as defined by the law of Christ, with Christ himself as the great exemplar (see on 5:6), then "love is not one virtue among a list of virtues, but the sum and substance of what it means to be a Christian" (Cousar, *Galatians*, 131). It is because of this equation of love and Christianity that Paul can stress in this very context that faith must work through love (5:6) and that it is none other than love that fulfills the law (5:14). For this reason, believers fulfill the law of Christ by bearing one another's burdens (6:2).

When Christians display such love, they become the most like Christ himself (each of the fruits of the Spirit represents Paul's "character sketch" of Christ). Love spells the end of "hatred, discord, jealousy, fits of rage, selfish ambition, dissensions, factions and envy." And so importantly, love can only be lived out in company of other people because by definition it is "non-self-centred existence" (Barrett, *Freedom*, 74). Love is Paul's antidote to the internecine strife of v. 15. It is just because of its social dimensions that love is greater than even faith and hope (1 Cor 13:13).[89]

Where love is present *joy* is sure to abound. Joy is so fundamental to the Christian way that John can write his first letter for the very purpose of making his readers' joy complete (1 John 1:4).

---

[89] See Fee, *Exegesis*, 169.

Joy is an emotion, but not one dependent on mere happenstance. Because it is generated by the indwelling Spirit, it can be experienced in spite of outward circumstances (Rom 5:2, 11). Biblical joy is rooted in the salvation-historical realities brought to light by the gospel. It is what the disciples felt when they realized that Jesus had been raised from the dead (Matt 28:8). Henceforth, of the essence of God's kingdom is no longer food and drink but righteousness, peace and joy in the Holy Spirit (Rom 14:17).

> God has brought us eschatological salvation. The future has already made its appearance in the present. God's people have already tasted the life that is to be. Already they have received full pardon, full forgiveness. By the Spirit they cry out *Abba* to the God who has loved them and given his Son for them. This is cause for joy, untrammeled, uninhibited joy, as "by the Spirit we eagerly await the hope of righteousness" (v. 5). The fruit of the Spirit is *joy*, joy in the Lord. What must begin at the individual level must also therefore characterize the believing community, among whom God still generously supplies the Holy Spirit (Fee, *Presence*, 448).

Joy is also future eschatological in that it looks forward in hope to the consummation of righteousness (5:5). For this reason, believers are to rejoice in their hope (Rom 12:12). Paul's message was initially received with great joy by the Galatians, but the circumcisers had managed to rob them of their delight in Christ by bringing them under bondage. Instead of joy in the Spirit and in one another, these people now know little but the bitterness of slavery. Paul's pastoral heart is grieved as he writes, because he knows that joy is vital and necessary if one is to persevere through the obstacle course that marks life this side of the resurrection. The restoration of joy thus becomes one of his prime mandates as he pens the words of this epistle.

Peace is naturally associated with love and joy (cf. Rom 14:17; 15:13, 32-33; 2 Cor 13:11). This term bespeaks the reconciliation that has occurred between God and his human creatures (Rom 5:1) and enables them to be reconciled to one another (Eph 2:14-16; 1 Thess 5:13). This means that peace is not merely inner tranquility, but quite pointedly is the realization of the bliss of the new creation, when Israel was expected to return from captivity (see on 1:3 and Beale, "Background," 37-38). At that time, according to Isa 32:1, 15-18, a king would reign in righteousness, the

Spirit would be outpoured and Israel would experience peace as a result of the renewal of the covenant (righteousness).

All these realities have come to pass with the preaching of the gospel in Galatia—this is *shalōm* in the comprehensive sense. It is surely significant that Paul can speak of Christ himself coming and preaching peace to those who are "far off," Gentiles, and those who are "near," Jews. He has brought down the wall that used to divide humanity into warring factions (Eph 2:14-16). But the Judaizers were busying themselves reerecting the wall and, in the process, were turning the peace of the new creation back into the discord of the old world. It was because of the influence of like-minded teachers that Paul exhorts the Roman believers: "Let us therefore make every effort to do what leads to peace and to mutual edification" (Rom 14:19).

Patience is not just a virtue akin to the three preceding ones; rather, it addresses the heart of the problems in the Galatian churches. The word is literally "long-tempered." It is, as defined by Trench, "A long holding out of the mind before it gives room to action or passion—generally to passion" (*Synonyms*, 196). Patience is thus the antithesis of the "fits of rage" (v. 20) and intolerance that characterize those who cater to the flesh. In some ways, remarks W. Barclay, patience is the greatest virtue of all. "It is not clad with romance and glamour; it has not the excitement of sudden adventurous action; but it is the very virtue of God himself" (*Flesh and Spirit*, 97).

Similar to patience is *kindness* (the two are also paired in 1 Cor 13:4; 2 Cor 6:6; Col 3:12). In words that certainly would have applied to the Galatian situation, Paul could say to the Ephesians, "Be kind to one another, tenderhearted, forgiving one another, as God in Christ forgave you" (Eph 4:32 [RSV]). The kindness of believers toward one another reflects God's kindness to them in Christ (Eph 2:7).

Goodness is a very general term and one which is exclusively biblical (Rom 15:14; 2 Thess 1:11), thus making it hard to define. In general, we may say that goodness is seeking the good of others (making it very much like love). W. Barclay compares this term with other words and concludes that "goodness" is specifically "generosity:" the good person is one who is generous to give what was never deserved; he openhanded and openhearted (*Flesh and Spirit*, 107). Rogers/Rogers agree that goodness is an "energetic principle." "It is the generosity which springs from the heart that is kind and will always take care to obtain for others that which is useful or beneficial" (*Key*, 431). Surely such a disposition is not only desirable but indispensable in maintaining the unity of the Spirit in the bond of peace.

If the real "pressure points" come at the beginning and end of this list, then *faith* occupies a position of special prominence. In a very real sense, this letter has been about faith. The readers began their Christian pilgrimage when they received the Spirit with "the hearing of faith" (3:5); they were justified by none other than faith in Jesus Christ (2:16). At this important juncture of his argument, then, Paul returns to the basic consideration of faith to reinforce the all-important link between the Spirit and faith. The fruit bearing of the Galatians is the product of the very same experience of the Spirit that initiated their existence "in Christ." "What the Spirit produces is not dedication to works of law or flesh, which was what the demands of the other missionaries amounted to, but the continued expression of that same faith which they as Gentiles had first experienced and exercised when they responded to the gospel Paul had preached" (Dunn, *Galatians*, 311). Their faith, in other words, should continue to be Christ-centered, not Torah-centered.

Yet faith is not one dimensional. It is unconditional trust in Christ alone, but our confidence in Christ continues to be expressed in our walk with him. Both the Greek and Hebrew words for "faith" (*pistis* and *'emunah*) are two-sided: faith and faithfulness. Given that a, if not the, fundamental issue in Galatians is perseverance, it is not surprising that Paul would list persevering trust in Jesus as one of the fruits of the Spirit. It is the Spirit who implants the seed of faith and then nurtures it to full fruition. It is just faith(fulness) working through love that will be consummated when we finally attain the righteousness that is now hoped for (5:5-6). But since Paul moves within the realm of the covenant with his faith-language, we may say that faith(fulness) pertains to the horizontal dimension of human relationships as well as to the vertical plane of divine/human intercourse. Faithfulness to our fellow Christians, as participants in the new covenant, will be the sure antidote to the distrust and suspicion so characteristic of the works of the flesh.

As one of the most recognizable biblical attributes (e.g., Ps 37:11; Zech 9:9; Matt 11:29; Eph 4:2) *gentleness* is integral to a mindset that would promote the peace of the new creation. Gentleness (or meekness) is frequently misunderstood and consequently mistaken as weakness. But precisely the opposite is true: gentleness is actually strength under control (W. Barclay, *Flesh and Spirit*, 111-21). This quality is "the power through which by the help of the Spirit of God the strong and explosive might of the passions is harnessed in the service of men and of God" (ibid., 121). In this context, gentleness is an eminently practical virtue, prominently because it is in a "spirit of gentleness" that correction of offenders is to be undertaken (6:1). In all likelihood, Paul is casting a glance in the direction of the opponents, who were anything but gentle in disposition and in their treatment of people (see on 6:1-5). It is significant that Jesus pronounces blessing on the "meek" (Matt 5:5 = Ps 37:11); it is they, not the Zealots, with their program of all-out violence, who will inherit the (new) earth. In calling for gentleness, Paul reverses his former values as one zealous for the traditions of the fathers (1:14). How he must have wished that the Judaizers would do the same.

Self-control was a quality widely prized even by pagan writers, not to say Judaism.[90] The term is quite broad and applies in principle to every area of life (cf. 1 Cor 6:12; 9:24-27). All of the works of the flesh, in point of fact, can be attributed to a lack of self-control. But if we keep in mind that there is a specificity to everything Paul writes in this portion of the letter, the factor of self-control has particular reference to community relations, as illustrated by the way in which errant Christians are to be restored (6:1-5). The circumcisers might have been exemplary as regards such things as impurity, drunkenness and sorcery, but woefully lacking when it came to correction in a spirit of gentleness. The "fruit" of their theology and example was nothing but biting, devouring, self-conceit and provocation of others (5:15, 26).

To nail down the point that the fruit of the Spirit is not simply a list of moral virtues detached from the Galatian situation, Paul reintroduces the law. If his gospel was being challenged by the law teachers, then he responds with the assertion that only those who bear the fruit of the Spirit will escape the condemnation of the law, because "the law is not against such as these."[91] The most natural biblical background for his language is the way the decalogue, in analogy with the Hittite Suzerain treaties, was deposited in the ark of the covenant to stand as a witness against Israel if the covenant

---

[90] See Longenecker, *Galatians*, 262-63; Betz, *Galatians*, 288; and especially Stowers, "Paul," 524-34. On self-mastery in Paul's letters, see ibid., 534-46.

[91] This is a better translation than "against such there is no law." The law in question is the Torah, not law in some indefinite sense. The Greek could also be translated, "against such things," that is, the fruit of the Spirit, not "against such persons." But at the end of the day, it makes little difference, because it is people who are characterized by these traits.

was broken by idolatry.[92] Of course, the nation did just that and suffered exile as a result, with the law bearing testimony. But now there is a new Israel, an Israel that fulfills the law by love and its accompanying attributes. The law does not testify against such fruit-bearing people, because they are the true covenant keepers. The Judaizing company, by contrast, is consigned to the curse of the law because of its inability to yield any harvest but corruption, due to their sowing to the flesh (6:8). The law does, in fact, bear witness against them. By definition, Paul includes in salvation those who have experienced the Spirit by the hearing of faith and excludes the opponents and their ilk. Following on from 3:10-13; 4:21-31, Paul again maintains that the real covenant breakers are those most zealous for the law. The irony of the situation is self-evident.

24 Paul's delineation of the fruit of the Spirit is topped off by a final glance at the flesh. "Those who belong to Christ Jesus," that is, those who bear the fruit of the Spirit, have done no less than nail the flesh, with its passions and desires, to the cross. This addendum to the fruit of the Spirit carries over from vv. 6 and 16 the important emphasis on the activism of faith as it follows suit with the leading of the Spirit (v. 18) and the Spirit-engendered virtues just listed. Dunn is surely right that in the Roman world the talk of crucifying the flesh is striking, to say the least. Crucifixion was such a horrific ordeal that a reference to it in any positive sense would have seemed almost obscene (*Galatians*, 314). Hays adds that the talk of crucifixion here is unexpected, since the Galatians are envisioned as the agents of their own crucifixion (*Galatians*, 328). But this is not the only place in the letter where Paul puts the cross to a surprising use. According to 2:20, he has been crucified with Christ, so that Christ now lives in him; and in 6:14 he has been crucified to the world and the world to him. The difference is that here "Christians are described not as the objects but as the

---

[92] See Kline, *Treaty*, 21. Most commentators point out that Paul's text here is matched word for word by a sentence in Aristotle's *Politics* (3.13.1284A). Equally, most are disinclined the think that Paul actually read Aristotle, yet they infer that the statement was common coinage in Paul's day as an ethical maxim or proverb which could be applied by various writers as they chose. However, the similarity of language could just be coincidental ("parallelomania"), and there is scant evidence that Paul is echoing an ethical proverb. In addition, none of the scholars who thinks Paul is drawing upon a common maxim has provided, in my view, an adequate explanation of what he precisely means in the present verse. It makes much more sense to read his words within the salvation-historical framework provided by the OT and assumed by this letter.

agents of this crucifixion" (Barclay, *Obeying*, 117). Or, as Martyn says, "The church...participates victoriously in the Spirit's apocalyptic war by participating in the victorious cross of Christ" (*Galatians*, 500). Such is in keeping with the believer's activity and passivity as regards the work of the Spirit in this chapter.

A superficial reading of the present statement might suggest that the crucifixion of the flesh is tantamount to a kind of perfectionism. But apart from other considerations, "flesh," in Galatians, continues to bear the connotations of the old creation, the era of the law. Paul is saying, then, that in a manner similar to Christ's own death (Rom 6:10), believers have in principle left the realm of sin's dominion and have dealt a deathblow to their innate passions. 5:17 makes it clear enough that struggle with the flesh is a dimension of this present life, but cruciform existence means that one's mind has been transformed by the Spirit, so that the old way of life no longer holds the same attraction as it did before. The tense of the verb "crucified" (aorist) takes us back to the decisive act of conversion and the commitment made to walk in newness of life from that point onward (Rom 6:4). And if we have died to sin, we have also died to the law (2:19; Rom 7:1-4). Crucifixion of the flesh entails, by the very nature of the case, abandonment of the law in favor of the Spirit-led and Spirit-empowered life of a new covenant and a new creation.

Borgen has a rather trenchant insight to offer. For Philo, circumcision was a symbol for the removal of the pleasures and passions of the flesh (*Migr. Abr.* 92; *Spec. Laws* 1.305; *Quaest. in Gen.* 3.48, 52). But for Paul, writes Borgen, the role of circumcision, removing pleasures and passions, has been transferred to the believer's crucifixion with Christ, to the exclusion of the observance of bodily circumcision itself. As he continues:

> At this point there is a basic difference between the anti-circumcision Jews, criticized by Philo in *De Migratione* 86-93, and Paul. Those Jews accepted and practised the ethical meaning of circumcision, but ignored the observance of bodily circumcision itself. Paul, on the other hand, transferred the role of circumcision to another event, namely the believer's crucifixion (and resurrection) together with Christ. Paul also rejected the observance of bodily circumcision, but gave

the ethical life a new and eschatological foundation in the death and resurrection of Jesus Christ.[93]

The irony of the situation is that the opponents claimed that departing from the desires of the flesh was the ethical meaning of circumcision. Paul agrees with that ethical meaning, but for him "their transition from the (pagan) desires of the flesh to a communal life in love was in an exclusive way tied to the believer's crucifixion with Christ, not to bodily circumcision and the jurisdiction of the Law of Moses" (Borgen, "Circumcision," 41). From this I deduce that *Paul still preaches circumcision, but without circumcision!*

25-26 In these verses, Paul brings full circle the argument of 5:13 up to this point. The words are slightly different, but the substance is the same. Verse 25 takes the form of a realistic condition: "Since we live by the Spirit, let us keep in step with the Spirit."[94] To live by the Spirit is to find our existence in him, now that we have died to the law, and conduct ourselves in accordance with his wishes (as articulated by the law of Christ, the "spiritual law" of Rom 7:14). If this is the tenor of our lives, then we ought as well to "keep in step with" the Spirit.

The verb here (*stoicheō*) recalls the believers "walk" in Christ (see on 5:16), but introduces the additional idea of "standing in line" or "keeping in step." It is a military term that carries with it the sense of an authority who is to be acknowledged and obeyed (like a drill sergeant). As Dunn explains, "Paul...does not see the Spirit as an anarchic power disruptive of all order, and continues to warn against treating the freedom given by the Spirit as a license for self-indulgence" (*Galatians*, 318).

---

[93] Borgen, "Circumcision," 40. Borgen further notes that in a similar way the role of circumcision in Col 2:11, 13 is transferred to the believers resurrection with Christ and reinterpreted on that basis. The circumcision "not made by hands" is the circumcision of Christ. "The meaning is the circumcision which belongs to Christ, and is brought about by union with him" (ibid.).

[94] The verse is also a chiasmus:
A If we live
  B by the Spirit
  B with the Spirit
A Let us keep in step.

It is worthy of notice that Paul's verb relates to the noun used earlier to depict the law as the "elements" (*stoicheia*) of the world (4:3, 9; Col 2:8; cf. Heb 5:12).[95]

> Paul is suggesting that the Galatians do not need to place themselves under any elementary principles of the universe, either pagan or Jewish ones precisely because they already live in and by the Spirit of God and should follow the Spirit's lead, staying in line with the Spirit, not the law.... The overtones then are that if the Galatians want to place themselves under a sort of martial law, all they really need to do is stay in step with the Spirit and they will receive all the guidance and discipline they need (Witherington, *Grace*, 413).

The converse of living by and keeping in step with the Spirit (v. 26) glances back to vv. 19-21 and provides a distillation of "the works of the flesh." The factor of "one another" is the outstanding feature. Life in the Spirit and the fruit of the Spirit receive their acid test in genuine and practical concern for one another. If we really love, then our thoughts and actions are directed toward the highest good of others rather than the promotion of self. But if anything marks the old life in the flesh, it is the "conceit" or "vainglory" (*kenodoxia*) that opens the floodgates to provocation of others and envy of others (cf. Phil 2:1-4). Such is the endeavor to "achieve unfounded respect by big talk, boasting, and ambition" (Rogers/Rogers, *Key*, 432). Such "vainglory" is no less than the self-consciousness and self-importance condemned by the central section of Paul's catalogue of vices. Significantly, he says "let us not become" (*genōmetha*) such people, as modeled after the Judaizers. Rather, we are to concentrate on becoming in practice what we were made in principle when we crucified the flesh with its passions and desires. This is the important interplay of the indicative and the imperative in Paul.[96]

---

[95] Semantically, *stoicheō* may a glance backward to *susstoicheō* in 4:25, to "align in parallel columns." If so, then Paul is warning the Galatians not to stand in the same column as the law.

[96] See Fung, *Galatians*, 278-83; Schlier, *Galater*, 264-67; Ridderbos, *Paul*, 253-58.

EXPOSITION OF GALATIANS

Section Note

19-21 Commentators have long sought to find an order to Paul's list of vices (although Betz thinks the list is chaotic, reflecting the chaotic nature of evil [*Galatians*, 283])! Witherington, in my view, comes closest to the mark as far as Paul's actual intentions are concerned. He argues that the first and last ones listed have to do with sins associated with the sort of *koinōnia* that went on in pagan temples, while those in the middle refer to sins that went on within the very different fellowship of the community of faith. This observation is followed with the comment: "There was danger from without and from within for the Galatians. Without there was the lure of the pagan environment, within there was the divisive teaching of the agitators urging the judaizing of these Gentiles. Both extremes must be combated, and countered with: (1) being led by the Spirit, which provides the primary answer to the pagan past; and (2) the Law of Christ which provides the primary alternative to the exhortation to follow the Mosaic Law" (*Grace*, 397).

Witherington ties into Ramsey's discussion of the vice-list (*Galatians*, 446-54). According to Ramsey, Paul addresses familiar social aspects of Galatian and Greco-Roman society: (1) vices connected with the national Anatolian religion; (2) vices associated with municipal life; (3) vices pertaining to customs of society in Hellenistic cities. Witherington wisely notes, though, that Paul does not specify one form of paganism in distinction to others; he critiques them all. More importantly, Paul is likely to have had in mind the effects of Judaizing on the Christian community in his list of the eight social sins (*Grace*, 397-98).

He goes on to suggest that the vices are structured according to the ABA pattern of Paul's letters.[97] The two "A" sections list sins associated with the audience's pagan past, while the "B" material has to do with sins against the community of faith, which is where Paul's emphasis lies (ibid., 399). Paul, as it were, holds up three mirrors to the Galatians in 5:19-23: "The mirror of the pagan past, the mirror of the present and possible future if dissensions and factions grow under the malignant influence of the agitators, and finally the mirror of the true Christian community" (ibid., 402). Thereafter he helpfully illustrates the pairs of antitheses resident in "the works of the flesh" and "the fruit of the Spirit:"

acts of hatred versus love (and joy)
discord versus peace
anger (quick temper) versus patience
fits of rage versus acts of kindness
acts of selfish ambition versus acts of generosity
dissensions leading to factions versus faithfulness to others

---

[97] See Feuillet, "plan;" Collins, "ABA."

acts of envy versus acts of considerateness.

With good reason, Witherington concludes: "Paul wishes his community of converts to be like neither the community centered on the pagan temple nor the community centered upon the Mosaic Law. Rather they are to be a community centered on Christ and in the Spirit" (ibid., 399-400).

GALATIANS CHAPTER SIX

(3) Freedom in Service to Others (6:1-10)

Paul now brings his argument respecting the responsibilities of freedom in the Spirit to a kind of climax with a pointed practical application or case study, namely, the restoration of Christians who fall into sin. The foregoing context makes it clear enough that he cares deeply about the crucifixion of the sinful self in its various manifestations. However, chief among his concerns is the flesh as it gives rise to self-importance, self-conceit and lack of love for others. Accordingly, he now undertakes to teach the Galatians in the concrete what it means to display the meekness and gentleness of Christ (2 Cor 10:1).[1]

Verses 1-5 are singular in Paul's letters. They stand out particularly because of the way they contrast with both the Judaizers' treatment of offenders and that of the Anatolian deities. The characteristics of the former will become apparent in the exposition that follows. I would only note here that some of Paul's opponents were not above slapping people in the face if they did not bow to their authority. To this, Paul retorts, "To my shame, I must say we were too weak for that" (2 Cor 11:20)! The passage likewise contrasts with the Anatolian inscriptions. Arnold affirms that this is a unique discussion in Paul's thought; and the occasional nature of this letter raises the question of why he would address this question at all. He recalls that the entire concern of the propitiatory inscriptions was precisely this question, namely, what to do when someone is caught in a transgression against the gods. Paul here commends a rather different approach than what the people were accustomed to in their pre-Christian religious environment. Paul's response is rooted in what he has already shared about the nature of his gospel. Accordingly, he commends a sensitive way of restoring fallen people to the community as based on the law of Christ ("Folk Belief," 449).

---

[1] For a detailed exposition of vv. 1-5, see my "Burden Bearing" (= *Essays*, 249-84). Hays (*Galatians*, 332) cites 1QS 5:24-6:1 as the closest parallel to the present passage. However, the difference is that the community was very tightly knit, and the attitude of correcting others in humility and charity extended only as far as the sect. Paul, by contrast, calls for something much more inclusive.

1 "Brothers," Paul says, "If a person is overtaken in any trespass..." (RSV). The verb here translated "overtaken" (*prolambanō*) signifies an inadvertent transgression. One does not intend to sin, but because of a lack of watchfulness one is caught "unawares" or is "surprised," in many cases by a "besetting sin." The term carries the sense of being "surprised" by sin rather than being "detected" in it. NEB translates: "If a man should do something wrong...*on a sudden impulse*," while NIV renders "if a man is *trapped* in any sin," and, according to NASB, "if anyone is *caught* in any trespass." The verb suggests that "the sinner has been forcibly laid hold of by sin before he was able to reflect" (Fung, *Galatians*, 284). Ridderbos agrees that the person was "caught hard upon the act of sin" (*Galatians*, 212). John Brown, then, is quite right that the reference is not to the "doer of sin" (1 John 3:6, 8), who is devoted to the old creation and its values, but rather to the one who, though committed to Christ, unintentionally falls into sin (*Galatians*, 316). In this light, Paul's portrayal of the offense as an entrapment has a significant bearing on the ensuing discussion. That is to say, the very fact that the sin in question was not premeditated ought to temper the way in which its rectification is approached.

The snare into which one may fall is a "trespass" (*paraptōma*). Burton's observation that Paul characteristically uses this word in the sense of "a falling beside, a failure to achieve" is to the point. He further suggests that "trespass" is an intended antithesis to the verb of 5:25 (*stoicheō*), "keep in step," "walk in a straight line," or "conform to a standard" (*Galatians*, 327). Paul does not specify any particular sin, but, in view of vv. 1c, 4, it is possible that underlying the sin is presumption, which in turn opens the way for the transgression itself. When combined with 5:15, 18-25, the implication may be that he is one who, out of vainglory and envy, considered himself to be superior to others.[2] One wonders if Prov 16:18 was in Paul's mind: "Pride goes before destruction, and a haughty spirit before a fall." In any event, "trespass" cannot be restricted to any particular misdeed. It is possible that the transgression in question may not be one which flagrantly flouts accepted standards, so that the community is brought into disrepute. At the same time, however, we should not reduce the scope of the term to a "wrong" (misdemeanor), because it is equally possible that the sin in question is particularly grievous.

---

[2] Cf. Mußner, *Galaterbrief*, 397.

Paul, then, envisages a situation which is clearly the fault of the brother/sister, but one which he understands and for which he has compassion. In point of fact, he is more concerned about how to deal with the problem than with the nature of the transgression itself. Barclay remarks: "The event should not be made an occasion for self-righteous condemnation of the sinner, which would only provoke or crush him. Rather it is an opportunity for spiritual people to display the fruit of the Spirit."[3] Accordingly, his counsel is to proceed with "a spirit of gentleness." As Burton notes, this phrase can mean one of two things. (1) "Spirit" is the Holy Spirit as possessed by the Christian, in which case "gentleness" denotes the effect of the Spirit's presence. The connection with the adjective "spiritual," then, would intimate that "those who possess the Spirit shall by virtue of that possession and the gentleness which it creates restore the offender" (*Galatians*, 328). (2) Alternatively, "spirit" is the human spirit as characterized by gentleness. In this instance, the preposition "in" marks "its object as that with which one is furnished and under the influence of which the action takes place" (ibid.). However, as is frequently the case with Paul's genitives (and datives), there is probably here a deliberate ambiguity. Since "gentleness" is one of the fruits of the Spirit (5:23), it stands to reason that (2) is inconceivable apart from (1). Consequently, the "gentleness of [that is, produced by] the Spirit," becomes the "spirit of gentleness" in the one who is filled with the Spirit: "The Galatians' manner of life in the community, including their treatment of offenders, must be an outworking of their obedience to the Spirit" (Barclay, *Obeying*, 157).

"Gentleness" ("meekness"), however, is not weakness. Indeed, the term connotes strength, but a strength which is under control (see on 5:23). This would account for the way in which "self-control" is placed side by side with "gentleness" in 5:23. Actually, "gentleness" stands between "faith(fulness)" and "self-control" and enables the Christian to correct the erring brother without arrogance, impatience or anger. This meekness has its basis in love and it cannot, therefore, think in terms of harsh punishment, even in relation to the disobedient. The "gentle" person is thus one who has learned to control his emotions, even in the face of disappointing, if not scandalous, behavior. Ultimately, "gentleness" is conformity to the image of Christ, the "meek and lowly" (Matt 11:29; 2 Cor 10:1).

---

[3] Barclay, *Obeying*, 157. Likewise Schlier, *Galater*, 270; Spicq, *Agapè*, 1.239-40.

Paul thus turns to the "spiritual" alone as being qualified to come to the aid of those who sin. It is possible that "spiritual" designates a segment of believers in the Galatian congregations to be distinguished from other Christians who have been more profoundly influenced by Paul's antagonists. Or, more likely, the "spiritual" constitute the genuinely Christian element in the churches, the possessors of the Spirit and the true brothers of Jesus, who said "I am meek and lowly in heart" (Matt 11:29). The others bear the image of the "false brethren" who "slipped in to spy out the liberty which we have in Christ" (2:4). In this case, "spiritual" serves to differentiate the adherents to the Pauline gospel from the circumcision party and its devotees. This identification is supported by the implied antithesis of "spiritual", that is, "fleshly," which refers to those who still follow the "desire of the flesh" and are "under the law" (cf. 1 Cor 3:1).[4]

The "spiritual," then, are those who bear the fruit of the Spirit: they and they alone are consistent with the principles of the new creation—faith working through love (5:6; cf. 6:15) and the service of one another through love (5:13). Otherwise put, the "spiritual," have, so to speak, learned to "beware of the leaven of the Pharisees" (Matt 16:6, 11), the "charter members" of the circumcision party (Acts 15:5). They are mindful that to the degree that the spirit of the Pharisees dominates in the church, to the same degree Christians will fail to mend the injured body of Christ. The "spiritual," then, are concerned that those for whom Christ died not be swallowed up by excessive grief (2 Cor 2:7).

Of the essence of spirituality is the restorer's cognizance that he himself is capable of falling. For this reason, says Paul, "Watch yourself, lest you too be tempted."[5] As a generalization, Fung is certainly correct that each one has the responsibility to exercise the strictest vigilance over himself, "Lest the would-be restorer become an offender himself. Such vigilance is necessary because 'anything can become a temptation' and because no one is above the possibility of succumbing to temptation. Awareness of this is conducive to the cultivation and manifestation of the spirit of gen-

---

[4] Lull notes that where "works of the law" stood in the nomists' claim, Paul substitutes "flesh" (*Spirit*, 104).

[5] The participle here may be either concessive ("although watch") or circumstantial ("all the while watching"). The difference is not particularly important. More significant is that "watch" means to "examine critically." Longenecker notes that in Greek literature it frequently bears the connotation of observing in order to avoid, which, he thinks, is certainly the nuance here: "'Watching yourself' in order to avoid the sins in question" (*Galatians*, 274).

tleness enjoined here" (*Galatians*, 286). Without denying the validity of this observation, however, Schlier's insight is more to the point, that is, the precise temptation is unjustifiable anger released by the sin of the offender.[6] The correctness of this is borne out by vv. 3-5, which elaborate the temptation of v. 1. Hence, the sin of anger is as serious as the sin into which the other person fell, as confirmed by 1 Cor 5:11, which places the "reviler" or "abusive person" in same company as the idolater, the sexually immoral, the thief and the alcoholic. Such a caution on Paul's part is an altogether appropriate response to the "theology of zeal" which motivated the Judaizers.

Paul's prime directive is to receive its due emphasis: "*Restore such a one.*" The verb "restore" (*katartizō*) in this setting signifies "repair" (to a former good condition), "To put a dislocated member of the body into its proper place."[7] "When a professed Christian falls into error or sin, he becomes, as it were, a dislocated member of the mystical body of Christ, incapable of properly performing its own functions, and occasioning pain and inconvenience to the other members of the body" (J. Brown, *Galatians*, 317). Paul's concern is for the individual, but it is equally for the church in its corporate dimension (cf. 2 Cor 2:1-10).[8] He calls upon the spiritual to perform pastoral surgery not simply for the sake of the one but also for the sake of the many.

The restorative process, as Brown again comments, involves use of the appropriate means of convincing the person of sin and of leading him to repentance. Among the means at one's disposal are: a faithful, but friendly, statement of the truth; a demonstration of the inconsistency of the sin in question with the law of Christ; an admonition about the evil consequences of the sin; a reminder of the grace of God, so that the offender will not be swallowed up by sorrow (ibid., 317-18). Of course, the exact words and methods chosen by us will vary according to individual circumstances. But whatever is said and done, it is surely vital that we attempt to understand *why* people are in the circumstances in which they find themselves. Christians, as anyone else, sin for reasons; and our

---

[6] Schlier, *Galater*, 271. Cf. Martyn, *Galatians*, 546, who cites 1QS 5:24-6:1 as a parallel.

[7] Probably something of the original medical usage of *katartizō* is retained here, that is, to "reset" a bone (Lagrange, *Galates*, 155; LSJ, 910; BDAG, 526).

[8] That Paul was the heir of notions of corporate identity and responsibility goes without saying. See Kaminsky, *Responsibility* (with other literature).

treatment of those who have sinned must be intelligent as well as compassionate.

The bottom line, then, is restoration. Without actually saying so, it is not unlikely that Paul was aware of the teaching of Jesus preserved in Matt 18:15-17. In fact, the probability of this is increased when we consider that, as argued by a number of scholars, "the law of Christ" to be fulfilled by Christians is rooted in the sayings of Jesus as preserved in the Gospels.[9] But whether or not he had this particular instruction in mind, the same principle applies to his exhortation to the "spiritual" in Galatia. That is to say, neither Jesus nor Paul envisages a mechanical process whereby the church may rid itself of undesirables: the goal is restoration, not excision. "When a member of the human body is dislocated, amputation is not immediately resorted to" (Brown, ibid., 317). The same is true of the body of Christ.

Here we see why the manner in which restoration is attempted is all-important. If our goal is the *recovery* of Christian brothers and sisters and the resumption of their walk in godliness, then nothing can be more paramount than the "spiritual" pursuit of that ambition. Our aim is not censure for the sake of self-aggrandizement, in the words of v. 4, boasting on account of our perceived superiority to our neighbor. It is, rather, for the sake of winning our brother or sister (Matt 18:15). If we may hear Calvin (*Galatians*, 108):

> Just as ambition is a particularly poisonous evil, so also great harm is done by unseasonable and excessive severity, which goes under the noble name of zeal but frequently springs from pride and from dislike and contempt of the brethren. For very many harass their brethren violently and cruelly, as if their faults were something to taunt them with. The reason is that they would rather scold than correct. Those who sin should be reproved, and it is often necessary to be severe and sharp. Therefore it is right to press them with rebukes even to the point of discourtesy; but the vinegar must be tempered with oil. Therefore he teaches us to show mildness in correcting the faults of brethren and says that no rebukes are godly and Christian which do not savour of meekness.

---

[9] See my "Burden Bearing," 173-76 (= *Essays*, 272-77); Das, *Paul and Jews*, 170.

2 The course of action outlined in v. 1 is only half the process, because one must be prepared to assume responsibility for the long-term effects of sin, even once repentance has been secured. This is why Paul adds: "Bear one another's burdens, and thereby fulfill the law of Christ" (NASB).

It is possible that the term "burdens" here is intended quite broadly, that is, the burdens of pain, suffering, inconvenience, finance, etc. But it should be kept in mind that in 6:1-5 Paul is pursuing a specific point, namely, how Christians are to respond to the "trespasses" of other Christians. Most likely, therefore, his counsel to the "spiritual," though capable of secondary applications, concerns particularly the *sin-burdens* of the one who has fallen (cf. Lagrange, *Galates*, 156). Burton is right to include in the "burdens" the factor of temptation, which may result in sin (*Galatians*, 329). "The *burdens* apparently in the first place refers to whatever oppresses man spiritually, threatens to induce him to sin, or to keep him in sin. This is pictured as a burden because one goes bowed under its weight and fears that he will succumb to its pressure" (Ridderbos, *Galatians*, 213). But how are such burdens to be borne? Assuming that "bear" is more than "tolerate," that the word entails "a willing, helpful, sympathetic sharing of the burden" (Burton, *Galatians*, 330), which results in effective assistance and relief, in what ways is the onus of sin to be borne?

For one, sin always has its consequences, its "burdens." Frequently, the consequences have a domino effect, meaning that problems can be multiplied and compounded almost indefinitely because of one foundational mistake. To "bear the burdens" of the other, in this case, is to *get involved in the difficulties occasioned by sin*. Sometimes, of course, these problems are intricate in the extreme, particularly where sexual sin is involved and families are broken as a result. Yet fulfilling the law of Christ may require involvement to this degree. In this light, the logic of 6:2, as it connects with the love-motif of 5:13-6:5, is self-evident: there can be no higher expression of love than bearing one another's burdens—this is *love going into action*. Witherington, following Hays, makes a strong case that Paul conceives of Christ as the ultimate burden bearer.[10] In giving himself for our sins (1:3-4; 2:20; 3:13-14), Christ bore our burdens in all their ugliness and complexity (1 Pet 2:24).

---

[10] Hays, "Christology and Ethics." Witherington, *Grace*, 423. Witherington asks if it is accidental that John 19:17 uses the verb "bear" in reference to the cross (ibid., 423, n. 20).

In the second place, we are to bear with the person himself/herself. Sin is not eradicated overnight. There may well be a period of time—even a lengthy period—during which the power of sin is being subdued. Since the process is not instantaneous, the original "trespass" may at intervals reappear. Therefore, to bear the burden of sin means to *forbear the person who has sinned*. Not that we are condoning sin itself, but we are telling the sinner that he is not rejected, either by Christ or by us. As Paul writes elsewhere: "I...beg you to lead a life worthy of the calling to which you have been called, with all lowliness and meekness, with patience, *forbearing one another in love*, eager to maintain the unity of the Spirit in the bond of peace" (Eph 4:1-3 [RSV]).

To bear one another's burdens in such a manner is not only to manifest a Godlike (1 Pet 5:7) or Christlike quality (1 Pet 2:24), it is to "fulfill the law of Christ." "The law of Christ" reminds us that the concluding injunctions of Galatians are very much connected with the letter as a whole, in which discussion of the law has dominated.[11] The exact phrase "the law of Christ" occurs only here in the NT. However, the idea contained in it is present in a similar combination of words in 1 Cor 9:21, according to which it is "the law of Christ" (*ennomos Christou*) which defines Paul's lifestyle as a Christian in contrast to what it used to be as a Jew. By virtue of this law, Paul can assert that he is not "under the law," as a Jew obliged to observe the Torah, but, at the same time, deny that he is "lawless" (*anomos*), a Gentile or apostate Jew who stood beyond the pale of the law of Moses. Paul is not lawless, but for him Christ, not the Torah, is the norm; he is now obliged to be obedient to Christ. He is, as a result, no longer bound by the distinctives of the old covenant, though, in order to win Jews, he frequently foregoes his liberty in Christ. Here clearly "the law of Christ" is set in opposition to the law of Moses: Christ's law has relieved Paul of the necessity of "living as a Jew" (Gal 2:14).

As for Galatians itself, even a casual reading of the epistle informs us that Paul continually contrasts Christ and his benefits with the Mosaic legislation. To make a long story very short, he informs the Galatians that what Israel assumed was her privilege by virtue of obedience to the law (divine sonship, the gift of the Spirit and justification) is to be found *in Christ*. Accordingly, the law of Christ embodies the freedom to which the Galatians have

---

[11] "These verses are not an independent or dispassionate account of Christian ethics tacked on to the end of an argumentative letter, but a continuation and completion of the argument" (Barclay, *Obeying*, 143).

been called (5:1). In order to be acceptable to God, one does not have to submit to circumcision and the other boundary markers of Israel's national identity. Therefore, the whole of the letter suggests most strongly that "the law of Christ," as in 1 Cor 9:21, is purposely set in contrast to the law of Moses. The opponents, for their part, would have perceived this phrase, "the law of Christ," as very much of an anomaly, just because for them Jesus the Messiah was the authoritative expositor of the Torah (much like Qumran's Teacher of righteousness).

There is thus an irony in Paul's phraseology. His opponents in Galatia were "nomists." For them the Torah in its entirety reigned supreme in every area of life, and fidelity to it insured blessing, life and the realization of the promises made to the patriarchs (Cosgrove, *Cross*, 85-101). But Paul speaks of "the law of Christ." He does so quite on purpose: "It is as though he said to his converts: if you must observe the law (as the agitators say), do so— only make sure that the law you observe is not Moses' law, but the law of Christ" (Fung, *Galatians*, 287-88).

Paul is not against law and the regulation of one's life by law. Quite the contrary.[12] But *what law?* For him the answer is clear: it is not that legislation which was valid only between Moses and Christ, but the expression of God's will which has come into being with the advent of Jesus the Messiah—the law of Christ. His law, in short, is what he has commanded (through the apostles) the church to observe until he comes (Matt 28:20). It is identifiable with the "form of teaching" to which the believer has been committed (Rom 6:17). Kuula is correct to suggest that "law" here comes close to the original Hebrew understanding of Torah as "instruction" (*Law*, 188). Yet this is not the instruction given by Moses to the Israelites, but the instruction given by Christ to his people. "For Paul, the principle of doing and obeying is not what makes the difference between covenantal nomism and Christian faith. *The crucial difference lies in the set of norms one complies to: the Mosaic law or the demands involved in the Christian message.*"[13]

---

[12] See Das, *Paul and Jews*, 173-80. My qualification is that it is not the Mosaic law as such that regulates the Christian life, but the law of Christ, which undoubtedly has retained elements from its predecessor. But Das is right that it is the law of Christ that the Spirit takes hold of (ibid., 184-86).

[13] Kuula, Law, 73, italics mine. One may agree with Winger that the Christian belongs to Christ and walks according to the Spirit rather than observe the Mosaic law ("Law of Christ"). However, to say that "the law of Christ" is only the Spirit is to evacuate that law of any content, quite in contrast to passages such as Matt 28:20 and Rom 6:17, not to mention Paul's paraenesis of Gal 5:13-6:10.

All this sets the stage for Paul's pronouncement that bearing one another's burdens *fulfills* the law of Christ. We have encountered many times the historical fact that the Judaism of Paul's day was very much concerned to remain within the boundaries set by the law. So, for Paul's Jewish contemporaries the law (of Moses) was "fulfilled," that is, achieved its purpose for being, when Israel was loyal to the covenant, when the people of God maintained their peculiar ethnic and religious identity. However, the mentality mirrored in Galatians went beyond a commitment to God, Torah and nation, which in itself was right and proper. Rather, the effect of the Judaizers' zeal was an ardent Torah-centricity, which gave disproportionate emphasis to those aspects of the law which marked them out as a distinct and chosen people, thereby minimizing the necessity of love.[14]

Consequently, these Jewish Christian missionaries insisted that Gentiles had to become as themselves before they could be reckoned among the people of God. Hand in hand with this demand went hatred for anyone unwilling to conform particularly to the Pharisaic conception of covenant life. Therefore, the law for these teachers was fulfilled not only by their allegiance to it but also by their hatred of all nonconformists to its standards. Not to hate would have been the same as compromising the honor of the God of Israel. In effect, *hatred was the fulfillment of the law*.

Over against his opponents and their conception of fulfilling the law, for Paul the very reason the law of Christ existed—just as the law of Moses existed—was to create a community of love (see on 5:14). Christ's law thus attains to its goal and its highest good when Christians exhibit the ideal of mutual help and forgiveness. God's design for his people, as expressed in the law of Christ, is achieved when they bear one another's burdens: it is their love which entitles them to be called "the Israel of God" (Gal 6:16). Gorman is quite right that lying behind the believer's fulfillment of the law of Christ is the story of Jesus' own cruciform love on behalf of others.

> Such concern for others is faith in action, love like that of Christ on the cross. For this reason Paul calls it ful-

---

[14] Cf. Dunn, *Romans*, 2.582-83, 593. Barrett contrasts circumcision and love in similar terms: "Circumcision is the sort of thing which, if abstracted from the rest of the law, can be performed as an end in itself.... Love, on the other hand, if it is rightly understood, cannot be performed as an end in itself; the moment it becomes such an end it ceases to be disinterested love—that is, it ceases to be love" (*Freedom*, 74).

filling (cf. 5:14) the "law of Christ." In the context this "law of Christ" is not something he issued but something he lived. It is the covenant "law"—or principle—of faith expressing itself in love (2:20; 5:6). If for Paul Jesus is a teacher (responding perhaps to the circumcisers), he is a teacher inasmuch as the story of his faithful, loving death is his lesson. The law of Christ is the narrative pattern of cruciform love that true faith engenders. Any who think themselves too important to love others in this way deceive themselves about possessing the Spirit (6:3). *The Spirit is the Spirit of cruciform love* (*Apostle*, 220, italics mine).

3 Restoration of the members of Christ's body places an onus directly on the one who engages in the work: if *restoration* is the actual goal, then the way in which one goes about the task is all-important. This is why correction is to be undertaken in a "spirit of gentleness" only by those who are "spiritual." We might think that this is enough, but for Paul it is not. The reverse side of the same coin is expressed by v. 1b: "But watch yourself, or you also may be tempted." In other words, a true spirit of gentleness is realistic in its assessment of self, because, at the end of the day, we are no less vulnerable than our brother/sister who has fallen. It is this pointedly admonitory dimension of Paul's counsel that is expanded in vv. 3-5.

Verse 3 sets before us the contrast of fact versus fiction. The fiction is one's belief that one is "something," while the fact is that he is actually "nothing." "Something," in the setting of Galatians 6, has reference to self-justification as regards the methods of one's recovery of fallen Christians. The one who is "something" claims to represent God and righteousness and will brook no contradiction as to the means employed in rectifying the wrong. In historical terms, to be "something" is, effectively, to sit in Moses' seat (Matt 23:2) and expect people to respond accordingly, as borne out by 2 Cor 11:5; 12:11, according to which the "super apostles" entertain very high views of themselves and their authority. In this regard, it is not irrelevant that those who sit in Moses' seat "bind heavy burdens, hard to bear, and lay them on men's shoulders; but they themselves will not move them with their finger" (Matt 23:4).[15] As

---

[15] Also of relevance is the polemic of Matt 23:15: a person converted by the Pharisees becomes twice as much a "child of hell" as they. McKnight comments: "Matthew's Jesus castigates these leaders for turning their converts into zealotic fanatics of the way of life being taught by the leaders. In the context of Matthew, this 'zeal' can only be construed as 'zeal for Torah minutiae'" (*Light*, 107).

applied to the Galatian situation, the Judaizers, who were so intent on imposing the outmoded burdens of the Torah, were not willing to bear the sin-burdens of those under their care.

Contrary to their self-perception, however, the "zealots" for righteousness are actually "nothing." That is to say, they are "unspiritual;" they do not exhibit the love which is the fruit of the Spirit. In Paul's own words elsewhere, "*if I have not love, I am nothing*" (1 Cor 13:2). Equally bad, such people "deceive" themselves. As Fung informs us, the verb translated "deceive" implies "a totally subjective delusion" (*Galatians*, 289-90). In other words, there is no objective (biblical) basis for entertaining such views of one's calling, authority and prerogatives: God has never conferred on anyone a ministry which violates both his law's reason for being and the humanity of those who sin *vis-à-vis* that law. Those who are "nothing" are well-advised not to try to restore others; they will only make matters worse, not better, and, at the end of it all, they will have an even more distorted self-perception.

This interpretation of Paul's terms is consistent with that of v. 1b, namely, the main temptation looming before the would-be corrector of others is excessive and unjustified anger, which is demonstrative of a spirit of "zeal" and results in "provoking one another" (5:26).[16] Paul does not have in mind Christians who fancy themselves to be without sin or weakness (e.g., Burton, *Galatians*, 330; Fung, *Galatians*, 290). It is highly doubtful that any such person has ever existed. Fung is right, though, that "Paul implies that those who imagine themselves to be somebody are unable to bear the burdens of others" (*Galatians*, 290), not because the "somebody," in this scenario, lays claim to perfection, but because he disclaims that his harshness and aggressiveness are uncalled for. In his view, his *modus operandi* is above reproach. In short, the "somebody," who is actually a "nobody," takes his stand on the authority of God and is, he imagines, beyond criticism in his treatment of the offender: his is the attitude denounced by 5:26 as "vainglorious."[17] This sort of person lacks sympathy and is unable to bear the burdens of others; he fails to fulfill the law of Christ. Given the particulars of this context, the principal reason for such insensitivity is that this kind of correc-

---

[16] It is significant that Paul's positive description of love in 1 Cor 13:4, that is, love is longsuffering and kind, is matched by the negative "is not zealous."

[17] Cf. Mußner, *Galater*, 400. Mußner takes the whole section 5:26-6:5 to be a warning against *kenodoxia* (ibid., 402).

tive process is the outworking of a "theology of zeal," not a "spirit of gentleness."

4 Paul now seeks to prevent the self-deception just depicted: "But each one must examine his own work, and then he will have reason for boasting in regard to himself alone, and not in regard to another" (NASB). The verb "examine" or "test" (*dokimazō*) is chosen quite on purpose. It means, in this setting, to put to the test for the purpose of determining worth.[18] If my "work" meets up to this standard, then—and only then—am I in a position to restore someone who has been overtaken in "any trespass."

The most emphatic element of the sentence is "his own work." In the broadest possible terms, the "work" can be interpreted as one's own endeavors to be obedient to God. Consequently, on this reading, "It is on his own conduct and performance that each person should concentrate, not the conduct and performance of others; he is to engage in self-assessment, not in critical evaluation of another" (Fung, *Galatians*, 290). Yet we are not to forget that the principal standard of the test is love, the immediate fruit of the presence of the spirit. Hence, even here the focus is not on "works" as such, but on love, which is the fountainhead of the believer's obedience, or, in the words of 5:6, *faith working through love*.[19] That such was Paul's consistent outlook is intimated by the like phrases "work of faith" and "labor of love" (1 Thess 1:3). To examine one's "work," accordingly, is to assess one's faith and love, the source all Christian exertion. It is, in other words, to take stock of one's faith (cf. 2 Cor 13:5).

The effect of such self-awareness, focused on love, rather than other-awareness, focused on sin, is that our boast will be in ourselves alone and not in someone else.[20] In other words, the reason for our boast will be sought in the "work" (= love) which we have done, not in the evil that others have done; then and only then will it be on a solid basis and not be pretentious. Boasting, then, should be grounded in positive, not negative, factors. We are

---

[18] "Christians are summoned to a test of their own accreditation" (W. Grundmann, quoted by Fung, *Galatians*, 290, n. 36). *Dokimazō* in 1 Cor 11:28 is used of the Christian's examination of his conscience.

[19] See the fine statements of Barrett, *Freedom*, 67, 71.

[20] That there is an appropriate "other-awareness" is indicated by the emphatic position occupied by "one another" in v. 2. When it comes to the "burdens" of sin, one ought primarily to consider others; but as regards love, or the lack thereof, one ought to think of oneself first and foremost.

to rejoice that we love; we are not to compare our avoidance of particular sins with Christians who have fallen into those sins and then think ourselves better by the comparison. Betz appropriately comments: "It was recognized [by Paul and others] that the most widespread illusions occur because of comparison of oneself with others. In playing this game, one can manipulate things at will so that the comparison always turns out in favor of oneself and to the disadvantage of the person with whom one compares oneself" (*Galatians*, 303). Such obedience is mechanical and—what is much worse—loveless.

For many readers, however, the idea of boasting presents a rather serious problem. Is Paul really saying that we should boast? The answer is yes, but with one significant qualification: the boasting of Gal 6:4 is not the kind that used to characterize Paul (Rom 2:17, 23; 1 Cor 1:26-31; 3:21; 2 Cor 11:21b-22; Gal 6:14), when his boast was in his standing as member of the chosen people and particularly in the degree of his dedication (as a Pharisee) to the purity of God's covenant with Israel (Gal 1:14; Phil 3:4-6). In their zeal for the Galatians (Gal 4:17), it is this sort of boasting in which the Jewish teachers still engage (Gal 6:13b) and which in turn breeds "vainglory" (Gal 5:26) and promotes harshness in response to human frailty. It is precisely because Paul's opponents continue to be enemies of the cross (Phil 3:18) and are scandalized by it (Gal 5:11; 6:12), boasting in things that are now passé, that they are intolerant of any and all violators of their standards.

Nevertheless, Paul the *Christian* continues to boast, because now his boast is in Christ and his cross (Gal 6:14; Rom 5:2). Thus, one may infer that boasting in "oneself," that is, in one's love, is legitimate, if it is *Pauline* boasting—and integral to Pauline boasting is *the cross*.[21] The statement of 6:14, "Not that I should boast, save in the cross of our Lord Jesus Christ, by whom the world has been crucified to me and I to the world," is matched by the earlier one of 2:20, "I have been crucified with Christ; it is no longer I who live but Christ who lives in me; and the life I now live in the flesh I live by faith in the Son of God, who loved me and gave himself for me." For Paul the cross, in which he now glories, was the most sublime display of the love of God for sinners. It was in light of the cross that Paul came to see that his

---

[21] Paul's boasting in his apostolic ministry is likewise to be tied to the cross Rom 15:17; 1 Cor 9:16; 2 Cor 1:12-14; Phil 2:16).

Pharisaic piety was nothing but excrement and that his boasting had been entirely misfocused (Phil 3:4-11).

The Christian's boasting, therefore, is a paradox—glory in the shame of Christ. The Christian must boast, but the "spiritual" in Galatia, as they boast in their "own work," are to remember that their love is the product of the love of God flowing from the degradation of the cross. Hence, to boast in one's "own work" is to glory, not in human flesh (6:13b, that is, circumcised converts to the Judaizers' "gospel") but in the cross of Christ, the very emblem of humility and selflessness; it is to assume the position of Jesus, the Servant, who gave himself for the sake of others (John 13:1-11; Phil 2:1-11). In this light, Schrage's conclusion is inevitable: "This self-sacrificing love for others is not only the heart and core but also the fundamental criterion of Pauline ethics" (*Ethics*, 212).[22] With this realization, the paradox of Christian experience is seen at its most poignant; and it is only when one thus glories in the cross of Christ that one can exhibit the "spirit of gentleness" necessary to understand and help others.

5 The necessity of boasting in one's self is highlighted by the account which each must give in final judgment. This is suggested by the (eschatological) future tense of v. 5, but more especially by the idea contained in Paul's warning that "each one will have to bear his own load." Some embarrassment has been occasioned by what appears to be a contradiction between v. 5 and v. 2. However, the contradiction is imaginary rather than real and is, in fact, only the product of the paradox of the situation: it is just because one has chosen to bear his own "load" (*phortion*) that he will bear the "burdens" (*barē*) of others. Whereas v. 2 refers to our help of the one who is unable to shoulder his sin-burdens by himself, v. 5 directs us forward to the account which every Christian must give to the Master before whom he stands or falls (Rom 14:4, 10-12).[23] Up to and including the last judgment, there is a load that one alone can bear;[24] and no one will be able to the escape censure of his own

---

[22] "Love...can be clumsily defined as non-self-centred existence" (Barrett, *Freedom*, 74).

[23] A near parallel is 4 Ezra 7:104-05. Written some years after the destruction of Jerusalem, "Ezra" warns his readers that in the last judgment no one will lay a burden on others, but will bear his own righteousness and unrighteousness.

[24] The "load" of v. 5 is "the traveler's own pack," that is, "The ineluctable duties of life that fall to each person, including answerability to God for one's own conduct and performance" (Fung, *Galatians*, 291). The "burdens" of v. 2, by contrast, are the unbearable weight of sin which cannot be supported alone. Possibly, the

wrongdoing by comparing himself with the sins of others. Christians who are cognizant of the gravity of their own responsibility will have neither the inclination nor the time constantly to turn the microscope on the lives of their fellow believers.

6 Some commentators are puzzled by the presence of v. 6 within this train of thought. It is thought that this is an independent piece of advise with no real links to the preceding or the following.[25] But most see the verse as a specific instance of burden bearing, pertaining directly to the ministry. It has also been suggested that Paul is reflecting on the charge of the Jerusalem apostles that he remember the poor (2:10), and now he is passing on that counsel to the Galatians (as in 2 Corinthians 8-9). Whatever its precise function in this context, this teaching is compatible with what Paul says about support for the ministry elsewhere (1 Tim 5:17).

7-8 The importance of bearing the burdens of others, as we put our own work to the test, is driven home by a pointed reminder of the day of judgment. Because this day looms on the horizon, Paul presses that the Galatians should not be deceived. He means either deceived by the Judaizers' theology and practice or self-deceived by their own inclinations. Either way, they must not persist down the path on which they have embarked, but rather return to the truth Paul first preached to them and now repreaches in his letter.

The wrongheadedness of their current attitudes is underscored by the fact that God "is not (or "cannot be" [NIV]) mocked." Paul is saying that their actions *are* a mockery to God, but God will not take that from them. The verb he employs means literally "to turn up the nose" so as to treat with contempt. "In a culture where face and honor and shame was very important, to turn up one's nose at someone was to shame them, it was to treat them as someone weak, as someone beneath one's own dignity, and as unworthy of one's respect" (Witherington, *Grace*, 431). Considering that the one despised is God, this is a scathing indictment indeed.[26] By their imitation of the fleshly deportment of the circumcisers, the Galatians were doing no less than thumbing their noses at God! And

---

singular "load" corresponds to the singular "work" in v. 4, in that it represents a summary of the requirements of the law of Christ.

[25] In other words, the verse would be a gloss, especially as it appears to interrupt the flow of thought respecting the last judgment in v. 5 and vv. 7-8 (cf. O'Neill, *Recovery*, 70). If not, it should be regarded as a parenthetical statement.

[26] Mockery of God is condemned especially in the wisdom literature of the OT (Job 22:19; Ps 44:13; 80:6; Prov 1:30; 11:12; 12:8; 15:5, 20; 23:9; cf. Ezek 8:17).

"one cannot act with impunity and not expect God to take notice or hold one accountable, even as a Christian" (ibid.).

Paul next apparently quotes a current proverb ("A man reaps what he sows"), though one with a biblical basis that extends into noncanonical literature as well (Job 4:8; Prov 22:8; Jer 12:13; 51:33; Hos 6:11; 8:7; Joel 3:13; Sir 7:3; *T. Levi* 13:6; *4 Ezra* 3:20; 4:28-32; 9:31; *2 Apoc. Bar.* 70:2). See also 2 Cor 9:6. In so doing, he draws on the metaphor of two soils into which one may sow. The one soil is that of the flesh. But to clarify that he is not speaking in the abstract, Paul writes literally "his *own* flesh." "Flesh" is used in a summary fashion and draws together the main emphases that have been attached to the word throughout the letter, and especially in chaps. 5-6. At heart, "flesh" is self-centered existence or the bent of fallen human nature to pander to itself. As such, the flesh can take many forms. In the present setting, however, the term denotes the self-gratification that manifests itself in the imperious treatment of those who have fallen; in brief, thinking that one is "something," when actually he is "nothing" (v. 3). The paradox of the situation is that the flesh assumes a religious guise or, more accurately, a sanctimonious demeanor that exalts self and despises others, especially "sinners" (*à la* Luke 15:2; 18:9-14).

It is just this cloak for the flesh that calls to mind again that the Judaizers have made much of their descent from Abraham, and most prominently the cutting of the flesh that signified their connection to the head of the Jewish race. In this light, as Martyn puts it so well: "To sow to one's own flesh is to be circumcised, under the illusion that, as the commencement of Law observance, circumcision of one's flesh is the antidote to the enslaving power called Flesh. To sow to one's flesh is then also to fall victim to the Flesh, precisely because nomistic circumcision of the flesh is impotent to curb the Flesh" (*Galatians*, 553). Indeed, this "very concentration on ethnic identity as alone giving legitimate part in the inheritance of Abraham put the other missionaries in direct antithesis and opposition to the Spirit of God" (Dunn, *Galatians*, 330).

This is so because the opponents' preoccupation with the flesh bred nothing but hatred and contempt for all uncircumcised and non-law-observant people. And it is just this attitude that spilled over into their loveless disregard of those who sin. The only harvest one may expect from such sowing is "corruption," evoking the image of a spoiled and rotten field at harvest time. Instead of being the "fruitful field," that is, the new creation people, of 5:22-23, those who cater to the flesh will prove to be nothing but the "thorns and thistles" of Earth under the curse (Heb 6:8 = Gen 3:18); they will be the fruitless vine of the old Israel (Isa 5:1-6; Jer 8:13; Hos 9:10; 14:6-7; Hab 3:17; Matt 21:18-22; 24:32-35 and pars.).

By contrast, those who have sown into the soil of the Spirit, that is, who have loved their fellow believers and have corrected them, when necessary, in a spirit of gentleness, will reap the harvest of eternal life.[27] In almost identical words, Paul can tell the Romans, "You have your fruit unto sanctification, and its end is eternal life" (Rom 6:22; also Rom 2:7; 5:21). The phrase "eternal life" is likewise qualified in this context by "the fruit of the Spirit." That is to say, the stress falls on the quality of life to be enjoyed forever by the latter-day Israel, whose discipleship to Christ is made evident by their love (John 13:35). Since the fruit of the Spirit is love and all the virtues flowing from it, the age to come is depicted by Paul as a world of love. In the eschaton, the law of Christ will be fully and perfectly fulfilled in a community that is established and maintained for all eternity by love.

Paul draws the same line of connection between love and final judgment in Romans 12 and 13. The love which is "unhypocritical" (12:9) will live peaceably with all and will never avenge itself, because (eschatological) vengeance belongs only to God (12:16-20). Such love will not be overcome with evil, that is, the evil of self-vindication, but will overcome it with good (12:21). Added to this is the love which does no harm to one's neighbor and thereby fulfills the law (13:8-10). For Paul the practice of love is all the more urgent because the night is far spent and the day is at hand; our salvation is nearer than when we first believed. Therefore, we are to cast off the works of darkness and walk becomingly as in the light, making no provision for the flesh (13:11-14). Paul knew that the day of judgment will be one of testing claims. The validity of *our* claims to be admitted to the eschatological kingdom of God will be weighed in the balances not of our talk, our "verbal orthodoxy," but of our love—precisely the logic of Matt 25:31-46. The awesome reality of this principle is not to be played down or explained away.

This scenario of the eschatological harvest finds its complement in the resurrection of the dead. Hays points to 1 Cor 15:42-

---

[27] The phrase "eternal life" appears late in the OT (Dan 12:2) and thereafter in intertestamental literature (2 Macc 7:9; *Pss. Sol.* 3:12; 1QS 4:7; 4 Macc 15:3; Philo, *Fuga.* 78).

58. In that passage, whereas the body is "sown" in "corruption" (*phthora*), it is raised to "immortality" (= eternal life). In like manner, Rom 8:9-13 opposes the death producing power of the flesh to the life giving power of the Spirit, which is linked to the resurrection of the body.

> Understood in this way, v. 8 encapsulates the message of the letter as a whole. It is not a moralistic warning against sensual self-indulgence; instead, it is a warning against placing confidence in anything that belongs to the realm of the merely human—particularly circumcision. Paul insists that only the Spirit of God has the power to confer life (*Galatians*, 337).

9 In keeping with the metaphor of sowing and reaping, Paul now exhorts the Galatians as hardworking farmers to sustain their labors with a view to the eschatological harvest (cf. 2 Tim 2:6). They will certainly luxuriate in the full harvest "at the proper time" (*chronō idiō*), that is, the time of God's appointment at the conclusion of this age, if they do not give up. But, for the time-being, they must wait for it. The realization of righteousness is still a hope (5:5), and while they are waiting, their faith must work through love (5:6). Literally translated, Paul writes "let us not grow weary doing the good." His words find a parallel in Rom 2:7, which maintains that glory, honor, peace and eternal life are to be attained "by endurance in good work." This is language reminiscent of Adam in the Garden. The first man was to complete the task assigned him, all the while maintaining faith with his Creator, and thereafter be confirmed in eternal life as the glorious image of God. As in biblical thought generally, "good" signifies the worship and service of God, while "evil" is tantamount to the service of the creature or idolatry (stemming from Gen 2:9, 17; 3:5, 22). And Adam's mandate is still set before the Christian. In doing "the good," we maintain faith with the Lord of the new covenant, and in the end we will reap the fruits of perseverance. It is to this end we strive, to lay hold of the prize of the upward call of God in Christ Jesus (Phil 3:12-16); and in the final judgment our lives will be appraised as a "good thing" (2 Cor 5:10) because we have worshipped and served the Creator rather than the creature.

Witherington underscores again that Paul envisages the possibility that those who name Christ might commit apostasy and give up the faith and thus miss out on eternal life. "Paul is not saying that a person is saved *by* good works, but he is saying that where there is time and opportunity for doing such things, one will not be saved without them. They are not optional extras in the Christian life" (*Grace*, 433). Longenecker concurs: "For Paul, the fruit of a spiritual harvest comes through the concurring actions of both God and the believer, with the believer's perseverance being generally in response to the Spirit's work in his or her life and specifically an expression of the virtue 'patience'" (*Galatians*, 282). In the Galatian setting, we recall that perseverance is in Paul's law-free gospel, while apostasy is to embrace law-centered "other gospel" of his opponents.

If we ask, What is the harvest? the answer is eternal life as the product of sowing into the "soil" of the Spirit (v. 8). But from a related vantage point, we might say that the harvest is the Spirit himself. If the Spirit has now been given as the "firstfruits" of and the "downpayment" on our inheritance (Rom 8:23; Eph 1:14; 2 Cor 1:22), then it is the Spirit who is the great reality to be experienced in fullness at the end of the age. The age to come will be *life in the Spirit* in all its blessings and ramifications, when the believer will have been given a "spiritual body" in which to enjoy all the Spirit's benefits (1 Cor 15:44; Phil 3:21).

10 Since our time in this life is to be occupied with "doing the good," then "let us work the good for all as we have opportunity" (literal translation). Our service of God the Creator in Christ ("the good") is to find its expression in helping other human beings as we are granted occasion to do so. In such activity we are fulfilling the law of Christ. It is to be noted again that Paul has no difficulty in connecting faith with "doing good" and "working good." This is another of many indications in this letter that Paul was not hostile to "doing" as such. The contrast of faith and works in Galatians is focused specifically on historical and christological matters: the time of "works of the law" is past, and now "the faith" has come (see on 2:16; 3:12, 23-25).

From one vantage point, doing good is a very broad notion, which Paul basically leaves undefined as to particulars. Nevertheless, doing good is reminiscent of "goodness" in 5:22. In the comments on that verse, it was suggested that goodness is seeking the good of others (making it very much like love). This being so, a couple of applications come to mind, especially given the particular content of this letter. One is the sharing of earthly goods with those who are in need. The early church was characterized by such selfless generosity (Acts 2:44-46; 4:32-37), and Paul made it his particular responsibility to fulfill the charge of the Jerusalem apostles to "remember the poor" (Gal 2:10; Rom 15:25-27; 1 Cor 16:3-4; 2 Corinthians 8-9). In principle, this includes providing for those who teach the Word of God (Gal 6:6). Another is that doing good comprehends an attitude: How do we deal with those with whom we disagree or those who fall into sin? In such cases, Paul's "golden rule" is: "Repay no one evil for evil," "never avenge yourselves," and "do not be overcome by evil, but overcome evil with good" (Rom 12:17, 19, 21). As a species of love (and forgiveness), doing good covers a multitude of sins (1 Pet 4:8; Jas 5:20). And whereas insistence on the circumcision of the flesh breeds hatred, contempt and division (5:15, 19-21, 26), the circumcision of the heart engenders the "spirit of gentleness" (6:1) that bears the burdens of others and so fulfills the law of Christ (6:2). Probably the finest commentary on Gal 6:10—doing good to the household of faith—is Rom 12:3-21.

This service is to embrace all people without distinction, but Paul expects that we will have an eye especially on "the household of faith" (NASB). He draws on the image of the church as a family or household (e.g., Eph 2:19; 1 Tim 3:15; Heb 3:5-6), with all its implications of mutual love, intimacy, care and help. But more in particular he has in view Israel as God's "house" (e.g., Num 20:29; 2 Sam 1:12; Ezek 3:4; Jdt 4:15; *Pss. Sol.* 17:42; 1QS 5:6; 8:5, 9; CD 3:19; 20:10, 13). Paul, then, takes over a predicate of the ancient people and applies it to the latter-day assemblies of Christ, constituted of uncircumcised Gentiles as well as Jews. In 6:16, he will go all the way and actually call such people "the Israel of God." Several commentators suggest that this phrase must have featured in the argumentation of the opponents, which would be consistent with the presence similar phenomena in the letter. In any event, the fact that Paul can term the church the household *of faith* is an indication of the primacy of faith in Christ as defining and delineating the new people. The phrase is especially striking in contrast to CD 20:10, 13, which denominate the Qumran community as "the house of the law."[28]

---

[28] Dunn may be correct in connecting "household of faith" with the expression "house of Israel" in the OT (*Galatians*, 333), although Hays expresses doubts (*Galatians*, 337).

Section Notes

1 One of the ironies of history is that the Pharisees, very likely, originated from groups who, during the Greek persecution of the Jews in the second century BC, self-consciously viewed themselves as the poor and oppressed people of God.[29] With the passage of time, however, the persecuted became the persecutors, with the Pharisees identifying themselves exclusively as Yahweh's true people and despising everyone unwilling to maintain their level of ritual purity and devotion to the traditions of the fathers (cf. John 7:49; Gal 4:29); they were the "righteous," while others were "sinners" (cf. John 9:24, 34) (see Dunn, *Jesus, Paul*, 61-88; id., *Partings*, 102-7). In effect, the Pharisees had forgotten their origins. In contrast, then, to the Pharisees who formed the circumcision party, the "spiritual" person remembers that he is "only a sinner saved by grace." Hence, his dealings with other sinners are always moderated by the recollection that, as "a person of like passions," he too can be tempted and fall. The "spirit of gentleness," therefore, is a spirit of realism.

2 When we compare v. 2 with John 13:34 (repeated in 1 John 2:7-11; 3:11, 23; 4:7-12, 17-21; 5:1-3; 2 John 5), "the law of Christ," for all practical purposes, is nothing other than Jesus' own "new commandment" to the church, the encapsulation of the Torah originally entrusted to the covenant people. In view of Gal 5:14 and Rom 13:8-10, the law of Christ is not love as an undefined commodity, because for Paul "the whole law" in all its particulars is summarized and accomplished by love. However, we are not to miss the obvious: the quintessence of the law of Christ is love, and without love there is no true obedience. Without love the commandments of God become a vehicle for spiritual exhibitionism and a club for subjugating sensitive consciences.

D. The Last Word (6:11-18)

In keeping with the customary practice, Paul pens the concluding paragraph in his own hand. But in the present case, he is not simply following convention but taking the opportunity to make one final impassioned appeal in the most personal manner possible. There is a very real sense in which this "last word" of the epistle is a summary of the whole, underscoring the matters closest to his

---

[29] See 1 Macc 2:29-38 and my treatment of the passage in *Obedience*, 114-118. Hengel comments that the Zealots, like the Essenes and the early Christians, may have regarded the name "poor" as an honorary religious title (*Zealots*, 335). See ibid., 335-36 (n. 121) for further references. At length on the origin of the Pharisees, see Neusner, *Traditions*; Kampen, *Hasideans*; Mason, *Josephus*; Saldarini, *Pharisees*; Stemberger, *Contemporaries*.

heart and removing any ambiguity as to where his own emphases lay. Betz affirms that 6:11-18 "becomes most important for the interpretation of Galatians. It contains the interpretive clues to the understanding of Paul's major concerns in the letter as a whole and should be employed as the hermeneutical key to the intentions of the Apostle" (*Galatians*, 313). In the same vein, Longenecker can say: "6:11-18 must be seen as something of a prism that reflects the major thrusts of what has been said earlier in the letter, or a paradigm set at the end of the letter that gives guidance in understanding what has been said before" (*Galatians*, 288-89). W. Harnish, then, is justified in maintaining that Paul's final death-life statement should be regarded as "nothing other than the central thesis of Paul's argumentation in Galatians."[30] Paul thus brings the whole letter full circle, because his opening paragraph likewise contains the entire letter in a nutshell; in it he telegraphs in advance the major themes with which he will deal throughout the letter. The epistle's beginning and ending thus serve to distill the content of the whole, "And this means that Paul's concluding remarks are the last thing interpreters can afford to neglect" (Hubbard, *Creation*, 191).

In his analysis of this paragraph, Weima has demonstrated a series of antitheses between Paul and those who have brought "another gospel:" (1) boasting in circumcision versus boasting in the cross; (2) seeking to avoid persecution for the cross versus willingly accepting such persecution and bearing the marks of the crucified one; (3) compelling people to be circumcised versus seeing circumcision or uncircumcision as an indifferent matter; (4) living under the influence of the old age versus living under the influence of the new creation. And the thing that especially upsets Paul about the agitators' message is that the offense and the sufficiency of the cross have been removed.[31]

---

[30] Quoted by Hubbard, *Creation*, 191. The theological significance of all of Paul's letter endings has traditionally been overlooked. However, see now Weima, *Endings*; id., "Gal. 6:11-18;" id., "Closings."

[31] Weima, "Gal. 6:11-18," 98-101; *Endings*, 157-74. See further Kuula, *Law*, 85-89; Matera, "Culmination;" Fee, *Exegesis*, 172. "It must be stressed that what the *peroratio* tells us is that the most fundamental thing Paul wants his audience to understand and embrace is not the experience of the Spirit or even justification but rather the cross. Justification is only possible, and the Spirit can only be experienced, because of the prior reality of the cross. For the agitators to neglect or downplay or vitiate the message of the cross is to cut off the very foundation of the faith, the very essence of the Gospel, the very means of salvation. Ultimately, neither circumcision nor uncircumcision matters to Paul, unless of course an emphasis on its necessity undercuts the heart of the Gospel. Then, the Holy Grail has

Yet of all the motifs that dominate the ending of the letter, the most outstanding is the new creation (v. 15). Functioning as the "life" side of Paul's death-life equation, new creation resonates back through the entire epistle and epitomizes the major thesis of the letter (Hubbard, *Creation*, 191). Hubbard's important discussion has yielded the conclusion that new creation is on Paul's mind from the earliest stages of Galatians and forms its culminating point here at the end (ibid., 191-232). In a very real sense, new creation is what Galatians is about. The root of the matter is that the new creation assumes a different shape than the old: the former things that used to identify the community of faith have now given way to the age of the Spirit.

11 If anyone thinks that Paul has not been serious in this letter, then the size of his handwriting should tell them otherwise! It has been proposed that this verse is evidence that Paul had an eye problem (in connection with 4:13, 15). Be that as it may, he wrote with large letters for the same reason that John Hancock did—to make a point! Paul's large letters are equivalent to boldface type in a modern book or double underlining in a manuscript. In making his point, Paul virtually ends the letter on the same note on which it began, with his apostolic authority (1:1). In short, he is saying "Pay attention: this is your mother in the gospel speaking!"

12 That this portion of the letter is a kind of summary of the whole is evident by the way Paul takes a parting shot at circumcision. "That Paul can thus once again sum up the goals of his Galatian opponents in the single objective of having Paul's Galatian converts circumcised confirms the tremendous symbolic power which this one ritual act had for Jews in general" (Dunn, *Galatians*, 336). His opponents want to make "a good showing in the flesh" (NASB). The verb he uses is literally "to have a good face." Since the face is that part of a person which most visibly mirrors feelings and responses, this is a way of saying that the Judaizers want to "put their best face forward" or make the most positive impression possible. In a society that placed such value on face and saving face, the people in question are after an "honor rating" with others. The irony, though, is that their favorable impression has to do with

---

been touched and Paul must respond with his whole arsenal. This, explains the tone, the polemics, the urgency we sense throughout this letter. It is because, in Paul's view, so much is at stake, that he must respond as he does. The message of the cross and the cruciform pattern of Christian life are non-negotiables for this apostle" (Witherington, *Grace*, 445).

the most unpresentable part of the body ("flesh" = the circumcised organ)! Paul speaks from the typically Jewish point of view that so highly valued circumcision as the distinctive mark of the chosen people.

As an illustration, the author of 1 Maccabees has nothing but contempt for those Jewish youths who removed the marks of their circumcision in order to be acceptable to the Greeks. In so doing, he says, they "abandoned the holy covenant" and "joined with the Gentiles and sold themselves to do evil" (1 Macc 1:15). What is particularly striking from this text is that to the Torah-true Jew the abandonment of circumcision meant apostasy from the covenant. But for Paul just the opposite is true: to embrace circumcision as the *sine qua non* of covenant membership is to apostatize from the new covenant; circumcision becomes the exit ritual out of Christ (see on 5:3).

From this standpoint, it is altogether understandable that the opponents were "trying to compel" the Galatians to submit to the knife. In historical perspective, they were not unlike John Hyrcanus, who about a hundred years earlier forcibly circumcised a company of Samaritans. George refers to the story of 1 Samuel 18, in which Saul demanded a hundred Philistine foreskins as the price for giving his daughter, Michal, to David as a wife. "Figuratively," says George, "Paul's opponents were doing the same thing David and his soldiers had done of old: presenting Gentile 'foreskins' as a mark of their own success and ingenuity as representatives of the Jewish Christian establishment" (*Galatians*, 434).

However, the circumcisers have an ulterior motive—the avoidance of persecution for the sake of Christ's cross. Paul knew such persecution well, both because he used to engage in it himself (Acts 8:1, 3; 9:1-2; 1 Tim 1:13) and had experienced it from the other end (Acts 13:45, 50; 14:2-5, 19-22; 17:5-9; 18:5-6; 19:28-41; 21:11, 27-36; 22:22-23; 23:12-15, 20-21; Rom 15:31; 2 Cor 11:23-26; Gal 5:11; 6:17; 2 Tim 4:14). Paul's implication is that if his opponents could only succeed in making proselytes by the normal Jewish route of circumcision and submission to the law, they would never incur the wrath of their fellow countrymen, and especially of the Zealot-types, who were so intent on resisting all foreign incursions into the covenant nation (see on 2:12).[32]

That the cross should be the focal point of the persecution is altogether significant. More than once Paul has contrasted his min-

---

[32] See further Longenecker, *Galatians*, xciii; Witherington, *Grace*, 447-49; George, *Galatians*, 435.

istry with that of the other missionaries precisely in terms of the cross (2:20; 3:1, 13; 5:11, 24; 6:14). For him, the gospel is circumcision-free and cross-centered—a combination sure to fill the Judaizers with contempt and loathing. And it was just by substituting circumcision for the cross that the troublers hoped to avoid the displeasure of all who were scandalized by the notion of a *crucified Messiah*—a blasphemous oxymoron to Jewish sensitivities. See on 5:11.

It is frequently said that Paul "attacks" his opponents motives or "vilifies" their character. However, it would be more accurate to say that he exposes their motives and character for what they really are. And Paul would know, because before the Damascus Road he was out to make "a good showing in the flesh," and certainly he would have never exposed himself to disfavor and hardships for the sake of the cross. What characterizes his language in Galatians is not vilification or demonization but "frank speech" (*parrēsia*). See the introduction to 3:1-5.

13 Paul not only calls his detractors' motivations into question, he throws kerosene on the fire by actually charging that these circumcised ones do not themselves keep the law! "Those who are circumcised" is somewhat ambiguous, but the phrase is best taken as a designation of the other teachers whose message and persons are marked by circumcision.[33] A perusal of Stern's *Authors* reveals that although other peoples practiced circumcision, the Jews preeminently were "the circumcised;" and perhaps Paul's language here is a tie-in to that perception. The accusation that they do not keep the law is likewise ambiguous and could mean more than one thing. It could be that they felt free to pick and choose from among the commandments, especially in a Gentile environment where strict Torah observance was, at best, a difficulty. This may be confirmed by 5:3, since it is conceivable that the opponents were allowing the Galatians some degree of flexibility concerning aspects of the law and perhaps were permitting themselves a similar freedom.

Most likely, though, we should understand Paul's allegation in light of 3:10-13 and 5:13-6:5 (see on both). According to 3:10-13, the Judaizers are denounced as idolaters and apostates because of their very devotion to the law; they are not obedient to the law in

---

[33] The present participle used by Paul (*hoi peritemnomenoi*) might conceivably refer to the Galatians who were in the process of getting circumcised (although some manuscripts [P46, B, F, G, L] have the perfect passive participle).

its eschatological design to point to Christ. It is just along these lines that Stephen could charge, "you who received the law as delivered by angels and did not keep it" (Acts 7:53). Rather, his contemporaries have turned the temple into a "house made with hands," a pagan temple (Acts 7:48)![34] In 5:13-6:5, the Judaizers do not keep the law because they have violated its most crucial and central principle—love (see on 5:6, 14). They do not, in point of fact, abide by "all things written in the book of the law," because they have cut the heart out of the covenant, love which fulfills the law. What other evidence could one want that they do not possess the Spirit?

The second part of the verse returns to the previous verse (the "good showing in the flesh"): the rival evangelists want to have the Galatians circumcised that they may boast in their flesh. Boasting, according to Paul, is the characteristic attitude of Second Temple Judaism in its consciousness of being the elect people, entrusted with the glory of God and the Torah (Bar 4:3-4; Rom 2:17, 23; 3:27; cf. 2 Cor 11:18; Eph 2:9; Phil 3:3).[35] From the perspective of the Judaizers, the more foreskins removed the more glory! In their own view, the glory would go to God and to Zion, but Paul observes them through the lens of his own experience, when all his zeal for the law and Israel was nothing but an extended ego-trip (Phil 3:4-6). By contrast to them, when he was converted to Christ, he put away his "confidence in the flesh" (Phil 3:4) and came to see his former righteousness as nothing short of excrement (Phil 3:8).

The irony of the troublers' boasting in the flesh is underscored by Paul in Phil 3:19. According to that verse, the opponents have made a god out of their belly, and their glory consists in their shame. Mearns has shown that "belly" (*koilia*) and "shame" (*aischunē*) are euphemisms for the male genitals ("Opponents," 198-200). Paul, then, is saying, no less, that the "god" and the "glory" of the Judaizers are their circumcised member! Paul is not opposed to boasting per se, but "let him who boasts, boast of the Lord" (2 Cor 10:17)! See the next verse.

---

[34] The charge of law-breaking was commonplace in Jewish intrasectarian rivalries (e.g., *Pss. Sol.* 4:1-8; *1 Enoch* 99:2; *Jub.* 6:33-38; 1QH 4:7-12; CD 1:10-21; 4Q267; 1QpHab; 4Q171). In each case, an author complains that other Jews have proven unfaithful to the law. The NT falls into line by its assertions that contemporary Israel has been faithless (Matt 23:3; John 5:45-48; 8:31-59; Acts 7:53).

[35] See Gathercole, *Boasting*, 37-111, 136-194 and the section note to this verse.

14 If the Judaizers boast in circumcised human flesh, then Paul goes on record that he can no longer share their attitude. In writing, "May I never boast," he means he cannot now be proud of Israel's election and the covenant privileges that used to be the ground of his rejoicing (Bar 4:3-4; Rom 2:17, 23). Hubbard (*Creation*, 220-21) calls attention to the important influence of Jer 9:23-25 on Gal 6:14 (and Rom 2:23-29). Jer 9:23-24 reads:

> This is what the LORD says: "Let not the wise man boast of his wisdom or the strong man boast of his strength or the rich man boast of his riches, but let him who boasts boast about this: that he understands and knows me, that I am the LORD, who exercises kindness, justice and righteousness on earth, for in these I delight," declares the LORD.

Yet Paul takes these verses in connection with what follows (vv. 25-26): "The days are coming," declares the LORD, "when I will punish all who are circumcised only in the flesh—Egypt, Judah, Edom, Ammon, Moab and all who live in the desert in distant places. For all these nations are really uncircumcised, and even the whole house of Israel is uncircumcised in heart."[36] Note how in this oracle of judgment Judah is placed second in the list of pagan nations! Circumcision really does count for nothing (5:6; 6:15; Rom 2:25-29)! In placing vv. 23-24 in connection with vv. 25-26 of Jeremiah 9, Paul links boasting in the flesh/boasting in the Lord with the rejection of external boundary markers such as "circumcision" and "uncircumcision."[37] Particularly when Rom 2:23-29 is brought into view, Paul is maintaining, no less, that *improper boasting is the result of an uncircumcised heart.*

Rather than boasting in the flesh (literally), as the circumcision party continues to do, Paul's boast is now in the Lord Jesus Christ

---

[36] The LXX reads that the nations are "uncircumcised in flesh," while Israel is "uncircumcised in their heart."

[37] Borgen ("Circumcision," 43) points to Philo, *Migr Abr.* 86-93, who maintains that the aim of avoiding persecution and gaining acceptance/fame can be given positive evaluation as part of scriptural Jewish convictions. It is a gift from God when people receive "a great name" and fame because they conform to the Law of Moses and thereby accept and keep the customs, fixed by divinely inspired men in the past. Those who ignore the observances of the feasts and circumcision are taught by the sacred word to have thought for good repute. In this way they can avoid being subject to censure and hostile plotting against them from the Jewish community.

(2 Cor 10:17), and particularly in his cross.[38] In the context of the ancient world, Paul could hardly have chosen a more peculiar or more scandalous thing to say. Crucifixion was looked upon with horror and disgust by cultured pagans, as evidenced by the fact that the cross was hardly mentioned in polite society. As Hengel characterizes it, "The heart of the Christian message, which Paul described as 'the word of the cross', ran counter not only to Roman political thinking, but to the whole ethos of religion in ancient times and in particular to the ideas of God held by educated people" (*Crucifixion*, 5). The bewilderment of the Greco-Roman world toward this message was only increased by the notion of a crucified God. Again Hengel: "The one whom Christians claim as their God is a 'dead God'—a contradiction in itself. And if that were not enough, he had been condemned justly, as a criminal, by his judges in the prime of life, i.e. before his time, to the worst form of death: he had to endure being fastened to the cross with iron nails" (ibid.).

Yet the cross was equally offensive to Judaism, because the notion of a crucified Messiah was simply unthinkable (see on 3:13). This was especially so of that segment of Judaism that held the cross to be reserved for traitors to Israel (see the section note to 3:13). No wonder, Paul could call the preaching of the cross foolishness to those who are perishing, both Jew and Greek (1 Cor 1:18). In brief, he has chosen to boast in something that no one in his day would have dreamed of doing, except like-minded Christians. But the significance of the cross, remarks Dunn, "Is not simply the revaluation of Jewish prerogative over Gentile, for that revaluation means a revaluation of the whole world" (*Galatians*, 340).

"World" is equivalent to the "present evil age" (1:4) in that it designates the totality of humanity in its idolatrous and unredeemed state, with its value system that is at such variance with the law of Christ. If the world has been crucified to Paul and Paul to the world, then the two are dead to each other and no longer have anything in common. This means that crucifixion to the world through the cross of Christ is all transforming. Cousar says eloquently that "the crucifixion of Christ remains not merely a part of Paul's memory to which he returns now and again, but creates a new and persisting situation whereby Paul's allegiance is radically changed, his identity revamped" (*Theology*, 143). Yet he proceeds to caution us that the "derived crucifixions" of Paul and other be-

---

[38] See further Cousar, *Theology*, 137-48.

lievers are not to be reduced to private and individual experiences. Rather, our crucifixions open up the possibility of new existence in a new world as eschatological event (ibid., 143-44).

The irony of the situation is that "world" includes and probably has special reference to Israel (in a manner akin to its usage in the Fourth Gospel, e.g., John 1:9-10; 7:7). It is this world to which the Judaizers still belong. But Paul abandoned that world when he died to the law (2:20) and crucified his flesh with its passions and desires (see on 5:24). It was only the excruciating death of the cross that could cause him to put away his previous values, commitments and way of life as a zealot for the traditions of the fathers (1:14). Only the agony of the cross could convince Paul of the glory of the cross.

Witherington is certainly correct that one can tell a lot about a person by what he boasts of. In Paul's case, "His conversion to belief in a crucified messiah entailed an enormous transvaluation of values, and an adoption of a new paradigm of what God was really doing in the world, how he was doing it, and therefore what the believer's life meant" (*Grace*, 450). With good reason, Martyn can likewise write: "He became as much of a stranger to his previous comrades—and indeed to all people who live in the world of the Law/the Not-Law—as their world became a stranger to him" (*Galatians*, 564).

Yet the cross has done more than effect the lives of individuals, because its effects are cosmic in proportion. The face of reality itself has been changed: the old world has passed away at the cross, and the universe has been reborn with the resurrection of Christ from the dead.

> In Paul's view the present evil age exists, but has been dealt a death blow by the crucifixion of Jesus. All of the world's basic values and assumptions and operating procedures have been put on notice that they are passing away (cf. 1 Cor. 7.31). What really matters are the new eschatological realities brought about because of the death of Christ. In Paul's view, even the Law, as well as other good things about the material world, are part of the things that are passing away or are fading in glory (cf. 2 Cor. 3). Having lost their controlling grip on a human life when Christ came and died, one must not submit to such forces again, but rather live on the basis of the new eschatological realities. The new age has already dawned and Christians should live by its

light and follow the path it illuminates (Witherington, *Grace*, 450).

15 In a virtual restatement of 5:6, Paul pens his final word on circumcision. The connection with the previous verse is noteworthy (as marked by "for"). Paul no longer boasts in things that used to be important simply because circumcision has become irrelevant as far as the new creation is concerned. The significance of circumcision for a Second Temple Jew can be taken for granted by this time (see on 2:3). Suffice it to say that Paul's proposition that "circumcision is not anything" would have appeared to many to be the most outrageous thing he has said in this letter—he has saved the worst for last!

An illuminating historical illustration of the offense that would have been given can be drawn from 1 Maccabees. King Antiochus IV had ordered that the Jews put away their distinctiveness as a people and obey him, and one of the focal points of his demand was circumcision. Says the author: "According to the decree, they put to death the women who had their children circumcised, and their families and those who circumcised them; and they hung the infants from their mothers' necks" (1:60-61). Given such an horrific scenario, Paul must have appeared to some as cavalier indeed. But for him the new creation is incomparably greater than this most famous boundary marker of Jewish self-definition. In blunt terms, circumcision is no longer worth dying for. On the other side, uncircumcision means nothing either; that is, Gentiles, who despised the rite of circumcision and considered it tantamount to castration, have no grounds for boastful superiority themselves (cf. Rom 11:13-24). In the new creation, the condition of a man's privates has no bearing whatsoever on his state of soul.

The phrase "new creation" appears also in 2 Cor 5:17, where it intended not merely in an individual sense (a "new creature") but cosmically as "the new world of the recreation that God has made to dawn in Christ, and in which everyone who is in Christ is included" (Ridderbos, *Paul*, 45). This is evident, says Ridderbos, by the neuter plural that follows: "The old things have passed away, the new have come." "It is a matter of two worlds, not only in a spiritual, but in a redemptive-historical, eschatological sense. The 'old things' stand for the unredeemed world in its distress and sin, the 'new things' for the time of salvation and the re-creation that have dawned with Christ's resurrection" (ibid.). Or, as Hays puts it, Paul is asserting that "the God who created the world has come to reclaim and transform it" (*Galatians*, 345). The same meaning holds true for the present passage, only Paul is making the more specific application that the new creation precludes circumcision or a lack thereof as marking the people of God.

The background to the "new creation" is Isa 65:17-25: "Behold, I will create new heavens and a new earth. The former things will not be remembered, nor will they come to mind" (v. 17), and Isa 66:22: "For as the new heavens and the new earth which I will make shall remain before me, says the LORD; so shall your descendants and your name remain" (RSV).[39] Paul thus announces in explicit terms what has been implicit in numerous passages in the letter, namely, the long-expected new cosmos, the return from exile, the outpouring of the Spirit and the definitive forgiveness of sins have come to pass in his lifetime and that of his readers. And preeminent among the "former things" that have now passed away is circumcision. What has taken its place in the new creation is "faith working through love" (5:6). This is ironically so, because Isa 66:23 goes on to say: "From new moon to new moon, and from sabbath to sabbath, all flesh shall come to worship before me, says the LORD." In Isaiah's day, this is precisely what would have been expected of the worshippers of God. But now new moons and sabbaths have become the lamented "days, months, seasons and years" (4:10) that the Galatians are being pressured into observing. The new creation brings an adjustment of values.

We may say that the new creation is synonymous with the new age and combines apocalyptic and anthropological elements. As for the first, Dunn can state:

> As the antithetical opposite [to "the present evil age"], the new creation must therefore mean the age to come (cf. Rom. 8.19-22 and 2 Cor. 5.17), that is, presumably the context of human existence made new, recreated, to serve as a fitting habitat for God's children (Rom. 8.21). The astounding claim of the first Christians is that the transition had already been made in effect for those "in Christ". Here indeed...are "two different

---

[39] Adams (*Constructing*, 226) points as well to: *Jub.* 4:26; *1 Enoch* 72:1; 91:15; Pseudo-Philo, *Bib. Ant.* 3:10; 16:3; 32:17; *4 Ezra* 7:75; *2 Apoc. Bar.* 32:6; 44:12 57:2; 1QS 4:25; Rev 21:1; 2 Pet 3:13. Hubbard's objection that if Paul had had in mind the well-defined Jewish expectation of the new heavens and earth he surely would have used the definite article "the new creation" (*Creation*, 224). But this fails to recognize that the more familiar a concept or term is the less need there is for definite articles. The outstanding example is the anarthrous *nomos* in Greek, reflecting the anarthrous *Torah* in Hebrew.

worlds"—the old world replaced through the apocalyptic shift of the cross by the new creation.[40]

Adams adds that as "new creation" occurs within the apocalyptic framework of this letter, it forms the antithesis to "world" and serves to as a tool for constructing a Christian social world separate from the Jewish community.

> Paul's converts must not become Jewish proselytes in an attempt to resolve their crisis of social identity, for to do so would be return to the *kosmos* from whence they came. Rather, in the knowledge that they belong to God's new creation, they are to construct for themselves a *new* social identity and develop a "positively valued distinctiveness" from Judaism (*Constructing*, 232).

I would qualify that Paul's concern goes beyond social identity to encompass nothing less than salvation itself, because, as Adams sates elsewhere, to assimilate to Judaism is to alienate oneself from the new creation (ibid., 228).

As for the anthropological dimension, Betz stresses that "through the Christ-event the Christian is enabled to participate in the new human existence 'in Christ' which in Galatians is described as 'the fruit of the Spirit' in all its manifestations" (*Galatians*, 320). Thus, to adapt Hubbard's comment, it is as accurate to speak of the new age entering the believer as the believer entering the new age (*Creation*, 224). Furthermore, Hubbard is accurate in saying that the new creation is not to be described so much in terms of ontological transformation as of *pneumatological restoration*. On this reading, new creation refers to the new inner dynamic of the Spirit which has begun the process of restoring the image of God marred by Adam's sin, and which enables those who rely on his power to fulfill the requirement of the law (Rom 8:4) (ibid., 235). The bottom line is that in the new creation the only circumcision that counts is that of the heart (Deut 10:16; 30:6; Jer 4:4; Rom 2:28-29; Col 2:11-13), an operation performed by the Spirit of God, who breathes life into the dead bones of Israel in exile (Ezek 37:1-14).

---

[40] Dunn, *Theology of Galatians*, 49-50. Hubbard objects that Jewish apocalyptic makes no mention of "shifting crosses" (*Creation*, 225). However, that is only to be expected, given the disdain of the cross generally in the ancient world and more especially among the Jews. The radical thing in Paul is precisely that it is the cross, of all things, that has effected the turning of the new age.

16 As this letter virtually began with an apostolic benediction, so now it practically ends with one too.[41] "Peace and mercy" are the precious possessions of "the Israel of God," which is now defined as all those who "walk by this rule" (NASB).[42] George notes that the conditional blessing at the end of the letter stands in marked contrast to the conditional curse with which Paul opened his epistle (*Galatians*, 439). This conditional blessing actually implies "a threat against those who, after having read the letter, do not intend to conform to Paul's rule and, consequently, fall under the curse" (Betz, *Galatians*, 321).

> Paul knew very well that he was writing to churches caught up in intense conflict over a serious theological matter. Rather than smoothing over the difficulty in the interest of a superficial harmony, Paul did the opposite: he emphasized the sharp differences between him and his opponents and forced the Galatians to make a choice. On the one side of that choice was the apostolic curse; on the other, the apostolic blessing (George, *Galatians*, 439).

Peace recalls the unfallen creation and its restoration by the work of the Servant of the Lord (see on 1:3). With the advent of the Messiah and the outpouring of his Spirit, *Paradise Lost* has been turned into *Paradise Regained*. The Galatians are privileged to be participants in this new creation by virtue of faith alone apart from works of the law. And if they have come to know God's peace in Christ, then they must be at peace with themselves as they bear the fruit of the Spirit (cf. Heb 12:14: "*pursue* peace"). Martyn (*Galatians*, 566) reminds us that Paul grew up in a home where he

---

[41] From a slightly adjusted point of view, Hays thinks: "Having begun the letter with a curse on the perverters of the gospel (1:8-9), Paul chooses to end it with a blessing on his readers in the hope that they will have been persuaded by his arguments to renounce circumcision and live as Gentiles under the direction of the Spirit" (*Galatians*, 345).

[42] It is frequently claimed that "peace" and "mercy" appear here in an illogical order; that is, mercy should precede peace, because the latter flows out of the former. However, Paul, as ever, is thinking in historical terms: both words have reference to Israel's return from captivity, at which time peace and mercy would simultaneously be conferred on the exiles. As in the relation of sonship and the Spirit in 4:6, Paul is not following a rigid *ordo salutis*. Some realities can be spoken of in one order or the other. The order of the "Blessing of Peace" of the *Shemoneh Esreh* is the same as Paul's.

was accustomed to hearing the pronouncement of blessing upon Israel (Ps 125:5; 128:6; *Pss. Sol.* 4:25; 6:6; 8:27-28; 9:8; 11:9; 13:12; 16:6; 17:45; 18:5; 11QPs^a 23:11).

Mention is usually made of the coda to the Eighteen Benedictions (*Shemoneh Esreh*), which actually reads: "May peace…and mercy…be upon us and upon all Israel thy people" (Babylonian Recension).[43] An inscription from the synagogue at Gerasa (2nd c. AD) also reads: "Peace be upon all Israel." The last two mentioned sources postdate the NT, but it is still attractive to think that Paul has formulated his sentence as a reference to such blessings, but with modifications as befits their application to a new people, notably the broadening of "Israel" to include Gentiles (see Betz, *Galatians*, 322).

Mercy (Greek *eleos*; Hebrew *hesed*) is God's covenant faithfulness and kindness. The classic passage is Exod 33:19-34:9, especially in context, the worship of the golden calf (Exodus 32). After Israel had so quickly forsaken Yahweh for an Egyptian idol (Exod 32:8; Deut 9:16), the Lord declares nonetheless: "I will have mercy on whom I will have mercy, and I will have compassion on whom I will have compassion" (Exod 33:19). Thereafter, he reveals his name to Moses: "The LORD, the LORD, the compassionate and gracious God, slow to anger, abounding in love and faithfulness" (Exod 34:6). Yahweh's name is the revelation of his character as the God who forgives sin and is gracious, "maintaining love to thousands, and forgiving wickedness, rebellion and sin" (Exod 34:7). That God's mercy is towards Israel is taken for granted by later OT texts (Ezra 3:11; Isa 44:23; 49:13; Ezek 39:25; Joel 2:13; Amos 5:15; Zech 1:12-17). Paul's echo of Exodus is especially appropriate because the Galatians themselves were in danger of "quickly" forsaking the Lord for an idol—the Torah. Nevertheless, Paul reminds them that the Lord is merciful and will receive them back for Christ's sake.

There are sufficient occurrences of both "peace" and "mercy" in the above mentioned sources to think that Paul may well have had them in mind. However, in a background study to this verse, Beale ("Peace") has demonstrated that the two terms appear together in Isa 54:10: "For the mountains may be removed and the hills may shake, But My *lovingkindness* will not be removed from you, And My covenant of *peace* will not be shaken, Says the Lord

---

[43] On the text, see Betz, *Galatians*, 321; Richardson, *Israel*, 79. Betz may be right that this blessing, the *Birkat ha-Shalōm* ("Blessing of Peace"), is at least as old as the time of Paul. However, the dating of the Benediction remains problematic.

who has compassion on you" (NASB). The LXX renders the key Hebrew terms of this text with the same words Paul uses here: "mercy" (*eleos* = *hesed*) and "peace" (*eirēnē* = *shalōm*). The peace and mercy of Isa 54:10 receive, in vv. 11-12, concrete expression in the coming conditions of the new creation at the time of Israel's restoration, when Jerusalem is going to be rebuilt of precious stones and thus become *in toto* a new temple (see on 4:27). In the broader context of Isaiah 54, it is God who is "making" Israel again (v. 5); he has "created" the nation that it might be restored (v. 16). Verses 9-10 then proceed to portray the coming restoration in terms of the renewal of the creation after Noah's flood and the necessity of cosmic dissolution which must precede the new creation. All of this material in Isaiah 54 is part of the larger pattern of new creation prophecies in Isaiah 40-66, which refers to the restoration of Israel from captivity as a new creation (ibid., 211).

The only other times when the two words appear in such close connection are Jer 16:5 and Ps 85:10 (LXX 84:10).[44] The former refers to God's removal of his "lovingkindness" and "peace" when Israel goes into exile, and the latter alludes to the return of these tokens of the divine favor when the nation is restored ("Love and faithfulness meet together; righteousness and peace kiss each other"). Earlier, in vv. 7-8 of Psalm 85, the two also occur in close proximity ("show us Your *lovingkindness*, O Lord, And grant us Your salvation. I will hear what God the Lord will say; For He will speak *peace* to His people, to His godly ones; But let them not turn back to folly" [NASB]). Beale notes that the promised condition of the peace and mercy of restoration is referred to as an "enlivening" in v. 6. Furthermore, the attributes surrounding mercy and peace are portrayed in the directly following verses as *fruits* of God's eschatological creative work (vv. 11-12). Psalm 85 thus has several points of affinity with Gal 6:16 in context. (1) "Mercy" and "peace" are pronounced "upon" Israel. (2) The notion of new life is associated with the salvation of God's people. (3) "Peace" is listed among other attributes which are part of fertility or fruit bearing in the new creation (ibid., 208-10).

Against this impressive OT backdrop of exile, restoration and new creation, we can see that Paul is claiming, no less, that the prophetic vision for the blissful future has been realized with his preaching of the gospel in Galatia and the influx of Gentiles into "the Israel of God," as he will come on to say momentarily (see the

---

[44] In noncanonical literature, the two are linked in *Jub.* 22:9 and 1QH 13:5.

section note to this verse). This people has become the fruit bearing vine of the eschatological new beginning in Christ.

The recipients of God's peace and mercy are those who "follow this rule." Paul draws again on the verb of 5:25 (*stoicheō*): the Galatians are to "stay in line" or "keep in step" with the new rule that defines the people of God. The "rule" (*kanōn*) is the "measuring rod," "chalk line" or "standard" by which persons should evaluate the genuineness of their Christianity. By "rule" Paul means the norm by which he lives and judges the "other gospel" of the opponents. It is certainly eye-catching that Josephus identifies the Torah as the "rule" of the Jewish faithful: "For all this our leader made the Law the standard and rule (*kanona ton nomon*), that we might live under it as under this father and master and be guilty of no sin through wilfulness or ignorance" (*Ag. Ap.* 2.174). One may assume that Josephus expresses an attitude typical in his day, which makes it all the more ironic that Paul disallows any lasting validity to the Mosaic law, and in particular to circumcision (v. 15). His "rule" evaluates people in their relation to the new creation, not in the absence or presence of foreskins.[45] And if circumcision no longer means anything, then indeed a new day has dawned in world history.

The concluding words of the verse read, according to NIV: "Even to the Israel of God."[46] The original is ambiguous enough that Paul could be referring to a different group of people than those who "walk by this rule" in the first clause: either non-Christian Jews or Christian Jews with whom he is upset at the moment.[47] But all in all, given that Paul has labored all the way through this letter to place uncircumcised Gentiles on an equal footing with Jewish believers, the "Israel of God" is none other than those people who adhere to the standard of the new creation—in plain terms, the Christian church or the renewed family of the Messiah.[48] Paul is saying pointedly that the people of God have been redefined and reconfigured. The assembly of Christ consists of Jew and Greek alike with no distinction between them: their

---

[45] This raises the possibility that Paul's "rule" forms a new *torah* or *nomos*, especially in light of his own phrase "the law of Christ" in Gal 6:2 and 1 Cor 9:21. In thought, at least, Paul was understood just this way by *Barn.* 2:6, which speaks of "the new law" (*ho kainos nomos*) of Christ.

[46] "Even" (*kai*) is here is equivalent to "that is."

[47] For advocates of both positions, see Hubbard, *Creation*, 228, n. 163.

[48] Likewise, Wright, *Perspective*, 114; Hays, *Galatians*, 346. For a different reading, see Hoch, *All Things*, 274-78.

identity is no longer derived from the Torah but from Christ and the Spirit.

This being so, converts to Christ do not have to be circumcised and made to submit to the law in order to belong to Israel—they are already in by faith alone. Weima is to the point: it is "difficult to believe that in a letter where Paul has been breaking down the distinctions that separate Jewish and Gentile Christians and stressing the equality of both groups, that he in the closing would give a peace benediction addressed to believing Jews as a separate group within the church."[49] The same applies to non-Christian Jews, who have never really been in his sights in this letter. Given that this final paragraph of the epistle is a distillation of the whole, the phrase "the Israel of God,"[50] although unique to this place, sums up Paul's whole body of teaching in Galatians respecting Jew/Gentile relations. Isa 54:5 says it all: "The Holy One of Israel is your Redeemer; he is called *the God of all the earth*."

Hubbard calls attention to the fact that most of the postscript of the letter has been occupied with rejecting the way of the law, circumcision, the flesh and all related criteria for defining the people of God. This, he says, is "a fair reflection of the dominant themes of Galatians" (*Creation*, 228). Yet an important corollary to the main point that faith and the Spirit now demarcate the latter-day people, not the law and circumcision, is that it is possible to speak of an "Israel of God" in contradistinction to "Israel according to the flesh" (1 Cor 10:18; cf. Rom 2:28-29; 9:3, 6, to which I would add 2 Cor 5:16). In the former, labels such as "Jew and Gentile, "male and female" or "slave and free" count for little, "for you are all one in Christ Jesus" (3:26-29). As he notes, this issue does not dominate the postscript, but it is "an obvious implication of the Christocentric soteriology of Galatians…" (ibid., 229).

17 It is the human being Paul who draws this letter to a close with a half-plea/half-command for certain people "from now on" to cause him no more troubles (or "labors," perhaps alluding to the "labor pains" of 4:19). The idiom "cause troubles" indicates that the upsets caused among the Galatian converts were almost like a

---

[49] Weima, "Gal. 6:11-18," 105. Likewise are Longenecker, *Galatians*, 298-99; B. W. Longenecker, "Defining," 96-97; Beale, "Peace," 205, 222; Sanders, *Paul, the Law*, 174; Barclay, *Obeying*, 98; Harvey, *Israel*, 225-26.

[50] Betz shows that the expression Israel *of God* finds analogies in the DSS, in which the Qumran sect can speak of itself as, for example, the "community of God" or the "assembly of God" (*Galatians*, 323, n. 112).

physical assault against himself, not to mention the actual punishment meted out by his enemies on various occasions. Paul has had enough of that, and he needs no more pains, "for" (*gar*) he bears the very marks of Jesus on his body—enough to last a lifetime!

These "marks" (*stigmata*) are primarily the scars resulting from the various beatings he had to endure, particularly at the hands of the Jews (2 Cor 6:4-5; 11:23-25; Acts 14:19; 16:23). Yet "the marks *of Jesus*" are an additional allusion to the cross, since victims of crucifixion were scourged beforehand (cf. Isa 53:5: "By his stripes we are healed"). Also, the verb "bear" (*bastazō*) itself possesses connotations of carrying the cross.[51] Paul, therefore, by bearing *these particular marks*, is being crucified to the world (6:14). Such marks of his identification with Jesus's own sufferings (Rom 8:17; 2 Cor 1:5; 4:8-10; Phil 3:10; Col 1:24) should be proof enough of the genuineness of his apostleship and the sincerity of his devotion to his master. Since "marks" were common in the ancient world for religious tattooing or slave branding (Davis, "*Proegraphē*," 208), Paul is likely suggesting as well that he is the possession of Christ and his slave (see Tsang, *Slaves*, 74-80). But besides "marks" in the sense of "stripes," Beale is right that Paul wants to be identified with the only mark of the new creation that there is—Messiah Jesus himself. His statement of v. 17 that he "bears on his body the brand-marks of Jesus" is another way of saying that he does not want to be identified by *the* badge of the old creation, circumcision, but wants to be identified with "the only sign of the new creation: with Jesus, and his suffering at the cross" ("Peace," 222).[52] He will accept a certain mark on his flesh, but only the mark of the cross.

---

[51] The idea of "carrying the cross" is from the Gospels (Matt 10:38 = Luke 14:27; Mark 8:34 = Matt 16:24 and Luke 9:23). Cf. Heb 13:13: we are to join Christ outside the camp by "bearing his reproach," an obvious reference to the crucifixion. The Greek verbs vary between the individual passages, but the idea is the same in each. Hengel shows that "carry the cross" was virtually a Zealot motto (*Zealots*, 260-61, 271), although in completely different sense than Paul's bearing of the cross of Christ.

[52] Judging from 2 Cor 11:21-12:10, Paul customarily appealed to his sufferings as the real "marks" of his apostleship. According to 12:12, the "the signs of a true apostle" (RSV, NRSV) (*ta men sēmeia tou apostolou*) were performed among the readers "in all perseverance." These were accompanied by other "signs and wonders and mighty works." So paradoxically, the genuineness of his ministry was attested by a twofold confirmation: the signs of Paul's weakness and the signs of God's power through him. Both are epitomized by 12:10: "*When I am weak, then I am strong.*" Cf. Hafemann, *2 Corinthians*, 467.S

18 All that remains is for Paul to confer one final benediction on his readers—"the grace of the Lord Jesus Christ be with your spirit." "Grace" is the most appropriate word he could have chosen as the crown of this epistle. From beginning to end, he has argued that God's covenant love and fidelity are the possession of the Galatians apart from the necessity of becoming Jews to enjoy the blessings of the family bond brought to realization in Christ (see on 1:3). Grace is thus specifically and eschatologically that of "the Lord Jesus Christ." The mention of the readers' "spirit" (singular) is perhaps a reminder that what bonded them together was the Spirit of God working in their spirit, rather than a law-centered identity as sealed by circumcision. After all, they do live in the age of the Spirit, not in the era of the Torah (3:3). And at the end of the day, they are still "brothers," members of the "household of faith" (6:10).

In light of everything said in this impassioned and yet pastorally sensitive letter, what else could Paul say but "amen?" He could only hope that the Galatians would add their own amen. By writing "may it be so," Paul is content to leave the entire matter in God's hands. "The letter thus ends where it began, with the invocation of God and God's will" (Witherington, *Grace*, 458).

Section Notes

13 Gathercole (*Boasting*) has amply demonstrated that boasting in the Judaism prior to and contemporary with Paul entails two elements: election/national privileges and actual performance of the Torah. His book serves as a useful and welcomed corrective to an imbalance on the part of some practitioners of the New Perspective. As he notes many times, there has been a tendency to play up sociological matters (Jewish distinctiveness and self-identity) and to play down the Torah's own requirement that one really and truly "do the law." Probably, the divide between the two on the part of certain notable scholars is not as stark as Gathercole would have us believe. Nevertheless, to the degree that he has redressed the balance in favor of a reading of Judaism and Paul that more accurately reflects the actual data, we are in his debt.

On the problematic side, Gathercole continues to perpetuate some of the same wrongheaded ideas about the character of Second Temple Judaism as his many of his predecessors. His approach to the sources is certainly an improvement over the imposition of terms like "legalism" and "works-righteousness" onto the Jewish materials by the likes of Schürer, Weber, Billerbeck, Bultmann, etc. But even so, his conclusions, in the end, are close enough to the "old school" approach to call for some criticism (see my review of Gathercole's book, *Defense*, 199-221). What he presents is a more enlightened and sensitive approach to the materials;

but, at the end of the day, Judaism remains a religion devoid of the Spirit and dependence on the grace of God. While avoiding some of the extremes of traditional Christian assessments of predestruction Judaism, essentially Gathercole's book is but another reassertion of the traditional understanding of the character of Paul's controversy with his Jewish contemporaries.

14 D. F. Watson ("Paul," 77) notes that Paul twice quotes Jer 9:23 in the context of boasting (1 Cor 1:31; 2 Cor 10:17). In Jer 9:23-24, God commands that boasting should not be in any sense anthropocentric. Boasting is not to be based upon wisdom, strength, or wealth, that is, upon the three major things in which humanity can place its trust other than in God and thereby promote itself (cf. 1 Cor 1:26-31). Boasting about one's fragile and uncertain life circumstances in which God is not taken into account is excluded (1 Kgs 20:11; Prov 25:14; 27:1). In fact, such boasting is foolish ungodliness (Pss 52:1; 94:3-4).

According to Watson (ibid., 78), "God commands rather that boasting be theocentric, with its basis in an intimate relationship with and knowledge of God. There is no room for boasting before God, who is the creator, sustainer, and judge (1 Sam 2:2-3; cf. Judg 7:2). Boasting in God's works is acceptable, particularly boasting about God's acts in sustaining the community of faith (1 Chron 16:28-29; 29:11; Pss 5:11; 89:15-18). As its incorporation into Psalms indicates (5:11; 89:15-18), such boasting is really worship and confession. Judaism continued this understanding of legitimate boasting as rooted only in God and God's work in the community of faith (Sir 17:9; 50:20), adding that boasting in the Law as God's gift was also legitimate (Sir 39:8). True boasting is in the fear of the Lord (Sir 1:11; 9:16; 10:22)."

As for the pagan environment, although self-boasting was generally thought repulsive, the conventions of Paul's era permitted such boasting in certain prescribed situations. To be specific: "Boasting was acceptable when speakers mentioned overcoming unfortunate circumstances as a tribute to ambition and as a way to cast aside pity; defended their name against charges stemming from envy; spoke against enemies or detractors who denounced their actions as discreditable; pleaded their case for justice with those that have mistreated them; demonstrated that to do the opposite of the conduct being criticized would have been shameful; mentioned their accomplishments in order to achieve a similar good; built up their character in order to invite the audience in a similar worthy endeavor; showed an advantage or further purpose like arousing ambition and inspiring the audience to emulation; subdued the headstrong; and swayed the audience from unsound policy. Boasting was unacceptable when it was motivated by ambition, fame, self-glorification, or relied on comparison in order to usurp praise rightfully belonging to others. It was also unacceptable to use boasting to refute the unfounded claims of others" (ibid., 81).

The classic instance of Paul boasting in the above described vein is 2 Corinthians 10-13. In Galatians, the only glimmer of a similarity is 6:4, but even that is not really parallel. It has to be remembered that Paul's Galatian opponents were boasting in their Jewishness; their "glory" was in the "flesh," specifically circumcised flesh. But by means of the starkest disparity conceivable, Paul finds his source of boasting in the dreaded and degrading cross, on which Jesus rendered all previous causes of boasting antiquated and illegitimate. Therefore, uncircumcised flesh is as "glorious" as circumcised.

16 Beale notes the LXX rendering of Isa 54:15: "Behold proselytes will come to you through me, and they will sojourn with you, and they will run to you for refuge." Here, God's promise of the Hebrew text to protect Israel from Gentile enemies and give the nation victory over their attackers is interpreted by the LXX as God's causing Gentiles to seek refuge in Israel. (This interpretation is strikingly similar to the LXX of Amos 9:11-12 and its use in Acts 15:15-18.) But even according to the LXX interpretative translation, believing Gentiles can enjoy eschatological blessings only as they confess and identify with the God of Israel and only as they identify with his people Israel by converting and becoming "proselytes" to the faith of Israel. "From the Septuagintal translator's perspective, the Gentiles cannot enjoy these blessings separately from Israel but only by becoming a part of national, theocratic Israel. Paul also likely does not see that Gentiles can enjoy endtime blessings separately from Jews because the only way that either can participate in such blessing is by identifying with Christ, the true Israel, the true "seed of Abraham." Gentiles no longer need to move to geographical Israel and find "refuge" there in order to convert to the faith of that theocratic nation and they no longer need to adopt the national signs of Israel (e.g., circumcision) to be considered true Israelites. Rather, now, in the new redemptive-historical epoch launched by Christ's death and resurrection, Gentiles merely need to move spiritually to Christ, find "refuge" in him, and convert to faith in him in order to become true Israelites" ("Peace," 215-16).

BIBLIOGRAPHY

Commentaries on Galatians

Betz, Hans Dieter. *Galatians: A Commentary on Paul's Letter to the Churches in Galatia*. Hermeneia. Philadelphia: Fortress, 1979.

Bligh, John. *Galatians: A Discussion of St. Paul's Epistle*. Householder Commentaries 1. London: St. Paul, 1970.

Brown, John. *An Exposition of the Epistle of Paul the Apostle to the Galatians*. Geneva Series of Commentaries. Edinburgh: Banner of Truth, rep. 2001.

Bruce, F. F. *Commentary on Galatians*. NIGTC. Grand Rapids: Eerdmans, 1982.

Burton, Ernest De Witt. *A Critical and Exegetical Commentary on the Epistle to the Galatians*. ICC. Edinburgh: T & T Clark, 1921.

Calvin, John. *The Epistles of Paul the Apostle to the Galatians, Ephesians, Philippians and Colossians*. eds. David W. Torrance and Thomas F. Torrance. Grand Rapids: Eerdmans, 1976.

Cousar, Charles B. *Galatians*. IBC. Louisville: John Knox, 1982.

Dunn, James D. G. *The Epistle to the Galatians*. BNTC 9. Peabody: Hendrickson, 1993.

Ebeling, Gerhard. *The Truth of the Gospel: An Exposition of Galatians*. Philadelphia: Fortress, 1985.

Fung, Ronald Y. K. *The Epistle to the Galatians*. NICNT. Grand Rapids: Eerdmans, 1988.

George, Timothy. *Galatians*. NAC 30. Nashville: Broadman and Holman, 1994.

Guthrie, Donald. *Galatians*. NCB. London: Nelson, 1969.

Hansen, G. Walter. *Galatians*. IVP New Testament Commentary Series 9. Downers Grove: InterVarsity, 1994.

Hays, Richard B. *Galatians. The New Interpreter's Bible.* 12 vols. Nashville: Abingdon, 2000, 11.181-348.

Hendriksen, William. *Galatians and Ephesians.* New Testament Commentary. Grand Rapids: Baker, 1979.

Jervis, L. Ann. *Galatians.* NIBCNT 9. Peabody: Hendrickson, 1999.

Lagrange, M.-J. *Saint Paul Epitre aux Galates.* EBib. Paris: Gabalda, 1950.

Lightfoot, J. B. *The Epistle of S. Paul to the Galatians.* Grand Rapids: Zondervan, rep. 1979.

Longenecker, Richard N. *Galatians.* WBC 41. Dallas: Word, 1990.

Lührmann, Dieter. *Galatians.* CC. Minneapolis: Fortress, 1992.

McKnight, Scot. *Galatians.* NIV Application Commentary. Grand Rapids: Zondervan, 1995.

Martyn, J. Louis. *Galatians.* AB 33a. New York: Doubleday, 1997.

Matera, Frank J. *Galatians.* SP 9. Collegeville: Glazier, 1992.

Mußner, Franz. *Der Galaterbrief.* HTKNT 9. 4th ed. Freiburg: Herder, 1981.

Ramsey, William M. *A Historical Commentary on St. Paul's Epistle to the Galatians.* Grand Rapids: Baker, rep. 1965.

Ridderbos, Herman N. *The Epistle of Paul to the Churches of Galatia.* NICNT. Grand Rapids: Eerdmans, 1953.

Schlier, Heinrich. *Der Brief an die Galater.* KEK. 5th ed. Göttingen: Vandenhoeck & Ruprecht, 1971.

Williams, Sam K. *Galatians.* ANTC. Nashville: Abingdon, 1997.

Witherington, Ben. *Grace in Galatia: A Commentary on Paul's Letter to the Galatians*. Grand Rapids: Eerdmans, 1998.

Ziesler, John. *The Epistle to the Galatians*. Epworth Commentaries. London: Epworth, 1992.

Other Literature

Abegg, Martin. "4QMMT, Paul, and 'Works of the Law.'" *The Bible at Qumran: Text, Shape, and Interpretation*. ed. Peter Flint. Studies in the Dead Sea Scrolls and Related Literature. Grand Rapids: Eerdmans, 2001, 203-16.

Adams, Edward. *Constructing the World: A Study in Paul's Cosmological Language*. SNTW. Edinburgh: T & T Clark, 2002.

Amir, Yehoshua. "The Term *IOUDAISMOS*: A Study in Jewish-Hellenistic Self-Identification." *Imm* 14 (1982): 34-41.

Anderson, A. A. *The Book of Psalms*. 2 vols. NCB. Grand Rapids: Eerdmans, 1972.

Arnold, Clinton E. "'I Am Astonished That You Are So Quickly Turning Away!' (Gal 1.6): Paul and Anatolian Folk Belief." *NTS* 51 (2005): 429-449.

Ashton, John. *The Religion of Paul the Apostle*. New Haven: Yale University Press, 2000.

Aune, David E. *The New Testament in Its Literary Environment*. LEC 8. Philadelphia: Westminster, 1987.

_____. *The Westminster Dictionary of New Testament and Early Christian Literature and Rhetoric*. Louisville: Westminster/John Knox, 2003.

Aus, R. D. "Three Pillars and Three Patriarchs: A Proposal Concerning Gal 2:9." *ZNW* 70 (1979): 252-61.

Avemarie, Friedrich. *Tora und Leben: Untersuchungen zur Heilsbedeutung der Tora in der frühen rabbinischen Literatur*. TSAJ 55. Tübingen: Mohr-Siebeck, 1996.

Bailey, Daniel P. "Jesus as the Mercy Seat: The Semantics and Theology of Paul's Use of *Hilastērion* in Romans 3:25." Ph.D. Dissertation, University of Cambridge, 1999.
_____. Dissertation summary, *TynBul* 51 (2000): 155-58.

Balch, David L. "Paul, Families, and Households." *Paul in the Greco-Roman World: A Handbook*. ed. J. Paul Sampley. Harrisburg: Trinity Press International, 2003, 258-92.

Bammel, Ernst. "The Poor and the Zealots." *Jesus and the Politics of His Day*. eds. E. Bammel and C. F. D. Moule. Cambridge: Cambridge University Press, 1984, 109-128.

Bandstra, Andrew John. *The Law and the Elements of the World: An Exegetical Study in Aspects of Paul's Teaching*. Kampen: Kok, 1964.

Banks, Robert. "The Eschatological Role of Law in Pre- and Post-Christian Jewish Thought." *Reconciliation and Hope: New Testament Essays on Atonement and Eschatology Presented to L. L. Morris on His 60th Birthday*. ed. Robert Banks. Grand Rapids: Eerdmans, 1974, 173-85.
_____. *Paul's Idea of Community: The Early House Churches in their Historical Setting*. Exeter: Paternoster, 1980.

Barclay, J. M. G. *Obeying the Truth: A Study of Paul's Ethics in Galatians*. SNTW. Edinburgh: T & T Clark, 1988.
_____. "Mirror Reading a Polemical Letter: Galatians as a Test Case." *The Pauline Writings*. The Biblical Seminar 34. eds. Stanley E. Porter and Craig A. Evans. Sheffield: Sheffield Academic Press, 1995, 247-67.
_____. *Jews in the Mediterranean Diaspora: From Alexander to Trajan (323 BCE-117 CE)*. Edinburgh: T & T Clark, 1996.

Barclay, William. *Flesh and Spirit: An Examination of Galatians 5:19-23*. Nashville: Abingdon, 1962.

Barrett, C. K. "Paul and the Pillar Apostles." *Studia Paulina*. ed. J. N. Sevenster. Haarlem: Bohn, 1953, 15-19.
_____. *The Signs of an Apostle*. Philadelphia: Fortress, 1972.
_____. "Shaliah and Apostle." *Donum Gentilicium: New Testament Studies in Honour of David Daube*. eds. C. K. Barrett,

Ernst Bammel and W. D. Davies. Oxford: Oxford University Press, 1978, 88-102.

_____. *Essays on Paul*. London: SPCK, 1982, 154-70.

_____. *Freedom and Obligation: A Study of the Epistle to the Galatians*. Philadelphia: Westminster, 1985.

_____. *The Acts of the Apostles*. 2 vols. ICC. Edinburgh: T & T Clark, 1998.

Bartchy, S. Scott. "Table Fellowship." *DJG*, 796-900.

Barth, Gerhard. *"pistis." EDNT*, 3.91-97.

Barth, Marcus. *Justification: Pauline Texts Interpreted in Light of the Old and New Testaments*. Grand Rapids: Eerdmans, 1971.

Barton, Stephen C. "Paul as Missionary and Pastor." *The Cambridge Companion to St Paul*. ed. J. D. G. Dunn. Cambridge: Cambridge University Press, 2003, 34-48.

Bassler, Jouette M. *God and Mammon: Asking for Money in the New Testament*. Nashville: Abingdon, 1991.

Bauckham, Richard J. "Barnabas in Galatians." *JSNT* 2 (1979): 61-71.

_____. "James and the Jerusalem Church." *The Book of Acts in Its First Century Setting. Volume 4: The Book of Acts in Its Palestinian Setting*. ed. Richard J. Bauckham. Grand Rapids: Eerdmans, 1995, 415-80.

Bayes, Jonathan F. *The Weakness of the Law: God's Law and the Christian in New Testament Perspective*. Paternoster Biblical and Theological Monographs. Carlisle: Paternoster, 2000.

Beale, G. K. "Isaiah VI 9-13: A Retributive Taunt against Idolatry." *VT* 41 (1991): 257-78.

_____. "Peace and Mercy Upon the Israel of God: The Old Testament Background of Galatians 6,16b." *Bib* 80 (1999): 204-223.

_____. ed. *The Right Doctrine from the Wrong Texts? Essays on the Use of the Old Testament in the New*. Grand Rapids: Baker, 1994.

_____. *The Temple and the Church's Mission: A Biblical Theology of the Dwelling Place of God*. New Studies in Biblical Theology 17. Downers Grove: InterVarsity, 2004.

_____. "The Old Testament Background of Paul's Reference to 'the Fruit of the Spirit' in Galatians 5:22." *BBR* 15 (2005): 1-38.

Beasley-Murray, G. R. *Jesus and the Kingdom of God*. Grand Rapids: Eerdmans, 1986.

Beker, J. Christiaan. *Paul the Apostle: The Triumph of God in Life and Thought*. Philadelphia: Fortress, 1980.

Belleville, Linda L. "'Under Law': Structural Analysis and the Pauline Concept of Law in Galatians 3:21-4:11." *JSNT* 26 (1986): 53-78.

Betz, Otto. "Jesus and the Temple Scroll." *Jesus and the Dead Sea Scrolls*. ed. James H. Charlesworth. New York: Doubleday, 1992, 75-103.

_____. and Dexinger, Ferdinand. "Beschneidung." *TRE*, 5.716-25.

Bickerman, Elias. *From Ezra to the Last of the Maccabees*. New York: Schocken, 1962.

Blomberg, Craig L. *Neither Poverty nor Riches: A Biblical Theology of Material Possessions*. New Studies in Biblical Theology. Grand Rapids: Eerdmans, 1999.

_____. *Contagious Holiness: Jesus' Meals with Sinners*. Downers Grove: InterVarsity, 2005.

Bockmuehl, Marcus. *Revelation and Mystery in Ancient Judaism and Pauline Christianity*. Grand Rapids: Eerdmans, 1990.

_____. *Jewish Law in Gentile Churches: Halakhah and the Beginning of Christian Public Ethics*. Edinburgh: T & T Clark, 2000.

Boda, Mark J. "Praying the Tradition: The Origin and Use of Tradition in Nehemiah 9." *TynBul* 48 (1997): 179-83.

_____. *Praying the Tradition: The Origin and Use of Tradition in Nehemiah 9*. BZAW 277. Berlin: de Gruyter, 1999.

BIBLIOGRAPHY

Boer, Willis P. de. *The Imitation of Paul: An Exegetical Study.* Kampen: Kok, 1962.

Boers, Hendrikus. *The Justification of the Gentiles: Paul's Letters to the Galatians and Romans.* Peabody: Hendrickson, 1994.

Bolt, Peter and Thompson, Mark, eds. *The Gospel to the Nations: Perspectives on Paul's Mission. In Honour of Peter T. O'Brien.* Leicester: Apollos, 2000.

Booth, Roger P. *Jesus and the Laws of Purity: Tradition History and Legal History in Mark 7.* JSNTSup 13. Sheffield: JSOT Press, 1986.

Borg, Markus J. *Conflict, Holiness, and Politics in the Teaching of Jesus.* 2nd ed. Harrisburg: Trinity Press International, 1998.

Borgen, Peder. "Paul Preaches Circumcision and Pleases Men." *Paul and Paulinism: Essays in Honour of C. K. Barrett.* eds. M. D. Hooker and S. G. Wilson. London: SPCK, 1982, 37-46.

Bornkamm, Günter. *Paul.* London: Hodder and Stoughton, 1971.

Brin, Gershon. *Studies in Biblical Law: From the Hebrew Bible to the Dead Sea Scrolls.* JSOTSup 176. Sheffield: Sheffield Academic Press, 1994.

Brinsmead, Bernard Hungerford. *Galatians—Dialogical Response to Opponents.* SBLDS 65. Chico: Scholars Press, 1982.

Brown, Raymond E. *The Death of the Messiah: From Gethsemane to the Grave. A Commentary on the Passion Narratives in the Four Gospels.* 2 vols. ABRL. New York: Doubleday, 1994.
_____. *An Introduction to the New Testament.* ABRL. New York: Doubleday, 1997.

Bruce, F. F. *The Spreading Flame: The Rise and Progress of Christianity from its First Beginnings to the Conversion of the English.* Exeter: Paternoster, 1958.
_____. "The Curse of the Law." *Paul and Paulinism: Essays in Honour of C. K. Barrett.* eds. M. D. Hooker and S. G. Wilson. London: SPCK, 1982, 27-36.

Bryan, Steven M. *Jesus and Israel's Traditions of Judgement and Restoration*. SNTSMS 117. Cambridge: Cambridge University Press, 2002.

Bryant, Robert A. *The Risen Crucified Christ in Galatians*. SBLDS 185. Atlanta: Society of Biblical Literature, 2001.

Byrne, Brendan. *'Sons of God'—'Seed of Abraham': A Study in the Idea of the Sonship of God of All Christians in Paul against the Jewish Background*. AnBib 83. Rome: Biblical Institute Press, 1979.

Calvert-Koyzis, Nancy J. "Abraham and Idolatry: Paul's Comparison of Obedience to the Law with Idolatry in Galatians 4.1-10." *Paul and the Scriptures of Israel*. eds. C. A. Evans and J. A. Sanders. JSNTSup 83. SSEJC 1. Sheffield: Sheffield Academic Press, 1993, 222-37.
_____. *Paul, Monotheism and the People of God: The Significance of Abraham Traditions for Early Judaism and Christianity*. JSNTSup 273. London: T & T Clark International, 2005.

Campbell, Douglas A. "The Story of Jesus in Romans and Galatians." *Narrative Dynamics in Paul: A Critical Assessment*. ed. Bruce W. Longenecker. Louisville: Westminster/John Knox, 2002, 97-124.

Carson, D. A. "The Vindication of Imputation: On Fields of Discourse and Semantic Discourse." *Justification: What's at Stake in the Current Debates?* eds. Mark Husbands and Daniel J. Treier. Downers Grove/Leicester: InterVarsity/Apollos, 2004, 46-78.
_____. and Moo, Douglas J. *An Introduction to the New Testament*. 2nd ed. Grand Rapids: Zondervan, 2005.
_____., O'Brien, Peter T. and Seifrid, Mark A. eds. *Justification and Variegated Nomism. Volume 1: The Complexities of Second Temple Judaism*. Grand Rapids: Baker, 2001.
_____., O'Brien, Peter T. and Seifrid, Mark A. eds. *Justification and Variegated Nomism. Volume 2: The Paradoxes of Paul*. Grand Rapids: Baker, 2004.
_____. "Mystery and Fulfillment: Toward a More Comprehensive Paradigm of Paul's Understanding of the Old and the New." *Justification and Variegated Nomism. Volume 2: The Paradoxes of Paul*. eds. D. A. Carson, Peter T. O'Brien and Mark A. Seifrid. Grand Rapids: Baker, 2004, 393-436.

BIBLIOGRAPHY

Carter, T. L. *Paul and the Power of Sin: Redefining 'Beyond the Pale'*. SNTSMS 115. Cambridge: Cambridge University Press, 2002.

Carter, Warren. *Matthew and Empire: Initial Explorations*. Harrisburg: Trinity Press International, 2001.

Chamblin, J. K. "Freedom/Liberty." *DPL*, 313-16.

Choi, Hung-Sik. "*PISTIS* in Galatians 5:5-6: Neglected Evidence for the Faithfulness of Christ." *JBL* 124 (2005): 467-90.

Christiansen, Ellen Juhl. *The Covenant in Judaism and Paul: A Study of Ritual Boundaries as Identity Markers*. AGJU 27. Leiden: Brill, 1995.

Ciampa, Roy E. *The Presence and Function of Scripture in Galatians 1 and 2*. WUNT 2/102. Tübingen: Mohr-Siebeck, 1998.

Clark, Gordon R. *The Word* Hesed *in the Hebrew Bible*. JSOTSup 157. Sheffield: Sheffield Academic Press, 1993.

Clements, Ronald. *Abraham and David: Genesis 15 and its Meaning for Israelite Tradition*. SBT 2/5. London: SCM, 1967.

Coenen, Lothar. "Church." *NIDNTT*, 1.291-307.

Collins, John J. "Chiasmus and the 'ABA' Pattern of the Text of Paul." *Studiorum Paulinorum Congressus Internationalis Catholicus*. 2 vols. AnBib 17-18. Rome: Biblical Institute Press, 1963, 2.575-83.

Cosgrove, Charles H. "The Law Has Given Sarah No Children (Gal 4:21-30)." *NovT* 29 (1987): 219-35.
_____. "Justification in Paul: A Linguistic and Theological Reflection." *JBL* 106 (1987): 653-70.
_____. *The Cross and the Spirit: A Study in the Argumentation and Theology of Galatians*. Macon: Mercer University Press, 1988.

Cousar, Charles B. *A Theology of the Cross: The Death of Jesus in the Pauline Letters*. Overtures to Biblical Theology. Minneapolis: Fortress, 1990.

Cranfield, C. E. B. "On the *Pistis Christou* Question." *On Romans and Other New Testament Essays*. Edinburgh: T & T Clark, 1998, 81-97.

Croft, Steven J. L. *The Identity of the Individual in the Psalms*. JSOTSup 44. Sheffield: Sheffield Academic Press, 1987.

Cross, Frank Moore, Jr. *The Ancient Library of Qumran*. 3rd ed. Sheffield: Sheffield Academic Press, 1995.

Crossan, John Dominic and Reed, Jonathan L. *In Search of Paul: How Jesus's Apostle Opposed Rome's Empire with God's Kingdom. A New Vision of Paul's Words and World*. San Francisco: HarperSanFrancisco, 2004.

Cullmann, Oscar. *Christ and Time: The Primitive Christian Conception of Time and History*. 2nd ed. Philadelphia: Westminster, 1964.

Cummins, Stephen Anthony. *Paul and the Crucified Christ in Antioch: Maccabean Martyrdom and Galatians 1 and 2*. SNTSMS 114. Cambridge: Cambridge University Press, 2001.

Dana, H. E. and Mantey, Julius R. *A Manual Grammar of the Greek New Testament*. New York: MacMillan, rep. 1955.

Das, A. Andrew. *Paul, the Law, and the Covenant*. Peabody: Hendrickson, 2001.
_____. *Paul and the Jews*. Peabody: Hendrickson, 2003.

Davies, Glenn N. *Faith and Obedience in Romans: A Study in Romans 1-4*. JSNTSup 39. Sheffield: Sheffield Academic Press, 1990.

Davies, W. D. *Torah in the Messianic Age and/or the Age to Come*. SBLMS 7. Philadelphia: Society of Biblical Literature, 1952.
_____. *Paul and Rabbinic Judaism: Some Rabbinic Elements in Pauline Theology*. 3rd ed. London: SCM, 1955.

_____. *The Gospel and the Land: Early Christianity and Jewish Territorial Doctrine.* Berkeley: University of California Press, 1974.

_____. "Paul: From the Jewish Point of View." *The Cambridge History of Judaism. Volume Three: The Early Roman Period.* eds. William Horbury, W. D. Davies and John Sturdy. Cambridge: Cambridge University Press, 1999, 678-730.

_____. *Christian Engagements with Judaism.* Harrisburg: Trinity Press International, 1999.

_____. and Allison, Dale. *Matthew.* 3 vols. ICC. Edinburgh: T & T Clark, 1988-97.

Davis, Anne. "Allegorically Speaking in Galatians 4:21-5:1." *BBR* 14 (2004): 161-74.

Davis, Basil S. "The Meaning of *Proegraphē* in the Context of Galatians 3.1." *NTS* 45 (1999): 194-212.

De Boer, Martinus. "Paul's Quotation of Isaiah 54.1 in Galatians 4.27." *NTS* 50 (2004): 370-89.

Deidun, T. J. *New Covenant Morality in Paul.* AnBib 89. Rome: Biblical Institute Press, 1981.

Derouchie, Jason S. "Circumcision in the Hebrew Bible and Targums: Theology, Rhetoric, and the Handling of Metaphor." *BBR* 14 (20040: 175-203.

Dempster, Stephen G. "Geography and Genealogy, Dominion and Dynasty: A Theology of the Hebrew Bible." *Biblical Theology: Retrospect and Prospect.* ed. Scott J. Hafemann. Downers Grove: InterVarsity, 2002, 66-82.

deSilva, David. *Introducing the Apocrypha: Message, Context, and Significance.* Grand Rapids: Baker, 2002.

_____. *An Introduction to the New Testament: Contexts, Methods and Ministry Formation.* Downers Grove: InterVarsity, 2004.

Dickson, John P. "Gospel as News: *euangel-* from Aristophanes to the Apostle Paul." *NTS* 51 (2005): 212-30.

Di Mattei, Steven. "Paul's Allegory of the Two Covenants (Gal 4.21-31) in Light of First-Century Hellenistic Rhetoric and Jewish Hermeneutics." *NTS* 52 (2006): 102-22.

Dodd, Brian. *Paul's Paradigmatic 'I': Personal Example as Literary Structure*. JSNTSup 177. Sheffield: Sheffield Academic Press, 1999.

Donaldson, Terence L. "The 'Curse of the Law' and the Inclusion of the Gentiles: Galatians 3.13-14." *NTS* 32 (1986): 94-112.
_____. "Zealot and Convert: The Origin of Paul's Christ-Torah Antithesis." *CBQ* 51 (1989): 655-82.
_____. "Zealot." *ISBE*. 2nd ed., 4.1175-79.
_____. *Paul and the Gentiles: Remapping the Apostle's Convictional World*. Minneapolis: Fortress, 1997.

Doty, William G. *Letters in Primitive Christianity*. GBS. Philadelphia: Fortress, 1973.

Downs, David J. "Paul's Collection and the Book of Acts Revisited." *NTS* 52 (2006): 50-70.

Dumbrell, William J. "Justification in Paul: A Covenantal Perspective." *RTR* 51 (1992): 91-101.

Dunn, James D. G. *Baptism in the Holy Spirit: A Re-Examination of the New Testament Teaching on the Gift of the Spirit in Relation to Pentecostalism Today*. SBT 2/15. London: SCM, 1970.
_____. *Jesus and the Spirit: A Study of the Religious and Charismatic Experience of Jesus and the First Christians as Reflected in the New Testament*. London: SCM, 1975.
_____. "Rom. 7,14-25 in the Theology of Paul." *TZ* 31 (1975): 264-73.
_____. *Unity and Diversity in the New Testament*. London: SCM, 1977.
_____. "The New Perspective on Paul." *BJRL* 65 (1983): 95-122.
_____. "Works of the Law and the Curse of the Law (Galatians 3.10-14)." *NTS* 31 (1985): 523-42.
_____. *Romans*. 2 vols. WBC 38 a, b. Dallas: Word, 1988.
_____. *Christology in the Making: An Inquiry into the Origins of the Doctrine of the Incarnation*. 2nd ed. London: SCM, 1989.

_____. *The Living Word.* Philadelphia: Fortress, 1987.

_____. *Jesus, Paul, and the Law: Studies in Mark and Galatians.* Louisville: Westminster/John Knox, 1990.

_____. "What was the Issue between Paul and 'Those of the Circumcision'?" *Paulus und das antike Judentum.* eds. Martin Hengel and Ulrich Heckel. Tübingen: Mohr-Siebeck, 1991, 295-317.

_____. "The Theology of Galatians: The Issue of Covenantal Nomism." *Pauline Theology. Volume 1: Thessalonians, Philippians, Galatians, Philemon.* ed. Jouette M. Bassler. Minneapolis: Fortress, 1991, 125-46.

_____. *The Partings of the Ways: Between Christianity and Judaism and Their Significance for the Character of Christianity.* London/Philadelphia: SCM/Trinity Press International, 1991.

_____. *Jesus' Call to Discipleship.* Understanding Jesus Today. Cambridge: Cambridge University Press, 1992.

_____. *The Theology of Paul's Letter to the Galatians.* New Testament Theology. Cambridge: Cambridge University Press, 1993.

_____. *Christian Liberty: A New Testament Perspective.* The Didsbury Lectures. Carlisle: Paternoster, 1993.

_____. "Judaism in the Land of Israel in the First Century." *Judaism in Late Antiquity Part 2: Historical Syntheses.* ed. Jacob Neusner. Leiden: Brill, 1995, 229-61.

_____. ed. *Paul and the Mosaic Law.* Grand Rapids: Eerdmans, 1996.

_____. "Neither Circumcision nor Uncircumcision, but..." (Gal 5:2-12; 6:12-16; cf. 1 Cor 7:17-20." *La foi agissant par l'amour.* ed. A Vanhoye. Rome: Abbaye de S. Paul, 1996, 79-110.

_____. "Once More, *PISTIS CHRISTOU.*" *Pauline Theology. Volume IV: Looking Back, Pressing On.* eds. E. Elizabeth Johnson and David M. Hay. SBLSymS 4. Atlanta: Scholars Press, 1997, 61-81.

_____. "4QMMT and Galatians." *NTS* 43 (1997): 147-53.

_____. "Paul's Conversion—A Light to Twentieth Century Disputes." *Evangelium, Schriftauslegung, Kirche: Festschrift für Peter Stuhlmacher zum 65. Geburtstag.* eds. Jostein Adna, Scott J. Hafemann and Otfried Hofius. Göttingen: Vandenhoeck & Ruprecht, 1997, 77-91.

_____. *The Theology of Paul the Apostle.* Grand Rapids: Eerdmans, 1998.

_____. *The Christ and the Spirit.* 2 vols. Grand Rapids: Eerdmans, 1998.

_____. "Paul: Apostate or Apostle of Israel? *ZNW* 89 (1998): 256-71.
_____. "Who Did Paul Think He Was? A Study of Jewish Christian Identity." *NTS* 45 (1999): 174-93.
_____. *Jesus Remembered. Christianity in the Making* 1. Grand Rapids: Eerdmans, 2003.
_____. *The New Perspective on Paul: Collected Essays*. WUNT 185. Tübingen: Mohr-Siebeck, 2005.

Eastman, Susan. "The Evil Eye and the Curse of the Law: Galatians 3.1 Revisited." *JSNT* 83 (2001): 69-87.

Ehrman, Bart D. *The New Testament: A Historical Introduction to the Early Christian Writings*. 2nd ed. New York/Oxford: Oxford University Press, 2000.

Eisenbaum, Pamela. "Paul as the New Abraham." *Paul and Politics: Ekklesia, Israel, Imperium, Interpretation. Essays in Honor of Krister Stendahl*. ed. Richard A. Horsley. Harrisburg: Trinity Press International, 2000, 130-45.

Elliott, J. K. "The Use of *Heteros* in the New Testament." *ZNW* 60 (1969): 140-41.

Elliott, Mark Adam. *The Survivors of Israel: A Reconsideration of the Theology of Pre-Christian Judaism*. Grand Rapids: Eerdmans, 2000.

Elliott, Susan, M. "Choose Your Mother, Choose Your Master: Galatians 4:21-5:1 in the Shadow of the Anatolian Mother of Gods." *JBL* 118 (1999): 661-83.
_____. *Cutting Too Close for Comfort: Paul's Letter to the Galatians in Its Anatolian Cultic Context*. JSNTSup 248. London/New York: T & T Clark International, 2003.

Ellis, E. E. *Paul's Use of the Old Testament*. Edinburgh: Oliver & Boyd, 1957.
_____. *Prophecy and Hermeneutic in Early Christianity*. Grand Rapids: Baker, 1993.
_____. *The Old Testament in Early Christianity: Canon and Interpretation in the Light of Modern Research*. Grand Rapids: Baker, 1992.

Engberg-Pedersen, Troels. "Paul, Virtues, and Vices." *Paul in the Greco-Roman World: A Handbook*. ed. J. Paul Sampley. Harrisburg: Trinity Press International, 2003, 608-33.

Enns, Peter. *Inspiration and Incarnation: Evangelicals and the Problem of the Old Testament*. Grand Rapids: Baker, 2005.

Erickson, R. J. "Flesh." *DPL*, 303-6.

Esler, Philip F. *Community and Gospel in Luke-Acts: The Social and Political Motivations of Lucan Theology*. SNTSMS 57. Cambridge: Cambridge University Press, 1987.
_____. *Galatians*. New Testament Readings. London: Routledge, 1998.

Evans, Craig A. *Noncanonical Writings and New Testament Interpretation*. Peabody: Hendrickson, 1992.
_____. "Predictions of the Destruction of the Herodian Temple in the Pseudepigrapha, Qumran Scrolls, and Related Texts." *Qumran Questions*. ed. James H. Charlesworth. The Biblical Seminar 36. Sheffield: Sheffield Academic Press, 1995, 92-150.
_____. and J. A. Sanders, eds. *Paul and the Scriptures of Israel*. JSNTSup 83. Studies in Scripture in Early Judaism and Christianity 1. Sheffield: Sheffield Academic Press, 1993.
_____. "Jesus and the Continuing Exile of Israel." *Jesus and the Restoration of Israel: A Critical Assessment of N. T. Wright's Jesus and the Victory of God*. ed. Carey C. Newman. Downers Grove: InterVarsity, 1999, 77-100.

Faber, Riemer A. "The Juridical Nuance in the NT Use of *Prosōpolēmpsia*." *WTJ* 57 (1995): 299-309.

Fairchild, Mark R. "Paul's Pre-Christian Zealot Associations: A Reexamination of Gal 1.14 and Acts 22.3." *NTS* 45 (1999): 514-32.

Fee, Gordon D. *God's Empowering Presence: The Holy Spirit in the Letters of Paul*. Peabody: Hendrickson, 1994.
_____. *Paul, the Spirit, and the People of God*. Peabody: Hendrickson, 1996.
_____. *To What End Exegesis? Essays Textual, Exegetical, and Theological*. Grand Rapids: Eerdmans, 2001.

Feuillet, André. "Le plan salvifique de Dieu d'apres l'Épître aux Romains." *RB* 57 (1950): 336-87, 489-529.

Finlan, Stephen. *The Background and Content of Paul's Cultic Atonement Metaphors*. SBL Academia Biblica 19. Atlanta/Leiden: Society of Biblical Literature/Brill, 2004.

Fiore, Benjamin. "Paul, Exemplification, and Imitation." *Paul in the Greco-Roman World: A Handbook*. ed. J. Paul Sampley. Harrisburg: Trinity Press International, 2003, 228-57.

Fitzgerald, John T. "Paul and Friendship." *Paul in the Greco-Roman World: A Handbook*. ed. J. Paul Sampley. Harrisburg: Trinity Press International, 2003, 319-43.

Fitzmyer, Joseph A. *Pauline Theology: A Brief Sketch*. Englewood Cliffs: Prentice-Hall, 1967.
_____. "Crucifixion in Ancient Palestine, Qumran Literature, and the New Testament." *CBQ* 40 (1978): 493-513.
_____. "The Biblical Basis of Justification by Faith: Comments on the Essay of Professor Reumann," in John Reumann, *Righteousness in the New Testament: "Justification" in the United States Lutheran-Roman Catholic Dialogue, with Responses by Joseph A. Fitzmyer and Jerome D. Quinn*. Philadelphia: Fortress, 1982, 193-227.
_____. *According to Paul: Studies in the Theology of the Apostle*. New York: Paulist Press, 1993.
_____. "Paul and the Dead Sea Scrolls." *The Dead Sea Scrolls After Fifty Years: A Comprehensive Assessment*. eds. Peter W. Flint and James C. Vanderkam. 2 vols. Leiden: Brill, 1998-99, 2.599-621.

Forbes, Christopher. "Paul and Rhetorical Comparison." *Paul in the Greco-Roman World: A Handbook*. ed. J. Paul Sampley. Harrisburg: Trinity Press International, 2003, 134-71.

Foster, Paul. "The First Contribution to the *Pistis Christou* Debate: A Study of Ephesians 3.12." *JSNT* 85 (2002): 75-96.

Foulkes, Francis. *The Acts of God: A Study of the Basis of Typology in the Old Testament*. London: Tyndale, 1955.

France, R. T. *Jesus and the Old Testament: His Application of Old Passages to Himself and His Mission*. London: IVP, 1971.

Franklin, Eric. *Christ the Lord: A Study in the Purpose and Theology of Luke-Acts*. Philadelphia: Westminster, 1975.

Fredrickson, David E. "Paul, Hardships, and Suffering." *Paul in the Greco-Roman World: A Handbook*. ed. J. Paul Sampley. Harrisburg: Trinity Press International, 2003, 172-97.

Fredriksen, Paula. "Judaism, The Circumcision of Gentiles, and Apocalyptic Hope: Another Look at Galatians 1 and 2." *The Galatians Debate: Contemporary Issues in Rhetorical and Historical Interpretation*. ed. Mark D. Nanos. Peabody: Hendrickson, 2002, 235-60.

Fridrichsen, Anton. *The Apostle and His Message*. Uppsala Universitets Årsskrift 3. Uppsala: A. B. Lundequistka, 1947.

Furnish, Victor Paul. *Theology and Ethics in Paul*. Nashville: Abingdon, 1968.

_____. *The Love Command in the New Testament*. Nashville: Abingdon, 1972.

Gärtner, Bertil. *The Temple and the Community in Qumran and the New Testament: A Comparative Study in the Temple Symbolism of the Qumran Texts and the New Testament*. SNTSMS 1. Cambridge: Cambridge University Press, 1965.

Gaffin, Richard B. *Resurrection and Redemption: A Study in Paul's Soteriology*. 2nd ed. Phillipsburg, NJ: Presbyterian & Reformed, 1987.

Garland, David E. *The Intention of Matthew 23*. NovTSup 52. Leiden: Brill, 1979.

_____. "Paul's Defense of the Truth of the Gospel Regarding Gentiles (Galatians 2:15-3:22)." *RevExp* 91 (1994): 165-81.

Garlington, Don. *'The Obedience of Faith': A Pauline Phrase in Historical Context*. WUNT 2/38. Tübingen: Mohr-Siebeck, 1991.

_____. *Faith, Obedience, and Perseverance: Aspects of Paul's Letter to the Romans*. WUNT 79. Tübingen: Mohr-Siebeck, 1994.

_____. "Righteousness." *New Dictionary of Christian Ethics and Pastoral Theology*. eds. David Atkinson, et al. Leicester: Inter-Varsity, 1995, 743-45.

_____. "Burden Bearing and the Recovery of Offending Christians (Galatians 6:1-5)." *TrinJ* ns 12 (1991): 151-83.

_____. "Oath-Taking in the Community of the New Age (Matthew 5:33-37)." *TrinJ* ns 16 (1995): 139-70.

_____. "Role Reversal and Paul's Use of Scripture in Galatians 3.10-13." *JSNT* 65 (1997): 85-121.

_____. "A Review Article: Jerome H. Neyrey, *Paul, in Other Words: A Cultural Reading of His Letters*." *Baptist Review of Theology* 4 (1994): 83-91.

_____. *Exegetical Essays*. Eugene, OR: Wipf & Stock. 3rd ed. 2003.

_____. "The New Perspective on Paul: An Appraisal Two Decades Later." *Criswell Theological Review* ns 2, no. 2 (2005): 17-38.

_____. *In Defense of the New Perspective on Paul: Essays and Reviews*. Eugene, OR: Wipf & Stock, 2005.

_____. "A 'New Perspective' Reading of Central Texts in Romans 1-4." http://www.thepaulpage.com.

_____. "Paul's 'Partisan *ek*' and the Question of Justification in Galatians," forthcoming.

Gaston, Lloyd. "Paul and the Law in Galatians 2-3." *Anti-Judaism in Early Christianity. Volume 1: Paul and the Gospels*. eds. Peter Richardson and David Granskou. Waterloo, ON: Wilfrid Laurier University Press, 1986, 37-57.

Gathercole, Simon J. *Where is Boasting? Early Jewish Soteriology and Paul's Response in Romans 1-5*. Grand Rapids: Eerdmans, 2002.

_____. "Torah, Life and Salvation: The Use of Leviticus 18:5 in Early Judaism and Christianity." *From Prophecy to Testament: The Function of the Old Testament in the New*. ed. C. A. Evans. Peabody: Hendrickson, 2004, 126-145.

Gaventa, Beverly R. "Galatians 1 and 2: Autobiography as Paradigm." *NovT* 28 (1986): 309-26.

_____. "The Maternity of Paul: An Exegetical Study of Galatians 4:19." *The Conversation Continues: Studies in Paul and John in Honor of J. Louis Martyn*. eds. Robert T. Fortna and Beverly R. Gaventa. Nashville: Abingdon, 1990, 189-201.

_____. "The Singularity of the Gospel: A Reading of Galatians." *Pauline Theology. Volume 1: Thessalonians, Philippians, Galatians, Philemon.* ed. Jouette M. Bassler. Minneapolis: Fortress, 1991, 147-59.

Georgi, Dieter. *Remembering the Poor: The History of Paul's Collection for Jerusalem.* Nashville: Abingdon, 1992.

Glueck, Nelson. Hesed *in the Bible.* New York: KTAV, 1975.

Goppelt, Leonhard. *Typos: The Typological Interpretation of the Old Testament in the New.* Grand Rapids: Eerdmans, 1982.

Gordon, T. David. "A Note on *PAIDAGOGOS* in Galatians 3.24-25." *NTS* 35 (1989): 150-54.
_____. "The Problem at Galatia." *Int* 41 (1987): 32-43.

Gorman, Michael J. *Cruciformity: Paul's Narrative Spirituality of the Cross.* Grand Rapids: Eerdmans, 2001.
_____. *Apostle of the Crucified Lord: A Theological Introduction to Paul and His Letters.* Grand Rapids: Eerdmans, 2004.

Gowan, Donald E. *Eschatology in the Old Testament.* Philadelphia: Fortress, 1986.
_____. *Theology of The Prophetic Books: The Death and Resurrection of Israel.* Louisville: Westminster/John Knox, 1998.

Green, Joel B. "Crucifixion." *DPL*, 197-99.
_____. "Death of Jesus." *DJG*, 146-63.

Gundry, Robert H. "The Nonimputation of Christ's Righteousness." *Justification: What's at Stake in the Current Debates?* eds. Mark Husbands and Daniel J. Treier. Downers Grove Leicester: InterVarsity/Apollos, 2004, 17-45.

Gundry Volf, Judith M. *Paul and Perseverance: Staying in and Falling Away.* Louisville: Westminster/John Knox, 1990.

Gunther, John J. *St. Paul's Opponents and Their Background: A Study of Apocalyptic and Jewish Sectarian Teachings.* NovTSup 35. Leiden: Brill, 1973.

Guthrie, Donald. *New Testament Introduction.* Downers Grove: InterVarsity, 1970.

Hafemann, Scott J. *Paul, Moses, and the History of Israel: The Letter/Spirit Contrast and the Argument from Scripture in 2 Corinthians 3.* Peabody: Hendrickson, 1995.
_____. "Paul and the Exile of Israel in Galatians 3-4." *Exile: Old Testament, Jewish, and Christian Conceptions.* ed. James M. Scott. Supplements to the Journal for the Study of Judaism 56. Leiden: Brill, 1997, 329-71.
_____. "The Spirit of the New Covenant, the Law, and the Temple of God's Presence: Five Theses on Qumran Self-Understanding and the Contours of Paul's Thought." *Evangelium, Schriftauslegung, Kirche: Festschrift für Peter Stuhlmacher zum 65. Geburtstag.* eds. Jostein Adna, Scott J. Hafemann and Otfried Hofius. Göttingen: Vandenhoeck & Ruprecht, 1997, 172-89.
_____. "'Because of Weakness' (Galatians 4:13): The Role of Suffering in the Mission of Paul." *The Gospel to the Nations: Perspectives on Paul's Mission. In Honour of Peter T. O'Brien.* eds. Peter Bolt and Mark Thompson. Leicester: Apollos, 2000, 131-46.
_____. *2 Corinthians.* NIV Application Commentary. Grand Rapids: Zondervan, 2000.

Hahn, Scott. "Covenant Oath and the Aqedah: *Diathēkē* in Galatians 3:15-18." *CBQ* 67 (2005): 79-100.

Hall, Robert G. "Arguing like an Apocalypse: Galatians and Ancient *Topos* outside the Greco-Roman Rhetorical Tradition." *NTS* 42 (1996): 434-53.

Hansen, G. Walter. *Abraham in Galatians: Epistolary and Rhetorical Contexts.* JSNTSup 29. Sheffield: JSOT Press, 1989.
_____. "Galatians, Letter to the." *DPL*, 323-34.
_____. "A Paradigm of the Apocalypse: The Gospel in the Light of Epistolary Analysis." *The Galatians Debate: Contemporary Issues in Rhetorical and Historical Interpretation.* ed. Mark D. Nanos. Peabody: Hendrickson, 2002, 143-54.

Harland, Philip A. "Familial Dimensions of Group Identity: 'Brothers' (*ADELPHOI*) in Associations of the Greek East." *JBL* 124 (2005): 491-513.

Harrill, J. Albert. "Paul and Slavery." *Paul in the Greco-Roman World: A Handbook.* ed. J. Paul Sampley. Harrisburg: Trinity Press International, 2003, 575-607.

Harris, Douglas J. *Shalom! The Biblical Concept of Peace.* Grand Rapids: Baker, 1970.

Harris, Murray J. *Jesus as God: The New Testament Use of Theos in Reference to Jesus.* Grand Rapids: Baker, 1992.
_____. *Slave of Christ: A New Testament Metaphor for Total Devotion to Christ.* New Studies in Biblical Theology 8. Downers Grove: Apollos, 1999.

Hartman, Lars. *'Into the Name of the Lord Jesus': Baptism in the Early Church.* SNTW. Edinburgh: T & T Clark, 1997.

Harvey, Graham. *The True Israel: Uses of the Names Jew, Hebrew and Israel in Ancient Jewish Literature and Early Christian Literature.* AGJU 35. Leiden: Brill, 1996.

Hauck, Friedrich and Bammel, Ernst. "*ptōchos.*" *TDNT*, 6.888-915.

Hays, J. Daniel. *From Every People and Nation: A Biblical Theology of Race.* New Studies in Biblical Theology 14. Downers Grove: Apollos, 2003.

Hays, Richard B. *The Faith of Jesus Christ: An Investigation of the Narrative Substructure of Galatians 3:1-4:11.* The Biblical Resource Series. 2nd ed. Grand Rapids: Eerdmans, 2002.
_____. "Christology and Ethics in Galatians: The Law of Christ." *CBQ* 49 (1987): 268-90.
_____. *Echoes of Scripture in the Letters of Paul.* New Haven: Yale University Press, 1989.
_____. "Notes on Galatians." *The HarperCollins Study Bible: New Revised Standard Version.* eds. Wayne A. Meeks, et al. New York: HarperCollins, 1993.
_____. "*PISTIS* and Pauline Christology: What Is at Stake?" *Pauline Theology. Volume IV: Looking Back, Pressing On.* eds. E. Elizabeth Johnson and David M. Hay. SBLSymS 4. Atlanta: Scholars Press, 1997, 35-60.
_____. "Justification." *ABD*, 3.1129-33.

———————. *The Conversion of the Imagination: Paul as Interpreter of Israel's Scripture*. Grand Rapids: Eerdmans, 2005.

Heiland, Hans-Wolfgang. *Die Anrechnung des Glaubens zur Gerechtigkeit: Untersuchungen zur Begriffsbestimmung von* hasab *und* logizesthai. BWANT 18. Stuttgart: Kohlhammer, 1936.
———————. "logizomai, logismos." *TDNT*, 4.284-92.

Hengel, Martin. *Judaism and Hellenism: Studies in Their Encounter in Palestine During the Early Hellenistic Period*. 2 vols. London: SCM, 1974.
———————. *Crucifixion: In the Ancient World and the Folly of the Message of the Cross*. Philadelphia: Fortress, 1977.
———————. *The Atonement: The Origins of the Doctrine in the New Testament*. Philadelphia: Fortress, 1981.
———————. *The Zealots: Investigations into the Jewish Freedom Movement in the Period from Herod I until 70 A.D.* Edinburgh: T & T Clark, 1989.
———————. *The Pre-Christian Paul*. London/Philadelphia: SCM/Trinity Press International, 1991.
———————. "The Stance of the Apostle Paul Toward the Law in the Unknown Years Between Damascus and Antioch." *Justification and Variegated Nomism. Volume 2: The Paradoxes of Paul*. eds. D. A. Carson, Peter T. O'Brien and Mark A. Seifrid. Grand Rapids: Baker, 2004, 75-103.
———————. and Schwemer, Anna Maria. *Paul Between Damascus and Antioch: The Unknown Years*. Louisville: Westminster/Knox, 1997.

Herbert, A. G. *The Throne of David: A Study of the Fulfilment of the Old Testament in Jesus Christ and His Church*. London: Faber, 1941.

Hess, Richard S. and Wenham, Gordon J., eds. *Zion: City of Our God*. Grand Rapids: Eerdmans, 1999.

Hester, James. "The Rhetorical Structure of Galatians 1:11-2:14." *JBL* (1984): 233-33.

Hill, David. *Greek Words and Hebrew Meanings: Studies in the Semantics of Soteriological Terms*. SNTSMS 5. Cambridge: Cambridge University Press, 1967.

Hillers, Delbert R. *Covenant: The History of a Biblical Idea.* Baltimore: The Johns Hopkins Press, 1969.

Hoch, Carl B., Jr. *All Things New: The Significance of Newness for Biblical Theology.* Grand Rapids: Baker, 1995.

Hoffman, Lawrence A. *Covenant of Blood: Circumcision and Gender in Rabbinic Judaism.* Chicago: University of Chicago Press, 1996.

Hofius, Otfried. "Paulus—Missionar und Theologe." *Evangelium, Schriftauslegung, Kirche: Festschrift für Peter Stuhlmacher zum 65. Geburtstag.* eds. Jostein Adna, Scott J. Hafemann and Otfried Hofius. Göttingen: Vandenhoeck & Ruprecht, 1997, 224-37.

Hooker, Morna D. *"PISTIS CHRISTOU."* NTS 35 (1989): 321-42.

Holmén, Tom. *Jesus and Jewish Covenant Thinking.* Biblical Interpretation Series 55. Leiden: Brill, 2001.

Hoppe, Lester J. *Being Poor: A Biblical Study.* Good News Studies. Wilmington: Glazier, 1987.

Horsley, Richard A., ed. *Paul and Empire: Religion and Power in Roman Imperial Society.* Harrisburg: Trinity Press International, 1997.
_____. ed. *Paul and Politics: Ekklesia, Israel, Imperium, Interpretation. Essays in Honor of Krister Stendahl.* Harrisburg: Trinity Press International, 2000.
_____. ed. *Paul and the Roman Imperial Order.* Harrisburg: Trinity Press International, 2004.

Howard, George. *Paul: Crisis in Galatia: A Study in Early Christian Theology.* 2nd ed. SNTSMS 35. Cambridge: Cambridge University Press, 1979.

Hubbard, Moyer V. *New Creation in Paul's Letters and Thought.* SNTSMS 119. Cambridge: Cambridge University Press, 2002.

Hultgren, Arland J. *Paul's Gospel and Mission.* Philadelphia: Fortress, 1985.
_____. "The *Pistis Christou* Formulation in Paul." *NovT* 22 (1980): 248-63.

Hurtado, Larry W. "The Jerusalem Collection and the Book of Galatians." *JSNT* 5 (1979): 46-62.

_____. *Lord Jesus Christ: Devotion to Jesus in Earliest Christianity*. Grand Rapids: Eerdmans, 2003.

Jeremias, Joachim. "Zur Gedankenführung in den paulinischen Briefen." *Abba: Studien zur Neutestamentlichen Theologie und Zeitgeschichte*. Göttingen: Vandenhoeck & Ruprecht, 1966, 269-76.

_____. Chiasmus in den Paulusbriefen." *Abba: Studien zur Neutestamentlichen Theologie und Zeitgeschichte*. Göttingen: Vandenhoeck & Ruprecht, 1966, 276-90.

_____. *New Testament Theology: The Proclamation of Jesus*. New York: Charles Scribner's Sons, 1971.

_____. *The Prayers of Jesus*. SBT 2/6. Naperville: Allenson, 1967.

Jewett, Robert. *Paul's Anthropological Terms: A Study of Their Use in Conflict Settings*. AGJU 10. Leiden: Brill, 1971.

_____. "The Agitators and the Galatian Congregation." *NTS* 17 (1970-71): 198-212.

_____. "Paul, Shame, and Honor." *Paul in the Greco-Roman World: A Handbook*. ed. J. Paul Sampley. Harrisburg: Trinity Press International, 2003, 551-74.

Jobes, Karen. "Jerusalem, Our Mother: Metalepsis and Intertextuality in Galatians 4:21-31." *WTJ* 55 (1993): 299-320.

Johnson, E. Elizabeth and Hay, David M., eds. *Pauline Theology. Volume IV: Looking Back, Pressing On*. SBLSymS 4. Atlanta: Scholars Press, 1997.

Johnson, Luke Timothy. *The Writings of the New Testament: An Interpretation*. 2nd ed. Minneapolis: Fortress, 1999.

Joubert, Stephan. *Paul as Benefactor: Reciprocity, Strategy and Theological Reflection in Paul's Collection*. WUNT 2/124. Tübingen: Mohr-Siebeck, 2000.

Käsemann, Ernst. "'The Righteousness of God' in Paul." *New Testament Questions of Today*. Philadelphia: Fortress, 1969, 168-82.

Kahl, Brigitte. "Hagar Between Genesis and Galatians: The Stony Road to Freedom." *From Prophecy to Testament: The Function of the Old Testament in the New*. ed. C. A. Evans. Peabody: Hendrickson, 2004, 219-32.

Kaminsky, Joel S. *Corporate Responsibility in the Hebrew Bible*. JSNTSup 196. Sheffield: Sheffield Academic Press, 1995.

Kampen, John. *The Hasideans and the Origin of Pharisaism: A Study of 1 and 2 Maccabees*. SBLSCS 24. Atlanta: Scholars Press, 1988.

_____. and Bernstein, Moshe J., eds. *Reading 4QMMT: New Perspectives on Qumran Law and History*. SBLSymS 2. Atlanta: Scholars Press, 1996.

Keck, Leander. "The Poor among the Saints in the New Testament." *ZNW* 56 (1965): 100-29.

Keesmaat, Sylvia C. *Paul and His Story: (Re)Interpreting the Exodus Tradition*. JSNTSup 181. Sheffield: Sheffield Academic Press, 1999.

Kern, Philip. *Rhetoric and Galatians: Assessing an Approach to Paul's Epistle*. SNTSMS 101. Cambridge: Cambridge University Press, 1998.

Kerrigan, Alexander. "Echoes of Themes from the Servant Songs in Pauline Theology." *Studiorum Paulinorum Congressus Internationalis Catholicus*. 2 vols. AnBib 17-18. Rome: Pontifical Institute, 1963, 2.217-28.

Kertelge, Karl. *"Rechtfertigung" bei Paulus: Studien zur Struktur und zum Bedeutungsgehalt des paulinischen Rechfertigungsbegriffs*. NTAbh 3. 2nd ed. Münster: Aschendorff, 1967.

Kilgallen, John. *The Stephen Speech: A Literary and Redactional Study of Acts 7,2-53*. AnBib 67. Rome: Biblical Institute Press, 1976.

Kilpatrick, G. D. "Galatians 1:18 *HISTORESAI KEPHAN*." *New Testament Essays: Studies in Memory of Thomas Walter Manson*. ed. A. J. B. Higgins. Manchester: Manchester University Press, 1959, 144-49.

Kim, Jung. *The Significance of Clothing Imagery in the Pauline Corpus*. JSNTSup 268. London: T & T Clark International, 2004.

Kim, Seyoon. *The Origin of Paul's Gospel*. WUNT 2/4. Tübingen: Mohr-Siebeck, 1981.
_____. *Paul and the New Perspective: Second Thoughts on the Origins of Paul's Gospel*. Grand Rapids: Eerdmans, 2002.

Klaiber, Walter. *Gerecht vor Gott: Rechtfertigung in der Bibel and Heute*. Biblisch-theologische Schwerpunkte 20. Göttingen: Vandenhoeck & Ruprecht, 2000.

Kline, Meredith G. *The Treaty of the Great King: The Covenant Structure of Deuteronomy. Studies and Commentary*. Grand Rapids: Eerdmans, 1963.
_____. *By Oath Consigned: A Reinterpretation of the Covenant Signs of Circumcision and Baptism*. Grand Rapids: Eerdmans, 1968.

Knibb, Michael. "The Exile in the Literature of the Intertestamental Period." *HeyJ* 17 (1976): 253-72.
_____. "Exile in the Damascus Document." *JSOT* 25 (1983): 99-117.

Koch, Dietrich-Alex. *Die Schrift als Zeuge des Evangeliums: Untersuchungen zur Verwendung und zum Verständnis der Schrift bei Paulus*. BHT 69. Tübingen: Mohr-Siebeck, 1986.

Köstenberger, Andreas J. and O'Brien, Peter T. *Salvation to the Ends of the Earth: A Biblical Theology of Mission*. New Studies in Biblical Theology 11. Downers Grove: Apollos, 2001.

Koperski, Veronica. *What Are They Saying About Paul and the Law?* New York: Paulist Press, 2001.

Kraus, Hans-Joachim. *Theology of the Psalms*. Minneapolis: Augsburg, 1986.

Kraybill, J. Nelson. *Imperial Cult and Commerce in John's Apocalypse*. JSNTSup 132. Sheffield: Sheffield Academic Press, 1996.

Kruse, Colin G. *Paul, the Law, and Justification*. Peabody: Hendrickson, 1996.

Kuula, Kari. *The Law, The Covenant and God's Plan. Volume 1. Paul's Polemical Treatment of the Law in Galatians*. Publications of the Finnish Exegetical Society 72. Helsinki/Göttingen: Finnish Exegetical Society/Vandenhoeck & Ruprecht, 1999.

Kwakkel, Gert. *According to My Righteousness: Upright Behaviour as Grounds for Deliverance in Psalms 7, 17, 18, 26, and 44*. *OTS* 46. Leiden: Brill, 2002.

Lambrecht, Jan. "Paul's Reasoning in Galatians 2:11-21." *Paul and the Mosaic Law*. ed. J. D. G. Dunn. Grand Rapids: Eerdmans, 1996, 53-74.

LaSor, W. S. "The *Sensus Plenior* and Biblical Interpretation." *A Guide to Contemporary Hermeneutics: Major Trends in Biblical Interpretation*. ed. D. K. McKim. Grand Rapids: Eerdmans, 1986, 47-64

Lincoln, Andrew T. *Paradise Now and Not Yet: Studies in the Role of the Heavenly Dimension in Paul's Thought with Special Reference to His Eschatology*. SNTSMS 43. Cambridge: Cambridge University Press, 1981.

_____. "Sabbath, Rest, and Eschatology in the New Testament." *From Sabbath to Lord's Day: A Biblical, Historical, and Theological Investigation*. ed. D. A. Carson. Grand Rapids: Zondervan, 1982, 197-220.

Longenecker, Bruce W. "Defining the Faithful Character of the Covenant Community: Galatians 2.15-21 and Beyond: A Response to Jan Lambrecht." *Paul and the Mosaic Law*. ed. J. D. G. Dunn. Grand Rapids: Eerdmans, 1996, 75-97.

_____. *The Triumph of Abraham's God: The Transformation of Identity in Galatians*. Nashville: Abingdon, 1998.

_____. ed. *Narrative Dynamics in Paul: A Critical Assessment*. Louisville: Westminster/John Knox, 2002.

Longenecker, Richard N. *Paul: Apostle of Liberty*. New York: Harper & Row, 1964.

_____. *Biblical Exegesis in the Apostolic Period*. 2nd ed. Grand Rapids: Eerdmans, 1999.

_____. "Graphic Illustrations of a Believer's New Life in Christ: Galatians 4:21-31." *RevExp* 91 (1994): 183-99.

_____. ed. *The Road from Damascus: The Impact of Paul's Conversion on His Life, Thought, and Ministry*. Grand Rapids: Eerdmans, 1997.

Lüdemann, Gerd. *Paul: Apostle to the Gentiles. Studies in Chronology*. Philadelphia: Fortress, 1984.

Lull, David John. *The Spirit in Galatia: Paul's Interpretation of Pneuma as Divine Power*. SBLDS 49. Chico: Scholars Press, 1980.

_____. "'The Law was our Pedagogue': A Study in Galatians 3:19-25." *JBL* 105 (1986): 481-98.

Lyonnet, Stanislas and Sabourin, Leopold. *Sin, Redemption, and Sacrifice: A Biblical and Patristic Study*. AnBib 48. Rome: Biblical Institute Press, 1970.

Lyons, George. *Pauline Autobiography: Toward a New Understanding*. SBLDS 73. Atlanta: Scholars Press, 1985.

McGrath, Alister E. *Studies in Doctrine*. Grand Rapids: Zondervan, 1997.

_____. "Justification." *DPL*, 517-23.

McKelvey, R. J. *The New Temple: The Church in the New Testament*. Oxford: Oxford University Press, 1969.

McKnight, Scot. *A Light Among the Gentiles: Jewish Missionary Activity in the Second Temple Period*. Minneapolis: Fortress, 1991.

_____. "The Warning Passages of Hebrews: A Formal Analysis and Theological Conclusions." *TrinJ* ns 13 (1992): 21-59.

_____. *A New Vision for Israel: The Teachings of Jesus in National Context*. Grand Rapids: Eerdmans, 1999.

_____. "Collection for the Saints." *DPL*, 143-47.

_____. "Jesus and the Twelve." *BBR* 11 (2001): 203-31.

_____. *Jesus and His Death: Historiography, the Historical Jesus, and Atonement Theory*. Waco: Baylor University Press, 2005.

McLean, B. Hudson. *The Cursed Christ: Mediterranean Expulsion Rituals and Pauline Soteriology*. JSNTSup 126. Sheffield: Sheffield Academic Press, 1996.

Malina, Bruce J. and Neyrey, Jerome H. *Portraits of Paul: An Archaeology of Ancient Personality*. Louisville: Westminster/John Knox, 1996.

Marshall, I. Howard. *New Testament Theology: Many Witnesses, One Gospel*. Downers Grove: InterVarsity, 2004.

Martinez, Florentino Garcia. *The Dead Sea Scrolls Translated: The Qumran Texts in English*. Leiden: Brill, 1994.

Matera, Frank J. "The Culmination of Paul's Argument to the Galatians: Gal. 5.1-6.17." *JSNT* 32 (1988): 79-91.

Martin, Dale B. *Salvation as Slavery: The Metaphor of Slavery in Pauline Christianity*. New Haven: Yale University Press, 1990.

Martin, Troy. "The Covenant of Circumcision (Genesis 17:9-14) and the Situational Antitheses in Galatians 3:28." *JBL* 122 (2003): 111-25.

_____. "Apostasy to Paganism: The Rhetorical Stasis of the Galatian Controversy." *The Galatians Debate: Contemporary Issues in Rhetorical and Historical Interpretation*. ed. Mark D. Nanos. Peabody: Hendrickson, 2002, 73-94.

_____. "Whose Flesh? What Temptation? (Galatians 4.13-14)." *JSNT* 74 (1999): 87-89.

Martin, Ralph P. *New Testament Foundations: A Guide for Christian Students*. 2 vols. Grand Rapids: Eerdmans, 1975, 1978.

Matlock, R. Barry. *Unveiling the Apocalyptic Paul: Paul's Interpreters and the Rhetoric of Criticism*. JSNTSup 127. Sheffield: Sheffield Academic Press, 1996.

Martyn, J. Louis. *Theological Issues in the Letters of Paul*. Nashville: Abingdon, 1997.

_____. "Events in Galatia: Modified Covenantal Nomism Versus God's Invasion of the Cosmos in the Singular Gospel: A Response to J. D. G. Dunn and B. R. Gaventa." *Pauline Theology*.

Volume 1: Thessalonians, Philippians, Galatians, Philemon. ed. Jouette M. Bassler. Minneapolis: Fortress, 1991, 160-79.

Mason, Steve. *Flavius Josephus on the Pharisees: A Composition-Critical Study.* Leiden: Brill, 2001.

Mearns, Chris. "The Identity of Paul's Opponents at Philippi." *NTS* 33 (1987): 194-204.

Metzger, Bruce. *An Introduction to the Apocrypha.* New York: Oxford University Press, 1957.

Millar, Fergus. *The Roman Near East: 31 BC-AD 337.* Cambridge, Mass: Harvard University Press, 1993.

Montefiore, C. G. and Loewe, H. *A Rabbinic Anthology.* New York: Schocken, rep. 1974.

Moo, Douglas J. "The Problem of *Sensus Plenior.*" *Hermeneutics, Authority, and Canon.* eds. D. A Carson and J. D. Woodbridge. Grand Rapids: Zondervan, 1986), 175-211.
_____. *The Epistle to the Romans.* NICNT. Grand Rapids: Eerdmans, 1996.

Moore, George Foot. *Judaism in the First Centuries of the Christian Era.* 3 vols. Cambridge, Mass: Harvard University Press, rep. 1966.

Morland, Kjell Arne. *The Rhetoric of Curse in Galatians: Paul Confronts Another Gospel.* Emory Studies in Early Christianity. Atlanta: Scholars Press, 1995.

Motyer, Steve. "Righteousness by Faith in the New Testament." *Here We Stand: Justification by Faith Today.* London: Hodder & Stoughton, 1986, 33-56.

Müller, H.-P. "*qahal.*" *TLOT*, 3.1118-26.

Murphy-O'Connor, Jerome. *Paul: A Critical Life.* Oxford: Oxford University Press, 1996.

Nanos, Mark D. *The Irony of Galatians: Paul's Letter in First-Century Context.* Minneapolis: Fortress, 2002.

_____. ed. *The Galatians Debate: Contemporary Issues in Rhetorical and Historical Interpretation.* Peabody: Hendrickson, 2002.

_____. "What Was at Stake in Peter's 'Eating with Gentiles' at Antioch?" *The Galatians Debate: Contemporary Issues in Rhetorical and Historical Interpretation.* ed. Mark D. Nanos. Peabody: Hendrickson, 2002, 282-318.

Newman, Judith H. *Praying by the Book: The Scripturalization of Prayer in Second Temple Judaism.* SBLEJL 14. Atlanta: Scholars Press, 1999.

Newton, Michael. *The Concept of Purity at Qumran and in the Letters of Paul.* SNTSMS 53. Cambridge: Cambridge University Press, 1985.

Neusner, Jacob. *The Rabbinic Traditions About the Pharisees Before 70.* 3 vols. Leiden: Brill, 1971.

Neyrey, Jerome H. "Bewitched in Galatia." *CBQ* 50 1988): 72-100.

_____. *Paul, In Other Words: A Cultural Reading of His Letters.* Louisville: Westminster/Knox, 1990.

Nicholas, Barry. "*Patria Potestas.*" *The Oxford Classical Dictionary.* eds. N. G. L. Hammond and H. H. Scullard. 2nd ed. Oxford: Clarendon, 1970, 789.

Nickelsburg, George W. E. "Abraham the Convert: A Jewish Tradition and Its Use by the Apostle Paul." *Biblical Figures Outside the Bible.* eds. Michael E. Stone and Theodore A. Bergen. Harrisburg: Trinity Press International, 1998, 151-75.

Nickle, Keith F. *The Collection: A Study in Paul's Strategy.* SBT 48. Naperville: Allenson, 1966.

Nolland, John. "Uncircumcised Proselytes?" *JSJ* 12 (1981): 173-94.

O'Brien, Peter T. "Justification in Paul and Some Crucial Issues of the Last Two Decades." *Right With God: Justification in the Bible and the World.* ed. D. A. Carson. Grand Rapids: Baker, 1992, 69-95.

_____. *Gospel and Mission in the Writings of Paul: An Exegetical and Theological Analysis.* Grand Rapids: Baker, 1995.

_____. "Fellowship, Communion, Sharing." *DPL*, 293-95.

_____. "Was Paul Converted?" *Justification and Variegated Nomism. Volume 2: The Paradoxes of Paul.* eds. D. A. Carson, Peter T. O'Brien and Mark A. Seifrid. Grand Rapids: Baker, 2004, 361-91.

O'Collins, Gerald G. "Crucifixion." *ABD*, 6.1207-10.

O'Neill, J. C. *The Recovery of Paul's Letter to the Galatians.* London: SPCK, 1972.

Onesti, K. L. and Brauch, M. T. "Righteousness, Righteousness of God." *DPL*, 827-37.

Oropeza, B. J. "Apostasy in the Wilderness: Paul's Message to the Corinthians in a State of Eschatological Liminality." *JSNT* 75 (1999): 69-86.

_____. *Paul and Apostasy: Eschatology, Perseverance, and Falling Away in the Corinthian Congregation.* WUNT 2/115. Tübingen: Mohr-Siebeck, 2000.

Ortlund, Raymond C. *Whoredom: God's Unfaithful Wife in Biblical Theology.* New Studies in Biblical Theology. Grand Rapids: Eerdmans, 1996.

Oswalt, John N. *The Book of Isaiah.* 2 vols. NICOT. Grand Rapids: Eerdmans, 1986, 1998.

Pancaro, Severino. *The Law in the Fourth Gospel: The Torah and the Gospel, Moses and Jesus, Judaism and Christianity According to John.* NovTSup 42. Leiden: Brill, 1975.

Pate, C. Marvin. *Communities of the Last Days: The Dead Sea Scrolls, the New Testament and the Story of Israel.* Downers Grove: InterVarsity, 2000.

_____. *The Reverse of the Curse: Paul, Wisdom, and the Law.* WUNT 2/114. Tübingen: Mohr-Siebeck, 2000.

Peace, Richard V. *Conversion in the New Testament: Paul and the Twelve.* Grand Rapids: Eerdmans, 1999.

Perry, Edmund. "The Meaning of *'emuna* in the Old Testament." *JBR* 21 (1953): 252-56.

Phillips, Elaine A. "*Nathan Naphshō*: Paradigms of Self-Sacrifice in Early Judaism and Christianity." *BBR* 9 (1999): 215-231.

Pietersma, Albert. "Kyrios or Tetragram: A Renewed Quest for the Original LXX." *De Septuaginta: Studies in Honour of John William Wevers on His Sixty-Fifth Birthday*. eds. Albert Pietersma and Claude Cox. Toronto: Benben Publications, 1984, 85-101.

Piper, John. *The Justification of God: An Exegetical and Theological Study of Romans 9:1-23*. 2nd ed. Grand Rapids: Baker, 1993.

Pobee, John S. *Persecution and Martyrdom in the Theology of Paul*. JSNTSup 6. Sheffield: JSOT Press, 1985.

Poorthuis, M. J. H. M. and Schwartz, J., eds. *Purity and Holiness: The Heritage of Leviticus*. Jewish and Christian Perspective Series 2. Leiden: Brill, 2000.

Porter, Stanley E. *Idioms of the Greek New Testament*. Sheffield: Sheffield Academic Press. 2nd ed. 1992.

Przybylski, Benno. *Righteousness in Matthew and His World of Thought*. SNTSMS 41. Cambridge: Cambridge University Press, 1980.

Qimron, Elisha and Strugnell, John, eds. *Discoveries in the Judean Desert X. Qumran Cave 4. V: Miqsat Maase Ha-Torah*. Oxford: Clarendon, 1994.

Rapa, Robert Keith. *The Meaning of the "Works of the Law" in Galatians and Romans*. Studies in Biblical Literature 31. New York: Peter Lang, 2001.

Rad, Gerhard Von. "Faith Reckoned as Righteousness." *The Problem of the Hexateuch and Other Essays*. London: SCM, 1984, 125-30.

_____. and Foerster, Werner. "*eirēnē*," etc. *TDNT*, 2.400-20.

Räisänen, Heikki. *Paul and the Law*. WUNT 29. Tübingen: Mohr-Siebeck, 1983.

Ramsaran, Rollin A. "Paul and Maxims." *Paul in the Greco-Roman World: A Handbook*. ed. J. Paul Sampley. Harrisburg: Trinity Press International, 2003, 429-456.

Rengstorf, Karl Heinrich. "*apostolos.*" *TDNT*, 1.414-20.

Reumann, John. *Righteousness in the New Testament: "Justification" in the United States Lutheran-Roman Catholic Dialogue, with Responses by Joseph A. Fitzmyer and Jerome D. Quinn.* Philadelphia: Fortress, 1982.

Richards, E. Randolph. *Paul and First Century Letter Writing: Secretaries, Composition and Collection*. Downers Grove: InterVarsity, 2004.

Richardson, Peter. *Israel in the Apostolic Church*. SNTSMS 10. Cambridge: Cambridge University Press, 1969.

Ridderbos, Herman N. *Aan de Romeinen*. Commentaar op het Nieuwe Testament. Kampen: Kok, 1959.
_____. *The Coming of the Kingdom*. Philadelphia: Presbyterian and Reformed, 1962.
_____. *Paul: An Outline of His Theology*. Grand Rapids: Eerdmans, 1975.
_____. *Redemptive History and the New Testament Scriptures*. 2nd ed. Grand Rapids: Baker, 1988.

Riesner, Rainer. *Paul's Early Period: Chronology, Mission Strategy, Theology*. Grand Rapids: Eerdmans, 1998.

Roetzel, Calvin J. *Paul: The Man and the Myth*. Columbia: University of South Carolina Press, 1998.

Rogers, Cleon L. Jr. and Rogers, Cleon L. III. *The New Linguistic and Exegetical Key to the Greek New Testament*. Grand Rapids: Zondervan, 1998.

Roth, S. John. *The Blind, the Lame, and the Poor: Character Types in Luke-Acts*. JSNTSup 144. Sheffield: Sheffield Academic Press, 1997.

Roth, Wolfgang M. W. "For Life, He Appeals to Death (Wis 13:18): A Study of Old Testament Idol Parodies." *CBQ* 37 (1975): 21-47.

Rowley, H. H. *The Biblical Doctrine of Election*. London: Lutterworth, 1950.

Russell, Walter Bo, III. *The Flesh/Spirit Conflict in Galatians*. Lanham: University Press of America, 1997.

Saldarini, Anthony. *Pharisees, Scribes and Pharisees: A Sociological Approach*. Wilmington: Michael Glazier, 1988.

Sampley, J. Paul. "'Before God I do not Lie' (Gal. 1.20): Paul's Self-Defense in Light of Roman Legal Praxis." *NTS* 23 (1977): 477-82.
_____. ed., *Paul in the Greco-Roman World: A Handbook*. Harrisburg: Trinity Press International, 2003.
_____. "Paul and Frank Speech." *Paul in the Greco-Roman World: A Handbook*. ed. J. Paul Sampley. Harrisburg: Trinity Press International, 2003, 293-318.

Sand, Alexander. "*sarx*." *EDNT*, 3.230-33.

Sanday, William and Headlam, Arthur C. *A Critical and Exegetical Commentary on The Epistle to the Romans*. ICC. Edinburgh: T & T Clark, 1895.

Sanders, E. P. *Paul and Palestinian Judaism: A Comparison of Patterns of Religion*. Philadelphia: Fortress, 1977.
_____. *Paul, the Law, and the Jewish People*. Philadelphia: Fortress, 1983.
_____. *Jesus and Judaism*. Philadelphia: Fortress, 1985.
_____. *Jewish Law from Jesus to the Mishnah: Five Studies*. Philadelphia: Trinity Press International, 1990.
_____. "Jewish Association with Gentiles and Galatians 2:11-14." *The Conversation Continues: Studies in Paul and John in Honor of J. Louis Martyn*. eds. Robert T. Fortna and Beverly R. Gaventa. Nashville: Abingdon, 1990, 170-88.

Schechter, Solomon. *Aspects of Rabbinic Theology*. New York: Schocken, rep. 1961.

Schlatter, Adolf. *The Theology of the Apostles: The Development of New Testament Theology.* Grand Rapids: Baker, 1998.

Schmidt, K. L. *"ekklēsia." TDNT*, 3.501-36.

Schmidt, Thomas E. *Hostility to Wealth in the Synoptic Gospels.* JSNTSup 15. Sheffield: JSOT Press, 1987.

Schmithals, Walter. *The Office of Apostle in the Early Church.* Nashville: Abingdon, 1969.

Schnabel, Eckhard J. "Israel, The People of God, and the Nations." *JETS* 45 (2002): 35-57.
_____. *Early Christian Mission.* 2 vols. Downers Grove: InterVarsity, 2004.

Schneider, Gerhard. *"agapē." EDNT*, 1.8-12.

Schnelle, Udo. *Apostle Paul: His Life and Theology.* Grand Rapids: Baker, 2005.

Schrage, Wolfgang. *The Ethics of the New Testament.* Philadelphia: Fortress, 1988.

Schreiner, Thomas R. *The Law and Its Fulfillment: A Pauline Theology of Law.* Grand Rapids: Baker, 1993.
_____. "Works of the Law." *DPL*, 975-79.
_____. *Paul: Apostle of God's Glory in Christ: A Pauline Theology.* Downers Grove: Apollos, 2001.

Schürer, Emil. *The History of the Jewish People in the Age of Jesus Christ.* eds. Geza Vermes, et al. 4 vols. Edinburgh: T & T Clark, 1973-87.

Schütz, John Howard. *Paul and the Anatomy of Apostolic Authority.* SNTSMS 26. Cambridge: Cambridge University Press, 1975.

Schweitzer, Albert. *The Mysticism of Paul the Apostle.* New York: Seabury, rep. 1968.

Scott, James M. *Adoption as Sons of God: An Exegetical Investigation into the Background of* HUIOTHESIA *in the Pauline Corpus.* WUNT 2/48. Tübingen: Mohr-Siebeck, 1992.

_____. "Paul's Use of the Deuteronomic Tradition." *JBL* 112 (1993): 645-65.

_____. "'For As Many as Are of Works of the Law Are under a Curse' (Galatians 3.10)." *Paul and the Scriptures of Israel*. eds. C. A. Evans and J. A. Sanders. JSNTSup 83. Studies in Scripture in Early Judaism and Christianity 1. Sheffield: Sheffield Academic Press, 1993, 187-221.

_____. *Paul and the Nations: The Old Testament and Jewish Background of Paul's Mission to the Nations with Special Reference to the Destination of Galatians*. WUNT 84. Tübingen: Mohr-Siebeck, 1995.

_____. "Paul's *'Imago Mundi'* and Scripture." *Evangelium, Schriftauslegung, Kirche: Festschrift für Peter Stuhlmacher zum 65. Geburtstag*. eds. Jostein Adna, Scott J. Hafemann and Otfried Hofius. Göttingen: Vandenhoeck & Ruprecht, 1997, 366-81.

_____. ed. *Exile: Old Testament, Jewish, and Christian Conceptions*. Supplements to the Journal for the Study of Judaism 56. Leiden: Brill, 1997.

Segal, Alan. *Paul the Convert: The Apostolate and Apostasy of Saul the Pharisee*. New Haven: Yale University Press, 1990.

Seifrid, Mark A. *Justification By Faith: The Origin and Development of A Central Pauline Theme*. NovTSup 68. Leiden: Brill, 1992.

_____. *Christ, Our Righteousness: Paul's Theology of Justification*. New Studies in Biblical Theology 9. Downers Grove: Apollos, 2000.

_____. "Righteousness Language in the Hebrew Scriptures and Early Judaism." *Justification and Variegated Nomism. Volume 1: The Complexities of Second Temple Judaism*. eds. D. A. Carson, Peter T. O'Brien and Mark A. Seifrid. Grand Rapids: Baker, 2001, 415-42.

_____. "Paul's Use of Righteousness Language Against Its Hellenistic Background." *Justification and Variegated Nomism. Volume 2: The Paradoxes of Paul*. eds. D. A. Carson, Peter T. O'Brien and Mark A. Seifrid. Grand Rapids: Baker, 2004, 39-74.

Shauf, Scott. "Galatians 2.20 in Context." *NTS* 52 (2006): 86-101.

Siker, Jeffrey S. *Disinheriting the Jews: Abraham in Early Christian Controversy*. Louisville: Westminster/John Knox, 1991.

Silva, Moisés. "The Law and Christianity: Dunn's New Synthesis." *WTJ* 53 (1991): 339-53.

_____. "Eschatological Structures in Galatians." *To Tell the Mystery: Essays on New Testament Eschatology in Honor of Robert H. Gundry*. eds. Thomas Schmidt and Moisés Silva. Sheffield: JSOT Press, 1994, 140-62.

_____. *Explorations in Exegetical Method: Galatians as a Test Case*. Grand Rapids: Baker, 1996.

_____. "Faith Versus Works of the Law in Galatians." *Justification and Variegated Nomism. Volume 2: The Paradoxes of Paul*. eds. D. A. Carson, Peter T. O'Brien and Mark A. Seifrid. Grand Rapids: Baker, 2004, 217-48.

Smiles, Vincent M. *The Gospel and the Law in Galatia: Paul's Response to Jewish-Christian Separationism and the Threat of Galatian Apostasy*. Collegeville: Glazier, 1998.

Smith, Dennis E. "Table Fellowship." *ABD*, 6.302-4.

Snaith, Norman H. *The Distinctive Ideas of the Old Testament*. London: Epworth, 1944.

Snodgrass, Klyne. "The Use of the Old Testament in the New." *Interpreting the New Testament: Essays on Methods and Issues*. eds. David Allen Black and David S. Dockery. Nashville: Broadman, 2001, 209-229.

Sohn, Seock-Tae. *The Divine Election of Israel*. Grand Rapids: Eerdmans, 1991.

Spicq, Celaus. *Agapè dans le Nouveau Testament: Analyse des textes*. 3 vols. Ebib. Paris: Gabalda, 1958-59.
_____. "*apostolos.*" *TLNT*, 1.186-94.
_____. "*pistis.*" *TLNT*, 3.110-16.
_____. "*sarx.*" *TLNT*, 3.231-41.

Stählin, Gustav. "*To Pneuma Iēsou* (Apostlegeschichte 16:7)." *Christ and the Spirit in the New Testament: Studies in Honour of Charles Francis Digby Moule*. eds. Barnabas Lindars and Stephen S. Smalley. Cambridge: Cambridge University Press, 1973, 229-52.

Stanley, Christopher D. "'Under a Curse': A Fresh Reading of Galatians 3.10-14." *NTS* 36 (1990): 481-511.
_____. *Paul and the Language of Scripture: Citation Technique in the Pauline Epistles and Contemporary Literature.* SNTSMS 74. Cambridge: Cambridge University Press, 1992.
_____. *Arguing with Scripture: The Rhetoric of Quotations in the Letters of Paul.* New York: T & T Clark International, 2004.

Stanton, Graham. "The Law of Moses and the Law of Christ—Galatians 3.1-6.2." *Paul and the Mosaic Law.* ed. J. D. G. Dunn. Grand Rapids: Eerdmans, 1996, 99-116.

Stein, Robert H. *The Method and Message of Jesus' Teaching.* Philadelphia: Westminster, 1978.

Stemberger, Günter. *Jewish Contemporaries of Jesus: Pharisees, Sadducees, Essenes.* Minneapolis: Fortress, 1995.

Stern, Menahem. *Greek and Latin Authors on Jews and Judaism.* Fontes Ad Res Judaicas Spactantes. 3 vols. Jerusalem: Israel Academy of Sciences and Humanities, 1976-84.

Stirewalt, M. Luther. *Paul: The Letter Writer.* Grand Rapids: Eerdmans, 2003.

Stockhausen, Carol K. "2 Corinthians 3 and the Principles of Pauline Exegesis." *Paul and the Scriptures of Israel.* eds. C. A. Evans and J. A. Sanders. JSNTSup 83. SSEJC 1. Sheffield: Sheffield Academic Press, 1993, 143-64.

Storkey, Alan. *Jesus and Politics: Confronting the Powers.* Grand Rapids: Baker, 2005.

Stowers, Stanley K. *Letter Writing in Greco-Roman Antiquity.* Library of Early Christianity. Philadelphia: Westminster, 1986.
_____. "Paul and Self-Mastery." *Paul in the Greco-Roman World: A Handbook.* ed. J. Paul Sampley. Harrisburg: Trinity Press International, 2003, 524-50.

Stuhlmacher, Peter. *Gottes Gerechtigkeit bei Paulus.* FRLANT 87. 2nd ed. Göttingen: Vandenhoeck & Ruprecht, 1966.
_____. *Revisiting Paul's Doctrine of Justification: A Challenge to the New Perspective.* Downers Grove: InterVarsity, 2001.

Sumney, Jerry L. *Identifying Paul's Opponents: The Question of Method in 2 Corinthians.* JSNTSup 40. Sheffield: JSOT Press, 1990.

Swetnam, James. *Jesus and Isaac: A Study of the Epistle to the Hebrews in the Light of the Aqedah.* AnBib 94. Rome: Biblical Institute Press, 1981.

Tan, Kim Huat. *The Zion Traditions and the Aims of Jesus.* SNTSMS 91. Cambridge: Cambridge University Press, 1997.

Thatcher, Tom. "The Plot of Gal 3:1-18." *JETS* 40 (1997): 401-10.

Thielman, Frank. *From Plight to Solution: A Jewish Framework for Understanding Paul's View of the Law in Romans and Galatians.* NovTSup 61. Leiden: Brill, 1989.
_____. *Paul and the Law: A Contextual Approach.* Downers Grove: InterVarsity, 1994.
_____. "Folk Belief and Persecution in Galatia: An Appreciative Response to Clinton E. Arnold." Paper delivered at the annual meeting of Institute for Biblical Research. Atlanta, November 22, 2003.
_____. *Theology of the New Testament: A Canonical and Synthetic Approach.* Grand Rapids: Zondervan, 2005.

Thompson, Michael B. *The New Perspective on Paul.* Grove Biblical Series. Cambridge: Grove Books, 2002.

Thomson, Ian H. *Chiasmus in the Pauline Letters.* JSNTSup 111. Sheffield: Sheffield Academic Press, 1995.

Tomson, Peter J. *Paul and the Jewish Law: Halakha in the Letters of the Apostle to the Gentiles.* CRINT 3.1. Minneapolis: Fortress, 1990.

Torrance, Thomas F. *The Doctrine of Grace in the Apostolic Fathers.* Grand Rapids: Eerdmans, 1959.

Trench, Richard C. *Synonyms of the New Testament.* Grand Rapids: Eerdmans, rep. 1953.

BIBLIOGRAPHY

Tsang, Sam. *From Slaves to Sons: A New Rhetoric Analysis on Paul's Slave Metaphors in His Letter to the Galatians*. Studies in Biblical Literature 81. New York: Peter Lang, 2005.

Udoh, Fabian E. "Paul's Views on the Law: Questions about Origin (Gal. 1:6-2:21; Phil. 3:2-11)." *NovT* 42 (2000): 214-37.

Urbach, Ephraim. *The Sages: Their Concepts and Beliefs*. Cambridge, Mass: Harvard University Press, 1987.

Wagner, J Ross. "Isaiah in Romans and Galatians." *Isaiah in the New Testament*. eds. Steve Moyise and Maarten J. J. Menken. New York: T & T Clark International, 2005, 117-32.

Walker, Peter W. L. *Jesus and the Holy City: New Testament Perspectives on Jerusalem*. Grand Rapids: Eerdmans, 1996.

Walker, William O, Jr. "Why Paul Went to Jerusalem: The Interpretation of Galatians 2:1-5." *CBQ* 54 (1992): 503-10.

Wallis, Ian G. *The Faith of Jesus Christ in Early Christian Traditions*. SNTSMS 84. Cambridge: Cambridge University Press, 1995.

Walters, James C. "Paul, Adoption, and Inheritance." *Paul in the Greco-Roman World: A Handbook*. ed. J. Paul Sampley. Harrisburg: Trinity Press International, 2003, 42-76.

Watson, Duane F. "Paul and Boasting." *Paul in the Greco-Roman World: A Handbook*. ed. J. Paul Sampley. Harrisburg: Trinity Press International, 2003, 77-100.

Watson, Francis. *Paul and the Hermeneutics of Faith*. London: T & T Clark International, 2004.

Wedderburn, A. J. M. "Some Observations on Paul's Use of the Phrases 'in Christ' and 'With Christ'". *New Testament Text and Language: A Sheffield Reader*. The Biblical Seminar 44. eds. Stanley E. Porter and Craig A. Evans. Sheffield: Sheffield Academic Press, 1997, 145-59.

Weima, Jeffrey A. D. "Gal. 6:11-18: A Hermeneutical Key to the Galatian Letter." *CTJ* 28 (1993): 90-107.

_____. *Neglected Endings: The Significance of the Pauline Letter Closings.* JSNTSup 101. Sheffield: Sheffield Academic Press, 1994.

_____. "The Pauline Letter Closings: Analysis and Hermeneutical Significance." *BBR* 5 (1995): 177-98.

Weiser, Artur. *The Psalms: A Commentary.* OTL. Philadelphia: Westminster, 1962.

Wengst, Klaus. *Pax Romana and the Peace of Jesus Christ.* London: SCM, 1987.

Wenham Gordon J. *Story as Torah: Reading Old Testament Narratives Ethically.* Grand Rapids: Baker, 2000.

Werline, Rodney Alan. *Penitential Prayer in Second Temple Judaism: The Development of a Religious Institution.* SBLEJL 13. Atlanta: Scholars Press, 1998.

Westerholm, Stephen. *Perspectives Old and New on Paul: The "Lutheran" Paul and His Critics.* Grand Rapids: Eerdmans, 2004.

_____. "The 'New Perspective' at Twenty-Five." *Justification and Variegated Nomism. Volume 2: The Paradoxes of Paul.* eds. D. A. Carson, Peter T. O'Brien and Mark A. Seifrid. Grand Rapids: Baker, 2004, 1-38.

Wevers, John William. *Notes on the Greek Text of Deuteronomy.* SBLSCS 39. Atlanta: Scholars Press, 1995.

White, John L. *The Apostle of God: Paul and the Promise of Abraham.* Peabody: Hendrickson, 1999.

White, L. Michael. "Paul and *Pater Familias.*" *Paul in the Greco-Roman World: A Handbook.* ed. J. Paul Sampley. Harrisburg: Trinity Press International, 2003, 457-87.

Wilcox, Max. "'Upon the Tree'—Deut 21:22-23 in the New Testament." *JBL* 96 (1977): 85-99.

Williams, David J. *Paul's Metaphors: Their Context and Character.* Peabody: Hendrickson, 1999.

Williams, Sam K. "Justification and the Spirit in Galatians." *JSNT* 29 (1987): 91-100.

Williamson, Paul R. *Abraham, Israel and the Nations: The Patriarchial Promise and Its Covenantal Development in Genesis.* JSOTSup 315. Sheffield: Sheffield Academic Press, 2000.

Wilson, Todd A. "Wilderness Apostasy and Paul's Portrayal of the Crisis in Galatia." *NTS* 50 (2004): 550-71.

Winger, Michael. *By What Law? The Meaning of* Nomos *in the Letters of Paul.* SBLDS 128. Atlanta: Scholars Press, 1992.
_____. "The Law of Christ." *NTS* 46 (2000): 537-46.

Winninge, Mikael. *Sinners and the Righteous: A Comparative Study of the Psalms of Solomon and Paul's Letters.* ConBNT 26. Stockholm: Almqvist & Wiksell, 1995.

Wintle, Brian C. "Justification in Pauline Thought." *Right With God: Justification in the Bible and the World.* ed. D. A. Carson. Grand Rapids: Baker, 1992, 51-68.

Wisdom, Jeffrey R. *Blessing for the Nations and the Curse of the Law: Paul's Citation of Genesis and Deuteronomy in Galatians 3.8-10.* WUNT 2/133. Tübingen: Mohr-Siebeck, 2001.

Witherington, Ben. *The Christology of Jesus.* Minneapolis: Fortress, 1990.
_____. *The Paul Quest: The Renewed Search for the Jew of Tarsus.* Downers Grove: InterVarsity, 1998.
_____. *The Acts of the Apostles: A Socio-Rhetorical Commentary.* Grand Rapids: Eerdmans, 1998.

Witulski, Thomas. *Die Adressaten des Galaterbriefes: Untersuchungen zur Gemeinde von Antiochia ad Pisidiam.* FRLANT 193. Göttingen: Vandenhoeck & Ruprecht, 2000.

Wright, N. T. "Righteousness." *New Dictionary of Theology.* eds. S. B. Ferguson, et al. Leicester: Inter-Varsity, 1988, 590-92.
_____. *The Climax of the Covenant: Christ and the Law in Pauline Theology.* Minneapolis: Fortress, 1991.
_____. *The New Testament and the People of God.* Christian Origins and the Question of God 1. Minneapolis: Fortress, 1991.

_____. *Jesus and the Victory of God*. Christian Origins and the Question of God 2. Minneapolis: Fortress, 1996.

_____. "Gospel and Theology in Galatians." *Gospel in Paul: Studies on Corinthians, Galatians and Romans for Richard N. Longenecker*. eds. L. Ann Jervis and Peter Richardson. JSNTSup 108. Sheffield: Sheffield Academic Press, 1994, 222-39.

_____. "Paul, Arabia, and Elijah (Galatians 1:17)." *JBL* 115 (1996): 683-92.

_____. *What Saint Paul Really Said: Was Paul of Tarsus the Real Founder of Christianity?* Grand Rapids: Eerdmans, 1997.

_____. "The Letter to the Galatians: Exegesis and Theology." *Between Two Horizons: Spanning New Testament Studies and Systematic Theology*. eds. Joel B. Green and Max Turner. Grand Rapids: Eerdmans, 2000, 205-36.

_____. "Paul's Gospel and Caesar's Empire." *Paul and Politics: Ekklesia, Israel, Imperium, Interpretation. Essays in Honor of Krister Stendahl*. ed. Richard A. Horsley. Harrisburg: Trinity Press International, 2000, 160-83.

_____. *The Resurrection of the Son of God*. Christian Origins and the Question of God 3. Minneapolis: Fortress, 2003.

_____. *Paul: In Fresh Perspective*. Minneapolis: Fortress, 2005.

Yadin, Yigael. *The Temple Scroll*. 3 vols. Jerusalem: Israel Exploration Society, 1983.

Yinger, Kent L. *Paul, Judaism, and Judgment According to Deeds*. SNTSMS 105. Cambridge: Cambridge University Press, 1999.

Young, Norman H. "*PAIDAGOGOS*: The Social Setting of a Pauline Metaphor." *NovT* 29 (1987): 150-176.

_____. "The Figure of the *Paidagōgos* in Art and Literature." *BA* 53 (1990): 80-86.

Zias, Joe, and Charlesworth, James H. "Crucifixion: Archaeology, Jesus, and the Dead Sea Scrolls." *Jesus and the Dead Sea Scrolls*. ed. J. H. Charlesworth. New York: Doubleday, 1992, 273-89.

Ziesler, J. A. *The Meaning of Righteousness in Paul: A Linguistic and Theological Enquiry*. SNTSMS 20. Cambridge: Cambridge University Press, 1972.